Moscow, Germany, and the West

from Khrushchev to Gorbachev

Moscow, Germany, and the West

from Khrushchev to Gorbachev

Michael J. Sodaro

Studies of the Harriman Institute

Cornell University Press

Ithaca and London

First published 1990 by Cornell University Press.

Library of Congress Cataloging-in-Publication Data

Sodaro, Michael J.
    Moscow, Germany, and the West from Khrushchev to Gorbachev / Michael J. Sodaro.
        p.   cm. — (Studies of the Harriman Institute)
    Includes index.
    ISBN 0-8014-2529-8 (Cloth : alkaline paper)
    1. Soviet Union—Foreign relations—Germany.   2. Germany—Foreign relations—Soviet
Union.   3. Soviet Union—Foreign relations—1953–1975.   4. Soviet Union—Foreign
relations—1975–1985.   5. Soviet Union—Foreign relations—1985–   I. Title.   II. Series.
DK282.S63   1991
327.47043—dc20   90-84233

Printed in the United States of America

♾The paper in this book meets the minimum requirements
of the American National Standard for Information Sciences—
Permanence of Paper for Printed Library Materials, ANSI Z39.48-1984.

To my parents
Joseph and Ellen Sodaro
with love and gratitude

Contents

vii

Acknowledgments

To acknowledge all the personal and intellectual debts I have amassed in the course of writing this book would require more pages than I have available, but a few individuals whose insights and encouragement have been particularly valuable deserve special mention. Herbert S. Dinerstein first impressed upon me the magnitude of Germany's importance in the Soviet Union's foreign policy toward Europe and the West in a seminar at the School of Advanced International Studies of The Johns Hopkins University. I pursued this interest at Columbia University under the direction of a stimulating team of specialists on the Soviet Union and Eastern Europe which included Seweryn Bialer, Zbigniew Brzezinski, Charles Gati, Robert Legvold, Peter C. Ludz, and Marshall Shulman. My colleagues at the Institute for Sino-Soviet Studies, the Department of Political Science, and the Elliott School of International Affairs at The George Washington University merit special thanks. Their advice, support, and tolerance of my absence from faculty meetings during the long years of my concentration on this project have been of inestimable value.

All or parts of the manuscript at various stages were read by Gert-Joachim Glaessner, Robert F. Goeckel, William E. Griffith, Johannes Kuppe, Robbin F. Laird, Elke Matthews, Norman Naimark, Fred Oldenburg, Bruce Parrott, Ilya Prizel, and Charles B. Skinner. I consider myself fortunate to have had such a constructive group of critics. They saved me from a potentially embarrassing number of errors, omissions, and redundancies. Of course they bear no responsibility for the final product, but they helped significantly to make this book much better than it might otherwise have been.

In addition to accumulating numerous intellectual debts from mentors and colleagues in the course of my career, I could not have written this book without the financial support of several exceptionally generous institutions. The German Academic Exchange Service and the Airlift Memorial Foundation of Berlin collaborated in funding two memorable years of research in West Berlin and another trip later on. The Ford Foundation enabled me to take a first look at some of the Soviet literature analyzed in this book with a "dual expertise" grant. Thanks to a sizable grant from the same foundation to the GDR Studies Association, I was able to take a timely research trip to Germany in the spring of 1989. The National Council for Soviet and East European Research provided me with vital assistance so that I could devote a full year to research and writing. IREX (the International Research and Exchanges Board) once again proved its responsiveness to scholars laboring in the Soviet field by generously awarding me a grant to conduct interviews in Moscow. (IREX obtains funding from the National Endowment for the Humanities and the United States Information Agency.) Finally, but no less gratefully, I have benefited over the years from research grants awarded by the Institute for Sino-Soviet Studies and the Graduate School of Arts and Sciences at George Washington. Naturally, none of these organizations is responsible for the views I have expressed.

The cooperation I received from colleagues at the Institute of the World Economy and International Relations (IMEMO) and the Institute of the Economics of the World Socialist System in Moscow deserves particular thanks. So does the cooperation I have received over the years from officials and academicians of the German Democratic Republic. My students, both graduates and undergraduates, who have been subjected to my discourses and digressions on Soviet-German relations have also been more helpful than they may realize in shaping my ideas and their presentation.

John Ackerman, my editor, deserves special accolades for piloting this book to completion in rapid order. It was a pleasure to work with him. Barbara Salazar skillfully edited the manuscript. Joan Barth Urban also played an important role in the book's publication. Leslie Auerbach of the Harriman Institute at Columbia University was very helpful in arranging for this book's inclusion in the Institute's series of volumes. Special thanks go to Thomas R. Wenner of the Library of Congress for indispensable bibliographic assistance. Thanks also to Charlene Gardella, Alice Krupit, Nancy L. Meyers (who prepared the index), Craig H. Seibert, Marcia Sleight, Suzanne Stephenson, and Dorothy Wedge. And most of all, thanks to Gloria, Paul, Alexandra, and Marshall, whose love and joie de vivre were a constant inspiration.

MICHAEL J. SODARO

Washington, D.C.

A Note on Transliteration

No system of transliterating Russian into English is completely satisfactory. In general I prefer *ya* to *ia, ei* to *ey, ii* to *iy, yu* to *iu* (and *ye* to *e* after vowels) in rendering the corresponding Russian sounds and letters in our own alphabet's rough equivalents. Consistency, alas, is not always possible. The popular press has familiarized us with certain usages that may depart from those we may prefer. Newspaper readers are thus accustomed to seeing Yeltsin and Yuri (instead of Eltsin and Yurii). In some instances I have adopted these commonly acccepted spellings (e.g., Yeltsin) while in others I have remained consistent with my own preferences (e.g., Yurii, Evropa). The problem of consistency is compounded by the fact that official English translations of Soviet journals, such as *International Affairs, Moscow News*, and *New Times*, use their own system of transliteration. In deference to the Soviet publishers, I have retained their rendering of Russian names whenever I cite them, even if their version differs from the way I transliterate the same names elsewhere in the text.

Abbreviations and Acronyms

CDU	Christlich-Demokratische Union (Christian Democratic Union)
CFE	Conventional Forces in Europe
COMECON	Council on Mutual Economic Assistance (Eastern bloc)
CPCz	Communist Party of Czechoslovakia
CPSU	Communist Party of the Soviet Union
CSCE	Conference on Security and Cooperation in Europe
CSU	Christlich-Soziale Union (Christian Social Union; FRG)
DA	*Deutsche Aussenpolitik*
EEC	European Economic Community
FAZ	*Frankfurter Allgemeine Zeitung*
FBIS	Foreign Broadcast Information Service, *Daily Report*
FDJ	Freie Deutsche Jugend (Free German Youth; youth movement of SED)
FDP	Freie Demokratische Partei (Free Democratic Party; FRG)
FRG	Federal Republic of Germany
GDR	German Democratic Republic
GLCM	ground-launched cruise missile
IA	*International Affairs*
ICBM	intercontinental ballistic missile
IMEMO	Institut Mirovoi Ekonomiki i Mezhdunarodnykh Otnoshenii (Institute of the World Economy and International Relations, Moscow)
INF	intermediate-range nuclear forces
MBFR	mutual and balanced force reductions
MEMO	*Mirovaya economika i mezhdunarodnye otnosheniya* (The world economy and international relations)
MIRV	multiple independently targeted reentry vehicle
MLF	Multilateral Force
NATO	North Atlantic Treaty Organization
ND	*Neues Deutschland* (daily newspaper of SED)

NPD	Nationaldemokratische Partei Deutschlands (National Party of Germany)
NPT	Nonproliferation Treaty
R&D	research and development
SDI	strategic defense initiative
SED	Sozialistische Einheitspartei Deutschlands (Socialist Unity Party of Germany; GDR)
SPD	Sozialdemokratische Partei Deutschlands (Social Democratic Party of Germany)
SSha	*USA*

Moscow, Germany, and the West

from Khrushchev to Gorbachev

Introduction

On November 9, 1989, the Berlin wall came open and East-West relations were suddenly transformed. Within a matter of weeks the breach in the barrier dividing the western and eastern sectors of this great city, a barrier that had symbolized for nearly three decades the ideological divisions between democracy and communism, would prove to be a breakthrough of revolutionary proportions. From East Berlin to Sofia, from Prague to Bucharest, communist party dictatorships that had seemed impregnable simply crumbled in an avalanche of spontaneous protest. These upheavals took place only a few months after the quieter but equally stunning decisions of the ruling parties of Hungary and Poland to relinquish total power by competing with noncommunists in open elections.

Nowhere were these transformations more important for the evolution of the European state system than in the German Democratic Republic. The virtually instantaneous collapse of the East German communist party was followed quickly by the disintegration of the GDR itself. The westward exodus of East German citizens, which had slowed somewhat after the opening of the inter-German borders in November, soon resumed its frenetic pace of the previous summer and early fall. In 1989 some 400,000 East Germans fled the GDR; as the new decade entered its first months, they were leaving at the rate of more than 2,000 a day. Revelations of official corruption, deep-seated fears of the state security apparatus, a rapidly depreciating currency, and a general sense that the political and economic systems of the GDR were simply beyond repair were among the factors that impelled people to pack up and get out. This accelerating stampede made it impossible for the East German government to stabilize the situation. Demands for unification with West Germany proliferated across the GDR,

2 / Moscow, Germany, and the West

confronting political leaders in both German states with no alternative but to draw up plans for economic and political union much more rapidly than many of them wished. In November 1989 unification had become a possibility; by February it was a foregone conclusion.

Responding to these uncontrollable events, the East German authorities advanced to March 18 the elections that had originally been scheduled for May 6. New political groupings sprang up like mushrooms in the GDR, but the campaign was dominated by affiliates of the leading West German party organizations, which provided prominent speakers, organizational skill, and policy advice to their sister parties in the East. A trio of parties allied with the West German Christian Democrats won a surprisingly large plurality with 48 percent of the vote. The East German Social Democrats garnered 22 percent, and a group of Liberals supported by the Federal Republic's Free Democrats got 5 percent of the total. All of these parties agreed on the necessity of unification, differing only on its timing and modalities. Parties opposed to unification were decisively rejected. Among them were the communists, whose Party of Democratic Socialism (formerly the Socialist Unity Party of Germany, or SED) received 16 percent of the vote. On April 12 a grand coalition government that included Christian Democrats, Social Democrats, and others took office in East Berlin and began to grapple with the task of phasing the German Democratic Republic out of existence. The monetary union of the two Germanies took effect on July 1, and legislators on both sides of the Elbe worked feverishly to prepare the way for East Germany's incorporation into the economic and legal systems of the Federal Republic. Formal unification came on October 3.

None of these things could have happened without the forbearance of the Soviet Union. The Gorbachev leadership's decision to refrain from intervention in the internal affairs of the Warsaw Pact states represented a radical departure from the practice of previous Soviet leaders, some of whom had not hesitated to intervene by force of arms or through more indirect machinations to assert Moscow's imperial sway over East-Central Europe. Whether the Soviet leaders and their advisers actually expected the East Europeans and the East Germans to break away so abruptly from communist influence is another question; it seems clear that they did not. Once the break came, however, Mikhail Gorbachev's unblinking inclination was to let it happen, irrespective of the consequences for local communist parties and for the socialist system itself. The fact that the Kremlin was even willing to permit the liquidation of the GDR and allow it to be incorporated into a greater Germany that would surely be attached to the West provided a particularly dramatic indication of Gorbachev's readiness to diverge from the straight and narrow paths set by his predecessors.

These dramatic developments highlight the differences between two competing views on Soviet foreign policy. One view has traditionally stressed the continuities in Soviet behavior. Its proponents have generally been quite skeptical of the Kremlin's capacity for substantial policy change, whether at home or in the international arena, and have tended to regard Soviet foreign policy as the product of relatively constant geopolitical interests (some of which go back to the tsarist era) and of equally unchanging Marxist-Leninist verities. By contrast, the other view has stressed the adaptability of Soviet foreign policy to shifting international and domestic conditions. Adherents of this notion have been particularly sensitive to variations in Moscow's international orientation from one leader to the next. Of course they recognize that all Soviet leaders have been keenly aware of geopolitical realities and ideological principles, but they point out that each of them, from Lenin and Stalin onward, managed to carve out sufficient latitude to interpret these overarching considerations in accordance with his own convictions and priorities.

Needless to say, the variations between Soviet rulers are glaringly obvious when one compares Gorbachev with his immediate predecessors. Subtle but important differences also distinguished Nikita Khrushchev from Leonid Brezhnev, however, and some of these differences were particularly evident in their German policy. These differences between Soviet leaders, moreover, have been accompanied by persisting policy disputes at lower levels of the foreign policy establishment, involving party and state officials, academicians, and journalists. In fact, internal divisions over policy toward Germany, and toward the United States and Western Europe more generally, have been visible in the Soviet elite under every leader from Khrushchev to Gorbachev. The intensity and openness of these policy conflicts have fluctuated over time, to be sure; the stultifying censorship system of the pre-Gorbachev decades required more oblique methods of articulating policy differences in public than is the case in the more liberated atmosphere of glasnost. Similarly, the range of policy options considered acceptable by the ruling hierarchy has narrowed or widened depending on the political inclinations of the leadership. Still, disagreements and debates over policy toward Germany and the Western alliance have been a constant feature of the Soviet political scene from the early 1960s to the onset of the 1990s.

Any effort to understand Soviet policy toward Germany and the West in these decades must therefore look inside the Soviet political system itself. It must delve into what may be broadly called the foreign policy formulation process. This is the process in which various members of the political elite discuss the prevailing trends of international life and shape their analyses into practical policy options. Such an approach aims above all to trace the domestic sources of Moscow's foreign policy behavior. It attaches considerable value to the way the Soviets themselves perceive the world, and it illuminates the variety of alternative policy choices that have been available to Soviet leaders at particular times. Of course this internally oriented mode of analysis must be highly sensitive to the elements of continuity that have linked Kremlin rulers from Khrushchev to Gorbachev in their dealings with the Western allies. Its main purpose, however, is to clarify their differences and explore the diversity of opinions that may be found within the various layers of the foreign policy elite. When focused on Moscow's German policy, this approach reveals not the constancy of Soviet attitudes but their flexibility; not a uniformity of thought but continuing debate; and not certitude over how to deal with German issues but a pervasive ambivalence.

By examining the internal dynamics of Soviet foreign policy making over more than twenty-five years we can fit the exciting developments of the Gorbachev years within a fairly broad historical canvas and acquire considerable insight into their origins and significance. After all, the Gorbachev phenomenon did not metamorphose overnight. The reforms that Gorbachev initiated both at home and abroad represented a response to a welter of problems that had been accumulating for many years. As far as Germany was concerned, Gorbachev inherited a legacy of failure in the principal political, economic, and military aspects of his precursors' policies.

On the political front, Gorbachev had to face the fact that the repressive neo-Stalinist system of government imposed on the population by generations of Kremlin hierarchs was a continuing source of alienation between the rulers and ruled in all the socialist countries. If this was the case in the Soviet Union (as Gorbachev doubtless believed), it was bound to be the case in the GDR and Eastern Europe. On the economic plane, Gorbachev recognized that the centralized planning system, whose contours had changed only marginally since the 1930s, had failed to match the leading market economies of the world in such vital sectors as high-technology innovation and basic material living standards. Once again, deficiencies that weakened the Soviet position could not help but weaken the GDR's. Finally, in the military sphere, Gorbachev had to confront the consequences of the vigorous conventional and nuclear arms buildups of the Brezhnev years. Not only had these expensive deployments failed to crack NATO's unity or give the Warsaw Pact a decisive military advantage; they had also shattered Moscow's fruitful détente with West Germany and landed the USSR in a deepening global isolation.

These failures did not make Gorbachev's breathtaking foreign policy turnabouts inevitable, to be sure, but they certainly paved the way for them. Our attempts to comprehend Gorbachev's actions must therefore wind back the threads of interconnected events to their sources in the Soviet past. These threads lead us back to Nikita Khrushchev's final year in office. After a decade of sharp conflict and desultory communications with Bonn, Khrushchev launched new initiatives in 1963 and 1964 to open up a dialogue with the FRG at the highest levels and to stimulate Soviet–West German economic contacts. Some members of the Soviet elite supported

Khrushchev's demarche but others argued vigorously against it. As opposition to the floundering Soviet leader mounted over a variety of issues, dissatisfaction with his German policy provided his critics with one more reason for removing him from power.

After Khrushchev's dismissal in 1964, the Brezhnev team put German policy on hold before responding to the opportunities for an accommodation with the Federal Republic that materialized in the late 1960s. As West Germany changed governments and reassessed its eastern policies, the Soviets went through a soul-searching process of their own, openly deliberating the advantages and dangers of a rapprochement with West Germany. In 1970 both sides were ready for major economic and political accords. Over the next two years the Soviet Union, the Federal Republic, and their principal allies put together a package of agreements intended to ease tensions and promote economic and humanitarian cooperation in the heart of Europe. By the middle of the decade détente was in full swing.

Even during the most relaxed phase of East-West cooperation, the Soviets were absorbed in continuing internal discussions about the implications of their new relationship with the FRG. Was Bonn becoming more independent of the United States, or was it still subordinate to its transatlantic ally? More broadly, could the ties uniting the Western allies be loosened only through a comprehensive relaxation of tensions, or could this eminently desirable goal be achieved in spite of mounting East-West confrontation? Disagreements over these and other issues bore directly on the question whether Moscow hoped to neutralize West Germany, a fear expressed by a number of concerned observers in the West.

Policy toward West Germany aroused considerably more contention at the start of the 1980s. While détente had brought palpable, if limited, political and economic rewards to both the Soviets and the West Germans, no significant progress had been made toward reducing the swollen military arsenals of the opposing alliance systems in Europe. Tensions surrounding the military square-off intensified in the late 1970s as the Soviets began to deploy a new generation of intermediate-range missiles in the European theater. As NATO moved to install new missiles of its own in response, the animosities still lingering in the East-West relationship escalated into one of the most bitter crises of the cold war. The Euromissile crisis also triggered an animated debate inside the USSR. The dispute centered around the tacit question of whether the West German government should be punished for its role in the missile controversy. Some Soviets were highly critical of Bonn's insistence on the new NATO missiles, and signaled their support for retaliation. Others essentially exonerated the FRG and blamed the United States for NATO's actions.

The implications of this debate extended well beyond the immediate question of penalizing Bonn. As subsequent events made clear, the larger point at issue was the very essence of the Brezhnev regime's conservative foreign policy. In many instances, opponents of a punitive policy toward Bonn were in effect arguing against the conservatives' conflictual characterization of détente and their confrontationist stance on a wide array of issues dividing the two alliances. By contrast, advocates of retaliation defended the hard-line premises of the conservative world view. The debate on Germany in the first half of the 1980s thus turned out to be a prelude to the wrenching reappraisal of Moscow's entire foreign policy course soon to be undertaken by Gorbachev and other Soviet reformers. It foreshadowed the coming clash between Brezhnevite "stagnation" and Gorbachev's "new political thinking" on the most vital questions of East-West relations.

Disagreements over German policy did not abate after Gorbachev came to power. If anything, they became even more explicit. Before November 1989, Gorbachev himself offered tantalizing hints of change on such things as the Berlin wall and the permanence of Germany's division, but he was cautiously ambiguous as to details. Senior officials and academicians took more forthright positions either for or against a reorientation of Moscow's German policy. Although the Soviet elite was manifestly engaged in a process of "new thinking" on Germany, however, the political leaders themselves had not yet settled on a clearly formulated new *policy* toward Germany when they were overtaken by the storm of popular revolt that rumbled through the GDR in the summer and fall of 1989. The improvisational character of Soviet positions on German unification after the Berlin wall was opened vividly demonstrated that the Kremlin was unprepared for the consequences of this extraordinary event. Even after agreeing in principle that Germany could be united, by the spring of 1990 Moscow was still scrambling for a coherent policy on the terms of unification, particularly as they related to the new Germany's relationship with NATO. Meanwhile, more conservative figures such as Yegor Ligachev were outspokenly critical of Gorbachev's failure to keep Germany divided. Only in mid-July, after shoring up his position against the conservatives at the 28th Party Congress, did Gorbachev formally acquiesce in Germany's membership in NATO after unification.

The position of the GDR in all these developments was of course crucial. Right up to its final collapse, the communist government in East Berlin had always sought to stake out its own vital interests in East-West politics. Quite obviously, its most elementary interest was simple survival. But though the GDR was dependent on Moscow for its very raison d'être, East German leaders did not always see eye to eye with their colleagues in the Kremlin. At various times both Walter Ulbricht and Erich Honecker were locked in open conflict with the Soviet leadership. Invariably these disputes centered on Moscow's policies toward Bonn. Ulbricht opposed the efforts of Khrushchev and Brezhnev to achieve a limited détente with the Federal

Republic. Ironically, Honecker sought to sustain détente with the FRG at a time when Brezhnev and his immediate successors, Yurii Andropov and Konstantin Chernenko, were more intent on pursuing the arms race. Gorbachev confronted Honecker with even more problems, applying strong pressures on the East Germans to adopt Soviet-style political reforms and to prepare for a more open relationship with West Germany than Honecker himself was ready to pursue. By the fall of 1989 these pressures from Moscow, combined with the surging popular unrest inside the GDR, became insurmountable. It was already much too late, however, to save a dying regime from complete collapse.

In order to evaluate East Germany's central role in the evolution of Soviet-German relations from the early 1960s to the edge of the 1990s, we need to submit it to the same kind of scrutiny as the Soviet Union. The internal mechanisms of policy formulation must be accorded as much attention as the GDR's external ties with the Soviet Union and West Germany. The differences and similarities between Walter Ulbricht's regime and Erich Honecker's must be clearly delineated, and so must the terms of policy debate among the East German elites. Although the scope and frequency of debate in the GDR were not so great as in the Soviet Union, a diversity of opinions on policy-related issues was plainly visible at several important junctures. The collision of opposing views was especially evident, for example, during the Euromissile crisis of the first half of the 1980s, as the East German elites went through the same agonizing debate over détente versus confrontation as their Soviet counterparts.

In sum, this book presents a comparative analysis of Soviet and East German policy and policy making with respect to West Germany during a clearly demarcated era in East-West relations. It begins with Soviet and East German efforts to maintain Germany's division in the aftermath of the construction of the Berlin wall; it ends with the failure of those efforts—and of the wall itself—in the final cataclysmic months of 1989. The advent of the 1990s marks the beginning of an entirely new epoch in Moscow's relationship with the German nation. Naturally, no one can predict exactly how this new relationship will evolve. But perhaps we can best appreciate its future possibilities by tracing its emergence from the not so distant past.

CHAPTER ONE

Analyzing Soviet-German Relations

F OR MORE than a century the relationship between Russia and Germany has had a critical impact on the course of war and peace in Europe. On two fateful occasions the strains in their rivalry as expansionist neighbors exploded into open warfare. At other times the achievement of a modus vivendi between the two powers has provided, however transiently, the basis of a more tranquil international order. More often than not, relations between Russia and Germany have occupied a shifting intermediate terrain between belligerence and actual trust. Particularly in the decades from the Bolshevik revolution to Hitler's invasion, the ties between the Soviet Union and a succession of German regimes tended to oscillate between intense confrontation and an almost irresistible proclivity to political, economic, and even military collaboration. The dividing line between these tendencies was often barely discernible; suspicion and duplicity coexisted precariously with the quest for accommodation and mutual advantage. The agreement to establish diplomatic relations reached at Rapallo in 1922 and the Nazi-Soviet pact of 1939, to cite two prominent examples, each fostered a relationship that may be characterized as one of cooperation between enemies or estrangement between partners.

The structure of Soviet-German relations of course changed substantially after World War II. As the international system evolved from world war to cold war, Moscow found itself dealing with two German states instead of one. In the Federal Republic, the Soviets faced an adversary that moved vigorously toward integration in the economic and military alliances of the West. The German Democratic Republic, by contrast, developed under the Kremlin's aegis into a tightly controlled communist party-state, the guarantor of Germany's division, and a forward deployment area for hundreds of thousands of Soviet troops.

Although the political allegiances of the two Germanies were firmly fixed from the earliest stages of the postwar period, the Kremlin's relationships with them were never a simple matter of unrelieved hostility toward West Germany and smooth collaboration with East Germany. At times Soviet leaders held out the hand of cooperation to the FRG, probing Bonn's interest in more harmonious relations and a more direct dialogue. These overtures invariably provoked the ire of the Kremlin's East German comrades, afflicting them with a near-permanent anxiety about the USSR's ultimate intentions in regard to the German question.

These crisscrossing patterns in Moscow's ties with the two Germanies were very much in evidence in the first ten years after the war, when talk of reunification was still in the air. At the Potsdam conference shortly after the Third Reich's surrender, the Soviets sought to retain Germany's status as a "single economic unit," largely in the hope of receiving generous reparations payments. Subsequently, the Kremlin on several occasions appeared to be dangling the prospect of a reunified Germany before the eyes of the West Germans. After a futile exchange of notes that went on for years among the Four Powers, Stalin on March 10, 1952, proposed the creation of a unified but neutral German state that would be allowed to have its own self-defense forces. Neither the Western powers nor Konrad Adenauer's government followed up the offer. Their decision still ignites controversy as to whether the West missed an opportunity to sound out Moscow's readiness for a deal on reunification.[1]

Another Soviet bid on reunification seems to have been in the offing a year later. After Stalin's death, Lavrentii Beria, the erstwhile state security boss, sought to advance his own cause in the Kremlin power struggle by setting the stage for renewed talks with the West on Germany. The scheme backfired before it could take concrete shape. Walter Ulbricht, chief of the SED, resisted Beria's pressures to mollify angry workers as a first step toward improving the atmosphere for negotiations. Ulbricht's intransigence sparked spontaneous workers' demonstrations in East Berlin and elsewhere in the GDR on June 17. Beria's rivals in Moscow quickly called out the tanks, the demonstrators were dispersed, and Beria himself was arrested and shot.[2]

Equally shadowy hints of movement in Moscow's position on the Ger-

---

1. For an example of the "missed opportunity" argument, see Rolf Steininger, *Eine vertane Chance: Die Stalin-Note vom 10. März 1952 und die Wiedervereinigung*, 2d ed. (Bonn: Dietz, 1986). For arguments against the notion that Stalin was seriously interested in reunification at this time, see Marshall D. Shulman, *Stalin's Foreign Policy Reappraised* (New York: Atheneum, 1965), pp. 191–92; Michael J. Sodaro, "France, Russia, and the European Defense Community," *World Affairs* 133 (June 1970): 29–46; and Gerhard Wettig, "Die sowjetische Deutschland-Note vom 10. März 1952: Wiedervereinigungsangebot oder Propagandaaktion?" *Deutschland Archiv*, no. 2, 1982, pp. 130–48.

2. For an insider's account, see Heinz Brandt, *The Search for a Third Way*, trans. Salvator Attanasio (New York: Doubleday, 1970), pp. 184–220.

man question surfaced in the spring of 1955. On the eve of West Germany's admission into NATO, the Kremlin suddenly withdrew its objections to a treaty providing for the withdrawal of occupation forces from Austria and for the creation of an independent and neutral Austrian state. Vague emanations from Moscow suggested that a similar arrangement might be worked out for Germany. Although the Soviets set up the Warsaw Treaty Organization at the same time, they continued to withhold the full legal attributes of sovereignty from the GDR, as if to imply that an agreement on reunification was still possible. When the West failed to pursue the latest Soviet overtures, Khrushchev invited Adenauer to Moscow. Adenauer turned aside the Soviet chief's plea to help him "have done with" the Americans and the Chinese. After several testy conversations, the two leaders agreed to establish diplomatic relations and widen trade ties, but no real détente emerged from the meetings.[3]

It is still not known just how serious Stalin, Beria, and Khrushchev may have been in their gestures toward reunification. In all probability their chief aim was to retard the process of West Germany's military integration into the Western alliance by playing on the West German public's widespread aversion to rearmament and its longings for reunification. Certainly the Soviet leadership never showed any inclination to sacrifice East Germany to the West by accepting Western proposals for reunification on the basis of free elections in both German states. From the time of Beria's ouster in the spring of 1953, if not sooner, Soviet leaders were probably resolved to keep Germany divided as long as they could not reach an agreement on reunification that would ensure at least some role for German communists in an all-German government.

In any event, their attempts to draw Bonn into their ambiguous designs got nowhere. After Adenauer's visit in 1955, relations between Bonn and Moscow settled into a frosty standoff, punctuated by sharpening frictions over Berlin. A lengthy crisis over the divided city began in November 1958 with Khrushchev's threat to sign a separate peace treaty with the GDR and to hand over to the East German government all responsibility for West Berlin. Deteriorating conditions in the GDR heightened Moscow's incentive to do something about the open border between the city's Eastern and Western sectors. Approximately 144,000 people left the GDR in 1959 and nearly 200,000 more followed in 1960. An additional 155,000 East Germans took flight during the first eight months of the following year, bringing the total number of emigrants since 1949 to roughly 2.7 million. The crisis came to a head on August 13, 1961, as East German authorities began installing makeshift barriers along the border with West Berlin. During the

3. Konrad Adenauer, *Erinnerungen, 1953–1955* (Frankfurt: Fischer, 1968), pp. 485–543, esp. 516.

next several months these barriers would take the more glowering shape of the Berlin wall.

With the construction of the wall Germany's partition was complete. Moscow's determination to keep it that way was now beyond dispute. The Soviets clearly regarded Germany's divided status as the bedrock of the international order in Europe and the precondition to peace and security for the socialist states for a long time to come. Even for many people in the West, the stability provided by the division of German was perfectly acceptable; others who deplored the situation increasingly considered it irreversible. Beneath the surface of this apparent stability, however, currents of change were constantly in motion.

For one thing, the West German government consistently refused to accept partition as a permanent condition. The constitution of the Federal Republic, framed in 1949, committed Bonn to seek national unity on behalf of the German people "in free self-determination." This commitment left open the possibility of reestablishing the German state within its borders of 1937, a sprawling geographical entity that would include not only East Germany but the territories taken over in the war's latter stages by the USSR and communist-led Poland. In the absence of a peace conference between the victors and the vanquished to settle the territorial terms of Hitler's defeat, the question of Germany's borders remained legally open as far as Bonn was concerned.

With hopes for reunification at least temporarily dashed at the Berlin wall, West Germany edged toward an accommodation with Moscow and East Berlin in the late 1960s and early 1970s with the aim of keeping the spirit of national unity alive by permitting closer contacts among Germans across the fortified divide. For Moscow, an accommodation of this kind was desirable only as long as it served as a substitute for reunification rather than its prelude. On this assumption, the Brezhnev regime agreed to sweeping trade-offs that opened up the GDR to millions of West German visitors every year and guaranteed the unhindered flow of civilian traffic to West Berlin. Though the SED got over its initial nervousness about these agreements and shared in the widening material benefits of détente, the East German population's expanding contacts with the West were bound to create political difficulties for the East German communist regime over time, eroding its efforts to create an independent national identity among the populace.

Economic factors spurred on these developments. The indisputable superiority of the West German economy gave Bonn considerable leverage in its dealings with Moscow and East Berlin. The chronic economic lability of the Soviet Union and East Germany, by contrast, had a direct impact on their respective policies toward the FRG, driving them ever closer toward economic cooperation with the West and at the same time undermining the

very basis of communist party authority at home. These economic relationships, though perhaps less dramatic than the diplomatic turning points and
confrontations that marked the years from 1963 to 1989, were a vital
source of change in Soviet-German relations throughout this period.

So too was the arms race. Ironically, the military rivalry in Europe
worsened as political and economic cooperation expanded. While NATO
looked to its own defenses, the Soviets primed the competition in weapons
systems with escalating tank and artillery deployments in the 1970s. The
resulting asymmetries in the Warsaw Pact's favor acquired a nuclear dimension with the installation of SS-20 missiles in the western USSR in the
second half of the decade. The Soviet military buildup and NATO's decision
in 1979 to install its own land-based missiles in Europe touched off a spiral
of conflicts between the opposing alliances and also within them. The
protracted Euromissile controversy derailed Moscow's détente with Bonn,
severely damaged Soviet–East German relations, and promoted the growth
of an active peace movement inside the GDR.

All these events helped lay the groundwork for the tumultuous occurrences of 1989. Along the way, they also prompted considerable discussion
and debate in the Soviet Union. How did the Soviets evaluate these processes and assess their policy implications? The search for answers to these
questions will not only reveal a great deal about Soviet policy toward
Germany; it will also clarify the basic factors that have shaped Soviet
foreign policy over the decades and indicate how they relate to the Soviet
political system itself.

Analytical Approaches to Soviet Foreign Policy

What are the driving forces of Soviet foreign policy? The controversy over *how* this question should be addressed has often been just as
spirited as the decades-old debate about what Soviet objectives themselves
actually are. The choice of research strategy is an important one; the
methods we use to investigate the Kremlin's international activities ultimately determine what we are able to find out about the subject and
directly affect the ways we use this information to explain the evolution of
Soviet behavior over time. Which modes of analysis, for example, best
account for the quantum leap in Soviet policy that took place between
Brezhnev and Gorbachev? Of course, few if any observers could have
predicted the astonishing scope of Gorbachev's compromises with the West,
and none but the truly clairvoyant could have foreseen the revolutionary
transformations that occurred in East-Central Europe at the end of 1989.
Still, some analytical approaches are particularly sensitive to the possibility
of change in the Kremlin's policies whereas others lean toward an emphasis
on their continuity.

Most specialists on Moscow's role in world politics can be grouped without too much oversimplification into two broad categories. One stresses the external dimensions of Soviet foreign policy, the other stresses its internal components. This distinction is familiar to students of international politics in terms of the "level-of-analysis" problem.[4]

Analysts who focus on the external aspects of the Soviet Union's international activity have often adopted—however implicitly—one variant or another of what international relations scholars call the "unitary actor" approach to foreign policy analysis. In this approach, the state is treated as a more or less unified whole, and the ruling elite is characterized as acting upon a commonly shared set of interests, goals, and perceptions of the world.

As applied to the Soviet Union, the unitary actor approach is typically more concerned with the outward behavior of the Soviet government in the international arena than with the internal formulation of Moscow's policies. The end product of the Kremlin's foreign policy decision-making process receives greater attention than the process itself. Usually the Soviet leadership is assumed to be essentially united on the USSR's fundamental aims in international affairs. The motivations that guide Soviet actions in this or that instance are frequently imputed to the Soviet government on the basis of certain broad guidelines that are regarded as part and parcel of every Soviet leader's basic world outlook—the historic traditions of Russian nationalism, say, or the "operational code" of Soviet behavior developed under Lenin and Stalin. Some of these analysts maintain that the USSR is basically just like other great powers of the past and present, and is therefore guided by traditional conceptions of realpolitik—such as the quest for security and the drive for power—rather than by ideological predispositions. In their view, the East-West rivalry is primarily a geopolitical conflict that transcends the obvious ideological differences.[5]

---

4. Seminal works on the level-of-analysis problem include Kenneth Waltz, *Man, the State, and War* (New York: Columbia University Press, 1959); David Singer, "The Level-of-Analysis Problem in International Relations," in *The International System*, ed. Klaus Knorr and Sidney Verba, pp. 77–92; (Princeton: Princeton University Press, 1961); and Graham T. Allison, *Essence of Decision* (Boston: Little, Brown, 1971).

5. Particularly representative of the externally oriented approach to the study of Soviet foreign policy are the works of Adam B. Ulam, esp. *Expansion and Coexistence* (New York: Praeger, 1968) and *Dangerous Relations: The Soviet Union in World Politics, 1970–1982* (New York: Oxford University Press, 1983). For an example of the view that the Soviet Union behaves like a typical great power, see Barry R. Posen, "Competing Images of the Soviet Union," *World Politics* 39 (July 1987): 579–97. Another work that stresses the great-power elements in Soviet policy and minimizes the impact of divergent foreign policy viewpoints in the Soviet elite, while relegating ideological considerations to a secondary level of importance, is Zbigniew Brzezinski, *Game Plan* (Boston: Atlantic Monthly Press, 1986). Henry Kissinger has also stressed the continuities in Soviet foreign policy, defining the USSR as a revolutionary power bent on achieving absolute security. See, e.g., *Nuclear Weapons and Foreign Policy* (New York: Harper, 1957), pp. 2–3, 325, 358–59; *American Foreign Policy* (New York: Norton, 1969), pp. 87–89; *Washington Post*, December 20, 1988, p. A25.

As a consequence, some scholars who take the unitary actor approach tend to accentuate the continuities in the Soviet Union's international orientation. Such themes as the tenacity of Moscow's hostility to the West, its periodic need for cooperation, its gnawing sense of vulnerability, and its aggressive impulse toward expansionism frequently emerge from analyses of this kind as the enduring hallmarks of Soviet policy.

While virtually all of the specialists who concentrate on the Kremlin's external activities readily agree that differences have of course been manifest in the foreign policies of such diverse figures as Lenin and Stalin, or Brezhnev and Gorbachev, many tend to attribute these variations to tactical shifts necessitated by changing international realities, or to idiosyncratic factors rooted in an individual leader's personal style. On the whole, however, these dissimilarities are regarded as less important than the underlying consistencies in Soviet strategy and behavior which serve to link one generation of Soviet leaders with another.

Moreover, the central focus of the unitary actor approach is on the actual behavior of the leading foreign policy decision makers rather than on their articulated perceptions of the world; actions, in this view, tend to speak louder than words. To the extent that words matter at all, the unitary actor method is concerned primarily with official pronouncements that have an immediate bearing on specific policy issues. Considerably less attention is accorded to the views of lower-level political officials, academicians, journalists, or other Soviet foreign policy specialists who are not immediately involved in the day-to-day conduct of foreign affairs. More generally, domestic influences on foreign policy tend to be given short shrift. Scholars who take the unitary actor approach may acknowledge linkages between international undertakings and domestic concerns, but they rarely explore such factors in depth.

The second group of experts emphasize the internal factors that go into the making of Soviet foreign policy decisions. Here the main accent falls on the pulls and tugs of the political process, which is often characterized, in the Soviet Union as in most states, by conflict, bargaining, coalition building, and prolonged indecisiveness on the part of the regime's decision-making elite. Not surprisingly, analyses of this type frequently stress the diversity of attitudes and policy preferences to be observed among Soviet leaders and other influential members of the foreign policy establishment. Though these scholars recognize the limits to policy differentiation in the Soviet Union imposed by historical and ideological factors, not to mention the censorship system, they nevertheless believe that there has always been greater room for disagreement and debate within the Soviet hierarchy than the unitary actor approach is likely to uncover. Evidence of such disagreement, to be sure, has been particularly apparent in the Gorbachev years, as the Soviet leadership has thrown open the doors to far greater public discussion of foreign policy issues than was possible at any other time in the recent past. Even in the pre-Gorbachev era, however, some Western scholars succeeded in peeling back the layers of mystification that enshrouded policy discussions and revealed considerable differentiation in the views of the Soviet elite on major foreign policy issues.

On the assumption that Soviet leaders, like their counterparts in other political systems, are able to choose from a panoply of policy options in pursuit of generally agreed-upon national and ideological interests, these scholars have employed a variety of analytical methods designed to spotlight divergences among key members of the Soviet elite. Some have focused exclusively on differences among the top leaders, using time-honored Kremlinological techniques. Others have used formal decision-making models to investigate such things as the connection between the views of various decision makers and their respective bureaucratic functions, or the risk-taking propensities of Soviet leaders. Others have extended the sweep of the analysis still further by examining the publications of prominent Soviet international relations scholars or journalists. And some scholars have made explicit efforts to examine additional domestic influences, particularly economic factors, on the formulation of Soviet foreign policy.[6]

The scholars in question invariably recognize that the Soviets whose views they are analyzing have been staunch defenders of Soviet interests, and rose to prominence largely by virtue of their professed adherence to certain prevailing axioms of Soviet foreign and domestic policy. Still, they assume that signs of disagreement among these key figures indicate genuine alternatives in the elaboration and conduct of Soviet foreign policy. When, for example, some Soviets appear to line up in favor of arms control with the West while others seem to be opposed; when some strike a militant stance with respect to Third World conflicts while others point out the disadvantages of the use of force—such evidences of divided counsels within the Soviet elite have been interpreted as signs that change in the direction of Moscow's foreign policy has always been possible.

As a consequence, many specialists associated with this second analytical approach attach considerable importance to the *perceptions* of international politics articulated in public forums by Soviet leaders and other

6. Examples of the Kremlinological approach include Carl A. Linden, *Khrushchev and the Soviet Leadership, 1957–1964* (Baltimore: Johns Hopkins University Press, 1966), and Michel Tatu, *Power in the Kremlin: From Khrushchev to Kosygin* (New York: Viking, 1969). The bureaucratic model has been applied by, among others, Jiri Valenta in *Soviet Intervention in Czechoslovakia, 1968* (Baltimore: Johns Hopkins University Press, 1979). For case studies of Soviet risk-taking, see Hannes Adomeit, *Soviet Risk-Taking and Crisis Behavior* (London: George Allen & Unwin, 1982). On the linkage between foreign and domestic policy, see Seweryn Bialer, ed., *The Domestic Context of Soviet Foreign Policy* (Boulder, Colo.: Westview, 1981); also Morton Schwartz, *The Foreign Policy of the USSR: Domestic Factors* (Encino, Calif.: Dickenson, 1975).

relevant members of the elite. What the Soviets say about the world is as useful a guide to the Kremlin's future behavior as what they do in actual practice.

While studies in this second category often feature finely detailed analyses of decision-making cases or elite perceptions, at times they are subject to the limitations that arise from the standard division of scholarly labor. Studies of Soviet decision-making, for example, usually concentrate on the top leaders. Only rarely do they take into account the views of academicians and other experts who may be at some remove from the corridors of power but who usually offer more elaborate rationales for Soviet policy in their publications than may be found in the utterances of the leading decision makers themselves. Case studies of Soviet decision-making also frequently focus on a narrow time frame, usually on a specific crisis confronting the leadership. Conversely, many analysts of elite perceptions confine themselves to elucidating the writings of Soviet scholars or journalists, but they do not seek to relate the various views they find in these sources to the perceptions and actual policy decisions of the Kremlin leadership. Lacking this policy-specific focus, they generally do not use the perceptions they analyze to explain a particular sequence of events.[7]

In other words, we have studies of policy decisions that do not look at perceptions and studies of perceptions that do not look at specific policies; we have studies that concentrate on the top decision makers and studies that focus exclusively on academicians. What we need is an attempt to unite these separate approaches. Specifically, we need to clarify the relationship between two key components of the Soviet (and East German) foreign policy elites: the leading decision makers (or the *primary* foreign policy elite), on the one hand, and lower-level officials, academicians, and journalists (the *secondary* elite), on the other.

Until 1990, the primary foreign policy elite consisted of the leading members of the Politburo and the Secretariat who had a special interest in foreign policy. The foreign minister and the defense minister are also included in this group, even if at times they did not happen to serve on these powerful party organs. The secondary elite includes Central Committee members, Foreign Ministry officials below the level of the minister himself, senior military officers, foreign trade functionaries, and the like. It also

7. For an example of a study of the relationship between Soviet behavior and the perceptions of Soviet decision makers, see Richard K. Hermann, *Perceptions and Behavior in Soviet Foreign Policy* (Pittsburgh: University of Pittsburgh Press, 1985). For examples of studies that focus on the perceptions of Soviet academicians, see Jerry F. Hough, *The Struggle for the Third World* (Washington: Brookings, 1986), and Gilbert Rozman, *A Mirror for Socialism* (Princeton: Princeton University Press, 1985). For a study treating the perceptions of Soviet military writers, see Mark N. Katz, *The Third World in Soviet Military Thought* (Baltimore: Johns Hopkins University Press, 1982).

includes important academicians who were usually connected with major international affairs research institutes in Moscow and East Berlin, such as the Soviet Union's Institute of the World Economy and International Relations (IMEMO) and the former Institute for International Relations in the GDR. The main journalists of interest are foreign affairs specialists who wrote for the leading daily and weekly newspapers. As a general rule, the members of the secondary elite who were in a position to write or speak out in public on foreign policy matters were sufficiently important that their views may be regarded as having a quasi-official character.

The connection between the primary and secondary elements of the Soviet foreign policy establishment has long been a subject of lively interest to analysts of Soviet foreign policy, but it has rarely been probed systematically.[8] Did the specialized literature produced by Soviet international affairs scholars and seasoned correspondents in the years between Khrushchev and Gorbachev have any relevance at all to what Soviet leaders actually did when they conducted foreign policy? Under what circumstances were foreign policy debates in the open press likely to flourish, and under what circumstances were they more likely to be circumscribed or channeled in officially desired directions? Such questions require us to be as specific as possible in delineating how foreign policy decisions taken at the highest levels of political power in the Soviet Union were related to the voluminous writings churned out by less highly placed foreign policy specialists.

In fact, throughout the period from 1963 to 1989 the views of Soviet (and, for that matter, East German) secondary elites provided a reasonably accurate indication of the opinions and policy alternatives under discussion at the very highest levels of political power. As a rule, disagreements on relevant foreign policy issues were most likely to surface among the secondary elite when the leading decision makers themselves were divided, or at least uncertain, about the directions they should follow and the policy choices they should make.

Of course, it is never possible to peer directly into the inner sanctum of policy discussions in Moscow or East Berlin, nor can we determine on the basis of published accounts exactly who said what to whom, or which academician or lower-level functionary influenced the views of which political leaders. While it is generally known that some members of the secondary elite are more influential than others, and may advise Kremlin political

---

8. For opinions on the relationship between academicians and policy makers in the Soviet Union, see William Zimmerman, *Soviet Perspectives on International Relations* (Princeton: Princeton University Press, 1969); Oded Eran, *Mezhdunarodniki* (Ramat Gan, Israel: Turtledove, 1979); Hough, *Struggle for the Third World*; Seweryn Bialer, *The Soviet Paradox* (New York: Knopf, 1986), pp. 294–95; Margot Light, *The Soviet Theory of International Relations* (New York: St. Martin's Press, 1988); and Allen Lynch, *The Soviet Study of International Relations* (Cambridge: Cambridge University Press, 1988).

leaders or Foreign Ministry officials, the details of these and other aspects of the "organizational process" in communist systems have usually been hidden from public view. This is one reason that it is extremely difficult to construct detailed representations of the Soviet foreign-policy-making process on the basis of interest-group theory or formal models of bureaucratic politics, efforts that will not be undertaken here.[9] Evidence of a connection between the opinions of the secondary elite and those of the primary elite is therefore indirect at best.

Our understanding of the views of the secondary elite is further clouded by the fact that these people, no matter how important, have not always been free to speak their minds in public; quite frequently—even in the relatively open atmosphere of the Gorbachev era—they must articulate the foreign policy line laid down by the Soviet leadership, even when they do not necessarily agree with it. As a general rule, the members of the secondary elite must fulfill two separate functions simultaneously. On the one hand, they are expected to be *advisers* to the political hierarchy, to provide the decision makers with objective analyses of the world situation and their own carefully considered recommendations for action. On the other hand, they are also expected to be *propagandists* (or apologists) for the prevailing policy line. Obviously, this duality of functions presents serious problems for the outside observer. As we shall see, however, clearly differentiated views among the secondary elite can indeed be discerned even when these differences are expressed in terms that do not directly challenge the main tenets of the official policy. The nature of esoteric communications in communist political systems permits people particularly skilled in its techniques to say one thing while appearing to say something else. As a consequence, some members of the secondary elite who at one time appeared to espouse one set of policies (the confrontationist course of the Brezhnev regime, for example) can emerge later on as advocates of a quite different set of options (such as Gorbachev's radical détente policy). A close examination of their writings and statements over the years, however, sometimes reveals greater consistency in their views over time than appeared at first glance. Especially when the primary elite itself is unsure of its course, members of the secondary elite have greater latitude to make their own policy preferences known in public, so long as they are careful not to reject directly the ruling hierarchy's chosen policy.

Despite the difficulties of obtaining hard information about the way foreign policy is formulated in communist systems (even in the considerably improved conditions of Gorbachev's more democratized political system),

9. For a review of writings on interest groups in the Soviet Union, see H. Gordon Skilling, "Interest Groups and Communist Politics Revisited," *World Politics* 36 (October 1983): 1–27. An extended treatment of the Soviet foreign policy process is provided in Vernon Aspaturian, *Process and Power in Soviet Foreign Policy* (Boston: Little, Brown, 1971).

we can still ascertain a great deal about the main assumptions, rationales, and alternative orientations underlying the policies of Soviet and East German decision makers by examining what the foreign policy elites in these countries have had to say about the relevant issues. What they say, in short, is just as important as what they do. It is equally possible to reconstruct the argumentation behind various policy choices from documentation in open sources. The pronouncements of the leaders themselves have always offered important clues as to their own basic attitudes and policy preferences, while the statements of the secondary elite have generally served as a semiofficial sounding board for various arguments and options that have been considered acceptable within the foreign policy establishment.

All of these considerations ultimately boil down to a single issue: Which method—the unitary actor approach or the elite differentiation approach—better explains Soviet (or East German) policy toward West Germany in the years 1963–1989? Basically the unitary actor method seems to be more suited to picking out those elements of continuity that remained visible in Soviet and East German policies in this period. Fears of a resurgent Germany and lingering mistrust of the capitalist West, for example, were much in evidence in those years.

The unitary actor approach is far less useful, however, when we try to account for variations in Soviet and East German policies. Although these variations may have been limited in scope, in fact there were clear differences between Khrushchev and Brezhnev and between Ulbricht and Honecker in their attitudes and actions with regard to the FRG. Even more strikingly, the policies of these leaders differed fundamentally from the approach adopted by Mikhail Gorbachev. These shifts in policy, whether modest or radical, did not occur spontaneously; all of them were rooted in discussions and debates among the primary and secondary elites of the Soviet Union and the GDR which took place throughout the entire period.

A full explication of Soviet and East German policy orientations therefore requires more than just a passing overview of these states' enduring national interests. It requires, to the greatest possible extent, an investigation of the internal process by which foreign policy was formulated, centering on policy differentiation among the relevant elites.

Explaining Foreign Policy in Moscow and East Berlin: External and Domestic Variables

All states must act within the context of an international system that they cannot entirely control. Geographical constants, the size and power of other states, and the structures of alliances and other multistate institutions are among the principal facts of life that any state must contend with as it shapes its international policies. Thus the policies of the Soviet Union and the GDR toward West Germany were always influenced by a host of external variables. These variables included the Federal Republic's economic and military potential; the domestic and foreign policy inclinations of its ruling elites and public opinion; the massive presence of the Atlantic alliance, and especially of the United States; and the impact of West Germany's relations with such sensitive areas as Eastern Europe and China. And of course the East Germans were deeply influenced by what the Soviets wanted, while the Soviets had to take the GDR's interests and attitudes into account in most questions pertaining to relations with West Germany.

While these features of the external setting necessarily conditioned Soviet and East German policy toward the FRG, there was nothing automatic about the way the ruling elites in Moscow and East Berlin responded to them. Although the USSR, like any other state, may always possess certain "objective" interests, such as the maintenance of security and the promotion of national ideals and well-being, those interests are ultimately defined and pursued by individual leaders. The leaders' *perceptions* of the international scene therefore play a critically important role in the shaping of most foreign policy decisions.[10] As the leaders change, perceptions and policies may change also. The importance of the leaders' attitudes underscores the fundamental significance of domestic factors in the elaboration of Moscow's foreign policy.

On the whole, the diplomatic and military dimensions of Soviet and East German policy toward the Federal Republic from 1963 to the end of 1989 can best be explained with reference to three interrelated variables: first, the nature of the decision-making regimes in Moscow and East Berlin; second, elite perceptions of the Federal Republic and of the FRG's role in East-West relations; and third, the main directions of Soviet and East German international economic policy, particularly as they relate to economic ties with West Germany. In one way or another, each of these variables is rooted in the internal system of the Soviet Union and the GDR. The nature of the decision-making regime is determined by the organization and policy orientations of the political leadership at the highest echelon; elite perceptions reflect discussions and disagreements within the foreign policy establishment, including the secondary elites; and East-West trade policy is intimately connected with domestic economic development strategy, and particularly with the vital question of economic reform.

A fourth variable is also relevant to Soviet and East German policy toward West Germany; namely, public opinion. Unfortunately, precious

---

10. On the importance of perceptions, see Robert Jervis, *Perception and Misperception in International Politics* (Princeton: Princeton University Press, 1976).

few data have ever been collected on popular attitudes toward Germany in the USSR.[11] The East German situation, however, has always been more transparent. Even before the explosion of unrest at the end of 1989, the population's impact on the government's foreign policy was significantly more acute in the GDR than in the Soviet Union. As Germans, the citizens of the GDR have always had an emotional stake in the improvement of inter-German ties. For many years before the Berlin wall was breached, growing numbers of East German dissidents, peace activists, youthful protesters, and ordinary citizens determined to leave the country looked to West Germany for support of one form or another, thereby compounding the pressures on the GDR's political authorities. These pressures could not help but exert some influence on the way East Germany's ruling elite conducted its policies toward the FRG.

The same four domestic variables, albeit in a more complicated fashion, also have a direct impact on foreign policy decisions in noncommunist systems, including Western democracies. Because of their particular salience in the Soviet Union and the GDR, however, the first three of these factors will occupy our attention here.

Decision-Making Regimes

That Soviet foreign policy is often a function of who is in charge in the Kremlin is a fact that has been amply demonstrated. The policy preferences and priorities of the top leader, the scope and limitations of his authority to pursue those objectives, and the influence of various bureaucratic players in the policy-making game (particularly the military) are among the factors that analysts have singled out as having a crucial bearing on the way the Soviet ship of state charts its course across the high seas of international politics. As some scholars have indicated, however, we need to systematize our approach to the connection between politics in the Kremlin and the Kremlin's behavior in international politics. In particular, we need to devise analytical categories and to formulate hypotheses designed to increase the level of generalization in regard to this critical nexus between power and policy.[12] This need has become all the more pressing in recent years, inasmuch as the amazing transformations in Soviet domestic

11. For public opinion surveys of Soviet attitudes toward West Germany, see Klaus Liedtke, *Der neue Flirt* (Hamburg: Stern, 1989).

12. One approach to this problem concluded that key aspects of Moscow's foreign policy behavior (such as policy consistency, coherence, responsiveness, and risk-taking) vary with the way power is distributed at the top of the Kremlin decision-making hierarchy. See Philip G. Roeder, "Soviet Policies and Kremlin Politics," *International Studies Quarterly*, vol. 28, no. 2 (June 1984), pp. 171–93.

and foreign policy engineered by Mikhail Gorbachev cannot be fully comprehended unless they are embedded within a fairly broad historical and analytical framework.

To begin with, variations in the conduct and public discussion of Soviet and East German foreign policy toward West Germany from 1963 to 1989 can be explained with reference to variations in the decision-making regimes. The first of these regimes may be called the *directive* decision-making regime. It is distinguished exclusively by the distribution of decision-making authority at the top. In fact, power in this regime is not so much distributed as it is monopolized by a single dominant leader who is able to impose his will on the party and state hierarchies. Though the leader may not necessarily be a dictator in the most literal sense, his authority in most areas of high policy is paramount, and his political predominance within the ruling hierarchy is virtually unchallengeable.

The other regimes are all characterized by a greater degree of power sharing among the leaders. In essence, they may be thought of as communist-style coalition governments. Each is composed of individuals who are joined together on the basis of certain common interests and outlooks but who may nevertheless differ on specific policies, whether for reasons of personal political "philosophy," bureaucratic self-interest, rivalry for power, or other considerations. The main distinction among these more collectively organized regimes lies in their predominant political orientation. Accordingly, they may be labeled the *conservative,* the *centrist,* and the *reformist* coalition regimes.

Although communist coalition regimes have been fundamentally oligarchic, they have by no means been leaderless. Communist political tradition places a high premium on personal authority. One individual (usually the chief of the party) has invariably emerged as the first among equals within the ruling coalition. As such, he has generally been accorded sufficient leeway by his colleagues to set the agenda for domestic policy and to pursue his preferred foreign policy initiatives. The party leader's discretion in these matters of high policy is usually further enhanced as he consolidates his power within the main organs of party and state.

What distinguishes the coalition regime from the directive regime is mainly the degree of the leader's power and authority. Coalitions tend to place tighter limits on the leader's primacy within the ruling hierarchy than directive regimes do, forcing the party chief to take full account of the views of the other members of the hierarchy when he shapes his policies. The party chief who heads a coalition regime does not always get his way. To an extent that varies with circumstances, coalition regimes also retain a greater ability than directive regimes to depose the party chief through internal political cabals. In sum, whereas directive regimes are built around the unquestioned authority of a preeminent leader, coalitions strike a greater balance between the efficiency of one-person rule and the informal checks and balances of collective leadership.

The prevailing political coloration of a coalition regime—whether conservative, centrist, or reformist—is therefore the result of a dynamic interaction between the leader's personal predilections and the collective's general consensus. The leader generally sets the tone for the regime's main political orientation. By definition, however, coalitions are multihued bodies that include individuals representing various shadings along the political spectrum. Centrists and even conservatives, for example, may thus participate in coalitions led by reform-minded leaders. What matters most in affixing the proper label to particular coalitions is the *predominant* tendency that emerges over time from the decisions taken by the governing elite. A coalition need not always be characterized by an exclusive tendency shared by all members of the Politburo and Secretariat.

As a consequence, the differences separating coalition regimes that are predominantly conservative, centrist, or reformist need not be very great. All of them, for example, have sought to retain the power of the communist party at home to the greatest possible degree, a task that even so radical a reformer as Gorbachev endeavored to pursue during his first few years in power, even as he transformed the party and opened up the political process to unprecedented levels of democratization.

In the realm of foreign policy, the various regimes that governed the Soviet Union and the GDR from 1963 to 1989 all hewed to the same general foreign policy strategy that had prevailed in Moscow since the 1920s: peaceful coexistence. Reduced to its essentials, peaceful coexistence was a policy of living with the West while at the same time opposing it. As sanctioned by Lenin himself, peaceful coexistence combined elements of both cooperation and rivalry in relations with the capitalist states, a combination that inevitably produced varying degrees of ambivalence and incoherence in Moscow's (and East Berlin's) foreign policy. Though Soviet and East German leaders differed in their tactical applications of this strategy, peaceful coexistence provided the overarching strategic rationale guiding foreign policy makers in the Soviet Union and the GDR throughout this period, up until the East European revolutions of 1989.

When all due account is taken of the similarities that narrow the gaps between these various regime types, the fact remains that identifiable differences indeed separated them. At times these differences were slight, representing merely a matter of degree or emphasis; at times they were quite substantial. Whatever the case, the distinctions that divided one decision-making regime from another made for noticeable variations both in the substance of their policy orientations and in key features of their decision-making processes.

The various decision-making regimes differed most strikingly with respect to four particular aspects of foreign policy activity. The first is the manner in which a given decision-making regime defined the *scope of détente*. Détente has traditionally been a tactical adaptation of peaceful coexistence strategy. As pursued by the Soviet and East German regimes, it represented above all an attempt to seek an accommodation with the West on outstanding political and military issues and to enlarge the possibilities of economic cooperation. In keeping with the tenets of peaceful coexistence, however, détente also implied a lingering undercurrent of conflict. Precisely how much cooperation and how much conflict the Soviet Union and the GDR were willing to pursue in their relations with the West (and above all with West Germany) varied from one regime to the next. The second factor that differentiated the foreign policy proclivities of the various decision-making regimes is *responsiveness* (or adaptability)—the decision makers' ability to recognize changes in the international environment and to adjust their policies accordingly. The third factor is *willingness to compromise* with foreign governments, and the fourth is *openness to internal debate*. This last factor is especially important in clarifying the relationship between decisions and perceptions in Soviet foreign policy. To place these factors in clearer perspective, let us look briefly at some of the ways in which they relate to the decision-making regimes.

As a result of the overwhelming power it confers on a single leader, a *directive* decision-making regime may move in any political direction its leader wishes—reformist, centrist, conservative, or any variant of them. With the final word on policy matters held indisputably by one individual, both the content of policy and the style of the policy-making process ultimately depend on the supreme leader. It is he who determines the regime's definition of the scope of détente. The degree of responsiveness displayed by this type of regime also rests largely on the leader's shoulders. If he is a resourceful and flexible person, his regime may be as responsive as any other; but if he is dedicated to the compulsive pursuit of an idée fixe, the result may be an exceptionally low level of adaptability and an equally diminished willingness to compromise with other governments, whether adversaries or allies. Furthermore, a leader driven by an exclusionary policy vision that admits of no alternatives is prone to close off public debate on the issues. Members of the primary and secondary elites are then reduced to parroting the official wisdom as proclaimed by the leader.

Walter Ulbricht's government was a prototypical directive regime. While Ulbricht was always limited in his options (as well as in his personal power) by what the Soviets were willing to allow, the primacy of the German communist leader was unchallenged within the leadership of the Socialist Unity Party of Germany from the late 1950s until shortly before his dismissal in 1971.

The reigning consensus in a *conservative* decision-making coalition in the period examined here rests on individuals and bureaucratic agencies devoted to the preservation of the domestic institutional status quo in its neo-Stalinist variant. Insistence on the party's monopoly of power, respect for the canons of central planning, and intolerance of dissent are among its chief internal characteristics. The representatives of this type of regime are united in their dedication to the unassailability of the leadership's authority at home and to the enhancement of Soviet power in the world. Most important, a cardinal element of the conservative regime is the enormous deference accorded to the military hierarchy. Though the military may not have veto power over all major foreign policy activities (and though members of the military establishment may differ on matters of policy), the wishes of the defense community are given exceptional weight in this type of regime whenever issues bearing on security policy come up.

The party leader himself may be either a centrist or an unreconstructed hard-liner; whatever the case, he is certainly not a reformer. His basic inclination is to make sure that the government's principal policy choices are acceptable to the more conservative members of the ruling coalition. He may at times have to do some bargaining and logrolling, but even so, the leader's personal predilections are not so far removed from those of the conservatives that internal compromises are unreachable.

The definition of détente agreed upon by a conservative coalition therefore tends to include, rather than repudiate, some of the more hard-nosed features of the conservatives' world view. The result can be a fairly high level of incoherence in the regime's foreign policy, at least as it appears to the outside world. The coalition's commitment to promoting a robust military development program, for example, may run counter to its formally stated desire for political and economic cooperation with the West.

Conservative regimes are not by nature incapable of adapting to observable changes in the international environment, nor are they averse to compromise. Both their responsiveness and their readiness to grant concessions, however, are subject to the limitations imposed by their reluctance to undertake major alterations in the status quo at Soviet expense, or to countenance a perceived diminution of Soviet power. Thus conservative decision-making coalitions may find it difficult to change course in the face of new opportunities or impending failures that demand a reevaluation of the main tenets of the prevailing consensus. These regimes may also be resistant to compromises that overstep the boundaries of the conservatives' most cherished principles.

Public discussion of policy issues in a conservative regime may be welcomed, but, as in other areas of the regime's operations, the field of tolerated activity is fairly narrow. Discussions of foreign policy issues must therefore confine themselves to opinions and options deemed acceptable by the decision makers. Policy debates may still go on within these prescribed parameters, but once the coalition's basic foreign policy orientation and its definition of the international situation is fixed, some academicians and journalists may tend to adjust their positions to conform with the official line. (Whether they do so independently of outside pressures or in response to instructions from above may be impossible to determine). If, as seems likely, the attenuation of open policy debate reduces the policy makers' ability to consider new ideas or policy approaches at variance with the prevailing consensus, the entire foreign policy establishment may end up saying and hearing only what the decision makers prefer to believe.

In sum, a conservative decision-making regime's paramount advantage over other regimes may be its ability to project strength both at home and abroad. Its chief deficiency may turn out to be that, when faced with mounting difficulties or new opportunities, it may not be able to adapt, back down, or even learn. The Brezhnev coalition constitutes a vivid example of this type of regime.

A *reformist* coalition in our period is defined by the determination of the principal leader and his closest allies within the leadership to make significant changes in Soviet policies. These changes necessarily concentrate on the domestic political system for the most part, but shifts in foreign policy soon become intertwined with them. Above all, a reformist regime may require a period of calm in the international environment (a *peredyshka*, or breathing spell) so that it may turn its attention more fully to the difficult business of bringing about internal transformations. In addition, reforms centering on the Soviet economy may require an expansion of trade and other economic contacts with the industrialized democracies. A redirection of resources to consumer-related sectors may require more stringent limits on military spending than a conservative regime would contemplate. These considerations, as well as a host of related ones, increase the Kremlin's willingness to seek compromises with its principal adversaries.

For the same reasons, a reformist decision-making regime also tends to take advantage of changes in the behavior of other states to promote a less hostile international climate, thus increasing its responsiveness. Meanwhile, a reformist regime is the most likely of these decision-making regimes to encourage a vigorous open discussion of policy-related issues, including matters of foreign policy. Although the reformist leadership may at times manipulate or censor such discussion with a view to promoting its own agenda for change, the range of what is permissible to enunciate in public forums is much wider than it is under other decision-making coalitions. Quite obviously, Mikhail Gorbachev's ruling coalition constitutes a prime example of the reformist type of decision-making regime.

The *centrist* decision-making regime is defined by the simple fact that it is situated between the conservative and reformist regimes. Though its exact complexion may vary from case to case, usually the centrist coalition combines relatively conservative political leaders with others who are either reform-minded, or, at the very least, highly flexible in their approach to domestic or foreign policy. Neither wing has an inalienable veto privilege in matters of high policy. The linchpin of this type of regime is an adaptable party leader who seeks to gain the confidence of both of these broadly defined groups by forging working majorities on policy decisions as they arise. The danger invariably arises, however, that—unless the party leader is particularly adroit at this kind of consensus building—the delicate balance that holds the centrist coalition together may collapse and oppositionist factions may conspire against the leader himself.

The definition of détente by a centrist regime in the 1963–1989 period tends to place roughly equal accents on cooperation and conflict with the West. The advantages of political and economic collaboration with Western states are counterbalanced by continuing reliance on ideological self-assertion and military strength. What most distinguishes a centrist regime, however, is that it consciously seeks to avoid the extremes to which the others may gravitate. A centrist regime eschews both the highly militarized, confrontationist foreign policy of the conservatives and the domestic reforms and accommodationist foreign policies of the reformists. Such policy extremes narrow the range of the centrist regime's foreign policy maneuver (in the case of confrontation) and threaten to disturb its domestic stability and international strength (in the case of reformism).

By virtue of these defining features, centrist coalitions should display a relatively high level of responsiveness and willingness to compromise with foreign governments. Indeed, the hallmark of the centrist regime is its ability to shift course whenever realities make a change in direction mandatory or desirable. What keeps these zigzags and apparent inconsistencies from getting out of hand is the fact that the center of political gravity in this type of regime is, precisely, the center. The span of opinion is not very wide from one end of the coalition to the other. Change, when it comes, tends to be marginal.

Open policy debate in a centrist regime should tend to reflect the alternative viewpoints considered acceptable by the members of the coalition. Foreign policy discussion, in particular, would presumably provide rationales for various policy choices under consideration by a decision-making elite that, within the limits specified by its centrist consensus, wishes to keep its options open.

Finally, some centrist regimes may gravitate more toward the conservative side of the spectrum, while others may lean more toward the reformist side. Nikita Khrushchev's regime provides a good example of a centrist-reformist coalition, while Erich Honecker's tenure as chief of the SED exemplifies the centrist-conservative type of coalition regime.

The terms "conservative," "centrist" and "reformist" are by no means intended to stand for absolute categories. They represent general tendencies and patterns, not rigid positions fixed in concrete. Like the terms "left," "center," and "right" as applied to Western political orientations, they are relational, representing points along a spectrum. Just as, in the West, some right-wingers may be more rightist than others, so some Soviet or East German conservatives may be more conservative than others. (In many respects, Ulbricht was more conservative than Brezhnev, who in turn was somewhat less conservative than certain members of his governing coalition. Gorbachev after a few years in power emerged as a considerably more radical reformer than Khrushchev.) Moreover, some individuals or coalitions may shift ground over time (usually only slightly), presenting themselves as more conservative or more reformist in some periods than in others.

The ability of any of these decision-making regimes to conduct an effective foreign policy depends to no small extent on the degree of its internal stability. A stable regime finds it easier to conceptualize and carry out an agreed-upon policy than one rent by constant disputes. By the same token, each of these regime types may traverse a series of phases, starting with a formative period, in which the internal distribution of power and its predominant political orientation are still taking shape, and continuing through a more mature period (one marked by greater stability) before proceeding on to a phase of degeneration, in which the prevailing premises of power and policy come undone.

These processes of genesis and decline may trigger tendencies of their own that affect the regime's approach to foreign policy. During either their formative or their degenerative phase, for example, coalition regimes can be expected to exhibit a low degree of clarity in their conception of East-West relations, a low degree of responsiveness to outside stimuli, and a corresponding reluctance to compromise. This occurs because the details of power sharing and policy direction have yet to be worked out in the initial phase of development, while these very details, which hold the coalition together during its mature stage, are increasingly called into question as the coalition falls apart. Open policy debate, however, may rise in either of these two phases, as the coalition in the making surveys the available options and the coalition in decline is no longer certain of its purposes. A directive regime has similar problems, but the precise way they are managed depends in the final analysis on the political authority and style of the leader.

These phase-related tendencies may reinforce the more mature characteristics of a decision-making regime in some instances and may counteract them in others. Thus a conservative coalition that already exhibits a relatively reduced willingness to compromise on certain international issues while at the peak of its power may become even less inclined to make major concessions as its internal coalescence evaporates. By contrast, a reformist regime that manifests a high willingness to compromise once it has firmly consolidated its domestic position may not be ready for serious compromises at the initial stages of its development or may become incapable of making them if it begins to disintegrate into warring factions. Indeed, a reformist regime is probably more susceptible to instability than any of the others, precisely because its very raison d'être is its resolve to alter existing structures in which entrenched political forces have a personal stake.

The decision-making regimes we have just examined have all had one thing in common: the communist party's monopoly of power. Although the Communist Party of the Soviet Union (CPSU) still dominates the political process in the USSR, it is increasingly factionalized and noncommunist elements are becoming ever more vocal. How the Soviet system develops over the coming years can only be a matter of conjecture, especially as new political institutions (such as the executive presidency) come into being and the prospect of a multiparty electoral system looms on the horizon. Even if the CPSU loses its preeminent place in the political system, however, it remains quite possible that decision making in the USSR will continue to follow some variant or another of the regimes described here. At least at the executive level of government, decisions are likely to be taken by some form of coalition regime (unless a heavy-handed dictator usurps power) and the policy directions the leaders choose may still be identifiable, *mutatis mutandis,* as predominantly conservative, centrist, or reformist. In all likelihood, therefore, the concept of decision-making regimes will continue to be applicable to the Soviet political system for an indefinite period of time.[13]

Perceptions of the FRG and Its Role in East-West Relations

What have been the aims of Soviet policy toward West Germany? This question invariably aroused controversy in the years before Gorbachev came to power, and divergent views on the subject continued to

13. These decision-making regimes and the policy orientations that define them can also be applied to other states that have been ruled by communist parties. Directive regimes include those headed by Stalin, Ceausescu, Castro, and Kim Il-sung. Conservative coalitions may be found in various East European countries after the postwar communist takeover of power, in Czechoslovakia before 1968 and between the Soviet invasion and the end of 1989, and in Vietnam until the second half of the 1980s. Centrist coalitions include various Polish regimes between 1956 and the elections of 1989, Kadar's regime in Hungary, China under Deng Xiaoping and Vietnam by the late 1980s. Reformist coalitions include the regimes that briefly held power before the Soviet invasions of Hungary in 1956 and Czechoslovakia in 1968, and Hungary again by the late 1980s.

surface even after Gorbachev embarked on his energetic détente and disarmament programs. Western specialists who have addressed it have come up with several alternative responses. One general tendency is to view Soviet policy toward Bonn, especially in the pre-Gorbachev period, as essentially hostile and manipulative. Some proponents of this view maintain that Soviet leaders have long sought to detach West Germany completely from its alliance with the United States, above all by achieving the withdrawal of American military forces from the Federal Republic. With this goal achieved, Moscow could then maneuver the West German government into a state of neutrality, whether official or undeclared. On the assumption that Gorbachev shared these aims, some analysts viewed his détente and arms-control policies with distrust.[14] This notion that Moscow has consistently sought—and may still seek—Germany's neutralization forms the centerpiece of the argument that what the Soviets have always wanted more generally is the Finlandization of all of Western Europe.[15]

Some analysts who stress the consciously manipulative purposes of Soviet policy are skeptical, however, as to whether Moscow has ever really tried to bring about a clear and permanent break between Bonn and Washington. They regard the Soviets as having generally been highly ambivalent about the desirability of a complete withdrawal of American troops from the FRG, inasmuch as the possible result of such a step might be a significant increase in West Germany's own military power. These analysts assume that Moscow may be even more alarmed by the prospect of a significantly expanded West German military posture than by the presence of American troops on the continent. Such fears would be compounded if Bonn were to compensate for the loss of American protection by gaining access to nuclear weapons.[16] Even after Germany's unification, the Kremlin may still harbor anxieties of this sort. One variation on this theme

14. Gerhard Wettig, "Germany, Europe, and the Soviets," in *Soviet Policy toward Western Europe*, ed. Herbert J. Ellison (Seattle: University of Washington Press, 1983), pp. 31–35; "The Soviet View," in *Germany between East and West*, ed. Edwina Moreton (Cambridge: Cambridge University Press, 1987), p. 39; and " 'New Thinking' on Security in East–West Relations," *Problems of Communism* 37 (March–April 1988): 1–4.

15. Robert Strausz-Hupe, "The European Policies of the Soviet Union," in *Soviet Foreign Policy toward Western Europe*, ed. George Ginsburgs and Alvin Z. Rubinstein (New York: Praeger, 1978), p. 245; and Hans-Peter Schwarz, "Die Alternative zum Kalten Krieg? Bilanz der bisherigen Entspannung," in *Entspannungspolitik in Ost und West*, ed. Schwarz and Boris Meissner (Cologne: Carl Heymanns, 1979), p. 303. Schwarz argues that by the late 1970s the Soviet Union had already succeeded in pulling West Germany into its orbit.

16. Thomas W. Wolfe, *Soviet Power and Europe, 1945–1970* (Baltimore: Johns Hopkins University Press, 1970), p. 288; Richard Pipes, "Détente: Moscow's View," in *Soviet Strategy in Europe*, ed. Pipes (New York: Crane, Russak, 1976), p. 23; Lawrence Freedman, "The United States Factor," in *Soviet Strategy toward Western Europe*, ed. Edwina Moreton and Gerald Segal, pp. 87–109 (London: George Allen & Unwin, 1984); F. Stephen Larrabee, "The View from Moscow," in *The Two German States and European Security*, ed. Larrabee (New York: St. Martin's Press, 1989), p. 193.

is the notion that the USSR has sought to "contain" the Federal Republic as its minimum goal while endeavoring to loosen its attachment to the United States as its maximum goal.[17]

Another group of analysts takes the view that in fashioning their policies toward West Germany (and toward the West more generally), the Soviets have basically tended over the years to act out of weakness. It is the failure of their own economy, in this view, that has impelled Soviet leaders to move toward accommodation and détente, even if greater economic dependence on the capitalist world may be the price the Kremlin has to pay for Western assistance. While economic considerations clearly prompted Gorbachev to improve Moscow's ties to the West, some analysts have emphasized the economic factors motivating Soviet détente policy ever since the 1960s.[18]

Most analysts who put forward these interpretations of the Kremlin's aims arrive at their conclusions by inferring the Soviets' motivations from their actions. Occasionally they support their observations with references to statements by Soviet leaders or writings by Soviet academicians. However, these allusions to Soviet elite perceptions are seldom investigated systematically. All too often, individual analysts are content to present what they conceive to be "the" Soviet position on West Germany, as though there were only one. Very few analysts have looked attentively at the variety of views that rise to the surface when the Soviets themselves discuss the Federal Republic in the open press.[19]

In fact, the Soviet foreign policy establishment advanced two broadly defined sets of views in regard to West Germany during the years under investigation. One view essentially favored overtures to Bonn for the purpose of exploring the possibilities of political accommodation or economic cooperation. It was based on a generally positive appraisal of the FRG's acceptability as a reliable partner in diplomatic or economic undertakings. The other view exhibited greater reluctance to engage in such direct ex-

17. Roland Smith, *Soviet Policy towards West Germany*, Adelphi Papers no. 203 (London: International Institute for Strategic Studies, 1985).

18. See, e.g., the chapters by Hillel Ticktin and Antonio Carlo in Egbert Jahn, ed., *Sozioökonomische Bedingungen der sowjetischen Aussenpolitik* (Frankfurt: Campus, 1975). The English-language version of this book is *Soviet Foreign Policy: Its Social and Economic Conditions* (New York: St. Martin's Press, 1978).

19. For analyses of variations in perceptions of West Germany within the Soviet secondary elite, see Hans-Heinrich Nolte, *Gruppeninteressen und Aussenpolitik* (Göttingen: Musterschmidt, 1979); Lena Jonson, "The Soviet Union and the Federal Republic of Germany: Soviet Policy Debate in the Press, 1975–1981," *Cooperation and Conflict* 21 (1986): 119–31; Wolfgang Pfeiler, *Deutschlandpolitische Optionen der Sowjetunion* (Melle: Ernst Knoth, 1988) and "Soviet Perceptions of the Federal Republic of Germany," in *East-West Conflict: Elite Perceptions and Political Options*, ed. Michael D. Intriligator and Hans-Adolf Jacobsen, pp. 128–49. (Boulder, Colo.: Westview, 1988). For a study that looks at Soviet and East German secondary elite images of the FRG, see Jörg-Peter Mentzel and Wolfgang Pfeiler, *Deutschlandbilder: Die Bundesrepublik aus der Sicht der DDR und der Sowjetunion* (Dusseldorf: Droste, 1972).

changes with the FRG. This perception was reflected in outspokenly negative images of West Germany's political, economic, or military ambitions. At times one or the other of these two images dominated public discourse about the FRG, but there were also periods when the division of opinion on West Germany was more conspicuous, reflecting serious debate within the Soviet elite. Much the same could be said about East German perceptions of the Federal Republic.

Policy disagreements of this kind were most in evidence at certain decisive turning points in Soviet-West German relations, when critical decisions had to be made. Should Khrushchev go to Bonn to meet with Chancellor Erhard in 1964? Should Moscow make special efforts to court the Social Democrats in the 1960s and 1970s? Should West Germany be penalized for deploying new intermediate-range American missiles in the early 1980s? Should Erich Honecker go to Bonn to meet with Chancellor Kohl in 1984? Should Gorbachev make significant concessions to West Germany on such things as the Berlin wall or the right of self-determination in the late 1980s? In these and other instances, some Soviets, and some East Germans, would have answered these questions by saying yes, while others would have tended to say no. At some times the main axis of disagreement fell between Moscow and East Berlin; at others the Soviet elite itself was most divided; and at still others the elites of both the USSR and the GDR were internally split into contending positive and negative camps.

These discussions usually revolved around positive or negative depictions of the West German government and its foreign policy orientation, particularly with respect to relations with Moscow and East Berlin. Was Erhard a potentially "businesslike" statesman, or was he just a reincarnation of the intransigent Adenauer? Could the Social Democrats be trusted to promote cooperation with the East, or were they just as perfidious as they had been in the 1920s? To what extent was Helmut Schmidt personally responsible for NATO's decision to install the new U.S. missiles in Western Europe? How should Helmut Kohl be evaluated? Such questions provided the context within which the Soviet and East German elites could openly debate West Germany's reliability as a negotiating partner.

In addition to providing assessments of Bonn's foreign policy aims in the short run, some specialists in the Soviet Union and the GDR were engaged in a continuing examination of the long-term tendencies of West Germany's international orientation. The crux of this discussion was the question of where the FRG fits into the evolving pattern of U.S.–West European relations. Is Bonn increasingly moving away from the United States in search of a more independent status in foreign affairs, or is it still firmly committed to following Washington's lead? Under what conditions can West Germany be encouraged to assert greater independence? Such long-range issues have been of central relevance to Soviet and East German policy toward the FRG throughout the decades extending from Khrushchev to Gorbachev. Indeed, they go right to the heart of the broader aims of Soviet policy as it relates not merely to West Germany but to the wider panorama of East-West relations.

Western observers have traditionally been divided in their interpretation of Moscow's ultimate aims with respect to the West. Some, as we have seen, have maintained that the Finlandization of Western Europe is what Soviet policy has always been about.[20] Others have suggested that Soviet policy has been concerned mainly with inducing the West Europeans to influence American policy toward the USSR and, when appropriate, vice versa. Some advocates of this position play down the Finlandization thesis while acknowledging that the Soviet Union has actively sought to promote and exploit conflicts between the United States and its West European allies.[21]

A few students of Soviet foreign policy have detected divisions within the Soviet establishment on the appropriate way of dealing with the Atlantic alliance. Jerry Hough, for example, has observed divergent orientations in Soviet writings on European security issues, including one that has favored emphasizing Western Europe as the primary target of Soviet diplomatic efforts and another that has favored direct contacts with the United States.[22] Reaching a roughly similar conclusion, Ernst Kux divided Soviet experts on East-West relations into "Yaltaists," who have preferred to deal with Washington, and "Rapalloists," who would rather work with Western Europe, and particularly with West Germany.[23] Hannes Adomeit observed three distinct analytical tendencies among Soviet experts: "Europeanism," which encouraged greater independence and neutralism on the part of the West European governments; "Atlanticism," which stressed Soviet-American cooperation, collusion, or bipolar "condominium" in dealing with Europe's problems; and "pan-Europeanism," a combination of elements of the first two approaches.[24]

20. For an extensive discussion of this theme, see Walter Laqueur, *The Political Psychology of Appeasement: Finlandization and Other Unpopular Essays* (New Brunswick, N.J.: Transaction, 1980).

21. See the chapters by Robert Legvold, Angela Stent Yergin, and John Lehman in Ginsburgs and Rubinstein, *Soviet Foreign Policy*. Also Robbin F. Laird, "The Soviet Union and the Western Alliance," in *The USSR and the Western Alliance*, ed. Laird and Susan L. Clark (Boston: Unwin Hyman, 1990), pp. 1–23. Also Neil Malcolm, *Soviet Policy Perspectives on Western Europe* (London: Routledge, 1989).

22. Jerry F. Hough, "Soviet Perspectives on European Security," *International Journal* 11 (Winter 1984–1985): 20–41.

23. Ernst Kux, "Moskaus Konfrontation mit Washington: Kontroversen im Kreml?" *Neue Zürcher Zeitung*, Sept. 12, 1981, pp. 3–4, and "Moskaus Attacken gegen Bonn," ibid., Aug. 4–5, 1984, pp. 3–4.

24. Hannes Adomeit, "Capitalist Contradictions and Soviet Policy," *Problems of Communism* 33 (May–June 1984): 1–18. Adomeit later refined these categories further by positing two "European" options in Soviet policy (the "Western European" orientation and the "pan-European" approach) and two hypothetical "Atlanticist" variants (the "Euro-Atlantic" orientation and the "condominium" or "collusion" scheme). See his "Soviet Policy toward the

Scholars who have attempted to discover and identify differentiated opinions within the Soviet foreign policy establishment have come up with a variety of schemes for classifying the various patterns of thought they have observed. One of the more common approaches is to divide Soviet positions into left and right orientations, with the left leaning toward a hard-line position and the right favoring a greater degree of accommodation.[25] A variant of this classificatory system groups Soviet foreign policy orientations into hard, moderate, and soft lines.[26] Several analysts who have examined Soviet writings on the United States have proposed additional categories for ordering contending Soviet views into distinct political tendencies.[27] Though all of these analysts agree that divergent opinions are in fact expressed in open publications in the Soviet Union, they may differ not only in the way they classify the various viewpoints but also in their assessment of the magnitude of these divergences. Some scholars maintain that for many years a fairly wide range of opinion has separated hard-liners from accommodationists in the Soviet Union, but others emphasize the commonalities that unite these two groups on fundamental issues (such as an essentially conflictual view of East-West relations).

In an earlier work I examined Soviet academic writings on U.S.–West European relations and proposed that they be divided into "marginal left" and "marginal right" perspectives.[28] Though the considerations that led me to these conclusions still seem valid in many respects, I have learned in the course of my research that those categories offer at best only a partial explanation of policy differentiation in the Soviet Union on these issues. It has become increasingly evident that four sets of views can be distinguished. Each addresses a question that is central to virtually all Soviet thinking about the West: To what extent are relations among capitalist states characterized by cooperation and unity, and to what extent are they disrupted by conflict and "intercapitalist contradictions"?

United States and Western Europe: 'Atlanticism' versus the 'Common House,' " in *Gorbachev and the Soviet Future*, ed. Lawrence W. Lerner and Donald W. Treadgold (Boulder, Colo.: Westview, 1988).

25. The terms "left" and "right," in this context, derive from Soviet political orientations of the 1920s and 1930s. For an example, see William Zimmerman and Robert Axelrod, "The 'Lessons' of Vietnam and Soviet Foreign Policy," *World Politics* 34 (October 1981): 1–24.

26. Robert W. Hansen, "Soviet Images of American Foreign Policy, 1960–1972" (Ph.D. diss., Princeton University, 1975), cited in Bialer, *Domestic Context of Soviet Foreign Policy*, pp. 404–5.

27. E.g., Stephen Gibert et al., *Soviet Images of America* (New York: Crane, Russak, 1977); Morton Schwartz, *Soviet Perceptions of the United States* (Berkeley: University of California Press, 1978); John Lenczowski, *Soviet Perceptions of U.S. Foreign Policy* (Ithaca: Cornell University Press, 1982); Franklyn Griffiths, "The Sources of American Conduct," *International Security* 9 (Fall 1984): 3–50; and Neil Malcolm, *Soviet Political Scientists and American Politics* (New York: St. Martin's Press, 1984).

28. Michael J. Sodaro, "Soviet Studies of the Western Alliance," in Ellison, *Soviet Policy*, pp. 259–65.

The significance of this issue can be traced to Lenin, who asserted that both cooperative and conflictual tendencies are always operative simultaneously in relations among capitalist states.[29] At any given period, however, one tendency may be dominant over the other. It is therefore the task of Soviet experts on international relations to assess the intensity of these centrifugal and centripetal forces and to chart their likely path. Lenin's thesis provides Soviet writers with a conceptual framework for discussing alternative approaches to the West, and prominent Soviet and East German leaders have taken sides on these issues, with clearly discernible implications for immediate policy decisions.

The *maximalist* orientation is the most unyieldingly hard-line of the four patterns. Its distinguishing feature is a generally unfavorable evaluation of Western governments and foreign policies. Usually this view tends to place greater emphasis on the forces that unite the capitalist world than on the contradictions allegedly tearing it apart. Even when advocates of this ultra-hard-line approach have acknowledged the existence of severe contradictions within the Western alliance, they have insisted that the West remains united in its hostility toward the socialist world.

The maximalist position has generally stressed the collaborative elements at work in relations between the United States and the Federal Republic, highlighting Bonn's willingly assumed role in "U.S. global strategy." Indeed, as far as West Germany is concerned, the maximalist perspective has been overwhelmingly negative. Maximalists could be expected to recommend an attitude of utmost circumspection in dealings with the FRG, whose "revanchist essence" is said to mark the policies of even the most pro-détente government in Bonn. They have warned against the dangers lurking in politically risky economic contacts with the West, and especially with the FRG. To the extent that the maximalist orientation has sanctioned cooperation with the West at all, it appears to have done so only on the basis of the maximum possible advantages for the Soviet Union and the GDR, with the minimum possible concessions or risks.

The *Europeanist* orientation is characterized by its accent on the primacy of Western Europe in Soviet policy toward the West. Analytically, it is rooted in the perception of a long-term trend in the direction of Western Europe's independence from the United States as the result of increasingly divergent political, economic, and military interests. The Europeanists have therefore attached greater significance to the "contradictions" corroding

29. Lenin wrote that in relations among capitalist states "two trends exist; one, which makes an alliance of all the imperialists inevitable; the other, which places the imperialists in opposition to each other—two trends, neither of which has any firm foundations": "Report on Foreign Policy Delivered at a Joint Meeting of the All Russian Central Executive Committee and the Moscow Soviet, May 14, 1918," in V. I. Lenin, *Collected Works* (Moscow: Progress, 1965), 27:369.

NATO's unity than to the elements of partnership that have held it together. They have further contended that Soviet policy can and should actively promote and take advantage of these contradictions. Most important, the preponderant emphasis of the Europeanist argument has fallen on the notion that Western Europe is more interested than the United States in détente with the socialist countries. Hence Europeanist analyses of the world scene have occasionally combined quite favorable impressions of selected West European governments with highly disparaging comments about U.S. foreign policy.

Most Europeanists, though by no means all, have generally presented positive images of West German foreign policy, drawing clear distinctions between "revanchist" and "realistic" forces in the FRG. These positive images, moreover, have not necessarily been confined to West German Social Democrats; they have also applied in varying degrees to certain Christian Democratic leaders, such as Chancellors Erhard, Kiesinger, and Kohl. Some outspokenly Europeanist analysts even appeared to favor efforts to preserve a positive working relationship with Bonn, as opposed to Washington, at times of acute East-West tension. Some Europeanists, by contrast, have appeared to place greater confidence in France than in the Federal Republic, thus suggesting that the Europeanist orientation is a bit more complicated than the term "Rapalloist" implies. In any event, the main policy prescriptions of the Europeanist tendency have emphasized expanded diplomatic and economic cooperation with Western Europe.

One implication of this view is that Moscow should give higher priority to influencing West European governments and public opinion than to dealing primarily with the United States. Thus Europeanists could be expected to regard a multipolar approach to the various Western capitals as potentially more rewarding than a bipolar relationship with the United States. Another implication is that the Soviet Union would probably be better off without the presence of American troops on the continent, a position sometimes justified by references to the obstacles standing in the way of West European military cooperation and West Germany's access to nuclear weapons. Finally, the Europeanist outlook would favor attempts to work primarily through the West Europeans as a "lever" designed to exert favorable influences on American policy.

The *Americanist* orientation rests on the assumption that the United States is not only the USSR's principal preoccupation in world affairs generally; more to the point, it is also Moscow's primary interlocutor in European affairs. The analytical premise underlying this notion is that, though contradictions between the United States and Western Europe may well be on the rise, the United States remains the preeminent power in the capitalist camp. As such it frequently succeeds in asserting its will over its European allies, or else acts unilaterally in blatant disregard of its allies' preferences. The Americanists have thus stressed the bonds of partnership that hold the NATO alliance together under American leadership. They have also been fond of pointing out that key West European leaders usually noted for their independent streak (such as Charles de Gaulle and Willy Brandt) have themselves been outspoken advocates of the Atlantic alliance.

As a consequence, the Americanists would probably argue in private that Moscow must either give prime consideration to Washington in the elaboration of policy toward the West or at least endeavor to strike a balance between the United States and Western Europe in its overall approach. They would also tend to favor working primarily through the United States to exert favorable leverage on West European policies whenever it is appropriate to do so. In contrast to the Europeanists, the Americanists would not be exceptionally predisposed to court the West Europeans in the hope of decisively increasing their independence from Washington. The Americanists would be more disposed than the maximalists, however, to pursue détente.

While this concept by no means precludes direct overtures aimed at improving relations with such countries as West Germany, the Americanist posture has tended to suggest that Bonn should not be entitled to special consideration, especially during periods of aggravated East-West discord. Consequently the Americanist orientation exhibits shifting positive and negative images of the FRG, depending on circumstances. Sometimes these images can be noticeably more negative than the Europeanists' outlooks. Moreover, the Americanist viewpoint is not entirely averse to a continuing American military presence in West Germany, on the grounds that an intensified West European—and above all West German—military effort in its absence might be much more detrimental to Soviet interests than a continuing American involvement on the continent.

Finally, the *Atlanticist* orientation lies between the Europeanist and Americanist orientations, and is characterized by a tendency to emphasize the centripetal and centrifugal forces in roughly equal measure. Analysts who employ this mode of argumentation have quite frequently portrayed the intense contradictions unraveling the U.S.–West European relationship in some areas (such as economic relations) as being counterbalanced by equally intense cooperation in others (such as the military sphere). In its policy prescriptions, the Atlanticist orientation appears to be the most ambiguous of the four, since its talmudic world view encompasses both distinct limits to Western Europe's prospective independence from the United States and exploitable opportunities for exacerbating the conflicts that separate Western Europe from the United States. On the whole, the Atlanticists have seemed to recommend opportunistic efforts to favor either Washington or Western Europe as the occasion demands, playing off one against the other without anticipating an apocalyptic breakup of the Western alliance in the foreseeable future.

In keeping with these outlooks, Atlanticists have regarded West Germany as a source of serious conflict with the United States, but have insisted that Bonn has sought to keep these conflicts confined to the framework of the Atlantic alliance. While the FRG may indeed be striving for greater auton-omy, its main purpose in doing so has been to improve its bargaining position, and hence its influence, within NATO. As a result, the Atlanticists have painted a mixed picture of the Federal Republic, with contrasting positive and negative images that reflect the complexities of Bonn's ambiva-lent relationship with the United States.

As I have just described them, these four orientations represent ideal types. In practice Soviet and East German writers present them with many caveats and nuances, as we shall see. With a few sporadic exceptions, however, Soviet foreign policy specialists in the years from 1963 to 1989 consistently rejected both the notion of Western Europe's potential neutral-ism (or Finlandization) and the notion of a potential U.S.–Soviet con-dominium that might be imposed over the heads of the Europeans. Even those writers most closely associated with the Europeanist view repeatedly acknowledged that Western Europe's drive for independence, however de-sirable from the Soviet point of view, has always been contained within the structures of the Atlantic alliance, and is likely to continue to be so in the foreseeable future. Similarly, writers who gave evidence of a pronounced Americanist bent invariably recognized that sharp contradictions did in-deed divide the various members of the alliance, so that a Soviet-American condominium would be self-defeating, if not impossible.

In short, both Europeanism and Americanism have had much in common with the Atlanticist viewpoint. Proponents of all three views admit the simultaneous presence of contradictions and partnership in U.S.–West Eu-ropean relations; all are acutely aware of the scope and limits of both tendencies. The differences that separate the three orientations tend to be marginal, reflecting divergent slants of emphasis. Whereas Europeanism emphasizes the need to cultivate Western Europe, Americanism provides reminders that the United States plays a vitally important role in European developments. The Atlanticist view, in effect, plays both ends up the middle.

Consequently, advocates of all three of these orientations would argue that the aim of Soviet policy should be to exploit and maximize the differ-ences among the Western allies without expecting either the collapse of the alliance or the reestablishment of American hegemony within it. In the process, Moscow should encourage the West Europeans to exert a favor-able influence on American policy and, depending on circumstances, it should maneuver the United States into influencing the West European governments in a positive manner. A pluralistic Atlantic alliance, not a monolithic or a disintegrated one, therefore emerged as the most realistic goal of Soviet policy from the writings of the leading Europeanist, Ameri-canist, and Atlanticist writers, at least until the end of 1989. Even in the new circumstances created by the unification of Germany, variants of Europeanism, Americanism, and Atlanticism may continue to guide Soviet discussions of East-West relations in Europe for some time to come.

As we shall see, Walter Ulbricht was fundamentally a maximalist in his outlook, while his successor, Erich Honecker, came to adopt a more Europeanist stance, in conformity with his efforts to broaden the GDR's cooperation with West Germany and the other states of Western Europe. (In view of the GDR's much more limited foreign policy goals and room for maneuver, the East German elite was less active than the Soviets in discussing the alternative variants of Europeanism, Americanism, and Atlanticism.) Soviet leaders have generally rejected maximalism in their foreign policy orientation. While Khrushchev, Brezhnev, and Gorbachev may have leaned now and then in the direction of either Europeanism or Americanism, ultimately all three tended to follow an Atlanticist course in their dealings with the nations of the Western alliance between 1963 and 1989. So did Andropov and Chernenko. This pursuit of an Atlanticist policy toward the West is a unifying thread that joins together all the ruling coalitions that wielded power in the Kremlin in those years, whether they were conservative, reformist, or centrist.

The various Soviet regimes have differed, however, in the tactics they have employed to conduct this Atlanticist policy. The conservative Brezhnev coalition, for example, adopted a relatively narrow conception of cooperation with the United States and Western Europe, in keeping with the conservative attitudes shared by leading members of the military establishment and other key figures in the primary elite. Gorbachev, by contrast, has pursued a considerably more active and flexible Atlanticist policy based on a greater propensity to compromise with the West on controversial military, economic, and human rights issues.

Soviet and East German Views on East-West Trade

The third main variable impinging on Soviet and East German policy toward the Federal Republic is the issue of East-West trade. As one scholar has shown in elaborate detail, the desirability of expanded trade and technology exchange with the West has been a subject of intense debate at all levels of the political establishment ever since the inception of the Soviet state.[30] It has also been a matter of controversy in the GDR. During the period under consideration here, the main question has not been *whether* the Soviets or East Germans should trade with West Germany but

30. Bruce Parrott, *Politics and Technology in the Soviet Union* (Cambridge: MIT Press, 1983).

how much, at what political price, and toward which domestic ends. These and related issues sparked lively debates within the Soviet and East German elites as well as between them.

In some instances, perceived weaknesses in the domestic economy prompted decision makers in Moscow and East Berlin to step up their economic contacts with the West Germans. Khrushchev, Brezhnev, Gorbachev, and Honecker all justified détente with Bonn on the basis of its recognized economic benefits, though their rationales sometimes differed. Khrushchev sought to combine expanded trade with various experiments aimed at decentralizing economic decision making. Brezhnev changed his mind on the issue, switching from relatively reserved support of intensified trade to enthusiastic advocacy. Brezhnev's conservative Politburo did not unanimously share his enthusiasm, however, and Brezhnev himself showed no inclination to enhance the opportunities for trade by undertaking needed reforms in the domestic economy. Honecker, too, favored economic cooperation with West Germany at least in part as a substitute for significant reform, but also out of sheer necessity. Gorbachev has been an even more vocal advocate of East-West trade, and has sought to widen its institutional scope with the aim of furthering his plans for the restructuring of the Soviet economy.

In contrast to these pro-trade views, some members of the Soviet and East German elites expressed fears that excessive long-term economic dependence on the West, and particularly on West Germany, might result in debilitating political dependence. This, in essence, was Walter Ulbricht's view. Scholars who have focused on the GDR in the years from 1963 to 1971 have largely overlooked the extent to which Ulbricht's opposition to détente with Bonn was partially motivated by economic trepidations. So great were his concerns, in fact, that Ulbricht spearheaded significant changes in East Germany's domestic economic policies largely in response to the challenges he perceived in East Germany's international environment.

Caveat Lector

Naturally, we cannot uncritically assume that the policy discussions and debates that are published in the Soviet or East German press represent exact duplications of the conversations that take place *in camera*. Inevitably, important details of the Soviet and East German policy-making process remain hidden behind a wall of secrecy. The best we can do is to identify, categorize, and compare alternative points of view among Soviet leaders and specialists as systematically as possible, and hold them up to the mirror of actual Soviet behavior to determine whether, or to what extent, the published Soviet sources provide reasonable explanations for the observed realities. Put more simply, we must read what the Soviets say and watch what they do, and compare the two.

Ultimately it is up to the investigator to figure out what the esoteric communications that are published in communist regimes are intended to mean. In the final analysis, the explication of communist texts is always a matter of interpretation. What one scholar makes of a given statement may differ from what another scholar gets out of it. Usually the intended meaning of a word or phrase cannot be determined without a close reading of the entire text. Accordingly, I have tried wherever possible to derive the messages being conveyed from the full context in which they appear. In my view, this form of what may be called contextual content analysis is preferable to other analytical techniques, such as quantitative content analysis, which leads the investigator to pick out selected words or phrases without always taking sufficient account of the various meanings they may acquire as part of a larger statement. In effect, I have let the Soviets and East Germans speak for themselves as much as possible.

Moreover, my efforts to categorize various elite communications focus mainly on thought tendencies rather than on groups or factions. To be sure, some individuals have consistently embraced only one of the four interpretations of U.S.–West European relations, and on occasion I describe them in blanket terms as "maximalists," "Europeanists," "Americanists," or "Atlanticists." Not all members of the elite have been so consistent, however. Some have changed their views over time; others cannot be readily classified at all. Analyzing their views in terms of thought tendencies rather than in terms of fixed groups of individuals establishes a stable backdrop against which changes in the positions of various personages can be more easily tracked.[31]

Generally I prefer to speak of "images" rather than "perceptions" when I refer to Soviet and East German characterizations of West Germany or of other aspects of the international scene. Strictly speaking, images are descriptions of phenomena; a perception is a mental cognition or interpretation of reality. Whereas images are spelled out in language, perceptions are locked away in the mind of the speaker or writer. In practice, analysts of published Soviet sources are unavoidably limited to interpreting what the Soviets say; we cannot be certain about what they may "really think." Typically, however, the general sense of Soviet perceptions can be inferred from the publicly expressed images, primarily because such images are often intentional political messages, deliberately contrived to convey distinct policy positions. Thus negative images of West Germany are normally

31. On this point see Franklyn Griffiths, "A Tendency Analysis of Soviet Policy Making," in *Interest Groups in Soviet Politics*, ed. H. Gordon Skilling and Franklyn Griffiths, pp. 335–77 (Princeton: Princeton University Press, 1971).

intended to signify a hostile policy orientation, whereas more positive images are usually expressions of a more forthcoming position.

Finally, I concentrate on issues that were topics of internal debate within the USSR and the GDR. I am less concerned with analyzing the foreign propaganda efforts of these two governments, which were directed mainly at influencing policy or public opinion abroad.

Sources

I have relied heavily on the leading foreign affairs journals and other relevant policy-oriented works published in the Soviet Union and the GDR. I have examined just about every relevant article that appeared between 1963 and 1989 in *Mirovaya ekonomika i mezhdunarodnye otnosheniya*, the monthly publication of the Institute of the World Economy and International Relations (IMEMO) in Moscow; *International Affairs*, the official English translation of *Mezhdunarodnaya zhizn*, a journal with close links to the Soviet Foreign Ministry; *SShA*, the journal of the Institute of the USA and Canada; *Kommunist*, the leading theoretical journal of the Communist Party of the Soviet Union; *Voprosy ekonomiki*; *Deutsche Aussenpolitik*, published until 1983 by the Institute for International Relations in the GDR; *Einheit*, the monthly journal of the Socialist Unity Party of Germany; and *Wirtschaftswissenschaft*. These periodicals may be regarded as representing the mainstream of public foreign policy discussion in the USSR and the GDR. In all, I have read more than three thousand articles in them. My reading of other journals, as well as of daily newspapers such as *Pravda, Izvestiya, Krasnaya zvezda,* and *Neues Deutschland,* has been extensive but more selective. I have also read a large number of books published in the Soviet Union and East Germany, most of which are identified in the notes.

I have also examined nearly all of the speeches addressing foreign policy issues in this period by the key members of the primary elite who spoke out on such issues with some regularity. In all of these efforts my research has been greatly facilitated by the *Daily Reports* published by the U.S. Foreign Broadcast Information Service. Finally, interviews with Soviet and East German academicians and journalists have helped to clarify my understanding of their views.

CHAPTER TWO

Khrushchev's Thwarted Initiative: 1963–1964

On October 14, 1963, Konrad Adenauer retired from the office of chancellor of the Federal Republic of Germany, capping a remarkable career as the guiding figure in West Germany's emergence from the ruins of war into a stable and prosperous democracy. His successor, Ludwig Erhard, quickly assembled a new cabinet drawn from the same coalition of Christian Democrats (representing the CDU and CSU) and Free Democrats (FDP) which had governed in Adenauer's final years in power. Erhard made it clear that his government, like Adenauer's, was solidly committed to NATO and to the continuing process of West European integration. Erhard was perhaps even more determined to reaffirm West Germany's ties to the United States than Adenauer, who had lately sought to forge a special bond with President Charles de Gaulle as a counterweight to exclusive reliance on Washington. At the same time, the new chancellor believed the time to be ripe for fresh initiatives toward fulfillment of West Germany's long-standing goal of reunification. To this end he indicated his interest in pursuing a more active eastern policy (ostpolitik) than his predecessor, one aimed particularly at "building bridges" to Eastern Europe and at resuming the long-dormant political dialogue with the Soviet Union.[1]

The new mood in Bonn did not go unnoticed in Moscow. Nikita Khrushchev responded positively to the Erhard government's signals, and exploratory contacts were initiated with the FRG starting in the first months of 1964 with a view to arranging a summit meeting in Bonn. In early September the West German government issued a formal invitation to the

---

1. On Erhard's motives and their background, see William E. Griffith, *The Ostpolitik of the Federal Republic of Germany* (Cambridge: MIT Press, 1978), pp. 108–25.

Soviet leader to visit the FRG at the start of the following year. The meeting, of course, never came off. On October 14, 1964, exactly a year after Adenauer's retirement, Khrushchev himself was replaced by a new team headed by Leonid Brezhnev and Aleksei Kosygin. Moscow's move in Bonn's direction was stopped dead in its tracks.

What had happened? Did Khrushchev's ouster have anything at all to do with his evolving German diplomacy? Although no new information has come to light which might put all speculation to rest on this score, a close look at the existing sources provides considerable insight into the forces at work both in Moscow and in East Berlin which impinged on this pivotal one-year period in Soviet–West German relations. Many of the central questions underlying Moscow's relationships with the two German states in later years were very much at issue in Khrushchev's last twelve months in office. If we are to understand developments in the late 1960s, 1970s, and 1980s, a microscopic examination of this critical year is essential.

Khrushchev's Decision-Making Regime

By the time Nikita Khrushchev began what proved to be his final year as first secretary of the Communist Party of the Soviet Union, he was already the scarred veteran of more than a decade at the helm of a fractious Kremlin coalition. After besting such initial rivals as Lavrentii Beria and Georgii Malenkov, Khrushchev was compelled to wage an unending struggle to maintain his authority as party chief and to effectuate his policies. In 1957 he was almost toppled in a palace coup.[2]

One of the main sources of these frictions was Khrushchev's determination to effect significant reforms in the institutions and operating procedures of Soviet political life. The most controversial of these endeavors included the de-Stalinization campaign and its accompanying cultural thaw and plans for the reorganization of the party apparatus. Though some aspects of these measures were demonstrably aimed at enhancing Khrushchev's personal power, they nonetheless represented sincere attempts to boost Soviet economic performance and to loosen up some of the rigidities of the repressive political system inherited from Stalin. Khrushchev was particularly intent on decentralizing the economic planning system. In a restless quest for new organizational procedures and labor incentives, Khrushchev in 1962 put his weight behind a package of reforms proposed

---

2. The classic accounts of Khrushchev's rule are Carl A. Linden, *Khrushchev and the Soviet Leadership, 1957–1964* (Baltimore: Johns Hopkins University Press, 1966), and Michel Tatu, *Power in the Kremlin: From Khrushchev to Kosygin* (New York: Viking, 1970).

by the economist Yevsei Liberman. The reforms sought to confer greater decision-making authority on enterprise managers and to introduce profits as a criterion for measuring success in place of gross output quotas. The new mechanisms were tried out on a limited basis but did not survive very long after Khrushchev's ouster. They nevertheless reflected Khrushchev's determination to improve the Soviet economy, an ambition that led him to improve relations with the West.

In retrospect, of course, none of Khrushchev's initiatives went nearly as far as the more radical political reforms undertaken by Mikhail Gorbachev some thirty years later. Still, Khrushchev's actions were considered significant enough in their day, and they seemed especially threatening to more conservative political rivals and bureaucratic interests fearful of losing their prerogatives and alarmed by the prospect of an erosion of the party's commanding role in Soviet society.

Khrushchev's efforts to shake up the domestic system were accompanied by shifts in military and foreign policy. Convinced that the nuclear age had rendered conventional infantry and naval forces less important, Khrushchev announced plans to reduce the army by more than a million men in the early 1960s and blocked the plans of senior naval officers for a vast expansion of the Soviet fleet. At the same time, the Soviet leader accorded special importance to the newly established Rocket Forces, thereby placing himself in the crossfires of interservice rivalries.

Meanwhile, Khrushchev's acknowledgment of the grim finality of nuclear devastation impelled him to seek a modus vivendi with the West based on the necessity of "peaceful coexistence." Without backing away from challenging the Western allies in a series of confrontations stretching from Europe to the Third World, Khrushchev insisted (contrary to Lenin) that war between capitalist and socialist states was no longer inevitable, and that the historic rivalry between the two systems could be played out through the peaceful processes of ideological and economic competition. The Soviet leader therefore coupled his occasionally saber-rattling rhetoric with appeals to Western leaders for "realism" and "sober-mindedness," and sought to pursue a continuing dialogue with the West on matters of sharp contention.

These leanings toward détente, however limited, were not universally shared within the Kremlin hierarchy. Some individuals (such as Frol Kozlov, a powerful party secretary) evinced more consistently hard-line attitudes. On occasion they took advantage of Khrushchev's foreign policy embarrassments (such as the U-2 incident in 1960) to strengthen their own hand at Khrushchev's expense and to press for a tougher stance on East-West relations.

In sum, Khrushchev may rightly be considered a moderate reformer by Soviet standards. Until October 1964 he also remained the triumphant "first among equals" within the Kremlin hierarchy. The oligarchical coalition he headed, consisting of staunchly conservative elements as well as centrists amenable to particular reforms, generally gave the first secretary sufficient leeway to promote his designs for internal reform and international détente. Throughout his tenure in office, Khrushchev was able to take the lead in setting the Kremlin's overall domestic and foreign policy agendas. The internal stability of this coalition, however, was always open to doubt. Opposition to his initiatives at times compelled Khrushchev to temporize in some areas of reform, or to backpedal in a more conservative direction in others. In the end, the decision-making regime that Khrushchev headed may therefore be characterized as a centrist-reformist ruling coalition, but one that exhibited a significant degree of incohesiveness owing to doubts about the substance of Khrushchev's policies and, as we shall see, dissatisfaction with his capricious leadership style.

No picture of Khrushchev's rule would be accurate, moreover, without a clear idea of the limits to his own quest for internal change and détente. In fact, Khrushchev shared many of the same assumptions about the primacy of party rule at home and the irrevocability of conflict with the West that motivated some of his more unyielding colleagues. While admitting that the Soviet economy was beset by serious problems, the first secretary displayed a naive faith in the USSR's capacity to outdistance the United States in nearly every facet of economic performance within a mere decade or two. (These convictions found their ultimate expression in the party program of 1961.) Though he was fully cognizant of the hair-trigger fragility of the nuclear balance, he took the bold gamble of putting missiles in Cuba. When in 1956 a reformist Hungarian party leadership declared its plans to withdraw from the Warsaw Pact and to install a multiparty electoral system, Khrushchev did not hesitate to reassert Moscow's imperial primacy in Eastern Europe in a bloody assault on the Hungarian population. Far more than Khrushchev's mercurial temperament or the give-and-take of Kremlin infighting was responsible for these policies. From first to last, Khrushchev remained typical of his generation of Soviet officials, a group of ruthless totalitarians whose political attitudes were shaped overwhelmingly by two powerful and traumatic experiences: Stalinism and World War II. Khrushchev himself had risen to prominence amid the terror of Stalin's purges; during the war, he lost a son at Stalingrad.

Among the many lessons to be learned from these formative experiences, several were to have a profound effect on the Khrushchev generation's outlook on international politics. One was that all capitalist states were class enemies, but the enemy at the gate was Germany. Another was that the East-West conflict was irreconcilable, but cooperation was at times a tactical necessity. Together these ideological axioms and experienced realities made a deep imprint on Soviet attitudes toward West Germany, spawning tendencies toward animosity and opportunism which at times proved contradictory.

Khrushchev's German Policy and the Soviet Debate on West Germany

By the end of 1963, the main tenets of Khrushchev's German policy were already well established. Foremost among them was the USSR's categorical opposition to Germany's reunification on Western terms. Although, as we have seen, the Soviets at various times under Stalin and Khrushchev expressed interest in a four-power deal on reunification, they never agreed to Western proposals for reestablishing German unity on the basis of free elections in both parts of the divided nation. As prospects for reunification faded, Moscow increasingly insisted on Bonn's need to recognize the postwar territorial status quo, meaning the incorporation of the large parts of prewar Germany into the USSR and Poland.

Inescapably, this policy also required Bonn's recognition of the GDR. Khrushchev himself had proved his commitment to the East German regime in 1953 by joining with other Soviet leaders in squelching the incipient workers' uprising of June 17. Ultimately Khrushchev blamed the unrest on Beria, and accused him of seeking to sell out the GDR.

In later years Khrushchev demonstrated his support for the East German leadership again in his policy on Berlin. In 1958 the Soviet leader launched a protracted crisis over the divided city by threatening to sign a separate peace treaty with the GDR unless the West came to terms. Although he repeatedly backed away from carrying out the threat (much to Ulbricht's chagrin), the crisis did not reach its catharsis until the Berlin wall was built in August 1961.[3] Having put an abrupt stop to the massive hemorrhage of East Germans to West Berlin, Khrushchev continued to assert that East Berlin was the capital of the GDR and that West Berlin was juridically separate from the Federal Republic.

Another cardinal principle of Khrushchev's German policy was his unswerving opposition to the development of West German military power. This issue assumed new urgency in the early 1960s, when the United States proposed the creation of a multilateral NATO naval force (MLF) to consist of nuclear-armed surface vessels manned by mixed crews from the NATO countries, including the FRG. Though West Germany would not have

---

3. On the Berlin crisis, see Jack M. Schick, *The Berlin Crisis, 1958–1962* (Philadelphia: University of Pennsylvania Press, 1971); Robert Slusser, *The Berlin Crisis of 1961* (Baltimore: Johns Hopkins University Press, 1973); Hannes Adomeit, *Soviet Risk-Taking and Crisis Behavior* (London: George Allen & Unwin, 1982), chaps. 11–15; and Curtis Cate, *The Ides of August* (New York: M. Evans, 1978).

decision-making authority over the use of the nuclear weapons aboard the multilateral fleet, the MLF's significance as a symbol of the FRG's growing military prominence provoked a vigorous Soviet propaganda campaign against it.

Meanwhile, Khrushchev balanced these ironclad Soviet security interests with a growing desire to promote trade with the West Germans. Contrary to Stalin, who had opted for virtual autarky, Khrushchev was open to the advantages of East-West trade. After Adenauer's visit to Moscow in 1955, the value of Soviet–West German trade increased gradually to more than $420 million by 1962. By far the most spectacular achievement during these years was a pipeline agreement concluded between the Soviet Union and three West German firms in October 1962. The agreement created an immediate uproar in Washington and among certain West German politicians who favored a more rigid embargo in technology transfers to the East. A month later, the Kennedy administration successfully pressured the West German government into canceling the deal. The Kremlin was infuriated, but Khrushchev remained determined to pursue additional trade agreements.[4]

Khrushchev also had more purely political motives in mind when he sought to open up a direct channel of communication with the government in Bonn. Although his foreign policy was generally predicated on the primacy of the U.S.-Soviet relationship, especially at a time when the United States clearly dominated the Atlantic alliance, Khrushchev was sensitive to the existence of disagreements between Washington and its NATO partners on a variety of issues bearing on East-West relations. A dialogue with West European leaders presented the most effective way to sound out America's allies on their own interests and outlooks, with a view to widening the opportunities for exploiting the rifts between Western Europe and Washington. It was these assumptions that had prompted Khrushchev to invite Adenauer to Moscow in 1955. Although this effort to probe for weaknesses in West Germany's links to the United States proved premature, the precedent for direct contacts with Bonn was now established. By the start of the next decade, Khrushchev's West European diplomacy began to intensify as the Kremlin began to court President de Gaulle and expanded its contacts with Italy, Britain, and Scandinavia.

Thus Khrushchev showed early signs of wishing to steer a flexible course between the United States and Western Europe. While he clearly recognized that the United States remained the paramount leader of the capitalist world and that Moscow could not avoid dealing directly with Washington on any significant issue confronting contemporary Europe, he was also alert

4. For details, see Angela Stent, *From Embargo to Ostpolitik* (Cambridge: Cambridge University Press, 1981), pp. 44, 47, 57–58, 79–81, 93–126.

to the potential advantages of having personal access to the key governments of Western Europe. The payoffs of such a policy were not immediately certain, given the evident unity of the Atlantic alliance at that time.
But Khrushchev seemed to agree with those Soviet analysts who pointed
out the inevitability of rivalry and "contradictions" in relations among
capitalist states, thereby holding out the hope of exploiting policy differences among the NATO allies. In this sense, then, Khrushchev may be
considered an Atlanticist in his overall foreign policy design. Without losing
sight of America's predominance, and without becoming entranced by the
unlikely prospect of enticing the West Europeans to abandon the United
States, the Soviet leader sought to widen the Soviet Union's scope of diplomatic maneuver within the interstices of the Atlantic alliance.

Soviet analysts, meanwhile, were by no means united in their assessments
of the latest developments in the FRG or in the broader framework of
Bonn's relations with the United States. Differences emerged among Soviet
specialists even before Erhard assumed power. Some analysts pointed to the
persistence of U.S.–West German unity.[5] Others, however, accentuated the
mounting problems for the United States created by France's growing
independence, or by the so-called Paris-Bonn axis cemented by de Gaulle
and Adenauer in the Franco-West German treaty of January 1963.[6] One of
the most forceful of these arguments came from Daniil Melnikov, a scholar
at Moscow's Institute of the World Economy and International Relations
who for decades had been one of the Soviet Union's leading specialists on
Germany.[7] In June 1963 Melnikov warned that "failure to pay equal
attention to each of the two tendencies of capitalist states outlined by Lenin
would lead to serious errors in the conduct of foreign policy." He then
proceeded to lay special stress on the contradictions that were currently
undermining Western unity. Describing the recent rapprochement between
France and the FRG as a danger to world peace, he also noted that it
"objectively" contributed to the decline of American influence in Europe.
Melnikov concluded with a plea for a "creative" application of Marxist-
Leninist foreign policy principles. His arguments provided support for a
flexible Soviet approach to Western Europe, calculated to play upon its
internal divisions and, above all, its differences with the United States.[8]

5. E.g., S. Beglov, V. Zhurkin, and M. Sturua, "Tekushchie problemy mirovoi politiki,"
Mirovaya ekonomika i mezhdunarodnye otnosheniya (hereafter *MEMO*), no. 7, 1963, p. 70.
   6. S. Madzoevskii, D. Melnikov, and N. Molchanov, "Evropeiskii uzel mezhimperialisticheskikh protivorechii," *MEMO*, no. 8, 1963, pp. 77–81; N. Inozemtsev, "Edinstvo
Zapada?" *MEMO*, no. 2, 1963, p. 69. Madzoevskii was the pseudonym of the British double
agent Donald Maclean.
   7. Melnikov was the nom de plume of Daniil E. Melamid. During World War II he
directed TASS propaganda broadcasts aimed at Germany.
   8. D. Melnikov, "Obostrenie mezhimperialistichekikh protivorechii na sovremennom
etape," *MEMO*, no. 6, 1963, pp. 18–31.

As we shall see, Melnikov was a consistent exponent of what I have called the Europeanist orientation of Soviet foreign policy. His article of June 1963 was fully in keeping with his earlier writings. In the wake of Adenauer's trip to Moscow, for example, Melnikov had joined with other Soviet academicians in extolling the benefits of Soviet–West German trade. Some Soviet writers in the years after Khrushchev's opening to Adenauer reinforced these views with explicit references to the Rapallo agreement of 1922.[9]

Rapallo, in fact, emerged as another favorite theme of members of the Soviet foreign policy establishment who hoped for a positive turnabout in Soviet–West German relations in the 1960s and later. In 1962, Soviet as well as East German academicians and journalists marked the fortieth anniversary of the Rapallo agreement with special conferences and publications.[10] In 1963 and 1964, documents and publications also appeared on the 1922 Genoa conference, which had enabled Lenin's government to expand its trade ties with the West and which led directly to the Soviet-German accord at Rapallo. As in earlier and later years, these positive references to Genoa and Rapallo invariably signaled support for broadened Soviet ties with Western Europe, and especially with West Germany.[11]

Shortly after Erhard assumed the post of federal chancellor, a parallel discussion broke out among Soviet academicians and journalists on the nature of the new cabinet in Bonn. The crux of the issue was whether Erhard represented a new departure in West German foreign policy, one directed toward a more accommodating relationship with the Soviet Union and its allies, or whether his government remained wedded to the anti-Soviet positions set by Adenauer. This debate continued throughout the entire year extending from Adenauer's retirement to Khrushchev's ouster. Some writers were highly critical of Erhard.[12] But a major essay that appeared in Kommunist in February 1964 not only proclaimed that Erhard was gradually moving away from Adenauer's policies but gave detailed evidence of changes in the attitudes of other leading West German politi-

9. See Melnikov's article in Znaniye, ser. 7, no. 3 (1956); I. Koblyakov, "Rapallo—Then and Now," New Times, no. 20, 1957; both cited in Stent, From Embargo to Ostpolitik, p. 261.

10. E.g., Rapallskii dogovor i problema mirnovo sosushchestvovaniya (Moscow: Izdatelstvo inostrannoi literatury, 1963). This volume consists of papers delivered at a conference organized by the Historians' Commission of the USSR and GDR and held April 25–28, 1962, to commemorate the fortieth anniversary of the Rapallo treaty. The German version, edited by Alfred Anderle, is Rapallo und die friedliche Koexistenz (East Berlin: Akademie, 1963). See also Alfred Anderle, Die deutsche Rapallo-Politik (East Berlin: Rütten & Löning, 1962).

11. See, e.g., the positive references to the Genoa conference in Pravda, Apr. 12 and 22, 1964, as well as other sources cited in Franklyn Griffiths, "The Sources of American Conduct," International Security 9 (Fall 1984): 7n, 8n.

12. "Tekushchie problemy mirovoi politiki," MEMO, no. 1, 1964, pp. 28–30, and no. 7, 1964, pp. 84–86.

cians in the FDP and the Social Democratic Party of Germany (SPD), whom it depicted as favoring an accommodation with Moscow and East Berlin. The *Kommunist* piece also emphasized the contradictions that were increasingly corroding Western unity, and portrayed the GDR as strong enough to conclude agreements with the West Germans, such as the Berlin pass agreement of December 1963, which permitted West Berliners to visit East Berlin over the Christmas holidays.[13] The appearance of such an unusually optimistic article about the FRG in the CPSU's leading theoretical journal just as Khrushchev was moving to resuscitate the Moscow-Bonn dialogue in all probability reflected attitudes associated with the first secretary himself.

In fact, by late 1963 and the first months of 1964 Khrushchev was laying the groundwork for his demarche toward Bonn. The first steps in this direction demonstrated that the Soviet leader was motivated particularly by economic concerns, but it quickly became apparent that political considerations were also high on his agenda.

The Soviet economy at this time was experiencing the latest in a series of agricultural problems. Poor harvests had required the Soviets to purchase wheat from the United States in the fall of 1963. An agreement to buy 300,000 tons of wheat from the FRG was initially held up by Adenauer, who demanded the destruction of the Berlin wall as a quid pro quo, but Erhard allowed the deal to go through shortly after becoming chancellor.[14] Part of the Soviets' problem stemmed from a shortage of chemical fertilizer. In December of the same year, Khrushchev addressed a Central Committee plenum on the need to revitalize the entire chemical industry. He placed special emphasis on the need to expand fertilizer supplies from both domestic production and foreign sources. Khrushchev sharply rejected any suggestion that the USSR would allow Western suppliers to attach political conditions to trade agreements, branding Adenauer as a "reactionary" in this regard. The Soviet Union, he insisted, planned to fulfill its current seven-year plan "by our own strength, making use of our own resources." In later years these phrases came back to haunt Khrushchev's successors, as Walter Ulbricht used them repeatedly in his efforts to block a further expansion of Soviet–West German trade. Khrushchev did not intend these boasts to be taken literally, however, as he went on to announce Moscow's readiness to purchase chemical equipment from abroad. He repeated his interest in borrowing technology from the capitalist countries in another speech before the Central Committee in February 1964.[15]

The Soviets followed up these declarations with an important agreement

13. P. Naumov, "Bonn: trevogi i poiski," *Kommunist*, no. 3, 1964, pp. 91–101.
14. Stent, *From Embargo to Ostpolitik*, pp. 122–24.
15. *Pravda*, Dec. 10, 1963, pp. 1–6; Feb. 15, 1964, pp. 1–6.

with the West Germans. In late March the Soviet Union contracted to buy an herbicide plant from Krupp. It was also agreed that the West German manufacturing giant would send a permanent representative to Moscow. Talks were soon under way on a new Soviet–West German trade agreement to replace the one that had expired in 1963. These economic undertakings came shortly after a secret conversation between Moscow's ambassador in Bonn, Andrei Smirnov, and Chancellor Erhard. Smirnov used the occasion to hand the chancellor an invitation from Khrushchev to meet in Moscow.[16] Smirnov later met with Erich Mende, the head of the Federal Ministry for All-German Affairs. This was the first time the Soviets had ever acknowledged the legitimacy of this politically sensitive ministerial post.[17] In addition, talks on Soviet–West German cultural exchanges were initiated.

Hopes for economic cooperation with the Federal Republic did not diminish Khrushchev's efforts to press for political advantages in his evolving diplomacy with the FRG. Speaking in Hungary in early April, he took up the theme of contradictions among the capitalist states, underscoring the presence of "splits, cracks, and breaches within the Western alliances." A week later, however, Khrushchev mounted a spirited attack on the Erhard government for its refusal to renounce West Germany's territorial claims and for its attempt to obtain access to nuclear weapons through participation in the proposed multilateral nuclear force. He also averred that the FRG's NATO allies were completely satisfied with Europe's current border arrangement.[18] Taken together, these two speeches revealed Khrushchev's political aims in any prospective talks with Erhard. On the one hand, the Soviet leader had an abiding interest in playing upon the divergences apparent within the Western alliance. On the other hand, he showed no signs of budging from the USSR's principled commitment to East Germany and the territorial status quo, or from its opposition to a nuclear role for the FRG. He also betrayed a desire to collude with the United States, Britain, and France in keeping Bonn's territorial revisionism in check.

Meanwhile, the first hints of internal opposition to Khrushchev's impending approach to the West German government sprouted to the surface. On March 7 a TASS statement savaged Erhard for failing to change Bonn's "revanchist and militaristic policy," and accused the FRG of pursuing a "double-dealing foreign trade policy."[19] While it is unclear whether Khrushchev personally disapproved of the statement, its tone was much harsher

---

16. Foreign Broadcast Information Service, *Daily Report* (hereafter FBIS): *USSR & Eastern Europe*, Mar. 26, 1964, p. BB15; Thomas W. Wolfe, *Soviet Power and Europe, 1945–1970* (Baltimore: Johns Hopkins University Press, 1970), p. 121.

17. *Handelsblatt*, Apr. 9, 1964, p. 1.

18. *Pravda*, Apr. 10, 1964, pp. 2–3; Apr. 16, pp. 1–3.

19. *Pravda*, Mar. 8, 1964, p. 4.

than Khrushchev's, and its timing, just one week before the Smirnov-Erhard meeting, was suspicious. So was the expulsion of the economic counselor of the West German embassy in Moscow on March 17 for no apparent reason. Much more graphic was the report of several Soviet journalists who visited the Federal Republic in April. Although one account of their meeting with Erhard published in *Izvestiya* was basically positive, subsequent articles in *Pravda* were uniformly derogatory of the West German economy and various political figures, who were described as pursuing the policies of "madmen."[20] One of the journalists on the trip, Shalva Sanakoyev, editor of *International Affairs*, later filed his own report. He derided Erhard for evading questions on nuclear proliferation and professed to see no differences whatever among the leaders of the major political parties on relations with the Soviet Union and the GDR, condemning their views as highly dangerous.[21] Sanakoyev's article offered a striking contrast to the essay that appeared in *Kommunist* earlier in the year.

East German Reactions

In the GDR, opposition to Khrushchev's opening to Bonn was unequivocal from the outset. Here the attack on Khrushchev's initiative was led personally by Walter Ulbricht, the strong-willed first secretary of the Socialist Unity Party whom Stalin had installed as his chief political operative in eastern Germany in the final weeks of the war. Ulbricht was entering the peak years of his power, having survived a lifetime of political challenges. With full Soviet backing, he now presided imperiously over a directive decision-making regime, flanked by trusted lieutenants who showed no signs of questioning his supreme authority. For nearly two decades Ulbricht had managed to hold East Germany in communist hands against all sorts of internal and external threats.[22] At various times he probably doubted Moscow's loyalty to East Germany, particularly during the years of four-power talks on the German question and during the crises of 1953 and 1961. It is quite likely that Ulbricht never got over his feelings of insecurity about the Kremlin's ultimate intentions. Accordingly, he now sought to acquire a veto right over future Soviet policy in regard to West Germany.

The East Germans lost no time indicating where they stood on the Erhard government. The SED leadership and contributors to the leading journals were unanimous in portraying the new chancellor as little more than a

20. See the article by M. Sturua in *Izvestiya*, Apr. 21, 1964, p. 2, and the articles by D. Kraminov, A. Lukovets, and P. Naumov in *Pravda*, May 17, p. 5, and May 18, p. 6.

21. Sh. Sanakoyev, "Peaceful Anschluss and Its Advocates on the Rhine," *International Affairs* (hereafter *IA*), no. 7, 1964, pp. 17–24.

22. Carola Stern, *Ulbricht: A Political Biography*, trans. Abe Farbstein (New York: Praeger, 1965).

reincarnation of Adenauer. East German analysts of Bonn's foreign policy routinely placed heavy stress on the FRG's continuing partnership with the United States, holding out little hope for capitalizing on contradictions between Bonn and Washington.[23] Particular attention was given to the bridge-building policy designed by West Germany's foreign minister, Gerhard Schröder. Schröder's attempts to establish trade missions in Eastern Europe were roundly condemned on the grounds that they were intended to "soften up" Warsaw Pact support for the GDR.[24] All of the evaluations of the Erhard cabinet published by the secondary foreign policy elite in the GDR echoed the SED decision makers, above all Ulbricht himself.

The East Germans also responded rapidly to Khrushchev's quest for expanded economic contacts with West Germany. Ever since the end of World War II the Ulbricht regime had endeavored to make East Germany economically indispensable to the Soviet Union and its allies in Eastern Europe. To be sure, the East Germans had little choice but to comply with Soviet dictates in economic matters, especially in the initial postwar period. According to one estimate, the Soviets may have extracted as much as $19 billion worth of goods and services from the East German economy between the end of the war and 1960.[25] Beyond the necessity of fulfilling Moscow's harsh demands, however, Walter Ulbricht recognized that close economic cooperation with the USSR was vital to the survival of the GDR. By enhancing East Germany's economic value to the Soviet Union, Ulbricht hoped to impress upon the Kremlin leadership the irreplaceable advantages to be gained from guaranteeing the existence of a strong and secure East German state. As a consequence, the SED chief went out of his way to bind the East German economy to the USSR and Eastern Europe, subordinating the domestic requirements of economic and social development to the overriding priority of reinforcing the GDR's utility to its allies.

23. Werner Kirchhoff, "Ist die 'Ära Adenauer' wirklich zu Ende?" *Deutsche Aussenpolitik* (hereafter *DA*), no. 1, 1964, pp. 41–48; Herbert Barth, "Vernunft und guter Wille notwendiger denn je," ibid., no. 3, 1964, pp. 169–75; Reinhard Klassen, Otto Schröder, and Kurt Voigtländer, "Parteitag wider die friedliche Koexistenz und den gesellschaftlichen Fortschritt," *Einheit*, no. 6, 1964, pp. 90–102; Heinz Geitzler, "Kuda idet Zapadnaya Germaniya?" *MEMO*, no. 6, 1964, pp. 116–23 (Geitzler was an East German academician). For a relatively positive evaluation of possible shifts in the foreign policy ideas of Willy Brandt and other prominent West German politicians not connected with the CDU or CSU, see Georg Neukranz, "Die Bewegung für eine Politik der friedlichen Koexistenz in Westdeutschland," *Einheit*, no. 5, 1964, pp. 75–87.

24. Günther Bühring and Gerhard Liebig, "Neue Methoden—alte Ziele," *Einheit*, no. 3, 1964, pp. 72–84; *Neues Deutschland* (hereafter *ND*), Apr. 18, 1964, p. 4.

25. Jean Edward Smith, *Germany Behind the Wall* (Boston: Little, Brown, 1969), p. 85. For additional data on the Soviet economic exploitation of East Germany in this period, see J. P. Nettl, *The Eastern Zone and Soviet Policy in Germany, 1945–1950* (Oxford: Oxford University Press, 1951), and Dietrich Staritz, *Die Gründung der DDR* (Munich: DTV, 1984), pp. 48ff.

This symbiotic relationship between foreign policy interests and internal economic policies extended not merely to resource allocation decisions; it also encompassed the very structure of the economy. In 1963 the GDR became the first country in the Soviet bloc to adopt on a broad scale a number of economic reforms that the Khrushchev leadership had discussed and partially approved. The "New Economic System of Planning and Management" in effect converted the East German economy into a laboratory for experiments with such concepts as decentralized decision making and profit incentives, concepts that were of great interest to the Soviets. Once again, for political reasons, the GDR under Walter Ulbricht undertook special efforts to perform an invaluable economic service to the Soviet Union while at the same time seeking to improve its own economy. The GDR also supported Khrushchev's plans for a more structured division of labor between the more industrially advanced members of the Council on Mutual Economic Assistance (COMECON), such as the GDR, and its less developed, more agriculturally oriented members, such as Romania, which resisted these plans.

At the same time, Ulbricht was sensitive to the long-term political hazards of excessive economic reliance on West Germany. Despite the fierce political hostilities underlying the FRG-GDR relationship, trade ties grew.[26] Although the GDR maintained a positive trade balance in these exchanges, much of what it imported consisted of manufactured goods in short supply in the GDR. Ulbricht and his colleagues in the SED were well aware that the GDR could not do without this trade line to the West; chronic shortages and bottlenecks in the East German economy required rapid access to foreign goods if plans were to be fulfilled and consumers' minimal needs met. This trade dependence entailed political risks, however, and the East German government was at pains to limit its scope. In the early 1960s, for example, the GDR launched the so-called *Störfreimachen* campaign, designed to make the East German economy "disturbance-free" from the potentially damaging effects of economic cooperation with the FRG. The campaign proved to be of short duration, as the GDR was still in no condition to forsake the benefits of doing business with West Germany. Nevertheless, the SED regarded the effort to reduce its reliance on the FRG as a long-term necessity.

It was not surprising, then, that Ulbricht took alarm at the prospect of a

---

26. By 1963, total trade turnover between the GDR and West Germany (including West Berlin) was over 1.8 billion valuta marks (VM), an amount that was approximately the same in West German deutsche marks (DM) at the time. Though this total was slightly lower than that of 1960, before the construction of the Berlin wall, it represented an increase of more than VM135 million over the total of 1962. See *Statistisches Jahrbuch der Deutschen Demokratischen Republik, 1965* (East Berlin: Staatsverlag der Deutschen Demokratischen Republik, 1966), p. 388.

revival of Soviet–West German economic contacts in 1964. Ulbricht made known his desire to tighten Soviet–East German economic cooperation in an article in *Pravda* in January, in which he called for the joint production of computer technology.[27] In February, speaking before a plenum of the SED Central Committee, Ulbricht revealed how deeply he had been affected by Khrushchev's December 1963 speech on the need to upgrade the Soviet chemical industry. He announced new plans to accelerate chemical production in the GDR, a decision that apparently did not sit well with various economic functionaries and scientists in the East German bureaucracy. Ulbricht openly acknowledged that some of these technocrats considered it "wrong" to accelerate chemical production. The SED chief was determined to move forward, however.[28] This would not be the last time that Ulbricht would insist on accelerating industrial growth for political purposes, even in the face of opposition from experts within the East German economic apparatus.

More direct indications of the Ulbricht regime's displeasure at Khrushchev's overtures soon followed. Barely two weeks after the disclosure of the Krupp deal, *Neues Deutschland* accused the West German government of blocking the sale of nitrogen fertilizer to the GDR for political reasons, a charge promptly denied by the FRG. In a remark patently aimed more at Moscow than at Bonn, the SED daily declared that "the GDR is not willing to sell its political rights to the revanchists for nitrogen or anything else."[29]

As it happened, the GDR found itself increasingly isolated within the Warsaw Pact on the issue of trade with the Federal Republic. In 1963 Poland, Romania, and Hungary had signed agreements with West Germany providing for the establishment of trade missions. Bulgaria followed suit in March 1964. Ulbricht had little alternative but to live with these agreements, though he continued to denounce West German trade missions as a "Trojan horse."[30]

It was the political implications of Khrushchev's initiatives, however, that most disturbed Ulbricht. The East German leadership moved quickly to assert a role of its own in the reopening of the Soviet bloc's contacts with Bonn, making it increasingly clear that any renewal of the Soviet–West German dialogue without meaningful talks between the GDR and the FRG was absolutely unacceptable to East Berlin.

On January 6 the GDR sent Bonn the draft of an inter-German treaty aimed at establishing a nuclear-free zone, accompanied by a letter from

27. *Pravda*, Jan. 9, 1964, pp. 3–4.
28. *ND*, Feb. 6, 1964, p. 3. For an analysis of the economic aspects of Ulbricht's speech, see Julius Götz, "Chemieprogramm in neuer Auflage," *SBZ-Archiv*, no. 6, 1964, pp. 87–94.
29. *ND*, Apr. 9, 1964, p. 1.
30. See the communiqué issued at the end of Ulbricht's visit to Budapest in *ND*, May 13, 1964, p. 1–2. For the remark about the "Trojan horse," see ibid., p. 5.

Ulbricht to Erhard calling for negotiations between the two German states.[31] Shortly before the Smirnov-Erhard talks in March, Anastas Mikoyan, an influential CPSU leader closely allied with Khrushchev, made a quick visit to East Berlin, possibly to apprise Ulbricht of the upcoming event. During Mikoyan's stay in the GDR, Albert Norden of the SED Politburo sharply rebuked Erhard for saying that he would be pleased to meet with Khrushchev but not with Ulbricht. Erhard was no different from Adenauer, Norden warned, adding that any understanding on the German question required talks between the FRG and the GDR.[32] Later, the East German government issued a formal note to the West complaining of alleged abuses by West Germany of the transit routes to West Berlin. In early April, East Germany forwarded another note to the American, British, and French governments asking them not to raise any objections to direct talks between the GDR and the FRG.[33] These actions coincided with a ten-day visit to the GDR by the Soviet defense minister, Rodian Malinovskii. Malinovskii's presence in East Berlin at this juncture (he was soon joined by Marshal Andrei Grechko) hinted that the SED leadership was trying to draw the Soviet military hierarchy into an alliance against Khrushchev's West German policy. The Soviet military already disgruntled by the latest cuts in the defense budget announced by Khrushchev, and Malinovskii's statements in East Germany condemning revanchism in the FRG appeared to offer a modicum of support for the SED's anti-Bonn position.[34]

Meanwhile, the SED displayed a certain reserve in its show of support for Khrushchev in his latest imbroglio with the Chinese leadership. Although the East Germans consistently backed the general lines of Khrushchev's China policy, they were visibly reluctant to repeat the Soviet charge that the Chinese were trying to exacerbate relations with the Soviet Union's allies. Quite probably the GDR did not wish to forgo the possibility of expanding its trade relations with the People's Republic, a concern indicated in the SED's statement on China issued on April 15. It is also possible that the SED leadership, in contrast to the Kremlin, hoped to avoid an irreparable break with the Chinese. Whatever the case, it was apparent that the GDR did not provide Khrushchev with an unqualified endorsement of his plans to expel the Chinese party from the ranks of the international communist movement.[35]

31. *ND* did not publish the documents until Jan. 16, 1964, several days after Ulbricht made a hastily arranged trip to Moscow.

32. *ND*, Mar. 12, 1964, pp. 4–5. Norden, a communist since 1920 and a Politburo member since 1958, was the SED secretary responsible for propaganda.

33. For the text of the first note, see *ND*, Apr. 2, 1964, pp. 1–2. For the second, see *ND*, Apr. 11., pp. 1–2.

34. See Malinovskii's speech in *ND*, Apr. 3, 1964, p. 3. Unlike Ulbricht, however, Malinovskii did not equate Erhard with Adenauer. See Ulbricht's speech in *ND*, Apr. 10, pp. 1–2.

35. On the GDR and China in 1964, see Carola Stern, "East Germany," in *Communism in Europe*, ed. William E. Griffith, 2:129–36. (Cambridge: MIT Press, 1966). Also I. Sp. [Ilse

It was Khrushchev's German policy, however, that most directly aroused the SED's apprehension. A *Neues Deutschland* editorial on May 4 professed incredulity at Erhard's stated desire for agreements with the USSR and other socialist countries, and declared that any such accords "can begin only with a normalization of relations with the GDR." It said that an inter-German agreement would be the true test of Erhard's seriousness and the "touchstone" of West Germany's policy. Ulbricht restated these ideas even more emphatically while he was in Hungary. In one speech he insisted that there was "no other way" to a peaceful solution of the German question than by inter-German negotiations; in another he affirmed that détente in Germany was possible only through talks between East Berlin and Bonn. Several weeks later Ulbricht reaffirmed his position in an arrogantly worded letter to Chancellor Erhard. Its key passage proclaimed that "no progress can be made on the German question" without direct inter-German negotiations.[36]

These official pronouncements were backed up by similarly trenchant comments in the leading East German journals. An article that appeared to be a last-minute insertion in *Deutsche Aussenpolitik* in April warned of the "repudiation of the spirit of Rapallo" currently prevailing in the FRG, and accused the Erhard government of continuing West Germany's "thirty-year war" against the USSR. The article pointedly called for the negotiation of agreements between the GDR and the Federal Republic before a normalization of Soviet–West German relations, alleging that Khrushchev himself believed that the German question could be solved only through inter-German talks. The article concluded by extolling economic cooperation between East Germany and the Soviet Union, and noted that it provided "essential help" to the Soviet economy.[37] An article in *Einheit* was consciously aimed at putting Khrushchev on the spot. While ostensibly congratulating the Soviet leader on his seventieth birthday, the unsigned essay lauded Khrushchev's action of 1953 in exposing "the traitor . . . Beria," who had wanted to "capitulate" to West Germany. Despite fulsome praise for Khrushchev's "personal" services on behalf of the GDR, the article's appearance in the context of the GDR's mounting cries of alarm about the

---

Spittmann], "Die SED und Peking," *SBZ-Archiv*, no. 16, 1964, pp. 248–54. For the official SED statement, see *ND*, Apr. 15, 1964, pp. 1–2. The same issue featured an article by Foreign Minister Otto Winzer denouncing Erhard and citing Khrushchev as having said in 1957 that the four powers had a "duty" to let the two German states solve their national question by themselves in direct negotiations (p. 5).

36. *ND*, May 9, 1964, p. 3; May 8, p. 4; May 28, pp. 1–2. The communiqué issued at the end of Ulbricht's stay in Hungary called for the normalization of inter-German relations but did not make it a precondition for détente with the FRG: *ND*, May 13, pp. 1–2.

37. "Die deutsch-sowjetischen Beziehungen," *DA*, no. 5, 1964, pp. I–XIV. The fact that the pages bearing this article were given Roman numerals and placed at the beginning of the issue attested to its hasty insertion just before publication. The issue's closing editorial date was Apr. 3.

current directions of Soviet policy could be interpreted only as a subtle warning to Khrushchev against following in Beria's footsteps.[38] In much the same admonitory spirit, East German and Polish historians staged a conference on the Locarno treaty in late May. There, an East German speaker drew ominous comparisons between the anti-Soviet implications of Germany's policy at Locarno and similar tendencies in Bonn's policies of the present day.[39]

By the end of May, the stage was thus set for an open confrontation between Ulbricht and Khrushchev on the conditions for talks with the FRG.

The Soviet–East German Treaty and Adzhubei's Visit

The emerging differences between Moscow and East Berlin stood out with even greater clarity during Ulbricht's twelve-day visit to the Soviet Union in June. During a week-long tour of Siberia, the SED leader repeatedly insisted on the necessity of FRG-GDR talks as a condition not merely for a normalization of inter-German relations but even for "peaceful coexistence" itself.[40] On June 11 the Soviet government handed Bonn a stiffly worded note warning the FRG against seeking a decision-making role in NATO's nuclear strategy.[41] On the next day, however, Khrushchev adopted a much more moderate tone than Ulbricht as the two leaders took turns in addressing the German question.[42]

Although Khrushchev staunchly defended the GDR's existence and called on Bonn to recognize the status quo in Europe, he did not criticize Erhard by name, and he proclaimed Moscow's interest in friendship and cooperation with the FRG. In Khrushchev's view, there was "only one way" to settle disagreements among states, and that was through peaceful talks and agreements. Reunification could come only after West Germany signed a peace treaty with the victorious powers and recognized the GDR (in that order). The CPSU chief also stated that not everyone in West Germany was revanchist, and acknowledged the "complicated and contradictory" nature of relations among *socialist* states.

38. "Zum 70. Geburtstag des Genossen Nikita Sergejewitsch Chruschtschow," *Einheit*, no. 4, 1964, pp. 14–15. The final editorial date of this issue was Apr. 6. Another article that ostensibly praises Khrushchev but cites him in support of East German policy positions is Peter Florin, "N. S. Chruschtschow—ein Mann des Friedens," *DA*, no. 4, 1964, pp. 279–83.

39. For a report on the conference, see Wolfgang Ruge, "Locarnopolitik führte nach München," *DA*, no. 7, 1964, pp. 668–70.

40. *ND*, June 2, 1964, p. 3; June 4, p. 2. See also Ulbricht's interview in *Combat*, reprinted in *ND*, June 3, p. 4.

41. The text appears in *Frankfurter Allgemeine Zeitung* (hereafter *FAZ*), June 14, 1964, p. 4.

42. Khrushchev's and Ulbricht's speeches appear in *Pravda*, June 13, 1964, pp. 1–5.

Ulbricht declared that Erhard's government had not changed West Germany's "revanchist" policy, and denounced the chancellor for failing to respond to his recent letter. Proclaiming what he now called the "German peace doctrine," Ulbricht further asserted that there was "no other way" to ensure peace but by normalizing relations between the GDR and the FRG and by signing a peace treaty (a noticeable reversal of Khrushchev's order). Ulbricht also implicitly disapproved of Moscow's renascent trade dealings with the FRG when he called for efforts to hold West German industry in check.

These speeches accompanied the unveiling of a new twenty-year Treaty of Friendship and Cooperation between the Soviet Union and the GDR. The treaty text came closer to Khrushchev's views than to Ulbricht's. It made two early appeals for a German peace treaty, but did not mention the need for inter-German negotiations until Article 7. Even then, the inter-German talks were described as a precondition for Germany's reunification, not for peaceful coexistence between the Soviet bloc and Bonn. As a whole, the treaty fell far short of what Ulbricht may have expected from a separate peace treaty with the USSR before the construction of the Berlin wall. To make matters still worse for the GDR, the Soviet Union delayed ratification of the treaty more than three months. The communiqué issued at the end of Ulbricht's visit hewed to the general contours of the treaty text and Khrushchev's speech. Interestingly, when calling on Bonn to recognize the GDR, the communiqué stated that the "only thing that is required is to recognize the existing situation," a formulation that did not seem to demand that Bonn extend de jure recognition to the GDR.[43]

The ink was scarcely dry on the June 12 treaty when, the very next day, Khrushchev held a lengthy meeting with West German Ambassador Horst Groepper in Moscow. The ambassador conveyed Erhard's willingness to meet with Khrushchev, preferably in Bonn, if the Soviet leader deemed such an encounter useful. *Pravda* on June 14 gave front-page prominence both to Khrushchev's meeting with Groepper and to a telegram from Ulbricht thanking the Soviets for their support. Meanwhile, Ulbricht insisted that the June 12 treaty contained "all the safeguards" of a Soviet–East German peace treaty. He further asserted that "détente" was possible only through West German recognition of the GDR, and stigmatized Erhard and other West German political figures for opposing it. Ulbricht also lavished praise on Soviet industrial and agricultural achievements, stressing their advanced technological foundations.[44] Khrushchev, for his part, now embarked on a three-week tour of Scandinavia. At various stops along the way he declared his interest in developing contacts with the Federal Republic, and admitted

---

43. The text of the treaty appears in *Pravda*, June 13, 1964, p. 1. Other aspects of the treaty are analyzed in I. Sp. [Ilse Spittmann], "1984," *SBZ-Archiv*, no. 12, 1964, pp. 177–78. The communiqué appears in *Pravda*, June 14, 1964, pp. 1–2.

44. *ND*, June 25, 1964, p. 3.

Soviet economic shortcomings and his desire for expanded trade with the West.

On July 19 the Soviet government released a statement reiterating its standard demands on West Germany and stressing its friendship with the GDR, as evidenced in the June 12 treaty. The statement also called for détente, however, and refrained from criticizing Chancellor Erhard.[45] A day later Aleksei Adzhubei arrived in West Germany as Khrushchev's special emissary. Adzhubei was the editor of *Izvestiya* at this time, and as Khrushchev's son-in-law he had close personal ties to the Soviet leader. During his first week in the FRG the Soviet visitor met with some of the leading captains of West German industry, including the directors of Krupp, Mannesmann, Thyssen, and Hoechst. He also met with representatives of the major political parties. After his long-awaited conversation with Chancellor Erhard and Foreign Minister Schröder, the Soviet envoy described Erhard as a man with whom one could talk, despite the differences between the Soviet and West German points of view. He even suggested the usefulness of a confidential correspondence between Erhard and Khrushchev, similar to the private exchange of letters then going on between the Soviet leader and President Kennedy. In several interviews conducted by the West German press, Adzhubei emphasized Moscow's desire for "a really big step" to improve political and economic ties with the FRG, and expressed the Soviets' willingness to resolve, together with the GDR, serious problems involving families separated by the division of Germany and Berlin. In reply to a remark about the difficulties of negotiating with Ulbricht, Adzhubei said that the East German party chief was suffering from cancer and would not live much longer.[46]

On the outstanding political issues dividing Bonn and Moscow, however, Adzhubei held fast to traditional Soviet positions. He called for a peace treaty with West Germany and an agreement between the two German states on normalizing their relations. He upheld Moscow's contention that West Berlin did not belong to the FRG and should be declared an independent entity; he also described the Berlin wall as simply a "border." Even more significant, Adzhubei communicated Khrushchev's view that the German question itself was to be off limits in his proposed meeting with Erhard, implying that such issues as the validity of Germany's present borders were non-negotiable. In addition, Adzhubei characterized West Germany's relationship with "the Anglo-Saxons" as unnatural, declaring that the latter possessed no "soul." "We Russians," he insisted, "are the only ones who can understand you Germans."

The SED leadership's reaction to Adzhubei's visit was swift and unequivo-

45. *Pravda*, July 19, 1964, p. 1.

46. The transcripts of Adzhubei's television interview of July 29 may be found in FBIS, *USSR & Eastern Europe*, July 31, 1964, pp. BB5–12, and those of his subsequent press conference in ibid., Aug. 3, pp. BB18–19. Also *Der Spiegel*, Aug. 3, 1964, pp. 17–20.

cal. At a gathering of Warsaw Pact leaders in Poland shortly after Adzhubei's arrival in the Federal Republic, Ulbricht openly attacked the West German government. His views were solidly backed by Wladyslaw Gomulka, who pledged Poland's "full and complete" support for the GDR. Khrushchev, by contrast, denounced West German "imperialists and revanchists" in ritualistic fashion, but scrupulously avoided impugning the Erhard government directly.[47] An even more chilling East German response to the Adzhubei visit came as the Soviet emmisary was winding up his stay in the FRG. On July 31 Albert Norden delivered a blistering attack on West Germany in a speech commemorating the anniversary of the outbreak of World War I. One of his chief targets was German capitalism. Norden asserted that such firms as Krupp, Mannesmann, and Thyssen had bled Germany to death in two world wars and were now "the present masters of West Germany," together with Hitlerite generals. In an obvious swipe at recent Soviet efforts to revive its oil and grain trade with the FRG, Norden recalled that German monopolies had forced Russia to surrender large amounts of oil and grain in the Brest-Litovsk treaty. He lambasted Chancellor Erhard as well as the SPD leadership for pursuing a policy of chauvinism and war, and called on West German workers to remove them from power.[48] Norden's philippic followed an earlier critique of the Erhard government by Foreign Minister Otto Winzer, who drew the now-familiar parallel between the FRG's refusal to accept its existing eastern borders and Germany's role in signing the Locarno pact of 1925.[49] When Adzhubei stopped in East Berlin on his way back to Moscow, the East German delegation sent to meet with him was headed by Norden and Winzer.[50]

The GDR next stepped up its diplomatic campaign aimed at portraying the West German government and economic system in the worst possible light.[51] In addition, an East German memorandum on the Soviet-GDR Treaty of Friendship and Cooperation called for "the recording in international law of the integrity of the state frontiers of the GDR," a demand that seemed to require more than just a de facto recognition of the "existing situation," as the Soviet–East German communiqué of June 12 implied. The memorandum's most severe broadsides against the FRG, together with its assertion that West Berlin "is legally part of GDR territory," were deleted from TASS's report on it.[52] The SED Politburo reinforced these views with

47. For Ulbricht's speech, see *ND*, July 22, 1964, p. 2; for Gomulka's, *ND*, July 23, pp. 3–4; for Khrushchev's, *ND*, July 23, p. 5.
48. *ND*, Aug. 1, 1964, pp. 3–4.
49. *ND*, July 19, 1964, p. 4. See also Otto Winzer, "Eine neue Etappe der Beziehungen zwischen der DDR und der UdSSR," *Einheit*, no. 7, 1964, pp. 3–17.
50. *ND*, Aug. 2, 1964, p. 1.
51. See the open letter addressed to the people of the FRG by the GDR's National Front, the multiparty organization controlled by the SED, in *ND*, Aug. 2, 1964, pp. 1 and 6, along with the National Front's "Declaration to the Peoples of the World," *ND*, Aug. 4, pp. 1–2. Both were promulgated on July 31.
52. *ND*, Aug. 5, 1964, p. 5; FBIS, *USSR & Eastern Europe*, Aug. 5, pp. BB 11–12.

references to West Germany's vassal-like subservience to the United States, views echoed in the leading East German journals.[53] Ulbricht himself spoke out on September 1. After reiterating the standard assaults on West German "monopoly capitalists" and directly linking them to the Erhard government, the SED chief intensified his emphasis on the necessity for inter-German talks. He now called for joint discussions between the GDR and the FRG for the purpose of elaborating a peace treaty proposal, which would then be submitted to the four powers. This idea further highlighted the contrast between Ulbricht's insistence on the priority of inter-German negotiations and Khrushchev's preference for an immediate resumption of the Soviet–West German dialogue, a topic that Ulbricht did not even mention. Willi Stoph, the GDR's head of government, followed Ulbricht's speech with a lengthy address alleging that in 1962 Chancellor Adenauer had personally approved the initiation of talks with the GDR based on East German proposals for improving political and economic ties. The talks never took place, Stoph said, because of the "Caribbean crisis" of October 1962. Stoph's claims, intended to establish a precedent for inter-German negotiations, were promptly denied by Adenauer.[54]

Adzhubei and Khrushchev presented quite different images of the FRG. Shortly after his return from the FRG, Adzhubei and other journalists who had accompanied him there published a series of articles in *Izvestiya*. While admitting that revanchism and fascism were still prevalent in the Federal Republic, they stressed the growing realism of some West German political and business leaders. They also suggested that Bonn's ruling circles should seek to revive the spirit of Rapallo as an example of "the realistic spirit" in Soviet–West German relations. At the same time, they insisted that Germany's postwar borders could not be the subject of negotiations or a political deal.[55]

Speaking in Prague in late August, Khrushchev condemned "revanchists"

53. See the SED theses in *ND*, Aug. 22, 1964, pp. 3–6, and the editorial in *ND*, Aug. 11, pp. 1–2. Also the following articles in *DA*: Volkmar Fenzlein, "Erhards Politik gegen Verständigung und friedliche Koexistenz," no. 5, 1964, pp. 349–56; Gerhard Kegel, "Die Decke wird immer dünner," no. 7, 1964, pp. 583–94; Herbert Kröger, "Bonn bestätigt den Bankrott der Hallstein-Doktrin," no. 7, 1964 pp. 595–600; Johannes König, "Die grosse Freundschaftsreise und ihre Ergebnisse," no. 8, 1964, pp. 697–703; Gerhard Dengler, "Das unrealistische Programm der Bonner Koalitionsparteien," no. 8, 1964, pp. 704–15; Wolfgang Schneider, "Das offene deutsche Gespräch und die friedliche Koexistenz der beiden deutschen Staaten," no. 9, 1964, pp. 809–15; and Bernhard Graefath, "Völkerrechtliche Aspekte des Freundschaftsvertrages," no. 10, 1964, pp. 906–16. For a relatively positive evaluation of "more realistic" elements in the views of such SPD leaders as Brandt and Bahr, mixed with critical comments about their "contradictoriness," see Hellmuth Kolbe, "Zur gegenwärtigen Deutschlandpolitik der SPD," *Einheit*, no. 7, 1964, pp. 72–81.

54. *ND*, Sept. 2, 1964, pp. 3–5. See also the Volkskammer's appeal to the three Western powers condemning the FRG in ibid., pp. 1–2. Adenauer's reply to Stoph's charges is reported in *FAZ*, Sept. 3, 1964, pp. 1, 5.

55. The articles, signed by Adzhubei, V. Lednev, N. Polyanov, and E. Pralnikov, are in *Izvestiya*, Aug. 9, 1964, p. 4; Aug. 11, p. 5; Aug. 13, p. 4; and Aug. 16, p. 4.

in the FRG in a general way, but again avoided applying this epithet to Erhard. He also voiced support for more East-West trade. The statement released at the end of Khrushchev's stay condemned Bonn's advocacy of the MLF and its refusal to regard the 1938 Munich treaty as invalid ab initio. But its proposal for a settlement of the German question placed the conclusion of a German peace treaty ahead of the normalization of inter-German relations. This priority was Khrushchev's, not Ulbricht's.[56]

In another curious development, it later became known that on August 29 the Soviet government had issued a decree rehabilitating the Volga Germans, a group persecuted by Stalin in 1941. The decree was not publicly revealed until January 1965, and by then the post-Khrushchev leadership had rescinded it. The Soviet Union's failure to disclose the decree when it was issued suggests that there may have been opposition to it at high levels. Under the circumstances, opposition to an effort that would have improved Soviet–West German relations was tantamount to opposition to the very idea of a rapprochement with Bonn.[57]

There matters stood when, on September 3, the West German government announced that it had formally invited Khrushchev to meet with Chancellor Erhard in Bonn. Though no date was set for the visit, it was expected to take place in early January 1965. It was also disclosed that agreement had been reached on an open agenda. Despite Adzhubei's earlier insistence that Khrushchev did not wish to discuss any aspect of the German problem, the Soviets now accepted Erhard's demands for an open-ended discussion.[58]

Khrushchev's Fall

The West German invitation marked the high point of Khrushchev's opening to Bonn. Thereafter, indications multiplied that Khrushchev was losing his grip on the rudder of Soviet foreign policy. On September 6 *Pravda* published an article by a West German communist party official attacking "some circles" for "trying to minimize the danger of the revanchist line of the West German imperialists." Though the attack was ostensibly directed at Mao Zedong, in all probability it repesented a veiled critique of Khrushchev, an impression reinforced by the article's critical allusion to the "cult of personality." Also on September 6 *Izvestiya* reprinted a map from a neo-fascist West German newspaper depicting West German and Chinese territorial claims on the Soviet Union.[59]

---

56. *Pravda*, Aug. 28, 1964, p. 3; Aug. 30, p. 3; Sept. 6, pp. 1–2. Khrushchev's order of priorities was confirmed in a Moscow radio talk on August 4 by Lev Bezymenskii, a Soviet specialist on Germany. See FBIS, *USSR & Eastern Europe*, Aug. 5, 1964, pp. BB12–13.
57. Tatu, *Power in the Kremlin*, p. 390.
58. FAZ, Sept. 4, 1964, pp. 1, 4.
59. The article accompanying the map was written by V. Lednev, one of the co-authors, along with Adzhubei, of the earlier *Izvestiya* articles that had praised the FRG. It cited right-

On the same day, a bizarre event dealt a serious blow to Soviet–West German relations. A West German technician attached to the FRG's embassy in Moscow, Horst Schwirkmann, was stabbed in the leg with an injection of mustard gas while attending church services in the monastery at Zagorsk. West German authorities did not reveal the incident for nearly a week in the hope of obtaining a quiet clarification from Moscow. The first Soviet comment did not come until September 16, when a Radio Moscow commentary expressed perplexity at what had "allegedly" happened at Zagorsk, without actually denying it.[60] Suspicions ran high in Bonn, where some officials interpreted the deed as a KGB counterintelligence operation (Schwirkmann's job was to check the embassy for electronic eavesdropping devices). Others saw it as an attempt by Khrushchev's foes to sabotage the meeting with Erhard.[61]

Over the next several weeks, both Khrushchev and Ulbricht continued to lobby on behalf of their contrasting views. Both visited Bulgaria and restated their positions. From there Ulbricht went on to Yugoslavia, but Tito refused to give him an official welcome for fear of jeopardizing Yugoslavia's ties with West Germany. Khrushchev, by contrast, continued to offer praise for the Federal Republic.[62]

Khrushchev's star was visibly plummeting, however, as both the Soviet and East German press intensified their thinly disguised sniping at his German policy. On September 11 *Kommunist* published an unsigned article criticizing the Chinese leadership for holding the view that Western Europe, spurred on by the "French and West German monopolies," was becoming increasingly independent of the United States. It was precisely this image of U.S.–West European "contradictions," of course, that Khrushchev and advocates of a more Europeanist orientation in the secondary elite had been projecting when they justified talks with Bonn. The author accused proponents of this view of moving toward "dubious political combinations."[63] The Soviet military stepped up its own criticisms of the FRG in the acrid tones normally employed by the East Germans.[64] And *Neues Deutschland* weighed in with another diatribe ostensibly aimed at China but laden with references to Chinese claims that the Soviet Union was disregarding East Germany's interests. It concluded by counterbalancing its support for

---

wing "revanchists" in the FRG as advocating closer ties with China, but the article did not attack the Erhard government.

60. The text is in FBIS, *USSR & Eastern Europe*, Sept. 17, 1964, pp. BB10–11.

61. *FAZ*, Sept. 14, 1964, pp. 1, 4; Sept. 15, p. 3; and Sept. 16, p. 5. Schwirkmann was flown back to the FRG and survived the attack.

62. *ND*, Sept. 19, 1964, p. 3; Sept. 20, pp. 1–3; Sept. 21, pp. 1–2; *FAZ*, Sept. 23, 1964, p. 2; *Pravda*, Sept. 20, 1964, pp. 1–2.

63. "Leninskaya politika mirnovo sosushchestvovaniya i klassovaya borba," *Kommunist*, no. 13, 1964, p. 56.

64. See, e.g., *Krasnaya zvezda*, Sept. 17, 1964, p. 4; Sept. 18, p. 4; Sept. 27, p. 3; Oct. 8, pp. 3–4; and Oct. 10, p. 4.

Khrushchev's planned trip to Bonn with the blunt assertion that "the GDR is not and never will be for sale."[65]

Then on September 24 and 25 a series of rapidly unfolding events appeared to spell doom for Khrushchev's overtures to West Germany. On the 24th the USSR formally rejected Bonn's accusations in the Schwirkmann affair as "false and provocative." Gromyko arrived in East Berlin to prepare for the ratification of the Friendship and Cooperation Treaty of June 12 by the Soviet and East German parliaments. Willi Stoph addressed the East German Volkskammer (People's Chamber), and indicated the latest economic and political responses of the GDR to Khrushchev's initiatives. In the economic sphere, he announced a "new, qualitatively higher level" of scientific-technical cooperation with the USSR, including the export of more than a hundred chemical installations to the Soviet Union. Politically, he scorned the peace talk of West German "imperialists" as designed "to deceive naive people," while at the same time blaming "malicious slanderers" for saying that the Soviet Union was responsible for "an alleged betrayal or surrender of GDR interests." Barely hours later, East German authorities announced that agreement had just been reached with the West Berlin Senate on a new visitor pass arrangement. The sudden withdrawal of certain East German objections to the text of the agreement, coming after nine months of arduous negotiations, suggested that the GDR may have withheld its approval until Moscow was ready to ratify the Friendship and Cooperation Treaty.[66]

On September 25 the USSR Supreme Soviet finally ratified the treaty. Addressing the assembly, Anastas Mikoyan declared that the Soviet Union would never seek to improve relations with West Germany at the GDR's expense. Deputy Foreign Minister V. V. Kuznetsov chimed in with a harsh assault on West Germany, thereby signaling that the Soviet Foreign Ministry had turned against Khrushchev's diplomacy. Other speakers, including delegates from the Ukraine and Georgia, also lashed out at the FRG. Mikhail Suslov, the party leadership's prestigious ideological specialist, spoke out against "revanchists and militarists" in the FRG, while Adzhubei expressed the more positive hope that "sober-minded and sane leaders" would prevail in West German political and business circles.[67] Meanwhile, a TASS broadcast criticized Erhard for the first time in months. Speaking on the same day, Ulbricht appeared to take deadly aim at Khrushchev: it was not enough to condemn the cult of personality, he said; "one must also draw the necessary conclusions from it." He then denounced those connected with "a go-it-alone policy and with underestimating the cold war measures of the adversary."[68]

65. *ND*, Sept. 20, 1964, p. 7. See also the speech by Paul Fröhlich, a member of the SED Politburo, attacking West German "monopolies," *ND*, Sept. 18, p. 5.
66. *ND*, Sept. 25, 1964, pp. 1, 3–5, 6; and Sept. 26, p. 2. See also *FAZ*, Sept. 25, pp. 1, 4.
67. *Pravda*, Sept. 25, 1964, p. 1, and Sept. 26, pp. 1–2.
68. *ND*, Sept. 26, 1964, pp. 3–5.

Khrushchev next spoke in public on September 28, but his remarks contained nothing controversial. More important, TASS on the same day announced that Brezhnev—not Khrushchev—would lead the Soviet delegation to the following week's ceremonies in East Berlin commemorating the establishment of the GDR.[69] Khrushchev was not entirely defeated yet, however. In late September he lectured the Central Committee on the hazards of autarky in a strong endorsement of scientific cooperation with the West, and *Izvestiya* followed up these remarks with an article implying that the GDR was not able to deliver all the chemical equipment it had promised.[70] These statements contrasted starkly with Ulbricht's insistence that "socialist teamwork" was the key to solving the problems encountered in all spheres of the economy.[71]

By early October, however, it was evident that the CPSU's ruling coalition had swung against Khrushchev's diplomacy toward Bonn. In what amounted to a snub, Willi Stoph failed to call on the embattled Soviet leader while he was briefly in the Soviet Union at the start of the month. On October 5 Suslov denied that Moscow was contemplating a commercial deal at the GDR's expense, adding that Soviet solidarity with East Germany was not for sale, not even for "all the gold in the world."[72] At the festivities celebrating the GDR's anniversary in East Berlin, Brezhnev warmly reaffirmed Soviet support for the GDR and the June 12 treaty, and warned West Germany against hoping for an agreement "behind the back of the GDR."[73] Ulbricht used the occasion to announce a greater emphasis on the chemical industry in the next annual economic plan, and bitingly compared "Professor Erhard" with Hitler, while at the same time denigrating the West German chancellor as a "small, completely barren episode in German history."[74]

On October 13 the Soviets forwarded another note to Bonn on the Schwirkmann affair, stating their willingness to supply more information but continuing to deny the FRG's version of the events.[75] Chancellor Erhard was determined to proceed with arrangements for Khrushchev's visit in any event, and on October 15 he informed the Bundestag of his plans to present the Soviet leader with a new reunification plan. The world did not learn until the next day that Khrushchev had already been removed from office on October 14.

69. *FAZ*, Sept. 17, p. 1.
70. *Pravda*, Oct. 2, 1964, p. 1; *Izvestiya*, Oct. 4, 1964, p. 2, cited in Bruce Parrott, *Politics and Technology in the Soviet Union* (Cambridge: MIT Press, 1983), p. 362n. The CPSU Central Committee appeared less than enthusiastic about Khrushchev's proposals, however, and *Pravda* published an article praising the East German economy on Oct. 3. See Parrott, pp. 149–50.
71. *ND*, Oct. 4, 1964, p. 3.
72. *Pravda*, Oct. 6, 1964, p. 3.
73. *Pravda*, Oct. 7, 1964, p. 3.
74. *ND*, Oct. 7, 1964, pp. 3–7. See also Ulbricht's interview in *Pravda*, Oct. 6, 1964, p. 1.
75. *FAZ*, Oct. 14, 1964, p. 3.

Conclusions

Precisely what impact Khrushchev's approach to West Germany in 1964 had on the decision to remove him from power still cannot be specified with any certainty. Although Soviet insiders have come forward in the Gorbachev years with various accounts of Khrushchev's ouster, none has yet clarified the role his German policy played in the decision to relieve him of office.[76] Nevertheless, the information available seems to argue against the notion that Khrushchev was about to sell out the GDR in some kind of grand bargain with Bonn. To begin with, there is no evidence to support such a proposition. On the contrary, Khrushchev's own statements and actions throughout the year displayed full support for the existence of the GDR and the established postwar territorial arrangement. Moreover, the Soviet leader had more than ample justification for going to Bonn short of trying to resolve the German question in a single master stroke. The value of playing on Western contradictions, the need to reiterate Moscow's case against the MLF, the desire to broaden economic contacts—these and related considerations were sufficient to prove the merit of opening a direct channel of communication between Moscow and Bonn. West German political leaders, too, entertained only modest hopes in connection with a Khrushchev visit. Though both sides wanted to talk, neither side was ready to yield on matters of principle.

It therefore seems likely that Khrushchev's opening to Bonn was not the decisive factor in his removal. Rather, the controversies it provoked in the Soviet Union and the GDR provided yet one more pretext among the many on which Khrushchev's opponents in the leadership seized in drawing up their brief against him. Thus Khrushchev's German initiative failed in part because Khrushchev failed more generally to stabilize his authority as a leader. Opposition to his domestic reforms, as well as to his cavalier decision-making style, ultimately spilled over into his foreign policy undertakings.

Indeed, the mounting frustration occasioned by Khrushchev's highly personalized style of leadership was clearly exacerbated by the first secretary's handling of policy toward Germany. Andrei Gromyko, for example, averred that Khrushchev had been toppled because he had sent Adzhubei to Bonn, plainly implying that the foreign minister should have been entrusted with this sensitive mission.[77] One account published in West Germany

---

76. One former Politburo member, Gennadii Voronov, said in 1988 that the plot to oust Khrushchev had been hatched a full year before it was carried out. *Izvestiya*, Nov. 18, 1988, p. 3. See also Petro Shelest's interview in *Argumenty i fakty*, no. 2, 1989, pp. 5–6, and the article by one of Khrushchev's former advisers, Fyodor Burlatskii, in *Literaturnaya gazeta*, Sept. 14, 1988, pp. 13–14. See also Fjodor Burlazki, *Chruschtschow: Ein politisches Porträt*, trans. Vesna Jovanoska (Düsseldorf: Claassen, 1990), and Sergei Khrushchev, *Khrushchev on Khrushchev*, trans. William Taubman (Boston: Little, Brown, 1990), pp. 132–33.

77. Cited in Tatu, *Power in the Kremlin*, p. 389.

reported that Adzhubei's trip had received the party hierarchy's endorsement, but that Khrushchev had aroused the ire of his colleagues when he personally debriefed Adzhubei upon his return without providing a similar opportunity for the rest of the collective leadership.[78]

Although we may therefore conclude that Khrushchev's German diplomacy ran into trouble because of growing opposition to Khrushchev himself, it would be a mistake to infer that this general dissatifaction with Khrushchev's leadership was solely responsible for the plainly articulated disapproval of his opening to Bonn. In fact, opposition to Khrushchev's German policy as such clearly existed. As we have seen, throughout Khrushchev's final year in power prominent members of the Soviet secondary elite explicitly argued that the West German government under Ludwig Erhard could not be regarded as a reliable partner in any prospective negotiations. Similar misgivings were also expressed about the Free Democrats and the leading opposition party, the SPD. These arguments evidently reflected the views of key members of the primary elite. Statements made by Brezhnev and Suslov in 1964, for instance, strongly indicated that these influential figures who helped engineer Khrushchev's fall had major reservations about dealing with the FRG at this time. Their chilly attitude toward West Germany over the next year or two appeared to confirm their personal doubts about engaging the Erhard government in a high-level dialogue.

Other members of the secondary elite quite openly supported Khrushchev's line. In short, the Soviet foreign policy establishment was seriously divided over policy toward the Federal Republic in 1963 and 1964. Obviously the public debates on German policy developed within the broader context of Khrushchev's headlong political decline, yet it was also apparent that important members of the Soviet foreign policy elite were in acute disagreement over the specific issue of détente with the FRG.

To be sure, the widening disapproval of Khrushchev over a variety of issues only heightened the significance of these divisions. It was virtually impossible for the Soviet government to make any kind of major foreign policy move until its internal leadership problems were straightened out. As the year progressed, Khrushchev's coalition bore all the characteristics of a decision-making regime in the throes of fragmentation. By September 1964, Moscow's commitment to exploring the possibility of détente with Bonn was transparently in doubt. The Kremlin's ability to demonstrate a measure of responsiveness to the openings offered by the Erhard government simply collapsed from within, as did its readiness for any kind of compromise, however limited, in its ties with West Germany. In the process, as Khrushchev's grip on the Soviet leadership weakened, the opportunities for debate on the wisdom of his German policy grew wider, permitting

---

78. *FAZ*, Oct. 21, 1964, pp. 1, 4.

advocates and opponents of his diplomacy to play their advisory role by enunciating their respective views in open forums with markedly greater explicitness than was usually the case in Soviet public discourse.

By way of contrast, the GDR under Walter Ulbricht clearly exemplified a directive decision-making regime led by a man of definitive views. Ulbricht's maximalist outlook left little room for détente with Bonn, and the GDR under his direction exhibited abysmally low levels of flexibility, readiness to compromise, and openness to internal debate. More than anything else, Ulbricht wanted to block any Soviet–West German dialogue behind East Germany's back. This was the principal message he had tried to convey with his insistence that inter-German negotiations had to precede or accompany, not follow, negotiations between Moscow and Bonn. Ulbricht also feared the long-term effects of an increase in Soviet-FRG economic relations.[79] In view of Khrushchev's determination to ignore these concerns, Ulbricht did not conceal his personal animus toward the Soviet leader once he was deposed. The SED chief charged that Khrushchev had "damaged and even abused the collectivity of the leadership."[80]

In the end, the Soviet leaders who ousted Khrushchev indicated that they were willing, at least for the time being, to give in to Ulbricht's demands for a halt to any Soviet–West German rapprochement. Ulbricht, in fact, had deftly taken full advantage of the Kremlin's internal disarray to press his views on the Soviet hierarchy. At the same time, however, it appeared doubtful that the anti-Khrushchev conspirators in Moscow shared Ulbricht's intransigence. Interestingly, neither Suslov nor Brezhnev voiced support for Ulbricht's letter to Erhard or for the SED chief's insistence that inter-German talks constituted a precondition to détente with Bonn. Brezhnev, in fact, did not criticize Erhard at all, but expressed the USSR's interest in settling its relations with the FRG. Kosygin also failed to echo Ulbricht's views in a speech delivered during Stoph's visit in October.[81]

---

79. In the immediate term, however, the GDR's trade with the FRG and West Berlin grew by over VM300 million in 1964: *Statistisches Jahrbuch der Deutschen Demokratischen Republik, 1965*, p. 388. See the statements favoring wider inter-German trade by leading East German foreign trade officials in FBIS, *USSR & Eastern Europe*, Aug. 5, 1964, pp. EE2, and *ND*, Sept. 6, 1964, p. 3. For an example of a more critical opinion, tying further improvements in inter-German trade to West German political concessions, see Erich Freund, "Der Handel zwischen beiden deutschen Staaten und der DDR mit Westberlin," *DA*, no. 9, 1964, pp. 816–29.

80. *ND*, Nov. 5, 1964, p. 3. Despite this criticism, the GDR's official comments on Khrushchev's ouster were tinged with a note of sympathy. The SED's first statement on the subject acknowledged Khrushchev's "merits in connection with Marxist-Leninist policies," and observed that his dismissal had "moved our party and people deeply": *ND*, Oct. 18, 1964, p. 1. Kurt Hager also stated that the removal of Khrushchev from office "caused a great emotional stir in our party," but went on to say that the deposed leader "acted willfully and was often guided by subjective considerations": *ND*, Dec. 4, 1964, p. 7. Paul Verner expressed roughly similar views: *ND*, Nov. 7, 1964, pp. 3–4.

81. *Pravda*, Oct. 4, 1964, p. 1.

These conspicuous efforts to distance themselves from Ulbricht's line strongly implied that the Soviet leaders who unseated Khrushchev had no intention of granting the GDR a veto over Soviet policy.

By the same token, neither did they have any immediate intention of reviving Khrushchev's German initiative. As the new Soviet leadership team under Brezhnev and Kosygin began settling into power, Moscow's relations with West Germany were summarily relegated to the back burner. The CPSU "theses" published on October 18 called for friendship and cooperation with the United States, Britain, France, and Italy, but urged West German workers to combat revanchism and militarism in the FRG.[82] Kosygin disclosed that he was too busy to go to Bonn, and the Soviet media soon resumed their customary propaganda assaults on the Federal Republic.[83] The Soviets also broke off negotiations on a new trade treaty with the FRG to replace the one that had expired a year earlier, citing Bonn's refusal to exclude West Berlin from its provisions. The next trade agreement would not be signed until 1972.

Clearly the Brezhnev-Kosygin team was not ready to deal with Bonn on the basis of the Erhard government's positions in 1964. Before too long, however, many of the issues raised in Khrushchev's abortive bid to resume the dialogue with Bonn would reemerge, confronting decision makers and policy analysts in Moscow and East Berlin with divisive new challenges.

82. *Pravda*, Oct. 18, 1964, p. 1.
83. *FAZ*, Oct. 21, 1964, pp. 1, 4.

CHAPTER THREE

Prospects for
Change in Europe:
1965–1967

THE MID-1960s was a transition period both in Soviet attitudes toward Western Europe and in West European attitudes toward the Soviet Union and its East European allies. For the most part, the impetus for these changing orientations came from the West Europeans. Charles de Gaulle's determination to forge a more independent role for France in East-West maneuverings and shifts in West Germany's posture toward the Eastern bloc opened up unanticipated new prospects for Soviet diplomacy on the continent. The newly established Brezhnev-Kosygin regime was still in its formative stages, however, and it reacted to these impulses for change mainly with caution and uncertainty. What stood out with growing clarity was the staunchly conservative nature of the new ruling coalition's stance on such issues as the division of Germany and the need for a substantial reinforcement of Soviet military strength. At the same time, the Brezhnev-Kosygin regime showed no inclination to allow Walter Ulbricht to tie Moscow's hands in any future bargaining that might develop with the Federal Republic. Although it offered its full support for the preservation of the GDR, the Kremlin was resolved to keep its options open as it waited for Bonn to make the decisive first move toward détente by recognizing the territorial status quo.

The Brezhnev Coalition in Search
of a Foreign Policy

Once installed in power, the Brezhnev-Kosygin team was initially more concerned with addressing problems at home than with breaking new ground in foreign policy. The first order of business was to undo some of the "hare-brained schemes" they accused Khrushchev of perpetrating. The ultimate division of foreign policy responsibilities within the CPSU Presidium (soon to be renamed the Politburo) had yet to be worked out. Initially Kosygin assumed the role of chief foreign policy spokesman. This was a position Brezhnev coveted for himself, but it was not until the late 1960s that he managed to eclipse Kosygin in foreign policy matters.

Meanwhile, as the post-Khrushchev leadership sought its bearings, its domestic orientations assumed a distinctly conservative cast. Brezhnev and Kosygin tangled over the question of economic reform in 1965, and the issue was resolved largely in favor of Brezhnev, who was unwilling to make significant alterations in the existing economic system.[1] Thereafter, efforts to improve consumer welfare did not involve significant reforms of industrial or agricutural structures. The trial of Yulii Daniel and Andrei Sinyavskii in early 1966 signaled a new toughness in the Kremlin's dealings with dissidents in the cultural community. De-Stalinization became a relic of the Khrushchev period.

Foreign policy also took on the mark of a conservative regime still in the process of sorting out its internal power structure and its political priorities. The new Kremlin leaders were not inclined to advance any major initiatives on Germany. Except for a few rare expressions of hope for a turnabout in Soviet–West German relations, such as Kosygin's remark that the youth of West Germany were not responsible for Nazism,[2] Soviet leaders generally tarnished the FRG with familiar charges of "revanchism" and "militarism."

At the same time, the Kremlin held its ground in a brief confrontation with both the Federal Republic and the GDR over the status of West Berlin. In April 1965 the West German Bundestag scheduled a plenary session in West Berlin. This demonstration of Bonn's assertion that Berlin was a constituent part of the Federal Republic provoked a warning from Moscow to the United States, Britain, and France of the USSR's determination to guarantee the inviolability of the GDR's borders. East Germany refused transit rights to Bundestag members on April 4, and followed up this order with periodic blockades of ground and waterway traffic to West Berlin during the week of the Bundestag's meetings in the divided city. As tensions mounted, however, the Soviets showed that they had no interest in a military confrontation. The GDR allowed armed American troop convoys to cross East German territory into West Berlin without incident and set up no further traffic blockades thereafter.

Reports in the West German press at the time of the Berlin imbroglio

1. Karl W. Ryavec, *Implementation of Soviet Economic Reforms* (New York: Praeger, 1975).
2. *Pravda*, May 8, 1965, cited in Thomas W. Wolfe, *Soviet Power and Europe, 1945–1970* (Baltimore: Johns Hopkins University Press, 1970), p. 283n.

suggested that the GDR had pressured Moscow into taking a confrontational approach to the situation, whereas the Soviets had favored greater caution.[3] There was also strong evidence that the GDR sought to take advantage of the incident by broadening its own claims of sovereignty over access routes to West Berlin. On June 24, 1965, Foreign Minister Otto Winzer declared for the first time that East Germany's legal authority extended to the air corridors over the GDR rather than just the surface routes. This claim flew squarely in the face of the USSR's rights over the air routes as one of the four occupation powers. It also implied that the GDR was seeking Moscow's permission to harass Western air traffic in future Berlin crises, a prerogative the Soviets reserved exclusively for themselves. By all available evidence, the Kremlin was not prepared to support the GDR's position, and East Germany did not mention its claim again for several years.[4]

Signs of renewed Soviet interest in dealing with Bonn in the fall of 1965 were mixed, to say the least. In the first week of September the West German government announced that Karl Carstens, at that time a minister of state in the Foreign Ministry, would visit Moscow later in the month to attend an international chemical trade fair. Several days before his scheduled arrival, Walter Ulbricht descended on the Soviet capital and announced his intention to plan joint measures with the Soviets "against West German aggression." Carstens was received in Moscow shortly after the Soviets had rebuked the West German ambassador for illegally transporting icons outside of the USSR, an allegation viewed in the Federal Republic as a deliberate affront.[5] During his brief stay Carstens met with Deputy Foreign Minister Semenov and First Deputy Foreign Minister V. V. Kuznetsov, and he returned to Bonn with the impression that the Soviets were interested in reviving commercial and cultural exchanges. He also reported interest in the idea of a mutual "nonaggression" agreement.[6] There was no talk of a summit meeting, however. The Carstens visit was given scant coverage in the Soviet press, and was completely overshadowed by the lavish welcome accorded Ulbricht. At a friendship rally held in Moscow the day after Carstens' talks ended, Brezhnev joined with the SED chief in denouncing West German "revanchism." Nevertheless, potentially significant variations could be detected in their speeches. While Brezhnev concentrated his attack on the FRG's reputed desire for nuclear weapons, Ulbricht inveighed against West German "monopolies." Ulbricht's suggestion that the GDR

3. *Der Spiegel*, Apr. 21, 1965, p. 31.
4. For an account of the 1965 Berlin incident, see Gerhard Wettig, *Community and Conflict in the Socialist Camp: The Soviet Union, East Germany, and the German Problem, 1965–1972*, trans. Edwina Moreton and Hannes Adomeit (London: C. Hurst, 1975), pp. 9–19.
5. *FAZ*, Sept. 18, 1965, p. 2; Sept. 21, p. 1.
6. Arnulf Baring, *Machtwechsel: Die Ära Brandt-Scheel* (Stuttgart: Deutsche Verlags-Anstalt, 1982), p. 226.

was still concerned about the possibility of a serious increase in Soviet–West German trade was underscored by the East German media, which warned that West Germany's economic strength conditioned its "quest for dominance."[7]

The ambiguous, not to say contradictory, signals sent by Moscow on the prospects for a thaw in Soviet–West German relations at the time of the Carstens visit were mirrored in the writings of academicians and journalists published in 1965. Two of IMEMO's leading experts on Germany, Daniil Melnikov and Mikhail Voslenskii, weighed in with emphatically negative critiques of the Erhard government's foreign policy.[8] The fact that Melnikov, who in earlier years had openly advocated improved ties with Bonn as a means of widening U.S.–West European contradictions, would sharply criticize the FRG at this time plainly demonstrated the limits of the Europeanist perspective. While leading Europeanists in the secondary elite clearly favored preferential relations with Western Europe, they did not necessarily favor major concessions as a means to achieve them. The main shifts in policy, it appeared, would have to come from Bonn.

Hopes that the West Germans might alter their positions in the future remained alive, however. A promising view emerged from an article on a debate that had taken place in West Germany between Rudolf Augstein, editor of *Der Spiegel*, and the conservative CSU politician Karl Theodor zu Guttenberg.[9] The Soviet commentator praised Augstein (an FDP member) for his "realism" in advocating a relaxation of tension in Central Europe and expanded East-West trade. He further noted that the Augstein-Guttenberg exchange testified to "the presence inside the West German bourgeoisie of serious disagreements, above all on the question whether the continuation of the revanchist policy of the cold war pays off." East German analysts tended to be more critical of the FDP.[10]

Precisely where the Social Democratic Party of Germany stood was a matter of open controversy at this time. East German commentators took a uniformly critical view of the Social Democrats, despite occasional references to hard-liners and more flexible elements within the SPD.[11] Soviet

7. See the editorials in *ND*, Sept. 24 and 25, 1965. Brezhnev's and Ulbricht's speeches appear in *ND*, Sept. 25, pp. 3–5.

8. D. Melnikov, "Dvadtsat let," *MEMO*, no. 5, 1965, pp. 3–16; M. Voslenskii, "Rezerv revanshizma," ibid., no. 6, 1965, pp. 116–20. Also D. Y. Melnikov, "The Pentagon-Bonn Axis," *IA*, no. 7, 1965, pp. 16–17. In the latter article Melnikov said that U.S.–West German solidarity was associated with periods of greater international tension, thus implying that détente would weaken it.

9. R. Fyodorov, "Politika revansha nanosit vryed samoi Zapadnoi Germanii," *MEMO*, 7, 1965, pp. 131–41.

10. Stefan Heymann, "Die FDP zu einigen Fragen der westdeutschen Aussenpolitik," *DA*, no. 7, 1965, pp. 776–86.

11. Martin Weiss, "Die Deutschlandpolitik der SPD," *DA*, no. 2, 1965, pp. 147–55; Bernhard Weissel, "CDU-Wahlsieg erhöht Kriegsgefahr," *DA*, no. 11, 1965, pp. 1264–67, and "Zapadnaya Germaniya nakanunye vyborov," *MEMO*, no. 9, 1965, pp. 116–21.

writers were a bit more divided. The authors of *MEMO*'s quarterly review of international affairs, for example, congratulated the SPD for favoring improved relations with the USSR during the 1965 election campaign, a position that, in their view, had evoked "understanding among significant sectors of the West German population."[12] Another Soviet writer quoted Willy Brandt favorably as saying that West Germans could no longer be pushed about "in a baby carriage"—presumably by the United States.[13] One Soviet writer, by contrast, observed that opposition within the FRG to U.S.-West German cooperation had "not been loud."[14] As for the daily press, *Pravda* and *Izvestiya* were far less negative in their characterizations of the SPD than *Neues Deutschland* when they assessed the results of the Bundestag elections of September 19.[15]

Meanwhile, Soviet and East German analyses of the broader trends of East-West relations displayed visible contrasts in 1965. Whereas Soviet writers advanced a variety of views, East German analysts tended to converge around an adamantly maximalist position.

The variety to be observed in Soviet writings was even more pronounced in 1965 than in 1964. Maximalist, Europeanist, Americanist, and Atlanticist views were all explicitly articulated. Shalva Sanakoyev, an opponent of Khrushchev's opening to Bonn in 1964, once again affirmed the maximalist notion that, despite the contradictions between the United States and its West European allies, all Western powers "in principle" pursued a common line against the socialist countries.[16] Other writers disagreed with this notion, however.[17]

Not surprisingly, analysts with a more Europeanist bent drew special attention to the difficulties currently exacerbating America's relations with France. A leading specialist on French politics, Yurii Rubinskii, noted that President de Gaulle had already withdrawn most French air and naval forces from the integrated NATO command, and that the French press was dropping "unambiguous hints about the possibility of withdrawal from NATO." While warning that NATO was by no means "doomed to liquidation in a short time," Rubinskii's article nevertheless offered one of the strongest affirmations thus far seen in the Soviet press of the view that the

---

12. "Tekushchiye problemy mirovoi politiki," *MEMO*, no. 10, 1965, p. 81.
13. N. Vladimirov, "West German 'Mafia' in Washington," *IA*, no. 9, 1965, p. 44.
14. N. Yuryev, "European Security and the German Question," *IA*, no. 10, 1965, p. 57.
15. *Pravda*, Sept. 22, 1965, p. 4, and Sept. 24, p. 5; *Izvestiya*, Sept. 21, 1965, p. 1; *ND*, Sept. 21, 1965, p. 1; Sept. 22, p. 7; Sept. 23, p. 2.
16. Sh. Sanakoyev, "Internationalism and Socialist Democracy," *IA*, no. 5, 1965, p. 22. Sanakoyev described U.S.–West European contradictions as "mere trends" whose importance should be neither underestimated nor overestimated: ibid., no. 7, 1965, p. 22.
17. D. Tomashevsky (Tomashevskii), "Lenin's Views on Socialist Foreign Policy," *IA*, no. 4, 1965, pp. 7–13. The author referred to the *Pravda* article of Apr. 12, 1964, which quoted Lenin's justification for Soviet participation in the 1922 Genoa conference, as an effort to "single out the pacifist wing in the bourgeois camp."

decline of American leadership was an "objective tendency" gaining in strength. At the same time, Rubinskii put forward two explanations to account for the "crisis of confidence" now undermining Western Europe's faith in its American ally. One was the attenuation of the fear of Soviet aggression among West European elites; the other was "the nuclear missile power of the Soviet Union," which increasingly put American territory at risk. Soviet writers were to use these arguments—the first emphasizing Moscow's peaceful intentions, the second justifying an expansion of Soviet strategic forces—with growing frequency over the coming years to explain the differences between the United States and Western Europe.[18]

Other Soviet writers also referred to the deterioration of U.S.-French ties in 1965, but balanced these references with reminders of continuing cooperation between Washington and Paris in certain areas of economic and even military policy.[19] For its part, the new post-Khrushchev leadership plainly regarded France as worthy of special attention. Gromyko visited Paris at the end of April, and the Kremlin reissued an earlier invitation to de Gaulle to visit the Soviet Union.

Meanwhile, evidence of a more outspokenly Americanist position also surfaced in the same year. An article in *International Affairs* set forth this view with remarkable clarity. While sharply critical of America's support for the MLF and of its general anticommunist posture, the author, T. Fyodorov, was considerably more hostile to West Germany. He portrayed the United States as seeking "to leave the way open for negotiations on a number of burning problems" and for "a certain relaxation of international tension." Curiously, Fyodorov noted that Washington's latest military actions in Southeast Asia were not intended "to come into direct military collision with the Soviet Union," a rather candid suggestion that the escalation of the Vietnam war should not be considered an obstacle to Soviet-American talks on Europe. Bonn, by contrast, was vilified for "striving to step up international tension by all possible means," especially in Europe, where the United States was "not willing to run too great a risk." Fyodorov provided several examples of American refusals to accept some of West Germany's positions on issues affecting European security. He concluded

18. Yurii Rubinskii, "Oslableniye sistemy imperialisticheskikh soyuzov," *MEMO*, no. 6, 1965, pp. 3–13. Rubinskii coupled his favorable comments on French policy with highly critical remarks on West Germany's pro-American stance. For another article highlighting Franco-American conflicts and calling for détente with Western Europe, see Y. Zhukov, "The Problems of European Peace and Security," *IA*, no. 6, 1965, pp. 3–9. For an additional example of the view that the United States' vulnerability to nuclear attack was undercutting its primacy in NATO, see "Zapadnaya Evropa i sovremenny kapitalizm," *MEMO*, no. 11, 1965, pp. 27–40.

19. L. M. Vidyasova, "Paris-Washington-Bonn," *IA*, no. 7, 1965, pp. 18–19. A critical view of French policy in the Third World was expressed by V. Lyubimova, "Frantszuskii gosudarstvenno-monopolisticheskii kapitalizm i kolonialnaya politika," *MEMO*, no. 7, 1965, pp. 29–42.

that, though the American stance on these issues was no less negative than Bonn's, "Washington, in principle, does believe that they could be negotiated [but] Bonn invariably refuses all discussion."[20] What was most noteworthy about his argument was that it specifically identified the United States, not the Federal Republic or even France, as Moscow's preferred negotiating partner in any talks on Europe's future.

Several other Soviet writers conveyed somewhat more variegated appraisals of the Western alliance, mixing examples of both conflict and cooperation in relations between the United States and Western Europe (and particularly between the United States and the FRG). This consciously balanced approach constitutes what I have defined as the Atlanticist orientation in Soviet writings on international affairs. Interestingly, several of these Atlanticist articles in 1965, while strongly anti-American, bluntly accused the Federal Republic of seeking to enhance its own power vis-à-vis the United States, either by forming a "nuclear pool" with Britain and France or by claiming an equal status with the United States in the event of France's withdrawal from NATO. In each case, the writer made it very plain that the disintegration of NATO's present structure would be a mixed blessing for the USSR, involving a serious danger if it led to a more potent West German military capability and greater latitude for Bonn to pursue its own foreign policy goals.[21]

East German academic writings on West German foreign policy shared the generally negative outlook of Soviet assessments of the Erhard government in 1965.[22] As we have seen, however, East German analysts tended to be more uniformly critical of the SPD and FDP than their Soviet counterparts. Moreover, the Europeanist, Americanist, and Atlanticist orientations were largely absent from the specialist press in the GDR. Although one article displayed some Europeanist leanings in its positive comments on de Gaulle's foreign policy, another lambasted French policy as merely an instrument of NATO aggression, a characterization that by now had virtually disappeared from the leading Soviet journals.[23]

20. T. Fyodorov, "Washington and Bonn—an Alliance against Peace," *IA*, no. 4, 1965, pp. 14–19.

21. I. Lemin, "Impaired Alliance: The Problem of 'Special Relationship' with U.S.A.," *IA*, no. 5, 1965, pp. 48–55; V. A. Matveyev, "U.S.A. and NATO," *IA*, no. 7, 1965, pp. 3–22; and N. Andreyev, "NATO and the War Danger in Europe," *IA*, no. 12, 1965, pp. 39–45.

22. E.g., Helmut Schnitter, "Die Bonner Ultras und die Atomstreitmacht der NATO," *Einheit*, no. 2, 1965, pp. 66–74; Wolfgang Schiel, "Gegen die Bonner Aggressionspolitik," ibid., no. 7, 1965, pp. 3–10; Stefan Heymann, "Bonns 'Europa-Plan'—ein weiterer Schritt der aggressiven Revanchepolitik," *DA*, no. 3, 1965, pp. 335–56; S. Doernberg, "Bonn's Atomic Ambitions," *IA*, no. 3, 1975, pp. 9–13.

23. For the more positive assessment of de Gaulle, see Siegfried Schwarz, "Veränderungen in den Beziehungen Bonn-Paris," *DA*, no. 9, 1965, pp. 1051–60; for the negative view, Willi Wilke, "Aspekte der Militärdoktrin des imperialistischen Frankreichs," *DA* no. 3, 1965, pp. 249–61.

A major exception to this lopsidedly maximalist approach in the GDR centered on the question of trade with West Germany. Despite Ulbricht's well-advertised aversion to excessive economic reliance on the Federal Republic, one writer expressed unconcealed interest in expanded trade with the FRG.[24] This was not a lonely view among East German economic specialists. It represented an attitude known as *Westdrall*, a tendency which favored continuing efforts to trade with the West (especially West Germany) for technology and other goods not readily available in the Soviet bloc. One of its leading proponents was the chief of the GDR State Planning Commission, Erich Apel. Apel was on record as advocating not only a broader trade relationship with the West but also an "active" détente policy and a serious effort to study the experiences of capitalist firms, without any "dogmatism."[25] At the end of 1965 Apel's fate took a tragic turn, quite possibly because of his policy stance. In December the GDR concluded a five-year trade pact with the USSR which obliged East Germany to commit well over half of its trade to the Soviet Union, on highly disadvantageous terms. Shortly before the pact was to be signed, Apel committed suicide. Although his motives were never fully clarified, many western observers attributed Apel's action to his opposition to the trade agreement. Hours after the tragedy, the GDR signed the pact.[26]

Soviet academicians were also divided on the issue of East-West economic exchange. This discussion was typified by two articles that took opposite positions on the state of contemporary capitalism. One writer insisted on the "incontestable advantages" of socialism over capitalism, pointing out that the COMECON countries enjoyed higher growth rates than the states of the West European Common Market.[27] The other took a much more positive view of the successes of Western capitalism in recent years, and warned against making "dogmatic formulations" about cyclical crises in capitalism without regard for concrete situations.[28] As developments were to show, these contrasting views on the status of capitalist economies were indicative of a broader debate on the desirability of promoting economic contacts with the West.

24. Gerhard Brendel, "Tauwetter im 'Ost-West' Handel," *DA* no. 2, 1965, pp. 121–33, and "Die sowjetischen Wirtschaftsbeziehungen mit Westdeutschland," *DA*, no. 8, 1965, pp. 908–19. For a positive view of trade with the West combined with criticism of the FRG, see Hermann Schwiesau, "Bonn und der Ost-West Handel seiner NATO-Partner," *DA*, no. 9, 1965, pp. 1073–80.

25. E.g., "Beratung Dr. Erich Apels mit Wirtschaftswissenschaftlern," *Wirtschaftswissenschaft*, no. 1, 1964, pp. 2, 5, 9.

26. On *Westdrall* and the Apel incident, see Thomas A. Baylis, *The Technical Intelligentsia and the East German Elite* (Berkeley: University of California Press, 1974), pp. 247–49. Also Joachim Nawrocki, *Das geplante Wunder* (Hamburg: Christian Wegner, 1967), pp. 172–84.

27. A. Alekseyev and Yu. Shiryayev, "Ekonomicheskoye sorevnovaniye dvukh mirovykh sistem i antikommunizm," *MEMO*, no. 8, 1965, pp. 3–15.

28. "Zapadnaya Evropa i sovremenny kapitalizm," *MEMO*, no. 10, 1965, pp. 3–17.

The 23d CPSU Congress

Though 1965 ended on a note of antipathy to the Erhard government in both the Soviet Union and the GDR, interesting nuances in attitudes toward the West could be observed among Soviet decision makers at the 23d Party Congress of the CPSU, which opened in late March 1966. Brezhnev, for example, referred explicitly to the aggravation of contradictions in U.S.–West European relations and to America's declining ability to direct the policies of its NATO allies. He seemed to hold out little hope for a change in West Germany's orientation, however, denouncing a speech by Erhard at a recent CDU congress as "revanchist." Similarly, the Soviet party chief made no mention of a possible breakthrough in Soviet ties with France. While noting a "coincidence of interests" between the USSR and the French government on several unspecified issues, Brezhnev listed France behind Finland, the Scandinavian countries, Turkey, and several Third World states when he identified countries with which the USSR currently enjoyed favorable relations.[29]

Foreign Minister Andrei Gromyko, however, balanced his criticisms of the FRG with more positive comments. He also prefaced his remarks on West Germany with a reminder to the United States of its obligations under the Potsdam agreement. References to the Potsdam meetings, which Gromyko himself had attended as a rising young official, appeared rather frequently in the foreign minister's speeches. Quite obviously they were intended to reassert the continuing responsibility of the four powers, and particularly the United States and the USSR, for German affairs. These allusions to Potsdam, together with a direct appeal to the United States "to take a close look at what is going on in West Germany" with respect to the FRG's territorial claims and demands for nuclear weapons, represented the Americanist aspect of Gromyko's approach to the Soviet Union's German policy.

From a practical standpoint, this Americanist tendency was evident in the Soviet Union's recent turnabout in its dealings with the United States on a treaty to halt the proliferation of nuclear weapons. After first indicating reluctance to pursue talks on this issue, Moscow took a more positive stance starting in January 1966.[30] Soviet statements on a nonproliferation treaty (NPT) made it plain that Moscow's first priority in the matter was to prevent the Federal Republic from acquiring nuclear weapons. As Lyndon Johnson's administration encountered mounting difficulties in forging a NATO consensus on MLF, the Soviets had good reason to believe that they could win American cooperation in blocking West Germany's nuclear am-

29. For Brezhnev's speech, see *Pravda*, Mar. 30, 1966, pp. 3–9.
30. Wolfe, *Soviet Power and Europe*, pp. 267–68.

bitions through an international ban on proliferation. Using the United States to influence West Germany in this manner constituted a prime example of the Americanist approach in action.

At the same time, however, Gromyko also gave evidence of a Europeanist orientation. In his speech before the 23d Congress, fully half of which dealt with Germany, the Soviet foreign minister was considerably more forthcoming than Brezhnev in expressing Moscow's hopes for an improvement in Soviet–West German relations. Like Brezhnev, Gromyko criticized Erhard's recent address at the CDU congress. He also repeated Brezhnev's blunt rejection of the Erhard government's "peace note" of March 25, 1966, which had declared Bonn's desire to conclude a renunciation-of-force agreement with any Warsaw Pact state except the GDR, without changing Bonn's positions on territorial issues.[31] Nevertheless, Gromyko went on to note "for the sake of fairness" that Konrad Adenauer had recently altered his traditional anti-Soviet stance by asserting that the USSR wanted peace. Accordingly, Gromyko assured his audience that the USSR did not wish to be permanently hostile to the FRG, but instead stood for an improvement in its relations with Bonn. "We know that far from all Germans are poisoned by the ideas of revanche," he added. "There are forces that come out for a resolute departure from the militaristic past."[32]

In short, Gromyko showed clear signs of favoring both Americanist and Europeanist approaches to West Germany. He appeared to indicate that the two orientations were not necessarily mutually exclusive, but were capable of being pursued sequentially or even simultaneously, as circumstances warranted. In this sense, Gromyko may be considered an Atlanticist in his foreign policy strategy toward the West at this time, having borrowed elements from both the Europeanist and the Americanist tendencies without committing himself exclusively to either.

In contrast to Gromyko, other speakers at the 23d Party Congress were predominantly negative in their references to West Germany. They included Ukrainian party chief Petro Shelest and Defense Minister Rodian Malinovskii. Predictably, Walter Ulbricht lashed out at the "Washington-Bonn axis."[33]

A noticeable diversity of opinion surfaced over the question of East-West economic relations. While Brezhnev spoke out in favor of trade with the West, his main emphasis fell on increased integration among the COMECON states. This position corresponded with his earlier statements contrasting the economic achievements of the USSR with the instability of capitalist economies, an optimism shared by such Politburo members as Mikhail

31. For details, see ibid., pp. 285–86.
32. *Pravda*, Apr. 3, 1966, pp. 4–5.
33. Shelest: *Pravda*, Mar. 31, 1966, pp. 2–3; Malinovskii: ibid., Apr. 3, p. 3; Ulbricht: ibid., Mar. 31, p. 6.

Suslov, Petro Shelest, and Andrei Kirilenko. Aleksei Kosygin, however, adopted a different stance, accentuating the need to broaden trade ties with the West, in keeping with his previous warnings about inadequate technological innovation in the Soviet economy.[34]

Military issues were also accorded due attention. As in the question of East-West trade, divergent views on this subject had already been expressed by key Politburo figures over the course of the previous year. Aleksei Kosygin and Nikolai Podgorny stood out as advocates of only limited increases in defense spending in 1965. Podgorny, in fact, went so far as to say that the Soviet population should no longer suffer "material restrictions" for the sake of strengthening the USSR's military capabilities.[35] Brezhnev, Mikhail Suslov, and Aleksandr Shelepin, however, firmly argued for further sacrifices for the sake of increased military spending. Kosygin cautiously defended his position, acknowledging the need to improve Soviet defenses in view of the Vietnam war, but advocating a "substantial reduction of military expenditures" if the international climate were to improve. Brezhnev and Rodian Malinovskii issued unequivocal calls to strengthen the USSR's defensive might, a proposition reiterated by Shelepin several months later.[36]

The communiqué issued at the end of the CPSU Congress took a generally hard-line position on virtually all of these issues. Its references to contradictions among the capitalist states made no mention of West European disaffection from the United States, but instead declared in a general fashion that "the exacerbation of its contradictions is driving imperialism to greater adventurism." Conceivably this rather combative formulation may have reflected uncertainty among Soviet decision makers about the wisdom of making overtures to France, West Germany, or other West European states at this time. As far as West Germany was concerned, the communiqué advanced a purely negative image, exclaiming that "the forces of revanchism and militarism are growing with the encouragement of the U.S. imperialists."[37]

Ultimately no clear and coherent strategy for dealing with Western Europe emerged from the 23d Party Congress. The Brezhnev Politburo was still in the process of forming a distinctive foreign policy of its own. The relative diversity of views to be found in the writings of the secondary elite reflected this search for viable options.

34. Bruce Parrott, *Politics and Technology in the Soviet Union* (Cambridge: MIT Press, 1983), pp. 185–88.
35. *Pravda*, May 22, 1965, p. 2.
36. Parrott, *Politics and Technology*, pp. 182–85. For Kosygin's speech, see *Pravda*, Apr. 6, 1966, pp. 2–7. For differences between Podgorny and Suslov on economic and defense issues, see Michel Tatu, *Power in the Kremlin* (New York: Viking, 1969), pp. 456–58, 499–503.
37. *Pravda*, Apr. 9, 1966, pp. 3–4.

The Inter-German Dialogue

Meanwhile, the question of overtures to the FRG was reaching a decision point. Nearly two months before the 23d CPSU congress, East Germany's Socialist Unity Party addressed an open letter to the SPD calling for talks between the two parties aimed at a reconciliation of the two German states.[38] The letter specifically proposed the elaboration of a united action program between the SED and the SPD for the purpose of promoting negotiations between the governments of the GDR and the FRG. These negotiations were then to be followed by a German peace treaty and reunification under a "really democratic" government. The SED open letter explicitly called on the SPD to abandon its support for the policies of the CDU. The SPD turned down the appeal for a unity-of-action program and proposed instead that members of the national parliaments of the two countries be allowed to discuss their views openly in both German states. The SED replied on March 25 with a counterproposal for an exchange of speakers from just the SED and the SPD. Here matters stood as the 23d CPSU Congress convened in Moscow.

It has been suggested that the impetus for the SED's initial proposal probably came from Moscow. It is also possible that the Soviets may have lost interest in a dialogue between the East Germans and the SPD before Ulbricht did.[39] Whether or not this was actually the case, the Soviet leadership did not appear inclined to press the issue in the months immediately after the party congress. It was also apparent, however, that Ulbricht's chief intention was to obtain SPD approval for the GDR's preferred scenario for a settlement of the German question. The plan outlined in the SED's open letter of February 7, placing inter-German negotiations ahead of the conclusion of a peace treaty, was precisely the sequence of events Ulbricht had proposed in 1964, when Khrushchev was trying to establish a Soviet dialogue with West Germany. Ulbricht had to know full well that the Social Democratic leadership in Bonn would reject this proposal out of hand. It is quite possible, therefore, that Ulbricht sought from the outset to maneuver the SPD into rejecting the conditions for a dialogue with the SED, with the ulterior motive of demonstrating to the Soviets that the West German Social Democrats could not be counted on to offer an acceptable alternative to the current CDU/CSU-FDP coalition government. Such a strategy would have been consistent with criticisms of the SPD appearing in the East German press.

In any event, in April the GDR began to retreat from its latest proposal for an exchange of speakers. A convenient pretext was provided by the consid-

38. The letter, dated Feb. 7, was published in *ND*, Feb. 11, 1966, pp. 3–4.
39. Wettig, *Community and Conflict*, p. 25.

eration of a "safe-conduct" law by the Bundestag. This law was actually intended to facilitate the visit of East German speakers to the Federal Republic by guaranteeing that no one from the SED would be prosecuted under existing West German legislation that prescribed penalties for certain categories of political crimes against the German people (such as the shooting by East German border guards of individuals trying to flee East Germany). In May the GDR protested the Bundestag's action, charging (incorrectly) that it was actually designed to place the SED speakers under legal liability. Immediately after the SPD concluded its own party congress, at which the notion of a working alliance with the SED was decisively rejected, the East German media on June 6 reverted to its traditional line that the SPD constituted no alternative to the Christian Democrats. On June 29, after a fruitless exchange of letters between Ulbricht and Willy Brandt, the SED formally withdrew its speaker exchange proposal.

The Kremlin leadership appeared to support Ulbricht's actions for now, apparently concluding that the time was not yet ripe for an opening to the Social Democrats. Before the year ended, however, events would show that the Kremlin was by no means so categorically opposed as Ulbricht to pursuing avenues of communication with the SPD leadership.

Soviet-French Relations and Their Consequences

For the moment, the Kremlin was more interested in France than in West Germany. De Gaulle's decision to withdraw French forces from the integrated military command by July 1966 was signaled in his press conference of February 21 and communicated to President Johnson in March. De Gaulle also announced his intention of visiting the Soviet Union in late June. With all eyes focused on these unprecedented events, the Kremlin kept its relationship with West Germany on hold. On May 17 the USSR finally presented its official response to Chancellor Erhard's "peace note," dismissing it as an indication of Bonn's refusal to abandon its "revanchist" policies.[40] Just before de Gaulle's arrival, the Soviets also spurned an attempt by the CDU leader Rainer Barzel to establish a Bonn-Moscow dialogue.

De Gaulle's bold initiatives prompted a heightened emphasis on U.S.–West European "contradictions" in Soviet foreign policy writings. One of the more effusive articles proclaimed that "a qualitatively new stage" in intercapitalist contradictions had now begun, with the transition from mere arguments among the NATO members to "real practical steps, . . . a regrouping of forces." De Gaulle was portrayed as being motivated by the

40. *Pravda*, May 19, 1966, p. 5.

absence of a Soviet military threat and by a desire for liberation from economic dependence on the United States. With the future of the American military presence in Europe viewed as increasingly uncertain, the article concluded that NATO was now experiencing "not simply a routine flare-up of disagreements but . . . a deep crisis" rooted in "objective conditions."[41] A similarly Europeanist article, by Dmitrii Tomashevskii, heartily approved of Soviet efforts to promote contradictions among capitalist states by cooperating with proponents of "a more moderate course" and "pacifists." Tomashevskii specifically referred to the Genoa conference of 1922, this time observing that it had demonstrated the possibility not only of trade but also of political agreements with these forces.[42]

One writer made an intriguing theoretical point when noting the "most remarkable fact" that the aggravation of international tensions tended to unify the capitalist states in the past, whereas now, "despite the existing tension of the international situation, the contradictions between the NATO members continue to deepen."[43] A different view, however, was put forward by the author of a major book on the question of intercapitalist contradictions, M. K. Bunkina. In an analysis that emphasized the economic conflicts dividing the West, Bunkina argued that the "relaxation of tensions" in international affairs was one of the prime factors accounting for the latest exacerbation of contradictions among the Western powers.[44] The question whether capitalist contradictions were more prevalent in periods of international tension or in periods of détente was to surface again in later years. In essence the opposing views appeared to group those Soviets who favored efforts to promote détente, particularly with Western Europe, against those who seemed less eager to make the compromises détente would entail, and who offered assurances that conflicts in the Western alliance would grow anyway, even without a relaxation of tensions. As subsequent events were to prove, this debate was of far more than purely academic interest. It capsulized perhaps the single most important question facing Soviet decision makers in their policy toward Western Europe over the next two decades: Would the effort to promote disunity among the Western allies require a broad-based relaxation of tensions, or could it permit (and perhaps require) a significant measure of confrontation?

Bunkina's book was also notable for its introduction of a new theme in Soviet writings on U.S.–West European relations. This was the notion that

41. "Tekushchiye problemy mirovoi politiki," *MEMO*, no. 7, 1966, pp. 90–94.
42. D. Tomashevsky (Tomashevskii), "The U.S.S.R. and the Capitalist World," *IA*, no. 3, 1966, pp. 13–17. See also Tomashevsky, "Lenin's Views."
43. B. Khalosha, "NATO: Krizis uglublyayetsya, ugroza octayetsya," *MEMO*, no. 10, 1966, p. 4.
44. M. K. Bunkina, *Razvitiye mezhimperialisticheskikh protivorechii v usloviyakh borby dvukh sistem* (Moscow: Moscow University Press, 1966), pp. 11, 18–19.

Western Europe was now emerging as "a special imperialist 'power center' " under the leadership of France and West Germany. Although the brunt of Bunkina's analysis fell on economic rivalries between the United States and the European Common Market, it held open the distinct possibility of "exploiting" the "interimperialist struggle" for the benefit of the socialist camp.[45] In later years the concept of "imperialist power centers" was expanded to include Japan, and was adopted by Brezhnev himself at the 24th Party Congress of the CPSU.

Meanwhile, several articles highlighted the notion of American and West German collusion against France, or described Bonn as exerting pressure on the United States to approve its military plans.[46] These essays were consistent with current attempts by the Soviet leadership to isolate both the United States and the Federal Republic from France during Moscow's blossoming relationship with de Gaulle. At the same time, other Soviet academicians took a more Atlanticist approach, mixing guarded approval of the French president's latest moves with warnings that his policies in no way constituted a complete rupture in Franco-American relations.[47] These varying accents, while not indicative of serious opposition within the Soviet elite to rapprochement with France, provide some evidence that the decision makers were discussing how far the rift between Paris and Washington (and, by implication, between the United States and Western Europe) could be expected to go.

As it happened, the Europeanist and Atlanticist tendencies underscored in these academic analyses appeared to provide the rationale for the Kremlin's next policy moves. At the time of de Gaulle's visit, Soviet decision makers and the party press intensified their efforts to stress the incompatibility between the "Bonn-Washington axis" on the one hand and the interests of France and certain other West European countries on the other. These endeavors bore mixed results. Though de Gaulle had every intention of pursuing a more independent foreign policy, he had no interest in a neutral one. The French leader's recognition of the Oder-Neisse line and his opposition to MLF did not vitiate his commitment to maintaining French troops in Germany or his refusal to recognize the GDR, which he was fond

45. Ibid., pp. 67–70. For another reference to the concept of "power centers," see "Aktualnye zadachi izucheniya problem mirovovo razvitiya," *MEMO*, no. 11, 1966, p. 18.

46. E.g., Y. Viktorov, "European Policy of the U.S.A.," *IA*, no. 3, 1966, pp. 38–42; D. Melnikov, "Confessions of a Learned Revanchist," ibid., pp. 60–62; "Tekushchiye problemi mirovoi politiki," *MEMO*, no. 1, 1966, p. 77; S. Filshtinskii," 'Povorot sudby' i bezopasnost Evropy," *MEMO*, no. 7, 1966, pp. 123–25; O. Bykov, "Vashington i Bonn: partnerstvo i protivorechiya," *MEMO*, no. 8, 1966, pp. 50–61.

47. I. Lemin, "Neravnomernost razvitiya kapitalizma i obostreniye mezhimperialisticheskikh protivorechiya," *MEMO*, no. 3, 1966, p. 52; "Zapadnaya Evropa i SShA," ibid., no. 11, 1966, p. 40. For a somewhat more Europeanist analysis noting elements of both partnership and conflict in U.S.–French relations, but stressing the latter, see Yu. Rubinskii, "Frantsiya i NATO," ibid., no. 12, 1966, pp. 27–37.

of calumniating as "la Prusse." The Brezhnev regime certainly had no interest in the Gaullist concept of an independent "Europe from the Atlantic to the Urals"—an open invitation to the countries of Eastern Europe to liberate themselves from Soviet dominance. De Gaulle's value to the Soviets lay primarily in his ability to disrupt NATO's military cohesiveness and perhaps to lead the rest of Western Europe away from the United States. The communiqué released at the end of his visit reflected these Europeanist predilections, emphasizing that "the problems of Europe should be considered first of all in a Europeanist framework."[48]

The Soviets scarcely skipped a beat after de Gaulle's departure before concretizing their renewed preoccupation with Western Europe in an authoritative Warsaw Pact policy statement. The Bucharest Declaration of July 5 declared that there could be "no doubt that the aims of U.S. policy in Europe have nothing in common with the vital interests of the European peoples and the tasks of European security." It accused Washington of seeking "to make Western Europe an instrument of U.S. global policy." Significantly, the communiqué distinguished between the "militarist and revanchist forces" in the FRG (whom it condemned for collaborating with "the American imperialists") and "circles in the Federal Republic of Germany which oppose revanchism and militarism" and who called for normalizing relations between the FRG and the GDR. The communiqué did not identify the members of either group, however, leaving open the question which category applied to the SPD leaders and other noncommunist West German politicians of potential interest to the Soviet Union. The document went on to denounce the MLF, the Bundeswehr, and West Germany's territorial demands. It called for a German peace settlement based on "a recognition of the fact of the existence of the two German states," but (contrary to Ulbricht's view) it did not make this settlement contingent on prior negotiations between the FRG and the GDR. As to the separate question of Germany's reunification, the statement called for a preliminary "rapprochement" between the two German states, which could then lay the groundwork for the creation of a "democratic" Germany.

The Bucharest Declaration's chief import consisted in proposals for the simultaneous dissolution of NATO and the Warsaw Pact, and for the convocation of a "general European conference" on security and cooperation in the spheres of economic, scientific-technical, and cultural exchanges. The proposal to dissolve the two alliance systems was made with an eye to the impending expiration of the Atlantic pact in 1969. The call for a European security conference, an idea first floated by the Soviets in the 1950s, was patently aimed primarily at the West Europeans. It was ambiguous, however, on the question of American participation. Though the tone

48. *Pravda*, July 1, 1966, p. 1.

and apparent aims of the Bucharest Declaration were avowedly European-
ist, Moscow was not yet ready for a more determined effort to exclude the
United States from discussions on a future "system of collective security in
Europe."[49]

Reactions to the Grand Coalition

Developments in Bonn soon drew Moscow's attention back to
West Germany. In late November the governing coalition of Christian
Democrats and Free Democrats under Ludwig Erhard fell apart. In a sharp
break with postwar precedent, the Christian Democrats for the first time
turned to the SPD to form a new federal government. The Grand Coalition
was formally established on December 1, 1966, with Kurt-Georg Kiesinger
(CDU) installed as chancellor and Willy Brandt (SPD) as foreign minister.

The new cabinet quickly announced a major initiative in West Germany's
ostpolitik. Henceforth Bonn would seek to establish diplomatic relations
with the states of Eastern Europe. This move took Schröder's bridge-
building policy a considerable step forward and signaled an abrupt departure from the "Hallstein doctrine," under which previous FRG governments had refused to normalize relations with states that formally recognized the GDR. At the same time, the FRG announced its willingness to
move toward a "regulated coexistence" ("*geregeltes Nebeneinander*") with
East Germany. This somewhat more positive attitude toward the GDR
stopped well short of normalized relations, however, and was intended
largely to facilitate humanitarian contacts with the East German population. The Kiesinger-Brandt government coupled these moves with pronouncements stressing Bonn's peaceful intentions and its desire for renunciation-of-force agreements with the East.

Despite the new look in West Germany's foreign policy, it preserved
important elements of the ostpolitik of the Adenauer and Erhard governments. Reunification on the basis of self-determination continued to be the
FRG's ultimate foreign policy goal. West Germany's claim to be the sole
legitimate representative of all Germans, including those living in East
Germany, remained in force. There was to be no formal diplomatic recognition of the East German regime, and the designation "German Democratic
Republic" was still anathema to many West German officials, who continued to refer to East Germany as the "Soviet Occupation Zone" or
"Mitteldeutschland." The FRG's constitutional provisions concerning the
status of Berlin were untouched. So was Bonn's commitment to NATO and
its hope for participation in some form of nuclear planning regime. Final

49. *Pravda*, July 9, 1966, pp. 1–2.

settlement of Germany's borders, in the Grand Coalition's view, would still have to be determined in a peace treaty with the four powers. Most important, it was evident that the new cabinet was determined to use diplomatic and economic leverage to encourage the East European states to relax their commitments to the GDR and abandon their hostility to Germany's eventual reunification. Only now Bonn regarded détente as a process that would precede reunification, whereas previous West German goverments had viewed détente as coming after reunification.[50]

Walter Ulbricht lost no time in denouncing the new government even before it was formally constituted. On November 29 he derided the Grand Coalition as simply another right-wing West German cabinet, and criticized the SPD for not joining forces with the Free Democratic Party. In mid-December, Ulbricht responded to Kiesinger's first policy declaration by asserting that the Grand Coalition offered no substantive changes in Bonn's policy, but resembled past CDU/CSU governments "as one rotten egg [resembles] another." The SED chief later coupled these attacks with the charge that the establishment of the Grand Coalition government heralded the end of the postwar period of "imperialist restoration" in West Germany and the advent of a new stage of "expansionism."[51] Over the coming weeks and months, the concept of West German expansionism was to become one of the main themes in the GDR's assaults on the Kiesinger-Brandt government, a theme propagated by SED decision makers as well as by academicians and journalists in the secondary foreign policy elite.[52]

In contrast to Ulbricht's quick repudiation of the Grand Coalition, Soviet reactions to the new cabinet displayed a studied ambivalence during its first month and a half in office. Positive comments alternated with negative ones, but no direct attacks were aimed at the new government as such until mid-January. Even the more critical remarks emanating from Moscow lacked the ferocity of the GDR's diatribes, and accusations of "expansionism" were scrupulously avoided.[53]

By and large, the Soviet military press tended to be more negative than *Pravda* in its initial evaluations of the new government in Bonn, but even

50. For the principal early policy statements of the Grand Coalition, see Kiesinger's government statement of Dec. 13, 1966, in *Bulletin der Presse- und Informationsamtes der Bundesregierung*, Dec. 14, 1966, pp. 1265–70; Brandt's speech before the West European Union, ibid., Dec. 16, pp. 1273–75; Kiesinger's Christmas Eve radio broadcast, ibid., Dec. 29, p. 1314; and his speech in Obershausen, ibid., Feb. 15, 1967, p. 122.

51. *ND*, Nov. 30, 1966, pp. 1–2; Dec. 16, pp. 6–7; Jan. 1, 1967, p. 1.

52. See, e.g., Dr. Herbert Barth, *Bonner Ostpolitik gegen Frieden und Sicherheit* (East Berlin: Staatsverlag der Deutschen Demokratischen Republik, 1969).

53. For examples of *Pravda*'s commentary on the Grand Coalition in its first weeks in office, see the issues of Nov. 28, 1966, p. 5; Nov. 30, p. 5; Dec. 1, p. 1; Dec. 3, p. 3; Dec. 14, p. 5; Dec. 16, p. 6; Dec. 17, p. 3; Dec. 18, p. 5; Dec. 20, p. 3; Dec. 21, p. 5; Dec. 23, p. 1; Dec. 24, p. 3; Dec. 26, p. 4; and Dec. 28, p. 4. For additional press reactions, see Wettig, *Community and Conflict*, pp. 33–37.

Krasnaya zvezda, the military's daily newspaper, was noticeably less op-probrius than the East German press or the SED leadership.[54] Not surpris-ingly, a favorite theme of the military press was the Grand Coalition's alleged striving after nuclear weapons.

Several leading Politburo and Secretariat figures addressed foreign policy issues in the weeks after the formation of the Grand Coalition. On the whole, their comments during December tended to be quite critical of West Germany's "revanchist" foreign policy and of the rise of the neo-Nazi National Democratic Party of Germany (NPD) in the Federal Republic. They generally refrained from attacking the Kiesinger-Brandt government by name, however.[55]

Some insight into the arguments that Soviet officials may have been weighing in the final months of 1966 is provided by the diverging assess-ments of West German foreign policy published in the specialist journals. Two articles in the October issue of *International Affairs* presented very sophisticated analyses of mounting contradictions between the United States and Western Europe. Though both placed heavy emphasis on cooper-ation between Washington and Bonn, each referred explicitly to conflicts in the U.S.–West German relationship.

The first of these articles, by A. Gorokhov, took due notice of cooperative as well as conflictual tendencies in NATO, and reminded its readers that France continued to adhere to NATO's political institutions. Gorokhov's main accent, however, fell decisively on the "centrifugal forces" now divid-ing the Western allies. As a result of a "new . . . Europeanism" manifest in "a growing tendency to regard alliance with the U.S. as an obstacle," U.S.–West European relations were entering a new stage characterized prin-cipally by the decline of U.S. hegemony and a desire in Western Europe for a "truly independent policy." Economic rivalries were also growing more intense, leading Gorokhov to the conclusion that it was now "imperative for the West European countries to expand their business contacts with socialist Europe," where they could expect greater understanding than across the Atlantic. Even West Germany was seen as at least potentially more independent of American tutelage. The infectiousness of de Gaulle's example, Gorokhov observed, was evidenced by increasing talk in West Germany to the effect that the country needed a "de Gaulle of its own" and should stop relying on the United States for everything. Accordingly, Gorokhov wrote, though some observers considered the prospects for

54. *Krasnaya zvezda*, Dec. 3, 1966, p. 5; Dec. 17, p. 5; Dec. 28, p. 3.

55. *Pravda*'s account of Brezhnev's speech in Hungary Dec. 2, 1966, p. 2, contained no references to West Germany at all. Kosygin's remarks while visiting France are in ibid., Dec. 3, p. 3, and Dec. 10, p. 2. See also *Pravda*'s accounts of the speeches by Ustinov, Dec. 9, pp. 1–2; Shelepin, Dec. 10, pp. 1–2; and Voronov, Dec. 11, pp. 1–2. *Krasnaya zvezda* published similar accounts of most of these speeches.

Gaullist-style cooperation with the socialist countries to be limited, "it is not the limited but the untapped possibilities of overall European cooperation that must be emphasized."[56]

Alongside these distinctly Europeanist arguments, Gorokhov included some observations of a more Americanist coloration. Significantly, they centered directly on Washington's role in restraining Bonn's military ambitions. Gorokhov acknowledged that the United States was increasingly reluctant to permit West Germany to have access to nuclear weapons. He further claimed that the United States justified its troop presence in Europe by persuading its allies to support NATO as "a force to contain West German militarism." These remarks strongly suggested that a continuation of some American military influence in Western Europe might not be such a bad thing for the socialist states. In the end, Gorokhov's subtle blend of Europeanist and Americanist views appeared to reflect Gromyko's double-edged Atlanticist policy of encouraging West European independence from the United States as well as American restraints on West Germany.

The second article, by V. Mikhailov, accentuated the prospects for change in West Germany's foreign policy. Mikhailov pointed to rivalries within the CDU/CSU between the "Europeanists" (such as Adenauer and Strauss, both of whom had pro-French proclivities) and the "Atlanticists" (such as Erhard and Schröder). He also echoed Gromyko's earlier reference to Adenauer's characterization of the USSR as a peace-loving nation. While underlining the tight cooperation that currently typified U.S.–West German relations, Mikhailov was exceptionally positive in his remarks about the SPD. He cited Herbert Wehner and an unnamed SPD leader as saying that the old clichés of West German policy no longer carried conviction, and that illusions were now being dismantled in the FRG concerning such questions as the eastern borders and reunification. Mikhailov praised the SPD for its negotiations with the SED the previous spring, and pointedly blamed the CDU leadership for preventing the exchange. In his view, the SPD leadership still favored the dialogue with East Germany.[57]

These views were in marked contrast to other analyses that appeared in Soviet and East German journals in 1966. Some critics of the SPD leaders held them responsible for blocking the proposed exchange of speakers with the SED.[58] The next issue of *International Affairs* for example, contained two articles strikingly different from the analyses of Gorokhov and Mikhai-

---

56. A. Gorokhov, "Western Europe, 1966," *IA*, no. 10, 1966, pp. 6–12.

57. V. Mikhailov, "Bonn between Past and Present," *IA*, no. 10, 1966, pp. 20–26, 60.

58. V. Levin, " 'Big Coalition' Passions," *IA*, no. 3, 1966, pp. 79–80; V. M. Khvostov, "Historic Significance of the German Democratic Republic," *IA*, no. 12, 1966, pp. 56–62; A. Chernyayev, "Sotsial-demokratiya pered litsom mezhdunarodnykh problem," *MEMO*, no. 8, 1966, pp. 14–26; Hans Schaul, "Der Dialog und der Dortmunder Parteitag der SPD," *Einheit*, no. 8, 1966, pp. 1027–37.

lov. N. Andreyev argued that the FRG would benefit from France's with-drawal from NATO military structures because it could then beef up its own military contribution to the alliance. Andreyev pursued his attack on the FRG by taking dead aim at the SPD leadership. He quoted Helmut Schmidt, the SPD's defense expert, as saying that France's military with-drawal would lower the atomic threshold, resulting in an earlier use of nuclear weapons along the FRG-GDR boundary than would otherwise be the case.[59]

The other article in the same issue took a consistently negative position on West Germany's domestic and foreign policy evolution. A. Kurchatov excoriated the "Right Social-Democratic leaders" for helping to smash political opposition to the ruling "monopolists" in Bonn. He stigmatized the FRG as an instrument of America's "global policy" and a bridgehead for U.S. troops in Europe. Kurchatov made no reference to contradictions within NATO, but insisted that the FRG's foreign policy was "supported, though not wholeheartedly, by the governments of the NATO states insofar as it meets their common class interests."[60] This sinister view of the western alliance signaled the presence of unwavering anti-Bonn attitudes in the Soviet secondary elite.

East German analyses of the FRG at this time tended to adopt similarly negative views, emphasizing West Germany's attempts to turn U.S.-French discord to its own advantage and denouncing the policies of the SPD leadership.[61]

As the year came to an end, signs of a close relationship between analysis and policy were very much in evidence in both the Soviet Union and the GDR. Divergent images of West Germany in the Soviet academic press coincided with obvious ambivalence and uncertainty in the CPSU Politburo about the future course of the Grand Coalition. A more pronounced bias against the Kiesinger-Brandt government found expression in both the Ulbricht-dominated SED hierarchy and the GDR's leading foreign affairs and party journals.

The Ulbricht Doctrine

The first direct criticism of the Grand Coalition by a Soviet official came on January 13, 1967, as Brezhnev declared that the new West

59. N. Andreyev, "Revanchism and the Atomic Bomb," *IA*, no. 11, 1966, pp. 74–78. The views expressed in this article were in many ways consistent with what Andreyev had written in 1965. See above, n. 21.
60. A. Kurchatov, "Aggressive Policy of West German Imperialism," *IA*, no. 11, 1966, pp. 45–50.
61. E.g., Heinrich Sperker, "Die Zuspitzung der Gegensätze zwischen den imperi-alistischen Hauptmächten," *Einheit*, no. 8, 1966, pp. 1058–67.

German government's program showed that "the goals of West German imperialism unfortunately remain unchanged." Despite his disapproving tone, the Soviet party chief did not criticize the SPD leadership. Rather he pledged that the Soviet Union would support "everything reasonable" that might permit a positive step in Bonn's direction. The tenor of his remarks suggested that Kremlin decision makers had by no means slammed the door on the Kiesinger-Brandt government, but remained hopeful that the new chancellor's words about mutual understanding would be converted into deeds.[62]

As the new year opened, it became apparent that Soviet leaders had two prominent concerns in mind when they formulated their policy toward West Germany. The first centered on the growing perception that the strains in U.S.–West European relations were intensifying significantly, offering the Soviets new opportunities for exploiting rifts among the NATO allies. Though France was taking the lead in this regard, the Federal Republic was inevitably the single most important country in Western Europe from the Soviet point of view. The key to Moscow's long-standing postwar goal of gaining the West's endorsement of the territorial and political status quo in Europe was held in Bonn, not in Paris or even Washington. Hence the Soviet leadership had to be attentive to the slightest possibility of change in the FRG's attitudes. Though the Grand Coalition government retained several of the cardinal elements of Adenauer's and Erhard's ostpolitik, important differences on some of these issues divided the leading figures of the ruling parties. The Social Democrats, in particular, were eager to probe Moscow's attitudes on a general accommodation, while the Christian Democrats were divided on the issue between relatively flexible types (such as Erhard, Kiesinger, and Barzel) and conservatives (such as Franz-Josef Strauss). Differences along much the same lines also existed on the question of Bonn's access to nuclear weapons.[63] Consequently, the Soviet Union had ample grounds for believing that a shift in Bonn's foreign policy, though not necessarily imminent, was at least a distinct possibility.

The second consideration underlying Moscow's German policy at this time revolved around Eastern Europe. Here the Soviets were confronted with two contradictory pressures. At one end stood Romania, which in the early 1960s had carved out a measure of foreign policy autonomy from the Soviet Union. Romanian party boss Nicolae Ceausescu made it clear that he was interested in normalizing relations with West Germany and in significantly expanding mutual trade ties. At the other end stood Walter Ulbricht, who emphatically opposed détente with the Grand Coalition. Meanwhile, as the Grand Coalition took office, Hungary and Czechoslovakia also

62. *Pravda*, Jan. 14, 1966, pp. 1–2.
63. On these points see William E. Griffith, *The Ostpolitik of the Federal Republic of Germany* (Cambridge: MIT Press, 1978), pp. 133–41.

signaled interest in Bonn's call for diplomatic relations and expanded economic cooperation, while Poland's Wladyslaw Gomulka provided faithful support for Ulbricht's intransigence.

These cross-currents within the Soviet alliance reached a watershed on February 1, when Romania established diplomatic relations with West Germany. The SED leadership made no secret of its alarm at the prospect of being isolated from its allies if other East European countries were to follow the Romanian example. On February 13 Ulbricht unleashed his most acrid attack yet on the Grand Coalition. But the speech appeared to be addressed primarily to the GDR's alliance partners rather than to Bonn. He warned that the West German government was currently attempting to reach "a kind of Locarno agreement" with Poland and Czechoslovakia, with the aim of isolating East Germany and the Soviet Union from its Warsaw Pact allies. Ulbricht seemed to be speaking directly to the Soviet leadership when he upbraided the SPD and rejected the notion of U.S.–West German contradictions:

> Some politicians maintain that they wanted to help the Kiesinger government and Mr. Brandt to separate West Germany from the United States and eliminate U.S. influence in Europe. So far, however, all the facts show that Kiesinger, Strauss, and Brandt are trying to strengthen the Bonn-Washington axis and create close relations. Brandt backs the payment of billions to the United States. He hopes that no U.S. troop reductions will be made. His policy adheres strictly to the Paris agreements, according to which the GDR is also to be incorporated into NATO.
>
> It is not true that there are leading politicians in Bonn who want to separate West Germany from the United States. On the contrary, Bonn wants to act as Washington's main ally.[64]

Ulbricht's remarks came less than a week after a hastily convened conference of Warsaw Pact foreign ministers held amid signs of disagreement among the participants.[65]

The GDR followed up its dire warnings about the Grand Coalition with efforts to reinforce its own claims to national sovereignty. On February 20 the Volkskammer enacted a law defining the conditions for a separate GDR citizenship.[66] East Germany also moved to solidify its ties with Poland and Czechoslovakia, its partners in Eastern Europe's so-called iron triangle. In March the GDR signed mutual assistance treaties with both countries. The texts of the two treaties, however, revealed the Czechs' reluctance to allow the treaty to exacerbate relations with the FRG, an impression confirmed in

64. The speech was printed as a special supplement to *ND* on Feb. 16, 1967.
65. The meeting, held February 8, produced no communiqué, an unusual occurrence. Romania was represented not by its foreign minister but by his deputy.
66. *ND*, Feb. 21, 1967, pp. 1, 3.

a speech by Antonin Novotny.[67] Gomulka firmly backed the GDR's demands against Bonn.[68] Hungary's Janos Kadar adopted views similar to those of Novotny when the GDR-Hungarian friendship pact was signed in May.[69]

It was Moscow's reaction, of course, that mattered most to the SED leadership. On January 25 the Soviets issued a declaration calling attention to the rise of neo-fascism in the Federal Republic, and followed it on February 7 by a note to the West German government rejecting its claim to sole representation of all Germans.[70] Both documents called on Bonn to recognize "the fact of the existence" of the GDR, a traditional demand but one that fell short of calling for full de jure recognition.

At the same time, leading Soviet decision makers were noticeably more equivocal than the SED leadership in their pronouncements on West Germany. Kosygin concluded that the new government in Bonn was no different from its predecessors on basic foreign policy questions. He added, however, that one could not exclude the possibility that the Grand Coalition leaders might recognize the results of World War II, in which case the USSR would without doubt make "an appropriate response." Podgorny took a similar position. Neither Kosygin nor Podgorny attacked the SPD. Brezhnev took up the theme of Bonn's growing isolation within the Western camp. He specifically noted a "broad concurrence of views" between East and West on denying the FRG access to nuclear weapons, a reference to the ongoing U.S.-Soviet discussions on a nonproliferation treaty. His characterization of the Grand Coalition, like Kosygin's and Podgorny's, mixed traditional criticisms of Bonn's current ostpolitik with explicit expressions of hope for a change of course. The Soviets, he said, "far from mechanically, by inertia, so to speak, transfer to the Kiesinger cabinet the attitudes we formed toward the former federal government," and he confirmed Moscow's interest in a substantial improvement in Soviet–West German relations. As in his speech of January 13, Brezhnev made no allusion to the "Bonn-Washington axis," and his only criticism of the SPD was confined to its support for the ban on the Communist Party of Germany. In another of his speeches at this time, Podgorny criticized West Germany for opposing détente, and added that the USSR would welcome it.[71]

67. The GDR-Czech treaty failed to mention the FRG in the *causus foederis* clause. The text is in *ND*, Mar. 18, 1967, p. 1. Novotny declared that the treaty was "aimed against no other state," and he failed to say that West German recognition of the GDR was a prerequisite to the normalization of Czech–West German relations.

68. *ND*, Mar. 16, 1967, pp. 3–4. See Hans Heinrich Mahnke, "Die Deutschland-Frage in den Freundschafts- und Beistandspakten der DDR mit Polen und der CSSR," *Europa Archiv*, no. 9, 1967, pp. 323–28.

69. *ND*, May 19, 1967, pp. 1, 4–5.

70. *Pravda*, Jan. 29, 1967, pp. 1–2; Feb. 9, 1967, p. 2.

71. *Pravda*, Mar. 7, 1967, pp. 1–2; Mar. 10, 1967, pp. 1–3; Mar. 11, pp. 1–3. Earlier Podgorny attacked the FRG and called for strengthening the Soviet military: ibid., Mar. 4, 1967, p. 3.

More exclusively negative images of the FRG were conveyed in speeches by Petro Shelest and Yurii Andropov.[72] Strictly negative views of West Germany were also expressed by the leading members of the Soviet military hierarchy in the spring of 1967.[73] These positive and negative images of the Grand Coalition seem to indicate that the leading Soviet decision makers and military brass had yet to form a final consensus on the likelihood or desirability of an accommodation with the West German government.

Perhaps the most striking differences that now emerged, however, were those between Brezhnev and Ulbricht. As the two leaders shared the dais at the Seventh SED Party Congress in April, Ulbricht used the occasion to fulminate at length against what he called the "Kiesinger-Strauss" government. He also denigrated the entire Social Democratic Party, insisting that its only real influence on West German policy lay in its support of Bonn's right-wing orientation. In remarks obviously intended for his Soviet listeners, Ulbricht noted that the GDR had seen through the new Bonn cabinet's rhetoric "from the beginning," and added a reference to the Erhard government's "middlemen on our side," a sardonic allusion to Khrushchev's abortive initiative in 1964. While acknowledging that there were contradictions in the Western alliance, Ulbricht declared that the FRG was seeking to resolve them through revanchism and expansionism. He also drew attention to the "Bonn-Washington axis" and to West Germany's alleged role in "U.S. global strategy."[74]

Brezhnev's speech at the SED congress also asserted that Bonn's foreign policy had not substantially altered under the Grand Coalition, and he condemned the FRG for seeking to strengthen its military power and divide the socialist states. Brezhnev went on to observe, however, that the capitalist states of Europe were dissociating themselves from these policies, and he did not repeat Ulbricht's contention that these contradictions were only making West Germany more expansionistic. Nor did Brezhnev refer to the "Bonn-Washington axis" or to "U.S. global strategy." The Soviet leader also failed to criticize the SPD. On the contrary, he seemed to go out of his way to voice hope for a change in West Germany's international outlook, stressing that he did not regard it as "something immutable, bearing the eternal

72. Shelest: *Pravda Ukrainy*, Mar. 10, 1967, p. 2. *Pravda* deleted Shelest's harsh words on West Germany in its coverage of his speech, Mar. 10, p. 2. In Shelest's speech of Jan. 25 he condemned West German "revanchists" without offering any more positive appraisals of the Grand Coalition. *Pravda Ukrainy*, Jan. 26, 1967, pp. 1–2. Andropov: FBIS, *USSR & Eastern Europe*, Mar. 7, 1967, p. DD28. *Pravda*'s account of Andropov's speech contained no references to his remarks about West Germany.

73. See the speeches by Andrei Grechko in *Pravda*, May 2, 1967, pp. 1–2, and May 9, p. 1. Grechko replaced Malinovskii as defense minister upon his death in March 1967. See also Aleksei Yepishev's article in *Sovetskaya Rossiya*, May 8, 1967, pp. 1–2.

74. *Protokoll der Verhandlungen des VII. Parteitages der Sozialistischen Einheitspartei Deutschlands* (East Berlin: Dietz, 1967), pp. 51–81, passim.

mark of Cain." Brezhnev followed up this biblical analogy with an assertion that Moscow had no interest whatever in rejecting in advance anything new that might appear in Bonn's external policies. Millions of West German citizens wanted peace, he concluded, and "these forces will increasingly influence West Germany's foreign policy."[75]

In addition to his lengthy diatribe against West Germany, Ulbricht used the SED congress as a forum for unveiling important ideological initiatives. The most significant of these announcements was the designation of the GDR as a "developed societal system of socialism" (*entwickeltes gesell-schaftliches System des Sozialismus*). Though this designation implied no substantial revision of orthodox Marxism-Leninism, it did amount to a reformulation, in terminology borrowed from systems theory and cybernetics, of the terms traditionally used to describe socialist systems in the USSR and Eastern Europe. The political significance of Ulbricht's ideological foray was potentially quite controversial. The very idea that the East German party chief would take it upon himself to announce a reconceptualization of socialist ideology, even one confined to terminology, constituted an arrogation of considerable authority. Traditionally, only the Kremlin had the right to make doctrinal pronouncements. Ulbricht's theoretical creativity provided a conspicuous contrast to the ideological torpor that had prevailed in the Kremlin ever since Brezhnev rose to power. Moreover, the GDR was visibly offering itself as a model of advanced socialism, with the evident intention of demonstrating to the other socialist states, including the Soviet Union, how they could learn from East Germany's experience.

Later that year Ulbricht went even further in the direction of theoretical innovation, this time departing explicitly from a time-honored tenet of Soviet doctrine. Marxist-Leninist orthodoxy held that communism would follow the stage of socialism after a relatively brief transition period, and in the course of a single historical process; Ulbricht rejected both propositions. Under current conditions, he maintained, socialism would be a more protracted historical phase than had been thought, and it constituted a "relatively independent socioeconomic formation," clearly demarcated from communism and therefore endowed with its own laws of development.[76]

Once again Ulbricht risked treading on Soviet sensitivities by advancing his own claims to ideological authoritativeness. And once again the SED chief was holding up the GDR as a model to be emulated throughout the Soviet bloc, an aspiration implicit in his assertion that the GDR had discovered some of the laws of advanced socialism in the course of its own

75. *Pravda*, Apr. 19, 1967, pp. 1–2.
76. *ND*, Sept. 13, 1967, pp. 3–6.

development. While the new doctrines had implications for the domestic political system (particularly in their reaffirmation of the "leading role of the party"), they also served important foreign policy functions. At a time when Soviet and East European leaders were starting to turn away from the GDR in the expectation of possible economic and political agreements with the Federal Republic, Walter Ulbricht felt it more necessary than ever to reinforce the GDR's value to its fraternal allies in every possible way. Though East Germany already made indispensable contributions to the Soviet bloc's military security and its economic development, Ulbricht saw a need to add an ideological dimension to this pattern of commitments. In addition, Ulbricht clearly believed that the East German model was potentially applicable to West Germany as well. The SED leader continued to dream that socialism would eventually prove its superiority over capitalism and that Germany would one day be united under a socialist system. Ulbricht's ideological convictions were deeply tinged with pan-German aspirations.

Immediately after the conclusion of the SED party congress, leaders of the various delegations from the Warsaw Pact countries (with the notable exception of Romania) traveled to Karlovy Vary for a meeting of European communist party representatives. A major purpose of the gathering was to reassert the bloc's solidarity behind the GDR in the aftermath of the normalization of Romania's ties with the Federal Republic. Accordingly, it was agreed at Karlovy Vary that no other East European states would enter into diplomatic relations with the FRG until Bonn recognized East Germany, a policy the Western press quickly dubbed the "Ulbricht doctrine." Despite this display of support for the GDR, however most participants held back from endorsing Ulbricht's maximalist program. Even Gomulka refused to echo the SED chief's most virulent criticisms of the FRG, and *Neues Deutschland* gave an expurgated and falsified account of the Polish leader's speech. Novotny indicated Czechoslovakia's continuing interest in economic relations with West Germany, and Kadar confirmed Hungary's hope for eventual diplomatic relations.[77]

Brezhnev's speech at Karlovy Vary showed that the Soviet leadership's main concern at this time was not to back Ulbricht's maximalist position to the hilt but rather to widen the rifts it perceived in U.S.–West European relations and to encourage the Grand Coalition to join in the movement toward a more independent posture. Brezhnev placed great stress on Western Europe's lack of support for the U.S. war effort in Vietnam and on the

77. Gomulka: *ND*, Apr. 28, 1967, pp. 4–5; Novotny: *ND*, Apr. 26, pp. 5–6; Kadar: *ND*, Apr. 28, p. 4. For a behind-the-scenes account of the Karlovy Vary conference by a defector who had earlier served as Gomulka's translator, see Erwin Weit, *Ostblock Intern* (Hamburg: Hoffmann & Campe, 1970), pp. 128–29, 148–49. For an English-language version, see *At the Red Summit* trans. Mary Schofield (New York: Macmillan, 1973).

"intensifying contradictions" between American and West European economic interests. "In place of pro-American policy concepts," he said, "new concepts that aim at transforming capitalist Europe into a force independent of the United States and capable of playing an independent role in the world arena are increasingly blazing a path for themselves." This was Brezhnev's most explicit articulation of the Europeanist aspect of Soviet foreign policy to date. He underlined it with an appeal for greater East-West economic cooperation in Europe and for the development of bilateral relations on the continent. Just as important, the CPSU chief counterbalanced his criticisms of the FRG's "revanchist demands" and close cooperation with the United States with a restatement of the USSR's readiness "to do everything" to improve ties with the present government in Bonn as long as it displayed "sobriety" in its foreign policy. Far from foreclosing any opportunity to work with the Social Democrats to this end, Brezhnev noted that the SPD had acquired "great possibilities for influencing the foreign policy course of West Germany." While expressing disappointment that the SPD had not exploited these possibilities thus far, the Soviet leader remained convinced that a growing number of Social Democrats in Western Europe were striving to jettison the ballast of the cold war. Once again Brezhnev avoided direct attacks on specific SPD leaders. As far as the GDR was concerned, he called for the "recognition of the existence of the two German states," and—remarkably—made no direct reference to the Ulbricht doctrine. Finally, Brezhnev reasserted the Warsaw Pact states' need "to raise their level of military preparedness."[78]

A comparison of Brezhnev's speech at Karlovy Vary with Ulbricht's speech on the same occasion reveals significant differences not only in their characterizations of West Germany and the SPD but in their analyses of U.S.–West European relations. Whereas Brezhnev underscored the contradictions undermining Western unity, Ulbricht emphasized "the coordinated general line of the leading imperialist powers." West Germany's ostpolitik, in his view, was part and parcel of the same "global strategy" that accounted for the American presence in Vietnam. While admitting that resistance to these policies was mounting in various NATO countries, Ulbricht's stress fell unmistakably on the "coordinated actions of imperialism," and above all on the "Bonn-Washington axis." Again he reminded the Kremlin that Germany had joined the Western powers at Locarno, and the result was the liquidation of the policy of Rapallo. And in a contemptuous reference to Romania, Ulbricht averred that Bonn's ostpolitik had lately "become stuck in some village street." Similarly, while acknowledging that elements of the SPD wanted an alternative to the FRG's present foreign policy, Ulbricht appeared to dash all hopes of expecting such a change from Willy Brandt

78. *Pravda*, Apr. 25, 1967, pp. 1–3.

and the other SPD cabinet ministers, whose main role was "to camouflage the expansionist policy of the monopolists." In view of these factors, Ulbricht insisted on "a policy jointly arrived at" among the Warsaw Pact members, and described recognition of the GDR as "the essential problem" of European security.[79]

Ultimately, the communiqué released at the end of the Karlovy Vary conference provided some reassurance to Ulbricht by requiring Bonn's "recognition of the existence" of the GDR as a precondition to further diplomatic accords with Eastern Europe. It did not, however, formally insist on de jure recognition, an issue that would sharply divide the Kremlin and the SED in years to come. Moreover, the document provided considerable backing for Moscow's Europeanist ambitions.[80]

Policy Discussions in the Secondary Elites

These differences between the Soviet and East German party chiefs were amply reflected in academic and journalistic analyses. Brezhnev's heightened emphasis on the Europeanist side of Soviet policy was reinforced and elaborated in the leading Soviet foreign affairs journals. At the same time, Brezhnev's ambivalence regarding the Grand Coalition apparently signaled the desirability of a debate in the specialized press on the government in Bonn and, in particular, on the SPD's role in it. Soviet writers advanced divergent views on these subjects in 1967, some taking a decidedly negative stance and others expressing a more ambiguous attitude. East German academicians and scholars, by contrast, tended to provide grist for Ulbricht's mill. His opinions were also echoed (with varying degrees of enthusiasm) by other SED Politburo members.

A growing number Soviet articles placed primary emphasis on the intensification of contradictions between the United States and Western Europe. Even when examples of countervailing tendencies of NATO cooperation were produced, as in the more explicitly Atlanticist analyses, a certain bias in the direction of Europeanist logic was often unmistakable.[81] Articles with a more Americanist orientation were remarkably few. Interestingly,

---

79. *Neues Deutschland*, Apr. 27, 1967, pp. 3–4.
80. For the text, see *Europa Archiv*, no. 11, 1967, pp. 259–66.
81. E.g., in *MEMO*, Yurii Shishkov, "Teoriya 'ultraimperializma' i sovremennost," no. 4, 1967, pp. 30–41; "Ucheniye V. I. Lenina ob imperializma i sovremennosti," no. 5, 1967, pp. 3–23; "Tekushchiye problemy mirovoi politiki," no. 7, 1967, pp. 97–99; D. Tomashevskii, "Nekotorye voprosy krizisa vneshnei politiki imperializma," no. 8, 1967, pp. 58–60; and in *IA*, S. Beglov, "Dialogue Goes Ahead," no. 3, 1967, pp. 44–49; Y. Rakhmaninov, "Alternative to a Divided Europe," no. 4, 1967, pp. 41–47; O. Bykov, "Atlantic Policy of the U.S.A. and European Security," no. 9, 1967, pp. 39–45.

though several writers criticized U.S.–West German cooperation, few referred to the "Bonn-Washington axis" or to the FRG's role in "U.S. global strategy."[82]

These articles accounted for the widening disparity between American and West European interests by such factors as economic rivalries, the failure of cold war policies, and the reputed decline of the "myth" of Soviet aggression in Western Europe. Significantly, some writers also pointed to the Soviet Union's growing military strength as a vital contributor to Western Europe's faltering confidence in Washington. One article in *International Affairs* spelled out this argument with striking candor. Yurii Shishkov maintained that ever since the USSR's first ICBM tests in 1957 had eliminated America's vulnerability to nuclear attack, the nuclear superiority of the United States and hence the American leadership of NATO had been "losing their importance." Shishkov argued further that the Cuban missile crisis had convinced many people in the West that in the event of war, the United States would try to "keep aside, and its 'nuclear umbrella' would hardly ever open." Moreover, the United States' adoption of the flexible reponse strategy, according to Shishkov, reinforced these feelings of abandonment in Western Europe. As a consequence, centrifugal tendencies were growing within NATO, as the West Europeans increasingly sought to "get out of all sorts of military pacts and blocs."[83] Though Shishkov's last point exaggerated the actual state of affairs in Western Europe, his other arguments had a certain basis in reality and provided considerable justification for the view that a buildup of Soviet strategic missile forces significantly exacerbated U.S.–West European contradictions. In later years, as we shall see, arguments of this kind underlay the Brezhnev coalition's prevailing view that a Soviet military buildup was not only compatible with détente but essential to it.

Soviet analysts' attitudes toward the Grand Coalition tended to be either ambivalent or hostile.[84] Opinions on the SPD were similarly divided. Several articles were quite critical of the Social Democrats' performance both

---

82. For exceptions, which did use these terms, see V. Matveyev, "Programma politicheskovo realizma," *MEMO*, no. 6, 1967, pp. 18–29; N. Polyanov, "Evropa: Voennoe protivosostoyanie i bezopasnost," ibid., no. 9, 1967, pp. 42–53.

83. Yurii Shishkov, "New Stage in Inter-Imperialist Contradictions," *IA*, no. 3, 1967, pp. 55–63.

84. Examples of the ambivalent tendency, which combined both positive and negative evaluations, include "Tekushchiye problemy mirovoi politiki," *MEMO*, no. 1, 1967, pp. 92–93; M. Voslenskii, "FRG: Pravitelstvo novoye: A politika?" ibid., no. 2, 1967, pp. 96–98; and D. Novoseltsev, "Ideological Precepts of West German Foreign Policy," *IA*, no. 1, 1967, pp. 71–78. Among the negative articles are "Tekushchiye problemy mirovoi politiki," *MEMO*, no. 4, 1967, p. 72; E. Busch (a Czech journalist), "Bonn in Search of New Tactics," *IA*, no. 1, 1967, pp. 37–41; A. Yefremov, "The True Face of the West German National-Democrats," *IA*, no. 4, 1967, 69–73; V. Mikhailov, "Bonn: The Old Road," *IA*, no. 8, 1967, pp. 38–45.

before and after they entered the government. Generally these articles took the SPD leadership to task for following CDU/CSU policies.[85] Several articles accused the SPD of torpedoing the dialogue with the SED in 1966, a reversal of the view held by other Soviet analysts.[86] A major book devoted to the contemporary SPD was unequivocally negative in its portrayal of the party's "rightist" leadership, which the author, V. S. Shumskii, accused of having "literally saved the CDU/CSU."[87] Two other books on West Germany published in 1967, however, advanced somewhat more balanced assessments of the SPD. The authors, Pavel Naumov and Mikhail Voslenskii, combined their critical comments about SPD support for Christian Democratic policies with more positive statements about the SPD-SED exchange of letters the previous year and relatively optimistic appraisals of the prospects for a favorable turnabout in the SPD's foreign policy. Naumov even made a positive reference to Rapallo, and spoke of "new generations" in the FRG which did not always follow "offical propaganda."[88]

Most of these Soviet evaluations of the FRG, paled in comparison with East German writings, whose critical tone was uncompromising. East German academicians and journalists vigorously assaulted the Grand Coalition's foreign policy as revanchist, militaristic, and expansionistic. Bonn's growing isolation was seen as merely intensifying these tendencies. Changes in Bonn's ostpolitik were regarded as strictly rhetorical, designed to mask the intention to make the East Europeans economically dependent on the FRG.[89] East German writers attacked SPD leaders by name, and placed little or no faith in the possibility of a change of course.[90] More broadly, as Soviet writers were paying increasing attention to the conflicts disrupting U.S.–West European relations, the East Germans emphasized the elements

85. N.a., "Tekushchiye problemy mirovoi politiki," *MEMO*, no. 10, 1967, p. 100; R. Fyodorov, "Politicheskii mekhanizm i soyuz predprinyatelei," ibid., no. 12, 1967, pp. 67–68; A. Baikalov and V. Ragnov, "Emergency Legislation in West Germany," *IA*, no. 4, 1967, pp. 73–76; Y. Panilov, "West Germany's Foreign Policy Impasse and the Big Coalition," *IA*, no. 5, 1967, pp. 9–14.

86. G. Sogomonyan, "Sotsial-demokratiya Evropy na raspute," *MEMO*, no. 10, 1967, pp. 54–67; P. Kryukov, "The German Question and the Present Situation," *IA*, no. 2, 1967, pp. 11–16.

87. V. S. Shumskii, *Politika bez budushchevo: Antikommunizm pravykh liderov SDPG* (Moscow: Mezhdunarodnye otnoshenia, 1967), p. 335.

88. Pavel Naumov, *Bonn: Siliye i bessiliye* (Moscow: Mysl, 1967), pp. 364–71, 395–99; Mikhail Voslenskii, *Vostochnaya politika FRG* (Moscow: Nauka, 1967), pp. 334–35, 387–89.

89. E.g., Günther Rose, "Bonns 'flexible' Osteuropa-Politik," *DA*, no. 2, 1967, pp. 198–207; Heinz Krusche, "Kernwaffenstreben der Regierung Kiesinger-Strauss bedroht Europas Sicherheit," *DA*, no. 3, 1967, pp. 267–277; Wilhelm Ersil, "Von der Restauration zur Expansion," *DA*, no. 4, 1967, pp. 398–413; Heinrich Sperker, "Die Zuspitzung der Gegensätze zwischen der imperialistischen Hauptmächten," *Einheit*, no. 12, 1967, pp. 1058–67.

90. Erich Hüttner, "Die Alleinvertretungsanmassung und die Bunkerkoalition," *DA*, no. 2, 1967, pp. 139–49; Herbert Häber, "Entwicklungen in Westdeutschland: Andere Szene—dasselbe Spiel," *Einheit*, no. 2, 1967, pp. 195–207.

of partnership within NATO. Special emphasis continued to be accorded the "Bonn-Washington axis" and the FRG's willingly assumed role in "U.S. global strategy."[91] The East Germans seemed to be warning the Soviets against the dangers of détente not only with the FRG but with the United States as well. These views scrupulously followed the line laid down in the writings of prominent SED officials.[92]

In the domain of East-West economic relations, analysts in the Soviet Union and the GDR devoted growing attention to the "scientific-technological revolution" in 1967. Writers in both countries tended to place a great deal of emphasis on the social problems afflicting capitalist countries as a result of technological progress. Here and there, however, voices were raised in favor of expanded trade with the West, albeit more often in the USSR than in East Germany.[93]

Moscow's Cautious Course

In contrast to the GDR's generally rejectionist positions, the Soviet Union went ahead in 1967 with negotiations with both the United States and the Federal Republic. Despite the tensions in U.S.-Soviet relations aroused by the Middle East war in June and the fruitless Glassboro summit meeting between Kosygin and Lyndon Johnson later in the month, Moscow and Washington came to a tentative agreement on a draft nuclear nonproliferation treaty in August.[94] News of the agreement created consternation in West Germany, especially among those Christian Democrats who still harbored hopes of a West German nuclear option. The SPD, however, was more inclined to accept a nonproliferation accord, seeing it as a basis for détente with the Soviet Union.[95]

Meanwhile, at Bonn's initiative, the USSR entered into a secret exchange of views on a Soviet–West German renunciation-of-force treaty. After a

91. Albrecht Charisius and Siegfried Zeimer, "Die NATO und das aggressive Programm des westdeutschen Imperialismus," *DA*, no. 3, 1967, pp. 278–91; Erich Hüttner, " 'Europäische Vorwärtspolitik'—Bonner Beitrag zur Globalstrategie," *DA*, no. 9, 1967, pp. 1064–75; the articles by Maretski, Gretschuchin (a Soviet academician), and Hinkel on "global strategy" in *DA*, no. 12, 1967; Gerhard Liebig, "Globalstrategie gegen Frieden und Fortschritt," *Einheit*, no. 8, 1967, pp. 963–71.

92. E.g., Werner Lamberz, "Der Teufelspakt Washington-Bonn," *Einheit*, no. 9, 1967, pp. 1187–96 (pt. 1), and no. 10, 1967, pp. 1299–1308 (pt. 2).

93. For a rare example of this pro-trade view in the GDR, see J. Kotkowski, "Die gegenwärtigen Bedingungen des ökonomischen Wettbewerbs der UdSSR und der USA," *Einheit*, nos. 10–11, 1967, p. 1327.

94. The draft did not include the all-important provision on inspection. See Wolfe, *Soviet Power and Europe*, p. 368.

95. On these points, see Helga Haftendorn, *Abrüstungs- und Entspannungspolitik zwischen Sicherheitsbefriedigung und Friedenssicherung* (Düsseldorf: Bertelsmann Universitätsverlag, 1974), pp. 157–87.

West German note in February outlined a treaty proposal, the Soviets pursued the talks through the spring and summer. No meeting of minds was reached, however. Bonn insisted on a renunciation-of-force accord with no conditions; on October 12 the Soviets demanded that Bonn conclude similar agreements with the GDR and the states of Eastern Europe. On November 21 the Kremlin raised new demands, calling for West German recognition of the existing borders and a repudiation of the FRG's constitutional provisions on Berlin, among other things. The November note also reminded Bonn of the USSR's special rights of intervention in German affairs under Article 53 of the United Nations charter. Nevertheless, the secret dialogue continued until mid-1968.[96]

Other contacts initiated by the Kiesinger-Brandt government were also without issue. The Soviets demurred at a West German proposal for wider trade ties in the summer, and refused to allow Ernst Majonica, one of the CDU's foreign policy experts, to meet with any ministerial-level officials during his visit to Moscow in September. An SPD politician, however, got to meet with Foreign Ministry officials.

Moscow closed out the year by steering a middle course between the Grand Coalition's overtures and Ulbricht's maximalism. On September 18 the GDR sent West Germany a draft treaty to be concluded between the two German states. It called for the normalization of inter-German relations and was accompanied by a harsh letter from Stoph denouncing West German expansionism.[97] On December 8 Moscow directed a strongly worded note of its own to the Federal Republic, denouncing neo-nazism in the FRG and identifying the CDU/CSU's policies with those of the National Democratic Party of Germany, a right-wing extremist grouping with pronounced neofascist tendencies. The note also acknowledged, however, that "considerable" numbers of West Germans had different political convictions.[98]

Four days later, at the conclusion of talks between Soviet and East German leaders in Moscow, an equally two-sided communiqué was released. Like the Soviet note of December 8, it condemned manifestations of neofascism while at the same time alluding to "healthy tendencies and forces" in the FRG. The communiqué more closely resembled Moscow's measured ambivalence toward the Grand Coalition than East Berlin's unambiguous opposition to it. It failed to attack the SPD or to refer to West Germany's alleged expansionism—themes still loudly trumpeted in the East German press—and made no mention of the GDR's draft treaty of September 18.[99]

96. Ibid., pp. 219–21.

97. *ND*, Sept. 20, 1967, p. 1. See also Stoph's letter to Kiesinger proposing inter-German negotiations, *ND*, May 12, 1967, pp. 1–2, and Sept. 20, pp. 1–2.

98. *Pravda*, Dec. 9, 1967, pp. 1–2.

99. For the text, see *ND*, Dec. 13, 1967, p. 1. The editor of *ND*, Günther Kertzscher, attacked Bonn's "expansionism" and the SPD leadership on Dec. 12, 1967, p. 6, and Dec. 13, pp. 3–4.

Conclusions

As the prospects for change in Europe began to take a promising turn in the mid-1960s, the Soviet leadership assumed a cautious wait-and-see attitude, shunning any dramatic overtures in Western Europe's direction. Moscow's caution reflected the conservatism of the post-Khrushchev leadership and its ambivalence in regard to U.S.–West European relations. On the one hand, the Brezhnev coalition clearly welcomed the independent course charted by de Gaulle, and signaled its attentiveness to the steps taken by the Grand Coalition to reevaluate the FRG's ostpolitik. On the other hand, the Kremlin adopted an essentially reactive posture with respect to these developments, appearing quite content to let Paris and Bonn take the initiative in exploring new approaches to East-West relations on the continent.

Moscow's responses to these overtures involved little more than cost-free diplomatic gestures and public proclamations favoring greater West European autonomy. These efforts, however, were noticeably short on specifics. Even the Bucharest Declaration of 1966, with its pronouncedly Europeanist pitch, provided no serious enticements to draw the West Europeans into cutting a grand bargain with Moscow. The Soviets surely had to realize that the declaration's proposal for the dissolution of NATO and the Warsaw Pact would fall on deaf ears; even de Gaulle, who remained faithful to the political institutions of the Atlantic alliance while withdrawing from its military component, rejected the idea out of hand. Similarly, in their initial diplomatic outreach to the Grand Coalition, the Soviets remained tentative and defensive, making it unmistakably clear to the West Germans that any political accord required Bonn's prior acceptance of the postwar territorial arrangement. As the Soviets proceeded with their courtship of Western Europe in these years, they offered flowers but no engagement ring.

The Soviet leadership's circumspection derived from its commitment to the main outlines of the European status quo—not merely to the division of Germany but also to Moscow's continuing hegemony over Eastern Europe. By the mid-1960s it was already evident that a broadening of détente with the West Europeans, in the direction of either France or West Germany, would awaken pro-Western sentiments among the East Europeans and would even spark demands for greater economic and perhaps political cooperation with Western Europe. These tendencies would have to be carefully controlled, a consideration that led Brezhnev to close ranks with Ulbricht in 1967, just as he had done in 1964. At the same time, however, Brezhnev had no plans to accord Ulbricht the right to veto Moscow's West German policy.

Another pillar of the European status quo which Moscow took for granted was the American military presence. Despite all its talk about West European independence, the Soviet leadership studiously refrained from embarking headlong on a strictly Europeanist path. Ample justification existed for a policy that conceded to the United States a major role in Europe. Some of these considerations were explicitly articulated by members of the secondary foreign policy elite. These views, in combination with a realistic appreciation of both the scope and the limits of West European self-assertiveness, dictated a flexible and manipulative Atlanticist approach to the U.S.–West European relationship.

The assumed endurance of the NATO alliance inevitably raised essential questions about the USSR's military posture. In this all-important category, too, the Brezhnev coalition made an early decision to move in a conservative direction. Although Khrushchev had built up Soviet nuclear forces in the European theater, he had tried to curb the Soviet military's appetite for across-the-board spending increases, and that was a policy Brezhnev was determined to reverse. Defense spending rose steadily in virtually all categories. Objections voiced by Kosygin and Podgorny were shunted aside.[100] By late 1966 there were signs that new plans were under way to strengthen Soviet conventional forces in Europe with a view to exploiting the possibilities inherent in Washington's flexible response doctrine, which assumed that any war that broke out in Europe could be a protracted affair in which the United States and the Soviet Union might conceivably avoid the use of strategic nuclear weapons.[101]

In sum, Soviet policy toward West Germany in this period mirrored the conservatism of the Brezhnev coalition in its initial stages of development. Moscow's definition of the scope of détente was nebulous at best; its responsiveness to the latest developments in Western Europe, though rhetorically warm, remained tepid in practice; its readiness for compromise had yet to be clarified. Rather active discussion of acceptable alternative foreign policy orientations abounded, however, as one might expect from a Soviet-style coalition still in the process of formulating its priorities. Most important, the Soviet secondary elite was sharply divided between those who favored a dialogue with the FRG and those who still harbored deep suspicions of all West German "bourgeois" politicians, including the Social Democrats.

In comparative terms, however, the Brezhnev regime's conservatism was not nearly so hidebound as Walter Ulbricht's. The SED chief's dominant— not to say domineering—presence made itself felt in an unambiguously maximalist orientation toward West Germany. As the unchallenged leader of a directive regime, Ulbricht did not deviate from his uncompromising antidétente strategy. With practically no exceptions, the secondary elite in

100. On Soviet military doctrine and force posture at this time, see Wolfe, *Soviet Power and Europe*, pp. 427–98, passim.

101. Michael MccGwire, *Military Objectives in Soviet Foreign Policy* (Washington: Brookings, 1987), pp. 28–42, 381–405.

the GDR obligingly echoed Ulbricht's propositions. Ulbricht even appeared eager to outdo the Soviets in boosting the rate of defense spending: at the end of 1967 the GDR announced a whopping 50 percent increase in military expenditures for the following year.[102]

The GDR was not entirely immune to international pressures for change, however; nor were the Soviets entirely resistant to a measure of flexibility. The reform movement that burst upon the scene in Czechoslovakia in 1968 would confront both Walter Ulbricht and Leonid Brezhnev with an ideological challenge of crisis proportions. It would also lead them to divergent assessments of the possibilities of détente with West Germany.

102. Wolfe, *Soviet Power and Europe*, p. 486.

CHAPTER FOUR

The Czech Crisis and
Ulbricht's Grand Design:
1968

THE CRISIS in Czechoslovakia dominated the attention of the Soviet Union and the GDR throughout 1968. In both states the reform movement that was ushered in with the ascendancy of Alexander Dubcek to the post of first secretary of the Communist Party of Czechoslovakia (CPCz) in January was perceived as a major challenge to ideologicial orthodoxy as well as to Soviet control of the Warsaw Pact bloc. On these points Soviet and East German leaders could readily agree. Beneath the surface of their common efforts to stifle the development of Czech reformism, however, a struggle was under way concerning the significance of the events in Czechoslovakia for policy toward West Germany.

Ulbricht sought to turn the Czech crisis to his own advantage in his efforts to quash any possibility of a rapprochement between Moscow and Bonn. The SED chief was particularly alarmed by the economic implications of the crisis. Recognizing that chronic economic stagnation was a primary source of the demands for change welling up in Czechoslovakia, Ulbricht was anxious to head off a rush in West Germany's direction not only by the Czech government but potentially by other East European countries as well. In the worst of cases, the Soviet Union itself might have to be discouraged from embarking on precisely such a westward course. Accordingly, as the crisis unfolded, Ulbricht proclaimed that economic dependence on the West had to be avoided at all costs, since its outcome could only be an intolerable level of political dependence. In the months after the August invasion, Ulbricht demanded that the Warsaw Pact states undertake a massive effort to promote economic modernization "by our own means." The GDR would lead the way in this effort by accelerating its own modernization plans.

The Soviet leadership did not follow this advice. Though Brezhnev and his Kremlin colleagues were just as concerned as Ulbricht by the prospect of a normalization of relations between Prague and Bonn, the Soviet-led invasion put an abrupt halt to movement along this path. The Kremlin oligarchy therefore emerged from the Czech crisis in a more confident frame of mind than Walter Ulbricht, convinced of its ability to protect the communist regimes of East-Central Europe from internal and external challenges. The "Brezhnev doctrine" promised similarly decisive intervention in the future, as necessary. Furthermore, Moscow's show of force in Czechoslovakia sent a terse message to Bonn: No rapprochement would be possible as long as it threatened to disturb Soviet dominance in Eastern Europe.

Accordingly, the Soviet leadership had reason to believe that, with the socialist community held firmly together, a Soviet–West German accommodation that would not prove destabilizing to communist orthodoxy in Eastern Europe might yet be worked out. In 1968 the Brezhnev regime made no effort to foreclose this option, either before or after the Czech invasion. Indeed, for political and, as developments would show, compelling economic reasons, the Soviet Union was increasingly interested in improving its relations with the Federal Republic.

These diverging interpretations of the lessons of the Czech crisis in Moscow and East Berlin were to sow the seeds of serious conflict between the two allies. The result was the development of markedly different approaches to economic and foreign policy over the next several years.

Initial Reactions to the Dubcek Reforms

The GDR publicly criticized the Dubcek government's policies earlier than the Soviet Union.[1] On January 30 Kurt Hager, the SED Politburo's ideological watchdog, indirectly impugned the proponents of reform in Czechoslovakia with an attack on Western convergence theory. Several weeks later, amid signs that Prague was backing away from the Ulbricht doctrine, Ulbricht visited the Czech capital along with other Soviet bloc leaders and warned his audience of West Germany's attempts to create "economic dependencies" among the socialist states. (Ominously, *Neues Deutschland* on the previous day carried an editorial on Soviet–East German military cooperation, calling it the embodiment of "our common responsibility for the security of Europe.") Erich Honecker followed up this

---

1. Gero Neugebauer, "Vom 'Eisernen Dreieck' zu der ostdeutschen Beteiligung an der Intervention in der CSSR: Der Wandel in den Beziehungen zwischen der SED und der KP der Tschechoslowakei, 1966–1968, und seine Ursachen" (manuscript, Otto-Suhr-Institut of the Free University, West Berlin, 1968–1969).

warning with a hard-hitting attack on West German foreign policy and the SPD leadership at a meeting of communist party delegations in Budapest. The Czech delegate used this forum to express hopes for improved ties with the FRG and looked to the Social Democrats for encouragement in this effort. As the Czechs continued to voice interest in better relations with Bonn, *Neues Deutschland* published oblique references to West German infiltration in Czechoslovakia's internal affairs, and portrayed events there as playing into Bonn's hands.[2]

In late March, Warsaw Pact political leaders (minus Ceausescu) gathered in Dresden to discuss the latest developments in Czechoslovakia with Dubcek. The communiqué issued at the end of the meeting placed heavy emphasis on economic issues, and praised the "constant upswing" of the socialist planned economies in contrast to the disturbances affecting capitalism. It was further noted that the participants at Dresden agreed to hold a high-level economic conference in the near future.[3]

This concern with economic issues reflected both Czechoslovakia's desire for immediate economic assistance from the Soviet Union (as the planning chief, Oldrych Cernik, apparently requested during his talks in Moscow on March 20) and Ulbricht's mounting anxiety about Prague's interest in expanded economic and diplomatic ties with Bonn. The Dresden communiqué also criticized the "latest steps" of the Grand Coalition against the GDR and other socialist states. This rebuke was mild, however, in comparison with the GDR's anti-Bonn tirades and its warnings of West German infiltration in Czechoslovakia. Ultimately the outcome of the Dresden meeting reflected Brezhnev's willingness to allow events in Czechoslovakia to take their course for the time being, without serious intervention from Moscow.[4]

Three days after the Dresden summit, the GDR escalated its attacks on the Czech reformers as Hager denounced the prevailing tendencies of Prague's foreign and domestic policies. He also upbraided Josef Smrkovsky, then a candidate for the presidency of Czechoslovakia, for fulfilling the hopes of the Grand Coalition and West Germany's Springer press.[5] Hager's charges prompted a formal protest by the Czech foreign minister, and *Rude Pravo*, the Czech party daily, invited the SED ideologist to read the far more moderate article on Czechoslovakia appearing in *Pravda* on March 27. (When *Neues Deutschland* reprinted this piece on March 29, it deleted

2. *ND*, Jan. 30, 1968, pp. 3–6; Feb. 3, p. 1; Feb. 20, p. 1; Feb. 23, pp. 1–2; Feb. 24, p. 3; Feb. 29, pp. 4–5; March 12, p. 7; Mar. 13, p. 7; Mar. 14, p. 7; Mar. 17, p. 7; Mar. 18, p. 7; Mar. 19, p. 7; Mar. 20, p. 7; Mar. 21, p. 7.
3. *ND*, Mar. 24, 1968, p. 1.
4. On the Dresden meeting, see Karen Dawisha, *The Kremlin and the Prague Spring* (Berkeley: University of California Press, 1984), pp. 15–46.
5. *ND*, Mar. 27, 1968, p. 7.

Pravda's references to the continuing solidarity of the CPSU and CPCz.)[6] Tempers soon cooled in Prague and East Berlin, but the respite proved to be only temporary.

Economic Issues and the Prague Spring

The salience of economic issues in the gathering storm over Czechoslovakia was next signaled in speeches by Brezhnev and GDR Premier Willi Stoph at the end of March. In an address devoted mainly to the need for greater ideological vigilance, Brezhnev on March 29 took issue with proponents of greater reliance on Western technology. "Some colleagues," he noted, "evidently underestimate the accomplishments of scientific-technical thought both here and in other countries of socialism. But at the same time, these people are prone to overestimate the achievements of science and technology in the capitalist world." Brezhnev specifically pointed to West Germany as a capitalist nation undergoing a severe economic crisis. His critical comments provided a clear indication that the CPSU leader was joining with conservatives in his ruling coalition who opposed an extensive increase in East-West trade. *Neues Deutschland* printed these excerpts from Brezhnev's speech on March 31.[7]

In the same edition, the SED newspaper also published a speech by Willi Stoph announcing new measures designed to reassert the decision-making authority of central planning organs in specific high-technology and related sectors. This decision represented a sudden reversal of the GDR's policy of economic decentralization, a policy initiated with the economic reforms of 1963 and confirmed as recently as January 1968.[8] Both the timing and the content of Stoph's announcement suggested that Ulbricht's warnings about the risks of economic dependence on the West were already having an impact on the GDR's domestic economic priorities. As later events would reveal, the SED leadership was now determined to accelerate growth in so-called structure-determining areas beyond the expectations of the 1966–1970 five-year plan, and was prepared to recentralize decision-making procedures in these areas to this end. Under the stimulus of the Czech crisis, both the plan goals and the command structure of the East German economy were now being significantly reshaped.

The speeches by Brezhnev and Stoph at the end of March represented only one side of the spectrum, however. At the other end were advocates of

6. *Osteuropäische Rundschau*, no. 4, 1968, pp. 16–18.
7. *ND*, March 31, 1968, p. 5.
8. In January 1968 regulations requiring enterprises to raise investment funds on their own went into effect, resulting in a further decentralization of the economy. See *Gesetzblatt der Deutschen Demokratischen Republik*, pt. 2, no. 68, 1967, pp. 459ff.

greater technological borrowing from the West. Among them were not only the reform-minded Czechs but prominent Soviet academicians, trade officials, and even such Politburo members as Kosygin. In the months before the invasion of Czechoslovakia, the debate over East-West technology exchange in the Soviet Union grew sharper, with Brezhnev increasingly siding with the more traditionalist advocates of limited trade with the West and Kosygin arguing for greater reliance on Western imports.

This debate was coupled with a contentious discussion of the possibility of entering into negotiations on strategic arms control with the United States. Once again Kosygin and Brezhnev appeared to be on opposite sides of the issue, at least initially. In February, Kosygin referred with obvious approval to the U.S.-Soviet draft agreement on nuclear nonproliferation, which, he said, "forecloses access by the West German revanchists to atomic weaponry." Kosygin also underscored the economic burdens imposed by the USSR's heavy defense expenditures, which were due to rise by 15.2 percent in 1968. Brezhnev at first seemed skeptical about arms talks, but by July he appeared to be gravitating toward acceptance of American feelers to start SALT negotiations. In this more approving stance Brezhnev was backed by Gromyko and such academicians as Nikolai N. Inozemtsev, the director of IMEMO, who also favored improved trade ties with the West. Mikhail Suslov, Aleksandr Shelepin, and senior members of the Soviet military displayed considerable coolness to the idea of arms talks and reductions in the growth of military spending, and presumably to the notion of significantly expanded trade with the capitalist countries as well.[9]

Against this background of serious differences of opinion in the USSR on vital economic and military aspects of East-West relations, both East Berlin and Moscow stepped up their pressure on the Czech government. This pressure was particularly evident after Oldrych Cernik, an advocate of greater involvement in the international economic system, was named prime minister on April 4. The need to integrate Czechoslovakia more fully into the world economy was one of the central points of the Czech "Action Program" issued the next day. This document also emphasized "the necessity of supporting the realistic forces in the Federal Republic," yet another sign of Prague's interest in promoting relations with Bonn. Statements by Cernik and the new foreign minister, Jiri Hajek, confirmed the impression that the new Czech government might not require Bonn's recognition of the GDR as a precondition to the establishment of diplomatic relations with the FRG.[10]

On April 10 the CPSU Central Committee issued a statement stressing

---

9. On all these points see Bruce Parrott, *Politics and Technology in the Soviet Union* (Cambridge: MIT Press, 1983), pp. 188–208.

10. For Cernik's speech, see *ND*, Apr. 25, 1968, p. 7; for Hajek's, see FBIS, *Eastern Europe*, Apr. 11, 1968, p. D3.

the "sharp aggravation of the ideological struggle between socialism and capitalism" and Western attempts to "undermine socialism from within," and calling for renewed efforts to combat the subversive effects of Western ideology. It also called for unity among the socialist states in the struggle against West German "revanchism, militarism . . . and imperialism." Interestingly, however, the Central Committee did not mention the Grand Coalition government by name, nor did it directly implicate the FRG in the events taking place in Czechoslovakia. In comparison with the anti-Bonn invective coming out of East Germany, much of it now aimed at the "Kiesinger/Strauss/Brandt/Wehner government," the CPSU's reference to the FRG was surprisingly mild.[11]

As *Pravda* now began pointing a finger at "antisocialist elements" in Czechoslovakia, the new cabinet ministers in Prague pursued their quest for economic assistance.[12] In late April, Ota Sik, the Czech government's principal architect of economic reform, announced that Czechoslovakia needed an immediate loan of approximately $500 million. If the money could not be obtained in Moscow, he suggested, Prague would have no choice but to seek it in the West. On May 4 Dubcek and Cernik went to the Soviet capital to discuss the matter. According to Smrkovsky, an eyewitness, even Kosygin expressed misgivings about Czechoslovakia's westward economic drift. Several days later, the leaders of Poland, Hungary, Bulgaria, and the GDR had a meeting of their own with the Soviets, during which Ulbricht reportedly pleaded for the stationing of Warsaw Pact troops inside Czechoslovakia.[13]

Although military maneuvers just outside Czech borders were initiated, the Moscow meeting reached no agreement on outright intervention, in part because of the reluctance of key Soviet decision makers. Brezhnev, Kosygin, and Podgorny even sent a warmly worded telegram to the Czech government expressing hopes for the strengthening of relations between the two countries. Meanwhile, in their remarks on West Germany later in the month, both Kosygin and Gromyko repeated the standard Soviet warnings about neofascism and the need to recognize postwar realities, but they conspicuously avoided blaming Bonn for mixing in Czechoslovakia's internal affairs. Soviet military figures were somewhat tougher in their references to Bonn, while *Izvestiya* on May 16 blasted the FRG's bridge-building policy.[14]

11. *Pravda*, Apr. 11, 1968, p. 1. The first open criticism of developments in Czechoslovakia to appear in the Soviet press surfaced Apr. 4, in *Sovetskaya Rossiya*. See Thomas W. Wolfe, *Soviet Power and Europe, 1945–1970* (Baltimore: Johns Hopkins University Press, 1970), p. 369. For an example of East German attacks on the SPD at this time, see *ND*, Apr. 20, 1968, pp. 6–7.

12. Parts of this *Pravda* article were published in *ND*, Apr. 15, 1968, p. 2.

13. Cited in Dawisha, *Kremlin and the Prague Spring*, pp. 73, 100.

14. For the sources, see ibid., pp. 106–10.

In this atmosphere of disagreement in the Soviet leadership, the GDR pressed its case against the Czech reform movement. On May 9 an East German newspaper, *Berliner Zeitung*, reported the presence of American military equipment in Prague, and alleged that U.S. troops were about to occupy Czechoslovakia. The Czechs lodged a protest with the East German government, noting that the military equipment in question was being used in the making of a film. On May 15 the same newspaper used the word "counterrevolution" in connection with developments in Czechoslovakia. *Neues Deutschland* published similarly ominous articles, and the East German government banned the distribution of German-language Czech newspapers in the GDR.[15]

Finally, on May 24, *Neues Deutschland* switched from its earlier practice of attacking selected reform groups or ideas to launching a full-scale broadside against the Czech Communist Party itself. The article, entitled "Bonn between Fear and Hope," concentrated its criticisms on Ota Sik's request for $500 million in hard currency to buy machinery from the West. This request, the article contended, would only help the capitalists direct their economic expansion against the socialist countries, a strategy attributed to Willy Brandt and World Bank chief Robert McNamara. The author then set forth the rationale for the GDR's current standpoint on East-West trade:

> Naturally socialist countries can buy machines, licenses, and complete plants in capitalist countries—as is well known, the GDR, which favors open world trade and wants such trade to serve world peace, does this, too. But, as all economic and political experience proves, that is not the principal way to strengthen the socialist commonwealth of states economically. Whoever wants to conduct a socialist policy must himself be economically strong . . . [and] must himself, together with his brother countries, strive toward a high international standard and seek to determine it.

A few days later Walter Ulbricht led a group of East German officials to Moscow for extensive talks on bilateral economic cooperation. The communiqué issued at the conclusion of these meetings asserted that "new forms" of economic and scientific-technical cooperation had been agreed upon. The SED leaders were even more enthusiastic in their evaluations of the trip upon their return home. At an SED Central Committee plenum held in early June, Hermann Axen described the outcome of the Soviet–East German talks as "the most comprehensive and far-reaching results in the history of relations between the GDR and the Soviet Union." Erich Honecker picked up this theme and denounced "manifestations of a one-sided

---

15. *ND*, May 17, 1968, p. 6; May 18, p. 1; May 21, p. 7. See also Ilse Spittmann, "Spekulation auf Frost in Prag," *Deutschland Archiv*, no. 3, 1968, p. 332; Neugebauer, "Vom 'Eisernen Dreieck' zu der ostdeutschen Beteiligung," p. 97.

and uncritical orientation toward the West" and "a neglect of Soviet scientific achievements." In Honecker's view, this was "a profoundly political question." Ulbricht strongly endorsed these remarks and warned that the socialist countries had already paid enough "tuition" (*Lehrgeld*) to the West. He coupled his announcement of a more Soviet-oriented, anti-Western economic emphasis for the GDR with a bitter denunciation of West Germany's alleged attempts "to develop economic relations in order to make the countries of the people's democracies dependent" on the FRG. In an undisguised reference to Czechoslovakia, the SED chief accused the Federal Republic of fomenting counterrevolution against the socialist countries.[16] This Central Committee plenum took place in the wake of the publication in Czechoslovakia of an alleged SED internal document calling for military intervention.[17]

The Czech Crisis and Relations with the FRG

The GDR's determination to use the Czech crisis as a pretext to scotch all chances for a rapprochement between Bonn and the other countries of the Warsaw Pact became unmistakable in mid-June, as the East Germans hardened their position on Berlin. For several months the GDR had been adamant in rejecting any institutional links between the Federal Republic and West Berlin, even refusing to allow West Berlin's mayor, Klaus Schütz, to leave West Berlin by car for an official trip to West Germany in April. On these and other occasions in 1968, the Soviet Union voiced support for East Germany's actions.[18]

On June 11 the GDR Volkskammer approved measures establishing passport and visa requirements for all West German travelers into the GDR, including those en route to West Berlin. (Up to this time, personal identity documents had sufficed to gain entry into the GDR, and no visa was required.) In addition, minimum currency exchange rates were raised and new taxes and controls of various kinds were imposed on goods transported on East German roads and waterways. The GDR justified these measures as a response to certain emergency laws in the FRG aimed at containing unruly political demonstrations.[19]

Although the Soviets lent quick public support to the GDR's action, their expressions of solidarity lacked enthusiasm. Indeed, it was reported that

16. *ND*, June 1–2, 1968, p. 1; June 7, p. 3; June 8, pp. 5–6; June 21, 1968, pp. 3–4. Ulbricht's speech was published nearly two weeks after it was delivered.

17. The document was published in *Literarny listy* on May 30.

18. For a sampling of Soviet and GDR views on West Berlin, see *ND*, Feb. 13, 1968, p. 3; Feb. 18, p. 7; May 2, p. 5; May 3, p. 6; June 1–2, p. 1.

19. *ND*, June 12, 1968, pp. 6–7.

Ulbricht had been pressing the Kremlin for permission to introduce the passport and visa regulations for at least two years, but Soviet leaders had balked at these suggestions.[20] Their willingness to go along with them now can perhaps best be explained by their growing sensitivity to the GDR's concerns in the light of events in Czechoslovakia. In any event, the Soviets made it plain that the new measures were not to exceed the limits specified in the Volkskammer decrees. There was to be no tampering with allied privileges on the routes leading to Berlin, a fact Ulbricht duly confirmed in an interview on Dutch television. Moreover, Kremlin spokesmen avoided echoing Ulbricht's assertion that West Berlin lay "on the territory of the GDR," a claim he repeated in the same interview.[21]

Moscow made its interest in limiting the dispute even more explicit as the Soviet ambassador to the GDR, Pyotr Abrassimov, received Willy Brandt in East Berlin. The West German foreign minister's presence in the city was a direct affront to East Germany, as Brandt was acting as a representative of the FRG government and did not show his passport. When the meeting was reported in the back pages of *Neues Deutschland* on June 20, both Brandt and Abrassimov were identified by their party functions (as chairman of the SPD and member of the CPSU Central Committee, respectively) rather than by their official titles. Ulbricht's pique at Moscow's decision to receive Brandt in Berlin was probably sharpened by reports that the Soviet envoy assured Brandt of Moscow's lack of interest in a new outbreak of hostilities over the divided city.[22] Reactions to the Volkskammer decrees were similarly muted in most of Eastern Europe, while the Czechs openly criticized the measures.[23]

Differences between the GDR and the Soviet Union continued to surface over the following weeks. Increasingly they centered on the GDR's recognition by West Germany, an issue whose importance for the GDR was magnified by the Czech government's obvious desire to normalize its relations with Bonn. On June 17 Foreign Minister Hajek made a quick trip to East Berlin to confer with Ulbricht. Upon returning to Prague, Hajek praised the GDR but stopped short of calling for its recognition by the FRG. On June 21 the GDR Staatsrat (the State Council, chaired by Ulbricht) declared that the "only peaceful way" to improve conditions in Germany was to conclude "treaties valid under international law on the normalization of relations." The declaration also made normalization contingent on Bonn's agreement to renounce the use of force, sign the nuclear non-proliferation treaty, recognize existing borders, and remove all nuclear

20. *Der Spiegel*, June 17, 1968, p. 27.
21. *ND*, June 14, 1968, pp. 1–2.
22. *Der Spiegel*, June 24, 1968, pp. 21ff.
23. For an East German comment, see *ND*, June 13, 1968, p. 6. See also Peter Bender, *Zehn Gründe für die Anerkennung der DDR* (Frankfurt: Fischer, 1968), pp. 105–6.

weapons from its territory. Its emphasis on strict compliance with international law was in effect an appeal for de jure recognition. Throughout the second half of June the GDR insisted repeatedly that the FRG accord it the full rights of state sovereignty.[24]

On June 27, however, Andrei Gromyko called on Bonn to recognize only "the existence of the GDR" and made no mention of de jure recognition. In a speech before the USSR Supreme Soviet, Gromyko also had some negative things to say about West Germany, condemning neo-Nazism in the FRG and reiterating the Soviet Union's time-worn demands for recognition of the borders and so forth. In an indirect reference to the Czech crisis, the Soviet foreign minister admonished the FRG against using "refined measures" to damage the unity of the socialist states, and warned that the latter were giving, and would continue to give, a "proper reply" to such efforts. He approved of the "appropriate measures" recently taken by the GDR concerning Berlin.

Along with these critical comments, however, Gromyko offered an explicit confirmation of Moscow's abiding interest in discussing a renunciation-of-force treaty with the FRG, predicated on Bonn's "clear-cut recognition of the situation existing in Europe." As he so often did, Gromyko once again referred to the Potsdam agreement. Though critical of Kiesinger, he made no mention of Brandt. In short, Gromyko's speech represented another example of a scrupulously balanced Soviet approach to the FRG, combining a firm restatement of Moscow's standing minimum demands on the German question with assurances that a change of policy in Bonn would be "welcomed" in the Soviet Union. At a time when the GDR was visibly trying to bar the way to détente with Bonn on any but the most stringent terms, Gromyko reaffirmed the Kremlin's desire to continue the dialogue with the FRG. He also called for better relations with the United States.[25]

Nevertheless, events in Czechoslovakia were now pushing Moscow toward a tougher stance. On June 27 the Czech National Assembly voted to abolish censorship, and a group of Czech reformists published 2000 Words, a program for further reform which advocated the purge of CPCz conservatives. (Ironically, these developments occurred on the same day as Gromyko's speech.) Soviet attitudes toward Czechoslovakia and East-West détente noticeably stiffened, both within the Politburo and in the press. Only a minimum of attention greeted the signature of the NPT on July 1, and the Kosygin-Gromyko line in favor of arms-control talks and other improvements in ties with the West came under attack, particularly in the

24. *ND*, June 19, 1968, pp. 1–2; June 21, p. 7; June 23, pp. 1, 3; June 13, p. 2; June 29, p. 4. On Hajek see also Peter Probst, "CSSR Aussenminister Hajek in Ostberlin," *Deutschland Archiv*, no. 4, 1968, p. 429.

25. *Pravda*, June 28, 1968, pp. 3–4.

military press. The Ukrainian party leadership under Shelest also appeared to be increasingly united in favor of intervention in Czechoslovakia.[26] Most important, approximately 16,000 Warsaw Pact troops, most of them from the USSR, entered Czechoslovakia in late June to conduct military maneuvers. Defense Minister Andrei Grechko and General Aleksei Yepishev, the commander of the Warsaw Pact, subsequently met with the GDR's defense minister, General Heinz Hoffmann, to assess the military situation.[27]

Suddenly, to the surprise of the Kiesinger government, *Izvestiya* on July 11 began to publish most of the notes exchanged between Moscow and Bonn in their secret dialogue on a renunciation-of-force treaty.[28] Significantly, the note of December 8, 1967, which was the most demanding of all the Soviet notes, was not among the ones published in the Soviet press. It had called on Bonn to conclude a renunciation-of-force treaty with the GDR "in a form corresponding to international law," whereas the final note sent to the FRG, as recently as July 5, 1968, had spoken only of Bonn's need to recognize "the existence of two independent German states." The texts of the notes gave evidence of the USSR's reluctance to require West Germany's de jure recognition of the GDR as a precondition to rapprochement with the USSR, a fact confirmed in the July 5 note, which was forwarded to Bonn less than a week before *Izvestiya*'s revelation of the exchange.

As the Soviet leadership intensified its pressures on Dubcek, the GDR pressed the Kremlin for decisive action against Czechoslovakia. At the same time, the East Germans redoubled their efforts to link the events in Czechoslovakia with the foreign policy designs of the Federal Republic. On July 13, in an issue that carried the texts of some of the Soviet–West German notes on the renunciation of force, *Neues Deutschland* published its most denunciatory commentary yet on the FRG's alleged political interference in Czechoslovakia's internal affairs. The article linked Bonn's bridge-building policy with similar concepts developed in the United States by Zbigniew Brzezinski and adopted by the Johnson administration. Another harshly worded piece appeared July 17. Entitled "Bonn's Massive Influence in the Internal Affairs of the CzSR," it took dead aim at Willy Brandt and the SPD for collaborating with like-minded reformists in Czechoslovakia, and denounced the visit to Prague of Karl Blessing, president of the Bundesbank.[29] Subsequent articles also took up the cudgels against the "Kiesinger-Strauss-

26. Dawisha, *Kremlin and the Prague Spring*, pp. 171–77; Wolfe, *Soviet Power in Europe*, pp. 369–72.

27. Jiri Valenta, *Soviet Intervention in Czechoslovakia, 1968* (Baltimore: Johns Hopkins University Press, 1979).

28. The notes were also published in *ND*, July 12, 1968, p. 7; July 13, pp. 1–2; July 14, pp. 1–2.

29. Blessing had visited Prague July 12 to discuss a possible credit arrangement. Other West German visitors to the Czech capital in 1968 included Egon Bahr in April, members of the Bundestag's Foreign Policy Committee in June, and Walter Scheel in July. On Sept. 4 *ND* alleged that Willy Brandt had met with Hajek on June 10 in Vienna.

Brandt" government's supposed embroilment in the Czech reform movement, stressing West Germany's role in "U.S. global strategy" and its alleged efforts to "hollow out" socialism from within by building relationships of economic dependence.[30]

Ulbricht reportedly spent most of his time lambasting West Germany in his speech at a hastily convened meeting of Soviet bloc leaders in Warsaw on July 14–15. Brezhnev deplored the situation in Czechoslovakia but had nothing to say about the FRG.[31] The meeting, which Dubcek had refused to attend, concluded with the issuance of an open letter to the Czech government. In addition to warning that the vital interests of the socialist states were endangered by the reform movement, the "Warsaw Letter" took note of Ulbricht's anxieties by accusing the FRG of taking advantage of the Czech events. Over the next two weeks, as the Soviets began military maneuvers on the Czech border together with East German and Polish troops, the SED kept up its propaganda barrage, repeatedly placing the onus of responsibility on Bonn for fanning the flames of counterrevolution in Czechoslovakia.[32]

The Soviet statement on Czechoslovakia's rejection of the Warsaw Letter's demands, while blunt, made no mention of West Germany. It was at this time, however, that *Pravda* began seriously inculpating Bonn in the Czech crisis.[33] Still, the Soviet statements were no match for the quantity and ferocity of East Germany's output. Moreover, as the Kremlin groped its way to a decision on intervention, it became apparent that most CPSU Politburo members were more exercised by the implications of the Czech crisis for ideological orthodoxy and ethnic solidarity at home and in Eastern Europe than by its foreign policy ramifications with respect to Bonn or Washington.[34] Moreover, the Soviets were still hopeful that their problems with Dubcek might be resolved at their forthcoming consultations with him scheduled for July 29 at Cierna nad Tisou.

The Importance of Economic Issues

On July 30 *Neues Deutschland* published one of its most devastating indictments of the Dubcek experiment. Just as important, the SED

30. *ND*, July 19, 1968, p. 1; July 20, p. 1.

31. Dawisha, *Kremlin and the Prague Spring*, p. 208, cites Erwin Weit's account.

32. Warsaw Letter: *ND*, July 18, 1968, p. 1; SED Central Committee statement: *ND*, July 20, p. 1; SED Politburo statement: *ND*, July 24, p. 6. The articles appearing in *ND* at this time are typified by those published July 20, p. 1; July 21, pp. 1 and 2; July 24, p. 1; and July 28, pp. 1 and 2.

33. *Pravda*, July 22, 1968, pp. 4, 5. The criticism of West German politicians visiting Prague provoked a protest by FRG Ambassador Georg Duckwitz. See also ibid., July 27, p. 4.

34. Dawisha, *Kremlin and the Prague Spring*, pp. 213–19. This was perhaps less true of Petro Shelest, whose criticisms of the Czech reformists combined ideological and ethnic themes

organ now summarized the GDR's principal foreign policy, economic, and ideological themes of the previous seven months, weaving into a coherent argument the separate strands of Ulbricht's grand design.

The unsigned article placed particular stress on the linkage between the East-West economic relationship and the political conflict between the capitalist and socialist states. It began with a pronounced emphasis on the "global strategy" of the West, a notion that contrasted starkly with the "interimperialist contradictions" so often mentioned in Soviet writings. The "European variant" of this general strategy, according to *Neues Deutschland*, was aimed at hollowing out the socialist countries by making them economically dependent. The article warned that the United States was deliberately extending its technological lead over its West European partners, leaving them to furnish inferior products to the socialist countries. In these circumstances, the East would be relegated to importing "third-rate technology" from the West, a "trap" in which the Czechs were about to be ensnared. The lesson was clear: "It means giving up speculation that socialism can be built with the help of the imperialists." In making this case, *Neues Deutschland* insisted that it was not advocating complete autarky. Rather, the point was to avoid such excessive reliance on Western economic assistance that the risk of political dependence would inevitably intensify. "Of course," the paper affirmed, "we are not against economic relations with the capitalist countries. We cultivate them, and we shall cultivate them further. But we also know what it means to be dependent on the deliveries of an imperialist state that wants to prove that socialism is not viable."

The article went on to recall how Lenin, while trading with the West, had nevertheless concentrated on developing the USSR's own economic strength. Drawing on this example, the author observed: "First our own strength must be mobilized. In the scientific, technical, and economic cooperation of the socialist countries there exist large reserves that are not as yet exhausted, not by a long shot." Moreover, in a message beamed squarely at the East Europeans, the article cautioned against waiting for Moscow "to come to our rescue" as a substitute for seeking credits in Bonn and Washington. "It is first of all a question of building on one's own strength."

This notion of "building on one's own strength" would soon emerge, in slightly reworded form, as Ulbricht's main battle cry in his campaign to reduce the Soviet bloc's quest for Western technology by intensifying its own technological development. As we have seen, the GDR by the end of March was already gearing up its own economy for this effort. In the view of the SED leadership, the acceleration of high technology development in

---

with attacks on West Germany, the United States, and Israel. See Grey Hodnett and Peter J. Potichnyj, *The Ukraine and the Czechoslovak Crisis* (Canberra: Australian National University, 1970), pp. 81–84.

the socialist camp was a pressing political necessity, made all the more urgent by the crisis in Czechoslovakia and by the dangers inherent in Prague's economic and political opening to West Germany.

In addition to explicitly linking foreign policy and economic questions, the July 30 *Neues Deutschland* article drew some related ideological conclusions. It roundly condemned the Czech reformers for seeking to introduce free-market mechanisms into the economy at the expense of central planning. Such efforts would ultimately undermine "the leading role of the party." The article concluded, with barely concealed self-satisfaction, that the Czechs would do better by imitating the GDR. "We do not think in terms of holding up the solutions we have found up to now as a model to the other socialist countries," it claimed. "But we believe that, for a socialist industrial state in our vicinity, the basic problems are surely to be looked at in the same direction."

Moving toward Invasion

On August 1 the Soviet-Czech negotiations at Cierna nad Tisou came to an end amid signs of agreement to defuse the situation. According to reports, Brezhnev and Suslov resisted Ulbricht's pleas for a more confrontationist attitude. On August 3 the Soviets pulled their remaining troops out of Czechoslovakia. High-level delegations from all the Warsaw Pact states except Romania gathered in Bratislava the same day for further discussions. The communiqué reflected Moscow's acquiescence in the Czech delegation's request for a conference to discuss economic issues. It also included, at the Czechs' insistence, a reference to West German forces "struggling against revanchism, militarism, and neo-Nazism," and it did not specifically include West German recognition of the GDR among the conditions for European security.[35]

A brief lull then ensued in East German and Soviet polemics on Czechoslovakia as leaders in both countries watched for signs that Dubcek would act decisively to control the reform movement. During this period, on August 9, Ulbricht spoke before the Volkskammer and, to the surprise of many listeners, raised the possibility of trade talks with West Germany.[36] This unexpected proposal, coming at the end of a speech laced with scathing criticism of the FRG, was confirmed on August 16, when the GDR officially communicated to Bonn its interest in starting the negotiations in late August or early September. Meanwhile, the East German press continued to reproach West Germany for interfering in Czech affairs.

35. Dawisha, *Kremlin and the Prague Spring*, pp. 259–61, 267; *Pravda*, Aug. 4, 1968, p. 1.

36. *ND*, Aug. 10, 1968, pp. 3–4.

The GDR's trade initiative, which became a dead letter after the invasion of Czechoslovakia, has been variously interpreted. One view suggested that the Bratislava meeting had resolved the Czech problem in Dubcek's favor, and that Ulbricht was shifting course accordingly. Another view held that, on the contrary, the Soviets had already decided to invade by August 9, and Ulbricht's gesture in Bonn's direction was designed to lull the West into thinking the crisis was over. A third interpretation contended that no final decision had been reached at Bratislava, and Ulbricht's overture was a hedge against possible Soviet approval of Czechoslovakia's westward orientation. Finally, a fourth view argued that Ulbricht was acting under pressure from technocrats in the GDR who favored more trade with the West.[37]

Though any assessment of Ulbricht's motives must be hypothetical, the most plausible explanation seems to be that the SED chief floated the trade negotiation proposal in order to exert pressure on Moscow to invade Czechoslovakia. A thorough reconstruction of the available evidence suggests that the CPSU Politburo did not reach a consensus on invasion until August 17.[38] Conceivably Ulbricht may have launched his trade initiative to show the Soviet leaders that if they failed to stop Dubcek's domestic and foreign policy revisionism, the GDR could make its own accommodation with the Federal Republic. The prospect of a separate inter-German rapprochement, especially one pursued by East Germany without Soviet supervision, would surely have challenged the Kremlin's control over the Warsaw Pact. Ulbricht may therefore have been signaling to Moscow the potentially chilling consequences of Soviet passivity in the Czech situation.

Whatever the case, Ulbricht also decided that a tête-à-tête with the Czech leadership was now imperative. On August 12 he led a large delegation of East German economic experts to Karlovy Vary to meet with Dubcek and assorted colleagues. At a rambling press conference the next day, Ulbricht lectured his hosts on the superiority of the East German economic system and reaffirmed his position that "European security" required diplomatic relations between the two German states. Dubcek did not echo this view.[39]

---

37. The varying interpretations of Ulbricht's demarche can be found in Melvin Croan, "Czechoslovakia, Ulbricht, and the German Problem," *Problems of Communism* 18 (January–February 1969), p. 4; Wolfe, *Soviet Power and Europe*, p. 416; Neugebauer, "Vom 'Eisernen Dreieck' zu der ostdeutschen Beteiligung," p. 121; Ilse Spittmann, "Die SED im Konflikt mit der UdSSR," *Deutschland Archiv*, no. 6, 1968, pp. 668–69; N. Edwina Moreton, *East Germany and the Warsaw Alliance: The Politics of Détente* (Boulder, Colo.: Westview, 1978), pp. 83–84; A. James McAdams, *East Germany and Détente* (Cambridge: Cambridge University Press, 1985), p. 88; and David Binder in *New York Times*, Aug. 28, 1968, p. 12.

38. Dawisha, *Kremlin and the Prague Spring*, pp. 282–90.

39. For the East German report on the press conference, see *ND*, Aug. 14, 1968, pp. 3–4. This report omits Dubcek's declaration that his country was capable of defending its own borders without outside help. See Neugebauer, "Vom 'Eisernen Dreieck' zu der ostdeutschen Beteiligung," p. 122. For the text of the Karlovy Vary communiqué, see *ND*, Aug. 13, p. 1.

Hence it is quite likely that Ulbricht passed on to the Soviets a very negative account of his consultations with the Czech leadership.[40] Meanwhile, Ulbricht and the East German press persisted in their polemical assaults on West German foreign policy both before and after the Karlovy Vary meeting, a clear sign that the GDR's proposal for inter-German trade talks was not about to be helped along by any reduction of rhetorical abuse.[41] As the Kremlin leadership pursued its final deliberations on the question of invasion, the Soviet press stepped up its own attacks on the FRG.[42] Finally, on August 20, *Neues Deutschland* extolled the virtues of Soviet-GDR cooperation.

Later that night, the invasion of Czechoslovakia began.[43]

Impact of the Czech Crisis on the GDR

In the course of the weeks and months that followed the invasion, a profusion of articles, editorials, and official statements filled the East German press with justifications for the military intervention. Although the proponents of reform in Czechoslovakia came in for unsparing criticism, even greater emphasis was placed on West Germany's responsibility for provoking the radical transformations in Prague's domestic and foreign policy orientations. *Neues Deutschland*, for example, averred that the invasion had been necessary to prevent the Federal Republic from changing the status quo in Europe.[44] Soviet press attacks on West Germany's putative role in the Czech events resumed somewhat later, toward the end of August. In early September, Moscow presented the Kiesinger government with a note sternly advising it to abandon its attempts to influence Eastern Europe.[45]

But whereas the Soviet Union's criticisms of the FRG centered heavily on Bonn's presumed attempts to alter the political-military balance between NATO and the Warsaw Pact by playing upon the turmoil in Czechoslovakia, the East Germans tended to accentuate economic themes. Typically, Bonn was accused of using its economic muscle to turn Czechoslovakia toward the West.[46] Although no specific agreement on economic coopera-

40. Dawisha, *Kremlin and the Prague Spring*, p. 279.
41. See *ND*, Aug. 13, 1968, p. 2; Aug. 14, p. 6; Aug. 16, pp. 1–2, and 7; Aug. 17, p. 7.
42. See I. Aleksandrov's article in *Pravda*, Aug. 18, 1968, p. 4.
43. The invasion forces included elements from two of the East German army's six divisions, most of which were soon withdrawn. See Thomas M. Forster, *The East German Army*, trans. Deryck Viney (London: George Allen & Unwin, 1980), pp. 92–93.
44. *ND*, Aug. 23, 1968, p. 1. See also *ND*, Aug. 25, pp. 1–2, 7; Aug. 27, pp. 1–2; Aug. 29, pp. 1–2; Sept. 2, p. 2; Sept. 6, p. 2; Sept. 9, p. 1; Sept. 10, p. 2.
45. Wolfe, *Soviet Power and Europe*, pp. 382–83, 415–16.
46. *ND*, Aug. 25, 1968, p. 7; Aug. 29, pp. 1–2, 7; Aug. 31, pp. 1, 7; Sept. 1, p. 5; Sept. 5, p. 6.

tion between Bonn and Prague was ready for signature at the time of the invasion, negotiations for this purpose were certainly under way.[47] Just as alarmingly, from the East German point of view, improved economic relations quite possibly would have paved the way to diplomatic normalization between the FRG and Czechoslovakia without Bonn's recognition of the GDR.[48]

In keeping with these images of the Czech crisis, Ulbricht and the SED leadership mounted a full-scale campaign to convince the Soviet Union and the other states of the Warsaw Pact to speed up their own economic development as a defense against Western economic enticements. To demonstrate the GDR's readiness to lead the way in this endeavor, Ulbricht in late September announced that the forthcoming five-year "perspective plan" for 1971–1975 would concentrate on the accelerated development of high technology and related "structure-determining areas." Affirming that the "main task" of the new plan would be "to strengthen the GDR further on all sides," Ulbricht referred specifically to the recent "imperialist threat" against Czechoslovakia, and concluded that arduous work on the East German economy was therefore necessary "precisely for political reasons."[49] Ulbricht's views on the need to concentrate investment resources in the structure-determining areas of science and technology in the 1971–1975 period were seconded by the chief of the State Planning Commission, Gerhard Schürer.[50]

Ulbricht strongly reinforced this outlook at the SED Central Committee plenum held in October. At this postmortem session on the Czech crisis, the SED chief spoke in no uncertain terms about the need to draw economic conclusions from the political upheavals of the preceding months. "Peak performance" (*Spitzenleistung*) in the East German economy, together with expanded cooperation among the COMECON countries, was seen as a vital necessity so that the confrontation with West German capitalism "may be successfully won." The first secretary then drew upon themes that had already been sketched out in the East German press during the preceding months in calling on the socialist states to develop their economic potential by their own means: *"In the embattled confrontation between socialism and imperialism on a worldwide scale, there crystallizes as a law of the class struggle between socialist and imperialist states the necessity of the socialist commonwealth of states to solve every important scientific-technical, military, economic, and other problem by their own skill and by their own means."* Ulbricht further professed that "the Soviet Union and the countries

47. *Industriekurrier*, July 18, 1968, p. 1.
48. *ND*, Sept. 1, 1968, p. 5.
49. See his speech before the Perspective Plan Commission, *ND*, Sept. 28, 1968, pp. 3–4.
50. Gerhard Schürer, "Das Neue bei der Ausarbeitung des Perspektivplanes 1971 bis 1975," *Einheit*, no. 12, 1968, pp. 1483–93.

allied with it are fully able to do this." However, as in 1964, when he acknowledged doubts among East German technocrats about his plans to accelerate the development of the chemical industry, Ulbricht admitted that questions were already being raised inside the GDR about the feasibility of the grandiose high-technology development plans now being drawn up. It would be necessary, he said, "to convince the scientists that our way is correct and necessary."[51] This candid remark provided yet another indication that Ulbricht's economic policies at this time reflected overriding political concerns rather than strict adherence to the demands of economic rationality.

Ulbricht also made it clear that the GDR was in no way advocating a complete cutoff of trade with the West. (In fact, at the end of 1968 the GDR was to conclude a trade agreement that would double imports from West Germany by 1975, to DM600 million.[52]) The ultimate purpose of his program was rather to avoid what he termed "dependence." "It goes without saying," Ulbricht stated, "that we cultivate economic and scientific-technical relations with monopoly-capitalistic states. But in the process we avoid falling into dependence on them." It was the Czech reformers, together with the leaders of Yugoslavia and "certain comrades" in the communist parties of Western Europe, who courted the risk of Western "economic penetration" by espousing expanded East-West trade ties, especially with West Germany. What these deluded individuals were seeking, in Ulbricht's view, was "a more comfortable way" of promoting economic growth than "the GDR's way," which stressed accelerated internal economic development and intensified cooperation with the USSR. Ulbricht buttressed these statements with a strong reaffirmation of the GDR's "developed societal system of socialism," which he now described as a "model" of advanced socialism.

The views expressed in Ulbricht's speech at the October plenum were approvingly reiterated by other SED Politburo figures, including Günter Mittag, the Politburo's leading economic specialist and a man usually regarded in the West as a pragmatic technocrat.[53]

The practical implications of these assertions had already been fore-shadowed in the spring and summer of 1968, as the East German government instituted measures to reinvest greater decision-making authority in centralized planning organs, as opposed to lower-level bodies, in the so-

51. *ND*, Oct. 25, 1968, pp. 3–4, 6; emphasis in original.
52. J. N. [Joachim Nawrocki], "Neue Verhandlungen im innerdeutschen Handel," *Deutschland Archiv*, no. 1, 1969, pp. 81–83.
53. For Mittag's speech, see *ND*, Oct. 27, 1968, p. 4. Mittag criticized the East German economist Günther Kohlmey for advocating a reduction of party control in economic matters. Though evidence supporting Mittag's charge was scarce, Kohlmey was known as an outspoken proponent of expanded trade with the West. See Günther Kohlmey, *Aussenwirtschaft und Wachstum* (East Berlin: Akademie, 1968).

called structure-determining areas. As we have seen, Stoph had signaled this change of direction in late March. Decrees issued in April and June gave effect to this announcement.[54] These recentralization measures were essentially intended to increase central supervision of Ulbricht's program to accelerate the GDR's technological growth "by its own means." Thus foreign policy considerations, rooted in Ulbricht's perception that technological backwardness vis-à-vis West Germany required a more vigorous economic response from the socialist states, were having a decisive impact not only in the resetting of the GDR's planned production targets but on the very organizational structure of its economy.

Recentralization went hand in hand with efforts to improve coordination and performance in the advanced technological sectors. Both of these domestic policies derived their main impetus from Ulbricht's explicitly articulated interpretation of the relationship between the exigencies of economic development and the dangers lurking in the international environment. The primacy of foreign policy in Ulbricht's domestic economic strategy had never been so precisely formulated or so extensively implemented as in these critical months of 1968.[55]

Even more explicit indications of the GDR's determination to push high-technology growth came in December, with the publication of the annual plan for 1969. As Table 1 indicates, the new plan targets exceeded the annual growth limits set in the currently operative 1966–1970 five-year plan in several categories. Not only was the net material product of the entire economy slated to grow at a higher rate; the pace for this overall advance was to be set by accelerated growth in high-technology areas. The 1969 growth targets in electronics and electromechanics, for example, were considerably higher than the annual growth rate projected in the five-year plan. (It should be noted that the goals of the 1966–1970 plan were finally promulgated only in 1967, more than a year behind schedule.) Schürer's speech to the Volkskammer explaining the 1969 plan guidelines made it obvious that the bulk of investment resources for that year would be channeled into the structure-determining areas.[56] Consumer goods and

---

54. *ND*, Apr. 23, 1968, p. 3; *Gesetzblatt der DDR*, pt. 2, no. 66, 1968, pp. 433ff. The "structure-determining areas" were defined to include computers, scientific implements, advanced construction equipment, synthetic fibers, and other high-technology products. See Angela Rüger, *Die Bedeutung "strukturbestimmender Aufgaben" für die Wirtschaftsplanung und -organisation der DDR* (West Berlin: Duncker & Humblot, 1969), pp. 12–13.

55. My interpretation of Ulbricht's economic policies at this time differs from that of Western scholars who regard the recentralization measures largely as an effort to keep East Germany's economic reforms from heading in the same market-oriented direction as those of Czechoslovakia. See, e.g., Konstantin Pritzel, "Warum Revision des NOS?" *Deutschland Archiv*, no. 4, 1970, pp. 344–45, and Joachim Nawrocki, "Vom NÖS zum Computer-Stalinismus," ibid., p. 348. Actually, the East German leadership had little to fear from market-style reformism, as the GDR's economic planning process was tightly controlled by the SED hierarchy.

56. *ND*, Dec. 14, 1968, p. 3.

Table 1. Annual growth rates in five sectors of GDR economy envisioned in three plans (percent)

Sector	1966–1970 plan	1968 plan	1969 plan
Net material product	5.0–5.7%	5.4%	6.0%
Industrial production	5.0–5.4	6.4	7.0
Electronics/electromechanics	10.4–10.8	NA	13.0
Chemical industry	8.4	NA	9.0
Labor productivity in industry	7.0–7.7	7.0	9.0

NA = not available.
Sources: *Gesetzblatt der DDR*, 1967, pt. 1, no. 8, pp. 65–87; *Neues Deutschland*, Dec. 16, 1967, pp. 5–7, and Dec. 14, 1968, p. 2; *Die Wirtschaft*, nos. 51–52, 1968, p. 3.

apartment construction once again got short-changed. The new plan provided dramatic evidence that in 1968 the GDR had decided to revise its plan goals in midstream, abandoning economic guidelines that had been adopted only the year before.

At the same time, the GDR moved to upgrade both the quantity and the quality of its economic cooperation with the Soviet Union. Statements by high-level East German trade and technology officials called for "genuine partnership" in Soviet-GDR economic relations, and for "equal research cooperation" between the two countries in high-technology sectors. Only on this basis, they insisted, could both the GDR and the USSR achieve international technological standards. The East Germans appeared to be saying that it was not in Moscow's interest to treat the GDR as an economic subordinate. Moreover, the GDR called on the Soviets to concentrate their own resources in the structure-determining areas, in accordance with the exhortation to develop socialism "by our own means."[57]

It was not immediately evident, however, that the Soviet Union went along with these appeals. Although the communiqué issued at the end of the meeting of the Soviet-GDR joint economic commission on December 20 announced long-term cooperative agreements in key high-technology areas, it did not mention several of the GDR's pet themes.[58] In particular, there was no reference to equality of partnership or to accelerated economic development "by our own means." As we have seen, the Soviet leadership was by no means united on the question of East-West trade in 1968, and it certainly did not move with the East Germans' decisiveness against ex-

57. *Die Wirtschaft*, no. 45, 1968, p. 2. See also the interview with Rudolff, general director of the GDR's Ministry of Foreign Trade, in ibid., p. 7. Also Günter Prey, "Mit der Sowjetunion gemeinsam die wissenschaftlich-technische Revolution meistern," *Einheit*, no. 11, 1968, pp. 1300–1308 (Prey was the GDR's minister for science and technology); Klaus Stubenrauch's article in *ND*, Dec. 29, 1968, p. 5 (Stubenrauch was Prey's deputy minister); and the article by Foreign Trade Minister Gerhard Fröhlich in *ND*, Sept. 28, p. 10.
58. For the text, see *ND*, Dec. 21, 1968, p. 1.

panded trade with the West. On the contrary, trends in Moscow were beginning to move in precisely the opposite direction.

Soviet and East German Debates

As in the past, East German analyses of the international scene appearing in the main foreign policy and party journals overwhelmingly supported the policy lines forged by the SED leadership. Once again relations among the leading Western countries were described primarily in terms of "U.S. global strategy." Special emphasis was placed on West Germany's role as the chief supporter of America's "aggressive" foreign policy. These lurid East German images of the West were quite patently intended to convey to Moscow the message that the chances of playing upon differences between the United States and West Germany were practically nonexistent.[59] By implication, they would presumably be nonexistent even under a government led by the SPD, as the SPD leadership was subjected to unceasing criticism.[60] A new ideological theme gained prominence as academicians and journalists in the GDR, taking their cue from the SED leadership, condemned "Social Democratism" in West Germany, frequently linking it with alleged proponents of convergence theory both in the West and in Czechoslovkia.[61] Finally, the question of international economic relations was treated almost exclusively in favor of greater cooperation among the Soviet bloc states. Indications of lingering *Westdrall* tendencies essentially disappeared from public view. Accordingly, East German journals tended to highlight the achievements of the Soviet economy and to disparage the economic performance of the FRG.[62]

59. See, e.g., Klaus Bollinger and Hans-Martin Geyer, "Ideologische Aspekte der USA-Globalstrategie," *DA*, no. 4, 1968, pp. 464–75; Willi Pater, "Die 'Zukunftsversion' der Bonner Globalstrategen," ibid., vol. 6, 1968, pp. 651–60; Siegfried Zeimer and Albrecht Charisius, "Die NATO zwischen den Tagungen von Brüssel und Reykjavik," ibid., pp. 661–74; Siegfried Schwarz, "Die besondere Rolle der westdeutschen Bundesrepublik in der NATO," ibid., pp. 1441–48; Genia Nobel, "Der Bankrott der USA-Globalstrategie in Asien und die Pläne des Franz-Josef Strauss," *Einheit*, no. 6, 1968, pp. 744–56.

60. See the review by Willi Schlegel of Willy Brandt's book *Friedenspolitik in Europa* in *DA*, no. 11, 1968, pp. 1381–83; Reinhard Klassen and Max Schmidt, "Die Strauss-Konzeption und die SPD-Minister," *Einheit*, no. 7, 1968, pp. 889–900; Hellmuth Kolbe, "Zu den zwei unterschiedlichen Linien in der westdeutschen Sozialdemokratie," *Einheit*, no. 8, 1968, pp. 1016–27.

61. For an analysis of this theme by a West German scholar, see Bernhard von Rosenblatt, *Die Auseinandersetzung mit der Konvergenztheorie in der DDR* (Eggenberg: Wissenschaft und Politik, 1970). Convergence theory was the notion that over time Western capitalist states and the more economically developed socialist states would become increasingly similar, ultimately converging on a model that combined socialist-style planning with Western-style concepts of democracy.

62. Gerhard Wyschka, "Die Bedeutung der Aussenwirtschaftsbeziehungen der DDR mit den sozialistischen Ländern," *DA*, no. 10, 1968, pp. 1185–93; Otto Raus, "Erfolgreiche

On all of these issues, Soviet academic writings were considerably less monotonous. A particularly lively exchange of opinion centered on the Atlantic alliance. Was Western Europe becoming more independent of the United States? While most Soviet analysts who addressed this question in 1968 recognized both conflict and partnership in U.S.–West European relations, thus taking the Atlanticist approach, a growing number of them —particularly writers who analyzed U.S. relations with France, Italy, and the Scandinavian countries—were inclined to stress the contradictions in these ties, strongly accentuating a more Europeanist outlook. The Americanist position faded from view.

Discussion of these issues became considerably more focused than it had been earlier, as IMEMO devoted an international conference and a collection of articles to contemporary Western Europe and published the first book ever released in the USSR on the subject of postwar U.S.–West European relations. The conference, held in late April 1968, brought together academic specialists on European security and politics from the Warsaw Pact countries and Yugoslavia. While the East German participants faithfully propagated the analytical and policy orientations of Walter Ulbricht, Soviet contributors displayed a greater variety of views. Several, such as N. N. Inozemtsev, Yurii Rubinskii, and Oleg Bykov, emphasized the "complexity" and "contradictions" increasingly evident in U.S.–West European ties; others, such as Vladimir Gantman, took due note of these contradictions but warned that the United States, far from making plans to leave Western Europe, was actually engaged in cementing Atlantic integration.[63] Gantman's analysis combined the balanced Atlanticist orientation with a hardline attitude toward the West in general.

A variety of views emerged in IMEMO's book on U.S.–West European relations. Bykov, for example, argued emphatically that in the context of the Vietnam war, the "disintegrative tendencies" in these relations were "stronger than the integrative tendencies." In view of these "deep, irreversible processes," Bykov contended, Western Europe now confronted the choice of either continuing its former alliance policy with the United States or elaborating a new approach to European security in cooperation with the socialist countries and "without the U.S.A."[64] This was one of the most forcefully argued examples of the Europeanist position yet seen in Soviet analytical writings. Other contributors to the IMEMO volume adopted a

Wirtschaftsentwicklung in der UdSSR," *DA*, no. 12, 1968, pp. 1419–31; Otto Reinhold, "Die westdeutsche Wirtschaft im Lichte der Marxschen Krisentheorie," *Einheit*, nos. 4–5, 1968, pp. 486–97.

63. For the contributions, see *MEMO*, no. 7, 1968, pp. 102–21, and no. 8, 1968, pp. 72–81. Gantman repeated these views when he wrote *MEMO*'s quarterly survey, "Tekushchiye problemy mirovoi politiki," no. 7, 1968, p. 98, and no. 10, 1968, p. 78.

64. D. E. Melnikov, ed., *Zapadnaya Evropa i SShA* (Moscow: Mysl, 1968), pp. 12–152, esp. 120, 132, 136.

more balanced outlook, however. While taking due account of conflictual tendencies in the NATO alliance, they did not repeat Bykov's suggestion that Western Europe might break away from the United States. They referred instead to continuing examples of transatlantic partnership.[65]

Similarly, Soviet specialists differed among themselves when they analyzed the strengths of centrifugal and centripetal forces at work in the Western alliance. Opinion even diverged on the Harmel report, a NATO document that called for the simultaneous pursuit of military modernization and détente. While some writers saw only its negative aspects, others stressed its more positive features.[66]

Where West Germany stood in all this was, of course, central to the issue of U.S.–West European relations. The majority of Soviet academicians who addressed the matter in 1968—even most of those who stressed the contradictions between the United States and Western Europe—stressed the abiding partnership of Bonn and Washington.[67] Very few of them, however, were as categorical as the East German writers in their analyses of this relationship. Most Soviet analysts tended to avoid such damning phrases as "the Bonn-Washington axis" and "U.S. global strategy" in 1968. On the contrary, some expressed the view that West Germany might eventually join the broader West European trend away from complete reliance on the United States. Daniil Melnikov, for example, declared with obvious approval that the SPD leadership and elements of the CDU/CSU had lately shown evidence of "*a shift in the direction of a 'European' conception.*" Though he warned that neither the Social Democrats nor the Christian Democrats had completely abandoned their old policies, Melnikov accorded special importance to the polarization evident in the West German political leadership on vital foreign policy issues.[68]

These views were basically consistent with Melnikov's contribution to the IMEMO book on relations between the United States and Western Europe, of which he was the editor. In a chapter co-authored with M. S. Zibirova, Melnikov surveyed the entire postwar history of U.S.–West German relations, highlighting the serious conflicts that divided Washington and Bonn despite their "common class interests." The essay concluded that

65. See the chapters by S. Madzoevskii on U.S.-British relations, ibid., pp. 153–211; by Yu. Rubinskii on U.S.-French relations, ibid., pp. 212–90; and by I. M. Ivanova on the concept of Atlanticism, ibid., pp. 348–405.

66. Centrifugal tendencies: L. Bashkin, "Mezhdu Bryusselem i Reikyavikom," *MEMO*, no. 5, 1968, pp. 68–71; centripetal tendencies: V. Vladimirov, "Sotsialisticheskiye strany i politicheskaya strategiya imperializma," ibid., no. 8, 1968, pp. 3–15. Harmel report: negative, V. Ardatovskii, "NATO: God dvadtsaty," ibid., no. 3, 1968, pp. 3–14; positive, Bashkin, "Mezhdu Bryusselem i Reikyavikom," p. 70. For an East German attack on the Harmel report, see Zeimer and Charisius, n. 59 above, p. 662.

67. E.g., P. Kryukov, "Bonn: New Stage, Old Ploy," *IA*, no. 3, 1968, pp. 14–21; L. Vidyasova, "NATO on the Eve of 1969," *IA*, no. 10, 1968, pp. 17–24.

68. *MEMO*, no. 7, 1968, p. 117; emphasis in original.

even the Grand Coalition government "demonstratively underlines its independence from the United States," and that further "sharp collisions" between the two NATO powers were "inevitable." The entire Atlantic alliance was thus "very unstable." He made it clear, however, that the FRG's quest for greater freedom of action was confined to the structure of the Atlantic alliance. Bonn, in Melnikov's view, showed no inclination to leave NATO.[69]

Melnikov in effect underscored a prevailing tendency among Soviet analysts of the Europeanist persuasion: Though they viewed Western Europe as distancing itself from the United States, they also perceived it as remaining fundamentally faithful to the Atlantic alliance. Thus the Europeanist outlook was not radically different from the Atlanticist orientation. The two approaches differed mainly in emphasis. While the Europeanists emphasized the West Europeans' palpable, albeit limited, desires for greater freedom of maneuver, the Atlanticists tended to lay roughly equal stress on Western Europe's quest for autonomy and its undiminished need for American protection.

In contrast to Melnikov, most Soviet specialists were highly critical of the Grand Coalition government in 1968, especially as the crisis in Czechoslovakia heated up. One writer even likened the contemporary Federal Republic to Hitler's Germany.[70] Several were particularly exercised at Bonn's military policies.[71] Nevertheless, one analyst noted that economic forces were compelling the Grand Coalition to make "relatively small expenditures on arms," and another suggested that the influence of right-wing radicalism would actually decline in an atmosphere of détente and international stability.[72]

Soviet writers were more clearly divided on the SPD. Several of them were highly critical of the Social Democratic leadership, both before and after the Czech invasion.[73] One assailed Brandt's proposal for balanced

69. Melnikov, *Zapadnaya Evropa i SShA*, pp. 291–347, passim. See also Melnikov, "Germanskaya natsiya i sudby Evropy," *MEMO*, no. 11, 1968, pp. 39–50, in which he refers to the "struggle" taking place within the West German ruling camp involving forces seeking to prevent a recurrence of the events that led to World War II. Such comments were particularly striking in view of their publication shortly after the Soviet intervention in Czechoslovakia.

70. Kryukov, n. 67 above, p. 14. See also A. Galkin, "Social Roots of Neo-Fascism," *IA*, no. 4, 1968, pp. 12–18; V. Mikhailov, "Bonn's Two Camps," *IA*, no. 8, 1968, pp. 70–76; "In Defence of Socialism and Peace," *IA*, no. 9, 1968, pp. 3–6.

71. "Tekushchiye problemy mirovoi politiki," *MEMO*, no. 4, 1968, p. 84; V. Shenayev, "V. I. Lenin o germanskom imperializme i sovremenny imperializm FRG," ibid., no. 12, 1968, pp. 16–30; V. Ilyin, "Bonn's Nuclear Ambitions," *IA*, no. 5, 1968, pp. 24–29.

72. E. Khelnitskaya, "Chto pokozal ekonomicheskii krizis v Zapadnoi Germanii?" *MEMO*, no. 4, 1968, p. 44; A. A. Galkin's remarks, ibid., no. 7, 1968, p. 107.

73. Y. Rzhevsky, "A Year of the Big Coalition," *IA*, no. 1, 1968, pp. 9–15, and "F.R.G. in the System of Western Alliances," *IA*, no. 12, 1968, pp. 24–29; A. Zalyotny, "F.R.G. and Developments in Czechoslovakia," *IA*, no. 11, 1968, pp. 22–27; and Kryukov, n. 91 above, pp. 14–21.

force reductions in Europe on the grounds that it displayed a pro-American bias.[74] Melnikov, however, referred in favorable terms to the discussions and decisions on the SPD platform that had taken place at the party's national congress in March. He noted in particular that the Social Democratic leadership had taken a positive stand on such issues as the nonproliferation treaty and a renunciation-of-force agreement with the GDR. Even Gantman, who was more wary than Melnikov of the evolving Europeanization of West German policy, took note of the "nuances" in Brandt's position at the SPD congress.[75] In any case, Soviet writers showed little, if any, inclination to follow the GDR's rhetorical blitz against "Social Democratism."

While these debates on West Germany were taking place, the broader issue of East-West trade and technology exchange continued to divide Soviet academicians. Some scholars, such as Inozemtsev, spoke up in favor of greater contacts with the West, a view supported by various Soviet trade officials. Others took a more jaundiced view of such efforts, undergirding their arguments with reminders of the current economic tribulations of capitalism and the perfidy of American and West German bridge-building policy.[76] None of these more negatively inclined specialists, however, took up Ulbricht's call for the socialist bloc's technological development "by our own means."

Conclusions

The Kremlin's actions in 1968 graphically demonstrated that when the Brezhnev Politburo was confronted with a severe challenge to Soviet authority in Eastern Europe, it would not flinch from military intervention. The invasion also reinforced conservative tendencies that were already apparent in key elements of the post-Khrushchev leadership's domestic and foreign policies. Leonid Brezhnev used the crisis to solidify his growing preeminence in foreign policy matters, enhancing his own conser-

74. Y. Novoseltsev, "Bonn's Eastern Policy and European Security," *IA*, no. 7, 1968, esp. pp. 30–32. This article also attacked Brandt's call for a "peace order in Europe," as outlined in his *Foreign Affairs* article of Apr. 1968.

75. *MEMO*, no. 7, 1968, p. 117, 96.

76. See N. Inozemtsev's contribution to the April 1968 IMEMO conference in *MEMO*, no. 7, 1968, pp. 103–6. For additional Soviet comments on wider economic ties with the West, see Parrott, *Politics and Technology*, pp. 194–97 and 202–6. Negative evaluations of trade with the West can be found in Vladimirov, "Sotsialisticheskiye strany i politicheskaya strategiya imperializma," *MEMO*, no. 8, 1968, p. 12; V. Cheprakov, "Lenin o sushchnosti natsional-nykh tipakh imperializma," *MEMO*, no. 9, 1968, pp. 16–26; G. Mekhanik, "Sotsialnye izder-zhki nauchno-tekhnicheskoi revolyutsii pri kapitalizme," *MEMO*, no. 12, 1968, pp. 31–41; Y. Sibirtsev, "The G.D.R. at a New Stage of Its Development," *IA*, no. 10, 1968, pp. 29–34; Zalyotny, "F.R.G. and Developments in Czechoslovakia," pp. 25–26.

vative credentials in the process. After taking a cautiously reserved position on the Czech events until late in the summer, the general secretary ultimately sided with the proponents of military action. He also expressed conservative opinions on East-West trade and military spending throughout the year.

The decision to invade was the result of a protracted consensus-building process among the top Kremlin decision makers which highlighted the Brezhnev regime's status as an oligarchical coalition. Differences were expressed within the primary elite on a host of other issues, including such vital questions as the pace of military development and the scope of economic cooperation with the West. However, as power relationships within the Politburo and Secretariat advanced beyond the formative stages of the previous three years and converged around Brezhnev's expanded authority, the regime's foreign policy approach assumed a generally conservative coloration. Economic cooperation with the West would increase only marginally, while defense expenditures would rise significantly. A coherent conception of détente had yet to emerge, and policy toward West Germany in 1968 did not progress very far beyond the reaffirmation of familiar demands on behalf of the territorial status quo. The Soviets exhibited at best a moderate level of flexibility in their approach toward Bonn, keeping their future options open while firmly reprimanding the Grand Coalition government for seeking to exploit the Czech events for "revanchist" ends. No clear indications of what kinds of compromises the Kremlin might be willing to make with the FRG came to the fore. Once again, the hesitancy and ambivalence of Kremlin leaders toward West Germany were strikingly confirmed by members of the secondary elite, who continued to offer openly divergent evaluations of the West German government's foreign policy inclinations.

While remaining extremely wary of Bonn's intentions, the Soviets were by no means ready to cut off their nascent dialogue with the Grand Coalition entirely. As if to underline the point, Soviet Ambassador Semen Tsarapkin called on Chancellor Kiesinger on the day after the Czech invasion to assure him of Moscow's undiminished interest in improved relations with Bonn. Gromyko met with Willy Brandt in New York on October 7, and the two foreign ministers agreed to make a fresh start in the Bonn-Moscow dialogue. Gromyko reiterated his support for a resumption of negotiations with the FRG in talks with Ambassador Helmut Allardt in December.

To no small extent, the Brezhnev regime's stunning exhibition of its willingness to use military force to preserve neo-Stalinist regimes in Eastern Europe ultimately strengthened its hand in its dealings with Bonn. The West Germans were now put on notice that Moscow would not tolerate any effort to undermine or skirt its control over its East European empire.

Various pronouncements suggesting that the USSR reserved the right to defend socialism by force even against internal challenges—pronouncements that collectively became known as the "Brezhnev doctrine"— reinforced this position.[77] Having reasserted their imperial domination over East-Central Europe, the Soviet leaders now felt themselves to be in a stronger position than before the invasion to deal with the Federal Republic on their own terms. They also probably felt that the invasion would reassure Walter Ulbricht of Moscow's resolve to use force to preserve the GDR too, if necessary. The East German leader would then have little reason to fear a regulated détente with West Germany.[78]

Nevertheless, East Germany was more settled than ever before on a decidedly maximalist course. Under the redoubtable leadership of Walter Ulbricht, the East German elite framed a broad-gauged antidétente policy that consciously integrated foreign policy priorities with domestic economic policies and ideological innovations to form a coherent grand design. Flexibility and willingness to compromise with Bonn on the GDR's explicitly stated positions remained at a low ebb. As if on cue, the East German secondary elite reiterated the arguments propounded by Walter Ulbricht and other prominent SED officials in support of the first secretary's authoritatively stated positions.

In the end, Soviet and East German responses to the Czech crisis of 1968 demonstrated that much more was at stake for both governments than just the question of political and economic reform in the socialist camp. The Czech crisis was also a proving ground for policy toward West Germany. The next two years would prove crucial in determining whether Moscow's cautious conservatism or Ulbricht's intransigent maximalism would best serve the interests of the Warsaw Pact alliance in response to the next developments in Bonn's ostpolitik.

77. On the Brezhnev doctrine, see Wolfe, *Soviet Power and Europe*, pp. 383–85.
78. Starting in 1968 the Soviets increased their troop levels in Central Europe from 26 divisions to 31 in the next decade. During the 1970s they stationed 519,000 troops in the region, 395,000 of whom were in the GDR. See *The Military Balance, 1979–1980* (London: International Institute for Strategic Studies, 1979), p. 109; John Collins, *U.S.-Soviet Military Balance: Concepts and Capabilities, 1960–1980* (New York: McGraw-Hill, 1980), pp. 540–41.

CHAPTER FIVE

Turning Points:
1969

THE DIFFERENCES between Soviet and East German attitudes toward West Germany which surfaced during the Czech crisis became magnified in 1969. As Brezhnev and other Kremlin leaders prepared themselves for the possibility that an SPD-FDP government might take power after Bundestag elections in the fall, Walter Ulbricht was more determined than ever to block any Soviet–West German arrangement that might diminish the GDR's exalted status within the Soviet bloc. While the SED leadership was probably most distressed at the prospect of a political deal behind East Germany's back (particularly one that fell short of full-scale de jure recognition of the GDR), economic considerations were also at the forefront of its concerns. Ulbricht was well aware that one of the chief determinants of the GDR's indispensability to the Warsaw Pact alliance was its invaluable contribution to Soviet and East European economic development. Any substantial increase in trade with the FRG by these countries could only reduce the GDR's preeminence among them and incline them to agreements with Bonn at East Germany's expense. As it happened, the drift of events was running against the GDR on this score. The widening economic gap between the socialist and capitalist states was pushing the Eastern bloc almost inexorably toward greater reliance on the West for highly valued goods, credits, and markets. As the year progressed, even Leonid Brezhnev joined the chorus of support for expanded East-West trade. Against this growing tendency, Walter Ulbricht pushed his scheme for accelerated development "by our own means" with renewed intensity. The resulting conflict between East Berlin and its Warsaw Pact allies glaringly exposed the economic underpinnings of the socialist camp's divided attitudes on détente. At the same time, it was also apparent that the Soviets themselves were still divided on policy toward Bonn.

Berlin, China, and the Debate on the SPD

Moscow's decision to keep itself open to possible agreements with the Federal Republic despite the Czech events became evident in the first months of the new year as a tug-of-war developed over Berlin. In early January 1969 the FRG decided to hold a meeting of the Federal Assembly (a joint session of the Bundestag and the Bundesrat) in West Berlin for the purpose of electing a successor to Heinrich Lübke as West Germany's president. The date for the election was set for March 5. From the outset Moscow made it very clear that it regarded the Federal Assembly's convocation in the divided city as a violation of the Soviet position that West Berlin was not legally part of the Federal Republic. The Soviets also made it known, however, that they wished to keep the confrontation from escalating into a crisis. Despite warnings of unspecified countermeasures if the March 5 meeting were to take place, *Pravda* and *Izvestiya* called attention to Soviet "self-restraint" and "patience" in the Berlin controversy.[1]

Moscow's readiness to discuss a deescalation of the dispute clashed with the GDR's attempts to exacerbate the conflict. On January 31 the Soviets signaled their interest in a negotiated outcome as Ambassador Abrassimov met with West Berlin Mayor Klaus Schütz and raised the possibility of a new holiday pass agreement permitting West Berliners to visit relatives in East Berlin over Easter. Abrassimov also proposed a new trade agreement with the FRG whose provisions would for the first time include West Berlin. While the Soviet envoy did not explicitly make these proposed agreements contingent on a decision to hold the Federal Assembly meeting elsewhere, FRG officials drew the logical inference that such a linkage was indeed intended.[2]

East Germany responded quickly. In rapid order the GDR issued menacing statements to the FRG and the government of West Berlin, followed by decrees barring members of the Federal Assembly from access to West Berlin. East Germany's note to Bonn insisted that West Berlin was located "on the territory of the German Democratic Republic." As tensions grew, Walter Ulbricht turned up unexpectedly in Moscow to discuss the situation.

A standoff ensued as the Soviets sought to assure the Kiesinger government of the GDR's willingness to arrange an Easter pass agreement for West Berliners while Ulbricht, much to Moscow's embarrassment, remained coolly unresponsive. A Soviet note advised Bonn against holding the electoral assembly in West Berlin, but balanced this warning with a restatement of Moscow's interest in "good-neighborly relations" with the FRG. The note also said that West Berlin was located "inside the territory" of the

---

1. *Pravda*, Dec. 20, 1968, p. 5; Jan. 18, 1969, p. 5; Jan. 27, p. 5; *Izvestiya*, Feb. 21, p. 2.
2. *FAZ*, Feb. 3, 1969, p. 1.

GDR, as opposed to East Germany's recent insistence that it was "on the territory" of the GDR, and it reaffirmed that the USSR had undertaken no commitments regarding West Berlin other than those entered into with the three Western occupation powers.[3]

Moscow's efforts to nudge the Ulbicht government into swapping Easter passes for the cancellation of the Federal Assembly meeting in West Berlin proved unavailing, however; the GDR showed no signs of wishing to resolve the dispute amicably.[4] On March 5, despite a final flurry of Soviet warnings, the Federal Assembly met in West Berlin without a hitch. Gustav Heinemann, a Social Democrat, was elected president of the FRG.

Meanwhile, the GDR let it be known that it rejected any tendency in Moscow to encourage the West German Social Democrats. Although *Izvestiya* on February 3 greeted Brandt's statement in favor of the nuclear nonproliferation treaty, *Neues Deutschland* warned on March 5 that "anyone who still has illusions that the Kiesinger/Strauss/Brandt/Wehner government conducts a policy other than that of the Adenauer and Erhard governments now knows better." Brandt himself was portrayed as walking "arm in arm" with Adolf von Thadden, chief of the neofascist NPD. In much the same spirit, the East German press provided occasional reminders that Brandt's coalition partner, Chancellor Kiesinger, had worked in the Nazi propaganda ministry, headed by Josef Goebbels.[5]

While the GDR thus bent all its efforts to poison Moscow's relationship with Bonn, the Soviets had other concerns to grapple with. Efforts to "normalize" the situation in Czechoslovakia were not completed until Gustav Husak's appointment as head of the CPCz in April; President Nixon's inaugural remarks about moving toward an "era of negotiations" needed to be assessed; and plans for a European security conference were still under consideration. Most critical of all, the Chinese attack on Soviet troops on the Ussuri River on March 2 required an immediate response. Ultimately, all of these issues impinged on Moscow's relations with the Federal Republic. Unlike the Ulbricht-dominated SED, the Soviet primary and secondary foreign policy elites were torn in conflicting directions by these developments.

To some extent the armed clash with China may have reinforced the arguments of those Soviets who already favored a more positive approach to West Germany. In this view, instability on the USSR's eastern flank justified special efforts to stabilize the situation on the western borders. This reasoning appeared to have an immediate policy impact, as the Soviets took the extraordinary step of briefing Kiesinger personally on the Ussuri River

3. *Pravda*, Feb. 16, 1969, p. 1.
4. For further details, see Gerhard Wettig, *Community and Conflict in the Socialist Camp* (London: C. Hurst, 1975), pp. 48–51.
5. Albert Norden compared the FRG with Hitler's Germany: *ND*, Feb. 22, 1969, p. 6.

fighting.[6] Though it is quite possible that opinions of this sort were uttered in private, they were never articulated publicly. Moreover, there is no conclusive evidence that the Brezhnev leadership sought a comprehensive agreement with Bonn *because* of the worsening conflict with China. As we have seen, key members of the Soviet decision-making elite had expressed an interest in improving relations with Bonn ever since the advent of the Grand Coalition government. But some people in the Soviet Union and the GDR referred to the conflict with China when they argued *against* détente with the FRG. Events would also show that the Kremlin was not inclined to abandon its minimum demands when it came to dealing with the FRG, regardless of tensions on the Chinese border. Thus China's impact on Soviet calculations with respect to détente with Bonn was multifaceted. While for some Kremlin leaders the clash on the Ussuri may have provided support for the notion of coming to terms with the West, it did not appear to be the decisive motivation for these efforts.

At the same time, the Ussuri River battles provided the occasion for a renewed debate on the SPD. The GDR initiated the discussions by directly linking the West German government with the Chinese border encroachments in *Neues Deutschland* on March 8. Scarcely a day went by without similar charges, often directly aimed at Willy Brandt's alleged connections with Beijing.[7] The Soviets also began to accuse West Germany of collusion with China.[8] Significantly, however, *Pravda* did not directly implicate the SPD leadership in relations with Chairman Mao's government. It was *Pravda Ukrainy*, the Russian-language newspaper of the Ukrainian party organization, that explicitly made this connection on March 9. This report followed earlier attacks on the SPD in the same newspaper.[9]

Pravda's next major article on the Bonn-Beijing connection came on March 18, but it again avoided referring to Brandt or other West German cabinet officials by name. Nevertheless, the next day a Radio Moscow broadcast accused Brandt of favoring expanded ties with China at a recent press conference, when in fact he had cautioned against embroilment in the Sino-Soviet dispute.[10] Other Soviet publications also accused Bonn of collaborating with the Chinese, including *Krasnaya zvezda* and *Trud*, the trade union newspaper under the general supervision of Shelepin.[11] A more frequent target of Soviet journalistic hostility at this time was Franz-Josef

6. *FAZ*, Mar. 17, 1969, p. 1. Ambassador Tsarapkin informed Kiesinger about the border clashes Mar. 11.

7. *ND*, Mar. 8, 1969, p. 7; Mar. 10, p. 5; Mar. 11, p. 2; Mar. 13, p. 7; Mar. 14, p. 7; Mar. 15, p. 2; Mar. 18, p. 7; Mar. 19, pp. 2, 7; Mar. 20, p. 7; Mar. 21, p. 7.

8. See the remarks by Leonid Zamyatin, the press spokesman of the Foreign Ministry, in *Pravda*, Mar. 8, 1969, p. 4.

9. *Pravda Ukrainy*, Mar. 4, pp. 2–3. Brandt favored economic ties with Beijing but opposed exploiting the Sino-Soviet conflict for the purpose of exerting political pressure on Moscow. See *Der Spiegel*, Mar. 17, 1969, p. 27.

10. *FAZ*, Mar. 28, 1969, p. 5.

11. *Krasnaya zvezda*, Mar. 19, 1969, p. 1; *Trud*, Mar. 11, p. 1. After being demoted by Brezhnev to the post of trade union chief in 1967, Shelepin presided over the transformation of

Strauss, who had openly advocated cooperation with China in his book *Challenge and Response.*[12]

Ultimately the Soviet central press was considerably less vocal in implicating the FRG in China's anti-Soviet foreign policy than the East German press, and was even more reluctant to criticize the SPD leadership in this respect. The same was true of Soviet leaders, with one major exception. On March 21 Petro Shelest condemned Bonn's alleged status as an "ally" of China, and noted that the recent border clash had occurred "at the moment of the exacerbation of the Berlin problem." Though he did not specifically allude to the SPD, Shelest denounced West German foreign policy in general as the work of "revanchists."[13]

The debate on the SPD took a more dramatic turn at the end of March, as Soviet bloc officials gathered in Moscow for celebrations commemorating the fiftieth anniversary of the founding of the Comintern. The main Soviet speaker was Mikhail Suslov, the CPSU's leading authority on ideological questions and generally reputed to be the number two man in the Soviet hierarchy, behind Brezhnev. Suslov's reputation as a hard-liner with solid Stalinist credentials (he had been entrusted with the brutal Sovietization of Lithuania after its annexation in World War II) gave his remarks a decidedly authoritative edge. It was therefore a matter of considerable consequence when Suslov announced a major revision of Soviet views on the role of the SPD in the 1928–1934 period. Admitting that the Comintern had made "mistakes," Suslov asserted that the "thesis that social democracy constituted the greatest danger, and that therefore the main blow had to be directed against it in a certain period, was wrong, and in essence led to sectarianism." This amounted to a repudiation of the Soviet-inspired policy adopted at the Sixth Comintern Congress in 1928, which had rejected German Communist Party collaboration with the SPD against Hitler and vilified the Social Democrats as "social fascists." Unquestionably Suslov's statement had more than just historiographical significance. It was an open signal of the Soviet leadership's interest in cooperating with the SPD if it came to power after the fall elections. This message was not lost on Ulbricht. After delivering a speech that upheld the traditional Soviet view that the Social Democrats were to blame for the failure of the German left to unite against Hitler, the SED chief abruptly left Moscow ahead of schedule, shunning the normally obligatory meeting with Brezhnev.[14]

Trud from a lackluster newspaper into a slick vehicle for his views. See Ilana Kass, *Soviet Involvement in the Middle East: Policy Formulation, 1966–1973* (Boulder, Colo.: Westview, 1978), p. 168.

12. See, e.g., Ernst Genrii's article in *Literaturnaya gazeta*, Mar. 12, 1969, p. 14. Genrii also criticized Egon Bahr in this regard. See also Lev Bezymenskii, "Eskalatsiya neveroyatnost," *Kommunist*, no. 4, 1969, pp. 104–14.

13. *Pravda Ukrainy*, Mar. 22, 1969, p. 2.

14. *ND* published excerpts from the speeches by Suslov and Ulbricht on Mar. 26, 1969, pp. 3–4. See also *ND*, Mar. 27, pp. 3–6. The full text of Suslov's speech is in *Kommunist*, no. 5, 1969, pp. 3–10.

Despite Suslov's clear signal, negative characterizations of the West German Social Democrats continued to find expression at this time, suggesting that Suslov's view was not unanimously shared within the Soviet foreign policy establishment. Starting in January, *Kommunist* published Comintern documents from the 1920s and 1930s which repeated the standard criticisms of the time concerning the SPD's "hypocrisy" and "capitulation" to fascism. An editorial in *Kommunist* in early March reiterated these charges, and made no reference to Comintern "mistakes."[15] At approximately the same time, *Voprosy istorii* published an article conceding that the Comintern had made mistakes when it attacked the German Social Democrats instead of enlisting their support for a united front against fascism. However, the article attributed these errors to the faulty application of a tactic that was itself essentially correct—the "class against class" line directed against the SPD leadership's "anticommunism, anti-Bolshevism, and anti-Sovietism."[16]

These somewhat more negative characterizations of the SPD in the Comintern era received authoritative support from Boris Ponomarev, a long-standing member of the CPSU Secretariat and, since 1955, the chief of the Central Committee's International Department. Ponomarev's speech at the Comintern anniversary meetings repeated Suslov's admission of mistakes. But unlike Suslov, Ponomarev followed this acknowledgement with a blistering attack on the SPD for pursuing "class collaboration" with the bourgeoisie in the pre-Hitler period and for using "all possible pretexts to refute every one of the Comintern's proposals designed to achieve unity of action." It was this "universally known fact," according to Ponomarev, that had shaped the Comintern's policy toward the SPD. Ponomarev echoed the criticisms of the SPD's "anti-Sovietism" appearing in *Voprosy istorii*, and added that when the Social Democrats were in power in the Weimar Republic, they were just as harsh as the bourgeois politicians in their "reprisals" against the communists.[17]

Precisely why Ponomarev's remarks diverged so explicitly from Suslov's in both tone and substance is not clear. As a former Comintern functionary, Ponomarev was perhaps defending his own past when he defended the Comintern's. It is also quite possible, however, that Ponomarev was signaling his disagreement with Suslov's openly pro-SPD stance. Differences between the two Politburo figures had arisen before. During the Czech

15. For the documents released by the Institute on Marxism-Leninism, see *Kommunist*, no. 2, 1969, pp. 3–12, and no. 3, 1969, pp. 3–14. For the editorial, see ibid., no. 4, 1969, pp. 3–10.
16. A. I. Sobolev, "Komintern i aktualnye problemy kommunisticheskovo dvizheniya," *Voprosy istorii*, no. 3 (Mar. 5), 1969, p. 5.
17. *Kommunist*, no. 5, 1969, pp. 11–28, esp. 24.

crisis, for instance, Ponomarev at one point had adopted a more hard-line position than Suslov.[18] The fact that these two influential members of the primary foreign policy elite, both of whom shared a well-deserved notoriety as ideological conservatives, were airing their differences on the SPD provides vivid evidence that policy toward West Germany was still a matter of debate in the upper reaches of the Brezhnev coalition. The GDR was quick to grasp the distinction between the two positions. The SED's theoretical journal, *Einheit*, published the text of Ponomarev's Comintern speech, but not Suslov's, and Albert Norden appeared to speak for the East German leadership in an article denouncing the SPD's policies during the Comintern era.[19]

At the same time, the main East German theoretical journals and party newspapers remained unremittingly hostile in their portrayals of the contemporary SPD.[20] Soviet scholars and journalists, however, transmitted both negative and positive images of the SPD in 1969, both before and after Brandt's installation as federal chancellor in October.[21]

The Budapest Appeal

As these discussions on the SPD were beginning to intensify in the wake of the first Sino-Soviet border skirmish in early March, the Soviets convened a gathering of the Warsaw Pact leadership in Budapest. In addi-

---

18. Karen Dawisha, *The Kremlin and the Prague Spring* (Berkeley: University of California Press, 1984), p. 228. Suslov also reportedly entertained hopes in 1968 of inviting the SPD to participate in an international conference of communist and workers' parties designed to pillory the Chinese Communist Party (ibid., p. 83).

19. *Einheit*, no. 3, 1969, pp. 259–90; Albert Norden, "Noske oder der Fall der Sozialdemokratie," ibid., no. 12, 1968, pp. 1420–44.

20. E.g., Harald Lange, "Die Bonner Ostpolitik und die Funktion Willy Brandts," *Einheit*, no. 3, 1969, pp. 358–67; Siegmar Quilitzsch, "Die sowjetische Aussenpolitik und die Bonner grosse Koalition," *DA*, no. 1, 1969, pp. 3–14.

21. For negative views, see Yu. Yurev, "Tekushchiye problemy mirovoi politiki," *MEMO*, no. 1, 1969, p. 87; L. Severyanin, "Disposistii zapadnogermanskoi reaktsii," ibid., pp. 61–63 (predicting a CDU/CSU victory in the Bundestag elections); A. Zholkver, "F.R.G.: Pre-election Carneval," *IA*, no. 5, 1969, pp. 35–42, and "FRG—Elections and After," *IA*, no. 12, 1969, p. 28; P. Kryukov, "Failure of Bonn's 'New Eastern Policy,' " *IA*, no. 7, 1969, pp. 43–44. More balanced portrayals of the SPD appear in G. Sogomonyan, "Sotsial-demokratiya: Massy i lidery," *MEMO*, no. 8, 1969, p. 59, which takes note of positive "nuances" among the SPD's "right wing" leaders; and D. Melnikov, "Istoriya predostregayet," *MEMO*, no. 9, 1969, pp. 28–38, which attacks Strauss but not the SPD, while referring to a "liberal-reasonable" group in the FRG. See also the favorable impressions recorded by *Izvestiya* correspondents V. Matveyev, M. Mikhailov, and M. Sagatelyan of statements by newly elected president Gustav Heinemann on Moscow radio's "International Observers' Roundtable," FBIS, *USSR*, Mar. 18, 1969, pp. A43–49. They quoted Heinemann as saying that the FRG must not link itself forever to the Atlantic bloc or permanently maintain the Bundeswehr.

tion to agreeing on various reforms of the military structure of the alliance,[22] the assembled leaders issued another statement aimed at promoting Western support for a European security conference. The "Budapest appeal," issued on March 17, confirmed the evident drift away from the maximalist preferences of the GDR.[23] Unlike the Bucharest declaration of July 1966 and the Karlovy Vary statement of April 1967, however, the Budapest appeal contained no derogatory comments about West German foreign policy, and it did not support the GDR's demand for recognition by Bonn as a precondition for the proposed security conference. Recognition of the GDR was mentioned as "one of the chief preconditions for the safeguarding of European security," but not for the conference itself. Moreover, the Budapest statement called specifically for "recognition of the existence of the GDR," rather than for full-fledged de jure recognition.

The content and tone of the Budapest appeal also marked it as a striking example of the Europeanist side of Moscow's generally Atlanticist foreign policy. In contrast to the Bucharest declaration, which was addressed to both Western Europe and the United States, the Budapest statement was directed specifically at the West Europeans. Its timing was determined at least in part by the impending expiration of the NATO pact in April. While it is highly doubtful that the Soviet leadership actually expected the NATO countries to decide against renewing their ties, for reasons to be examined below, they certainly perceived an opportunity to play upon the conflicts they detected in U.S.–West European relations. With the United States bogged down in the Vietnam conflict, they also detected an opportunity to exploit Washington's presumed inattentiveness to European affairs. Accordingly, members of the Soviet secondary elite suggested openly throughout the year that the United States and Canada were not to be invited to the "all-European conference" Moscow had in mind.[24] Soviet decision makers, however, were somewhat more ambiguous on this point. The possibility that the United States might indeed be included in a future conference on European security was raised on May 5, as the government of Finland formally proposed the convocation of such a meeting in Helsinki, with American and Canadian participation.

While the Soviets thus appeared to be uncertain about just how to deal with the United States in their evolving European diplomacy, they were noticeably disinclined to make any significant policy decisions at this time in response to President Nixon's call for negotiations with the United

---

22. See Christopher D. Jones, Soviet Influence in Eastern Europe (New York: Praeger, 1981), pp. 132–33.

23. For the text, see Pravda, Mar. 18, 1969, p. 1.

24. See, e.g., the statement by Izvestiya correspondent N. Polyanov, attesting to the fact that the Budapest appeal "did not address itself to NATO at all, but to Europeans, and it intends a reply from Europeans": FBIS, USSR, Apr. 2, 1969, p. A23.

States. Aside from an agreement in October to begin SALT negotiations, an issue that was still a matter of controversy inside the USSR, U.S.-Soviet relations did not advance very far in 1969.[25] Western Europe enjoyed a distinct priority in Soviet foreign policy at this time.

For Walter Ulbricht, the upshot of all this was that the Kremlin's commitment to obtaining West German recognition of the GDR was now clearly subordinate to the broader Soviet goal of promoting disunity within the Western camp. In this respect, the clock was now turned back to 1964. All that was needed to duplicate Khrushchev's European diplomacy of that year was a direct overture to Bonn. As the continuing Soviet debate on the SPD indicated over the next several weeks, such an overture was very much under consideration in Moscow.

As it happened, initial Soviet commentary on the Budapest appeal displayed a mixture of positive and negative portrayals of the Grand Coalition government and its reactions to the latest Warsaw Pact proposal.[26] East German reactions were decidedly less equivocal. In a curious departure from normal practice, the SED media and leadership did not officially comment on the latest Warsaw Pact declaration for several days. When Ulbricht finally spoke out on March 22, he interpreted the Budapest appeal's message with a sharpness that was completely out of tune with the moderation of the actual text.[27] Over the next few weeks the East German press and government officials conducted a strident campaign accentuating the GDR's insistence on equality of status with the FRG as a participant both in the proposed European security conference and in its preparatory meetings.[28] Additional press commentary stressed the need for full de jure recognition, and drew attention to the refusal of Brandt and other SPD leaders to go along with it.[29] These efforts flew in the face of Soviet

25. See Raymond L. Garthoff, *Détente and Confrontation* (Washington, D.C.: Brookings, 1985), pp. 69–75.

26. *Izvestiya*'s editorial of Mar. 30 on the Budapest appeal was more critical of the Grand Coalition than *Pravda*'s editorial of the same day. *Trud*'s editorial of Mar. 19 was less harsh on the FRG than *Izvestiya*'s but contained a reference to the Locarno Pact and a "Germany thirsting for revenge" on its eastern borders. Vladimir Mikhailov, *Pravda*'s Bonn correspondent, adopted a more scrupulously equivocal tone. On Mar. 25 he quoted Brandt as praising the Budapest statement and communicating his desire to ratify the NPT, but he criticized the SPD cabinet ministers for failing to condemn CDU/CSU efforts to block ratification. A similar view was expressed by *Izvestiya*'s Polyanov on "International Observers' Roundtable": FBIS, *USSR*, Mar. 18, 1969, p. A23.

27. *ND*, Mar. 23, 1969, pp. 3–6. For reports of Ulbricht's displeasure at the Budapest appeal, see *FAZ*, Mar. 19, 1969, p. 5, and Mar. 24, p. 1.

28. See Ulbricht's statement in *ND*, Mar. 25, 1969, p. 1, and Winzer's statement in *ND*, Apr. 1, p. 6. Also ibid., p. 1.

29. *ND*, Mar. 24, 1969, pp. 1, 2; Mar. 26, pp. 1, 2; Mar. 28, p. 1; Apr. 10, p. 7; Apr. 17, pp. 1–2. For additional commentary emphasizing the SPD's support for NATO and its desire to transform the GDR from within, see *ND*, Apr. 17, p. 7; Apr. 18, p. 6; Apr. 19, p. 5; Apr. 20, p. 2.

assurances to Brandt that West German recognition of the GDR, or even of the existing borders, would not be a precondition to the convening of a European security conference.[30] Most important of all, Ulbricht in late April stated more forcefully than ever that de jure recognition of the GDR by West Germany was the only possible basis for normalizing relations between the two German states.[31]

Conflict over Economic Relations with the FRG

The GDR's opposition to a Soviet rapprochement with Bonn was by no means limited to political and diplomatic issues. As we have seen, Ulbricht's policy was multifaceted, involving scrupulous attention to the economic components of East-West relations. In the first half of 1969, the campaign to develop the Soviet bloc's economic potential "by its own means" was energetically promoted by the East German media, economic specialists and party and state officials.[32] Members of the secondary elite who addressed this theme reiterated Ulbricht's earlier admonition that socialist economic progress "by our own means" was a "law of the class struggle," dictated by West German attempts to entrap the socialist states in relations of economic dependence, to be followed by political dependence. Once again the linkage between the political and the economic dangers ostensibly emanating from détente with the FRG was spelled out in graphic detail.[33]

As it happened, however, neither the Soviet Union nor any of the East European states appeared ready to heed the GDR's advice. At ceremonies held in East Berlin to commemorate COMECON's twentieth anniversary, the deputy chairman of the GDR Council of Ministers, Gerhard Weiss, drew no positive response to his suggestion that "the socialist commonwealth of states must solve every important scientific, technical, military, and economic problem through its own strength and by its own means." On the contrary, the Soviet chairman of COMECON, Nikolai Fadeyev, averred that "individual countries are no longer in a position to work out the most

30. Lawrence A. Whetten, *Germany's Ostpolitik* (London: Oxford University Press, 1971), pp. 75–77. See also Wettig, *Community and Conflict*, pp. 52ff.

31. *ND*, May 8, 1969, pp. 4–5. This speech was delivered Apr. 30. See also Honecker's call for de jure relations in *ND*, Apr. 29, p. 7.

32. For examples in the economic specialist press, see *Die Wirtschaft*, no. 1, 1969, pp. 12 and 22, and no. 3, 1969, p. 1. Erich Honecker explicitly endorsed the campaign to promote the socialist bloc's economic development "by our own strength" in a speech before the SED Central Committee. See *ND*, Apr. 29, 1969, p. 4.

33. See the article by Günter Kertzscher, editor of *ND*, in the issue of Apr. 9, 1969, p. 9. Also Werner Friedrich, "Die WTR und die Notwendigkeit der allseitigen Festigung der Gemeinschaft der sozialistischen Länder," *Wirtschaftswissenschaft*, no. 4, 1969, pp. 641–51.

important scientific-technical problems through their own strength alone." Whereas Weiss had denounced the Federal Republic, Fadeyev conspicuously refrained from condemning West Germany's foreign policy, and instead chided the West for not permitting trade with the Soviet bloc to grow even faster than at the current rate.[34]

Similarly, at the next regular COMECON session, held in late April, the GDR received little visible support for its proposals to intensify intrabloc coordination of industrial cooperation and scientific-technical research and development. These proposals had been publicly discussed in the GDR, along with East Berlin's traditional appeals for a rational "division of labor" within COMECON, a policy that was patently intended to favor East Germany's advanced economy. Differences of opinion on these and related issues among the COMECON members were apparently sharp. Most important, however, the communiqué made no allusion to development "by our own means," but instead called for expanded trade ties with other nations of the world, regardless of their social system.[35]

Even more worrisome for East Berlin was the turnabout in Poland's position on West Germany the following month. On May 17 Gomulka announced what amounted to a new set of conditions governing Poland's approach to the FRG. Departing from custom, the Polish leader now placed West Germany's acceptance of the Oder-Neisse line ahead of recognition of the GDR when he listed the main preconditions for a Polish–West German understanding. Gomulka thus reversed the order of priorities he had observed earlier, no doubt in deference to Ulbricht. More pointedly, Gomulka dropped Poland's former demand that recognition of the GDR constituted a precondition for the start of negotiations between Warsaw and Bonn, and he made no reference to de jure recognition of East Germany. Furthermore, the Polish party chief went out of his way to praise Willy Brandt for his views on the need to recognize Poland's western borders.[36]

This volte face in Poland's attitude was attributable at least in part to economic factors. The country was once again in the throes of an economic slump, a fact Gomulka candidly admitted in early April.[37] Rather than run the political risk of domestic belt-tightening and greater production demands on Polish workers, Warsaw opted to widen its trade ties with the

34. For Weiss's speech, see *Die Wirtschaft*, no. 4, 1969, pp. 3–4; for Fadeyev's, ibid., pp. 4–6.

35. See Friedrich, n. 33 above, pp. 650–51; *FAZ*, Apr. 28, 1969, p. 5; *Pravda*, Apr. 27, 1969, p. 1. Ulbricht implicitly acknowledged the meagerness of the COMECON meeting's results when he referred to Western reports of its unsatisfying outcome. See his speech of Apr. 29 in *ND*, May 8, 1969, p. 4.

36. *ND* published excerpts from Gomulka's speech on May 18 but omitted the passages in praise of the SPD. For an official Polish report on the speech, see FBIS, *Eastern Europe*, May 19, 1969, pp. G7–13.

37. Nicholas Bethell, *Gomulka* (Harmondsworth: Penguin, 1972), pp. 270–74.

Federal Republic. Shortly after Gomulka's May 17 speech, West Berlin Mayor Schütz and a leading West German trade official, Klaus Dieter Arndt, were invited to the upcoming Polish trade fair in Poznan. There the Polish foreign trade minister informed them of his government's plans for a massive upsurge in economic cooperation between the two countries. The Poles expressed hopes of tripling the current volume of trade over the next few years, and unveiled lavish schemes for inviting West German firms to erect plants on Polish territory, especially in such sectors as chemicals and electronics. The somewhat astonished West German visitors gained the distinct impression that Warsaw was interested in reducing its dependence on the GDR for high-technology goods.[38] Meanwhile, the Poles failed to support the GDR's "by our own means" formula during talks held earlier in East Berlin.[39] The East German press responded by stepping up its warnings of West Germany's—and the SPD's—invidious designs on Poland.[40]

As Poland moved to improve its economic ties with Bonn, the Soviet Union took a major stride in the same direction. Foreign Trade Minister Nikolai Patolichev attended the Hanover trade fair in May, and while there the Soviets agreed to purchase wide-diameter steel pipe from the West German manufacturing firm Thyssen.[41] Patolichev met with Karl Schiller, the West German minister of economics, and discussed an exchange of Soviet oil and natural gas for West German pipe as well as the construction of a Soviet–West German pipe factory outside Moscow. To pursue these possibilities, Schiller dispatched State Secretary Klaus von Dohnanyi to the Soviet capital later in the month.

Just as Dohnanyi was about to arrive in Moscow, however, an inflammatory article in *Krasnaya zvezda* charged West Germany with profiting handsomely from the sale of arms to Mao's China.[42] Two days later *Izvestiya* claimed that the West German embassy in Moscow was infested with Nazi-trained spies and racketeers. While taking note of recent signs of an upturn in Soviet–West German relations, including the Patolichev-Schiller conversation, the *Izvestiya* article, which was particularly critical of Bonn's economic functionaries, insisted that no other Western embassy contained such a large number of political and economic espionage agents.[43] The article was an embarrassment for the Soviet officials who received Dohnanyi, and they reportedly expressed their regrets. Though the two articles could not be traced directly to higher authorities, their publication at a

38. On these developments, see *Der Spiegel*, June 9, 1969, p. 34, and June 16, 1969, p. 31.
39. For the communiqué, see *ND*, Apr. 12, 1969, p. 1.
40. *ND*, May 20, 1969, p. 7; May 29, p. 7.
41. Angela Stent, *From Embargo to Ostpolitik* (Cambridge: Cambridge University Press, 1980), p. 166.
42. *Krasnaya zvezda*, May 22, 1969, p. 3.
43. *Izvestiya*, May 24, 1969, p. 6. The authors were identified as B. Alekseyev and I. Moskvin.

sensitive time in Soviet–West German relations suggested that the Soviet political leadership was not yet unified behind a course of political or even economic cooperation with Bonn. Nevertheless, Brezhnev himself showed up at a West German industrial exhibit in Moscow at this time and praised the quality of the goods on display.[44]

The gap between Brezhnev and Ulbricht on these issues was visibly widening. In early June the two party leaders presented very divergent assessments of the international situation at a mammoth international conference of communist and workers' parties convened in Moscow mainly for the purpose of ostracizing the Chinese party leadership. Ulbricht's speech centered squarely on the interaction between politics and economics in the strategy of "world imperialism" in general and of the FRG in particular. While acknowledging the West's "temporary economic advantage" over the socialist states, Ulbricht trotted out his old warnings about Bonn's Trojan horse strategy of promoting the Soviet bloc's "economic dependence." West Germany, he proclaimed, was using science and technology as "decisive weapons" in the East-West struggle. Consequently, the SED chief advised his listeners that mastering the scientific-technical revolution was of critical foreign policy importance for the socialist countries, which, in his view, already possessed "everything necessary" to close the economic gap between West and East. Ulbricht rounded out his speech with laudatory references to the GDR's "developed societal system of socialism."[45]

In contrast to Ulbricht's blanket condemnation of Western imperialism, Brezhnev opened his speech with references to the "contradictions" undermining the NATO alliance. He did not mention the FRG at all. Thus the Soviet leader in effect signaled Moscow's interest in exploiting divisions among the Western allies without specifically excluding cooperation with the Federal Republic for this purpose. The CPSU chief was even more forthcoming in identifying "a more moderate wing" in the Western camp, whose views the USSR took into account. With respect to economic issues, Brezhnev was downright gloomy in his assessment of the current predicament of the socialist states. After admitting that the capitalist states were guilty of exerting economic pressure on the socialist countries, Brezhnev cautioned that the USSR's economic achievements "have not made us lose sight of the shortcomings that exist in our work and the serious problems confronting us." He observed that there could be no minimizing the scientific and technological strength of socialism's competitors, adding tersely, "Here a long and hard struggle lies ahead." Not surprisingly, Brezhnev did not repeat the GDR's exhortation to master the scientific-technical revolu-

---

44. FBIS, *Soviet Union*, June 5, 1969, p. A19. See also *FAZ*, May 23, 1969, p. 1; May 27, p. 3; and May 29, p. 4.

45. *ND*, June 10, 1969, pp. 3–5.

tion "by our own means," but called instead for mutually beneficial trade and scientific-technical cooperation with the West. The Soviet leader also held out the possibility of improved relations with the United States.[46]

The main statement issued at the end of the Moscow conference reflected conflicting views on a variety of issues. On the question of relations among capitalist states, it mentioned on the one hand that, "in spite of growing contradictions," the NATO countries were unifying their efforts as the United States endeavored to forge a "common policy" against the socialist camp. This line of reasoning implied that the chances of weakening the attachments of West Germany (or any other West European state) to the United States were slim at best. On the other hand, the statement later proclaimed that "the anti-imperialist forces take account of all contradictions in the capitalist camp, and strive to deepen and take advantage of them." Similarly, the document reflected both East Germany's view that the scientific-technical revolution had become a decisive battleground of the East-West competition and Brezhnev's affirmation of the value of East-West economic cooperation. Interestingly, the statement also called for Bonn's recognition of the GDR "on the basis of international law," a term the GDR usually employed to signify de jure recognition. Given the equivocal nature of this final document, both Ulbricht and Brezhnev were later able to quote relevant portions of it to justify completely divergent policies.[47]

In the weeks after the Moscow meeting, the GDR intensified its efforts to persuade the Soviets to hold back from widening their economic ties with West Germany and to deepen their cooperation with East Germany instead. At a meeting of high-level Soviet and East German government officials in East Berlin, Premier Willi Stoph made it known that the GDR was interested in concluding new treaties with Moscow aimed at promoting cooperation in research and development. However, the communiqué issued at the end of the meetings made no mention of Stoph's proposal. Later both Stoph and Ulbricht announced that the Soviets had agreed to their proposals "in principle," but indicated that the matter had been referred to study commissions for further consideration.[48]

On July 7 a large group of leading party and government officials from the GDR, including representatives of key economic organs, arrived in Moscow for an extraordinary series of consultations lasting an entire week. (Ulbricht had planned to lead the delegation himself, but was unable to do so for reasons of ill health.) While the Soviets escorted their guests on a tour of research institutes and offered profuse assurances of Moscow's high

46. For the text, see *Kommunist*, no. 9, 1969, pp. 46–78.

47. See, e.g., the GDR's official interpretations of the document in *ND*, June 19, 1969, pp. 1–2, and June 25, p. 1. For a CPSU appraisal, see *Pravda*, June 27, p. 1. The text of the communiqué is in *Kommunist*, no. 9, pp. 5–33.

48. *ND*, July 2, 1969, pp. 1–2; July 5, p. 1; July 21, p. 4; Aug. 1, p. 3.

regard for the economic achievements of the GDR, it was nevertheless clear that the Kremlin was still reluctant to commit itself on several of the Ulbricht government's chief demands. Many of the themes voiced in public by East German spokesmen, such as appeals for a "closer intertwining" of the two economies, for "full equality" in bilateral relations, and for "jointly" mastering the scientific-technical revolution, found no resonance in Soviet pronouncements.[49] Above all, no Soviet official seconded the East German delegation's call for socialist economic development "by our own means." The Joint Declaration issued at the end of the negotiations was similarly mum on the GDR's pet economic themes.[50] As if to underline the actual score for the East Germans, Patolichev began talks in Moscow with an executive of Thyssen Pipe Works, Ernst Mommsen, on the same day as the signing of the Soviet-GDR joint declaration.

Speeches by Ulbricht and Hermann Axen, the SED secretary responsible for relations with foreign communist parties, made it plain that the GDR was deeply troubled by the prospect of major economic accords between the USSR and the Federal Republic. This anxiety explained the East German leadership's almost desperate determination to reinforce the GDR's indispensability to the USSR as its chief economic partner. At the same time, the East Germans reissued their warnings about the SPD. Relying on his seniority among the leaders of the Soviet bloc, Ulbricht insisted that "we older ones" had become acquainted with the SPD's duplicity in the days of the Weimar Republic. Politburo member Hermann Matern joined in the latest chorus of invective against the Social Democrats.[51]

Poland's turnabout was also a matter of mounting concern to the GDR. In late July, Albert Norden seemed to be addressing the Gomulka government directly in a speech bristling with criticism of West German policies toward Poland. In keeping with the latest barrage of scorn for the SPD, Norden singled out Willy Brandt and Herbert Wehner for special abuse.[52]

Moscow Moves toward Détente

Despite the GDR's best efforts, the Soviet leadership in midsummer decided to make another major pronouncement in favor of improved

---

49. Compare, e.g., the remarks of Stoph and Brezhnev in *ND*, July 8, 1969, p. 3, and the speeches of GDR Deputy Staatsrat Chairman Gerald Götting and Kosygin, *ND*, July 9, p. 2. See also the speeches by Stoph, *ND*, July 10, p. 4, and Mittag, *ND*, July 12, p. 3. Also Kertzscher's article in *ND*, July 14, p. 4. See also Honecker's speech in the Soviet Union linking the Federal Republic with China and with U.S. "global strategy," *ND*, July 9, pp. 3–4, and his speech in Kiev attacking Brandt and calling for de jure recognition, *ND*, July 14, pp. 3–4.

50. *ND*, July 9, 1969, p. 2; July 15, pp. 1–2.

51. *ND*, July 30, 1969, p. 4; Aug. 1, p. 3; July 18, pp. 4–5.

52. *ND*, July 22, 1969, p. 5.

relations with the Federal Republic. On July 10 Andrei Gromyko announced the Soviet government's readiness to resume negotiations with Bonn on a renunciation-of-force treaty. Despite the presence of the East German economic delegation in the Soviet Union, Gromyko asserted the USSR's interest in economic and technological cooperation with the FRG, acknowledging bluntly that East-West economic ties were "an important basis for political cooperation." He repeated Moscow's call for an "all-European conference," but did not press either for prior recognition of the GDR by Bonn or for the GDR's full legal equality with the FRG as preconditions for holding the conference. By the same token, Gromyko was silent on the United States' possible participation in the conference.[53]

Together with these ostensibly Europeanist remarks, Gromyko reiterated the Kremlin's interest in commencing SALT talks with the United States. In a gesture that demonstrably linked the Europeanist and Americanist tendencies in Soviet foreign policy, Gromyko called for talks with the United States, Britain, and France on the Berlin problem. The Soviet foreign minister was well aware that one of Bonn's chief demands in any long-term rapprochement with the USSR would involve an amelioration of conditions surrounding West Berlin. As was his custom, he also formally acknowledged the "responsibilities" of the Western powers in this regard. None of these considerations was expected to sit well with the GDR. Indeed, Gromyko appeared to be distancing himself even further from the East German position that West Berlin lay "on the territory" of the GDR when he stated somewhat elliptically that West Berlin was located "in the heart of" the GDR, a juridically meaningless statement. Thus the Soviet foreign minister confirmed his desire to improve Soviet relations with both West Germany and the United States simultaneously, once again combining Europeanist and Americanist orientations in an Atlanticist synthesis.

Gromyko's standpoint did not appear to be universally shared in the Soviet Union, however. Once again Petro Shelest registered his disquiet. Speaking at a reception in Kiev for Erich Honecker and the traveling East German delegation only three days after Gromyko's speech, the Ukrainian party chief made no reference to Gromyko's initiative, but instead impugned the FRG in general terms for its "revanchism" and "militarism." Interestingly, however, Shelest did not echo the GDR's exhortation to develop socialism "by our own means."[54]

The GDR responded quickly to Gromyko's initiative on Berlin. Less than a week after his speech, the East German Foreign Ministry protested President Heinemann's forthcoming visit to the divided city, adding that West

53. *Pravda*, July 11, 1969, pp. 2–4.
54. Shelest's speech was published in *ND*, July 14, 1969, p. 3. For additional examples of anti–West German sentiment in the Ukrainian party organization at this time, see *Pravda Ukrainy*, July 13, p. 1, and July 15, pp. 1–2.

Berlin was located "in the middle of the German Democratic Republic and on its territory."[55] On September 24 East Berlin's delegates to the East German Volkskammer participated in the vote ratifying the nonproliferation treaty. This was the first time the GDR had violated the West's legal position that the East Berlin delegation had no right to take part in Volkskammer activities.

As the West German election campaign entered its most intense phase, the East German press aimed a steady stream of polemics at the SPD. Meanwhile, *Pravda* and *Izvestiya* presented conflicting positive and negative images of Willy Brandt and other SPD leaders throughout the summer, while the Soviet military press issued dire warnings of West Germany's—and the SPD's—military ambitions.[56] As for the Soviet leadership, it left little doubt as to its own electoral preferences. The Soviets received FDP leaders Walter Scheel, Hans-Dietrich Genscher, and Wolfgang Mischnick in Moscow in July, and Willy Brandt and Helmut Schmidt of the SPD in August. On September 13 the Kremlin sent a note to the West German government announcing its readiness for talks on a renunciation-of-force agreement, presumably with any government that might emerge victorious from the elections.[57]

Reactions to the Brandt-Scheel Government

When the election results of October 3 became known, the Soviet leaders were barely able to conceal their satisfaction. Speaking at the GDR's anniversary celebrations on October 6, Brezhnev labeled the SPD-FDP victory "an undoubtable success on the part of the democratic forces in the FRG," and gave assurances that Moscow "would welcome a change toward realism in the policy of the Federal Republic."[58] Ulbricht adopted a considerably less conciliatory posture, reemphasizing his demands for de jure recognition and stiffening his terms for a rapprochement between the two German states to include "the development of democracy in West Germany."[59] *Neues Deutschland* deleted Brezhnev's more favorable comments about the FRG in its edition of October 7, and *Pravda* returned the favor by omitting Ulbricht's broadsides against West Germany on the same day.

55. *ND*, July 17, 1969, p. 2.
56. Critical views of the SPD include those in *Izvestiya*, July 9, 1969, p. 2; *Pravda*, Aug. 31, p. 4; *Krasnaya zvezda*, Sept. 14, p. 3. More positive or mixed views are found in *Literaturnaya gazeta*, July 2, p. 15; *Pravda*, Aug. 12, p. 5, and Sept. 25, p. 4; *Izvestiya*, Sept. 12, p. 2. See also *Krasnaya zvezda*, July 13, p. 1, and July 15, p. 3.
57. Arnulf Baring, *Machtwechsel* (Stuttgart: Deutsche Verlags-Anstalt, 1982), p. 243.
58. *Pravda*, Oct. 7, 1969, p. 3.
59. *ND*, Oct. 7, 1969, pp. 3–7.

On October 28 Brandt delivered his maiden speech as chancellor, and adumbrated a significantly new approach to West Germany's ostpolitik. Acknowledging the existence of "two German states in one German nation," Brandt said that the FRG was now ready to enter into formal negotiations with the GDR for the purpose of moving from a "regulated coexistence" to a state of "living together" (*Miteinander*). Brandt strictly ruled out de jure recognition of the GDR, however, calling instead for relations "of a special type." He also called for renunciation-of-force agreements with the USSR and other Warsaw Pact states, and for a settlement of the problem of access rights to West Berlin on the basis of four-power negotiations.[60]

Within days of Brandt's speech, the Warsaw Pact foreign ministers gathered in Prague. The communiqué issued October 31 signaled another setback for the GDR. It proposed two topics to be discussed at an all-European security conference: the safeguarding of security through renunciation-of-force agreements and the expansion of economic cooperation among the states of Europe, "with the goal of developing political cooperation among the European states." The Prague declaration also endorsed both bilateral and multilateral agreements on these issues.[61]

The substance and tenor of the Warsaw Pact's latest statement revealed the Soviet leadership's intention of rapidly including the new West German government in its evolving diplomacy on the proposed all-European security conference. A positive response to the Soviet initiative had already been signaled before the elections by Brandt and the FDP leadership.[62] In his first governmental statement as chancellor, Brandt asserted that such a conference would be "useful," provided that it led to reduced armaments in Europe. Although Bonn and Moscow still differed widely on the main purpose of the conference, with Brandt stressing the need for arms reductions and the Soviets emphasizing recognition of the postwar status quo, the Kremlin could derive some satisfaction from the fact that Brandt and the new foreign minister, Walter Scheel, appeared to be more receptive to a European security conference than the Christian Democrats had been.[63]

60. *Bulletin der Presse- und Informationsamtes der Bundesregierung*, Oct. 29, 1969, pp. 1121–28.

61. *Pravda*, Nov. 1, 1969, p. 4.

62. On April 24, 1969, Brandt in his capacity as foreign minister announced four conditions for West Germany's participation in a European security conference: (1) no preconditions with respect to convening the conference; (2) thorough preparation; (3) U.S. and Canadian participation; and (4) realistic prospects for success. In May, Brandt called for prior talks between the FRG and the GDR to determine the conditions for joint participation. On these points, together with a discussion of the FDP's views, see Helga Haftendorn, *Abrüstungs- und Entspannungspolitik zwischen Sicherheitsbefriedigung und Friedenssicherung* (Düsseldorf: Bertelsmann Universitätsverlag, 1974), pp. 306–8.

63. See Yurii Zhukov's positive reference to Brandt's statement that the GDR should participate in the security conference, *Pravda*, Nov. 11, 1969, p. 5. For accounts of dissension within NATO on the Soviet proposal for a European security conference, see ibid., Dec. 8, p. 5, and *Izvestiya*, Dec. 8, p. 2.

Ulbricht was scarcely consoled by these prospects. Foreign Minister Otto Winzer brusquely rejected the idea of bilateral agreements between the individual Warsaw Pact states and the Federal Republic. Later Winzer and the East German press reiterated the view that the GDR must participate in the European conference "on an equal basis" with all states. In addition, *Neues Deutschland* insisted that full de jure recognition of the GDR was a prerequisite for any improvement in inter-German relations. "Only in this way," the paper stated, was a rapprochement possible between the two German states. Finally, the GDR reacted to the Prague communiqué's call for expanded bilateral economic agreements with the West European states by emphatically stating its preference for multilateral accords. Foreign Minister Winzer asserted that "no large all-European project can be realized without or against the GDR."[64] This statement also revealed the GDR's sensitivities over the Soviet–West German pipeline negotiations, which were now nearing completion.

The GDR's open discontent after the Prague meeting led to another gathering of Warsaw Pact leaders starting on December 1 in Moscow. The communiqué issued December 4 reflected the efforts of the GDR's allies to allay some of Ulbricht's trepidations. For the first time the Warsaw Pact formally advocated de jure recognition of the GDR, although this was stated as a general preference and not as a precondition to improved relations with Bonn. Most important of all from the GDR's point of view, the members of the Soviet alliance agreed to "consult" one another regarding all important international problems, and to pursue their policies in a "coordinated" fashion.[65] For the GDR, this meant a public commitment by its allies not to negotiate behind its back with the FRG.

Unfortunately for East Germany, on matters of substance the Moscow statement did not endorse Ulbricht's hostile views on future cooperation with Bonn short of full de jure recognition. On the contrary, the new SPD-FDP government was applauded for its "tendencies in the direction of a realistic policy," and especially for its decision on November 28 to sign the Nuclear Nonproliferation Treaty.

The SED was barely more satisfied with this latest Warsaw Pact statement than with the Prague declaration. Ulbricht interpreted the Moscow document in accordance with his own preferences and priorities. In a speech replete with vitriolic attacks on SPD and FDP leaders, Ulbricht remained adamant in his view that inter-German relations necessitated "full equality and mutual recognition under international law." This position was rigidi-

64. *ND*, Nov. 4, 1969, p. 2; Nov. 9, p. 1; Nov. 20, p. 5; Nov. 30, p. 5. The Nov. 9 article also said that Bonn's recognition of the GDR would have to follow the European security conference rather than precede it, thus reversing Ulbricht's proposed sequence of 1967. Conceivably this shift in Ulbricht's position may have been imposed on him by Moscow, as it was included in the Prague communiqué.

65. *Pravda*, Dec. 5, 1969, p. 1. And see Robin A. Remington, *The Warsaw Pact: Case Studies in Communist Conflict Resolution* (Cambridge: MIT Press, 1971), p. 124.

fied even further when Winzer declared that the GDR would not even negotiate with the FRG except on the basis of de jure recognition.[66]

Finally, as the year drew to a close, the GDR submitted a new draft treaty to the Federal Republic. Its terms were considerably stiffer than those of the 1967 draft treaty with respect to the question of recognition. The new treaty proposal called explicitly for normalization on the basis of international law and for the exchange of ambassadors in Bonn and "Berlin." In addition, it omitted the earlier draft's call for "rapprochement" (*Annäherung*) between the two German states and for economic and trade agreements, referring instead simply to a "regulated coexistence."[67]

Promoting Ulbricht's Grand Design

These bold assertions of the GDR's political interests were accompanied by equally assertive measures in the domestic economic system. As the results of the economy's performance in 1969 became known and plans were elaborated for the following year, the SED leadership was determined to forge ahead with its efforts to accelerate growth in the so-called structure-determining areas beyond the goals originally laid out in the 1966–1970 five-year plan. Once again Ulbricht and other spokesmen justified their actions by the need to promote the socialist bloc's economic development "by its own means." As in late 1968, the foreign policy pressures impinging on the East German regime were having an immediate impact on decisions regarding the allocation of domestic resources.

The fact that the economic policy choices now being adopted by the GDR were motivated not by strict calculations of economic rationality but rather by political considerations was evident in the SED's own evaluations of the economy's shortcomings, and even of its successes. To begin with, the elevated growth rates that had been targeted for 1969 in such key areas as the chemical industry and electronics were not met. Indeed, the projected 6 percent growth rate for the economy as a whole could not be attained, as the 1969 growth figure for net material product amounted to 5.2 percent. These results should have argued for more realistic targets in 1970. On the contrary, however, the SED leadership decided to boost plan targets in the important industrial sectors even higher, calling for an overall growth rate in net material product of 6.3 percent for 1970.

Meanwhile, the 1969 plan results, while falling short of the projected goals, were by no means lamentable. In fact, the growth levels reached in all of the structure-determining categories except the chemical industry actu-

---

66. *ND*, Dec. 14, 1969, pp. 1, 4–9; Dec. 17, p. 4.
67. Submitted to Bonn on Dec. 17, the treaty was published in *ND*, Dec. 21, 1969, p. 1.

ally conformed to or even exceeded the annual growth rates originally projected in 1967, when the 1966–1970 perspective plan was first introduced. Rather than rest content with these results, the SED decision makers, no doubt prodded by Walter Ulbricht himself, were resolved to stimulate development even further. Accelerated growth, not growth per se, was the new imperative of the East German hierarchy.

At the same time, the SED Politburo was well aware of the structural inadequacies of the East German economy. In a critical review of economic performance at a Central Committee plenum in December, Günter Mittag openly admitted that the GDR suffered by comparison with prevailing international standards in production techniques and in research and development.[68] Significantly, Mittag also acknowledged that harsh weather had exacerbated the GDR's problems in 1969, straining energy resources and food supplies. He even hinted at rising popular discontent in East Germany as the result of insufficient supplies of home heating fuels. Moreover, the need to import grain and other commodities had swelled the GDR's external debt. In addition to all of these difficulties, Mittag made it known that objections had been raised within the GDR by proponents of a more "equilibrated" approach to economic growth, one less concentrated in the advanced industrial sectors.

Despite these harsh realities, Mittag vowed to press on in pursuit of still higher growth rates in 1970, to be concentrated overwhelmingly in the structure-determining areas. The 1970 plan would achieve a "dynamic" proportionality "through concentration." Investment resources were to be channeled primarily into modernizing such sectors as the electronics industry, data processing, and chemical production. Spending on consumer goods was due to rise by only 3.8 percent in 1970.

The purpose of these almost frantic attempts to speed up the pace of the GDR's technological modernization was fully in keeping with Walter Ulbricht's campaign to reduce the socialist bloc's economic reliance on the West to the maximum feasible extent. To be sure, Ulbricht was only too well aware how much the GDR still needed West German assistance. In 1969 East German imports from the FRG rose by 42.5 percent, thereby doubling the GDR's deficit in inter-German trade. Plans to develop trade relations with the FRG even further were in the works.[69] In spite of this trade dependence (and indeed perhaps because of it), Ulbricht insisted that the

68. *ND*, Dec. 15, 1969, pp. 3–7. Ulbricht himself had stated earlier that labor productivity rates in the GDR lagged 20% behind West German standards: *ND*, Mar. 23, 1969, pp. 3–6.

69. Ulbricht and Stoph discussed inter-German trade with Otto Wolff von Amerongen, a prominent West German industrialist and advocate of expanded East-West trade, at the Leipzig fair at the end of 1969. See J. Nawrocki, "Überraschung in Leipzig," *Deutschland Archiv*, no. 4, 1970, pp. 414–16.

Soviet bloc needed to undertake urgent efforts to diminish its economic reliance on the West. What the SED chief envisaged was not an immediate cutoff of Western assistance but rather a long-term program designed to free the socialist states from the politically debilitating effects of economic inferiority to the West, above all in the critical fields of advanced technology. While recognizing that the members of the bloc still had a long way to go before they reached this goal, he felt that they already had the capacity to accelerate technological growth at faster rates than was generally thought possible. The GDR's latest economic plans were intended to serve as a vivid example of the feasibility of this strategy.

Significantly, however, Ulbricht's continuing emphasis on concentrated development did not go unchallenged. By late 1969, East German economists were boldly contradicting the assumptions of "dynamic proportioning." One of them was Harry Maier, a prominent official in the GDR's Central Institute of Economics. At a conference sponsored by the East German Academy of Sciences in October, Maier dismissed "the principle of concentration on high priorities" as injurious to stable economic growth. His talk was also noteworthy for its endorsement of expanded trade with the West.[70] These views ran directly counter to Ulbricht's economic priorities and served notice of the lingering presence of *Westdrall* sentiments in the East German secondary elite. As we shall see, the publication of Maier's remarks in January 1970 testified to serious misgivings about the soundness of Ulbricht's economic policies within the SED leadership as well.

Closely connected with these economic considerations were the GDR's ideological ambitions. Ulbricht had broken new ground in this area in 1967, with the introduction of the "developed societal system of socialism" and his theory of socialism as an autonomous phase of history, and these concepts received further elaboration with the publication in September 1969 of a massive textbook titled *The Political Economy of Socialism and Its Application in the GDR*.[71] The fanfare that accompanied the release of the book left no doubt as to its intended purpose of providing a comprehensive exposition of the East German model of advanced socialism. Walter Ulbricht, who was singled out for having "decisively influenced the book's theoretical substance," opined that the tome would be "of interest to readers outside the GDR."[72] Another commentator said that its concepts were applicable "in all socialist countries."[73] In 1970 the book was translated into Russian.

70. Harry Maier, "Probleme des intensiven ökonomischen Wachstums im Sozialismus unter den Bedingungen der wissenschaftlich-technischen Revolution," *Wirtschaftswissenschaft*, no. 1, 1970, esp pp. 4, 18, 22.
71. *Politische Ökonomie des Sozialismus und ihre Anwendung in der DDR* (East Berlin: Dietz, 1969).
72. ND, Sept. 23, 1969, pp. 3, 1. See also Mittag's remarks in praise of Ulbricht on p. 1.
73. DA, no. 2, 1970, pp. 303–4.

The volume's content revolved mainly around the concept of the GDR as a "total system," together with a strong defense of more orthodox notions, above all that of "the leading role of the party." Like Ulbricht's ideological forays of 1967, these ideas represented an attempt to dress up contemporary Marxist-Leninist ideology in systems-theory jargon while retaining such critical elements of othodox Marxism-Leninism as centralized political control and economic planning, concepts essential to a neo-Stalinist regime. Ulbricht regarded this effort as particularly urgent in light of the demands of the "scientific-technical revolution" and the ideological heresies that circulated in Czechoslovakia in 1968. The volume also included a ringing endorsement of socialist economic development "by our own means." As a summary statement of the GDR's current politial and economic doctrines, it represented an authoritative ideological component of Ulbricht's grand design.

Policy Debates in Moscow and East Berlin

Although Ulbricht's political, economic, and ideological initiatives were thus aimed at enhancing the GDR's value to its allies, in fact East Germany was becoming increasingly isolated within the Soviet bloc, especially with respect to its ties with Moscow. While Brezhnev and his associates were in all likelihood still uncertain about the kind of political agreement that might eventually be concluded with the Brandt-Scheel government, they had greater room for optimism than ever before about prospects for achieving the principal aims of their German policy. These aims included above all the desire to take advantage of "contradictions" within the Western camp, and especially those affecting Bonn's relationships with its major allies; the need to expand trade and technology imports from the West, and particularly from West Germany; and, most important, the abiding necessity of obtaining the FRG's recognition of the territorial and political status quo in Europe. On each of these points a lively debate flourished within the secondary foreign policy elite of the Soviet Union both before and after the Bundestag elections of October 1969. These debates provide documentary evidence that members of the Soviet foreign policy establishment were still divided in their assessments of critical aspects of the Soviet Union's German policy.

Debate continued, for example, over whether the main trend in current U.S.–West European relations resided in partnership or in "contradictions." The centrality of this question for Soviet foreign policy was underscored by Nikolai Inozemtsev, the director of IMEMO, at a conference devoted to international relations theory. While appealing for a realistic, "scientific" approach to the study of international politics, Inozemtsev attached special importance to the question "What is the relationship of centripetal and centrifugal tendencies in the camp of imperialism in our times?"[74] Of the specialists who inquired into this relationship in 1969, several placed unmistakable emphasis on the contradictions eating away at NATO's unity. As in earlier years, Daniil Melnikov, Oleg Bykov, and Yurii Rubinskii were among the chief advocates of this view. While clearly articulating this Europeanist position, however, all three either stated or intimated that the Western alliance was by no means ready to disintegrate.[75] Once again the West Europeans' drive for "independence" from the United States was seen as designed to enhance their influence within the Atlantic alliance rather than as an effort to break out of it.

Other writers, while freely acknowledging the presence of intercapitalist contradictions, emphasized the elements of unity that continued to make NATO a cohesive and dangerous adversary. As in 1968, V. I. Gantman was a vocal proponent of this view. At a conference of foreign policy specialists, Gantman quoted a passage from the June 1969 Moscow meeting of communist and workers' parties in support of his position on the "primacy" of intercapitalist unity. The next article in the same issue, however, contradicted this view, arguing that the participants at the June meeting held that the presence of some elements of unity "in no way eliminates the sharp contradictions between the imperialist states."[76] Like Gantman, writers on military affairs stressed U.S.–West European partnership as opposed to disunity.[77]

Once again the question of West Germany's position in the tangled web of U.S.–West European relations was pivotal. The FRG's weight in Western Europe was growing not only because of the new dynamism in its own foreign policy but also because of Charles de Gaulle's departure from the political scene. (The French president resigned from office in April 1969.) As in earlier years, West Germany's course continued to be a matter of controversy among Soviet scholars and journalists. Several prominent ana-

---

74. *MEMO*, no. 9, 1969, p. 90. Inozemtsev added that Soviet foreign policy was guided by "the effort to look the truth squarely in the eye, to proceed in its policy from what in fact is, and not from what we would like to see in the world arena" (p. 91).

75. See, e.g., the views presented by D. E. Melnikov at an IMEMO roundtable discussion on the theme "Where Is Western Europe Heading?" *MEMO*, no. 6, 1969, pp. 103–5; O. N. Bykov, ibid., pp. 106–8; Yu. Rubinskii, ibid., pp. 112–14. See also O. Bykov, "Evolyutsiya 'Atlantizma,'" ibid., no. 8, 1969, pp. 28–36, and "Obshchaya strategiya imperializma, 'globalizma' i 'Evrotsentrizma,'" ibid., no. 11, 1969, pp. 83–85. For similar views, see F. Silin, "Tekushchiye problemy mirovoi politiki," ibid., no. 4, 1969, pp. 80–85. One specialist suggested that it was an "undoubtable law" that the integration process among the West European states actually slackened in periods of détente. See D. E. Menshikov, ibid., no. 6, 1969, p. 116.

76. For Gantman's views, see *IA*, no. 9, 1969, pp. 55–57; for the opposite view, see V. Sushchenko, ibid., pp. 57–59. See also Gantman's article in *Literaturnaya gazeta*, Feb. 5, 1969, pp. 1, 14.

77. E.g., N. F. Zaletni, *Militarizm FRG* (Moscow: Nauka, 1969).

lysts clearly emphasized the growing contradictions in U.S.-FRG ties in 1969. Curiously, while Brandt and the SPD were usually portrayed as wanting greater independence from the United States than the Christian Democrats, some writers, such as Melnikov, also drew attention to the anti-American aspects of the policies of Franz-Josef Strauss, the conservative leader (whom Melnikov otherwise denounced as a "chauvinist").[78] Along these lines, an article in *Kommunist* noted that though the "Bonn-Washington axis" was still strong, the demands for greater independence articulated by Kiesinger, Strauss, and Brandt were making Bonn "increasingly less controllable" as an American ally. Brandt in particular was cited as holding views whose "logical conclusion" would result in support for Soviet proposals on European security. The article concluded that it was now "impossible to stop the centrifugal currents" in NATO.[79]

On the opposite side of the argument, several articles placed their primary accents on U.S.–West German collaboration, especially military collaboration. Adherents of this view were particularly critical of the SPD's continuing loyalty to NATO, both before and after the October elections.[80] As might be expected, the Soviet military press was highly exercised at the cooperative aspects of U.S.–West German relations. Several articles published in *Krasnaya zvezda* and *Izvestiya* after the Bundestag elections, in fact, portrayed the new government's defense minister, Helmut Schmidt, as an inveterate proponent of strengthening the Bundeswehr.[81]

While the Soviet secondary elite was therefore openly divided in its assessments of the current path of the Atlantic alliance as a whole and of

78. See Melnikov's remarks in *MEMO*, no. 6, 1969, p. 105. For an elaboration of Melnikov's views, based on a recent trip to the Federal Republic, see his book (co-written with three other authors), *Gamburg—Bonn—Myunkhen* (Moscow: Mezhdunarodnye otnosheniya, 1969). The authors rejected the notion that no changes had occurred in the psychology or ideology of the West German bourgeoisie (a view ascribed to other Soviet writers) and pointed specifically to important "nuances" in the SPD's position (pp. 42–51).

79. N. Polyanov, "Alians bez budushchevo," *Kommunist*, no. 12 (Aug. 12), 1969, pp. 98–109. This issue marked a shift in Polyanov's position from a more pronounced emphasis on U.S.–West German cooperation earlier in the year. See "Bonn's Challenge to Europe," *IA*, no. 1, 1969, pp. 21–28. For a book that emphasized U.S.–West German cooperation but also referred to statements by Strauss and Brandt on the need for greater independence from the United States, see N. N. Sofinskii, *Bonn i Vashington* (Moscow: Nauka, 1969), pp. 144–46. The author quoted Brandt as saying that the FRG was an economic giant but a political dwarf. Another writer was highly critical of Strauss but hopeful of a change for the better with Brandt. See the articles by Ernst Genrii in *Literaturnaya gazeta*, Mar. 12, 1969, p. 14; June 25, pp. 14–15; and Jan. 14, 1970, p. 14. For another predominantly negative view of Strauss, see L. Istyagin, "Bonnskii militarizm i bavarskii 'Evropizm,'" *MEMO*, no. 2, 1969, pp. 138–41.

80. For negative views of Brandt stressing his support for NATO, see the remarks of I. Manfred in *MEMO*, no. 6, 1969, p. 111; A. Zholkver, "FRG—Elections and After," *IA*, no. 12, 1969, p. 28. See also A. Gorokhov, "NATO: 20-Year Balance Sheet," *IA*, no. 3, 1969, pp. 20–26.

81. *Krasnaya zvezda*, Sept. 14, 1969, p. 3; Oct. 10, p. 3; Dec. 12, p. 3; Dec. 13, p. 3. Also *Izvestiya*, Nov. 1, 1969, p. 3; Dec. 2, p. 2.

West Germany in particular, one conclusion was certain: None of these analysts expected the breakup of the alliance in the foreseeable future. This view was shared even by the Europeanist analysts, who otherwise tended to emphasize their prognosis of growing West European independence of the United States. The apparent consensus within the secondary elite on the durability of the Western alliance system placed a number of the recent foreign policy decisions taken by the primary elite in a highly revealing light. In effect, the secondary elite's portrayal of the "common class interests" that continued to bind the Western allies together, even as their "contradictions" mounted, ran directly counter to the rationale that appeared to guide the Budapest appeal and other official statements issued at this time. Ostensibly these statements urged the governments of Western Europe to loosen their attachments to Washington, dissolve the opposing alliance systems, and join with the socialist states in creating a new "all-European" framework for mutual security. Contrary to the evident aims of these Soviet appeals, the analyses published by the Soviet secondary elite suggested that the prospects for a serious rupture between the two sides of the transatlantic partnership were minimal at best.

Unless one assumes that the primary and secondary foreign policy elites in the Soviet Union were diametrically opposed in their assessments of U.S.–West European relations—a decidedly unlikely occurrence, given the sensitive political links connecting the two elites—it appears that the main implication of this apparent disharmony is that the Soviet leadership did not really take very seriously the possibility that Western Europe would accept the Warsaw Pact's call for the dissolution of NATO. The preponderance of analytical opinion in the Soviet elite argued decisively against such a possibility. What is most likely is that the Brezhnev regime advanced this offer mainly to test its propaganda effect on West European public opinion. The decision makers in the Kremlin probably held out little hope for drawing the governments of Western Europe into an "all-European" dialogue that explicitly excluded American participation. While the effort was surely worth a try, the Brezhnev coalition's moves in the direction of a more exclusively Europeanist foreign policy were halfhearted at best. Ultimately the Brezhnev regime remained committed to a generally Atlanticist policy direction, encouraging West European aspirations for greater cooperation but in the end entertaining no serious expectations of prying the West Europeans loose from their alliance commitments.

Meanwhile, the discussion on trade and scientific-technical exchange with the West was also quite animated among Soviet specialists in 1969. Several of them openly endorsed a broadening of trade ties with the capitalist states. In support of this view, some scholars noted the recent successes of capitalist economies, and one of them, A. G. Mileikovskii, went so far as to advise studying the "objectively progressive tendencies" present in certain capitalist systems.[82] Other experts warned against exaggerating the achievements of capitalism and argued, either explicitly or by implication, against excessive East-West trade.[83] Significantly, however, none of these more traditionalist experts ever explicitly endorsed the GDR's injunction to develop socialism's economic potential "by our own means." In fact, the only support for the SED leadership's economic views to be found in the leading Soviet specialized journals in 1969 was supplied by East German authors.[84]

Finally, there was a brief exchange among Soviet writers on the form Bonn's recognition of the GDR should take. While some stressed recognition "in accordance with international law," the prevailing euphemism for de jure recognition, others spoke merely of the need to recognize "the fact of the existence" of the GDR.[85]

We have already seen how various figures in the CPSU and SED leadership circles tended to gravitate toward one or the other of the alternative viewpoints at issue in these discussions among Soviet analysts before the Bundestag elections in the fall of 1969. As the year ended with the formation of the new SPD-FDP government in Bonn, contention over these questions continued to be evident both between the CPSU and SED primary elites and among the Soviet decision makers themselves.

In the vital area of U.S.–West European relations and West Germany's role in them, Brezhnev's emphasis fell decisively on the contradictions disrupting intercapitalist relations. Not only did he make this point at the international communist party conference in June; he repeated it in his statement welcoming the electoral victory of the SPD and FDP, thereby placing on the record his awareness of the possibilities of conflict between Bonn and Washington. At the same time, however, the Soviets were moving cautiously toward exploring the possibilities of détente with the United States. The most significant landmark in this direction in 1969 was reached in October, when the two superpowers formally agreed to begin SALT

82. *MEMO*, no. 9, 1969, pp. 16–27. See, e.g., the remarks of D. G. Tomashevskii in ibid., p. 95, and A. Gavrilov, "Cherez obshcheevropeiskoye soveshchaniye—k bezopasnosti kontinenta," ibid., no. 6, 1969, p. 7.

83. See the book by M. F. Kovaleva and other sources cited in Bruce Parrott, *Politics and Technology in the Soviet Union* (Cambridge: MIT Press, 1983), pp. 237–38.

84. Otto Reinhold, "Nauchno-tekhnicheskaya revolyutsiya i borba dvukh sistem," *MEMO*, no. 4, 1969, pp. 113–17, and K. Dohmdey's article in *Ekonomicheskaya gazeta*, no. 39, 1969, p. 21.

85. De jure recognition: A. Zholkver, "F.R.G.: Pre-Election Carneval," *IA*, no. 5, 1969, p. 39; V. Mikhailov, "Bonn's Variant of European Security," *IA*, no. 10, 1969, p. 16; Lt. Col. M. Ponomarev in *Krasnaya zvezda*, Oct. 30, 1969, p. 3. De facto recognition: Gavrilov, n. 82 above, p. 7; I. Koloskov, "Evropeiskaya bezopasnost: Realnosti i illyuzii," *MEMO*, no. 10, 1969, p. 46.

negotiations. Thus the Soviets were advancing haltingly in two directions at once, toward Western Europe and toward the United States, a dualistic Atlanticist approach articulated most explicitly by Gromyko.

In contradistinction to these policies, Walter Ulbricht emphatically rejected efforts to cooperate with either Bonn or Washington unless he were rewarded with de jure recognition at a minimum. These views found expression in the SED chief's continuing fulminations against the FRG's role in "U.S. global strategy." Ulbricht reiterated these ideas after the formation of the Brandt-Scheel cabinet, declaiming that the United States had now decided "to fight against the socialist states primarily through the Social Democrats."[86] As in previous years, this conception of U.S.–West German unity was faithfully echoed by the East German secondary elite.[87] So were Ulbricht's harangues about the failures of capitalism and the machinations of Bonn's economic diplomacy.[88]

But the Soviet leadership itself was by no means unified in its outlook on the new government in Bonn. Shelest and Marshal Grechko were especially vocal in their negative characterizations of West German foreign policy after the formation of the Brandt-Scheel governing coalition. Speaking in Kiev on October 17, Shelest warned that the United States was placing "its main stake on increasing West Germany's military-economic capacity," and charged that militarism, revanchism, and neo-Nazism constituted "state policy" in the FRG. In Shelest's view, Bonn aimed at "tearing off this or that piece from the socialist camp." His remarks on the recent Bundestag elections completely ignored the SPD and FDP and concentrated on the votes gathered by the neofascist party.[89] Grechko admitted that there were mounting contradictions in the Western alliance, but he insisted that these very contradictions were increasing the West's "adventurism." Pointing specifically to American and West German attempts to fuel the arms race, Grechko insisted that the USSR was therefore "obligated to do everything to maintain the Soviet state's defensive might."[90] Quite obviously, Grechko's views held out no hope whatever of luring Bonn away from NATO.

86. *ND*, Dec. 14, 1969, p. 7.
87. E.g., Klaus Bollinger and Hans Maretzki, "Was ist die USA-Globalstrategie?" *DA*, no. 1, 1969, pp. 22–28; Eberhard Heidmann, "Die konzeptionellen Auffassungen Henry A. Kissingers zur Aussenpolitik der USA," *DA*, no. 5, 1969, pp. 535–46; Klaus Linger, "Das Jahr 2000 im imperialistischen Sicht," *DA*, no. 9, 1969, pp. 1044–68; Siegfried Thomas, "Die Expansionspolitik der deutschen Imperialismus—Von der Restauration zur Aggression," ibid., pp. 1069–83; and Horst Hemberger and Karl-Heinz Schwank, "Ursachen und Erscheinungsformen der Aggressivität des westdeutschen Imperialismus," *Einheit*, no. 8, 1969, pp. 1005–17.
88. Elfriede Blunk, Joachim Klatte, and Heinz Kretzschmar, "Das wissenschaftliche Potential der westeuropäischen Hauptmächte," *DA*, no. 6, 1969, pp. 706–22; Joachim Klatte, "Imperialistische Aussenpolitik und wissenschaftlich-technische Revolution," *DA*, no. 9, 1969, pp. 1088–90.
89. FBIS, *USSR*, Oct. 21, 1969, pp. B13–14.
90. *Krasnaya zvezda*, Nov. 27, 1969, pp. 1–3. For a Soviet military officer's uncharac-

In keeping with these conservative attitudes, it appeared that the Soviet leadership was moving toward a consensus on the need for further increases in military spending. Brezhnev advocated devoting "large resources" to defense in his June speech at the international meeting of communist and workers' parties. Even Podgorny, once an outspoken critic of excessive military spending, now acknowledged the need to "maintain the necessary level of the USSR's defense power."[91] Accordingly, Soviet defense spending in 1969 rose by nearly 9 percent over the previous year's substantial 15.2 percent increase. After the invasion of Czechoslovakia, the Soviets left some 60,000 troops in that country to augment their standing forces in Europe. The Brezhnev coalition's resolve to pursue a course of robust military development was especially evident at the strategic level. As the decade ended, it was apparent to many Western observers that the USSR had already acquired a strategic missile force fully capable of maintaining the second-strike capability required for adequate deterrence. The deployment of heavy missiles aimed at the United States continued to proliferate, however, and the testing of antiballistic missile systems proceeded apace. Having spent the second half of the 1960s erasing America's large superiority in strategic weaponry, the Soviet Union was now raising serious questions about its willingness to settle for relative strategic parity with its super-power rival.

Soviet leaders also debated the desirability of expanded East-West trade in 1969. While Shelest and Suslov were reluctant to broaden these economic exchanges in 1969, Kosygin continued to favor them. A major turning point came when Brezhnev shifted his stance on this issue, adopting a position more amenable to trade with the West.[92] The culminating event in this gradual transformation came on December 15, when the CPSU chief delivered a stinging critique of Soviet economic performance at a secret Central Committee plenum. As news of the speech trickled out into the Soviet press in the following weeks, it became clear that Brezhnev had berated Soviet functionaries for the shortcomings of the economy, in the process acknowledging that the USSR confronted serious economic difficulties. From this point forward Brezhnev emerged as a consistent proponent of expanded trade and technology ties with the capitalist states.[93] The

teristically positive view of cooperation with those Western social democrats "who are struggling against imperialism not in words but in deeds," see Lt. Col. N. Ponomarev's article in *Kommunist vooruzhenikh sil*, no. 24, 1969, pp. 9–16. This article may have been intended to prepare the Soviet military for a future détente with the SPD-led government in the FRG.

91. *Pravda*, Nov. 7, 1969, p. 3. Podgorny added, however, that the USSR had already advanced a number of proposals to reduce the arms race so that the "enormous resources" devoted to it could be used to increase "the welfare of the people."

92. Parrott, *Politics and Technology*, pp. 232–36.

93. *Pravda* published an editorial on Brezhnev's speech on Jan. 13, 1970. See Christian Duevel, "Brezhnev's Secret Report," *Radio Liberty Research*, CRD 29/70 (Jan. 29, 1970).

result was a blunt repudiation of Ulbricht's "by our own means" strategy. Furthermore, not even Ulbricht's putative allies in the Soviet primary elite, such as Shelest and Grechko, ever publicly repeated this pregnant phrase that represented the economic cornerstone of Ulbricht's grand design.

Conclusions

By the end of 1969, therefore, key members of the Soviet decision-making hierarchy had converged on a position favoring a resumption of the dialogue with Bonn which they themselves had indefinitely postponed upon taking power some five years earlier. Brezhnev now added an economic rationale to his efforts to exploit intercapitalist contradictions. Suslov, while unenthusiastic about East-West trade, clearly perceived that advantages might be gained from cooperation with the SPD. Kosygin was guided by economic considerations and apparently to a greater extent than either Brezhnev or Suslov by hopes for arms-control agreements of some kind. Podgorny also voiced concern about the burdensome opportunity costs of the arms race. The leading supporter of détente with Bonn outside the Politburo, Foreign Minister Gromyko, combined support for economic cooperation and arms control with a keen sense of the connections linking détente with West Germany to détente with the United States. Meanwhile, several leading personages—notably Grechko, Shelest, and Ponomarev—appeared to be still unreconciled to the prospect of a serious accommodation with the Federal Republic. Once again, these differences within the decision-making elite coincided with a lively exchange of views among the secondary elite.

Precisely what kind of détente might emerge from contacts with the new Brandt-Scheel government was of course uncertain. Moscow's negotiating flexibility and its readiness for compromise were still untested. The outlines of a generally conservative approach to relations with the FRG, however, were gradually coming into focus. At a minimum, Bonn would have to recognize the territorial status quo; upgraded economic relations would not be allowed to alter the basic structures of the USSR's command economy; and a significant military détente in Europe would remain unlikely for an indeterminate period. The discussions in the Soviet press generally conformed to these conservative expectations. Moreover, the separate elements of this emerging Soviet consensus all rested on the assumption that the Federal Republic would have to be dealt with as a powerfully important member of the NATO alliance. This notion effectively ruled out any realistic prospects for dissolving Bonn's military ties with the United States or for reducing the FRG to a state of benign neutrality.

The GDR's policy toward the Federal Republic continued to reflect the maximalist priorities of Walter Ulbricht's directive regime. The SED chief pursued an all-encompassing antidétente strategy that admitted of little flexibility or willingness to compromise. The East German secondary elite provided ringing endorsements of this obstinate stance, although faint stirrings of doubt about the wisdom of Ulbricht's breakneck economic policies were beginning to be heard above the din of orchestrated approval.

In their final outcome, the events of 1969 had shown above all that the relationship between foreign policy and the domestic economy in the USSR was now essentially the reverse of what it was in the GDR. For the Soviet Union, as indeed for the leading states of Eastern Europe, the need for economic modernization was increasing the pressure for détente. For the GDR, the prospect of détente was increasing the pressure for accelerated economic modernization.

CHAPTER SIX

Building Détente:
1970

WILLY BRANDT assumed the office of federal chancellor with a grand design of his own. Unlike Ulbricht's, Brandt's strategy called for a comprehensive East-West détente aimed at unifying Germany on the basis of freedom and self-determination. The immediate task of the West German government was therefore to engage the Soviet Union and its allies in a process of dialogue and rapprochement, above all to remove the barriers of hostility and mistrust that still divided the combatants of World War II. Brandt believed that West Germany had not yet done enough to convince its eastern neighbors of its desire for reconciliation. His ostpolitik rested on an emotional core of *Versöhnungspolitik*, a "policy of reconciliation" that touched sentiments deeply rooted in Brandt's past as an expatriate from Nazi Germany and that reflected his conviction that special efforts were still needed to overcome the residual antagonisms of the war. A central element of this world view was the notion that the FRG had to take more energetic measures than in the past to convince the Soviets and the East Europeans that they had nothing to fear from Germany, not even from a united Germany.

From this starting point, Brandt envisaged a five-part scenario. First, political accords were to be worked out with the Soviet Union and its major allies based on Bonn's renunciation of the use of force with respect to the existing borders. Efforts to resolve the particular problems of Berlin through four-power negotiations would accompany these accords. Second, and simultaneously, economic agreements between West Germany and the Soviet bloc nations would begin to create the framework for economic interdependence between the two parts of Europe. Third, a process of military disengagement would follow, starting with mutual reductions of troops and weaponry in a way that would preserve a military equilibrium on the continent at reduced force levels and within the existing context of NATO and the Warsaw Pact. Fourth, in tandem with these endeavors, Bonn would negotiate with the GDR on *"menschliche Erleichterungen"* (humanitarian measures) to ease the situation of Germans separated by the physical and psychological barriers of partition. Efforts to renew direct contacts between citizens of East and West Germany would also serve to maintain the cultural unity of the German people. These notions were encapsulated in Brandt's insistence that, despite the existence of two German states, there still existed one German nation. Finally, after the success of these measures had created a self-sustaining European "peace order" of trust and cooperation, Germany would be unified.[1]

Brandt was also heavily influenced by the concept of "change through rapprochement" (*Wandel durch Annäherung*) developed by his foreign policy adviser, Egon Bahr. This was the notion that, over time, détente between the two German states would tend to liberalize the East German regime.[2]

Viewed from East Berlin, the theoretical and practical aspects of the new West German government's foreign policy program formed a ganglion of intolerable threats. Recognition of the existing borders on anything but a de jure basis was inherently impermanent. A four-power agreement on Berlin would infringe on the GDR's claim to sovereignty over the access routes and hamper its ability to restrict traffic when it wished to do so. A significant expansion of economic, scientific, and technological ties between West Germany and the Soviet bloc threatened to undermine the GDR's indispensability to Eastern Europe and the Soviet Union, and risked subjecting all the socialist countries to political manipulation by the FRG. Agreements widening the opportunity for contacts between the two German states ran the risk of eroding popular support for the SED regime at home, already tenuous enough, even further. Most important of all, the Federal Republic's outspoken hope for reunification inevitably implied the eventual liquidation of the German Democratic Republic.

For all of these reasons, Walter Ulbricht was resolved to oppose Bonn's

1. On Brandt's foreign policy designs, see Willy Brandt, *A Peace Policy for Europe*, trans. Joel Carmichael (New York: Holt, Rinehart & Winston, 1969); Peter Bender, *Die Ostpolitik Willy Brandts* (Reinbek bei Hamburg: Rowohlt, 1972); David Binder, *The Other German: Willy Brandt's Life and Times* (Washington, D.C.: New Republic, 1975); Claudia von Braunmühl, *Kalter Krieg und friedliche Koexistenz* (Frankfurt: Suhrkamp, 1973).

2. Bahr outlined his initial conceptualization of this notion in his speech before the Evangelical Academy in Tützing on July 15, 1963. The text is in *Deutschland Archiv*, no. 7, 1973, pp. 862–65. See also Walter F. Hahn, "West Germany's Ostpolitik: The Grand Design of Egon Bahr," *Orbis* 16 (Winter 1973): 859–80. The concept was further developed by the publicist Peter Bender in *Offensive Entspannung: Möglichkeit für Deutschland*, 4th ed. (Cologne: Kiepenheuer & Witsch, 1965), and *Zehn Gründe für die Anerkennung der DDR* (Frankfurt: Fischer, 1968).

diplomatic and economic initiatives. He was equally resolved to present his own grand design as an alternative to détente. As for the Soviet Union, the challenge of these competing West and East German comprehesive strategies required the clarification of its own foreign policy orientation, a process that came to a head in 1970 with the Brezhnev coalition's achievement of an internal consensus on the scope—and limits—of détente with the Federal Republic.

The Kremlin vs. Ulbricht:
The Economic Dimension

After initiating contacts in December 1969, the Soviets and the new Brandt government agreed in mid-January to commence negotiations. Bonn's special emissary for the talks, State Secretary Egon Bahr, arrived in the Soviet capital on January 28. Meanwhile, the FRG began pressing both Moscow and East Berlin for talks between the two German states, with Brandt declaring before the Bundestag on January 14, "There must, there can and ultimately there will be negotiations between Bonn and East Berlin."

Anticipating these developments, the GDR in early January reemphasized its insistence on full de jure recognition. The East German press touted the GDR's recently submitted draft treaty as its "minimum program" for inter-German relations, a claim that flatly contradicted the hopes of those West Germans who assumed that the GDR was merely staking out an initial maximum program for bargaining purposes.[3] Walter Ulbricht restated this position on January 19 at a press conference, the first one at which he fielded questions from Western journalists publicly since shortly before the construction of the Berlin wall in 1961. Emphasizing that diplomatic relations in full accordance with international law constituted "the only possibility" for normalizing the inter-German relationship, Ulbricht shunted aside Brandt's talk of the unity of the German nation and instead described the GDR as "a socialist German national state." To the astonishment of many listeners, Ulbricht also declared that there existed no residual four-power authority over the GDR or its capital, "Berlin." On a more positive note, Ulbricht hinted that the GDR would be willing to engage in direct talks on "specific problems" with the FRG without requiring a prior agreement on the terms of the 1969 draft treaty. (In fact, direct talks between the FRG and the GDR had already taken place in September 1969 on such questions as postal fees and river transit rights.) However, Ulbricht plainly

---

3. *ND*, Jan. 6, 1970, p. 2; Jan. 12, p. 5. See also *ND*, Feb. 24, p. 2.

intimated that such weighty matters as a renunciation-of-force treaty were not appropriate topics for these purely technical discussions.[4]

Evidence that Moscow was already wavering in its support for Ulbricht's demands surfaced even before Ulbricht's press conference. At a reception for the diplomatic corps in East Germany, Pyotr Abrassimov, Moscow's ambassador to the GDR and an early advocate of negotiations with an SPD-led government, urged Bonn to recognize "the fact of the existence of two sovereign German states." He also noted approvingly that acceptance of this view was gaining ground in West Germany.[5] Ulbricht's speech on the same occasion reiterated the necessity for mutual de jure recognition. Over the course of the following weeks, the East German press and leading figures such as Otto Winzer, Paul Verner, and Hermann Axen relentlessly pursued the theme of de jure relations as "the only possible way" to reach an inter-German understanding. On February 11 Willi Stoph affirmed this position yet again in his reply to Brandt's letter of January 22 proposing talks. With pressures for an early beginning to inter-German negotiations now virtually insurmountable, however, Stoph agreed to an exchange of views with Brandt, proposing a meeting in East Berlin in the latter half of February.[6]

By this time the Soviet–West German negotiations were already showing signs of progress. A harbinger of things to come was the announcement on February 1 of a major economic accord. After eight months of negotiations, Moscow and the FRG had come to terms on an exchange of 1.2 million metric tons of West German steel pipe for 52 billion cubic meters of Soviet natural gas. In addition, four West German banks agreed to extend $400 million in credit to the Soviet Union at the favorable interest rate of 6.25 percent.[7] The deal amounted to the largest East-West trade agreement ever consummated up to that time. While no specific quid pro quo was linked to it, the accord could not help but have a salutary effect on Bahr's negotiations with the Soviets.

Curiously, Soviet commentary on the implications of expanded economic dealings with the West at this time continued to be mixed. Within

4. *ND*, Jan. 20, 1970, pp. 3–6. *Pravda*'s coverage of the press conference (Jan. 20, p. 5) did not report Ulbricht's dismissal of four-power prerogatives.

5. *ND*, Jan. 10, 1970, p. 2. Through intermediaries, Abrassimov had communicated to Willy Brandt his wish for an SPD-FDP government in 1966, together with the suggestion that there were people in Moscow who would be favorably disposed to such a government. See Arnulf Baring, *Machtwechsel* (Stuttgart: Deutsche Verlags-Anstalt, 1982), pp. 243–44.

6. *ND*, Jan. 10, 1970, pp. 1–2; Jan. 23, p. 2; Jan. 24, p. 1; Feb. 7, p. 6; Feb. 19, p. 3; Feb. 13, p. 3.

7. For the terms of the agreement, see Robert W. Dean, *West German Trade with the East: The Political Dimension* (New York: Praeger, 1974), p. 215. Also Angela Stent, *From Embargo to Ostpolitik* (Cambridge: Cambridge University Press, 1980), p. 167.

days of the pipeline agreement, one writer hailed it for demonstrating the "unused opportunities and potential resources" of Soviet–West German economic relations. Several days later, however, another article attempted to refute Brezhnev's recent criticisms of the Soviet economy, insisting on its inherent strength.[8] As we shall see, Soviet specialists as well as members of the leadership remained divided on this issue over the ensuing months.

East German reactions were by no means so equivocal. Once word was out that the pipeline accord was imminent, Otto Winzer issued a ringing denunciation of West German capitalism, pointedly casting aspersions on the West German banking industry. Similar assaults on the "expansionist" nature of West German economic policy in general and on bankers in particular were published after the February 1 agreement was signed. One of these articles assailed the Thyssen and Mannesmann firms, both of which had lately agreed to provide steel pipe to the Soviet Union.[9]

The impending clash between the GDR and the Soviet Union over the question of trade with West Germany had been prefigured only days before the conclusion of the pipeline agreement at a conference of Soviet-bloc social scientists. An East German delegate, Herbert Kröger, acknowledged differences among the socialist countries, especially in economic matters. Nevertheless, he voiced the GDR's hope for "a close economic alliance with the Soviet Republic," a necessity he considered all the more urgent in view of the East-West confrontation under the conditions of the scientific-technical revolution.[10] However, one of the chief Soviet participants, Oleg Bogomolov, placed even greater stress on the disparity of national interests among socialist countries, and announced that this was not only inevitable but healthy. Bogomolov, a leading expert on Eastern Europe, recalled that Lenin himself had cautioned against "an artificial, mechanistic unity of countries." Bogomolov hit the nub of the matter when he pointed to differences in the various socialist countries' approach to economic relations with capitalist states. Lauding such ties as "an important means of guaranteeing international security," the Soviet delegate forcefully endorsed "buying needed goods and the latest technology" from the West, despite the capitalist states' attempts to "pull the socialist states into their technological-economic sphere of influence."[11]

The vital connection between East Germany's foreign policy predicament and its domestic economic priorities now came to the fore once again. On

8. *Sotsialisticheskaya industriya*, Feb. 6, 1970, p. 3; *Literaturnaya gazeta*, Feb. 11, 1970, cited in Stent, *From Embargo to Ostpolitik*, p. 171.

9. *ND*, Jan. 24, 1970, p. 6; Feb. 20, p. 6; Feb. 24, p. 7; Hans Tanner, "Die ökonomische Konzentration im System imperialistischer Expansionsstrategie," *Einheit*, no. 1, 1970, p. 2.

10. *Einheit*, no. 3, 1970, pp. 303–4.

11. *Kommunist*, no. 8, 1970, pp. 14–25. The speech was reprinted in *Einheit*, no. 4, 1970. Bogomolov expressed similar views in an article he wrote with V. Terekhov, "Lenin i razvitiye mirovovo sotsialisticheskovo sodruzhestva," *Voprosy ekonomiki*, no. 2, 1970, pp. 3–15.

February 9 Walter Ulbricht returned to this preoccupation in a speech titled "The Lessons of History and the Year 2000."[12] Issuing stern warnings about West Germany's aggressive designs, Ulbricht asserted, "In view of these plans on the part of the adversary, it is more necessary than ever to accelerate the pace of the GDR's socialist development." He portrayed the GDR on the threshhold of the next millennium as one of the most productive and technologically advanced countries in the world. Ulbricht combined this futuristic rodomontade with reminiscences of his meeting with Lenin in bygone days ("He invited us to a discussion"), in yet another transparent attempt to bolster the GDR's standing within the socialist bloc as well as his own prestige as one of the founding fathers of the communist movement.

At approximately the same time, Willi Stoph also drew attention to the linkage between the struggle against "imperialism" and the socialist camp's economic might, reasserting the GDR's thesis that the socialist states possessed the capability of solving the problems posed by science and technology "with our own strength and by our own means."[13] A member of the GDR Academy of Sciences elaborated upon these notions, offering further confirmation of the fact that the GDR was fashioning its economic and ideological policies primarily with foreign policy purposes in mind.[14]

Once again Ulbricht and those who echoed his views were broadcasting their fear that an extensive, long-term trade relationship involving significant transfers of high technology from West Germany to the USSR and Eastern Europe would ultimately undermine the GDR's economic importance to its allies. While the SED chief knew full well that East Germany was in no position to compete with West German technology at present, his visions of the year 2000 revealed his hope that eventually the GDR would emerge as the main supplier of advanced technological products within the socialist bloc, after the Soviet Union itself. The fulfillment of this dream, Ulbricht knew, required initimate collaboration with Soviet scientists and R&D specialists. It also required efforts to advance the productive capacities of the East German economy in a hurry.

Accordingly, several weeks later Ulbricht unveiled yet another campaign to speed up the GDR's economic development. Spearheaded by the slogan "overtake without catching up," the campaign zeroed in on the GDR's lagging rates of labor productivity. This was a problem Brezhnev had designated the previous December as one of the principal determinants of the Soviet economy's sluggish performance. Ulbricht's announcement of a new crash program to raise productivity in direct response to Brezhnev's

12. *ND*, Feb. 11, 1970, p. 4.
13. *Einheit*, no. 1, 1970, p. 4.
14. Werner Hänisch, "Probleme der internationalen Stellung der DDR," *DA*, no. 2, 1970, pp. 185–98.

concerns bore a striking resemblance to his decision to upgrade the GDR's chemical industry in response to Khrushchev's concerns in 1964. Just as in 1964, he was seeking to deflect the Soviets' inclination to deal with their economic problems by borrowing technology from the West.

That the new campaign was conceived in the wake of the Soviet–West German pipeline deal of February 1 was evident from Ulbricht's opening remarks. Citing recent statements by Walter Scheel concerning the USSR's economic backwardness, Ulbricht accused both the Federal Republic and the United States of exploiting the Soviet Union's "supposed technological difficulties" in order to extract political and economic concessions. After conceding that the phrase "overtake without catching up" was not meant to be taken literally, he suggested that the socialist states should now aim to raise their labor productivity "by leaps and bounds," moving so rapidly that, hypothetically, they would eventually overtake the West without even appearing to stop long enough to "catch up." Ulbricht offered no precise details as to how this hyperbolic goal was to be reached, asserting only that "wholly new technological processes" and "hitherto unknown methods" would be necessary. Indeed, the SED chief openly acknowledged that the technicians charged with implementing the new program had already warned that the GDR lacked the technological capacity to accomplish the breakthroughs he demanded.[15]

Nevertheless, Ulbricht was adamant about pressing forward with the project, insisting that it was "correct, necessary, and realizable." Speaking before the Staatsrat in mid-March, he reaffirmed his commitment to the new campaign, and remarked that the purpose of the GDR's accelerated economic efforts was to counteract the political designs of the Federal Republic.[16] He hammered away at this theme again at the end of the month, this time justifying plans to accelerate growth in the chemical industry with explicit references to the October 1968 SED Central Committee plenum, which had brought the linkage between foreign policy and domestic economic strategy to the forefront of the East German leadership's concerns.[17] Over the course of the next several months, "overtake without catching up" became the watchwords of the East German econ-

15. The speech was published Feb. 26, in *Die Wirtschaft*, no. 9, 1970, pp. 8–9. A West German study published in 1970 calculated the GDR's lag behind the FRG in industrial labor productivity at more than 30%. The figure was higher in specific industries, such as electronics (32%), chemistry (48%), and metallurgy (57%). See Deutsches Institut für Wirtschaftsforschung, "Arbeitsproduktivität in der Industrie der DDR und der Bundesrepublik—ein Vergleich," *Wochenbericht*, no. 20, 1970, pp. 140–41.

16. *ND*, Mar. 14, 1970, p. 3. Ulbricht stated in Abrassimov's presence that the GDR expected to speed up its efforts to compete in world markets: *ND*, Mar. 2, p. 2. At approximately the same time, Ulbricht wrote that the competition between "imperialism" and socialism now "takes place primarily in the field of economics and the field of scientific-technical progress": *Einheit*, no. 4, 1970, p. 395.

17. *ND*, Mar. 28–29, 1970, p. 4.

omy, headlining a profusion of articles in the specialized press. Invariably the aim of the campaign was attributed explicitly to the international confrontation with the FRG.[18]

To give effect to this latest twist in the GDR's economic policy, various measures were introduced in March to increase the technological resources made available to specific economic sectors.[19] Then, starting in April, a series of draft regulations for the proposed restructuring of the East German economic system was released for discussion among planning officials. The injunction to "overtake without catching up" received top priority in these documents. So did the concept of "dynamic proportioning," the euphemism for the lopsided concentration of investment resources in specific "structure-determining" industries.[20] These measures and proposals, and the context in which they were elaborated, provided still more evidence that the SED leadership's perceptions of the international political situation were instrumental in determining the priorities of East Germany's domestic economic policies at this time.

In the USSR, meanwhile, some Soviet officials were still not convinced of the wisdom of Brezhnev's economic opening to the West. In the spring, Aleksandr Shelepin, Pyotr Demichev, and Petro Shelest expressed critical views about capitalist economies, reinforcing them with optimistic comments on the Soviet economic system which were very much at odds with the line adopted by Brezhnev at the December plenum. Shelepin and Shelest, in particular, punctuated these statements with belligerent attacks on Western foreign policies.[21] Thus Brezhnev's inclination to promote

---

18. *ND*, Apr. 1, 1970, p. 1; Klaus Stubenrauch and Dietrich Austel, "Überholen ohne einzuholen," *Einheit*, no. 6, 1970, pp. 733–41; Edelgard Göhler, "Höchste Arbeitsproduktivität—entscheidend für den Sieg des Sozialismus," *Einheit*, no. 7, 1970, pp. 967, 973; Karl-Heinz Stiemerling, "Zu einigen Bedingungen des stabilen ökonomischen Wachstums in der vorwiegend intensiven erweiterten sozialistischen Reproduktion," *Wirtschaftswissenschaft*, no. 1, 1970, p. 28; Dieter Bergner and Berndt P. Löwe, "Philosophische Probleme des Kampfes gegen die Globalstrategie," *Deutsche Zeitschrift für Philosophie*, no. 9, 1970, p. 1052.
19. *ND*, Apr. 17, 1970, p. 3.
20. On "dynamic proportioning," see, e.g., Harry Maier, "Probleme des intensiven ökonomischen Wachstums im Sozialismus unter den Bedingungen der wissenschaftlich-technischen Revolution," *Wirtschaftswissenschaft*, no. 1, 1970, pp. 22–23; Herbert Wolf, "Die Dynamik der erweiterten sozialistischen Reproduktion und ihre planmässige Umsetzung durch die Strukturpolitik," *Einheit*, no. 3, 1970, p. 279; Erich Wappler, "Komplexe sozialistische Automatisierung—eine gesellschaftliche Aufgabe," *Einheit*, no. 2, 1970, p. 131. For the draft regulations, see *Die Wirtschaft*, supp. 14, no. 18, 1970; suppl. 15, nos. 19–20, 1970; suppl. 16, no. 27, 1970. I am indebted to Maria Haendcke-Hoppe for pointing out to me the existence of these draft proposals.
21. See Shelest's speech of Mar. 26 in FBIS, *USSR*, Mar. 30, 1970, pp. BB1–10, and his speech of Apr. 17 in ibid., Apr. 20, pp. B6–23. See also Bruce Parrott, *Politics and Technology in the Soviet Union* (Cambridge: MIT Press, 1983), pp. 240–43. In March reports were published in the Western media, based on Yugoslav sources, about criticism of Brezhnev's economic policies by Shelepin, Suslov, and Kirill Mazurov. See FBIS, *USSR*, Mar. 12, 1970, p. B1.

economic agreements with the FRG, while certainly the ascendant policy within the CPSU leadership, was not without opposition. Nevertheless, Brezhnev renewed his criticisms of the Soviet economy in a speech at Kharkov on April 13. In a passage that sounded like a response to Ulbricht's latest exhortations, the Soviet chief affirmed that the USSR was indeed "catching up with and surpassing" the West in many areas, but not in labor productivity.[22]

The Bahr-Gromyko Talks and the Inter-German Dialogue

The prominence attached to economic relations with the FRG by both Moscow and East Berlin in 1970 was more than matched by the political aspects of the relationship. Although another controversy over the FRG's ties to West Berlin developed in January, the Soviets did not let it mar the opening rounds of Bahr's negotiations with the Soviet negotiating team headed by Andrei Gromyko. Nor did they echo East Germany's repeated assertion that West Berlin was "on the territory" of the GDR. With the prospect of talks on Berlin now in view, the Kremlin was increasingly distancing itself from Ulbricht's attempts to intrude upon a possible four-power agreement. At the same time, as West German parliamentarians assembled in West Berlin for official meetings, the USSR issued its traditional protests against such activities, while the GDR obstructed traffic into the divided city.

Amidst proliferating signs of disagreement between the Soviet Union and the GDR over the reliability of the Brandt-Scheel government as a negotiating partner, Bahr and Gromyko pursued their talks.[23] During the early stages, Gromyko called for Bonn's de jure recognition of the GDR. How seriously Gromyko intended this demand is difficult to assess, in light of the fact that in the past he had usually called merely for Bonn's recognition of the "existence" of the GDR. In any event, Gromyko quickly dropped the demand in February, as Bahr reminded him that the FRG lacked the legal competence to confer de jure recognition on the GDR owing to four-power

22. *Pravda*, Apr. 14, 1970, pp. 1–2.
23. At the French Communist Party Congress in early February, the Soviet delegate Andrei Kirilenko (a close associate of Brezhnev's) stated that "changes have taken place" in the leadership of the FRG; by contrast, Hermann Axen of the SED said that the Brandt-Scheel government was no different from the CDU/CSU: *ND*, Feb. 6, 1970, p. 6, and Feb. 7, p. 6. See also the violent attack on the FRG's economic and ideological challenges by Honecker, *ND*, Feb. 22, pp. 4–5, and by Defense Minister Heinz Hoffmann, *ND*, Feb. 24, p. 2. For other sharp East German criticisms of the SPD-FDP government, with frequent allusions to the Czech crisis, see *ND*, Feb. 23, p. 2; Feb. 28, p. 9; Mar. 9, p. 2; Mar. 6, p. 6. By contrast, *Pravda* on Feb. 21 attacked leftist and rightist deviations from Marxism in Europe but made no mention of the SPD. The article was reprinted in *ND*, Feb. 24, p. 4.

prerogatives in the German question. Reportedly Gromyko appeared to be taken aback by this suggestion that de jure recognition would actually infringe upon Soviet rights. As a veteran of the Potsdam negotiations and other seminal postwar discussions, however, the Soviet foreign minister was well aware of the merits of Bahr's argument. Bahr himself later said that he would have broken off the talks if the Soviets had stuck to their insistence on de jure recognition.[24]

As this breakthrough in the Soviet–West German dialogue developed, Gromyko shuttled to East Berlin in late February. Although initially scheduled to spend two days conferring with the East German leadership, he stayed four. During his stay, Foreign Minister Otto Winzer reminded his Soviet counterpart of the perfidy of Western "global strategy," and declared that the current situation required the "harmonization and coordination" of Soviet and East German policy. Winzer staunchly defended the GDR's 1969 draft treaty, and insisted that recognition of the GDR's sovereign equality was "an absolute necessity." Gromyko made no mention of de jure recognition in his published remarks while in East Berlin, and in an interview printed in *Neues Deutschland* he actually admitted that socialist states did not have unified national interests. At the time of his visit, SED Politburo members Verner and Norden, as well as various writers for *Neues Deutschland*, offered incessant reminders of the FRG's alleged "expansionism" and of the indispensability of de jure recognition.[25]

The communiqué issued at the end of Gromyko's stay suggested a Soviet victory. East Germany confirmed its readiness to conduct relations with the FRG on the basis of "sovereign equality," but there was no specific reference to de jure relations. The communiqué also expressed the GDR's support for Soviet efforts to improve the West Berlin situation, and took note of "tendencies in favor of a realistic and reasonable course" in the FRG.[26]

After the Gromyko visit, the Soviets increasingly backed away from the provisions of the GDR's draft treaty of December 1969, stating perfunctorily that it "could" be useful in improving inter-German relations, but carefully refraining from endorsing the document as the only basis for a normalization of FRG-GDR ties.[27] Moscow's waning support for the draft treaty, and particularly for its insistence on de jure recognition, was further signaled in an article by G. A. Deborin, a professor at the Soviet School of Diplomacy, published in *Deutsche Aussenpolitik*. In an ironic twist, De-

---

24. Baring, *Machtwechsel*, pp. 256, 260, 272, 275.

25. *ND*, Feb. 26, 1970, p. 2; Feb. 24, p. 6; Feb. 26, pp. 2, 7; Feb. 27, pp. 3–4. Gromyko's interview was originally published in the USSR in *Ogonyok*.

26. *ND*, Feb. 28, 1970, p. 1.

27. *Pravda*, Mar. 1, 1970, p. 1. See also the Soviet statements reprinted in *ND*, Mar. 3, pp. 1–2, 7; Mar. 4, p. 7.

borin made no reference to the 1969 draft treaty, but instead expressed full approval of Walter Ulbricht's "peace doctrine" of 1964, which had called only for "recognition of the equality of both German states." Deborin also noted the peace doctrine's commitment to Germany's reunification, a concept that had all but dropped out of Ulbricht's political vocabulary by 1970.[28] Precisely how this article came to be published in East Germany's leading foreign affairs journal at this time is uncertain, but its publication probably reflected either Soviet pressure or receptiveness to the Soviet view on the part of at least some East Germans, or perhaps both. Whatever the case, the message was decidedly opposed to Ulbricht's current policy line.

Meanwhile, in another departure from Ulbricht's maximalist position, Moscow's paramount interests in a Berlin settlement at this time also assumed practical dimensions as the quadripartite negotiations began on March 26.

Despite Gromyko's arm-twisting mission in the GDR, the path to an early meeting of East and West German heads of government was still not entirely cleared. East Germany refused to proceed with planning for the Brandt-Stoph encounter when Brandt announced his intention to make a stopover in West Berlin on his way back from East Berlin, where the talks were initially set to take place. Even after the FRG proposed a new location for the talks, the GDR stalled for several days before finally agreeing on March 12 to hold the first session in Erfurt one week later. Ulbricht and Norden foreshadowed the tone of the coming negotiations with blunt reaffirmations of East Germany's demand for de jure recognition, and *Neues Deutschland* announced fatalistically that, barring an agreement to this effect, the talks would inevitably fail.[29]

As the first of the "Willy-Willi" talks took place on March 19, amid spontaneous pro-Brandt demonstrations, it was apparent that the two sides were engaged in a *dialogue des sourds*. Stoph faithfully reiterated the GDR's standing demands for de jure recognition in accordance with the 1969 draft treaty, and actually raised East Germany's demands on the FRG by calling for a mutual 50 percent reduction in military spending and a settlement of the GDR's war damage claims. He also insisted that neither the GDR nor its capital, "Berlin," was subject to four-power authority. Brandt contradicted virtually all of Stoph's central propositions, calling for "between-German [*zwischendeutsche*] relations of a special type" that would preserve the unity of the nation. He defended the FRG's ties with West Berlin, and explicitly linked the achievement of détente to an agreement on the Berlin problem. In addition, Brandt expressed his hope for a

28. *DA*, no. 3, 1970, p. 361.
29. *ND*, Mar. 7, 1970, p. 3; Mar. 8, pp. 2, 3; Mar. 9, p. 2.

continuing dialogue on relaxing restrictions on the travel of citizens of the two states across their mutual border.[30]

Perhaps the only agreement reached in Erfurt was the decision to hold another round of talks in Kassel in late May. Reportedly the SED leadership agreed in advance with Moscow to hold one more Brandt-Stoph encounter, while adhering to its position on de jure recognition.[31] The GDR used the intervening period largely to confirm the maximalist course set by Stoph in Erfurt. Ulbricht, Stoph and Winzer continued to place primary emphasis on the absolute necessity of de jure recognition. Only after the conclusion of a treaty to this effect would the GDR be prepared to discuss "questions of detail" with the Federal Republic. East German journalists and academicians further poisoned the pre-Kassel atmosphere with a barrage of attacks on "Social Democratism" and the SPD leadership.[32]

In April, Walter Ulbricht used the occasion of the Lenin centenary celebration in Moscow to rail against Weimar Germany's repudiation of the Rapallo treaty, and to remind his Soviet listeners once again of his personal contacts with Lenin.[33] Later Ulbricht was given the opportunity to restate his position in *Kommunist*. The article summarized the main themes of Ulbricht's foreign policy, complete with ominous references to the FRG's role in U.S. "global strategy," the perfidious actions of West German firms and banks, and the historical lessons of Locarno. The SPD came in for scathing criticism, its policies likened to those of the CDU/CSU and even the Nazis. Brandt was personally vilified for pursuing "an absolutely unrealistic policy in the style of Stresemann." The SED chief called repeatedly for de jure recognition by Bonn, as well as for recognition of the postwar borders as "immutable."[34]

Why the Soviets allowed Ulbricht to showcase his views in the pages of *Kommunist* at this time is not clear. Perhaps they were acting out of a certain grudging respect, letting the faithful old German communist have

30. For a side-by-side comparison of the two speeches, see Anita Dasbach-Mallinckrodt, *Wer macht die Aussenpolitik der DDR?* (Düsseldorf: Droste, 1972), pp. 295–329.

31. Gerhard Wettig, *Community and Conflict in the Socialist Camp: The Soviet Union, East Germany, and the German Problem, 1965–1972*, trans. Edwina Moreton and Hannes Adomeit (London: C. Hurst, 1975), pp. 71, 73. This might explain occasional Soviet statements at this time in favor of de jure recognition. See, e.g., Abrassimov's statement in *ND*, Apr. 1, 1970, p. 6.

32. *ND*, Mar. 21, 1970, pp. 3–4; Mar. 9, pp. 3–4; Mar. 22, p. 1; Mar. 26, p. 1; Mar. 30, p. 2; Apr. 3, p. 2; Apr. 5, p. 2; Apr. 14, p. 2; Apr. 18, p. 2; Apr. 27, p. 2; Otto Winzer, "Die Leninsche Politik der friedlichen Koexistenz und ihre Anwendung in der Aussenpolitik der DDR," *Einheit*, no. 5, 1970, esp. p. 592; Stefan Doernberg, "Das politische Programm des Helmut Schmidt," *Einheit*, no. 2, 1970, pp. 180–87.

33. *ND*, Apr. 22, 1970, p. 8.

34. Walter Ulbricht, "Dvadtsatipyatiletiye osvobozhdeniya," *Kommunist*, no. 7, 1970, pp. 91–105.

his say before compelling him to submit to their dictates. In the past, however, the Soviet press had shown no misgivings about deleting unpalatable remarks by the SED chief; hence this explanation cannot be accepted at face value. It is quite possible that there were forces in the CPSU still opposed to détente with Bonn on anything less than maximalist terms, and that these forces favored giving Ulbricht a hearing in the party's most important journal.

Indeed, Soviet academicians and journalists continued to express skepticism about the Brandt government throughout the spring of 1970. The leading foreign affairs journals published several articles that were quite critical of Brandt's "vagueness" and his loyalty to NATO. These were counterbalanced by more positive images of the SPD-FDP government in other articles, including one that referred favorably to Rapallo. As in late 1969, Soviet writers differed as to whether the GDR should be recognized on a de jure basis.[35] Additional signs of a policy debate surfaced in May, when a serious discussion broke out on a chapter of a recently published book which had extolled Lenin's criticism of Bolsheviks who opposed the 1918 Brest-Litovsk peace treaty with Germany. Soviet critics of the chapter strongly implied that Germany could not be trusted to keep its agreements, thereby raising serious doubts about the desirability of a renunciation-of-force treaty with the FRG.[36]

In any event, the Kassel meetings that began on May 21 produced no significant changes in the position of the two German governments. Brandt summarized the FRG's stance in twenty points, all of which had already been advanced earlier. Stoph also adhered to the well-trod paths of East German diplomacy, proposing at the end of the talks a "pause for thought" in the inter-German dialogue.[37]

As the Kassel meetings were in progress, the Bahr-Gromyko discussions were reaching a decisive stage. On May 22 Soviet and West German negotiators reached tentative agreement on the draft of a reununciation-of-force treaty. The "Bahr paper," as it came to be known, explicitly affirmed the validity of prevailing four-power agreements on Germany and dismissed the possibility of de jure recognition of the GDR by the Federal Republic.

35. Negative images of the FRG were in Y. Rzhevsky, "European Security and the Stability of Frontiers," *IA*, no. 5, 1970, pp. 80–84; A. Aleksandrov, "Tekushchiye problemy mirovoi politiki," *MEMO*, no. 7, 1970, pp. 88–93. See also A. Sverdlov, "GDR, FRG i OON," *MEMO*, no. 5, 1970, pp. 79–81, calling for de jure recognition of the GDR. Positive images were in G. Andreyev, "Lenin and Peaceful Soviet Foreign Policy," *IA*, no. 5, 1970, pp. 3–14 (which refers to Rapallo), and E. Novoseltsev, "Europe Twenty-five Years Later," *IA*, no. 7, 1970, pp. 15–22 (calling for recognition of the GDR merely on the basis of "generally accepted international rules").

36. *Voprosy filosofii*, no. 11, 1970, pp. 166–73, cited in Parrott, *Politics and Technology*, p. 389n.

37. For the texts, see *Deutschland Archiv*, no. 6, 1970, pp. 621–48.

West Germany was now prepared to conclude an agreement with the GDR which would have "the same binding force customary between states," and would act "to shape its relations with the GDR on the basis of full equality of rights, nondiscrimination, and respect for the independence and autonomy of each of the two states" regarding internal matters.[38] The document also referred to the "inviolability" (*Unverletzlichkeit* in German, *nerush-imost* in Russian) of Germany's postwar borders. This wording represented a victory for Bahr, who had objected to Gromyko's earlier preference for "irrevocability" (*nezyblimost*). In addition, Bahr drafted a letter declaring that the treaty as drafted did not prejudice the FRG's goal of achieving German unity on the basis of free self-determination, and he obtained the Soviet delegation's consent to accept such a letter at the appropriate time without contradicting its contents.[39]

The Bahr-Gromyko text soon became a matter of intense discussion in the West German Foreign Office and cabinet over the ensuing weeks,[40] and evoked considerable controversy when parts of it were leaked to the Springer press on June 12. The full text was published on July 1 in two popular West German magazines. As it happened, prominent Soviet officials and writers also had occasion to discuss Soviet–West German relations in public forums during the spring and early summer months.

Soviet Discussions on the FRG

Immediately before and after the negotiations on the Bahr paper, a number of Kremlin leaders registered their views on the current international situation. An analysis of these speeches reveals some interesting differences in the way prominent officials assessed the latest events, and also provides some clues as to the consensus that was taking shape on political, economic, and military issues within the Kremlin hierarchy.

Speaking in Kharkov in mid-April, Brezhnev surveyed the international scene and took issue with those who claimed that no changes were occurring in world politics. On the contrary, Brezhnev asserted, "very considerable" changes were in fact taking place. He then elaborated on Soviet proposals on the territorial status quo in Europe and on economic and technological exchanges with the West. Brezhnev also affirmed that the USSR would do "all in its power" to see that the SALT talks would prove useful. A week later he coupled his commitment to cooperating with the

---

38. For the text, see ibid., no. 9, 1970, pp. 250–60.
39. Baring, *Machtwechsel*, pp. 317–18.
40. See Günther Schmid, *Entscheidung in Bonn: Die Entstehung der Ost- und Deutsch-landpolitik, 1969/1970* (Cologne: Wissenschaft und Politik, 1979).

West and negotiating a halt to the arms race with a pledge to "continue to strengthen our country's defense and equip our army with the most up-to-date weapons." Interestingly, he also acknowledged that cooperation among *socialist* states did not arise "automatically," and that "difficulties and contradictions" sometimes manifested themselves in these ties. Brezhnev repeated his commitment to strengthening Soviet defense forces in late May, shortly after the Bahr paper was negotiated.[41]

On June 12, on the eve of the elections to the USSR Supreme Soviet, Brezhnev specifically addressed the recent negotiations with West Germany, noting that the Soviet Union was ready "to bring them to a positive conclusion." In a similarly affirmative vein, the Soviet leader voiced approval of "realistic" forces in the United States, and called for an improvement in U.S.-Soviet relations. He appealed for "the greatest possible vigilance" to prevent a war from breaking out, however, and insisted once again on the need to strengthen the defense capacity of the USSR and the entire socialist community.[42] In sum, the CPSU general secretary demonstrated a personal commitment to negotiations with both the FRG and the United States on a variety of issues, but offered an equally strong endorsement of enhanced Soviet military capabilities. He made no mention of West German or U.S. proposals for force reductions in Europe.

Kosygin also took a positive view of the negotiations with the FRG, indicating that they would be continued. He described "revanchists" as "just living corpses" whose ideas were "dangerous but futile." Suslov was critical of American foreign policy but silent on the FRG. As the number two man in the Politburo, however, and a known advocate of cooperation with the SPD, he is unlikely to have been displeased by the Bahr-Gromyko talks. Meanwhile, Suslov seconded Brezhnev's commitment to "improve" Soviet military power. Podgorny proclaimed that West German foreign policy was now "heavily influenced by forces that regard the state of affairs soberly and realistically," rejecting militarism and revanchism. He also praised East-West economic cooperation, and said that it could lead to agreements on nuclear weapons. By June 1970 it was therefore evident that the four most prominent voting members of the CPSU Politburo were in favor of continuing the talks with the FRG on the basis of the Bahr paper of May 22. Of the nonvoting Politburo members likely to be influential in foreign policy discussions, Yurii Andropov added his weight to these views with a statement advocating a European security conference to promote the renunciation of force and East-West trade.[43]

Among the principal bureaucratic figures likely to have an interest in the

41. *Pravda*, Apr. 14, 1970, pp. 1–2; Apr. 22, pp. 2–5; May 27, pp. 1–2.
42. *Pravda*, June 13, 1970, pp. 2–3.
43. *Pravda*, June 11, 1970, p. 2; June 10, p. 10; June 12, p. 2; June 2, p. 2.

Soviet Union's German policy, senior trade and technology functionaries such as D. M. Gvishiani, the deputy chairman of the USSR State Committee for Science and Technology, expressed their support for expanded East-West economic contacts at this time.[44]

Not all senior-level Soviet political figures were positive in their characterizations of the prospects for détente at this critical juncture, however. Among the voting members of the Politburo, Petro Shelest was not recorded as having had anything positive to say about the FRG in the spring of 1970. According to *Pravda Ukrainy*, Shelest devoted "a considerable part" of his Supreme Soviet election speech to foreign policy matters, but nothing specific was published on this score. In his earlier speeches, however, Shelest had uttered harsh pronouncements against Western "imperialism." At the same time, Shelest remained a consistent advocate of increased military spending. Aleksandr Shelepin also took a dim view of Western "imperialism," but in his June election speech he concentrated his ire on the United States rather than on the Federal Republic. However, the trade union newspaper he supervised, *Trud*, was an occasional critic of the FRG that spring. (*Neues Deutschland* reprinted a *Trud* article calling for de jure recognition of the GDR.) Though Shelepin rarely made public comments against the FRG, his views opposing excessive trade ties with the West, together with *Trud*'s generally hard-line orientation, cast him as a possible doubter about the desirability of extensive détente with Bonn.[45]

A more outspoken critic of West Germany at this time was Boris Ponomarev, who warned that "forces of revanchism and reaction continue to act in the FRG." He did not counterbalance this shibboleth with any positive comments about West Germany. Ponomarev also defined the effort to strengthen Soviet defenses as "the most important international task of the CPSU."[46] Although Ponomarev was not a member of the Politburo at this time, his position on the Secretariat and his role as head of the International Department conferred considerable credibility on his opinions on foreign policy, and his influence may have been especially strong within the Central Committee apparatus.

Significantly, the Soviet Union's leading military officials were consistently negative in their images of the FRG in the first half of 1970. Though none was on the Politburo or Secretariat at this time, their views on foreign policy were not to be easily dismissed by the civilian political leadership. Some three months after the Brandt government had signed the Nuclear Nonproliferation Treaty, for example, Defense Minister Grechko presented

44. *Sotsialisticheskaya industriya*, Jan. 10, 1970, p. 2; *New Times*, no. 3, 1970, pp. 7–9.
45. Shelest: *Pravda Ukrainy*, Mar. 26, 1970, p. 2; Apr. 18, pp. 2–3; May 9, pp. 1, 4; June 2, pp. 1–2. Shelepin: *Pravda*, June 5, 1970, p. 3; *ND*, Mar. 25, 1970, p. 1.
46. *Pravda*, June 3, 1970, p 2.

a sinister view of West Germany as "the main hotbed of danger in Europe." Grechko placed heavy emphasis on military collaboration between the United States and the FRG, and coupled his warnings with a call for Soviet "superiority in the economic, scientific-technical, . . . and military fields."[47]

Other prominent Soviet military figures were equally harsh in their portrayals of West Germany at this time. In May, General Aleksei Yepishev, chief of the military's Main Political Directorate, castigated "the most aggressive detachments of imperialism" in the United States and the Federal Republic for seeking "revenge." Consequently, he wrote, the USSR was "taking all steps to strengthen the country's defense capability." Marshal Ivan Yakubovskii, commander in chief of the Warsaw Pact forces, claimed that the FRG still refused to recognize the established borders in Europe and was therefore "intensifying the aggressiveness of the North Atlantic alliance." These and other statements by members of the Soviet high command conformed to the generally harsh image of the enemy projected by military figures in 1970.[48]

Meanwhile, as the Soviet political leadership edged closer to a renunciation-of-force treaty with Bonn, an article in *Krasnaya zvezda* voiced an unusually strong plea for attentiveness to the military's political views. Published on July 30, in the midst of sensitive negotiations between the Soviets and the West Germans on the final wording of the treaty, it bluntly asserted the military's right to a political role. The article quoted Lenin as saying that the army "cannot and must not be neutral," and added that the notion that the military should not be involved in politics was "the slogan of hypocritical servants of the bourgeoisie." The article underscored the relevance of these statements to the current negotiations with the FRG by citing the SED's Hermann Axen on the "economic war of the main imperialist powers" against the GDR.

By early summer, at any rate, the constellation of interests and personal preferences within the primary foreign policy decision-making elite tilted heavily—but not unanimously—in the direction of political and economic agreements with the Federal Republic of Germany. This was manifestly not the case with respect to military questions, however. Here the preponderant emphasis fell on the further "strengthening" of Soviet military forces, with no positive agreement apparent with respect to the Brandt government's feelers on force reductions in Europe.

47. *Kommunist*, no. 3, 1970, pp. 51–64. See also Grechko's article in *Pravda*, Feb. 23, 1970, p. 2; his speech in Minsk of Mar. 15 in FBIS, *USSR*, Mar. 16, 1970, pp. E5–6, and his speech as reported in *Pravda*, May 9, 1970, pp. 2–3.

48. *Militarsko-istoricheskii zhurnal*, May 1970, pp. 14–22; *Pravda*, May 14, 1970, p. 4; *Krasnaya zvezda*, Jan. 11, 1970, p. 1; Jan. 20, p. 3; Jan. 24, p. 1; Feb. 20, p. 4. See also the sources cited in Hans-Heinrich Nolte, *Gruppeninteressen und Aussenpolitik* (Göttingen: Musterschmidt, 1979), pp. 102–4.

The Renunciation-of-Force Agreement
and East German Reactions

The first hints of policy differences within the SED leadership began to emerge by mid-June. In a speech before the Central Committee, Walter Ulbricht for the first time spoke in public about the possible benefits of de facto recognition by Bonn. Although de facto recognition would "not suffice" to settle all the problems affecting inter-German relations, he said, it might prove useful in influencing other governments to recognize the GDR. Ulbricht also toned down his criticism of Brandt's foreign policy by attributing its harshest aspects to pressure from the CDU/CSU, and by characterizing Brandt's offer to conclude a renunciation-of-force treaty with the GDR as a distinct change from the positions of earlier West German governments. Ulbricht reminded the Central Committee that ultimately the "most important" element in the GDR's political success was its economic strength, and he carefully counterbalanced his remarks on de facto recognition with strong statements in favor of full diplomatic relations with the FRG and the admission of both German states to the United Nations.[49]

By contrast, Albert Norden and Willi Stoph blasted the FRG's putatively aggressive designs on the GDR. Both echoed Ulbricht's insistence on full diplomatic relations, but neither repeated his musings on de facto recognition.[50]

For the time being, the hints of change in Ulbricht's speech remained only hints. But it was clear that events were spinning increasingly out of the GDR's control. At the end of June the foreign ministers of the Warsaw Pact states gathered in Budapest. Neither the communiqué nor the memorandum issued at the end of their deliberations called for de jure recognition of East Germany. Significantly, the memorandum explicitly approved of U.S. and Canadian participation in the proposed European security conference.[51] This approval, which had already been signaled by Soviet officials in January, represented a marked shift from the Kremlin's earlier intimations that the conference should be confined to European states. The Kremlin was now overtly linking détente in Europe to détente with the United States, a connection already operative in the four-power Berlin negotiations.

It was perhaps ironic that just as the Kremlin was about to seal an unprecedented political agreement with West Germany, with the express intention of exacerbating the "contradictions" between Bonn and Washington, it was also moving to include the United States more formally in the emerging diplomacy of European détente. To no small degree this step was

49. *ND*, June 16, 1970, pp. 3–4.
50. *ND*, June 15, 1970, pp. 6–8; June 16, p. 5.
51. *Pravda*, June 24, 1970, p. 4; June 27, p. 4.

prompted by the Brandt government's terms for a Soviet–West German rapprochement. Just as Brandt had declared that an amelioration of the Berlin situation was a sine qua non of a bilateral détente, he insisted that the FRG would participate in a European security conference only if the United States participated as well. Thus the very context of Moscow's Europeanist diplomacy nudged the Soviet leadership once again toward an explicitly Atlanticist approach. At least for the present, the Soviets found that they could effect no improvement in their ties with Western Europe without dealing directly with the United States on vital European issues. This realization spelled, if not the end, then at least the postponement of Soviet efforts to deal with the states of Western Europe independently of their transatlantic ally, a tendency that had been evident, however modestly, ever since de Gaulle's break with NATO in 1966.[52]

Nevertheless, the Soviets continued to show little inclination to act on West Germany's appeals for a discussion of mutual force reductions at the proposed European conference. The Budapest statement suggested that the issue of force reductions could be discussed either in a separate organ created at the conference or in another suitable forum. These discussions, however, were to be confined exclusively to the question of reducing "foreign troops on European territory," a formula evidently meant to apply only to American forces. Thus Moscow was still averse to the concept of "mutual" force reductions in Europe.[53]

Events now moved rapidly toward a denouement in the Soviet–West German negotiations. In July, as the debate on the Bahr paper spilled out into public forums in the FRG, Gromyko announced that the terms of the draft were final. The West German government insisted on modifications, however, and on July 26 Foreign Minister Walter Scheel led a delegation to Moscow. The initial going was tough. The Soviets refused Scheel's request to include a passage stating that the treaty was valid only until the conclusion of a peace treaty. The West Germans also insisted on more explicit language affirming that Bonn's recognition of the territorial status quo applied only to the concept of the renunciation of force. The FRG thereby hoped to avoid any implication that its acceptance of Germany's present borders was final. Scheel also suggested a separate letter on German unity. At first the Soviets demurred. Gromyko said that gaining internal acceptance of the May 22 document in the Soviet Union had been a complicated

---

52. Appropriately, Valentin Falin, who headed the Third (European) Section of the Soviet Foreign Ministry and who was a participant in the Bahr-Gromyko negotiations, later remarked that in 1970 it was still too early to loosen the FRG's ties to the Atlantic alliance. See Baring, *Machtwechsel*, p. 219.

53. See Helga Haftendorn, *Abrüstungs- und Entspannungspolitik zwischen Sicherheitsbefriedigung und Friedenssicherung* (Düsseldorf: Bertelsmann Universitätsverlag, 1974), pp. 306–13, 319–22.

and painful process, and warned that demands for changes in its text only raised questions about Bonn's seriousness. Valentin Falin, a highly placed Soviet Foreign Ministry official who specialized in German affairs, also opposed altering the Bahr paper, and suggested that if it were to be defeated in the Bundestag as written, then the time was simply not yet ripe for a Soviet–West German accord. Scheel was ready at this juncture to return home empty-handed.

Matters were quickly resolved, however, starting with meetings in Gromyko's dacha on August 2. The Soviets agreed to link the notion of the inviolability of the borders to the clause on renunciation of force. They also agreed to remove a passage referring to the FRG's willingness to conclude an agreement with the GDR and to work for the admission of both German states to the United Nations. Most important, Gromyko accepted Scheel's text of a separate letter acknowledging West Germany's right to seek reunification. Finally, the Soviet foreign minister, who refused to discuss the Berlin question on the grounds that it was strictly a four-power matter, made a statement at the FRG's request confirming that the treaty did not violate four-power prerogatives regarding Berlin. On August 7 Scheel and Gromyko initialed the historic agreement.[54]

The Soviet–West German Renunciation of Force Treaty was signed in Moscow by Brandt, Scheel, Kosygin, and Gromyko on August 12. Shortly before the signing, a West German embassy official delivered the "Letter on German Unity" to the Soviet Ministry of Foreign Affairs.[55] Only in April 1972, as the Bundestag was debating ratification of the treaty, did the Soviets publicly acknowledge the letter's existence.

While in Moscow, Chancellor Brandt informed Brezhnev that the treaty could not be ratified before the Berlin problem was settled. Although the Soviets never formally consented to this *"Berlin-Junktim"* (Berlin connection) as a quid pro quo for ratification, they fully appreciated its importance for the West German government. Bahr himself had communicated this message to Gromyko in their initial discussions.[56] Moreover, the Soviets realized that ratification would be difficult enough in the best of circumstances, given the SDP-FDP coalition's slender twelve-vote majority in the Bundestag and opposition to the treaty by key Christian Democratic leaders, as well as some Free Democrats.

The GDR's first reaction to the treaty was one of guarded approval. It was not long, however, before East German leaders, including Ulbricht,

---

54. For an inside account of the negotiations based on Scheel's private papers, see Baring, *Machtwechsel*, pp. 332–49. For the texts of the treaty and the "Letter on German Unity," see Lawrence Whetten, *Germany's Ostpolitik* (London: Oxford University Press, 1971), pp. 224–25, 227.

55. Baring, *Machtwechsel*, p. 342.

56. Ibid., p. 322.

began beating the drum once again for de jure recognition. On August 14 the GDR Council of Ministers issued a statement describing normal diplomatic relations with the FRG as "logically necessary" to the fulfillment of the treaty's obligations.[57] After a quick meeting of the Political Consultative Committee of the Warsaw Pact, which praised the Moscow-Bonn agreement, Hermann Axen declared that formal relations of this kind were necessary to prevent a war. Even more caustically, *Neues Deutschland* published China's recent charge that the USSR had committed "treason against the sovereignty of the GDR."[58]

At the same time, both the primary and secondary elites in the GDR mounted a new offensive against the West German political leadership. Ulbricht fired the first volley in July, but tended to focus his attack on neo-Nazis and other right-wing forces in the FRG who were out to obstruct the Brandt government's efforts to achieve an East-West understanding. The dominance of this rightist cartel, Ulbricht warned, "would mean preparation for war." The Council of Ministers' statement of August 14 took up this theme, pointing to a state of "permanent tensions" and a possible military conflict as a result of rightist opposition to the treaty. The apogee of the campaign was reached at the end of the year with *Einheit*'s publication of a virulent attack on alleged opponents of the Bonn-Moscow treaty in West Germany. Strangely, these opponents included the Brandt government, which was "striving further toward the greatest degree of similarity with the CDU/CSU" and was defending the August 12 treaty only "halfheartedly."[59]

This sinister view of politics in the FRG conflicted with the prevailing tone of Soviet commentary, which generally maintained a reserved but upbeat attitude on developments in West Germany at this time. *Pravda*, for example, noted that those accustomed to regard the FRG as a tool of aggression now found it difficult to "reconcile themselves to the fact that West Germany, like any other state, has its own interests, and wishes to pursue a policy that takes into consideration the real situation and real possibilities." Other Soviet press reports called on the Brandt government to ratify the treaty, and criticized the treaty's CDU/CSU opponents without accusing them of thirsting for war. The Soviets also offered public assurances of their support for the GDR, both verbally and by organizing Warsaw Pact military exercises on East German territory.[60]

57. *ND*, Aug. 12, 1970, p. 2; Aug. 15, p. 1. *Pravda* on Aug. 15 deleted the controversial passages from the Council of Ministers' statement.

58. For the Warsaw Pact statement, see *Pravda*, Aug. 21, 1970, p. 1; *ND*, Sept. 14, 1970, p. 3, and Sept. 22, p. 6. Beijing's accusations were published in *People's Daily* Sept. 13.

59. *ND*, July 17, 1970, pp. 3–4; Stefan Doernberg and Harald Lange, "Der Vertrag UdSSR-BRD und seine Gegner in der Bundesrepublik," *Einheit*, no. 12, 1970, pp. 1549–60.

60. *Pravda*, Aug. 18, 1970, p. 5; "Nash drug GDR," *Izvestiya*, Sept. 20, 1970, p. 2; W. I. Popow, "W. I. Lenin und die aussenpolitischen Verbündeten sozialistischer Staaten im Kampf gegen den Imperialismus," *DA*, no. 5, 1970, pp. 683–86. On the military exercises, see *Krasnaya zvezda*, Oct. 7, 1970, p. 1.

These assurances notwithstanding, in the first months of the year the SED leadership exerted enormous pressure on Moscow to pay greater attention to East German interests. Ulbricht called for full recognition by Bonn in an article in *Pravda*.[61] After mending fences with Romania, the GDR reinforced its ties with the conservative Czech leadership under Gustav Husak in late October.[62] A month later Ulbricht failed to show up at the Hungarian party congress, and a low-level Politburo official, Friedrich Ebert, was sent to head the SED's truncated delegation. Ulbricht's absence was interpreted as an intentional rebuke of the Soviet hierarchy. Gromyko was quickly dispatched to East Berlin, where he conferred with Ulbricht and other East German leaders. *Neues Deutschland*'s uninformative account of the talks omitted the standard reference to the "unanimity of views" that usually accompanied such high-level meetings.[63]

One of the chief targets of Ulbricht's pique was the four-power Berlin parley. By mid-October Moscow had dropped its demand that the legal status of West Berlin had to be discussed before talks on transit rights to the city could begin. By separating the tortuous issue of status from the more negotiable issue of access, the Soviets removed a major obstacle to a mutually satisfactory aggreement. On November 4 new Soviet proposals signaled even greater flexibility. Abrassimov, who headed the Soviet delegation, spoke optimistically about the prospects of a settlement.[64]

Not so Ulbricht, who sought assurances that any Berlin agreement would meet with the GDR's satisfaction. On November 8 the SED leader repeated an earlier offer to discuss the Berlin transit question directly with the FRG. However, he insisted on the termination of all activity in West Berlin that violated "the interests of the GDR and other socialist states," a condition that could apply not only to the FRG but to the three Western powers as well. Despite Brezhnev's promises to protect the GDR's legitimate interests, on November 29 East German authorities blocked traffic into West Berlin to protest meetings of the CDU/CSU Bundestag delegation in the divided city. Though the Soviets did not veto the action, it is questionable whether they had initiated it. Several days later, at a meeting of the Political Consultative Committee of the Soviet alliance in East Berlin, Ulbricht reportedly lashed out at Brezhnev, accusing the Soviets of undermining the GDR's existence and of validating China's claims of treason through their concessions to the West on Berlin.[65]

61. *Pravda*, Oct. 7, 1970, pp. 4–5.

62. The long-delayed GDR-Romanian Friendship Treaty was signed Oct. 1. For the text, see *ND*, Oct. 2, 1970, pp. 1, 7. For the GDR-Czech communiqué, together with the speeches of Ulbricht, Stoph, Honecker, and others, see *ND*, Oct. 23, pp. 4–5; Oct. 24, pp. 3–4; Oct. 25, pp. 1–2.

63. *ND*, Nov. 20, 1970, p. 1.

64. *ND*, Nov. 7, 1970, p. 2; Wettig, *Community and Conflict*, pp. 82–84.

65. *ND*, Nov. 9, 1970, p. 3; Nov. 25, 1970, p. 3; Nov. 30, p. 4; Wettig, *Community and Conflict*, pp. 87–88.

The GDR's manifest discontent evidently made its mark on the Soviet leadership. The communiqué released at the end of the East Berlin meetings specified that any agreement on Berlin had to correspond to the GDR's "legitimate interests and sovereign rights." The SED Central Committee issued an unusually warm endorsement of the proceedings, and *Neues Deutschland* declared triumphantly, "It is clear: No basic question in Europe can be solved without the participation of the GDR." Ulbricht himself averred that the East Berlin session had "produced clarity and answered complicated questions," and he resumed his adamant stance on de jure recognition by the FRG.[66] The source of the GDR's satisfaction became visible on December 10, as Abrassimov reverted to the Soviet Union's earlier intransigent posture on West Berlin's status at the four-power negotiations. The Soviet media reinforced the new uncompromising tone over the next several weeks. On December 19 the East Germans began obstructing the passage of SPD officials to West Berlin, and on January 12, 1971, in an unusual move, the Soviets blocked Western military traffic bound for the divided city.

It was evident that the GDR had won its point in Moscow. The Kremlin had decided to halt progress toward a Berlin settlement, at least temporarily. Ulbricht gained a further reprieve from Soviet pressures for détente as Moscow's attentions turned toward Poland. In late December, only weeks after the conclusion of a renunciation-of-force treaty between Bonn and Warsaw, Gomulka was removed from office after an outburst of strikes and demonstrations. In view of these events, the Soviets were probably willing at this time to placate Ulbricht, who could always be counted on as the reliable guardian of East Germany's internal stability. Ironically, however, just as Gomulka had fallen victim to Poland's chronic economic misfortunes, Ulbricht's own domestic position was now in the process of falling apart, a result of the incontestable failure of his greatly overextended economic ambitions.

Economic and Ideological Adjustments in the GDR

Indications that the SED's plans to accelerate industrial growth were running into more trouble surfaced in the spring. In March the minister of the chemical industry confessed that the goals that had been set for his sector for 1970 were not going to be met. Günter Mittag admitted

---

66. *ND*, Dec. 3, 1970, p. 1; Dec. 12, p. 1; Dec. 5, p. 1; Dec. 10, pp. 3–4. *Pravda*'s account of Ulbricht's speech Dec. 11 deleted his comments about East German sovereignty over the transit routes to Berlin.

that "some scientists" in the GDR were complaining that the proposed new growth targets and related demands existed "nowhere in the world." The SED Politburo's chief economic specialist nevertheless insisted that the need to overtake the West demanded efforts to "realize what at present does not exist."[67] As of late March, however, fully two-thirds of the next perspective plan's targets in the crucial structure-determining areas had still not been specified, owing in large part to mounting criticism by economists and technocrats of the government's excessively high expectations.[68]

Severe weather in 1969 and 1970 exacerbated these problems. But proponents as well as critics of the current plan targets also blamed other factors. Mittag, in his midyear report on the economy, offered vivid examples of enterprises that failed to conform to the government's economic directives. He also acknowledged complaints that "the plan is too high and must be 'relaxed.' " To remedy this situation, Mittag announced new concentration measures aimed at enhancing the central planning authorities' supervision of lower-level economic bodies. He also emphasized the "class confrontation especially with West German imperialism" as the inspiration for these spirited economic efforts, including the need to "overtake without catching up."[69] As in 1968, East German officials provided unmistakable evidence that foreign policy factors were having a decisive impact on both the resource allocations and the very structure of the East German economy. It was Walter Ulbricht, moreover, who was personally setting the economy's priorities.

What Mittag failed to mention was that these very priorities were responsible for many of the problems he had enumerated in June. By the end of July, the inability of the economy to perform at the levels demanded of it could no longer be denied. Growth in the structure-determining areas was down a full 10 percent from the gains registered the previous year.[70]

These stark realities prompted a thorough reappraisal of the SED's economic course. The first signs of a turnabout emerged on September 8, as the SED Politburo announced another major recentralization of the economy. Unlike previous measures of this kind, the latest effort gave clear indications that the government was abandoning its accelerated development program. The very next day, *Neues Deutschland* admitted the existence of

67. *ND*, Mar. 20, 1970, pp. 3, 4.

68. Werner Halbritter, "Zur Systemcharakter der Verwirklichung der ökonomischen Gesetze," *Einheit*, no. 3, 1970, p. 273. Halbritter was a candidate member of the SED Politburo. For a debate on the "contradictions" arising from the concentration of resources in key sectors, see Autorenkollektiv, "Lenin und die wissenschaftliche Leitung der sozialistischen Gesellschaft (Thesen)," *Wirtschaftswissenschaft*, no. 7, 1970, pp. 961–91.

69. *ND*, June 11, 1970, pp. 3–6; June 12, pp. 3–4.

70. *ND*, July 24, 1970, pp. 3–4; Deutsches Institut für Wirtschaftsforschung, *Wochenbericht*, no. 38, 1970. See also Hans-Dieter Schulz, "Überforderte Planwirtschaft," *DA*, no. 7, 1970, pp. 782–83.

fundamental economic difficulties, and cited West German assessments of the "overexertion" (*Überforderung*) of the East German economy and of "faulty evaluations on the part of the planning organs." Though the paper denounced these sources as "anticommunists," its publication of these criticisms was a sign that similar views were shared within the SED elite.

The article was also notable for its failure to mention "overtaking without catching up" or "dynamic proportioning." Both of these ideas quickly vanished from sight. Similarly, the concept of mastering the scientific-technical revolution "by our own means" was replaced by "plan-based [*planmässige*], proportional development." The essence of this notion was the very opposite of the ideas that animated the accelerated growth campaign of 1968. Emphasis was shifted from development of the structure-determining areas to a more equilibrated scheme that acknowledged the GDR's economic limitations and took account of vital economic tasks that tended to be neglected in the all-out drive for concentrated growth. The demand for proportionality became a central theme of the party journal *Einheit*, while the former strategy of concentrated development was either ignored altogether or buried under an avalanche of criticism.[71]

It was not long before the policy transformations heralded in the journals were implemented. Starting in late September, the term "plan-based, proportional development" or its equivalent appeared in most of the resolutions, decrees, and regulations that now came down from the GDR's central policy-making organs.[72] Even more important, leading SED and government officials took up the concept. At the Central Committee plenum in December, Paul Verner delivered the main report of the Politburo and called for "plan-based, proportional development of the economy" as a means to "correct certain exaggerated ideas and wishes that do not correspond to the material possibilities." In effect, he repudiated Ulbricht's economic agenda of the past two years. Prime Minister Stoph repeated Verner's appeal for proportionality, and offered the extraordinary admission that the heavy concentration on structure-determining areas had produced both disproportions and a reduced rate of development. The resulting problems could be solved only "in the course of many years." Planning chief Gerhard Schürer supported the emerging shift toward proportional development.

71. Werner Kalweit and Otto Reinhold, "Der gesellschaftliche Charakter der Arbeit im Werk Friedrich Engels," *Einheit*, no. 11, 1970, p. 1398; Gerhard Schulz, "Die wissenschaftlich-technische Revolution sozialistisch meistern," ibid., pp. 1402, 1406; Harry Maier, "Höchste Effektivität und Arbeitsproduktivität erfordern umfassende Zeitökonomie," ibid., no. 12, 1970, pp. 1522–25; Rosemarie Winzer, "Ökonomisches Denken sozialistischer Arbeit," ibid., pp. 1507–15.

72. See, e.g., the Council of Ministers communiqué in *ND*, Sept. 24, 1970, pp. 1–2; and the new guidelines for the economy published Dec. 1, in *Gesetzblatt der DDR*, 1970, pt. 2, p. 731.

Table 2. Planned and actual annual growth rates in five sectors of GDR economy, 1966–1971 (percent)

Sector	1966–1970 plan	1969 Plan	1969 Results	1970 Plan	1970 Results	1971 plan
Produced national income	5.0–5.7%	6%	5.2%	6.3%	5.2%	4.9%
Industrial goods production	6.5–7.0	7	8.0	8.5	6.4	5.6
Electronics/ electromechanics	10.4–10.8	13	11.9	15.1	11.0	10.7
Chemical industry	8.4	9	7.6	11.3	8.3	7.3
Labor productivity in industry	7.0–7.7	9	8.0	9.4	5.0	5.4

Source: *Gesetzblatt der Deutschen Demokratischen Republik*, no. 8, pt. 1, 1967, pp. 65–87; *Neues Deutschland*, Dec. 14, 1968, p. 2; Dec. 16, 1970, p. 3; Jan. 22, 1971, pp. 3–4; *Die Wirtschaft*, nos. 51–52, 1968, p. 3, and no. 1, 1970, suppl. 2; *DDR-Wirtschaft: Eine Bestandsaufnahme*, 1974, pp. 355–56.

Moreover, in an open affront to Ulbricht, Schürer claimed that "too many people are working on the elaboration of general documents for the year 2000 and too few on the production and technology of 1971."[73]

Accordingly, the economic plan targets set for 1971 offered a striking contrast to the plans for 1969 and 1970.[74] The goals established for the coming year were quite modest, with both aggregate and sectoral targets, particularly in the structure-determining areas, set well below the norms of the entire previous five-year period (see Table 2).

Another disappointment to the GDR in 1970 lay in relations with the COMECON states, above all with the Soviet Union. As we have seen, the GDR accompanied its appeals for development "by our own means" with repeated calls for intensified cooperation among the COMECON partners, especially in what the East Germans liked to call "international large-scale research." No agreement on this key issue was reached at the COMECON meetings of 1970, however, and the Soviets gave no signs of accepting the GDR's proposals for intensified cooperation in R&D, to be centered on "joint research collectives." In fact, an article in *Einheit* lodged an explicit complaint to this effect.[75]

With the failure of Ulbricht's acceleration program, the economic component of his grand design collapsed. The implications of this collapse for Ulbricht's tenure as first secretary of the SED were ominous. It was therefore not surprising that the SED chief confined himself to foreign policy

73. *ND*, Dec. 10, 1970, p. 5; Dec. 11, pp. 3–5; Dec. 13, p. 5.
74. *ND*, Dec. 16, 1970, p. 3.
75. *ND*, May 15, 1970, p. 2; Stubenrauch and Austel, n. 18 above, p. 741.

issues at the December Central Committee plenum, skirting the thicket of economic problems. As Verner, Stoph, and even Mittag joined in the rising chorus of criticism of the economic course of 1968–1970, many other speakers did not even mention Ulbricht by name, a rare occurrence. The same thing happened at the December Volkskammer meeting, at which Ulbricht did not speak at all.

Ulbricht's ideological schemes were also encountering resistance. On September 22 *Pravda* published a critical review of his *Political Economy of Socialism and Its Application in the GDR.* At a conference in Prague the following month, Soviet and other socialist-bloc ideologists criticized Ulbricht's theory of socialism as an independent historical formation. Moreover, the Soviets showed little interest in Ulbricht's plea in November for greater collaboration on theoretical problems.[76]

Meanwhile, a new wrinkle in East Germany's campaign against the SPD and "Social Democratism" developed in the fall, and it was not Ulbricht who first articulated it. On September 13 Hermann Axen, chief of the SED Central Committee's International Department, declared the GDR's firm resolve "to further delimit [*abgrenzen*] our workers-and-peasants' state from the imperialist Federal Republic in all areas." Willi Stoph repeated this pledge three weeks later. Rejecting Brandt's talk of the "unity of the nation," Stoph said that in relations between the two German states "there inevitably occurs an objective process of delimitation [*Abgrenzung*] and not of rapprochement." Erich Honecker spoke in similar terms.[77] Though the *Abgrenzung* theme was consistent with Ulbricht's anti-SPD rhetoric, it would later be used by the post-Ulbricht leadership as an ideological defense against West Germany once Soviet détente policy made inter-German cooperation inevitable. Whether Axen, Stoph, and Honecker were already planning for this eventuality in the fall of 1970 cannot be determined with any certainty. It is quite possible, however, that they and other SED officials saw the handwriting on the wall by this time, and recognized that Moscow fully intended to repulse Ulbricht's last-ditch efforts to block a settlement with the FRG. In fact, it was Stoph who apprised Brandt in October of the GDR's willingness to resume the dialogue with the FRG without first requiring de jure recognition. Despite Ulbricht's efforts to stall these talks by tying them to the Berlin issue, they began on November 27, quite probably at Moscow's insistence.[78]

76. *Probleme des Friedens und Sozialismus,* no. 11, 1970, p. 1662. Other speakers in Prague, including one from the Soviet Union, supported the East German position: ibid., pp. 1653–54; ND, Nov. 15, 1970, p. 3. I am indebted to Klaus Lehmann for pointing out the *Pravda* review to me.

77. ND, Sept. 14, 1970, p. 3; Oct. 7, 1970, p. 4; and see Honecker's article in *Pravda,* Sept. 30, 1970, p. 4; also ND, Oct. 17, 1970, pp. 3–4. See also Norden's speech in ND, June 15, pp. 6–8.

78. William E. Griffith, *The Ostpolitik of the Federal Republic of Germany* (Cambridge: MIT Press, 1978), pp. 201–2.

In any event, by the end of the year the bases of Ulbricht's authority were profoundly shaken. This fact further weakened his position vis-à-vis Brezhnev, whose own domestic power was reinforced by a gathering consensus on détente with Bonn.

Soviet Conceptualizations of Détente at the End of 1970

After the Soviet–West German renunciation-of-force treaty was signed on August 12, most Soviet press commentary praised the agreement. Credit for the treaty tended to be attributed to the consistency of Soviet policy throughout the postwar period. In this view, it was the Federal Republic, not the USSR, that had changed its policy, having finally come to terms with the "realities" of the war's consequences.[79] Indeed, there was considerable merit to this argument. The terms of the August 12 treaty did in fact reflect a fundamental shift in West Germany's willingness to accept the territorial status quo in a formal agreement. Explicitly or implicitly, and through a variety of formulas, this is precisely what Moscow had been demanding over most of the post-1945 period. The Kremlin had never adopted a rigid commitment to de jure recognition of the postwar situation as the sine qua non of détente with Bonn. As we have seen, Khrushchev, Brezhnev, Gromyko, and other high officials had usually demanded the FRG's recognition of "the fact of the existence" of the GDR and its territorial status. In acceding to the Brandt government's refusal to consider de jure recognition, the Soviets were not significantly retreating from past policy positions. On this question, at least, Moscow's policy was essentially reactive to developments in West Germany's foreign policy.

The Soviets were somewhat more prone to alter their policies when it came to economic relations with the FRG. The extent of trade with the West had long been a matter of contention within the Soviet primary and secondary elites. Once Brezhnev came around to the view that more extensive technology imports from Western countries were highly desirable, Soviet economic policy toward the FRG shifted accordingly. In the final months of 1970, the predominance of this view was reflected in the nonacademic press as well as in the leading specialized journals.[80]

79. See, e.g., the article by V. Mikhailov in *Pravda*, Sept. 20, 1970, p. 4, and V. Gantman, "Tekushchiye problemy mirovoi politiki," *MEMO*, no. 10, 1970, p. 59. See also Brezhnev's remarks to this effect in *Pravda*, Aug. 29, 1970, p. 2.

80. A number of articles accentuated the deleterious impact on the United States of intensified Soviet–West European economic cooperation. See, e.g., *Pravda*, July 29, 1970, p. 4, and Oct. 6, p. 4. Also D. Melnikov's article in *Literaturnaya gazeta*, Sept. 2, 1970, p. 4. Others suggested that improved Soviet–West European trade ties might permit the United States to reconsider its embargo policies. See, e.g., *Sotsialisticheskaya industriya*, Sept. 3, 1970, p. 3.

The military aspect of policy toward the FRG, however, ran counter to these policies of diplomatic and economic cooperation. The Soviet military press leveled a constant stream of criticism at the FRG in the months after the August 12 accord was signed. These attacks took aim at the "aggressive essence" of Bonn's foreign policy in general and its "militarist" security policies in particular. Neither orientation was regarded as having changed very much in spite of the renunciation-of-force treaty.[81] *Krasnaya zvezda's* editorial on the treaty consisted mainly of phrases borrowed from *Pravda's* commentary, together with negative references to opponents of the treaty in the FRG.[82] No mention was ever made of the Brandt government's clearly articulated hopes of extending détente to the military sphere, above all through an accord on mutual force reductions in Europe. Nor was there any mention of Bonn's plans to reduce its own military spending in order to devote more funds to social priorities.[83] On the contrary, Soviet military spokesmen at this time openly emphasized the growing importance of nuclear weapons in theater warfare, with unmistakable references to the European front. The need to develop new missile technologies for use in a variety of battlefield situations was a central element of this strategy.[84]

What is especially striking about these pleas for continued military vigilance is that they were shared by Brezhnev and Suslov. Speaking in Baku on October 2, Brezhnev coupled his remarks about the "indisputably" favorable effects of the Soviet–West German renunciation-of-force treaty with grave warnings about the "aggressive forces of imperialism." In view of the West's promotion of the arms race, Brezhnev demanded "constant concern for the reliable defense of the country." At the annual observances of the Bolshevik revolution in November, Suslov adopted views virtually identical to those of Marshal Grechko. Both men characterized the Bonn-Moscow treay as "important," noting that it offered opportunities for improvement

---

Articles calling for more East-West trade included N. Inozemtsev, "Leninskaya teoriya imperializma i revolyutionnye sily sovremennosti," *MEMO*, no. 5, 1970, pp. 3–25, and G. Prokhorov, "V. I. Lenin i novy tip mezhdunarodnykh ekonomicheskikh otnoshenii," *Voprosy ekonomiki*, no. 7, 1970, pp. 15–22.

81. E.g., *Krasnaya zvezda*, Sept. 11, 1970, p. 3; Sept. 18, pp. 2–3.

82. *Krasnaya zvezda*, Aug. 14, 1970, p. 3. Compare this article, which noted some opposition in the FRG press to the treaty, with the article in *Pravda*, Aug. 17, 1970, p. 3, which commented that the general tone of the West German press was not unfavorable to the treaty.

83. On the Brandt government's spending priorities, see Haftendorn, *Abrüstungs- und Entspannungspolitik*, p. 323. Military spending in the FRG, in current dollars, rose from $8.53 billion in 1969 to $8.74 billion in 1970 and $9.61 billion in 1971. Adjusted for inflation, however, real spending actually fell from 1969 to 1970, before rising slightly in 1971. These dips were reflected in the figures for the military budget's share of gross national product (3.6% in 1969, 3.3% in 1970, and 3.4% in 1971), and its share of total government expenditures (28.3% in 1969, 25.9% in 1970, and 26.1% in 1971). See U.S. Arms Control and Disarmament Agency, *World Military Expenditures and Arms Transfers, 1968–1977* (Washington, D.C.: U.S. Government Printing Office, 1979), p. 43.

84. See, e.g., the article by Lt. Col. I. Zavyalov in *Krasnaya zvezda*, Oct. 30, 1970, pp. 2–3.

in Soviet–West German relations. With this statement Grechko in essence formally acknowledged his acceptance of the treaty. The Soviet Union's leading military figure had now signed on to Brezhnev's rapprochement with Bonn. But both Grechko and Suslov also described "imperialism" as aggressive, in Europe as well as in the United States, and warned that forces of revanchism and militarism still existed in the Federal Republic. Accordingly, both officials called for efforts to strengthen the Soviet armed forces, with Suslov vowing that the USSR "will constantly perfect and arm the Soviet army and navy with the most up-to-date weapons." Neither speaker referred to the issue of force reductions in Europe.[85]

Official figures on Soviet defense spending for the 1971 plan period revealed an increase over the previous year. This was the sixth consecutive annual increase since Brezhnev had assumed the helm of the CPSU.[86] Meanwhile, the Soviet government had yet to formulate a definitive policy on strategic arms negotiations with the United States. While a serious debate on arms-control issues took place among influential members of the military and civilian secondary elites, the SALT negotiations did not get under way until November 2, following months of preliminary wrangling.[87] The period following the signature of the renunciation-of-force agreement also witnessed vigorous Soviet efforts to arm Egypt with surface-to-air missiles for use against Israeli bombardments.

In short, the prevailing view of the Soviet leadership in 1970 seemed to favor political and economic détente with the Federal Republic, but there were no clear signs in Moscow of a serious desire for military détente in Europe. Nor was there to be any ideological détente, a position repeatedly affirmed by Brezhnev and other Soviet leaders in their disquisitions on peaceful coexistence.[88]

This differentiated approach to détente was reflected in the major Soviet journals. Several articles underscored the desirability of political and economic agreements with West Germany while bluntly attesting to the limits of such cooperation. One of them, by Dmitrii Tomashevskii (a consistent advocate of political and economic cooperation with the West), was pub-

85. *Pravda*, Oct. 3, 1970, pp. 1–2 (Brezhnev), Nov. 7, 1970, pp. 1–3 (Suslov, Grechko).
86. According to official American sources, Soviet military spending, measured in constant (1976) dollars, rose from $104.6 billion in 1969 to $107.2 billion in 1970 and $109.6 billion in 1971. As a percentage of GNP, however, Soviet defense spending fell from 14.7% to to 13.8% in those years, while also falling as a share of total central government outlays (from 72.6% in 1969 to 64.5% in 1971). See *World Military Expenditures*, p. 61. The International Institute for Strategic Studies provides a figure of 11% of GNP for 1969 and 1970. See *The Military Balance, 1972–1973* (London, 1972), p. 70.
87. On the Soviet arms-control debate during the SALT I period, see Samuel B. Payne, Jr., *The Soviet Union and SALT* (Cambridge: MIT Press, 1980).
88. This view was shared by the SPD, which on Nov. 14, 1970, adopted a resolution reaffirming the sharp distinction between social democracy and communism (cited in Baring, *Machtwechsel*, p. 358).

lished in *Kommunist* immediately after the conclusion of the August 12 treaty. The suasive tone of the essay suggests that its main purpose was to convince erstwhile opponents of rapprochement with Bonn—particularly those in the party apparatus, who were among the most likely readers of *Kommunist*—of the "Leninist" nature of this policy. Tomashevskii noted, for example, that Lenin had "sharply criticized those who do not see or do not want to see new developments, and who cling to the notions of yesteryear." Recalling Lenin's impatience with the leftist conceptions of Bukharin and Trotsky, Tomashevskii pleaded for "political realism," and referred to Lenin's prescription for the "skillful use" of the contradictions between capitalists who seek military solutions to problems and those who "lean toward pacifism." The Soviet Union was therefore justified in making the "compromises that are necessary in the field of foreign policy." Significantly, however, these compromises were acceptable only to the extent that the Soviet government "knew how to find that limit before which it was necessary to demonstrate sobriety." It was imperative, for example, never to lose sight of "the aggressive anti-Soviet efforts of the imperialists." In short, Tomashevkii's article made a strong case for détente with the Federal Republic, even at the price of Soviet concessions, while offering reassurances that this policy implied no retreat from a hard-boiled, conflictual view of East-West relations. A similar article appeared in *Kommunist* a month later.[89]

Other articles zeroed in on Bonn's military policies more directly. Both before and after the conclusion of the August 12 treaty, the main Soviet foreign policy journals printed articles sharply critical of the Bundeswehr under the Brandt-Scheel government. Defense Minister Helmut Schmidt was at times portrayed as enjoying even higher esteem among the West German military than his Christian Democratic predecessors in that office.[90] An article by Daniil Melnikov drew the distinction between the favorable aspects of political-economic relations with the FRG and the unfavorable tendencies of the military relationship with particular sharpness. After a strongly positive assessment of the Soviet–West German treaty and the prospects for economic cooperation, Melnikov harshly denounced Helmut Schmidt, whom he described as "clearly linked with the military-industrial complex."[91] The fact that Melnikov, who had been a persistent

89. D. Tomashevskii, "Leniniskii printsip mirnovo sosushchestvovaniya i klassovaya borba," *Kommunist*, no. 12 (Aug. 13), 1970, pp. 101–13; Peredovaya, "Leninskaya vneshnyaya politika Sovetskovo Soyuza," no. 14 (Sept. 22), 1970, pp. 3–14.

90. L. Khodovskii and L. Istyagin, "Bonnskie alternativy," *MEMO*, no. 1, 1970, pp. 77–84; L. Istyagin, "Gorizonty bonnskoi voenshchiny," ibid., no. 8, 1970, pp. 27–38; N. Glazunov, "The Bundeswehr in FRG Political Life," *IA*, no. 8, 1970, pp. 42–47.

91. D. Melnikov, "Sovetsko-zapadnogermanskii dogovor i razmezhevaniye politicheskikh sil v FRG," *MEMO*, no. 12, 1970, pp. 15–24. For Melnikov's views on Rapallo, see his interview in *Der Spiegel*, Jan. 19, 1970, pp. 90–100. Melnikov believed that there were fundamental differences between Brandt, whom he viewed positively, and Schmidt, whom he regarded as a "rightist" (personal communication, Moscow, June 1987).

advocate of the Europeanist orientation, should make this stark distinction provided additional evidence that Soviet Europeanists had a keen eye for the limits inherent in Bonn's quest for greater independence from the United States. At the same time, Melnikov's insistence on the need to separate Bonn's positive ostpolitik from its negative military alliance with the United States appeared to reflect a crucial distinction in the Soviet leadership's own thinking. In effect, Melnikov's article provided an analytical rationale for the Kremlin's decision to move forward with major agreements with the West Germans on the diplomatic and economic fronts while simultaneously eschewing major European arms-control accords and actually building up Soviet military forces in the European theater. In this sense, the Melnikov article accurately mirrored the emerging consensus within the Soviet decision-making elite on policy toward Bonn in the context of the recently signed renunciation-of-force treaty.

Meanwhile, discussion of U.S.–West European relations continued throughout 1970. Soviet international relations journals published quite a few articles that stressed the ever-sharpening contradictions undermining the Atlantic alliance. Western Europe's growing economic strength and its interest in cooperation with the Soviet bloc received particular notice. Several of these essays adopted a distinctly anti-American tone, frequently conveying a strong Europeanist bias.[92] M. K. Bunkina, who in 1970 published another book on Western Europe's emergence as one of the "power centers" of world capitalism, expressed very similar views. Bunkina appraised this development as a "qualitatively new phenomenon in the world arena" and stressed Western Europe's differences with the United States over a host of economic and political-military issues, especially East-West trade.[93]

An interesting divergence of opinion was evident among these writers, however, on the critical question how U.S.–West European contradictions could be promoted most effectively. Some (such as Tomashevskii and Bunkina) argued that a relaxation of international tensions and an increase in East-West economic cooperation provided the best means for multiplying conflicts among the NATO allies. Others maintained that frictions within the Western alliance could also occur in periods of tension and confrontation. Analysts who pursued this line of argument included Vladimir Gant-

92. E.g., I. Ivanova, "Antikommunizm i kontseptsiya 'atlanticheskovo soobshchestva,'" *MEMO*, no. 6, 1970, pp. 3–10; O. N. Bykov in ibid., no. 10, 1970, pp. 120–21; Yu. V. Shishkov in ibid., pp. 121–22; V. Shavkov, "How to Solve Europe's Vital Problems," *IA*, no. 1, 1970, pp. 11–15; V. Matveyev,"European Security and NATO," *IA*, nos. 2–3, 1970, pp. 88–92, 137; V. Trukhanovsky, "Lenin's Ideas and Contemporary International Relations," *IA*, no. 4, 1970, pp. 13–18, 23; and E. Novoseltsev, "Europe Twenty-five Years Later," *IA*, no. 7, 1970, pp. 15–22.

93. M. K. Bunkina, *Tsentry mirovovo imperializma: Razvitiye i rasstanovka sil* (Moscow: Mysl, 1970), pp. 4, 214–18. At the same time, Bunkina took note of divergences *within* Western Europe, and warned of Bonn's attempts to subordinate the EEC to "aggressive West German interests" (p. 268).

man, who earlier had tended to stress the elements of partnership holding NATO together.[94] The difference between the two positions was of considerable practical importance. Their respective policy implications led in diametrically opposite directions. Soviet decision makers who, like Brezhnev, referred explicitly to the contradictions in U.S.–West European relations would ultimately have to come to their own conclusions as to whether these conflicts were best fostered by détente or by confrontation.

Another policy conundrum that surfaced that year centered on the degree of Western Europe's independence from the United States and the consequences of a more independent stance. In essence, this was a continuation of the "contradictions versus partnership" debate. While the writers just cited clearly favored a Europeanist approach, another line of argumentation was less optimistic about the prospects for Western Europe's autonomy and less positive about its possible repercussions.

Arguing from a Europeanist perspective, L. Vidyasova observed that there was a growing realization in the United States that "over the long haul" West Germany's quest for greater influence within NATO "could well lead to Bonn's abandonment of the policy agreed with the USA." She was further convinced that the settlement of the postwar border question and related issues ultimately "would result in the elimination of problems whose existence itself determined the FRG's orientation towards the USA and NATO." This was an exceptionally blunt articulation of the notion that the prevailing trend in U.S.–West German relations was toward greater separation, a trend that Vidyasova believed could be greatly encouraged by the process of détente now developing between Bonn and Moscow. At the same time she acknowledged the FRG's success in displacing Britain as America's "privileged ally" and in its efforts to gain access to NATO's nuclear planning organs. Vidyasova recommended continuing attention to the "explosive material within the capitalist camp," but she stopped short of predicting or advocating West Germany's eventual neutralization.[95]

A less hopeful perspective was advanced by S. I. Beglov in *SShA*, the new foreign policy journal published by the Institute of the USA. Beglov stressed the Nixon administration's determination to maintain U.S. troops in Europe and to keep its NATO allies "on a common leash." Hence, he argued, it would be "extremely difficult" for Western Europe to free itself from its transatlantic partner. Beglov was especially critical of West Germany, warning of alleged plans by Schmidt and Strauss, in concert with West European "Atlanticists," to establish a European nuclear force within NATO. On a

94. M. Bunkina, "Novy etap mezhimperialisticheskovo sopernichestva," *MEMO*, no. 9, 1970, p. 56; D. G. Tomashevskii, ibid., no. 10, 1970, p. 120; Gantman, ibid., p. 125; Rubinskii, ibid., p. 127.
95. L. Vidyasova, "Shifts in the Alignment of Forces in the Imperialist Camp," *IA*, no. 10, 1970, p. 22.

more promising note, Beglov suggested that Western Europeans who recognized "existing realities" and favored a European security conference were urging the United States to do likewise. He thus suggested that a desirable and realistic goal of Soviet policy should be to get the Europeans to influence American policy in favorable directions. In sum, Beglov's article was essentially America-centered. By drawing attention to the continuing commitments of the United States in Western Europe and to the negative consequences of a more assertive West Germany, it provided arguments against the likelihood or even the desirability of splitting off the FRG from the United States.[96]

The analyses presented by foreign policy specialists in 1970 therefore supplied alternative characterizations of where West Germany might be heading in its relationship with the United States and of the conditions under which U.S.-FRG "contradictions" could be expected to grow. Their ultimate conclusion was that West Germany was unquestionably demonstrating growing autonomy in foreign policy but that its ties to NATO remained strong. Through their explicit endorsement of both propositions, most writers who displayed Europeanist and Americanist inclinations showed how close their views were to the Atlanticist position, which most clearly approximated the outlook of the Soviet leadership.

Conclusions

As the year ended, the Soviet Union could look with satisfaction at the results of its improved relations with Western Europe (Georges Pompidou was another visitor in Moscow in 1970), and especially with the Federal Republic. A consensus seemed to prevail within the leadership on the value of the renunciation-of-force treaty and of expanded Soviet–West German economic ties. But there was an equally visible reluctance to extend détente with Bonn into the military domain, at least for now. Brezhnev stepped forward as the principal architect of this consensus, combining a strong public advocacy of political and economic détente with the Federal Republic with a clear endorsement of strengthened Soviet military capabilities. As in 1969, the general secretary forged this coalition by garnering support for the separate facets of this policy among the leading mem-

---

96. S. I. Beglov, "SShA-Zapadnaya Evropa: Nekotorye aspekty vzaimootnoshenii," *SShA*, no. 6, 1970, pp. 3–13. Another article in *SShA* in its inaugural year noted "an absence of notable enthusiasm" in the Nixon administration for the Soviet–West German renunciation-of-force treaty, but cited a West German newspaper's report of an increasing realization in Washington that efforts to obstruct Soviet–West German relations would only damage U.S. ties with Bonn and NATO. See the unsigned article "Posle podpisaniya dogovora mezhdu SSSR i FRG," ibid., no. 10, 1970, pp. 63–65.

bers of the decision-making elite. Suslov, Kosygin, Podgorny, and Gromyko were on record as favoring political accords with Bonn; Kosygin and Gromyko were equally outspoken on the desirability of greater East-West trade. The decision to defer agreement on arms-control measures while building up Soviet forces, both in Europe and in the strategic balance with the United States, was supported most vocally by Suslov and Grechko. Out of this mesh of diverging preferences Brezhnev was able to weave a coherent consensus that took account of the main policy priorities of each of these key figures while gaining their assent for elements of his policy that some of them might otherwise have opposed. (Suslov and Grechko, for example, did not seem to be especially keen on expanding trade with Bonn, while Kosygin and Podgorny, as we have seen, had expressed greater hopes for arms control.)

As this policy coalition took shape, the most prominent Soviet skeptics of détente with Bonn in 1970 continued to be Shelest and Ponomarev. Shelepin, as noted earlier, may also have voiced concern about the rapprochement with the FRG, but if so, he kept his misgivings out of public view. In the end, all three may have supported the renunciation-of-force treaty. Certainly they would all have supported substantial efforts to beef up the Soviet military.

The result of this internal decision-making process was a conservative conception of détente with West Germany, resting on the fundamental pillars of the postwar political status quo, foreign trade without domestic reform, and the continuing development of Soviet military strength. To be sure, the renunciation-of-force agreement, with its implicit de facto acceptance by Bonn of Germany's eastern borders, was viewed in Moscow as sufficiently important to warrant a certain amount of flexibility in the Soviet negotiating position. However, the Kremlin's decision not to insist on de jure recognition of the GDR did not represent a major departure from past Soviet policy. Likewise, Moscow's reluctance to publicize the "Letter on German Unity" revealed its abiding resistance to Germany's reunification. Still, by signing the August 12 treaty, the Soviets signaled their willingness to consider future concessions to the FRG. The precise nature of these quid pro quo's would become clearer over the next two years.

Meanwhile, discussion and debate continued within the same permissible parameters as in earlier years. Writers who favored Europeanist and Americanist views stressed one or the other of the two sides of the Western alliance while sharing the main assumptions of the Atlanticist position. There were no signs that Soviet specialists on these matters foresaw Western Europe's neutralization or favored a bilateral Soviet-American condominium. While quite a few expressed approval of détente with Bonn, echoes of more hard-line views provided an undercurrent of suspicion and distrust about the FRG's ultimate intentions. The fact that leading exponents of détente with the FRG in the Soviet secondary elite (such as Daniil Melnikov) could underscore the image of a continuing West German military threat, even in the unprecedently convivial atmosphere prevailing in the aftermath of the renunciation-of-force treaty, provided a clear indication that the Kremlin did not intend to relax its ambitious efforts to modernize and enlarge its military forces in the European theater, regardless of this historic turnabout in Soviet–West German relations. On the contrary, the steady expansion of the USSR's conventional and nuclear capabilities on the continent over the next several years was to demonstrate quite sharply that the landmark achievements of 1970 were never meant to extend to the terrain of military confrontation.

Indeed, the conclusion is practically inescapable that the Brezhnev coalition deeply feared the potential political effects of comprehensive disarmament in Europe. After all, the openly proclaimed strategy of the West German government, as articulated explicitly by Willy Brandt, was to achieve the unification of Germany as the end result of a successful process of détente and East-West military disengagement. While a withdrawal of troops and weaponry from the continent might well reduce America's role in Europe substantially, it would also emasculate the Kremlin's controls over Eastern Europe. A West German government that could no longer be portrayed as a serious threat to the security of the region would only accelerate the East Europeans' desire to free themselves from Soviet domination. The Brezhnev leadership was just not ready for that eventuality, especially after having sent troops to Czechoslovakia only two years earlier. To risk potentially irresistible pressures to establish a unified and powerful German state, while at the same time risking the disintegration of Moscow's security buffer in Eastern Europe, would be to jeopardize virtually everything Leonid Brezhnev and his generation of Soviet leaders had fought for in World War II and immediately afterward. The uncertainties of a future of this kind were simply not attractive in comparison with the more clear-cut assurances of a Europe divided into two counterpoised military and ideological blocs.

The year 1970 thus came to a close with markedly different assessments of the situation in the Western community and in Moscow. Many Western observers expressed optimism, at times bordering on euphoria, over the prospects for an end to the cold war in Europe; others offered grim warnings of Soviet machinations aimed at Finlandizing West Germany. The Soviet leadership shared neither of these expectations. For Moscow, the continuation of cold war confrontation was far preferable to a serious military détente. Moreover, the FRG's firm anchorage in the NATO alliance was a perfectly acceptable reality, given the uncertainties of a more independent West German foreign policy course.

As for the GDR, Walter Ulbricht turned out to be the main casualty of the year. With Moscow retaining the last word in policy toward the West, the SED chief was forced to acknowledge the reality of a major rapprochement between the Soviet Union and West Germany. At the same time, the collapse of Ulbricht's technological acceleration program removed the props from under his grandiose scheme for the Soviet bloc's economic development by its "own means." Ulbricht's maximalist grand design was unraveling, and so was his domestic power base. The combination of the Soviets' irritation at his foreign policy intransigence and the East German elite's dissatisfaction with his economic excesses sent unmistakable signals to the other leading members of the SED hierarchy to begin distancing themselves from the first secretary's shattered policies. By the end of 1970, Walter Ulbricht's directive regime was openly disintegrating.

CHAPTER SEVEN

Extending Détente:
1971–1972

THE 24TH Soviet Party Congress confirmed the general consensus on policy toward West Germany which had emerged in 1970. It also confirmed Brezhnev's personal ascendancy to the role of the Soviet Union's principal foreign policy spokesman, a position he had gradually consolidated over the course of three to four years. Brezhnev's style, however, was primarily that of a coalition-builder rather than that of a bold policy innovator forcefully implementing his own design. More specifically, Brezhnev's policy toward the Federal Republic involved a reaffirmation of traditional Soviet commitments to the territorial status quo; a reversal of his own previous views on economic ties with the West; and an acute sensitivity to the preferences of the Soviet military.

Taken together, these strands of Brezhnev's evolving détente policy came together in the Soviet Union's "Peace Program," which the general secretary enunciated at the 24th Party Congress. Brezhnev's speech on March 30 was particularly notable for his renewed emphasis on the "contradictions" at work among capitalist states.[1] The CPSU chief even elaborated on the concept of the "imperialist power centers" advanced earlier in Soviet academic writings. Noting that neither economic integration nor common "class interests" had been able to stem the tide of conflict among the capitalist powers, Brezhnev asserted that the tripartite division of the capitalist camp into separate American, West European, and Japanese power centers had only just emerged as a distinguishable trend in the early 1970s. Brezhnev added that the competition among these three centers was not confined to economic affairs, but increasingly involved political questions.

1. The full text of the speech is in *Pravda*, Mar. 31, 1971, pp. 2–10. See also his additional remarks in ibid., Apr. 10, pp. 1–2.

The resolution adopted at the conclusion of the 24th Congress reiterated this emphasis on intercapitalist contradictions, adding that it was "important to utilize the opportunities" they presented.[2] This represented a marked shift away from the position adopted in the resolution of the 23d Party Congress, in 1966. That document, it will be recalled, specified that the contradictions affecting intercapitalist relations only made the capitalist states more aggressive; it did not mention "opportunities" to be exploited. The new resolution obviously reflected the events of the previous year. It provides textual evidence that the Soviet leadership justified its détente policy at least in part as an effort to take advantage of the political and economic conflicts between Western Europe and the United States.

At the same time, Brezhnev provided a carefully balanced evaluation of West Germany, drawing attention to both "revanchists" and neo-Nazis in the FRG and the "substantial shift" in Soviet–West German relations. He reaffirmed the continuity of the USSR's position "over the whole postwar period" on the inviolability of Germany's borders, and warned that a delay in the ratification of the August 12 treaty by the Bundestag would create a new crisis of confidence in Soviet ties with the FRG, causing the political climate to deteriorate. Brezhnev followed up this warning, however, with the assertion that the problems associated with West Berlin must also be settled. This close juxtaposition of the issues of ratification and Berlin seemed to imply the Kremlin's acknowledgment that the two questions were indeed related. While Brezhnev did not formally accept the Brandt government's Berlin *Junktim*, neither did he explicitly reject it. At the same time, the Soviet leader referred to West Berlin's "special status," rather than to the standard Soviet designation of West Berlin as an "independent political entity."

Brezhnev called on Bonn to "establish relations of equal rights" with East Germany, "based on generally accepted norms of international law." This formula was palpably designed to take account of Walter Ulbricht's repeated insistence on international law as the fundament of inter-German relations, without exactly echoing Ulbricht's more explicit insistence on de jure recognition.

Interestingly, Brezhnev announced Moscow's willingness to consider a reduction of troops and armaments in Central Europe, including "local" (Soviet and other Warsaw Pact) forces, as well as measures to prevent accidental wars. He further declared that the USSR was ready to come to terms on a reduction of military expenditures by the major states. These and other passages in his remarks at the 24th Congress strongly suggest that the Soviet general secretary was aware of the significance of arms-control agreements in the general structure of East-West détente. Moreover,

2. *Pravda*, Apr. 10, 1971, p. 3.

Brezhnev's endorsement of higher investments in agriculture and other branches of the consumer sector of the economy implied a commitment to seek reductions in heavy industry, perhaps with the eventual aim of reducing the rate of growth in military spending. He may have had something of this sort in mind when he observed that a successful SALT agreement would make it possible "to free substantial resources for constructive purposes." Nevertheless, Brezhnev offered no specific proposals for force reductions in Europe or for a cutback in military spending in East and West. He was equally vague as to the current round of strategic arms negotiations with the United States. Soviet behavior at the bargaining table at this time further suggests that the contours of a SALT accord had yet to be worked out in Moscow. In short, Brezhnev appeared to be inching toward some level of military détente with the West, but remained uncertain as to how far he could move in this direction without encountering significant resistance from the Soviet military. For the next several years, Brezhnev would continue to walk this fine line between the desirability of some measure of arms control and his equally firm determination to keep the military on his side and to build up the power and capabilities of Soviet military forces.[3]

Finally, Brezhnev took due note of the successes of the Soviet economy but criticized its shortcomings, especially in science and technology. Accordingly, he renewed his appeals for increased technology transfers from the West.[4]

Gromyko generally hewed to the lines of Brezhnev's scrupulously balanced presentation. After making his customary reference to the Potsdam accords, the foreign minister insisted that West Germany's ratification of the renunciation-of-force treaty, the European security conference, and the four-power Berlin talks must all proceed "in parallel, without waiting for the end of proceedings in one direction before passing on to another." This artfully worded statement appeared to reject Brandt's Berlin *Junktim* without actually doing so unequivocally. Like Brezhnev, Gromyko was noncommittal in his comments on the United States, describing an improvement in U.S.-Soviet relations as possible but denouncing the "zigzags" in American negotiating positions.[5]

Of the known hard-liners, both Shelest and Grechko refrained from making any direct comments about the FRG at the 24th Party Congress. Their silence on the German question appeared to signal that current Soviet

3. For an account of Brezhnev's military and economic priorities at the 24th Congress, see Peter M. E. Volten, *Brezhnev's Peace Program* (Boulder, Colo.: Westview, 1982), pp. 58–75.

4. Some party leaders echoed Brezhnev's call for technology exchanges, but others saw dangers in them. See Bruce Parrott, *Politics and Technology in the Soviet Union* (Cambridge: MIT Press, 1983), pp. 248–50. See also Erik P. Hoffmann and Robbin F. Laird, *The Scientific-Technical Revolution and Soviet Foreign Policy* (New York: Pergamon, 1982), p. 187.

5. *Pravda*, Apr. 4, 1971, p. 4.

policy toward Bonn, at least for now, was a settled matter. Both flailed away at the United States, however, and Grechko proclaimed that the "constant strengthening of the armed forces is an objective necessity."[6]

According to West Germany's ambassador in Moscow, Helmut Allardt, Shelest throughout 1971 remained opposed to abandoning the standard image of West Germany as a hotbed of revanchism.[7] Indeed, the Ukrainian press and local political authorities did their utmost to keep this negative image of the FRG alive. Shelest invariably laced his speeches with reminders of the ferocity of the German invasion, while the press reported on the discovery of Nazi execution sites in the Ukraine in September and December 1970 and demanded that the West German government hand over the perpetrators.[8] In March 1971 the Ukrainian courts tried and sentenced a group of wartime collaborators. Latvian party publications raised similar charges at this time. None of these accusations was carried in the central CPSU press, however, nor did the Soviet government take them up with the West German authorities.[9]

Significantly, neither Shelest nor the Latvian party chief, Arvid Pelshe, openly criticized the West German government in the immediate aftermath of the renunciation-of-force treaty. In fact, Shelest ascribed "great importance" to the treaty in his speech at the Ukrainian Party Congress on March 17.[10] What seems to have motivated the displays of anti-German sentiment in the Ukraine and Latvia was fear that a relaxation of traditionally hostile portrayals of West Germany—and indeed of the West generally—might undermine the party's rationale for rigid controls on the population and for the sacrifices required by military service and high levels of military spending. Moreover, the authorities had always relied on grim memories of the war to bolster popular support of the Communist Party as the mobilizer of the great patriotic victory over the Germans. This propaganda function took on particular significance in the non-Russian republics that had suffered under the Germans, as it was used in an attempt to build emotional ties not only between the party and the population but also between the non-Russian communities and the Russian-dominated central political hierarchy. Whether the Soviet authorities were very successful in these efforts is of course questionable.

To be sure, the central authorities in Moscow were not unaware of the significance of this kind of propaganda; they had used it themselves for

6. *Pravda*, Apr. 1, 1971, pp. 3–4; Apr. 3, pp. 5–6.

7. Helmut Allardt, *Moskauer Tagebuch* (Düsseldorf: Econ, 1973), p. 381; cited in Gerhard Wettig, *Community and Conflict in the Socialist Camp* (London: C. Hurst, 1975), p. 91.

8. *Radyanska Ukraina*, Dec. 26, 1970, p. 3; cited in *Digest of the Ukrainian Soviet Press*, no. 2 (February), 1971, pp. 26–27.

9. Wettig, *Community and Conflict*, pp. 100–101n.

10. *Pravda Ukrainy*, Mar. 18, 1971, pp. 2–4.

decades, and for much the same reasons. Brezhnev's reference at the 24th Party Congress to the existence of revanchists and neo-Nazis in the Federal Republic is a case in point. It may well have been intended to assure people who had a vested interest in a negative image of the FRG that the Kremlin leadership was not about to ignore the dark side of West Germany in its quest for political and economic cooperation. In any case, Brezhnev and his entire generation of Soviet citizens had their own harsh memories of the war. These powerful personal experiences could not help but color Soviet attitudes toward Germany, and particularly the attitudes of the political and bureaucratic elite, most of whom were old enough to have lived through the war as adults.

Meanwhile, Walter Ulbricht was almost sheepish in his remarks at the 24th Party Congress. He avoided his usual inflammatory rhetoric and devoted the main portion of his speech to the theme of East Germany's loyalty to the USSR and its other allies. Ulbricht specifically disavowed any attempt to forge a special "German road to socialism," and did not refer to the "developed societal system of socialism" even once. Nevertheless, Ulbricht displayed his pique at the Soviet leaders in more subtle ways, indulging once again in his reminiscences of Lenin, failing to condemn China, and neglecting to mention Brezhnev's name in the SED's message of greetings to the CPSU.[11]

By the beginning of April, however, it was increasingly evident that Ulbricht's speech would be his last appearance at a Soviet party congress. With Brezhnev's position at the helm of Soviet foreign policy clearly established and with Poland restored to order under Edward Gierek, the Soviet Union was now ready to resume its pursuit of a diplomatic accord on Berlin.

Ulbricht's Removal from Power

During the first three months of 1971 Walter Ulbricht tempered his anti-Bonn polemics only slightly and persevered in his efforts to derail the Berlin negotiations. The importance he attached to preventing an agreement on rights of access to West Berlin, an agreement that would inevitably have inhibited the GDR's ability to interfere with the transit routes, became visible once again at the beginning of the year. In January and February the GDR initiated a series of traffic hindrances as West German political figures journeyed to West Berlin to conduct party and parliamentary business there. The Soviets initially joined in these efforts, imposing restrictions on

11. *ND*, Apr. 1, 1970, pp. 1–2. Note that the SED's greetings to the CPSU did mention the "developed societal system of socialism" in the GDR.

Western military traffic on January 11 and 12. They also offered verbal support for the GDR's actions at the end of the month. East Germany followed up these efforts with proposals to discuss the Berlin situation, including a possible Easter pass arrangement, with the West Berlin authorities.[12] Once these talks got under way in March, however, the GDR made it clear that it wanted to discuss the touchy issue of West Berlin's legal status, a matter the West regarded as the exclusive preserve of the four powers.[13]

The Soviets now began a slow retreat from their earlier show of support for the GDR on Berlin. On February 8 Soviet representatives at the quadripartite negotiations were more conciliatory than they had been in weeks. And in mid-February, with Ulbricht in Moscow, East German authorities put up no traffic obstructions to the SPD Executive Committee as it traveled to Berlin for a formal meeting.[14] Despite these hints of movement toward a Berlin settlement, the Soviets nevertheless remained entrenched in an intransigent negotiating position at the four-power talks, as reflected in Abrassimov's proposals of March 26.

While reports circulated in the West that Ulbricht was trying to make common cause with Soviet officials who were unsympathetic to détente at this time, such as Shelest,[15] the SED chief kept up his barrage of propaganda assaults on West Germany. His targets included not just neo-Nazis and the opponents of the renunciation-of-force treaty in the CDU and CSU (who were also stigmatized in the Soviet press) but also the leaders of the SPD (who were not).[16] Ulbricht also reiterated his demand for de jure recognition, a demand that was not repeated in the communiqué issued by the Warsaw Pact foreign ministers at the end of their meeting in Bucharest in late February.[17]

Ulbricht proved to be just as unrelenting in his ideological convictions as he was in his opposition to détente with Bonn. Speaking at a Central Committee plenum at the end of January, Ulbricht unveiled the agenda for the next SED party congress, scheduled for mid-June. The main address, to be delivered by Ulbricht himself, was to be titled "The Developed Societal System of Socialism in the 70s." Erich Honecker was also scheduled to address this topic. Elaborating on these plans, Ulbricht restated the importance of the GDR's conceptualization of socialism as a "total system," and hinted at the development of another of his pet ideological themes, the

---

12. See Stoph's letter to Schütz, ND, Feb. 26, 1971, p. 1.
13. Honoré M. Catudal, Jr., *The Diplomacy of the Quadripartite Agreement on Berlin* (West Berlin: Berlin Verlag, 1978), p. 151.
14. Wettig, *Community and Conflict*, p. 92.
15. Ibid., pp. 91–92.
16. See, e.g., Ulbricht's speech of Dec. 17, 1970, in ND, Jan. 14, 1971, p. 4. *Pravda*'s account of the speech deleted passages offensive to the SPD.
17. See Ulbricht's remarks in ND, Jan. 1, 1971, p. 1, and Jan. 10, p. 2. The Bucharest communiqué is in *Pravda*, Feb. 20, 1971, p. 1.

"socialist community of man."[18] Ulbricht's failure to mention the concept of *Abgrenzung* lent substance to the notion that this term implied the GDR's eventual acceptance of some kind of rapprochement with Bonn.

Though his ideological pretensions remained undiminished, Ulbricht nevertheless signaled a retreat from his economic ambitions. Acknowledging "serious disproportions" in the East German economy, Ulbricht in January threw his weight behind efforts to safeguard the "plan-based, proportional development" of the GDR's economic system. Without pointing to his own responsibility in promoting the very distortions he now admitted, Ulbricht in effect practiced an implicit form of self-criticism when he conceded that the principle of proportionality had been "damaged," and that economists had warned against excessive concentration on specific sectors the previous year.[19]

To be sure, the failure of Ulbricht's economic concentration program was his Achilles' heel. Together with his obstreperousness on foreign policy and his assertiveness in matters of Marxist doctrine, both of which rankled the Soviet leadership, it made the SED chief's political survival increasingly problematic. No doubt sensing the danger, Ulbricht on February 8 began a series of trips to the USSR to consult with Soviet leaders. During his five weeks there he conferred personally with Brezhnev on at least three occasions. (On returning home from one of these trips on March 14, Ulbricht was welcomed in East Berlin only by Albert Norden and state security chief Erich Mielke, the two most outspoken hard-liners in the SED Politburo.) Precisely when Moscow finally decided to depose him cannot be pinpointed, but it was probably during the first twelve days of April.[20] This timing would seem to confirm the notion that the 24th CPSU Congress had agreed to proceed with Brezhnev's détente policy toward West Germany. Ulbricht's failure to accompany Honecker, Stoph, Verner, and Axen on a quick tour of Soviet cities in early April provided the Soviets with an opportunity to discuss Ulbricht's removal with the SED's other leading personalities. In the course of their travels, the East Germans made statements that differed markedly from Ulbricht's favorite themes. Honecker, for instance, denounced Mao Zedong and alluded to the GDR's "common coordinated policy" with the USSR. Stoph insisted that East Germany was "learning from the experience of the CPSU."[21] None of them mentioned Ulbricht.

On April 3 *Pravda* listed Honecker's name behind Stoph's, in accordance

18. *ND*, Jan. 29, 1971, p. 1; Jan. 30, p. 4.
19. *ND*, Jan. 30, 1971, pp. 3, 5. Axen discussed the GDR's economic difficulties in even greater detail than Ulbricht at the January plenum. See *ND*, Jan. 29, 1971, p. 3.
20. Myron Rush, *How Communist States Change Their Rulers* (Ithaca: Cornell University Press, 1974), p. 199.
21. *ND*, Apr. 5, 1971, p. 3; Apr. 6, 1971, p. 3.

with Soviet-bloc protocol. The next day, however, Honecker was suddenly listed ahead of Stoph, a sure sign of the SED secretary's political elevation in Soviet eyes. As other indications of Ulbricht's impending demise multiplied,[22] the embattled SED leader delivered a spirited defense of the "developed societal system of socialism" in a speech bearing the valedictory title "The Historical Mission of the Socialist Unity Party of Germany." It was to be his penultimate public appearance. After a visit to Moscow set for April 26 was abruptly canceled, Ulbricht on May 3 delivered his resignation speech before the SED Central Committee. Claiming that his advanced age compelled him to place the party leadership "in younger hands," Ulbricht nominated his long-designated heir apparent, Erich Honecker, as his successor. "Frankly," Ulbricht said, "my decision did not come lightly."[23]

Honecker Takes Over

Erich Honecker's assumption of the office of first secretary of the SED represented a personal triumph for a man who had devoted a lifetime to the cause of German communism. The son of working-class communists from the Saarland, Honecker had spent ten years in Hitler's prisons before taking his place beside Walter Ulbricht and other party leaders. After earning his stripes as the head of the SED's youth movement, Honecker rose through the upper ranks of the party as one of Ulbricht's most favored protégés. It was Honecker who was entrusted with the sensitive task of overseeing the construction of the Berlin wall.[24]

Honecker's close ties to Ulbricht did not result in any particular loyalty to Ulbricht's political legacy once power changed hands, however. The rapidity with which the SED leadership repudiated the cardinal tenets of Ulbricht's economic and ideological policies was truly astonishing. Moreover, the acerbic tones adopted by Honecker and other Politburo figures in denouncing these policies, at times bordering on mockery, suggested that a number of Ulbricht's personal initiatives had been held in disrepute by his colleagues for quite some time before his ultimate departure from office.

Honecker, in fact, appeared to be distancing himself from Ulbricht as early as 1970, if not sooner. To be sure, he had frequently echoed Ulbricht's call for de jure recognition (and continued to do so even after Ulbricht's

22. See N. Edwina Moreton, *East Germany and the Warsaw Alliance* (Boulder, Colo.: Westview, 1978), p. 185; William E. Griffith, *The Ostpolitik of the Federal Republic of Germany* (Cambridge: MIT Press, 1978), p. 205.

23. *ND*, Apr. 22, 1971, p. 4; May 4, 1971, p. 1. A new, largely ceremonial post was created for Ulbricht, that of chairman of the SED. He was also allowed to retain his positions in the Politburo and as head of the Staatsrat.

24. For a biography, see Heinz Lippmann, *Honecker and the New Politics of Europe*, trans. Helen Sebba (New York: Macmillan, 1972).

removal, as we shall see) and he had explicitly linked the GDR's economic policies of 1969 and 1970 to the challenges emanating from West Germany, lending his own voice to the "by our own means" campaign. Nevertheless, Honecker tended to back away from such slogans as "overtake without catching up." And while he had joined in the SED's vehement anti-SPD rhetoric, Honecker's adherence to the notion of *Abgrenzung* at the end of 1970 probably signaled his acceptance of a normalization of inter-German relations that would fall shy of de jure recognition.

Certainly by early 1971 Honecker was making conscious efforts to pull away from Ulbricht and ingratiate himself with Moscow. In his speech before the SED Central Committee in January, Honecker went out of his way to place more emphasis on the GDR's "firm integration in the socialist commonwealth" than Ulbricht was prone to do. Honecker also failed to mention the "developed societal system of socialism"—a central theme of Ulbricht's speech—and referred instead to the "further development of socialist society" in the GDR. Subsequently, in an article for the March issue of *Einheit*, Honecker called for "realistic" economic policies and did not even mention Ulbricht's name.[25]

The extent of his rejection of Ulbricht's legacy became all the more apparent in Honecker's speech at the Eighth SED Party Congress in June. The new SED chief acknowledged "disproportions" in the GDR's recent economic development, and warned that the East German economy "cannot manage too many miracles outside the plan," promising instead a "realistic appraisal of our strengths and possibilities." In a backhanded critique of Ulbricht's "overtake without catching up" campaign, Honecker cautioned that labor productivity "will not grow by leaps and bounds." Honecker also redefined the "main task" of the next five-year plan. Whereas Ulbricht had once proclaimed this task in terms of "strengthening the GDR on all sides," in accordance with his goal of accelerated technological development, Honecker now characterized the plan's principal aim as the "further increase in the material and cultural standard of living of the people." This new emphasis on the East German consumer represented a sharp break with Ulbricht's priorities, and also reflected the urgency of raising living standards in the GDR so as to gird the population against the coming influx of better-off West Germans once an agreement on normalizing inter-German relations was reached. Appropriately, Honecker reiterated his commitment to the "plan-based, proportional development of the economy." Not coincidentally, Leonid Brezhnev used virtually identical words in describing the economic requirements facing all the socialist countries in his own speech before the Eighth SED Congress. Honecker also substituted the Soviet-inspired term "developed socialist society" for the

25. *ND*, Jan. 31, 1971, pp. 3–4; Erich Honecker, "Unsere Partei—die grosse umgestaltende Kraft der Gesellschaft," *Einheit*, no. 3, 1971, pp. 243–50.

now discredited "developed societal system of socialism" as the official formulation of East Germany's current phase of development. In addition, he explicitly repudiated Ulbricht's theory of socialism as a relatively independent historical formation.[26]

Further renunciations of Ulbricht's economic and theoretical ideas followed in October in a lengthy speech by Kurt Hager, the SED Politburo's preeminent authority on ideology. Hager ridiculed the systems-theory jargon of the "developed societal system of socialism" as "phrasemongering" (*Wortgeklingel*), charging that it had led to confusion in the economy and digressions from Marxism-Leninism. In adopting the more acceptable notion of the "developed socialist society," Hager announced that the GDR was now "in full harmony" with the CPSU. Significantly, Hager also stepped away from Ulbricht's excessive optimism about the economic potential of socialism. After noting that labor productivity in socialist states does not grow automatically, but can "temporarily stop" growing, Hager took an unusually positive view of capitalism. "We do not overlook the fact," he said, "that imperialism still commands a significant scientific-technical potential; nor the fact that, in the course of the last decade, its scientific-technical progress has accelerated in various domains."[27] This statement not only aligned the SED leadership behind Brezhnev and other Soviet proponents of greater East-West economic cooperation; it also signaled the SED's approval of a more westward-looking economic orientation for the GDR in the coming years. Finally, Ulbricht's *Political Economy of Socialism and Its Application in the GDR* was withdrawn from circulation and replaced by the German translation of a more orthodox Soviet tome.

The Berlin Settlement

The extraordinary efforts to cast aside Ulbricht's economic and ideological policies were duplicated, albeit somewhat less dramatically, in the realm of foreign policy. The first indication of a shift in Moscow's direction came in Honecker's maiden speech as first secretary on May 3. The new SED chief adopted a considerably less obdurate stance on Berlin than his predecessor, referring to West Berlin merely as a "city with a special

---

26. For Honecker's remarks, see *Protokoll der Verhandlungen des VIII. Parteitages der Sozialistischen Einheitspartei Deutschlands* (East Berlin: Dietz, 1971), pp. 57, 61–62, 110. For Brezhnev's comments, see ibid., p. 178.

27. Kurt Hager, *Die entwickelte sozialistische Gesellschaft* (East Berlin: Dietz, 1972), pp. 12, 25–28, 43, 61. See also Walter Völkel, "Das Problem der ideologischen Integration: Anmerkungen zur Sozialismusdiskussion in der DDR und der Sowjetunion," *Deutschland Archiv*, no. 10, 1973 (special issue), pp. 64–73.

political status" rather than as an "independent political entity," Ulbricht's customary phrase. As the Soviets picked up the pace of the four-power talks in July and August (perhaps prodded by news of Henry Kissinger's forthcoming trip to Beijing, announced in mid-July), Honecker conferred on several occasions with Soviet officials. After his meeting with Brezhnev in the Crimea, the Soviets on August 11 informed the West of their desire for a speedy resolution of outstanding differences in the negotiations. As the quadripartite talks plunged somewhat frantically into their final phase, the East Germans remained in close contact with Gromyko and Abrassimov.[28] On August 23 Abrassimov informed the Western negotiators of Moscow's approval of the treaty text.

Only one brief flap now arose to delay the signature of the agreement. While working out the details of an accord regulating civilian traffic between the FRG and West Berlin, a team of West German negotiators led by Egon Bahr reported that the East Germans had deliberately mistranslated a section of the quadripartite treaty. The English language version of the accord specified that "ties" between West Berlin and the Federal Republic would be maintained and developed; the East Germans had substituted the word *Verbindungen* for *Bindungen* in their own text of the agreement. (*Verbindungen* implies somewhat looser ties than *Bindungen*.) The Western powers delayed the signing ceremony in hopes that the dispute could be resolved. It could not, however, and ultimately the FRG and the GDR agreed to disagree on the matter. The four powers signed the quadripartite agreement on September 3.

These events, as well as the legal implications of the Berlin agreement, have been amply treated elsewhere.[29] Let it suffice here to make a few observations about the implications of the treaty for Moscow's relations with the GDR and the Federal Republic.

Though Ulbricht's forced resignation removed a major barrier—perhaps *the* major barrier—to Moscow's readiness to come to terms with the Western powers on Berlin, it did not follow that Erich Honecker regarded the terms of the quadripartite accord with equanimity. Honecker was surely aware that the final four-power agreement placed serious constraints on the

28. See the notice issued at the end of Gromyko's visit to East Berlin, *ND*, Aug. 20, 1971, p. 1.
29. See Catudal, *Diplomacy of the Quadripartite Agreement*, pp. 166–91, 233–76; Wettig, *Community and Conflict*, pp. 104–17; Griffith, *Ostpolitik*, pp. 206–8. See also Dennis L. Bark, *Agreement on Berlin* (Washington, D.C.: American Enterprise Institute, 1974); Richard L. Merritt and Anna L. Merritt, *Living with the Wall: West Berlin, 1961–1985* (Durham, N.C.: Duke University Press, 1985); Ronald A. Francisco and Richard L. Merritt, *Berlin between Two Worlds* (Boulder, Colo.: Westview, 1986); and David M. Keithly, *Breakthrough in the Ostpolitik: The 1971 Quadripartite Agreement* (Boulder, Colo.: Westview, 1986). For a Soviet view, see G. M. Akopov, *Zapadny Berlin* (Moscow: Mezhdunarodnye otnosheniya, 1974).

GDR. By declaring that civilian traffic would be "facilitated" and given "preferential treatment," the treaty drastically curtailed East Germany's ability to hinder access to West Berlin. By reasserting four-power prerogatives, it undermined the GDR's claims to sovereignty over the access routes. By requiring an inter-German agreement on transit issues, it compelled East Germany to acknowledge Bonn's authority to negotiate matters pertaining to Berlin. And by pledging that citizens of West Berlin would be able to visit East Berlin under ordinary conditions, rather than on the basis of specially negotiated arrangements, it required the GDR to grant visiting rights to West Berlin residents as a matter of course. These were serious reverses for the GDR. What had changed with Ulbricht's departure was not East Germany's interests but its willingness to challenge Moscow openly. Honecker lacked Ulbricht's personal standing in the councils of the Soviet bloc. While he may indeed have argued against elements of the emerging quadripartite accord in his consultations with the Soviets,[30] in the end he succumbed rather quickly to Soviet pressures for an agreement.

Furthermore, the overwhelming impression conveyed by the East German leadership during Honecker's first months in power was one of willing subordination to Soviet preferences. When Ulbricht spoke of the need to maintain the solidarity of the Soviet alliance, his primary aim was to rally Soviet and East European support for his own conceptions, whether in foreign policy, economics, or ideology. Honecker abjured this approach, and not merely because Moscow would not permit him to do otherwise. His retrenchment from Ulbricht's economic and ideological policies had visible support within the SED leadership even without Soviet prodding. Similarly, it was in the SED's interest to declare a truce with Moscow in order to restore the working consensus that Ulbricht's nonconformity had disrupted. Acceptance of Moscow's foreign policy preferences was essential to stability at the top of the East German hierarchy.

As for the Federal Republic, the four-power accord revealed Moscow's willingness to compromise on Berlin for the sake of gaining ratification of the renunciation-of-force treaty in the Bundestag. Although the Soviets clung to their traditional position on the vital question of the city's status, they took large strides in Bonn's direction when they agreed to permit the FRG to maintain a permanent liaison agency in West Berlin and to conclude international treaties in the city's behalf. Moreover, the agreement to facilitate visits by West Berliners to East Berlin was a significant example of the *menschliche Erleichterungen* the Brandt government was pledged to obtain from its dealings with the East. Questions of interpretation of the treaty's provisions of course remained, and important matters of substance were left untouched by the accords. Nevertheless, the quadripartite agreement

---

30. See Moreton, *East Germany and the Warsaw Alliance*, pp. 187–90.

on Berlin was an achievement of historic proportions. In effect it removed the city from its precarious position as one of the most volatile trouble spots of the postwar world. Meanwhile, it inevitably raised Moscow's expectations of the speedy ratification of the Soviet–West German treaty of August 1970.

The Ratification Process

Several weeks after the conclusion of the four-power Berlin agreement, Willy Brandt met with Leonid Brezhnev at the Soviet leader's Crimean vacation retreat in Oreanda. While Brandt sought to impress his host with West Germany's commitment to unification, Brezhnev announced that the quadripartite accord would not take effect until after Bonn's ratification of the treaties, in effect establishing a reverse *Junktim*. This position was later restated by Gromyko. The communiqué issued on September 18 announced the two leaders' support for a European security conference (with American and Canadian participation), negotiations for mutual force reductions, and the eventual admission of the FRG and the GDR into the United Nations.[31] The Soviets were quite probably cheered by Brandt's statement on his return to West Germany that the FRG was "forming its own opinion" on important international issues, and by the fact that Brandt had not consulted with the United States before accepting the invitation to Oreanda.

The shaky condition of the SPD-FDP's Bundestag majority increasingly jeopardized chances for the smooth ratification of Bonn's treaties with Moscow and Warsaw, however. By mid-October 1971, defections from the ranks of the ruling parties had reduced the government's Bundestag majority from twelve votes to five. Several of these switches of party affiliation were due to misgivings about the ostpolitik pursued by Brandt and Scheel.[32] The alarming dissipation of the government's majority made further Soviet guarantees of progress on Berlin and on inter-German relations imperative.

Accordingly, the Soviets undertook a series of exceptional measures aimed at shoring up support for the treaties in the Bundestag. The first of these efforts occurred in late October, as Brezhnev made an unscheduled stop in East Berlin at a time when the Honecker government was attempting to delay the conclusion of agreements with Bonn and West Berlin on transit matters. These inter-German talks had begun on September 6, but they quickly bogged down over East Germany's refusal to discuss the travel

---

31. For the communiqué, see *Pravda*, Sept. 19, 1971, p. 1. For Brandt's account of the meetings, see his *People and Politics* (Boston: Little, Brown, 1978), pp. 345–55.
32. Arnulf Baring, *Machtwechsel* (Stuttgart: Deutsche Verlags-Anstalt, 1982), pp. 397–99.

rights of West Berliners with the Federal Republic's representative, Egon Bahr. Another problem centered on the GDR's attempt to deny access to West Berlin to various categories of undesirable people, above all those who had fled the GDR. After Brezhnev's personal intervention, Honecker announced his hopes for a "positive conclusion" of the transit talks, and a more forthcoming East German negotiating posture followed.[33] To speed things along, Scheel visited Moscow in November and proposed the simultaneous settlement of the FRG-GDR transit negotiations and the ratification of the treaties in the Bundestag. The Soviets agreed only to study the matter, but were impressed with Scheel's warnings of the possible collapse of the SPD-FDP government. After two more weeks of hard bargaining, the FRG on December 17 came to terms with the GDR on a transit agreement covering traffic between the Federal Republic and West Berlin.[34]

Despite this successful outcome, ratification of the treaties in West Germany was still by no means assured. Additional defections from the SPD and FDP lowered the government's voting edge in the Bundestag to three by the end of April 1972. The Christian Democrats, meanwhile, were embroiled in a debate over their own stance on ratification. Rainer Barzel, Kiesinger's successor as chairman of the CDU, leaned toward ratification, but others, including Strauss, were more inclined to vote against the treaties. The Soviets decided to keep communications open with the CDU, and received Gerhard Schröder in Moscow in January 1971 and Barzel at the end of the year. As the Christian Democrats moved toward a vote of confidence in the Bundestag in the conviction that they could topple the Brandt-Scheel government, the Kremlin continued its efforts to win over the treaties' opponents. Among other things, Moscow agreed to include West Berlin within the provisions of a new trade agreement with the Federal Republic. On April 12, 1972, Gromyko divulged the contents of the "Letter on German Unity" to the Supreme Soviet, and the letter's existence was disclosed for the first time in the Soviet press and on television. Moscow also continued to pressure the GDR for a more accommodating attitude in its current negotiations with West Germany. The East Germans were once again dragging their feet, this time in their talks with the FRG on a general agreement regulating travel between the two states. On April 18, however, Honecker retreated from his earlier demands for diplomatic recognition and an exchange of ambassadors with the FRG, and instead adopted a more ambiguous call for "normal relations."[35] On April 26 a preliminary agreement was reached between the two German states on certain elements of a traffic agreement.

33. *ND*, Nov. 2, 1971, p. 3.
34. For a detailed account, see Catudal, *Diplomacy of the Quadripartite Agreement*, pp. 192–217.
35. See Honecker's statement in Sofia in *ND*, Apr. 19, 1972, p. 3.

The next day the Christian Democrats' confidence motion failed by two votes to unseat the Brandt-Scheel government. In a subsequent Bundestag vote, however, the government lost its majority and fell to exactly the same number of votes as the Christian Democrats.

At this point the Christian Democrats were in a position to demand a parliamentary resolution clarifying disputed points in the treaties with the USSR and Poland. As Barzel (CDU), Strauss (CSU), Genscher (FDP), and Horst Ehmke (SPD) labored over the resolution's text, Moscow's new ambassador in Bonn, Valentin Falin, remained in constant contact with the negotiators in a series of consultations that were quite probably unprecedented in diplomatic history. A resolution acceptable to the four main West German parties was finally drafted on May 9. Its main provisions affirmed that the renunciation-of-force treaties created no legal precedent for the existing borders, which were to be fixed in a peace treaty, and that they did not infringe on four-power responsibilities for Germany as a whole or for Berlin as a whole. After the Soviets initially appeared reluctant to accept these terms, Falin informed Scheel of Moscow's approval of the text on the same evening.

Meanwhile, as the Soviets were taking special steps to gain the Christian Democrats' approval of the treaties, the United States was exerting its own influence in the matter. The Nixon administration, eager for a smooth ratification of the treaties before the president's forthcoming trip to Moscow, informed Christian Democratic leaders of its preference for a favorable vote on the treaties.[36] For the Soviets, the incident presented a striking example of how the United States could use its leverage on its West European allies to adopt policies favored by the Soviet leadership. Even at a time when the West Germans were taking the lead in promoting improved ties with the Kremlin, Washington could at times provide useful support for these endeavors. This fact no doubt reinforced the arguments of Americanists and Atlanticists in the Soviet elite, who generally argued that the United States still had a positive role to play in European affairs, and that Moscow should therefore avoid exclusive reliance on the West Europeans.

As it happened, none of these outside pressures on the Christian Democrats proved effective. Just when Barzel and the government appeared to have the basis for a bipartisan ratification of the treaties wrapped up, Strauss backed out of the deal under strong pressure from expellee organizations. Hopelessly divided, the Christian Democrats decided to abstain from the vote on ratification. This vote took place on May 17, with ratification passing by a margin of 248 to 10, with 238 abstentions.[37]

With the ratification of the treaties, the way was now open for other

36. Baring, *Machtwechsel*, p. 431.
37. For a detailed account, see ibid. pp. 405–47.

important East-West understandings. On May 26 the FRG and the GDR came to terms on an agreement to regulate travel between the two German states by their respective citizens. This accord in turn led to the conclusion of the Basic Treaty between the FRG and the German Democratic Republic on December 21.[38] As this process of inter-German détente unfolded, the SPD and FDP coalition decisively reestablished its parliamentary majority in the Bundestag elections of November 19. Just two days before the elections, Moscow reaffirmed its own support of the Brandt government by agreeing to a $1 billion deal with West German firms to build a steel mill in Kursk.

These events took place within a broader framework of improved relations between the Soviet Union and the United States. On May 14, 1971, Leonid Brezhnev declared that the Soviet Union was now ready to begin negotiations on force reductions in Europe. The quadripartite agreement on Berlin lent an additional impulse to the germinating superpower détente. Negotiations on a strategic arms treaty gathered steam during the following spring, and the SALT accord was signed during President Nixon's visit to Moscow in May 1972. In September the United States and the USSR agreed to start preliminary consultations on a European security conference and on separate negotiations dealing with what the United States called "mutual and balanced force reductions" in Europe (MBFR).

Policy Discussions in the GDR and the Soviet Union

The events just surveyed inspired considerable analysis on the part of Soviet and East German academicians and journalists. As in earlier years, the accents tended to differ between Soviet writings and those published in the GDR (although the reasons for these differences changed somewhat with the replacement of Walter Ulbricht by Erich Honecker). By and large, however, East German analysts showed few signs of disagreement once this transfer of power was completed. Under Honecker as under Ulbricht, the specialist literature on foreign policy in the GDR tended to reflect the main themes and policies laid down by the SED leadership in 1971 and 1972. Soviet analysts, by contrast, once again displayed considerable variety in their interpretations of the occurrences of these years. The main line of division, now more pronounced than ever before, centered on Europeanist as opposed to Americanist orientations, with continuing evidence of manifestly hard-line (or maximalist) views bucking the tide of détente. Moreover, in a pattern of marked continuity with analyses that

38. For an account, see Ernest D. Plock, *The Basic Treaty and the Evolution of East-West German Relations* (Boulder, Colo.: Westview, 1986), pp. 62–87.

appeared in 1970, several Soviet analysts offered favorable evaluations of political and economic cooperation with the Federal Republic together with unfavorable characterizations of Bonn's military policies.

As long as Ulbricht still held formal power in the GDR, assessments of the international and domestic scene appearing in *Deutsche Aussenpolitik* and *Einheit* were divided between Ulbricht's preferences and those that would soon be promoted by First Secretary Honecker. Divergences within the East German secondary elite thus mirrored discussions at the pinnacle of the SED leadership. In two issues that went to press before Ulbricht's retirement, for example, *Deutsche Aussenpolitik* published articles that clearly reflected Ulbricht's attitudes toward West Germany and toward the foreign policy implications of East Germany's "developed societal system of socialism." (One of them was written by Defense Minister Heinz Hoffmann.)[39] The next issues, prepared in mid-April, printed several articles stressing the harmony of East German and Soviet interests, a favorite theme of Honecker's.[40] During these same months, *Einheit* seemed to be under Honecker's control already, as indicated by an article by Honecker himself and by proponents of Soviet-GDR unity and "proportional" development in the economy.[41]

After Honecker's accession to power, both journals overwhelmingly conformed to the foreign policy, economic, and ideological agenda set by the new first secretary. To begin with, direct attacks on the SPD leadership noticeably abated. Now the concept of "adaptation" (*Anpassung*) was trotted out to explain why elements of the West German ruling class, including "right-wing" Social Democratic leaders, had come around to realizing the utility of peaceful coexistence with the socialist states and were therefore willing to make important "concessions."[42] At the same time, "Social Democratism" as an ideology was sharply attacked, along with West German culture, in keeping with the Honecker leadership's *Abgrenzung* doctrine.[43]

39. Heinz Hoffmann, "Erfolgreiche Militärpolitik der Sozialistischen Einheitspartei Deutschlands," *DA*, no. 2, 1971, pp. 226–37; Werner Hänisch and Joachim Krüger, "Zur Dialektik von Innen- und Aussenpolitik in der Strategie und Taktik der SED," ibid., pp. 433–50.

40. See, e.g., the articles in *DA*, no. 4, 1971, by Peter Florin (pp. 646–61), Harry Ott (pp. 662–80), and Gerhard Brendel (pp. 681–92).

41. Honecker's article is cited in n. 25 above. See also Karl-Heinz Stiemerling, "Planmässige, proportionale Entwicklung, Effektivität und Stabilität," *Einheit*, no. 3, 1971, pp. 269–80; Paul Markowski, "Die internationale Politik der SED," ibid., no. 4 (Mar. 26), 1971, pp. 383–94; and Gerhard Schilling and Horst Steeger, "Proportionalität in unserer sozialistischen Planwirtschaft," ibid, no. 5 (Apr. 26), 1971, pp. 539–50.

42. Otto Reinhold, "Der Imperialismus der BRD," *Einheit*, no. 6, 1971, pp. 758–68; Lutz Maier, "Dialektik der Anpassung," ibid., no. 4, 1972, pp. 514–24.

43. Dieter Ulle and Klaus Zierman, "Zur Kulturkonzeption des Imperialismus der BRD," *Einheit*, nos. 7–8, 1971, pp. 890–900; Friedrich Richter and Vera Wrona, "Ideologie des Sozialismus in der Gegenwart," ibid., no. 2, 1972, pp. 221–27. See also the articles under the theme of "coexistence and the class struggle" in ibid., no. 8, 1972, pp. 972–1004.

Although East German analysts (and policy makers) tended to devote more attention to the ideological dangers of the SPD than their Soviet counterparts, their strident *Abgrenzung* campaign was nevertheless in full conformity with the general Soviet position that there could be no ideological détente between socialism and capitalism. Conformity between Soviet and East German views was also observed in the treatment of West German military policy. Like many Soviet writers, authors in the GDR expressed dire warnings that the West German military danger remained undiminished, despite Bonn's acceptance of peaceful coexistence in other areas.[44] Indeed, the dominant theme in East German specialist writings now was the unity of Soviet and East German positions in every aspect of policy. As suggested earlier, whereas Ulbricht had demanded greater solidarity *against* Moscow's détente policies, Honecker promised greater solidarity *with* Soviet policy. The literature published in the GDR's leading journals duly registered this shift.[45]

Soviet analysts, as usual, were not so monotonous. Diverging accents between Europeanist and Americanist orientations were particularly noticeable. By and large, the Europeanists continued to place primary emphasis on the contradictions eating away at the fabric of Western unity, and above all on Western Europe's growing "independence" from the United States. What was especially striking about the Europeanist argument in 1971 and 1972, however, was a tendency to be outspokenly critical of American foreign policy. Coming at a time when cooperation between the United States and the Soviet Union was progressing toward a postwar high, these harsh critiques of U.S. policy were jarringly out of tune with the prevailing tenor of Soviet foreign policy.

IMEMO's Oleg Bykov, for example, berated the Nixon administration's notion of an "era of negotiations" in 1971, denouncing it as indistinguishable from confrontation. Western Europe, by contrast, was pursuing "a more independent line." Despite the United States' attempts to strengthen its dominance in NATO, the West Europeans, in Bykov's view, were manifesting their readiness "to meet the socialist states halfway" on European security. In the spring of 1972 Bykov again confirmed Western Europe's growing independence and averred that by trying to turn a future European

44. Reinhold, "Imperialismus der BRD," p. 767; Werner Hübner, "Ideologische Klarheit und Wehrbereitschaft," *Einheit*, no. 10, 1972, pp. 1305–13.
45. E.g., Gerhard Brendel, "Die Aussenwirtschaftsbeziehungen der DDR mit den RGW-Ländern unter den Bedingungen der sozialistischen ökonomischen Integration," *DA*, no. 6, 1971, pp. 1058–67; Siegmar Quilitzch, "Die UdSSR—Hauptkraft des sozialistischen Weltsystems," *DA*, no. 2, 1972, pp. 240–55; Gerhard Hahn, "Das sowjetische Friedensprogramm in Aktion," *DA*, no. 6, 1972, pp. 1045–55; Gerhard Schulz and Heinrich Swoboda, "Ein neues Werk zur politischen Ökonomie des Sozialismus," *Einheit*, no. 12, 1971, pp. 1409–14. *DA* and *Einheit* also published quite a few articles by Soviet writers in 1971 and 1972.

security conference to its own advantage, the United States was "isolating itself" from the Europeans. Later he portrayed American cold warriors as concerned about a "loss of control" over the détente process in Europe.[46] Daniil Melnikov expressed similar notions. In an article that went to press at the end of 1971 he argued that the process of West European economic integration enhanced Western Europe's independence from the United States, producing "polycentrism" within the capitalist camp. After criticizing American policy as designed solely to strengthen NATO as a "superbloc" and to create a "position of strength" vis-à-vis the Soviet Union, Melnikov took a much more optimistic approach to Western Europe. Noting that peaceful coexistence was a "universal" principle applicable to all states in the world, Melnikov stated that it had a "special meaning" in Europe. This was tantamount to saying that Europe should be the main focus of Soviet détente policy. Melnikov also quoted Brezhnev's remarks at the 24th Party Congress concerning the three centers of capitalist rivalry—the United States, Western Europe, and Japan.[47]

In a piece published in May 1972, Melnikov looked more specifically at the U.S.–West German relationship. After noting that the FRG's membership in NATO "limited" its independence in foreign policy, Melnikov stressed that Bonn's political role in the Western community had "grown significantly." In particular, West Germany's economic disagreements with the United States could not help but affect political relations between the two states, while Bonn's recent treaties with the socialist countries had "broadened West Germany's room for maneuver" in its dealings with the United States. Melnikov noted that Washington had greeted the news of these treaties "guardedly," while Dean Acheson, George Ball, and many American newspapers had openly expressed disagreement with Brandt's ostpolitik. Melnikov then quoted a recent speech by Brezhnev signaling the USSR's hopes for an SPD-FDP victory in the forthcoming Bundestag elections.[48]

Despite these singularly favorable remarks about the current West German government's general political and economic orientation, Melnikov took strong exception to Bonn's military policies. He was particularly critical of Helmut Schmidt, whom he characterized as seeking close military collaboration with the United States and a "more effective" West German military role in NATO. Given these contrasting images, Melnikov's position

46. O. Bykov, "O nekotorykh chertakh vneshnepoliticheskoi strategii SShA," *MEMO*, no. 4, 1971, pp. 53–64; his remarks in ibid., no. 5, 1972, pp. 100–102; and "Zaokeanskoye 'prisutstviye,'" ibid., no. 11, 1972, p. 48.
47. D. Melnikov, "Zapadnoevropeiskii tsentr imperializma," *MEMO*, no. 1, 1972, pp. 14–30.
48. D. Melamid [D. Melnikov], "Vozmozhnosti i perspektivy 'vostochnoi politiki' V. Brandta," *MEMO*, no. 5, 1972, pp. 95–98. Ball was under secretary of state for European affairs in the Johnson administration.

once again seemed to favor political and economic détente with Bonn, but not a serious military détente. He made no mention, for example, of the Brandt government's repeatedly articulated hopes for a significant reduction of forces in Europe. Melnikov had nothing positive to say about the upcoming Nixon visit and the attendant warming trend in U.S.-Soviet relations. This evident bias against the United States only accentuated his outspokenly Europeanist inclinations.

Another article attributing great significance to U.S.–West German differences appeared in April. Asserting that the United States was actually exercising pressure on the FRG to hinder the rapid entry into force of the treaties with the USSR and Poland, the author contended that the Brandt-Scheel government had "guaranteed the FRG greater independence than before in its relations both with the West and with the East." He quoted Willy Brandt's statement after the Oreanda meeting on Bonn's new-found freedom to deal with the Russians without having to go through other Western powers, and he even cited Helmut Schmidt favorably as saying that the United States was having a difficult time getting used to the new situation.[49]

The Europeanist orientation is also evident in other articles published in 1971 and 1972.[50] Curiously, not all of them placed West Germany at the forefront of their analyses of Western Europe's growing self-assertiveness. Several of them conspicuously listed France in first place, ahead of the FRG. At times these efforts to accord Soviet-French relations a certain pride of place were accompanied by warnings that one must have "no illusions" about NATO or about West Germany's unabated military buildup.[51] These arguments suggested that, even in the early 1970s, not all Europeanist analysts gravitated primarily toward Bonn.

An additional topic pursued by various advocates of Europeanism was the notion that trade relations between the Soviet bloc countries and Western Europe aided the West Europeans in their efforts to decrease their dependence on the United States.[52]

Though all of these Europeanist writings expressed considerable opti-

49. G. Ponomarev, "Novy etap borby za evropeiskoye soveshchaniye," *MEMO*, no. 4, 1972, pp. 3–14.

50. E.g., N. Polyanov, "European Realities and Prospects," *IA*, no. 9, 1971, pp. 3–10, 18; E. N. Novoseltsev in *IA*, no. 11, 1971, pp. 69–70; M. Bunkina, "Protivorechiya atlanticheskovo partnerstva: Ekonomicheskii aspekt," *MEMO*, no. 11, 1972, pp. 55–65.

51. V. Gantman and L. Sergeyev, "Tekushchiye problemy mirovoi politiki," *MEMO*, no. 4, 1971, pp. 90–110; V. Gantman, "Tekushchiye problemy mirovoi politiki," ibid., no. 1, 1972, pp. 72–90; V. Matveyev, "Borba za mir v menyashchemsya mire," ibid., no. 12, 1971, pp. 3–12; Ye. Primakov, "Sushchnost kursa na evropeiskuyu bezopasnost," ibid., no. 5, 1972, pp. 84–87.

52. S. Losev and L. Sergeyev, "Tekushchiye problemy mirovoi politiki," *MEMO*, no. 1, 1971, pp. 74–93; Yu. Shishkov, "Problemy ekonomicheskovo sotrudnichestva," ibid., no. 5, 1972, pp. 89–93.

mism about Western Europe's growing independence, none cast any doubt on the continued strength of the region's ties to the United States. Greater independence *within* the alliance, not neutralism outside of it, was regarded as the driving aim of West European political leaders.

Against these analyses of Western Europe's relative independence from the United States were others that focused on the United States' continuing predominance within the Atlantic alliance, despite the proliferation of "contradictions" in U.S.–West European relations. This tendency was likely to continue, according to these analysts, because the United States was unlikely to withdraw its troops from Europe.

One of the most prominent spokesmen for this view was Anatolii Gromyko, son of the foreign minister. Writing in *International Affairs* in early 1971, the younger Gromyko admitted that the United States was indeed losing its influence over France, Italy, and "to some extent" West Germany, but he cautioned that the advocates of a continuing U.S. troop presence in Europe were "firmly entrenched in Washington."[53] Earlier, at a conference organized by the Institute on the USA in November 1970, Anatolii Gromyko noted that the United States was actually pulling back some of its forces from Europe. While many Americans opposed further cuts, he pointed out, those who favored additional withdrawals also advocated greater military efforts on the part of Western Europe. This step would lead to the further militarization of the NATO bloc, he warned, and would thereby create "the basis of a united militarist military-industrial complex in Western Europe." Some West Europeans advocated precisely such an outcome, young Gromyko added. This stark image conveyed the distinct impression that greater West European military independence from the United States might not necessarily be beneficial to Soviet interests.[54]

In 1972 Anatolii Gromyko observed that contradictions in economic and political relations between the United States and its allies at times bordered on "crisis." "However," he suggested, "it does not therefore follow that one should overestimate the influence of this factor on U.S. foreign policy." On the contrary, he noted, the White House occasionally acted with little regard for the reactions of its allies when it shaped its policies. Although he accused the Nixon administration of inconsistency, he drew a positive balance of recent U.S.-Soviet agreements and negotiations, and he expressed approval of Nixon's upcoming visit.[55]

Most speakers at the November 1970 conference sponsored by the Institute of the USA stressed that the Nixon doctrine by no means signaled the

53. Anatoly Gromyko, "U.S. Heavyweight in the European Ring," *IA*, no. 2, 1971, pp. 16–23.
54. See Gromyko's contribution to the discussion on "Doktrina Niksona: Deklaratsii i realnost," *SShA*, no. 2, 1971, pp. 34–36.
55. Anat. A. Gromyko, "Sovremennye tendentsii vneshnei politiki SShA," *SShA*, no. 4, 1972, pp. 40–47.

abandonment of America's global role. Several participants drew attention to the enduring presence of U.S. troops in Europe, despite some cutbacks. One of them maintained that the Nixon doctrine's devolution of greater responsibility on countries defended by the United States did not apply to Western Europe. Of the eleven speakers cited, only one accentuated the aggravation of contradictions between the United States and Western Europe. The predominant opinion was that the United States was still the main force to be reckoned with in the capitalist world.[56]

Other exponents of Americanist logic noted the salutary effect of the quadripartite Berlin agreement on U.S.-Soviet relations (rather than simply on Soviet–West German relations) and the "groundlessness" of American assumptions that the USSR wanted to push the United States out of Europe by excluding it from a European security conference. These views in essence suggested that Soviet policy toward the United States and Soviet policy toward Western Europe were linked, and they were not accompanied by references to Western Europe's alleged "independence."[57]

These Europeanist and Americanist modes of argumentation by no means accounted for all the views put forward on U.S.–West European relations in the Soviet specialized press in 1971 and 1972. Some articles adopted a mixed (Atlanticist) approach, noting the presence of both contradictions and partnership within the Atlantic alliance as a whole, or in U.S.-FRG ties more specifically.[58] Others took a hard-line position on current trends in world politics, arguing against the prevailing Soviet view that the pendulum had swung toward détente. The most consistent of these analysts was Shalva Sanakoyev, editor of *International Affairs*. He and other authors also expressed dogmatically critical views on West Germany, including Brandt and the SPD, and unequivocally emphasized the negative aspects of West German partnership with the United States as opposed to the contradictions in this relationship. These articles served notice of the abiding presence of suspicion and hostility toward Bonn within the Soviet foreign policy establishment in 1971 and 1972.[59] This maximalist approach could be seen also in the brusque rejection of Western MBFR proposals by various Soviet writers.[60]

56. *SShA*, no. 2, 1971, pp. 18–48.
57. Yu. A. Kotov and A. A. Sayanov, "Vazhnoye soglasheniye," *SShA*, no. 11, 1971, pp. 58–61; M. F. Petrov, "Pered nachalom mnogostoronnykh konsultatsii v Khelsinkii," ibid., no. 11, 1972, pp. 57–62.
58. E.g., V. Shein, "NATO: The Price of Mature Partnership," *IA*, no. 2, 1972, pp. 50–56; D. Melamid [D. Melnikov], "Vozmozhnosti i perspektivy 'vostochnoi politiki' V. Brandta," *MEMO*, no. 5, 1972, pp. 95–98.
59. For Sanakoyev's views, see *IA*, no. 6, 1971, pp. 8–15; no. 11, 1971, pp. 64–66; no. 4, 1972, pp. 3–10; no. 12, 1972, pp. 7–15. See also R. Faramzyan, "Sovremennost i militarizm," *MEMO*, no. 6, 1971, pp. 27–38; G. Sogomonyan, "Sotsial-demokratiya i problemy evropeiskoi bezopasnosti," *MEMO*, no. 7, 1972, pp. 45–56; and Y. Zakharov, "An Important Condition for Detente in Europe," *IA*, no. 12, 1972, pp. 27–33.
60. See, e.g., the views of Yu. Kostko in *MEMO*, no. 6, 1972, pp. 87–89, and no. 9, 1972, pp. 17–25.

In sum, Soviet foreign affairs specialists presented the decision makers with a varied menu of policy orientations in 1971 and 1972. The policy decisions adopted by the Brezhnev Politburo in these years, however, fell decisively on linking détente in Europe with détente in Moscow's relations with the United States. To a significant degree, as we have observed, the Brandt government itself wanted this linkage. It was Brandt who told the Soviets that there could be no ratification of the 1970 treaty without a four-power agreement on Berlin, no European security conference without American participation, and no lasting détente in Europe without mutual and balanced force reductions within the framework of NATO and the Warsaw Pact. Meanwhile, the Soviets recognized that détente with the United States could bring its own rewards. Hence the Kremlin leaders proceeded with negotiations on SALT and received President Nixon in Moscow despite a sudden escalation of American bombing in Vietnam. The Soviets also looked forward to a major increase in trade with the United States. And in a remarkable gesture, Brezhnev in Tbilisi announced his support for force reduction talks only days before a vote in the U.S. Senate on a bill sponsored by Senator Mike Mansfield to withdraw American troops from Europe. Brezhnev's curious timing was widely interpreted as a sign of Moscow's preference for an American military presence on the continent, at least for the foreseeable future, as opposed to the unknown consequences of a sudden pullout.[61]

Thus in 1971 and 1972 Soviet decision makers opted for a carefully balanced Atlanticist policy toward the West, borrowing elements from both the Europeanist and the Americanist orientations while committing themselves exclusively to neither. At the same time, the Kremlin hierarchy chose a measure of accommodation with the West as opposed to maximalist intransigence. These choices seem to have garnered the support of the overwhelming majority of the Soviet decision-making elite, with Brezhnev now assuming a commanding public presence as the principal orchestrator of this policy. The removal of Petro Shelest from his sinecure as chief of the Ukrainian party organization in the spring of 1972 was generally regarded as a personal foreign policy success for Brezhnev, in view of Shelest's opposition to detente with the United States.[62]

And yet these choices left ample room for ambiguity as to how far the Soviet leadership was willing to take détente. The decision to enter into discussions on force reductions in Europe, for example, was hardly the same as an agreement on this sensitive issue. Moscow's position in the

61. Raymond L. Garthoff, *Détente and Confrontation* (Washington, D.C.: Brookings, 1985), pp. 115–16.

62. In November 1971 Shelest had suddenly adopted a conciliatory posture toward West Germany, but a Western analyst later suggested that this cosmetic statement did not represent a significant change in Shelest's basic anti-Bonn position. See Grey Hodnett, "Ukrainian Politics and the Purge of Shelest," unpublished paper, cited in Parrott, *Politics and Technology*, pp. 254, 386n.

matter had yet to be tested. In 1972 the Soviets were not yet ready to receive NATO's emmisary, Manlio Brosio, for exploratory discussions on MBFR talks.[63] Just as significant, one of the themes that ran like a thread through virtually all of the foreign policy orientations that surfaced in the specialized press in 1971 and 1972 was the enduring—indeed growing—danger of West German military strength. None of the Soviet academic writings produced in these years appeared to hold out much hope for a serious breakthrough in reducing arms on the continent. On the contrary, they seemed to signal Soviet obduracy, justified in terms of West German "militarism."

Conclusions

Ultimately, Soviet attitudes toward the FRG in 1971 and 1972 continued to be those of a conservative ruling coalition. Although flexible enough to effect significant compromises on Berlin and on the prickly question of West Germans' access to the GDR, the Brezhnev team was still unwilling to extend its emerging political and economic détente into the military sphere.

The GDR, meanwhile, was embarking on a process of internal transformation. While Erich Honecker lacked Walter Ulbricht's majestic political authority, he certainly had Moscow's backing. How power would ultimately be distributed within the SED hierarchy was a question yet to be answered, however. For the time being, there were no serious signs of policy differences among the leading decision makers, nor did the specialized press give any hint of significant debates on foreign policy. Although a Soviet-style decision-making coalition might be expected to exhibit a relatively wide array of opinions in its formative stages, little variety was in evidence within Honecker's regime in 1971 and 1972. Quite possibly this relative absence of debate was due to the overriding necessity of acceding to Moscow's wishes in foreign policy and to the equally compelling need to rectify the disproportions engendered by Ulbricht in the domestic economy.

Before too long, however, policy makers in East Berlin and Moscow alike would be faced with the delicate business of putting détente with West Germany into practice. In the process, the Brezhnev regime would reinforce the more conservative aspects of its internal consensus. Erich Honecker and his colleagues, by contrast, would gradually steer a more centrist foreign policy course.

63. Helga Haftendorn, *Abrüstungs- und Entspannungspolitik zwischen Sicherheitsbefriedigung und Friedenssicherung* (Düsseldorf: Bertelsmann Universitätsverlag, 1974), pp. 334–35.

CHAPTER EIGHT

Defining Détente:
1973–1977

THE PERIOD extending from 1973 to the end of 1977 bridges two very distinct phases in Soviet–West German relations. It constitutes a transition period between the détente of the early 1970s and the bitter clash of wills over arms deployments in the first half of the 1980s. As the Brezhnev leadership became increasingly committed to enlarging Soviet military forces, in keeping with its conservative outlook, the Honecker regime edged toward a more centrist position aimed at stabilizing a cooperative relationship with West Germany.

The Brezhnev Consensus

As the rapprochement between Bonn and Moscow and between the two German states took shape from 1970 to 1972, a consensus emerged within the Soviet leadership on the broad contours of the meaning of détente in Europe. This consensus rested on three sets of propositions. Politically, it held that Bonn's de facto recognition of the territorial status quo was an acceptable substitute for full-scale de jure recognition as long as it was understood that the "German question" was now closed and the juridical status of Berlin unchanged. In the economic sphere, the consensus maintained that the Soviet Union needed to broaden its economic ties with the West, and particularly with the FRG, without necessarily reforming the structure of the Soviet economy. And in the military domain it held that, while some form of arms control might be advisable (particularly in the strategic relationship with the United States), the USSR and its Warsaw Pact allies must nevertheless continue to strengthen their overall military potential despite the cooperative features of political and economic détente.

In the mid-1970s this conceptualization of détente crystallized into a comprehensive world view that spelled out the nature of the forces at work in contemporary East-West relations and prescribed, with barely concealed frankness, the main outlines of what Soviet policy should be in the light of these carefully drawn images. In essence, the years 1973–1977 witnessed the further elaboration of foreign policy perceptions and preferences that had already found expression in the pronouncements of Soviet leaders and academicians during the first three years of the decade.

The Soviet détente doctrine that developed during the peak years of the Brezhnev era in the 1970s can be summarized as follows:

1. While détente constituted the "main tendency" of contemporary world politics, the "main contradiction of our epoch" continued to be the historic confrontation between socialism and capitalism. Détente itself was a "special form of the class struggle."

2. No détente was possible in the realm of ideology. This precept applied not only to the general ideological dichotomy between capitalism and socialism but also to such particular aspects of it as the enduring incompatibility between Leninist socialism and Western social democracy. On a global scale, there could be no compromise of Soviet support for "national liberation movements" in the Third World.

3. Détente had come about largely for three reasons: (*a*) the "correlation of forces" in the world had shifted to the advantage of socialism; (*b*) more particularly, the capitalist states had been forced to reconcile themselves to the "economic and defense might" of the USSR and its allies; and (*c*) the "cold war strategies" of the West had failed to roll back communism from the countries it governed and to impose political outcomes on the socialist states "from a position of strength." As a consequence, the leading states of the West had found themselves "compelled" to come to terms with the USSR and its allies in the early 1970s.

4. The "myth of the Soviet threat" was in decline in the West, and especially among West European publics and political leaders. Thus the West had an additional incentive to seek détente.

5. Long-term economic cooperation provided important benefits for both capitalist and socialist states. It was primarily the capitalist states, however, that were to blame for the failure of East-West trade to realize its full potential.

6. Despite the cooperative aspects of détente and the growing realism of certain Western leaders, the "aggressive essence of imperialism" remained unchanged. Moreover, opponents of détente continued to exert their influence in Western countries whose governments had lately embraced it.

7. Political détente needed to be supplemented with military détente. NATO was responsible for obstructing this process by consistently raising military expenditures, however, with the United States and the FRG setting the pace.

8. The socialist states therefore had to observe continuing "vigilance" against the intrigues of antidétente forces in Western Europe and the United States, and needed to maintain and strengthen the defense might of the Warsaw Pact.

This explanation of the origins, scope, and limits of détente was carefully calculated to appeal to key elements of Brezhnev's ruling coalition. It was articulated in such a way as to emphasize the vital contribution of Soviet military power in both creating and sustaining the conditions for détente with the West. The enhancement of Soviet military capabilities, far from being viewed as incompatible with détente, was in fact regarded as its very precondition.

Moreover, the Brezhnev regime's international outlook placed heavy emphasis on the ideological nature of the East-West confrontation. Rather than constituting a strictly geopolitical conception of global politics, the Brezhnev coalition's world view was rooted in the perception that the unceasing conflict between socialism and capitalism was the axis around which all international political activities ultimately revolved. Détente itself was never intended to surmount these fundamentally irreconcilable differences. Thus the Soviet Union could in no way be regarded simply as a typical great power; its "image of the enemy" was conceptualized in profoundly ideological terms.

Furthermore, the Soviet leaders now in power were of the generation that derived its outlooks on both domestic and international politics from the macabre world of Stalinist Russia; in their totalitarian conceptions of political power, these leaders were truly Stalin's successors.[1] In addition, their attitudes toward the West, and particularly toward West Germany, could not help but be indelibly stamped by the experiences of World War II. The Brezhnev regime was also acutely sensitive to its status vis-à-vis the other superpower. Memories of the humiliation suffered at the hands of the United States in the Cuban missile crisis, which took place at a time of overwhelming U.S. nuclear superiority, still scraped a raw nerve in the Soviet leadership. The Kremlin was determined to gain Washington's acknowledgment of the USSR's equality with the United States as a global power, and it vehemently denounced American attempts to deal with Moscow "from a position of strength."[2]

In view of the wide constituency for these attitudes, it is perhaps not surprising that no significant debate emerged into public view over the détente doctrine as a whole during the 1970s. While there were some signs of differentiation in the way various individuals discussed particular aspects

---

1. Seweryn Bialer, *Stalin's Successors: Leadership, Stability, and Change in the Soviet Union* (New York: Cambridge University Press, 1980).

2. On this point see William B. Husband, "Soviet Perceptions of U.S. 'Positions-of-Strength' Diplomacy in the 1970s," *World Politics* 31 (July 1979): 494–517.

of it, these differences had more to do with shadings of emphasis than with outright rejection of the doctrine itself.

Brezhnev generally took the high road in his public utterances on détente, stressing the indispensability of world peace and the reciprocal advantages to be gained from economic collaboration. But Brezhnev was also a persistent advocate of military "vigilance" and the strengthening of Warsaw Pact armed forces. These themes, prominent in his speech before the 25th CPSU Congress in February 1976, continued to dominate the general secretary's pronouncements in the mid-1970s.[3]

Kosygin tended to concentrate on promoting East-West economic relations, but in deference to the dominant consensus he also referred to the need for "vigilance." In 1975 he coupled these themes with a reference to the "lessening of the danger of war," perhaps as a sign of his commitment to arms control and restraint in Soviet military spending. Podgorny, once an outspoken advocate of reduced military expenditures, generally stressed the cooperative aspects of détente but also drew attention to rising NATO (particularly West German) military spending. He tended to stop short of calling openly for the "strengthening" of Soviet military power, however, focusing instead on the need to develop Soviet economic strength. Gromyko usually joined with Brezhnev, Kosygin, and Podgorny in highlighting the positive features of East-West political and economic cooperation, but he also added his weight to appeals to "strengthen the defense might" of the Soviet armed forces.[4]

Against these upbeat (but carefully balanced) characterizations of East-West relations, other Soviet leaders stressed the sinister side of Western intentions. Marshal Grechko led the charge. On several occasions the Soviet defense minister warned that, despite the recent improvements in the international climate, the NATO states were actively engaged in "material preparations for war." Grechko invariably concluded that the USSR and its Warsaw Pact partners must therefore "further strengthen" their military capabilities. These stark allusions to the ever-present dangers of war were seconded by Boris Ponomarev, who similarly urged constant attention to enhancing the Warsaw Pact's military potential. At the same time, Ponomarev also commended efforts to promote East-West economic cooperation. Another exponent of the more negative features of the composite Soviet détente doctrine was Mikhail Suslov. While occasionally supportive of long-term economic cooperation with the West, Suslov pressed the themes of ideological and military vigilance even more vigorously, and frequently

3. *Pravda*, Feb. 25, 1976, pp. 2–4. See also ibid., Aug. 16, 1973, pp. 1–2; Sept. 25, 1973, pp. 1–2; Oct. 27, 1973, pp. 1–3; Oct. 29, 1974, p. 2; June 14, 1975, pp. 1–2.
4. Kosygin: *Sovetskaya Rossiya*, Nov. 15, 1973, pp. 1–3; *Pravda*, June 13, 1974, pp. 1–2; June 12, 1975, pp. 1–2. Podgorny: *Pravda*, June 14, 1974, pp. 1–2; June 13, 1975, pp. 1–2; Nov. 11, 1975, p. 4. Gromyko: *Pravda*, June 11, 1974, p. 2; June 3, 1975, p. 2.

laced his pronouncements with stern reminders about the evils of capitalism and the blessings of socialism.[5]

In sum, the most important participants in the foreign policy decision-making process espoused a multidimensional détente policy that consisted of both cooperative and conflictual elements. While some stressed the cooperative elements and others stressed the conflictual, all appeared to accept the policy as a whole. Meanwhile, the general secretary stepped forward as the most articulate spokesman for both features of the détente doctrine, consolidating his position of preeminence within the Soviet hierarchy in the process.

Personnel shifts in the Kremlin in the mid-1970s reinforced Brezhnev's leadership. In April 1973 Gromyko and Grechko were elevated to full membership in the Politburo (along with KGB chief Yurii Andropov), while Shelest and G. I. Voronov were removed. Shelepin was dismissed from the Politburo and his remaining satrap as trade union chief in 1975. Upon Grechko's death in April 1976, the post of defense minister fell to Dmitrii Ustinov, a long-time Brezhnev associate. Ustinov quickly took up the cudgels in support of continuing Soviet military deployments. In the spring of 1977 Brezhnev engineered the ouster of Podgorny from the Politburo, and soon garnered for himself the latter's position as chief of state. Meanwhile, as Brezhnev's image in official propaganda acquired all the luster of a full-fledged cult of personality, Suslov quietly solidified his own authority as the party's second secretary.

Defining Détente in the Secondary Elite

The writings of Soviet academicians and journalists in the leading periodicals offered consistent support for this broadly conceived Brezhnev-era conceptualization of détente. Like Soviet leaders, the commentators combined a generally favorable evaluation of political accommodation and economic cooperation with a rather hard-hitting assessment of the role of Soviet military might in constraining the West to accept détente in the first place and in preserving vigilance against the West even as détente evolved.[6]

5. Grechko: *Krasnaya zvezda*, Jan. 30, 1974, p. 3; June 5, 1974, p. 2; Jan. 29, 1975, pp. 1, 2; *Pravda*, June 4, 1975, p. 2; and his article in *Problems of Peace and Socialism*, reprinted in FBIS, *Soviet Union*, Apr. 23, 1975, pp. R5–17. Ponomarev (who had become a candidate member of the Politburo in 1972): *Pravda*, June 11, 1974, p. 3; June 5, 1975, p. 2; *Krasnaya zvezda*, Jan. 29, 1975, p. 3; and *Kommunist*, no. 11, 1975, pp. 11–28. Suslov: FBIS, *Soviet Union*, July 16, 1973, pp. J1–17; Dec. 6, 1973, pp. R1–12; *Pravda*, June 12, 1974, p. 2; June 10, 1975, p. 2; Sept. 18, 1976, p. 2. See also *Kommunist*, no. 11, 1975, pp. 3–10, and no. 14, 1977, pp. 13–28.

6. The writings of Dmitrii Tomashevskii of IMEMO are particularly illustrative of the Brezhnev-era concept of détente. See, e.g., "Mirnoye sosushchestvovaniye: Novy etap,"

Public discussion of military issues was especially one-sided. Writers who dealt with security questions in the leading foreign affairs journals generally confined themselves to ominous portrayals of NATO defense spending and to categorical rejections of western MBFR proposals. While most commentators paid lip service to the general desirability of military détente—a constituent element of the official détente doctrine—several underscored the difficulties standing in the way of progress in this area. One authoritative military affairs specialist at IMEMO, Daniil Proektor, blamed NATO for seeing to it that the achievement of military détente was bound to be a "complicated and protracted process"; in 1976 Proektor rejected any possibility of military détente "without a substantial improvement in the political climate." Another author also viewed military détente primarily as a consequence of political détente, rather than vice versa. This view, of course, conflicted with Willy Brandt's conception of East-West accommodation, which prescribed significant steps in the direction of military détente as a vital precondition to further improvements in political ties. Even Yevgenii Primakov, a future foreign policy adviser to Mikhail Gorbachev, blamed the West for blocking military détente and rejected Western concepts of deterrence.[7]

One aspect of Soviet conceptualizations of security issues at this time would prove to be seriously flawed. The Brezhnev consensus affirmed that the "myth of the Soviet threat" was on the wane in Western Europe. At the same time, the détente doctrine also specified that continued efforts to strengthen Soviet armed forces were fully justified under the prevailing conditions of East-West relations. In effect these two assertions implied that the Soviets could build up their military forces virtually without limit while continuing to assure themselves that Western Europe's fears would progressively diminish. It would soon be revealed, however, that the Soviets could not have it both ways. Eventually the quantity and quality of Soviet weapons deployed on the European continent would arouse the concern of

---

MEMO, no. 10, 1973, pp. 3–16; "Na puti k korennoi perestroike mezhdunarodnykh otnoshenii," ibid., no. 1, 1975, pp. 3–13; "Shirokiye gorizonty leninskoi politiki mira," ibid., no. 6, 1976; and "How the West Is Reacting to Détente," *International Affairs*, no. 11, 1976, pp. 34–43. See also Tomashevskii's book *Leninskiye ideii i sovremennye mezhdunarodnye otnosheniya* (Moscow: Politizdat, 1971), published in English as *Lenin's Ideas and Modern International Relations* (Moscow: Progress, 1974), and his briefer study *Politika, otvechayushchaya korennym interesam narodov* (Moscow: Politizdat, 1972). See also V. V. Zagladin, ed., *The World Communist System: Outline of Strategy and Tactics* (Moscow: Progress, 1973).

7. Daniil Proektor, "Military Détente: Primary Task," *IA*, no. 6, 1976, p. 35; A. Migolatyev, "Who Is Speeding Up the Arms Race and Why?" *IA*, no. 11, 1977, p. 90; Yevgenii Primakov, "Politicheskaya razryadka i problema razoruzheniya," *IA*, no. 10, 1975, pp. 3–12. Primakov, an IMEMO scholar, broached a future theme of the Gorbachev years when he spoke of the "interdependence" of political and military détente, noting that neither was possible without the other.

leaders of nearly all the major West European parties and growing segments of the general public as well. For the moment, the inherent contradiction between these central elements of the Soviet world view was allowed to pass unnoticed in the statements of key decision makers and in the publications of foreign policy specialists.[8]

Soviet analyses of economic matters were more nuanced than discussions of security questions. Most academicians and journalists who addressed economic issues strongly supported the notion of expanded economic cooperation.[9] Nevertheless, discordant notes continued to be registered. At a conference sponsored by the journal *Mezhdunarodnaya zhizn* in early 1973, for example, one specialist echoed one of Walter Ulbricht's favorite themes by warning that the capitalist countries were still working to make the COMECON states economically dependent on them. Greater efforts at deepening integration among the socialist countries were therefore indispensable if this "aggressive" Western design was to be resisted. A far more positive assessment of East-West economic cooperation was voiced by another participant in the conference.[10]

Evidence of an ongoing debate on economic ties with the West accumulated over the next several years.[11] Generally, those who favored widened international trade and technology exchanges spoke openly about the benefits to accrue from such activity, while those with a contrary (or, at the very least, a skeptical) attitude on the subject emphasized such themes as the economic failings of capitalism, the advantages—indeed, the superiority—of socialism, and the dangers of making political concessions in exchange for Western economic benefits. The chorus of critical commentary on the nature of capitalism grew particularly resonant after 1974. In the wake of attempts by the U.S. Congress to link economic cooperation with the USSR to human rights issues such as Jewish emigration—efforts that culminated in the passage of the Stevenson amendment to the Export-Import Bank bill in September of that year and the Jackson-Vanik amendment to the U.S.-Soviet trade agreement in December—Soviet specialists stepped up their

8. See, e.g., "Evrope—bezopasnost," *MEMO*, no. 8, 1973, pp. 3–13, which argues that the "defense might" of the USSR was one of the factors contributing to détente, while the "myth of the Soviet threat" had all but disappeared from Western Europe. For similar kinds of reasoning, see D. Proektor, "Evropeiskaya bezopasnost, nekotorye problemy," ibid., no. 9, 1973, pp. 88–89, and A. Svetlov, "Razoruzheniye—nasushchaya zadacha borby za mir," ibid., no. 7, 1976, pp. 3–16.

9. E.g., M. Maksimova, "Vsemirnoye khozyaistvo i mezhdunarodnoye ekonomicheskoye sotrudnichestvo," *MEMO*, no. 4, 1974, pp. 3–20; N. Inozemtsev, "XXV sezd KPSS i problemy sovremennovo mirovovo razvitiya," ibid., no. 11, 1976, pp. 3–20; V. Yevgenev, "Important Areas of Interaction in Europe," *IA*, no. 8, 1976, pp. 62–69.

10. See the remarks by V. Knyazhinsky and V. Shchetinin in *IA*, no. 4, 1973, pp. 17–18 and 21–22.

11. For additional evidence of this debate from 1973 to 1975, see Bruce Parrott, *Politics and Technology in the Soviet Union* (Cambridge: MIT Press, 1983), pp. 256–75.

denunciations of the capitalist system and Western (especially American) foreign trade policy. These negative portrayals of the Western economies were darkened even further by gloomy images of the economic crisis that rocked the United States and Western Europe as a result of the sudden spurt in world oil prices.[12]

Not all of these analysts were entirely opposed to expanded East-West trade per se. Some combined their assaults on contemporary capitalism with acknowledgments of the reciprocal benefits of cooperation.[13] The message conveyed by these analysts seemed to be that, while trade with the West certainly had its benefits, the Soviet Union should not expect too much from its economic dealings with the capitalists and should under no circumstances make extensive political concessions in exchange for trade favors or overlook the tasks that needed to be resolved through the existing framework of the Soviet economic system. It was this position that most accurately reflected the Brezhnev consensus on East-West trade.

While Brezhnev himself was vocal in his support for economic cooperation with the West, he wanted no part of the U.S.-Soviet trade agreement once the congressional amendments tying it to Jewish emigration were passed.[14] (The Soviet government renounced the trade agreement in January 1975.) Neither did Brezhnev show any inclination to restructure the Soviet economy so as to facilitate joint ventures or other cooperative undertakings with Western firms, many of which chafed under the rigidities of the Soviet planning system. On the other side of the debate, Suslov displayed little enthusiasm for trade with the West, but he went along with it anyway. Although Suslov may have been a skeptic on this issue, he was certainly no Walter Ulbricht.

While several prominent foreign affairs specialists in the Soviet secondary elite directly addressed these military and economic policy issues, others

12. E.g., I. Gurev, "Obshchii krizis kapitalizma i evo dalneisheye uglubleniye," *MEMO*, no. 10, 1975, pp. 26–69; A. Manukyan, "Vzryv protivorechii kapitalisticheskovo vosproizvodstva," ibid., pp. 40–55; Yu. Shishkov, "EEC: Trudnaya dilemma," ibid., pp. 56–69, and "Krizis mekhanizma ekonomicheskikh otnoshenii kapitalisticheskikh stran," ibid., no. 1, 1977, pp. 25–39; A. Mileikovskii, "Sovremenny etap krizisa burzhuaznoi politekonomii," ibid., pp. 70–82; A. Shapiro, "Kapitalizm 70-kh godov. Osnovoi antagonizm: modifikatsiya i uglubleniye," ibid., no. 8, 1976, pp. 53–72. Also *Izvestiya*, Jan. 14, 1975, p. 4, and *Pravda*, Apr. 3, 1975, p. 4. The Stevenson amendment placed a $500 million cap on loans the Export-Import Bank could guarantee to the Soviet Union without congressional approval. It dashed Soviet hopes for large loans to finance Siberian energy development plans. The Jackson-Vanik amendment tied most-favored-nation status for the Soviet Union to greater Jewish emigration.

13. E.g., A. Anikin and E. Kirichenko, "Aktualnye voprosy sovetsko-amerikanskikh ekonomicheskikh otnoshenii," *MEMO*, no. 2, 1977, pp. 27–40; N. Shmelyev, "Mirnoye sosushchestvovaniye i ekonomicheskoye sotrudnichestvo," ibid., no. 4, 1976, pp. 26–36; V. Kudrov, "The Economic Competition between the Two Systems," *IA*, no. 1, 1977, pp. 32–41.

14. Brezhnev explicitly rejected the notion of exchanging political concessions to the West for economic benefits in 1974. See *Pravda*, June 15, 1974, pp. 1–3.

were preoccupied with the wider context of international relations in the 1970s. As in earlier years, the U.S.–West European relationship generated extensive commentary, stimulating a wide-ranging discussion about the relative weight of "contradictions" and partnership within the Atlantic alliance.

Once again several distinct patterns could be discerned in these discussions. While evidence of an exceptionally hard-line maximalist view diminished as the "relaxation of tensions" emerged as the proclaimed policy of the Brezhnev coalition, some writers seemed to accept the détente line only grudgingly. Such specialists as Shalva Sanakoyev of *Mezhdunarodnaya zhizn* and *Izvestiya* correspondent Vikentii Matveyev, while cognizant of the benefits of détente and the rise of U.S.–West European conflicts in recent years, continued to present ominous images of the West, as if to warn the Soviet leadership against losing sight of the intractable nature of Western anti-Sovietism.[15] Other writers, however, adopted more pronouncedly Europeanist, Americanist, or Atlanticist positions.

The Europeanist strain was especially well represented. Europeanist authors viewed the 1970s as a turning point in America's relations with its leading West European allies, as contradictions between the two poles of the Atlantic alliance intensified on an unprecedented scale. One observer, L. Vidyasova, professed to see a "qualitatively new stage" in the scope and severity of conflicts among the Western partners, leading "almost to the point of armed conflict" among them.[16] Although other analysts were not so prone to exaggeration, many agreed that the West Europeans were showing Washington an independent streak "unique" in the postwar era. Not only were economic rivalries sharpening as the West European and Japanese "imperialist power centers" mounted a vigorous challenge to American commercial and financial predominance; even more upsetting to Washington was the realization that economic conflicts were increasingly accompanied by differences over sensitive political and military issues.[17]

15. Sanakoyev: "Meeting with FRG Journalists," *IA*, no. 3, 1973, pp. 90–91; "An Important Factor behind Positive World Developments," *IA*, no. 4, 1973, pp. 3–6; "USSR-FRG: A Turn toward New Relations," *IA*, no. 8, 1973, pp. 12–17. Matveyev: "The Strategy and Tactics of the Champions of the Cold War," *IA*, no. 11, 1973, pp. 20–24; "NATO: Back to Old Positions," *IA*, no. 9, 1974, pp. 102–5; "'Trekhstoronaya strategiya' i ee evolutsiya," *MEMO*, no. 3, 1977, pp. 14–24.

16. L. Vidyasova, "Crisis of Imperialist Foreign Policy," *IA*, no. 1, 1973, pp. 56–63; "The Détente and Inter-Imperialist Contradictions," *IA*, no. 11, 1973, pp. 14–17; "Inter-imperialist Contradictions and Western Foreign Policy," *IA*, no. 3, 1976, pp. 98–108; and, for the reference to "armed conflict," "Inter-Imperialist Struggle Is Aggravating," *IA*, no. 8, 1976, p. 39.

17. M. K. Bunkina, *USA versus Western Europe: New Trends*, trans. Jane Sayer (Moscow: Progress, 1979), pp. 35–36. This is the English translation of a revised version of the original, which appeared in the USSR in 1976 under the title *SShA–Zapadnaya Evropa: Novye tendentsii v sopernichestve*. The emphasis on contradictions in U.S.–West European relations

Several authors pointed to the events of 1973 as providing ample confirmation of these tendencies. Western Europe's rejection of Henry Kissinger's proposal for a "new Atlantic Charter," the refusal of key NATO allies to permit the United States to use its bases in Europe to assist Israel during the October war, and Britain's entry into the Common Market were all regarded as symptomatic of a secular trend in the direction of West European self-assertiveness in the face of American efforts to dominate the alliance. Centrifugal forces, in this view, were clearly gaining ascendancy over centripetal tendencies within the Atlantic world.[18]

The Europeanist point of view assigned a prominent role to the USSR's détente policy in encouraging Western Europe's growing independence. Convinced that political leaders and public opinion in Western Europe were more amenable than their American counterparts to cooperation with the socialist states, Europeanist writers dropped unmistakable hints that it was in Moscow's interest to promote these advantageous trends by cultivating the West Europeans. Not only would such an approach widen the rifts within NATO, but Western Europe could be expected to exert a beneficial effect on American policy toward the socialist states as well.[19]

Another theme taken up by Europeanist authors centered on the integration process in Western Europe. The Soviet government refused to enter into formal relations with the European Economic Community and appeared to be concerned that Western Europe's integration could result in an excessively powerful economic—and perhaps military—union. Nevertheless, several writers took a positive view of the EEC on the grounds that it would enhance Europe's competitive position vis-à-vis the United States. At the same time they offered assurances that relations among the leading West European states were themselves subject to intercapitalist contradictions, which would reduce the likelihood of Western Europe's emergence as a united superpower equal in strength to the United States or the Soviet Union. In the same vein, a trio of IMEMO's leading West European specialists dismissed prospects for an integrated British–French–West German military force in the near future as improbable, thus implying that greater

also prevailed in A. Kirsanov, *The USA and Western Europe: Economic Relations after World War II*, trans. David Skvirsky (Moscow: Progress, 1975). Another predominantly Europeanist publication at this time was the collection of essays by IMEMO scholars edited by D. E. Melnikov, *Mezhdunarodnye otnosheniya v Zapadnoi Evrope* (Moscow: Mezhdunarodnye otnosheniya, 1974).

18. References to 1973 may be found in A. E. Yefremov, *Evropeiskaya bezopasnost i krizis NATO* (Moscow: Politizdat, 1975), pp. 256–61. Yefremov's book is essentially Atlanticist in orientation, mixing both Europeanist and Americanist positions. On the predominance of centrifugal trends, see S. Madzoevskii, "Mezhimperialisticheskiye protivorechiya v usloviyakh mirnovo sosushchestvovaniya dvukh sistem," *MEMO*, no. 5, 1974, pp. 36–44.

19. On West European influence on American policy, see V. Zhurkin, "Krupny vklad v uprocheniye mira," *MEMO*, no. 8, 1974, p. 5.

West European autonomy need not pose a new military threat to the USSR.[20]

Counterbalancing these Europeanist arguments were analyses reflecting more Americanist inclinations. Writings of this kind typically emphasized the continuing primacy of the United States in the capitalist world and occasionally maintained that unifying factors rather than centrifugal forces were now the dominant tendency.[21] The effort to establish détente with the United States was therefore valuable not only for its own sake but also because the United States had the capacity to influence West European policies favorably.[22] Others pointed out that the United States was still trying to revamp the concept of the "Atlantic community" to make it more palatable to Western Europe.[23] Americanist authors also poured cold water on the Europeanist notion that Western Europe's expanding independence from the United States was an accelerating, perhaps irreversible process. A scholar writing in *SShA,* the principal forum for the Americanist position, claimed that Bonn had actually drawn closer to the United States ever since Helmut Schmidt became chancellor in 1974, and was now "the right hand of the USA."[24] On the whole, however, relatively few articles with a distinctly Americanist flavor appeared in the mid-1970s, in all probability because the bloom was fading from U.S.-Soviet détente as a result of the tensions surrounding Third World conflicts and human rights issues.

The most pronounced tendency in Soviet discussions of "West-West" relations in this period was the Atlanticist orientation. Quite a few publications placed roughly equal stress on the presence of cooperative as well as conflictual trends at work within the Atlantic alliance. One variant of this approach suggested that, whereas centrifugal tendencies were paramount

20. Bunkina, *USA versus Western Europe,* pp. 184–85; S. Madzoevskii, D. Melnikov, and Yu. Rubinskii, "O politischeskikh aspektakh zapadnoevropeiskoi integratsii," *MEMO,* no. 9, 1974, pp. 50–61. See also M. Bunkina, "Zapadnaya Evropa i SShA: Partnerstvo i sopernichestvo," *MEMO,* no. 10, 1973, pp. 34–35, and G. Kolosov, "Zapadnoevropeiskii Soyuz: Funktsii i perspektivy," *MEMO,* no. 3, 1975, pp. 139–41. See also Christopher H. Binns, "From USE to EEC: The Soviet Analysis of European Integration under Capitalism," *Soviet Studies* 30 (April 1978): 237–61.

21. For an analysis that concluded that Western Europe could not attain political independence from the United States without closing the large technological gap now in America's favor, see V. Gromeka, "The United States–Western Europe: Scientific and Technological Competition," *IA,* no. 6, 1974, pp. 33–40. On the primacy of unifying factors, see A. Shapiro, "Tri tsentra imperializma i mezhimperialisticheskiye protivorechiya," *MEMO,* no. 12, 1977, pp. 91–95.

22. V. Nikitin, "Peaceful Coexistence and Soviet-U.S. Relations," *IA,* no. 6, 1974, pp. 3–9, 114.

23. I. M. Ivanova, *Kontseptsiya 'atlanticheskovo soobshchestva' vo vneshnei politike SShA* (Moscow: Nauka, 1973), and A. Utkin, " 'Atlantizma' 70-kh godov," *MEMO,* no. 5, 1975, pp. 83–92.

24. F. I. Novik, "Bonn-Vashington: Trudnosti partnerstva," *SShA,* no. 10, 1975, pp. 14–22.

in U.S.–West European relations in the early 1970s, centripetal forces were now reasserting themselves. Rather than specifying the advantages to be gained from working primarily through either the West Europeans or the Americans, the Atlanticist argument implied that the Soviet government could move back and forth between these approaches as circumstances allowed.[25]

One of the most conspicuous features of the Atlanticist argument was its close resemblance to the world view of the conservative Brezhnev coalition. Just as Soviet officials drew a clear distinction between the desirability of cooperation with the West in the political and economic spheres and the need for "vigilance" and "strengthening" in the military sector, scholars and journalists made a similar distinction using pronouncedly Atlanticist arguments. Contradictions between the United States and Western Europe, they observed, were growing over sensitive political issues and economic competition, but cooperation and American hegemony still prevailed in NATO's military activity.[26] This analysis established a theoretical underpinning for efforts to build up Soviet military power, despite the tendencies that were viewed as splitting the seams of Western unity in other areas.

Just as important, even Europeanist-oriented specialists frequently took note of these persisting evidences of NATO unity on the military front. While they steadfastly insisted that contradictions of various kinds constituted the main tendency within the Atlantic alliance, they were careful to make at least passing reference to continuing military cooperation between even the most pro-détente governments in Western Europe (such as the FRG) and the United States.[27] In another example of the prevailing convergence on the Atlanticist position, Oleg Bykov, an IMEMO scholar noted for his Europeanist leanings, was moved to observe that the two superpowers had a "special responsibility for the fate of the world."[28] This was a view more likely to be expressed by Americanists. Similarly, Americanist arguments that stressed the unabated predominance of the United States within the Atlantic alliance and maintained that the West Europeans themselves had set limits to their quest for independence also recognized that

25. A. I. Utkin, "O novykh yavleniyakh v mezhatlanticheskikh otnosheniyakh," *SShA*, no. 4, 1977, pp. 12–23; "Printsip mirnovo sosushchestvovaniya v deistvii," *MEMO*, no. 7, 1973, p. 9. For a book-length version of the Atlanticist position, see Yefremov, *Evropeiskaya bezopasnost*.
26. A. Antonov, "NATO in Conditions of Détente," *IA*, no. 2, 1974, pp. 34–41; N. Khomutov, "The Atlantic Relationship 25 Years Later," *IA*, no. 5, 1974, pp. 37–45.
27. E.g., Vidyasova, "Inter-imperialist Struggle Is Aggravating," *IA*, no. 8, 1976, p. 39, and "Peaceful Coexistence and International Cooperation," *IA*, no. 3, 1977, pp. 69–78; N. Turkatenko, "Inter-imperialist Contradictions and the Strategy of Atlanticism," *IA*, no. 2, 1976, pp. 82–91.
28. O. Bykov, "SShA i realnosti mezhdunarodnoi razryadki," *MEMO*, no. 8, 1976, p. 34.

contradictions between the two parts of the alliance had lately risen to unprecedented heights.[29]

We may therefore conclude that both the Europeanist and Americanist modes of argumentation were very close to the Atlanticist position at this time. In effect, the Atlanticist view constituted a central axis of consensus from which the other two orientations diverged only marginally. The differences between these tendencies were mainly a matter of emphasis. Whereas the Europeanist outlook emphasized U.S.–West European contradictions and the Americanist viewpoint stressed U.S.–West European partnership, the two orientations shared the Atlanticist notion that both of these forces were powerfully represented in relations between the United States and Western Europe.

Moreover, none of these three Soviet perspectives appeared to foresee the imminent breakup of the Atlantic alliance. All of them acknowledged that, at least for now, the development of sharp conflicts between the United States and its European allies was essentially contained within the alliance's existing structure. Rather than seeking to quit the alliance, therefore, the West Europeans were regarded as concerned mainly with expanding their own role and influence within it.

It was this balanced Atlanticist approach, furthermore, that most closely conformed to the Brezhnev coalition's weltanschauung and to its actual behavior in its dealings with the West. Over the course of the mid-1970s the Kremlin was engaged in a seesaw relationship with both the United States and Western Europe, and did not appear to favor one side over the other with any demonstrable consistency. While the Kremlin continued to deal with France and West Germany, for example, Richard Nixon was welcomed in Moscow only months before his resignation, and talks on SALT II proceeded at a deliberate pace with the administrations of Gerald Ford and the newly inaugurated Jimmy Carter. In addition, these ties involved a calculated mixture of cooperative and conflictual elements, in keeping with the ruling coalition's articulated perspectives on East-West relations.

Meanwhile, exponents of all the major analytical tendencies offered explicit support for the chief tenets of the Brezhnev coalition's détente doctrine. Such notions as the West's need to accept détente because of the "economic and defense might" of the socialist states, the declining "myth of the Soviet threat," and so on received the clear endorsement of most Soviet

29. E.g., Yurii Davydov, "USA–Western Europe: A 'New Relationship,'" *IA*, no. 1, 1974, pp. 35–41, and Anat. Gromyko and A. Kokoshin, "US Foreign Policy Strategy for the 1970s," *IA*, no. 10, 1973, pp. 15–22. Yurii Davydov was a specialist on U.S.–West European relations at the Institute of the USA and Canada, and Gromyko had earlier expressed Americanist attitudes on the positive features, from the Soviet point of view, of the U.S. military presence in Europe. See chap. 7, n. 53.

foreign policy specialists at this time, regardless of their predominant orientation.[30] Virtually no real debate rose to the surface on these issues. As Brezhnev's conservative coalition solidified its power and clarified its policy positions, differentiation within the secondary elite corresponding to the separate strands of Europeanism, Americanism, and Atlanticism was allowed to proceed, but the opportunities for serious open disagreement on matters of theory or substance appeared to be seriously diminished.

One issue that once again contained the seeds of potential controversy, however, was how the Soviet Union could best promote contradictions among the western allies. As in previous years, some authors insisted that détente—the "relaxation of tensions"—would be a powerful stimulus to the development of conflicts within the West, particularly between the United States and Western Europe. As we have seen, however, a contrary view suggested that U.S.–West European conflicts could also grow in periods of East-West confrontation. Echoes of this view were still being sounded.[31] Moreover, the official concept of détente placed a high value on Soviet military power as the sine qua non of a greater "relaxation of tensions." This view, too, was seconded by most international affairs specialists.

Thus the all-important issue of the compatibility of détente in Europe with a persistent Soviet military buildup was never addressed explicitly. Contrasting views on the most effective means of promoting contradictions in the West, however, suggested that divergent opinions on this matter existed within the secondary foreign policy elite. Perhaps a more open airing of the issue might have compelled the Soviet leadership to confront the contradictions in its policies more directly. The primary elite showed no interest in such a debate, however, and remained wedded to the notion that political and economic détente could go hand in hand with a dynamic expansion of military power. This assumption would prove to be illusory, especially in regard to West Germany.

Soviet Images of the FRG

The course of Soviet–West German relations from 1973 to 1977 was quietly uneventful in comparison with the remarkable accomplishments of the preceding three years. The main resolvable issues had essentially been resolved; no new breakthroughs came into view on the diplo-

---

30. In addition to the sources cited above, see "Uspekhi leninskoi politiki mira," *MEMO*, no. 6, 1973, pp. 3–14, and "Evrope—bezopasnost," ibid., no. 8, 1973, pp. 3–13.

31. Bykov, for example, claimed that "national liberation movements" supported by the USSR promoted contradictions among the Western allies. See D. E. Melnikov, ed., *Zapadnaya Evropa i SShA* (Moscow: Mysl, 1968), p. 89.

matic horizon. On the political level, both sides tended to concentrate on carrying out and interpreting the treaties and understandings already agreed upon. On the economic level, trade and other forms of cooperation increased appreciably, but progress in this area actually fell short of expectations in both countries. As officials in both Bonn and Moscow settled in for the next phase of détente, it soon became apparent in both capitals that there were distinct limits not only to the economic aspects of cooperation but to its political dynamics as well.

Perhaps the most dramatic development of these years provided a troubling indication of what these limits could entail. On May 7, 1974, Willy Brandt resigned as federal chancellor after the arrest of Günter Guillaume, a close political aide, for espionage on behalf of the GDR. Brandt's replacement by Helmut Schmidt resulted in a subtle but noticeable change in Bonn's attitude toward the USSR. Schmidt's crisp, businesslike manner offered a brusque contrast to the moral engagement of Brandt, whose Eastern policy had always been suffused with the emotional overtones deriving from his personal responses to the tragedies of twentieth-century Germany. Above all, Schmidt lacked the prestige Brandt enjoyed in the East as an elder Social Democrat steeped in the antifascist and working-class traditions of his party.

Moreover, by virtue of his own professional inclinations and the nature of the problems confronting the FRG in the mid-1970s, Schmidt presided over the demotion of ostpolitik from its earlier status as the SPD-FDP government's number one foreign policy priority. As a former finance minister, Schmidt eagerly plunged into the economic problems arising from the upsurge in oil prices which jolted the world economy after the Middle East war of October 1973. Though ostpolitik was still of considerable importance for the FRG in these years, it inevitably took a back seat to the politics of energy interdependence, monetary instability, and stagflation in the West. In addition, Schmidt's recent tenure as defense minister and his career-long interest in security issues made him particularly sensitive to the implications of the military balance. In a book published in 1969 he displayed a fascination with the subtleties of military strategy and their political ramifications in East-West relations.[32] This attentiveness to the military dimensions of foreign policy became a distinguishing characteristic of the right wing of the SPD, which Schmidt spearheaded along with Georg Leber (the new defense minister) and Hans Apel (a future holder of the same office). It accounted for the strong personal interest Schmidt took in the accretion of Soviet military power as it progressed steadily during the 1970s and into the 1980s.

32. Helmut Schmidt, *Strategie des Gleichgewichts* (Stuttgart: Seewald, 1969). The English version is *The Balance of Power*, trans. Edward Thomas (London: Kimber, 1971).

Though the Kremlin had to accommodate itself to the shift from Brandt to Schmidt, Soviet leaders and political analysts displayed extraordinary continuity in their attitudes toward West Germany throughout the 1973–1977 period. The themes of the desirability of economic cooperation and the need for unabated military "vigilance" proved to be fully consistent with Soviet actions with respect to the West German government in these years. Once again policy closely approximated images.

In addition, Soviet decision makers and political commentators were unanimous in the defense of Moscow's official interpretation of the quadripartite agreement on Berlin. Efforts by the West German government to implement its own understanding of the treaty's provisions concerning the maintenance of institutional "ties" between the Federal Republic and West Berlin were categorically denounced whenever they violated the Soviet interpretation of the treaty text. Moscow's strict adherence to its position on Berlin, however, did not exceed the boundaries of diplomatic firmness. Though the Soviets occasionally backed up their verbal protests with action (as we shall see), they did not escalate their rhetoric or their behavior to a level suggesting that all other aspects of the Soviet-FRG relationship depended on the Berlin issue. Moscow even found a way to include West Berlin in some agreements signed with the Federal government.[33]

All these themes abounded in public discourse. Brezhnev customarily took the lead in expressing the Kremlin's views. On several occasions he affirmed his commitment to economic cooperation and scientific-technical exchanges with the West Germans. This was his central message during his visit to the FRG in May 1973, immediately after the ratification of the FRG-GDR Basic Treaty in Bonn. In meetings with West German officials and business leaders and in various public forums, Brezhnev ebulliently proclaimed his hopes for the development of large-scale, long-term industrial cooperation, and he did so again when Schmidt visited the USSR in October 1974.[34]

Yet Brezhnev never lost sight of the FRG's negative features. Several months after his 1973 visit to Bonn, the Soviet leader drew a pointed reference to "certain circles" in West Germany who still refused to accept the GDR. This was a direct allusion to Christian Democratic leaders who had recently challenged the legality of the Basic Treaty before the West German constitutional court in Karlsruhe. (The court upheld the treaty but

33. In May 1973 two Soviet-FRG agreements were extended to include West Berlin on the basis of an agreement negotiated by West German Foreign Ministry official Paul Frank and Ambassador Falin. The Soviets refused to apply the same principle in other cases regarded as appropriate by Bonn, however. See David M. Keithly, *Breakthrough in the Ostpolitik* (Boulder, Colo.: Westview, 1986), pp. 188, 195.

34. Angela Stent, *From Embargo to Ostpolitik* (Cambridge: Cambridge University Press, 1980), pp. 191–95; *Pravda*, Oct. 29, 1974, p. 2.

ruled that it did not vitiate the FRG's traditional claims to sole representation of Germans in both German states.) Brezhnev coupled these criticisms with a general attack on proponents of unrestrained military growth in the West. He took another swipe at opponents of détente in the Federal Republic during Schmidt's visit to Moscow the next year, and openly criticized Bonn's positions on Berlin and MBFR. Brezhnev reiterated all of these themes during a visit to Moscow by Willy Brandt in July 1975.[35] Finally, in his lengthy tour d'horizon at the 25th Party Congress, Brezhnev escalated his direct criticism of the Schmidt government by claiming that it was actually succumbing to the pressure of right-wing forces in certain aspects of its policy. In sum, Brezhnev took a studiedly mixed view of the FRG in his public statements during the 1973–1977 period, blending appeals for economic cooperation with explicit, if restrained, criticism of Bonn's policies in other areas.

Andrei Gromyko's references to the Federal Republic in these years were distinguished mainly by their blandness. While the foreign minister made the usual approving remarks about the important agreements on Germany concluded at the start of the decade, he invariably conferred greater prominence on the United States and France in his commentary on Soviet foreign policy. (At one point Gromyko stated that the "greatest experience of cooperation under conditions of détente has been with France.") Gromyko's comparatively perfunctory references to the FRG, viewed in the context of his past remarks on the enduring importance of the Potsdam accords, offered further evidence of his ambivalence toward Bonn.[36]

Other Soviet leaders who addressed foreign policy issues in the 1973–1977 period tended to subsume their thoughts on the FRG under the more general rubric of détente with the West. Advocates of trade with the capitalist states, such as Kosygin, clearly included West Germany in this category, while critics of NATO military spending surely cast a cold eye on the Bundeswehr. Of the lesser officials, such foreign trade specialists as Nikolai Patolichev spoke explicitly in favor of economic cooperation with the FRG.[37] But Patolichev remained firmly opposed to the idea of reforming the Foreign Trade Ministry's monopoly on trade dealings with the West.

On the whole, the images of West Germany to be found in the leading foreign policy journals conformed to the same calculated mix of positive

35. *Pravda*, Aug. 16, 1973, p. 2; July 4, 1975, p. 2; July 6, 1975, p. 4.
36. *Pravda*, June 11, 1974, p. 2; Nov. 7, pp. 1–3. See also Gromyko's article in *Kommunist*, no. 14, 1975, pp. 3–20.
37. E.g., see Patolichev's remarks in *Izvestiya*, June 14, 1973, p. 2; also the remarks of Vladimir Novikov, deputy chairman of the Council of Ministers, in FBIS, *Soviet Union*, Feb. 16, 1973, p. F2, and Mar. 26, 1974, p. E8. Novikov was the chief delegate to the Soviet-FRG Joint Commission on Scientific, Technical, and Economic Cooperation. Also the remarks by Nikolai Tikhonov, first deputy chairman of the Council of Ministers, in *Izvestiya*, June 5, 1977, p. 3.

and negative perceptions conveyed by the decision makers. Once again the preponderance of positive attitudes fell on economic cooperation, while the principal focus of negative views was Bonn's alleged military dynamism. Schmidt's contributions to shoring up pro-NATO governments in Italy, Portugal, and Turkey with significant economic aid were also highlighted.[38] The leading newspapers presented similarly split images of the FRG. *Pravda* and *Izvestiya* placed roughly equal stress on the positive aspects of Soviet–West German economic cooperation and the negative features of West Germany's military strength.[39] In keeping with their own bureaucratic perspectives, publications dealing with economic issues generally stressed the former theme and *Krasnaya zvezda* stressed the latter.[40]

Soviet Policy toward the FRG

Soviet policy toward the FRG in the years 1973–1977 generally followed the paths indicated by these contrasting images. The political-diplomatic side of the relationship oscillated between cordiality and contention. Both governments repeatedly affirmed their favorable intentions

38. Examples of positive views of the FRG include G. Sokolnikov, "Vozmozhnosti i problemy sovetsko-zapadnogermanskikh ekonomicheskikh svyazei," *MEMO*, no. 10, 1973, pp. 17–25; A. Chubaryan and Yu. Leonidov, "Strana sovetov i mir kapitalizma," ibid., pp. 28–42; T. Sosnovskaya, "Soviet Union–FRG: Possibilities and Prospects," *IA*, no. 2, 1974, pp. 47–52; V. Rostovtsev, "USSR-FRG: Developing Relations," *IA*, no. 7, 1974, pp. 45–54; A. Grigoryev, "USSR-FRG Economic Relations," *IA*, no. 10, 1974, pp. 47–53; A. Voronov and G. Rozanov, "A Tour of West German Cities," *IA*, no. 2, 1977, pp. 105–13. Negative views can be found in S. Yefimov, "Evrogruppa NATO," *MEMO*, no. 4, 1976, pp. 126–28; G. Sogomonyan, "Sotsial-demokratiya i sovremennost," *MEMO*, no. 5, 1977, pp. 23–35 (a critical appraisal of the SPD); and G. Kirilov, "West Berlin: Past and Future," *IA*, no. 7, 1976, pp. 75–80. A mixture of positive and negative accents can be found in L. Istyagin, "Partii i politicheskaya borba v FRG," *MEMO*, no. 4, 1974, pp. 117–25; Y. Zakharov, "Support for the Policy of Realism," *IA*, no. 2, 1973, pp. 71–74; and in Daniil Melnikov's article in *Literaturnaya gazeta*, May 29, 1974, p. 14. For a sophisticated mix of positive and negative opinions, see Ilya S. Kremer, *FRG: Vnutripoliticheskaya borba i vneshnyaya orientatsiya* (Moscow: Mysl, 1977).

39. Economic cooperation: *Pravda*, May 20, 1973, pp. 1, 4; Nov. 2, 1974, p. 1; Apr. 3, 1975, p. 4; Mar. 5, 1977, p. 4; and *Izvestiya*, Feb. 11, 1973, p. 2; Apr. 12, 1973, p. 4; May 20, 1973, pp. 1, 2; Sept. 17, 1974, p. 4; Feb. 9, 1975, p. 2; Aug. 10, 1975, p. 2; June 2, 1977, p. 4. Military policy: *Pravda*, Aug. 13, 1973, p. 3; Dec. 19, 1973, p. 5; Aug. 14, 1976, p. 5; Dec. 18, 1976, p. 5; and *Izvestiya*, Jan. 24, 1976, p. 3, and Feb. 12, 1977, p. 3.

40. For positive views on trade with the FRG, see *Ekonomicheskaya gazeta*, no. 15, 1975, p. 19; *Sotsialisticheskaya industriya*, Aug. 12, 1976, p. 5. For a reference to war dangers in an article that made no reference to East-West economic cooperation, see *Sotsialisticheskaya industriya*, Apr. 9, 1975, p. 3. For typical examples of *Krasnaya zvezda's* commentary, see May 24, 1973, p. 1 (an editorial on "vigilance" published shortly after Brezhnev's return from Bonn); June 10, 1973, p. 3; Mar. 30, 1974, p. 3; Jan. 10, 1976, p. 3; Mar. 28, 1976, p. 3; Aug. 27, 1976, p. 3; Sept. 19, 1976, p. 3; July 12, 1977, p. 3; and July 20, 1977, p. 3. On the whole, *Krasnaya zvezda* refrained from attacking Chancellor Schmidt in this period, but equated the SPD's military policy with that of the CDU.

and pledged to conduct their relations on the basis of détente. The height of this cooperative spirit was reached at the time of Brezhnev's visit to the FRG in the spring of 1973. The goodwill generated by the trip carried over into 1974 and permitted Bonn to wrap up its efforts to normalize relations with Eastern Europe. After Walter Scheel's visit to Moscow in the fall of 1973, the Soviets acted to remove the last hurdles in the way of a rapprochement between the FRG and Czechoslovakia. Bonn and Prague agreed to establish diplomatic relations on December 11.[41] This agreement opened the way to the normalization of the FRG's relations with Bulgaria and Hungary. With these accords the energetic first phase of the SPD-FDP coalition's ostpolitik drew to a close. A new phase of economic cooperation opened, however, as the Schmidt government expanded its economic cooperation with Eastern Europe, particularly Poland and Hungary.

Still, the feeling in Bonn that a turning point had been reached in the FRG's relations with the East became unmistakable with Brandt's resignation. The circumstances surrounding his withdrawal from office sent a shock through the West German body politic, providing incontrovertible evidence that détente, for all its achievements, did not signify an end to such traditional forms of East-West friction as espionage. Though reports circulated that neither Brezhnev nor Honecker had been aware of Guillaume's actual identity—Ambassador Falin averred that Brezhnev had been furious on first learning of the incident—serious damage had been done to the spirit, if not the letter, of détente.[42]

The Soviets greeted Schmidt's ascension to power with an outward display of hopefulness, giving wide play to his declarations in favor of détente, but it was not long before the new chancellor was embroiled in his first altercation with Moscow. In the summer of 1974 the West German government set up a West Berlin branch office of the Federal Environmental Agency, in accordance with its view that the quadripartite agreement permitted the development of such institutional ties between the Federal Republic and West Berlin. The Soviet Union and the GDR quickly protested the measure as a violation of the 1971 four-power treaty. On July 26 the GDR set up roadblocks and interrogated drivers from the FRG about their

---

41. As early as 1971 Moscow had backed away from insisting on Bonn's formal acknowledgment that the 1938 Munich treaty had been invalid ab initio. Last-minute hitches concerning the status of West Berlin arose in the course of the West German–Czech negotiations in 1973, but compromise language was found to circumvent the difficulty. See William E. Griffith, *The Ostpolitik of the Federal Republic of Germany* (Cambridge: MIT Press, 1978), pp. 220–23.

42. Arnulf Baring, *Machtwechsel* (Stuttgart: Deutsche Verlags-Anstalt, 1982), p. 740. Soviet media never referred to Guillaume's role in Brandt's resignation, which was blamed on a variety of internal political factors, including, in one account, the alleged intrigues of a CDU/CSU "fifth column" inside the SPD. See Ye. Grigorev's article in *Pravda*, May 12, 1974, p. 5.

246 / Moscow, Germany, and the West

affiliations with the environmental office. One official of the agency was turned back. As the Soviet government and the three Western powers responsible for Berlin exchanged notes, Moscow and East Berlin showed that various other pressures could be brought to bear on West Germany. In early August a group of ethnic Germans went on trial in Estonia for participating in a protest demonstration earlier in the year. The GDR arrested West Berliners accused of "trafficking in human beings" (that is, trying to smuggle East Germans out of the GDR). More than forty people, including GDR citizens, were convicted of such charges in East German courts by late August. As the confrontation continued, the United States in late July broke off talks with the GDR on establishing diplomatic relations.

Tensions abated by early September as the Soviets and East Germans backed away from further escalation of the dispute. Neither Moscow nor East Berlin, having made its point, wished to jeopardize economic and other contacts with the FRG over the juridical status of Berlin, a perennially intractable problem. Bonn went ahead with the Environmental Agency's West Berlin office, the United States and the GDR agreed to normalize relations, and ill feelings were sufficiently smoothed over in time for a visit by Gromyko to Bonn in mid-September.

Schmidt visited Moscow in late October, and joined with his Soviet hosts in reasserting the mutual benefits of regular political consultations and long-term economic cooperation.[43] But the Berlin incident had left its mark. The Schmidt-Brezhnev encounter was not without its strains, and disagreements over Berlin prevented agreement on scientific-technical cooperation and other matters. Over the ensuing months, Soviet–West German relations grew appreciably cooler.[44]

Thus the glitter of détente was already beginning to fade by the time the Conference on Security and Cooperation in Europe (CSCE) concluded its work in midsummer 1975. The final act of the conference was signed by the representatives of thirty-five states in Helsinki on August 1. The two-year negotiation of the agreement had been a classic exercise in East-West diplomatic wrangling. The Soviets had wanted the conference to confirm the territorial status quo in Europe, in effect supplementing the ostpolitik accords with the institutional (though not juridical) equivalent of the ever-elusive post–World War II peace treaty. They could not reach anything resembling this long-sought goal, however, without agreeing to the extensive human rights provisions spelled out in what became known as "Basket III" of the final document. The Schmidt government was not interested in a protracted quarrel over human rights issues, but it strongly supported the Basket III provisions, above all because they could be used in dealings with

43. See the communiqué in *Pravda*, Oct. 31, 1974, p. 2.
44. Dettmar Cramer, "Bonn und Moskau: Distanzierter," *Deutschland Archiv*, no. 4, 1975, pp. 358–61.

the GDR on such subjects as family reunification. Bonn also worked closely with the Ford administration to elicit Soviet acceptance of a clause permitting the peaceful change of the existing borders in such a way as to leave open the possibility of Germany's reunification.[45]

Although the Soviets valued their dialogue with Bonn in spite of the latest difficulties, they showed no signs of making the Federal Republic the exclusive focus of their West European policy. France continued to occupy a special place in Moscow's priorities. Brezhnev visited Paris twice in this period (in 1974 and 1977), and President Georges Pompidou and his successor, Valéry Giscard d'Estaing, each journeyed to the USSR. During Giscard's visit in October 1975, the two sides concluded a wide-ranging friendship declaration. A similar document was concluded a month later with Italy.[46] For Moscow, these efforts to broaden its ties with other leading West European states had more than merely economic motivations, important as these were. They served as a counterweight to relations with Bonn, which soured even further as Schmidt visited China in the fall of 1975.

Despite the "considerable difficulties" Soviet leaders saw in their relations with the West German government at this time, they manifestly preferred the SPD-FDP cabinet to the Christian Democrats.[47] Although the Soviet press occasionally reported favorable shifts in the attitudes of such CDU politicians as Helmut Kohl and Kurt Biedenkopf, the Soviets continued to castigate most Christian Democrats as "enemies of détente." (Kohl himself, the Christian Democrats' standard-bearer in the upcoming elections, was somewhat rudely treated during a visit to Moscow in September 1975.)[48] Accordingly, Moscow sought to intervene in the Bundestag election campaign of 1976. On May 22 the Soviet government released a twelve-point statement lambasting anti-Sovietism in West Germany. As Brezhnev himself later admitted, the statement was targeted at the Christian Democrats, who were sharply critical of central elements in the government's ostpolitik. The Schmidt government also came in for criticism just before the elections, however, as *Pravda* accused it of "inconsistency" and foot-dragging in its foreign policy. Although the Soviets welcomed the SPD-FDP coalition's victory in October, *Pravda* again denounced the two parties for adhering to NATO's military "dogmas" and for sharing the Christian Democrats' view that the Warsaw Pact's latest defense measures were excessive.[49]

45. For details, see John J. Maresca, *To Helsinki* (Durham, N.C.: Duke University Press, 1985), pp. 110–16.
46. *Pravda*, Oct. 18, 1975, p. 2; Nov. 21, pp. 1, 4.
47. The phrase was Podgorny's. See *Pravda*, Nov. 11, 1975, p. 4.
48. Kosygin twice postponed his meeting with Kohl, and *Pravda* embarrassed him by printing an attack on CSU chief Strauss during Kohl's stay in the Soviet capital. See the German Press Agency accounts in FBIS, *Soviet Union*, Sept. 25, 1975, p. E7; Sept. 26, p. E8; Sept. 29, pp. E6–7; Sept. 30, pp. E7–8; Oct. 1, p. E6. Also *Pravda*, Sept. 25, 1975, p. 5.
49. *Pravda*, May 22, 1976, pp. 1, 4; Sept. 28, p. 4; Dec. 18, p. 5.

In September 1976, in the heat of the election campaign, it was announced that Brezhnev would make a second visit to Bonn. (The trip was delayed until May 1978, in large part because of worsening Soviet–West German frictions.) Appropriately, in his comments on the Bundestag elections, Brezhnev observed that relations with the United States and the FRG had "slowed down lately."[50] In view of the deteriorating trends in East-West relations, this remark would soon come to be regarded as an understatement.

Meanwhile, it was the economic component of the Soviet-FRG relationship that most sustained the fragile détente between Moscow and Bonn.[51] On the positive side of the ledger, total trade turnover between the two countries rose from $1.1 billion in 1972 to $4.6 billion by the end of 1977. Among the various economic agreements signed in this period, the most significant included a ten-year accord on industrial and technical cooperation concluded during Brezhnev's visit in 1973; another long-term agreement of a similar nature in January 1974; and a barter deal in October 1974 providing for the exchange of Soviet natural gas for West German steel pipe (the third since 1970). This arrangement was followed by another natural gas deal involving Iran in 1975. On the government-to-government level, the Soviet-FRG Commission on Economic and Scientific-Technical Cooperation, inaugurated in 1972, met at least once a year, while on the private level the USSR established contacts with more than a hundred West German firms and signed contracts for such large-scale projects as the construction of an electromagnetic combine and several chemical plants. Although the Schmidt government decided in 1974 not to subsidize artificially low interest rates for the socialist states, West German banks provided nearly $4 billion in insured credit to the USSR by 1977.

Not all negotiations ended in agreement. Failure to agree on the inclusion of West Berlin held up the signing of an accord on scientific-technical cooperation. Berlin also complicated talks on the construction by West German firms of a nuclear power plant in Kaliningrad. (Ultimately the project was abandoned because of American and East German objections.) Meanwhile, West German businessmen complained of inherent barriers to the expansion of cooperation attributable to bureaucratic hindrances in Moscow, the absence of currency convertibility, and the USSR's undeveloped internal market.

Both sides were keenly aware of the political hazards of excessive economic dependence. Opponents of the gas-for-pipe deals in the FRG warned

50. *Pravda*, Oct. 26, 1976, pp. 1–3.
51. The following account is based on Stent, *From Embargo to Ostpolitik*, chaps. 8 and 9; Klaus Bolz, Hermann Clement, and Petra Pissulla, *Die Wirtschaftsbeziehungen zwischen der BRD und der Sowjetunion* (Hamburg: Weltarchiv, 1976); and E. Yordanskaya, "SSSR-FRG: Nauchno-tekhnicheskoe sotrudnichestvo," *MEMO*, no. 7, 1976, pp. 120–24.

that Moscow could threaten to cut off gas supplies in exchange for political concessions, a possibility dismissed as unlikely by the SPD-FDP government. (By the late 1970s, the FRG was getting about 15 percent of its natural gas from the USSR, and the government believed this figure could be doubled without undue risk.) Critics of extensive economic ties with the Soviets both within and outside West Germany additionally argued against providing Moscow with advanced technology that could be used for military purposes. It was on this basis that the United States and Britain had objected to the Kaliningrad nuclear power plant. Little, if anything, in the way of sensitive high technology was actually transferred to the Soviet Union in these years, however, as the Schmidt government in principle shared NATO's concerns.[52] As for the West German economy's trade dependence, it was officially estimated that as many as 300,000 jobs hinged on trade with the East, but the net figure was below 100,000 when account was taken of jobs lost as the result of Soviet and East European imports. Though the impact of *Osthandel* was considerable in certain manufacturing sectors, in the aggregate it constituted little more than 2 percent of the FRG's total world trade.

The Soviets were themselves fully cognizant of the political risks of economic cooperation. While various writers in the USSR lamented the fact that Soviet–West German trade had in no way "exhausted its possibilities" (a phrase Brezhnev echoed), even proponents of trade cautioned against political concessions and the instabilities of capitalism (again, views shared by Brezhnev). Economic relations became increasingly important for both sides, but they did not override decisive political priorities.[53]

It was in the military sector that the Brezhnev coalition's policies most directly contradicted its stated goal of promoting détente with the FRG. To the Schmidt government, Moscow seemed determined to expand its arsenals beyond its needs for defense.[54] Particularly disturbing was the Warsaw Pact's burgeoning superiority in tanks and conventional artillery in northern and central Europe.[55] The Soviets evinced little inclination to reach an

52. West German electronic products generally made up less than 5% of the FRG's annual exports to the Soviet Union in this period, and less than 3% of total Soviet imports from West Germany. See Bolz et al., *Wirtschaftsbeziehungen*, pp. 57, 270, 273. On the FRG and NATO's embargo policies at this time, see ibid., pp. 147–52, 295–300, and 474–75.

53. Stent, *From Embargo to Ostpolitik*, p. 232.

54. See *The Military Balance*, the annual report published by the International Institute for Strategic Studies in London. Also John M. Collins, *U.S.-Soviet Military Balance: Concepts and Capabilities, 1960–1980* (New York: McGraw-Hill, 1980), pp. 291–339; and Phillip A. Karber, "To Lose an Arms Race: The Competition in Conventional Forces Deployed in Central Europe, 1965–1980," in *Soviet Power and Western Negotiating Policies,* ed. Uwe Nerlich, 1:31–88 (Cambridge, Mass.: Ballinger, 1983). For official West German views, see the *White Paper* published annually by the Ministry of Defense.

55. In 1970 the Warsaw Pact had approximately 14,000 main battle tanks in this area as against 5,500 for NATO. By mid-1978 the figures were 20,500 for the Warsaw Pact and 7,000

250 / Moscow, Germany, and the West

early accord with the West on these or other conventional forces in the area. The MBFR negotiations quickly bogged down over widely disparate NATO and Warsaw Pact estimates of existing force structures. Soviet negotiators at the Vienna talks displayed a marked interest in achieving a reduction of the Bundeswehr, but their proposals for reductions on their own side fell far short of satisfying the West.[56]

Meanwhile, the FRG made important contributions to the modernization of various NATO weapons systems in these years (such as the advanced Leopard tank and Tornado aircraft), but real military spending rose by little more than 3 percent in the FRG between 1973 and 1977.[57]

These concerns over the conventional weapons balance became considerably magnified as the Soviets began to deploy their new intermediate-range missile, the SS-20. This advanced nuclear delivery system was vastly superior to the aging SS-4 and SS-5 rockets it was designed to replace. It boasted of an extended range (3,100 miles), a multiple payload (three independently targetable warheads), and tactical mobility (it was launched from a truck). Chancellor Schmidt raised his objections to the new missile in conversations with Brezhnev as early as October 1974, at a time when the SS-20 was still being tested.[58] The Soviets deployed their first SS-20s in the western USSR in 1977, and continued to install them at a peak rate of two per week for the next several years.

Conceivably Moscow may have been encouraged to deploy the new missiles by the United States' refusal to include European-based nuclear delivery systems in the SALT II negotiations, a position confirmed by President Ford at the Vladivostok summit in November 1974. It is equally plausible, however, that the Soviets were intent on modernizing their intermediate-range missile capabilities in any event. A move in this direction would

for NATO. (The French had an additional 325 tanks stationed in the FRG and 485 in eastern France.) In conventional artillery the two sides were about equal at the start of the decade, but by mid-1977 the Warsaw Pact had more than 5,600 of these weapons in the same battle area against approximately 2,700 for NATO. A year later the Warsaw Pact figure jumped to more than 10,000 while NATO's remained the same. See *Military Balance, 1970–1971*, pp. 93–94; *1976–1977*, p. 101; *1977–1978*, pp. 106–7.

56. On the MBFR talks see John G. Keliher, *The Negotiations on Mutual and Balanced Force Reductions* (New York: Pergamon, 1980), and Jonathan Dean, *Watershed in Europe* (Lexington, Mass.: Lexington Books, 1987), pp. 153–84. The USSR's accelerating deployments appeared all the more ominous in the light of Soviet strategic writings in this period, with their emphasis on lightning breakthroughs and rapid escalation to nuclear warfare. For a review, see Joseph D. Douglass, Jr., *Soviet Military Strategy in Europe* (New York: Pergamon, 1980).

57. Measured in constant (1976) dollars, the FRG's real military expenditures in this period rose from $14.98 billion in 1973 to $15.46 billion in 1977. Bonn's defense spending held steady at about 3.5% of GNP in these years, but its share of central government expenditures actually dropped, from 25.7% in 1973 to 22.4% in 1977. See U.S. Arms Control and Disarmament Agency, *World Military Expenditures and Arms Transfers, 1968–1977* (Washington, D.C.: U.S. Government Printing Office, 1979), p. 43.

58. See Schmidt's memoirs, *Menschen und Mächte* (Berlin: Siedler, 1987), p. 61.

certainly have been consistent with the Brezhnev coalition's general commitment to military "vigilance" and to the "further strengthening" of Soviet military might. The conviction that West Germany would remain a powerful component of a powerful Atlantic alliance for a long time to come, a view confirmed by nearly all the members of the secondary elite who addressed this question, provided a further argument in favor of a major modernization of Soviet missile forces in the European theater. At the same time, the Soviets were well aware of the "contradictions" that had been building up over the years in Washington's military relationship with its allies as a result of America's presumed reluctance to risk its own destruction in a nuclear war now that the USSR enjoyed strategic parity. This consideration probably convinced many Soviet strategists that the enhancement of Soviet nuclear capabilities targeted on Western Europe could aggravate these contradictions even further. By improving Moscow's capability to deliver sharply pinpointed nuclear strikes aimed at the FRG, for example, the SS-20s would increase the likelihood of the rapid nuclearization of an armed conflict in the European theater, thereby increasing the risk to both Bonn and Washington. In these circumstances, the U.S.–West German defense link might be effectively decoupled, and West Germany could be held permanently hostage to a modernized Soviet intermediate-range rocket force, backed up by the Warsaw Pact's growing conventional arsenals.[59]

The decision to deploy large numbers of SS-20s was also in conformity with Soviet military doctrine at the time, which lacked a conceptual determination of reasonable limits to defense procurements.[60] Even though the USSR's economic problems appeared to necessitate reductions in the annual growth of military spending starting in 1976, these budgetary constraints did not impinge upon Moscow's determination to go ahead with production and deployment of SS-20s.[61]

Most significant, the Soviet leadership repeatedly rejected appeals by Schmidt and other NATO leaders to halt development of the new missiles even when it became abundantly clear to Moscow that relations with Bonn could only deteriorate under the strain of the Soviet weapons deployments. By the end of 1977, the outlines of an impending Soviet–West German confrontation over the military balance in Europe were very much in

59. For an explicit Soviet reference at this time to the importance of the USSR's military strength in weakening the credibility of the U.S. nuclear umbrella in Western Europe, and to West German criticisms of U.S. flexible response strategy, see Yefremov, *Evropeiskaya bezopasnost*, pp. 42ff., 76, 116–17.

60. Benjamin S. Lambeth, "Trends in Soviet Military Policy," in *Soviet Policy toward Western Europe*, ed. Herbert J. Ellison (Seattle: University of Washington Press, 1983), p. 221.

61. The CIA estimated that Soviet defense spending grew at about 4% per year until 1976 but fell to an annual growth rate of approximately 2% per year between 1976 and 1982. See Richard F. Kaufman, "Causes of the Slowdown in Soviet Defense," *Soviet Economy* 1 (January–March 1985): 9–31. See also the remarks by John Steinbrunner and David Holloway in ibid., pp. 32–41.

evidence. Chancellor Schmidt was instrumental in galvanizing U.S. and West European support for the long-term modernization of NATO forces, an idea that won NATO's endorsement in May. Schmidt also agreed to consider a Carter administration proposal for the future deployment of enhanced radiation weapons (the so-called neutron bomb), designed to augment NATO's antitank forces. In October Schmidt gave a much-publicized speech in London calling for a NATO response to the problems raised by the Soviet military buildup in the European theater.[62]

The battle lines were now being drawn for a controversy that would cast a pall over Soviet–West German relations for the next ten years.

The GDR Defines Détente

In 1973 the GDR continued to sound the defensive tone that had characterized its attitudes toward West Germany in the immediate aftermath of Honecker's accession to power, at a time when Moscow was pressuring the East German leadership into moving ahead with détente. To be sure, the positive results of East Germany's recognition by the Federal Republic and by a host of other states were touted with unconcealed pride. Recognized by only 55 states at the end of 1972, the GDR would maintain diplomatic relations with 100 states by the end of 1973. In September 1973 East Germany was admitted to the United Nations, along with the Federal Republic. But with millions of West Germans poised to enter the GDR under the liberalized visitation procedures, and with the West German government's next moves toward East Berlin still uncertain, the Honecker government adopted a combative stance that was clearly intended to warn Bonn against taking undue advantage of the GDR's vulnerabilities.

A combination of positive and negative images of inter-German relations came across quite vividly in statements by Erich Honecker and Hermann Axen, who increasingly stepped forward as the SED's most authoritative spokesman on international relations after Honecker himself. On the positive side, both noted that the diplomatic blockade against the GDR was finally broken, and that East Germany was now making its own "positive contribution" to détente. In more negative terms, however, both leaders stated that the ideological struggle with the West was actually growing sharper, a theme closely related to the GDR's *Abgrenzung* campaign. Honecker observed that détente was by nature a "contradictory" process in which sudden reversals were to be expected. He even warned that any

---

62. Schmidt said that in order to "maintain the balance of the full range of deterrence strategy," NATO would have to "be ready to make available the means to support its present strategy." See *Survival,* January–February 1978, pp. 3–10.

attempt by the West to denigrate the GDR's sovereignty would result in a reduction of East Germany's economic ties with the capitalist states. Meanwhile, both Honecker and Axen reaffirmed the need for "vigilance" in the Warsaw Pact's military posture. More one-sidedly negative images of the FRG were presented by such hard-liners as Albert Norden and Heinz Hoffmann.[63]

The practical implications of this hostile rhetoric became particularly visible toward the end of 1973. In November the GDR raised the minimum currency exchange required of visitors to the GDR arriving from the FRG and West Berlin. The decision was officially justified by the need to provide additional services to the stream of visitors now pouring into the country. A transparent purpose of the new rule, however, was to gain more hard currency for the GDR and, not incidentally, to discourage West Germans from visiting East Germany. At the same time, the new currency edict was meant as a signal to Bonn that the GDR, far from being weakened by détente, was still able to protect its own interests and to impose costs on the FRG for policies it regarded as unacceptable (such as those concerning Berlin's status or the GDR's sovereignty).[64]

Within less than a year, however, the GDR rescinded the most irritating provisions of the currency exchange ordinance. Indeed, relations with the Federal Republic underwent a progressive improvement over the course of 1974. Although polemical attacks against Bonn remained harsh in the first months of the year, the East German authorities were evidently stung by the implications of Brandt's resignation in May. Perhaps out of concern that the Guillaume affair might create an anti-GDR backlash in West Germany, Honecker reiterated his commitment to détente and noticeably muted his attacks on the Bonn government in his first public comments after Helmut Schmidt's assumption of the chancellorship. He did not rule out a meeting with Schmidt later in the year.[65]

The strains that arose over the FRG's determination to establish a West Berlin branch office of the Federal Environmental Agency were not allowed to dissipate East Germany's resurgent interest in establishing a cordial relationship with the Federal Republic. As East Berlin and Moscow decided not to press the issue, Honecker and Schmidt exchanged letters in early September. The opening of this direct channel of communication at the highest level set the stage for the GDR's announcement in late October that

63. Axen: FBIS, *Eastern Europe,* Feb. 21, 1973, pp. E7–8; *Pravda,* Mar. 7, 1973, p. 4; *ND,* May 8, 1973, p. 3. Honecker: *ND,* May 29, 1973, pp. 3–7; Oct. 23, pp. 1–2; and Nov. 1, pp. 3–5. Norden: *ND,* Jan. 14, 1973, p. 6; July 11, p. 6; Oct. 3, pp. 3–5; Oct. 28, p. 5. Hoffmann: *ND,* Mar. 1, 1973, p. 3; May 30, p. 3; Oct. 16, p. 5.

64. Fred Oldenburg, "Ostberlin wieder auf härterem Kurs," *Deutschland Archiv,* no. 11, 1973, pp. 1121–29. Helmut Schmidt has suggested that the Soviet Union prompted the GDR to raise the currency exchange requirement at this time: *Menschen und Mächte,* p. 51.

65. *ND,* May 13, 1974, p. 3; also June 4, pp. 3–4.

the currency exchange requirement would be reduced. In December the GDR took the additional step of absolving visiting pensioners of any currency exchange obligation.

What accounted for the GDR's turnabout? One factor had to be the fact that the East German authorities were now confident that the GDR could withstand the influx of nearly eight million Western visitors a year without experiencing serious social unrest.[66] The long-feared possibility that détente with West Germany might lead to political instability in the GDR had simply failed to materialize.

A more pressing factor, however, was the economic situation. By the second half of 1974 it was increasingly evident that the GDR was being severely affected by the fluctuations in world oil prices. Increases for oil imports from OPEC countries were already costing the GDR an additional 400 million valuta marks a year.[67] An even more direct source of adverse economic influences was the Soviet Union. In 1974, the Soviets informed their COMECON partners that the prices of Soviet oil would double in 1975, and in subsequent years would be based on a five-year average that took world market prices into account. Since the GDR obtained roughly 90 percent of its petroleum from the USSR, it now faced spiraling oil bills for the remainder of the decade.

These external economic constraints threatened to slow the Honecker government's efforts to improve social benefits for GDR citizens. With production bottlenecks and shortages still endemic features of the East German economy, and with the need for hard currency reserves rising rapidly in view of skyrocketing prices for energy, technology, and other items purchased on world markets, it was clearly to the GDR's advantage to maintain and even widen its economic contacts with the Federal Republic.[68] In fact, one of the reasons that the GDR had come to terms on the currency exchange controversy was that the Schmidt government had threatened to cancel future "swing" credits unless the GDR exhibited a more forthcoming approach to this issue.[69] The threat provided a sharp reminder of East Germany's continuing reliance on West Germany's economic assistance.

Not everyone within the SED Politburo appeared to approve of the more positive turn in Bonn's direction. As on other occasions in the past, Albert

66. Honecker noted that between January 1972 and the end of 1974, between 7 and 8 million visitors from capitalist countries had visited the GDR each year, most of them from the FRG and West Berlin. More than 33 million had used the transit routes between the Federal Republic and Berlin in the same period: *ND*, Dec. 13, 1974, p. 3.

67. *FAZ*, Oct. 16, 1974, p. 14.

68. Horst Lambrecht, "Aussenhandel der DDR 1974: Im Zeichen internationaler Preissteigerungen," *Deutschland Archiv*, no. 7, 1975, pp. 852–56.

69. The "swing" was a credit arrangement, dating back to the 1960s, which enabled the GDR to finance short-term purchases in the FRG. In December 1974 a new five-year swing agreement was reached, setting the annual amount of credit available at the equivalent of DM850 million for the 1976–1981 period.

Norden raised the red flag of resistance to extensive economic dealings with the FRG in December. The spirit and letter of Norden's remarks clashed markedly with the latest utterances of Honecker and Axen, both of whom offered justifications for the West's growing interest in trade with the socialist countries.[70] Reports reaching West German journalists at the end of 1974 pointed to dissension within the SED Politburo over the inter-German relationship, as well as to Soviet uncertainty about how far East Germany planned to go in its next moves toward Bonn.[71]

The decision to expand economic ties with West Germany and other capitalist countries proved to be irrevocable, however. Over the next several years the Honecker government entered into an expanding net of trade and other agreements with the West, running up a trade deficit of nearly 4 billion deutschemarks. (This figure contrasted with a total trade surplus of 5 billion valuta marks in the 1963–1970 period.) By mid-1976 the GDR had accumulated a net debt to the West of approximately $3.5 billion.[72]

As the Schmidt government continued to offer various forms of economic assistance to the GDR in the hope of encouraging East Berlin's cooperation over a broad range of issues, the Honecker government seized its opportunities. In addition to the swing credits, visa fees, and other payments made by West German visitors, East Germany profited from a series of agreements on such things as lump-sum road toll payments and highway construction. Between 1970 and the end of 1977 these various transactions amounted to more than DM7.5 billion. In 1976 the GDR's trade with the capitalist world surpassed 28 percent of its total trade turnover, an all-time high; by the following year, more than a third of this trade was with the FRG and West Berlin.[73] A veritable two-currency system developed in East Germany after the government's decision in 1973 to permit GDR citizens to receive gifts of hard currency from Western contacts. Much of this cash was spent in the state-owned Intershops, a network of relatively high-quality stores that proliferated throughout the GDR to funnel hard currency into the national treasury. By the late 1970s the GDR was netting nearly DM700 million a year from these cash transfers.[74]

70. Norden: *ND*, Dec. 14, 1974, p. 5; *Deutschland Archiv*, no. 2, 1975, pp. 191–98, linking the FRG with the Maoist regime. Honecker and Axen: *ND*, Dec. 13, 1974, pp. 3–8; Dec. 14, p. 7.

71. FBIS, *Eastern Europe*, Dec. 11, 1973, pp. E4–5; Gerhard Wettig, *Die Sowjetunion, die DDR und die Deutschland-Frage, 1965–1976: Einvernehmen und Konflikt im sozialistischen Lager* (Stuttgart: Bonn Aktuell, 1976), p. 143.

72. Hartmut Zimmermann, "The GDR in the 1970s," *Problems of Communism* 27 (March–April 1978): 23.

73. Calculated from official West German figures in *Deutschland Archiv*, no. 5, 1978, pp. 529–33, and from data in *Statistisches Jahrbuch der Deutschen Demokratischen Republik, 1979* (East Berlin: Staatsverlag der Deutschen Demokratischen Republik, 1979), p. 232, and Deutsches Institut für Wirtschaftsforschung, *Handbuch DDR-Wirtschaft* (Reinbek: Rowohlt, 1977), p. 233.

74. Hans-Dieter Schulz, "Vor dem Einkauf schnell zum Bank," *Deutschland Archiv*, no. 5, 1979, p. 452.

In return for Bonn's largesse, the GDR came forward with concessions in several areas. The quota of East Germans allowed to visit West Germany on urgent family business rose to more than 40,000 annually; a growing number of family reunification cases was resolved; and direct telephone links between the two parts of Germany, severed during the height of the cold war, were restored. In this spirit, Hermann Axen noted that "compromises" on the part of the socialist states were a necessary element of peaceful coexistence.[75]

The brimming self-confidence that animated the East German leadership in this period was put on display during the closing ceremonies of the Conference on Security and Cooperation in Europe. In effect, the CSCE represented the GDR's international coming-out party, and the buoyant Honecker clearly relished his debut as world statesman. In addition to meeting in Helsinki with President Ford and other Western dignitaries, the SED chief had two sessions with Helmut Schmidt to discuss proposals for future inter-German cooperation. Honecker emphatically restated his commitment to further economic cooperation with the FRG in an interview with the *Saarbrücker Zeitung* in February 1977.[76]

Cooperation by no means represented the only trend in the GDR's approach to inter-German relations in these years, however. East German leaders repeatedly warned of the mutability of détente, with cooperative tendencies alternating abruptly with sharp conflicts. Honecker remarked that the dual characteristics of realism and "adventurism" in Western foreign policy were often visible in one and the same individual, an unconcealable personal reference to Chancellor Schmidt.[77] These artfully balanced images of West Germany showed their negative side on several occasions during the mid-1970s. On the sensitive issue of Berlin's status, for example, the GDR continued to be unyielding.[78] Efforts to fortify the borders with the FRG and West Berlin also continued unabated, and two shooting incidents in 1976 attracted worldwide attention.

Meanwhile, the GDR's internal propaganda organs continued to inculcate "hatred" for the FRG, in keeping with the ongoing policy of *Abgrenzung*. Some SED officials continued to speak of the FRG and the GDR as two separate "nations," in keeping with the SED's earlier formulation of this notion. (Honecker himself appeared to back off from the "two nations" concept in 1973, however.)[79] Some of the SED's sensitivities in these mat-

75. *ND*, Oct. 4–5, 1975, pp. 3–5.
76. Reprinted in *ND*, Feb. 22, 1977, pp. 3–5. Honecker admitted that the GDR's need for hard currency was "greater than is generally supposed."
77. *ND*, Sept. 12, 1975, p. 4.
78. At one point *ND* resurrected Ulbricht's notion that West Berlin lay "on the territory of the GDR," a position that, as before, failed to elicit Moscow's endorsement. See Wettig, *Sowjetunion*, p. 139.
79. A. James McAdams, *East Germany and Détente* (Cambridge: Cambridge University Press, 1985), pp. 143–44. The notion that the FRG and the GDR were two German "nations"

ters stemmed from lingering fears that détente would enlarge Bonn's opportunities to interfere in East Germany's domestic affairs. The CSCE Final Act, which the SED had bravely published in *Neues Deutschland,* inevitably aroused the regime's anxiety with its Basket III provisions concerning the free mobility of the population and improved working conditions for foreign journalists. According to Western estimates, the number of East German citizens petitioning for the right to emigrate to the West swelled to nearly 200,000 within a year after the signing of the Final Act.[80]

The growing prominence of East German dissidents fueled these official concerns. The most sensational case involved Wolf Biermann, a popular Marxist balladeer noted for his lyrical criticisms of the East German government. Biermann was deprived of his GDR citizenship while performing in West Germany in 1976. A month later, a prominent West German journalist reporting from the GDR was summarily expelled. Stricter visa and passport regulations were imposed on all visitors from West Berlin soon afterward. These measures were accompanied by frequent reminders that the FRG was still an "imperialist foreign country," where the enemies of détente had not ceased their intrigues.

While coupling these positive and negative attitudes toward the Federal Republic, the Honecker leadership was also careful to balance its emerging détente with Bonn with reassurances of its undiminished loyalty to Moscow. One of the most conspicuous examples of this special relationship was the new Friendship and Cooperation Treaty signed by the two allies on October 7, 1975. A key provision of the document implied that the GDR might have to provide military assistance to the Soviets in conflicts that arose outside the European theater (in China, for example).[81] East Germany also bolstered its declarations of solidarity with the Kremlin with tangible economic and military assistance.

The GDR continued to be the USSR's number one trading partner throughout the decade, remaining a valuable source of machinery, chemicals, and other industrial products. The two partners also collaborated in setting up "production associations" in their respective economic systems.[82]

East Germany's military contribution to the Soviet alliance system in these years was just as vital. Figures on defense spending published by the East Germans themselves revealed a 73.5 percent increase from 1969 to 1977, reflecting an annual growth rate of 7 to 8 percent. Per capita military spending rose from 372 marks to 654 marks in the same period. While these

---

was first advanced by Albert Norden in 1972. See Ilse Spittmann, "Ulbricht als Sündenbock," *Deutschland Archiv,* no. 8, 1973, p. 787.

80. Werner Volkmer, "East Germany: Dissenting Views in the Last Decade," in *Opposition in Eastern Europe,* ed. Rudolf L. Tökes (London: Macmillan, 1979), p. 121.

81. *ND,* Oct. 8, 1975, p. 1.

82. Leslie Holmes, *The Policy Process in Communist States* (Beverly Hills, Calif.: Sage, 1981).

official figures suggested that the GDR's defense efforts were quite substantial, they probably understated the actual amount of East Germany's military outlays.[83]

The GDR performed other important "services" for the USSR. Starting in the mid-1970s, East Germany assumed an expanding role in the Third World, providing various forms of assistance to key Soviet clients in the Middle East, Africa, and Latin America.[84] The SED also played a leading role in the bloc's relations with controversial West European communist parties. Honecker, Axen, and other officials met periodically with Portuguese party leaders during the tumultuous post-Salazar years, and they were active participants in the occasionally testy dialogue with the Eurocommunist parties of Italy, Spain, and France. These efforts were rewarded when East Berlin was chosen as the site for a major conference of European communist parties in June 1976.

In each of these activities the Honecker leadership pursued three related aims. The first was to reassure the Soviets of the GDR's reliability. To this end, the GDR adopted the Brezhnev coalition's views on East-West relations. Like their Soviet counterparts, SED leaders combined their favorable remarks about détente and East-West trade with stern admonitions about Western aggressiveness and the need for intensified military vigilance.[85] Honecker's second goal was to enhance the visibility and prestige of the GDR in the eyes of the world and, just as important, in the eyes of its own citizens. These efforts served to confirm the SED regime's international and domestic legitimacy, still its leaders' most fundamental goals.

These two efforts promoted Honecker's third aim: to win from Moscow greater latitude to expand the GDR's cooperative relationship with West Germany. By offering repeated demonstrations of the GDR's continuing value to Moscow, the Honecker leadership in all probability sought to trade off its contributions to Soviet foreign and security policy interests for permission to take greater advantage of the special economic benefits made possible by the GDR's unusual relationship with the Federal Republic. Although the Brezhnev coalition was committed to broadening its own economic ties with the FRG, it was not necessarily inclined to savor the GDR's preferential relations with the West European Common Market or its easy access to Western currency.[86] It is not unreasonable to suspect that

83. Karl Wilhelm Fricke, "Der Verteidigungshaushalt der DDR," *Deutschland Archiv*, no. 2, 1977, pp. 160–68.

84. See Michael J. Sodaro, "The GDR and the Third World: Supplicant and Surrogate," in *Eastern Europe and the Third World*, ed. Michael Radu, pp. 106–41 (New York: Praeger, 1981).

85. See, e.g., Honecker's speeches in *ND*, Sept. 14, 1974, p. 3, and May 19, 1976, pp. 3–13.

86. Moscow reportedly instructed the GDR to waive its special status vis-à-vis the Common Market in 1977, to no avail. (East Germany's trade with West Germany was not subject to Common Market trade barriers.) See *Der Spiegel*, Mar. 22, 1977, pp. 51–54. In 1978 the

the Soviet Union, along with other Warsaw Pact states, was jealous of these East German prerogatives. Moreover, as the Soviet–West German relationship darkened over the issue of the military balance in Europe in the latter half of the 1970s, the future of détente was increasingly in doubt. The GDR had a growing economic stake in cooperation with Bonn, and was not likely to favor a new round of confrontation in Europe which might jeopardize further improvements in inter-German relations. A potential difference of opinion with Moscow over the implications of a breakdown of détente now loomed on the horizon.

Thus as the decade advanced, the GDR's relationship with Moscow was not without its tensions or its ironies. Whereas Walter Ulbricht had fought to deflect the Soviet Union's interest in détente, Erich Honecker increasingly sought to sustain it. At a time when the USSR was heading toward renewed conflict with the FRG, Honecker was moving toward greater collaboration with it. And in perhaps the most ironic twist of all, at the very time that the Federal Republic was offering substantial economic incentives to secure East Germany's cooperation, the Soviet Union, through its energy policies and its military demands, was imposing new hardships on the East German economy. Bonn, in effect, was enhancing East Germany's internal stability by bolstering its economic underpinnings, while Moscow—without ever wavering in its basic commitments to the GDR—was actually hindering the SED's efforts to shore up its domestic bases of legitimacy.

Foreign Policy Discussions in the GDR

The shifts and strains in the Honecker regime's foreign policy in the mid-1970s were amply reflected in the leading theoretical journals. Quite a few authors faithfully adhered to the general line on East-West relations put forward by Erich Honecker and Hermann Axen, stressing both the positive and the negative features of détente, inter-German relations, and East-West trade. These mixed images of the world scene duplicated the Soviet Union's general line on East-West relations.[87] As in the

---

Soviets apparently tried to pressure Honecker into restricting the right of East Germans to receive cash from Western contacts, but the GDR authorities did not rescind this right entirely. See Dettmar Cramer, "Abschied vom Intershop?" *Deutschland Archiv*, no. 9, 1978, pp. 897–98.

87. E.g., Hartwig Busse and Klaus Lingner, "Die Politik der friedlichen Koexistenz in den Beziehungen zwischen sozialistischen und kapitalistischen Ländern," *DA*, no. 6, 1973, pp. 1315–34; Hartwig Busse and Werner Hänisch, "Friedliche Koexistenz—Grundprinzip der Aussenpolitik der DDR," *DA*, no. 1, 1974, pp. 18–39; Werner Hänisch, "Aktuelle Probleme der Dialektik von Innen- und Aussenpolitik der DDR," *DA*, no. 9, 1975, pp. 1293–1310; Günter Kühne, "Im Interesse des Friedens und sozialer Fortschritt," *DA*, no. 2, 1977, pp. 5–14.

Soviet Union, however, writers were free to emphasize either the positive or the negative aspects of the prevailing official position. This ability to choose was something of a novelty for the East German secondary elite. Under Ulbricht they had had little opportunity to depart from the SED leader's unyieldingly maximalist outlook. Honecker's Politburo, however, was more of an oligarchical coalition than a directive regime. Accordingly, various members of the Politburo now had somewhat greater room to articulate their political preferences by highlighting specific facets of the omnibus general line, whose overall validity was accepted in principle by all of them.

Thus Honecker and Axen had their differences with Albert Norden over the question of economic cooperation with the Federal Republic. Norden, in fact, maintained a consistently hard line on relations with West Germany. Kurt Hager, the ideological watchdog, generally supported the Honecker-Axen line, but concentrated on the demands of political and cultural *Abgrenzung*. Defense Minister Heinz Hoffmann, who joined the SED Politburo as a full member in 1973, stressed the ominous side of West Germany's foreign policy. He drew attention to the existing "war danger" and called repeatedly for the strengthening of Warsaw Pact forces, while referring to Soviet military superiority over the West. Security chief Erich Mielke also took a hard line on the FRG. Paul Verner and Werner Lamberz tended to accentuate similarly negative themes, such as Bonn's violations of the spirit of détente.[88]

Willi Stoph, who lost and then regained his chairmanship of the Council of Ministers in this period, generally conformed to the evenly balanced Honecker line. So did Günter Mittag, who also staged a comeback after being demoted by Honecker from his position as the Secretariat's leading specialist on economics. Another supporter of the composite Honecker position was the new foreign minister, Oskar Fischer, who replaced Otto Winzer in January 1975. All of these individuals favored broadened economic ties with West Germany, as did certain lower-level functionaries such as Foreign Trade Minister Horst Sölle.[89]

88. Norden: *ND*, Jan. 14, 1973, p. 6, and Oct. 28, 1973, p. 5; "Orientierungsversuche im Dschungel der Krise des Kapitalismus," *Einheit*, no. 7, 1975, pp. 732–41. Hager: *ND*, Jan. 19, 1974, pp. 3–4, and Nov. 25, 1977, pp. 3–7; "Grundrichtungen der gesellschaftswissenschaftlichen Forschung," *Einheit*, no. 2, 1975, pp. 136–43. Hoffmann: *ND*, May 30, 1973, p. 3; Oct. 16, 1973, p. 5; Oct. 18–19, 1975, p. 2; May 20, 1976, pp. 8–9; Nov. 23, 1977, p. 5. Mielke: *ND*, Sept. 26, 1974, pp. 1–2; Feb. 8–9, 1975, p. 3. Verner: *ND*, Dec. 15, 1973, pp. 3, 5. Lamberz: *ND*, May 26, 1977, pp. 3–4. Verner was now the party secretary responsible for internal security matters; Lamberz was the secretary in charge of agitation and propaganda.

89. Stoph: *ND*, May 8, 1974, p. 3; Nov. 28, 1975, p. 3; Dec. 16, 1976, pp. 3–4. Fischer: "Along the Common Course toward Peace and Security," *IA*, no. 4, 1976, pp. 12–19. Sölle: *ND*, Mar. 12, 1975, p. 3. In 1973 Mittag was demoted from secretary for economics to first deputy chairman of the Council of Ministers. At the same time Stoph was moved from his slot as chairman of the Council of Ministers to the less important post of chairman of the Staatsrat, or State Council. Both men regained their former positions in October 1976, apparently because the GDR's dire economic circumstances required their expertise at the highest eche-

Variations in the discussion of East-West issues among the East German secondary elite tended to follow the same paths taken by the decision makers. Some writers placed heavy stress on the threatening side of West Germany's ostpolitik; Willy Brandt and the SPD were attacked in a continuing campaign against *Sozialdemokratismus*.[90] In the same spirit, analysts specializing in security issues excoriated West Germany's military policies and underscored Bonn's role as a favored NATO partner of the United States.[91] Other negatively oriented writers threw a harsh light on economic issues. Without condemning East-West trade ties per se, they conspicuously refrained from speaking out in favor of them. Their denunciations of capitalism, combined with their impassioned defense of socialism, suggested that they had deep misgivings about the wisdom of risking further economic dependence on the FRG or other capitalist countries.[92] By contrast, a number of prominent writers (including Otto Reinhold, who had once championed Ulbricht's motto of economic development "by our own means") argued in favor of widened trade relations with the West.[93]

lon. For an account, see Ilse Spittmann, "Die NÖS-Mannschaft kehrt zurück," *Deutschland Archiv*, no. 11, 1976, pp. 1121–24.

90. E.g., Hans Leichtfuss, "Die Klassenfunktion der sozialen Demokratie," *Einheit*, no. 4, 1973, pp. 416–21; Karl-Heinz Schwank, "Imperialistische Wirtschaftstheorien zwischen Wunschbild und Realität," ibid., pp. 422–29; Eberhard Fromm and Werner Paff, "Das veränderte Kräfteverhältnis und der Antikommunismus," ibid., no. 5, 1974, pp. 521–31; Kurt Tiedke, "Die Politik der friedlichen Koexistenz und die Verschärfung des ideologischen Kampfes," *DA*, no. 5, 1974, pp. 1062–75; Siegfried Schwarz, "Imperialistische Aussenpolitik im Zwang zur Anpassung," *DA*, no. 1, 1975, pp. 68–80 (pt. 1) and no. 2, 1975, pp. 227–44 (pt. 2); and Horst Köhler, "Die 'Europa'-Ideologie des Imperialismus der BRD: Entwicklung und kulturelle Variante," *DA*, no. 2, 1976, pp. 245–63.

91. E.g., Albrecht Charisius, "NATO gegen Entspannung und Abrüstung in Europa," *Einheit*, no. 4, 1973, pp. 484–91; "Günter Frenzel, "Friedliche Koexistenz und Schütz des Sozialismus," ibid., no. 2, 1974, pp. 189–97; Helmut Geidel, "NATO gegen Frieden und Sicherheit," ibid., no. 6, 1974, pp. 741–49; Werner Hübner, "Militärische Macht des Sozialismus im Kampf um die Sicherung des Friedens," ibid., no. 7, 1974, pp. 849–57; Albrecht Charisius and Klaus Engelhardt, "Militarismus heute—Hauptfeind von Entspannung und Sicherheit," ibid., no. 6, 1977, pp. 729–36; Wilhelm Ersil, "Zur Westeuropa-Politik der BRD," *DA*, no. 3, 1973, pp. 650–65 (pt. 1) and no. 4, 1973, pp. 895–909 (pt. 2); Ingo Oeser, "Kampf sozialistischer Staaten für praktische Ergebnisse der Wiener Verhandlungen," *DA*, no. 6, 1976, pp. 805–17; Albrecht Charisius and Wilhelm Ersil, "Die NATO und die Bukarester Deklaration 1976," *DA*, no. 3, 1977, pp. 102–15. Oeser led the GDR delegation at the MBFR talks; Colonel Charisius worked at the Military History Institute of the GDR; Ersil was at the GDR's Institute on International Relations.

92. E.g., in *Einheit*, Karl-Heinz Domdey, "Aus dem Schulbuch des Imperialismus," no. 2, 1973, pp. 219–26; Günter Kalex, "Neues Image für Kapitalisten gesucht," no. 3, 1973, pp. 261–65; Dieter Klein, "Die Grenzen des Kapitalismus in der wissenschaftlich-technischen Revolution," no. 1, 1975, pp. 93–101; Caspar Schirmeister, "Inflation—chronisches Gebrechen des heutigen Kapitalismus," no. 1, 1977, pp. 94–104.

93. In *Einheit*, Otto Reinhold, "Internationale Auseinandersetzung und wirtschaftliche Beziehungen zwischen Sozialismus und Kapitalismus," no. 11, 1973, pp. 1300–1316, and "Die kapitalistische Krise und die ökonomische Zusammenarbeit zwischen sozialistischen und kapitalistischen Ländern," no. 8, 1975, pp. 906–15; Gerhard Weiss, "Die DDR—fester Bestandteil des RGW," no. 1, 1974, pp. 24–33; and in *DA*, Wolfgang Nikolai, "Wirtschaftsbeziehungen zwischen sozialistischen und kapitalistischen Staaten," no. 5, 1973, pp. 1051–62,

Meanwhile, signs of differentiation in the East German evaluation of U.S.–West European relations made their first appearance in the theoretical literature. In a marked departure from the standard depiction of the "Bonn-Washington axis" that prevailed during the Ulbricht era, some writers turned their attention to the contradictions that made the U.S.–West German relationship a complicated phenomenon rather than a seamless web of anticommunist unity. Arguments of a Europeanist nature, similar to those propounded by Soviet writers, gave evidence of a growing sophistication among East German analysts.[94] As in the USSR, the reference to inter-capitalist contradictions provided a rationale for efforts to promote various forms of cooperation with the West, as Honecker's own statements and actions testified.[95]

Conclusions

During the mid-1970s the Soviet leadership under Brezhnev displayed the principal features of a stable conservative coalition. Its definition of détente emphasized the necessity of Bonn's acceptance of the territorial status quo and Washington's acceptance of the Soviet Union's status as a highly competitive global superpower. Ideological considerations, rooted in the persisting antagonism of capitalism and socialism, continued to play a fundamental role in shaping the Soviet leadership's world view. Economic cooperation with the West was pursued within the confines of the existing Soviet central planning system. This narrowly construed concept of détente was accompanied by a major effort to modernize and enlarge Soviet conventional and nuclear weaponry, both in Europe and in the larger strategic context. It was this commitment to expanded military power beyond what was considered sufficient in the West for Soviet security that gradually became the primary foreign policy preoccupation of the Brezhnev leadership. This decidedly conservative tendency threatened to eclipse the cooperative features of Moscow's relations with the Federal Republic and other Western states. Faced with increasingly explicit warnings from Bonn

---

and "Realitäten und Möglichkeiten der ökonomischen Zusammenarbeit in Europa," no. 12, 1975, pp. 1791–1807; Gerhard Brendel and Hans-Joachim Dubrowsky, "Der Aussenhandel der RGW-Länder unter den Bedingungen der sozialistischen ökonomischen Integration," no. 6, 1974, pp. 1320–44; Gerhard Huber, "Zur Wirtschaftskooperation der RGW-Länder mit kapitalistischen Staaten," no. 10, 1975, pp. 1478–94.

94. E.g., Karl-Ernst Plagemann, "Zur Westeuropa-Politik der USA-Regierung," DA, no. 6, 1974, pp. 1367–84; M. S. Siborowa, "Neue Tendenzen in den Beziehungen USA-BRD," DA, no. 10, 1975, pp. 1523–39 (pt. 1) and no. 11, 1975, pp. 1711–22 (pt. 2).

95. See, e.g., Honecker's speech in ND, July 6, 1974, pp. 3–5. See also Hager's call for a "more differentiated" analysis of relations among the capitalist states on the part of East German social scientists in Einheit, no. 2, 1975, p. 142.

that Moscow's unrestrained military growth could not go unchallenged, the Brezhnev regime displayed low levels of adaptability and an equally low readiness to compromise on this issue.

Policy discussions in the Soviet press during this period reflected the dominant foreign policy consensus of the Politburo. Europeanist and Americanist views tended to converge on the Atlanticist outlook preferred by the regime. No voices were raised on behalf of either the potential Finlandization of Western Europe or a joint Soviet-American condominium over Europe. Professional foreign policy analysts, moreover, largely conformed to the postulates of the Brezhnev regime's eight-point conceptualization of East-West relations, with its fundamentally conservative outlook. In the process, they quietly pursued their role as advisers while never losing sight of their obligation to serve as public propagandists for the official policy line, elements of which they broadly shared.

Meanwhile, Erich Honecker moved the SED decisively away from Ulbricht's discredited maximalism. The GDR increasingly shared the main tenets of Brezhnev's conception of détente, with its double-edged tactic of cooperation and conflict with West Germany. However, as the decade progressed and the Brezhnev coalition hunkered down into an increasingly militant foreign policy posture, the GDR groped toward a more balanced approach that would permit a widening of economic contacts with the FRG while reaffirming East Berlin's fundamental loyalties to its Soviet ally. This manifest shift toward a more centrist position was accompanied by increasing responsiveness to Bonn's cooperative initiatives, together with a growing willingness to compromise on some inter-German issues. Public discussion of foreign policy in the GDR also began to open up, reflecting a cautious balance between positive and negative opinions on détente with the FRG. Though the GDR had not yet undertaken any dramatic efforts to differentiate itself from the Brezhnev regime's lapidary conservatism, it was certainly moving toward a more centrist orientation.

For both the Soviet Union and the GDR the mid-1970s seemed to end on a successful note. The Soviets could congratulate themselves on having secured West Germany's de facto reaffirmation of Europe's postwar borders and its willingness to widen its economic ties with the East without giving up their commitment to building up Soviet military forces. The GDR had not only survived the onslaught of West German visitors but actually profited from its economic exchanges with the Federal Republic. In the process it finally emerged on the diplomatic scene as a duly recognized member of the international community. The concluding festivities at the Conference on Security and Cooperation in Europe in 1975 marked the apogee of the Soviets' and East Germans' efforts to build a stable détente with the West which would preserve their security and contribute to their economic well-being.

These outward successes would turn out to be hollow. Moscow's problem was in part conceptual: the Brezhnev coalition's world view contained fundamental inaccuracies and inconsistencies in its evaluation of Western détente policy. The regime's reluctance to permit a more explicit discussion of these issues closed off the possibility of questioning the wisdom of its chosen policy path. The Soviet leadership was particularly blind to the possibility of a Western backlash against the unrestrained expansion of Soviet military power. Meanwhile the conservatives in the Kremlin paid little heed to the country's mounting economic difficulties. Instead they paraded the USSR's military might before the world while camouflaging the magnitude of its economic decline. They also used East-West trade, however meager, as a substitute for urgently necessary economic reforms.

East Germany's achievements were similarly deceptive. The GDR's internal stability and international prestige masked severe political and economic weaknesses both at home and in its relationship with the Federal Republic. The most critical problem was that the SED had yet to instill an enduring sense of national identity in its own population. The regime's lack of confidence in this regard was plainly evident in its *Abgrenzung* campaign and above all in its refusal to tear down the barriers that walled off the GDR from West Germany. The human rights provisions of the Helsinki Final Act made the SED's legitimacy-building problems even more transparent and intractable. So too did the GDR's persisting economic inferiority vis-à-vis the Federal Republic. Luckily, the Honecker regime could count on the West German government's forbearance and assistance. Bonn had no desire to precipitate a political upheaval in East Germany, an event that might end badly for the population there. On the contrary, the SPD-FDP government, together with a growing number of Christian Democrats, was in favor of improving living conditions for the people of East Germany as much as possible and widening the opportunities for face-to-face contacts across the borders through a cooperative and generous détente.

Moreover, the political and economic advantages were overwhelmingly on Bonn's side. The SED's only effective trump card was its control over the fortified borders, which allowed it to determine who got out of East Germany and to influence (through its manipulation of the currency exchange requirements) how many got in. Whereas Bonn's bargaining position rested squarely on its economic strength and the attractiveness of its freedoms and prosperity to millions of East Germans, East Berlin's resided almost entirely in the keys it held to a garrison state.

Over the next several years the conflicts lying just beneath the surface of Soviet-German relations would overpower the fragile structure of détente. Moscow's conservative policies would place severe strains not only on its ties with Bonn but also on its relationship with the GDR. Just as striking would be the deep internal divisions displayed by both the Soviet and East German elites over the implications of the Kremlin's foreign policy course.

CHAPTER NINE

In the Shadow
of the Missiles:
1978–1984

T HE SOVIETS' deployment of SS-20 missiles triggered the most
serious confrontation between the USSR and West Germany since the
prolonged Berlin crisis of the Khrushchev era. It also set off a remarkable
debate within the Soviet establishment on policy toward West Germany.
Opinions openly diverged on the question of Bonn's responsibility for the
deterioration of East-West détente in general and for NATO's decision to
rearm the West in particular. Some members of the foreign policy elite
sharply criticized the FRG while others spared Bonn from attack and
shifted the blame to the United States. The debate provided striking evidence that the Soviets were quite divided in their assessments of the situation. Whereas one group appeared ready to punish the FRG, another group
displayed considerable reluctance to renounce the political and economic
benefits that Moscow stood to gain from a more harmonious working
relationship with the West German government. More broadly, the debate
on Germany in the first half of the 1980s signaled deep misgivings over the
confrontationist course pursued by Brezhnev, Andropov, and Chernenko.

Meanwhile, the same debates were taking place in the GDR. As Erich
Honecker followed Moscow's lead in the anti-NATO campaign while keeping the door open to wider cooperation with Bonn, the East German elites
were openly divided between those who emphasized West Germany's perfidious role in the missile issue and those who stressed the advantages of
inter-German détente. Ultimately Honecker shifted the GDR's focus toward the détente side of this Janus-like policy and reinforced the centrist
elements within his ruling coalition. As *Westpolitik* in East Berlin and
Moscow tilted dramatically in opposite directions, it was obvious that, in
the GDR as in the Soviet Union, opposition was growing to the intransigent

foreign policy stance adopted by a succession of conservative coalitions in the Kremlin.

The INF Tangle

Soviet spokesmen justified Moscow's decision to deploy SS-20 missiles primarily in military terms. In their view, the new rockets represented only a modernization of an aging intermediate-range missile force due for replacement. The Soviets insisted, moreover, that the new deployments did not exceed the limits of the NATO-Warsaw Pact nuclear equilibrium. For Moscow, the SS-20s constituted an antidote to American forward-based nuclear delivery systems in Western Europe. Moreover, the Soviets probably had reason to believe that the emplacement of SS-20s did not violate any agreements with the United States on nuclear force modernization. As the 1980s wore on, the Soviets could also point to expanding arsenals of French and British nuclear forces.[1]

From the outset, however, political calculations rather than purely military ones played a central role in shaping Kremlin policy in the missile controversy. One transparent aim of the modernization program was to keep open the possibility of exploiting "contradictions" between Bonn and Washington. Although Soviet strategists did not seem to hold out much hope of neutralizing the Federal Republic decisively, they clearly perceived opportunities to promote conflicts between the two partners on vital matters of NATO strategy.

The notion that West Germany might be ripe for Finlandization was not supported by Soviet leaders or foreign affairs analysts. On the contrary, the SS-20 deployments came at a time when both the primary and secondary echelons of the Soviet foreign policy establishment were essentially united in the perception that the NATO alliance remained strong, and that the Western allies, irrespective of the disputes that divided them, were still indissolubly bound together by their "common class interests." This bond was regarded as especially solid between the United States and West Germany. Bonn was viewed as actually strengthening its ties with Washington in these years, as the Schmidt government worked to enhance the FRG's political clout and military contribution within the NATO partnership. This

1. On possible Soviet motives for deploying the SS-20s, see Raymond L. Garthoff, *Détente and Confrontation* (Washington: Brookings, 1985), pp. 870–86. For a comparison of U.S. and Soviet views on the INF balance in Europe early in the decade, see *Washington Post*, Nov. 22, 1981, p. E1. The United States claimed that the Western allies (including France) had 924 launchers and approximately 1,229 warheads in the region and that the Warsaw Pact had 2,537 launchers and about 3,787 warheads. According to the official Soviet estimate, the West had 1,031 launchers and 1,483 warheads in the European theater, while the Warsaw Pact's figures were 1,055 and 2,035.

image of U.S.-FRG solidarity, a condition that was expected to last well into the future, was articulated with particular forcefulness by the most conservative elements of the Soviet elite, above all by the military establishment. It was not the weakness of West Germany's alliance commitments that dominated the expressed perceptions of the Soviet elite in this period but its enduring strength.

Nevertheless, the Soviets were intensely aware of the conflicts that continued to vex U.S.–West European relations in a variety of areas. Doubts about Washington's willingness to come to the rescue of its allies in the event of a Soviet attack in Europe had been expressed repeatedly by influential West Europeans, whether explicitly or tacitly, for more than a decade. As we have seen, Soviet commentators were fully cognizant of these West European concerns, and they did not hesitate to attribute them to American (as well as to European) apprehensions about the Soviet Union's achievement of strategic parity with the United States and its "growing military might." It is therefore quite probable that key members of the Soviet elite argued that the deployment of a new generation of missiles aimed at Western Europe could only exacerbate these tensions among the NATO partners by preserving, and perhaps even increasing, the likelihood that any war in Europe would quickly go nuclear. In these circumstances, NATO's flexible response strategy, which was predicated on the desirability of delaying escalation to the nuclear threshold as long as possible, would be rendered rapidly inoperative and thus would require some painful decisions in Washington. By maintaining the nuclear threat to Europe, the SS-20s would undercut the credibility of America's nuclear pledge to its allies, further aggravating the "crisis of confidence" in NATO. If NATO could not be broken up, at least it could be kept in permanent political disarray. From the Soviet point of view, a divided NATO was more achievable—and in many respects more desirable—than a shattered one.

Similarly, a Western alliance that was perpetually at odds over its military strategy was decidedly more achievable than victory in an actual war. Moscow's SS-20 deployments were hardly intended to provide the Soviet government with a foolproof capability to wage and win an all-out nuclear exchange in Europe. In spite of the hair-raising assertions by Soviet military writers of Moscow's determination to resort to nuclear weapons at the very outset of military hostilities on the continent, in fact Soviet strategists also acknowledged the futility of turning Europe into a "heap of ruins."[2] Moreover, Moscow could not be entirely certain how the Western powers would react to a real attack. For all their insistence on the West Europeans' lack of confidence in their American partner, the Soviets in all likelihood did not

---

2. Soviet military authors are quoted in Joseph D. Douglass, Jr., *Soviet Military Strategy in Europe* (New York: Pergamon, 1980), pp. 163–65.

make the assumption that the Atlantic allies would be paralyzed into inaction by an assault on NATO territory or by the threat of one. Here again, the writings of the overwhelming majority of Soviet analysts provide insight into actual Soviet perceptions. Their incessant reminders of NATO's military potential called attention not only to American nuclear arsenals in the European theater but also to the growing military capabilities of Britain, France, and (in the conventional domain) West Germany. These pointed references offered direct evidence that Soviet military affairs analysts viewed the Western allies as formidable foes in any potential confrontation. For the Soviets as for most Western experts and politicians, a war in Europe would be simply too dangerous to constitute a rational policy option.

Other political factors reinforced the Kremlin's reasoning. In keeping with their comprehensive world view, Soviet leaders were convinced that the enhancement of the USSR's military strength per se had already brought a cornucopia of political dividends. Presumably these rewards would multiply as Soviet power grew. Moreover, the fortification of the Soviet Union's image of strength vis-à-vis the West had an important value for its own sake, particularly to the extent that it countered American efforts to dictate terms to Moscow "from a position of strength." Consequently, some Soviet officials may have blithely assumed that when it came to providing a convincing rationale for military procurements, the general principle "more is better" was as good as any. Here again the Kremlin was driven by perceptions of the abiding power of the United States and of the NATO alliance, not by notions of their weakness.

Perhaps the single most important factor underlying Moscow's decision to modernize its intermediate-range nuclear forces (and to build up conventional arms) was the Brezhnev coalition's commitment to the political status quo in Europe. In the eyes of Kremlin conservatives, the maintenance of Soviet hegemony in Eastern Europe and of Germany's divided status remained the irremovable cornerstones of the Soviet Union's position on the continent. Any challenge to these realities had to be effectively resisted. As the events of the past decade had clearly revealed, the most serious external threat to Moscow's grip on East-Central Europe did not come from the United States or from NATO as such, it came from West Germany. Bonn's challenge, moreover, was essentially political rather than military. Ever since the Grand Coalition government, West Germany's ostpolitik had sought to normalize relations with Eastern Europe and to open up East Germany to direct contacts with the Federal Republic. The express aim of these efforts was to create a climate of trust in Europe which would one day prove strong enough to permit reunification.

Bonn's principal weapon in pursuit of these aspirations was not military intimidation but wide-ranging cooperation. Only a Germany that was perceived throughout Europe as irreversibly committed to peace stood any chance of being allowed to regain its national unity. But a peaceful Germany that posed no threat to the East could not help but undermine the very raison d'être of the Warsaw Pact. A comprehensive relaxation of tensions, particularly one that resulted in major force reductions for both alliance systems, would eventually require the Kremlin to relax the controls that held its postwar empire together. The main threat to Moscow's imperium was not military aggression but military détente.

Accordingly, the leading Kremlin authorities felt it necessary to retain a significant element of confrontation in their relations with the NATO allies despite their commitment to a modicum of cooperation. When faced by the fundamental choice of modernizing and expanding Soviet weapons systems or reducing them by agreement with the West, they opted unequivocally for modernization and expansion. In doing so the Soviets were arming less against the military dangers of war than against the political dangers of disarmament.

Finally, the Soviets may also have assumed that the West would not respond to the SS-20s with a major rearmament scheme of its own. This calculation was grounded in the perception that the "myth of the Soviet threat" was declining in Western Europe, making public opinion, if not the governments themselves, less willing than in the past to shell out large sums of money for defense. West Germany's desire for détente, particularly in its relations with the GDR, was seen as reinforcing these antimilitary sentiments. The adverse reaction of many West Germans to the neutron bomb had recently provided an instructive confirmation of these perceptions.

In sum, Soviet decision makers and political analysts had a long list of reasons to justify the modernization of intermediate-range nuclear forces. Depending on the individual, some of these arguments probably carried more weight than others. In all likelihood the chief decision makers were motivated mainly by general political considerations while military planners were especially sensitive to the strategic and technical aspects of the issue. On the whole, however, the list was long enough to attract a broad consensus on the new missiles as the policy formulation process unfolded behind closed doors.[3]

Helmut Schmidt had his own views on the matter. With his long-standing concern for balance and stability in the East-West military face-off, Schmidt was first of all troubled by the Warsaw Pact's superiority in tanks and artillery, which had swelled to even greater proportions in the 1970s. Consequently he had taken the lead in convincing the United States and other NATO allies of the advisability of raising annual defense spending in

3. For a discussion of various models of Soviet defense decision-making, see Stephen M. Meyer, "Soviet National Security Decisionmaking: What Do We Know and What Do We Understand?" in *Soviet Decisionmaking for National Security*, ed. Jiri Valenta and William Potter, pp. 255–97 (London: George Allen & Unwin, 1984).

each country by 3 percent, at a time when yearly growth in U.S. military expenditures had fallen below that figure. The 3 percent goal was accepted by the Carter administration and adopted by NATO in 1977 and 1978.[4]

The SS-20s posed special problems. Schmidt was disturbed by the absence of medium-range nuclear weapons from the SALT II agenda. He was also averse to the Carter administration's decision to trade off cruise missiles, a newly developed delivery system of potential usefulness in Western Europe, against Soviet ICBMs aimed principally at the United States. Europe, in his view, was being relegated to a "gray area" that was inadequately covered either by arms-control negotiations or by efforts to restore what he viewed as a disequilibrium that was increasing in the USSR's favor.

Schmidt was above all determined to avoid giving Moscow any impression of a possible decoupling of the U.S.–West German security partnership. The SS-20s, in his judgment, appeared to pose a particularly serious challenge in this regard. Their extensive range and their MIRV capability significantly increased the number of West European targets that the Soviets were now able to strike with medium-range weapons based in the USSR. Moreover, the mobility and relatively low-yield payloads of the SS-20s provided Moscow with a greater capacity than ever before to pinpoint specific targets. A small-scale Soviet nuclear strike on a limited area in Europe might conceivably be less likely than a full-blown assault on U.S. forces or major population centers to trigger a reprisal by the United States.

This possibility made the troublesome question of credibility increasingly serious. Any doubts about America's willingness to defend its European allies would presumably give the Soviets a psychological advantage over the West Europeans which Moscow could exploit. In Schmidt's view, the SS-20s significantly enhanced the Kremlin's ability to engage in such manipulative nuclear diplomacy, exposing Western Europe (and particularly a nonnuclear power like West Germany) to the prospect of political blackmail. As a consequence, the West German government came to the view that the United States needed to take some kind of action to reinforce the credibility of its extended deterrence doctrine in the face of the SS-20 deployments.

Initially the Carter administration was not disposed to respond to the Schmidt government's concerns by placing new missiles in Western Europe. The feeling in Washington in 1977 was that the Europeans were sufficiently protected by U.S. missile-carrying submarines detached to NATO and by other American forces arrayed across Western Europe.[5] Although the

---

4. See Foreign Policy Research Institute, *The Three Per Cent Solution and the Future of NATO* (Philadelphia, 1981).

5. Ibid., pp. 854–57. Zbigniew Brzezinski, Carter's national security adviser, did not initially favor new land-based missiles in Europe. See his memoirs, *Power and Principle* (New York: Farrar, Straus & Giroux, 1983), pp. 307–8.

United States had been funding and testing the Pershing II missile since the early 1970s as a potential successor to the Pershing IAs that were already based in the Federal Republic, the administration was still far from making a decision on its deployment.[6] In 1978, however, continuing pressures from the Schmidt government and other European allies, backed by supporters of their views in the United States, convinced the Carter administration that a new land-based deterrent located in Western Europe was critical to reaffirming the durability of the American nuclear umbrella.

At a summit of alliance leaders held in Guadeloupe in January 1979, President Carter formally proposed the installation of Pershing II and cruise missiles in the FRG. Schmidt insisted that West Germany should not be the only country to deploy the new weapons. After a series of additional conferences, it was agreed at the NATO meetings held in Brussels in December 1979 that, beginning in 1983, 108 Pershing IIs would be installed in the FRG and 464 ground-launched cruise missiles (GLCMs) would be placed in West Germany and other NATO countries willing to accept them.[7] (Britain and Italy quickly agreed to take a share of GLCMs; Belgium and the Netherlands also agreed in principle to deploy them, but parliamentary objections held up final approval for several years.) The Brussels meeting also affirmed NATO's willingness to engage the Soviets in immediate discussions on the missile issue in hopes of persuading Moscow to halt its SS-20 deployments. Just as important, the negotiating track of the dual-track decision was designed to allay the West European public's fears of an unbridled nuclear arms race that threatened to escalate beyond control. Chancellor Schmidt was particularly interested in exploring every available opportunity to induce the Soviets to accept a negotiated settlement of the INF problem.

From the outset, Soviet leaders professed dismay at NATO's evolving plans for the new missiles. On the eve of a state visit to West Germany in May 1978 (the visit that had been originally scheduled for 1976), Leonid Brezhnev said in an interview with the SPD newspaper *Vorwärts* that only a "pathologically perverted imagination" could conceive that the USSR was building up a military capability that exceeded the needs of defense.[8] As the NATO states moved closer to their INF decision, the tone of Soviet commentary on West Germany's security policy grew sharper. Throughout much of 1978 and into 1979, *Pravda* and *Izvestiya* had characterized the West German government as favoring détente in principle while contradict-

6. Garthoff, *Détente and Confrontation*, pp. 799, 862, 879.
7. The Pershing II was a single-warhead mobile missile capable of reaching targets within a range of 1,125 miles in approximately six to fourteen minutes. The Tomahawk cruise missile had a range of 1,560 miles and a speed of less than 500 miles an hour, and was designed to fly at altitudes low enough to evade radar detection.
8. Reprinted in *Pravda*, May 4, 1978, p. 1.

ing it in practice by impugning the USSR's defense policy. By the spring of 1979, however, the same newspapers were attacking Helmut Schmidt and Foreign Minister Hans-Dietrich Genscher directly for departing from their stated commitment to arms control and for allegedly yielding to the Christian Democrats' pressures for rearmament.[9] Meanwhile, Brezhnev and other top-level Soviet officials stuck to their guns in reiterating the need for "vigilance" and further "strengthening" in the military sphere. Gromyko asserted that the Soviets would "not relax" their defense efforts in the face of NATO's actions. An attitude of hard defiance on military issues characterized the Soviet foreign policy decision-making hierarchy throughout 1979.[10]

The next salvo in what would soon broaden into a massive campaign to pressure the West German government into abandoning its support for new U.S. missiles came in October. Speaking in East Berlin on the thirtieth anniversary of the GDR, Brezhnev declared that the USSR was prepared to "reduce" the number of its intermediate-range missiles facing Europe, provided that no new missiles were deployed by NATO. As a sign of good faith, the Soviet leader announced the unilateral withdrawal of 20,000 Soviet troops and 1,000 tanks from East Germany within a year. Brezhnev accompanied this gesture with a warning to the FRG of unspecified "consequences" in the event of any new NATO missile deployments, and pointedly accused the FRG of joining with the United States in such plans. He also threatened to refuse to negotiate on INF if NATO decided on new deployments.[11]

From NATO's perspective, Brezhnev's speech offered little of substance. The general secretary's proposal to reduce medium-range missiles from the western USSR had not specifically mentioned the SS-20s, leaving open the possibility that it applied exclusively or in part to the obsolescent SS-4s and SS-5s. It also refrained from specifying whether the mobile ss-20s would be destroyed (as NATO demanded) or simply removed eastward to areas from

9. See, e.g., the articles by A. Grigoryants in *Izvestiya*, June 1, 1979, p. 5, and by V. Mikhailov in *Pravda*, June 3, 1979, p. 5.

10. See Brezhnev's speech calling for an agreement on no first use of nuclear weapons and on an East-West nonaggression pact, while at the same time advocating "considerable means to strengthen the country's security": *Pravda*, Mar. 3, 1979, pp. 1–2. See Gromyko's speech in ibid., Feb. 27, p. 2. Suslov's hard-line speech, containing no references to East-West trade, is in ibid., Mar. 2, p. 2. See also his remarks in ibid., Sept. 19, p. 2. Other appeals for strengthening of Soviet defense were expressed by Ponomarev, ibid., Feb. 17, p. 2, and Ustinov, ibid., Feb. 23, p. 3; Feb. 24, p. 2; and Sept. 8, p. 2. Curiously, Yurii Andropov called for "consolidating" Soviet military power, a term that fell short of "strengthening": ibid., Feb. 23, 1979, p. 2.

11. *Pravda*, Oct. 7, 1979, p. 1. Brezhnev also claimed that the new Soviet INF deployments actually reduced the number of intermediate-range Soviet launchers in the European area and their nuclear yield. At the time, this claim was technically correct. See Raymond L. Garthoff, "Brezhnev's Opening: The INF Tangle," *Foreign Policy*, no. 41 (Winter 1980–1981), pp. 82–94.

which they could be easily transported back to forward deployment zones for use in wartime. (The Soviets did little to clarify this matter when Valentin Falin told *Der Spiegel* that the SS-20s would be moved "so far away that you will no longer be able to see them with the naked eye.")[12] The troop and tank reductions were considered nugatory in view of the USSR's huge concentrations of personnel and armor in the GDR. In the end, the Schmidt and Carter governments viewed the October speech as a transparent effort to play upon West German public opinion and to derail the impending NATO decision on INF deployments. A quick visit to Bonn by Gromyko in late November failed to dispel these perceptions, and the Brussels decision was formalized on schedule.[13]

The damage to East-West relations that resulted from the INF conflict widened appreciably when, barely two weeks after the dual-track decision, the Soviet Union invaded Afghanistan. The invasion destroyed what little remained of détente between Moscow and the United States. The Soviets had never really warmed up to Jimmy Carter, whose human rights campaign needled the Kremlin at its most sensitive domestic nerve point. Carter's alternately amicable and hostile comments on the Soviet Union made it difficult for Soviet leaders to draw a bead on the American president. Although Carter himself was committed to détente and arms control out of both political and moral conviction, the administration's denunciation of Soviet activities in Africa, its open courtship of China, and its attempts to close the USSR out of the Camp David peace process in the Middle East only exacerbated what was from the outset an uncomfortable relationship. The signing of SALT II in Vienna in June 1979 constituted the principal highlight of the Kremlin's dealings with Carter, but the cordiality displayed at this summit meeting soon evaporated when it became obvious that the treaty was in serious trouble in the Senate. An anti-Soviet mood was perceptibly growing among the American public, fueled by conservatives' warnings of declining American military strength and by widening disappointment in Carter's effectiveness as a leader even among many Democrats. Many Americans saw the collapse of the Shah's regime in Iran as a gain for Moscow, and the USSR's unsympathetic attitude during the embassy hostage crisis in Tehran further soured the national temper. The incursion into Afghanistan was the last straw, giving Carter little choice but to withdraw the SALT treaty from Senate consideration.

With its relationship with Washington now in tatters, the Kremlin turned to Western Europe in hopes of avoiding complete international isolation. Brezhnev personally spearheaded this effort, making explicit references to

12. See the interview with Falin and Vadim Zagladin in *Der Spiegel,* Nov. 5, 1979, pp. 38–63.

13. While in Bonn, Gromyko hinted that the "impulses" behind NATO's impending INF decision came from the FRG, and not just the United States: *Pravda,* Nov. 25, 1979, p. 4.

Western Europe's special role in preserving détente and blaming the United States for "imposing" the INF decision on the West Europeans.[14] His meetings with Giscard d'Estaing and Helmut Schmidt in the spring of 1980, at the height of American attempts to organize a unified Western reaction to the Afghan invasion, created considerable consternation in Washington. The Carter administration bristled when, before going to Moscow, Chancellor Schmidt proposed a three-year moratorium on INF deployments. Schmidt's intention was to enjoin the Soviets to halt the emplacement of new SS-20s while NATO was waiting for the Pershing II to become operational, in keeping with the two-track decision. On the advice of National Security Adviser Brzezinski, President Carter wrote to Schmidt warning him against abandoning the decision reached at Brussels and accusing him of risking West Germany's neutralization. After a tense meeting with Carter and Brzezinski in Venice, Schmidt visited Moscow on June 30.

In an unusual departure from protocol, Schmidt was allowed to address a group of senior Politburo figures and to meet with the Soviet chief of staff, Marshal Nikolai Ogarkov. According to his own account, Schmidt reaffirmed in no uncertain terms his objections to the SS-20s and his full support for the NATO dual-track decision. Brezhnev responded with an offer to hold talks with the United States on intermediate-range missiles without any preconditions.[15] These talks opened in Geneva later in the summer, but they were soon suspended in view of the presidential election campaign and the Reagan administration's reassessment of the U.S. position.

It was by now apparent that both Moscow and Bonn were caught in an inescapable quandary. The Kremlin's problem stemmed from the Brezhnev coalition's fundamental assumption that Moscow could pursue political and economic cooperation with Western Europe simultaneously with a vigorous military development program. As the INF controversy intensified, the Soviets remained determined to move in both directions at once. Although Brezhnev himself admitted while in West Germany in 1978 that commercial relations with the FRG were encountering difficulties (largely because of administrative problems on the Soviet side, a fact he did not mention), he had a personal stake in expanding Moscow's economic ties with the West. However, if the INF entanglement were to cause Soviet–West German relations to deteriorate, as Brezhnev had plainly implied in October 1979, the economic side of the relationship might be jeopardized. Any effort to punish Bonn for its role in the missile question would presumably include economic sanctions aimed at hurting those sectors of the West German economy that were heavily involved in trade with the East. But a

14. See, e.g., his speeches in *Pravda*, Jan. 13, 1980, p. 1; Feb. 23, 1980, pp. 1–2; and Aug. 30, 1980, pp. 1–2.

15. Helmut Schmidt, *Menschen und Mächte* (Berlin: Siedler, 1987), pp. 113–23.

reduction in commercial and scientific-technological exchanges with the FRG would unavoidably hurt the Soviets as well. While some members of the Soviet elite might not lament this development (Suslov, among others, had evinced little enthusiasm for doing business with the capitalists), Brezhnev and his pro-trade supporters were sure to be disappointed by a diminution of economic ties with the USSR's most favored trading partner in the West. Thus the leaders of the Brezhnev coalition found themselves hooked on the horns of a dilemma of their own making: to punish West Germany would be to punish themselves.

Helmut Schmidt was similarly cornered. Détente had brought tangible benefits to the Federal Republic. While the blossoming of citizen-to-citizen exchanges with the GDR was the gain most widely noticed among the West German populace, the growth of trade with the Soviet Union and its allies was duly appreciated by both the business community and organized labor. Moreover, a decade of ostpolitik had changed the psychological climate of East-West relations in West Germany. Détente had tapped a groundswell of popular longing for an end to the tensions and personal sacrifices experienced for more than three decades by a country poised on the front lines of the cold war. The emergence of a new generation of West Germans into public life reinforced widespread feelings that a page had been turned in the FRG's postwar history. Hopes for a more relaxed international climate were especially strong among younger voters, most of whom had little or no personal recollection of West Germany's vital dependence on the United States in the aftermath of World War II and during the years of sharp confrontation with the Soviets over Berlin. A desire for greater independence from the United States was especially evident on the left, building a strong constituency for détente within the still largely pro-NATO left wing of the SPD and stimulating more pronouncedly anti-NATO sentiments in the new Green party.[16]

In addition to being keenly aware of these shifts in the West German body politic, Chancellor Schmidt was personally committed to keeping détente alive. In his view, West Germany could best serve its interests by drawing the Soviets into long-term economic and cultural interactions with a view to increasing their stake in cooperation. Only a cooperative relationship with the USSR seemed to provide any hope of the future unification of Germany. Furthermore, Schmidt rejected efforts to stigmatize the Soviets publicly for their human rights abuses as unduly provocative and less likely to achieve results than quiet diplomacy. He also regarded trade embargoes designed to punish Moscow for international misconduct as ineffective and self-

16. See Stephen F. Szabo, "West Germany: Generations and Changing Security Perspectives," in *The Successor Generation: International Perspectives of Postwar Europeans*, ed. Stephen F. Szabo, pp. 43–75 (London: Butterworth, 1983).

defeating. Instead of isolating the Soviet Union in times of stress, Schmidt favored a continuing dialogue that would permit Western leaders to air their objections to troublesome aspects of Soviet behavior in frank and direct exchanges with the top Kremlin officials. Talks of this kind, in his view, were all the more necessary in periods of high tension. Together with these positions, Schmidt emphatically embraced George Kennan's concept of a patient but persistent containment of Soviet expansionism as the fundamental starting point of Western policy toward the USSR.[17]

On the basis of these guiding conceptions, Schmidt ultimately moved to separate the political and economic aspects of Bonn's relations with the USSR from the military side of the relationship. Faced with the Brezhnev Politburo's determination to make the same distinction, Schmidt coupled his commitment to NATO's nuclear rearmament with a resolve to encourage more pliant Soviet behavior over the long run by providing significant economic incentives to cooperate. In this spirit, Schmidt proposed the elaboration of a twenty-five-year "framework accord" on economic cooperation with the Soviet Union. This accord was signed during Brezhnev's visit to Bonn in 1978.[18]

After his trip to Moscow in 1980, the chancellor revealed that plans were in the works for a new Soviet pipeline that would siphon natural gas from Siberia to Western Europe. Bonn's obvious interest in the project roiled the Carter White House, which was pressing its reluctant allies to join in a blocwide economic embargo against the Soviets in response to the invasion of Afghanistan. The pipeline project, which Moscow heralded as "the deal of the century," touched off an even more rancorous dispute between the United States and its largest NATO partners in the first two years of the Reagan administration. In the summer of 1981 the Soviet Union signed an agreement with Mannesmann for more than half a million tons of steel pipe for the project. The first in a series of credit arrangements with West German banks was also concluded at this time. After additional pipeline-related contracts were awarded to French, British, and Italian firms over the last four months of the year, a new shock jolted East-West relations. On the night of December 12–13, the Polish government under General Wojciech Jaruzelski proclaimed martial law and banned the Solidarity trade union.

17. For Schmidt's views on the expansionist tendencies of Russian and Soviet foreign policy, see his *Menschen und Mächte*, pp. 28–39.

18. For the details, see Angela Stent, *From Embargo to Ostpolitik* (Cambridge: Cambridge University Press, 1980), pp. 205–7. For an analysis of Moscow's trade with the FRG in this period, see Heinrich Machowski, "Soviet–West German Economic Relations: The Soviet Perspective," in *Economic Relations with the Soviet Union: American and West German Perspectives*, ed. Angela Stent, pp. 49–67 (Boulder, Colo.: Westview, 1985). Machowski concludes that trade with the FRG brought real benefits to the USSR, but not significant dependence. Soviet imports from the FRG made up only 0.4% of the USSR's distributed national income by 1982. See also Jochen Bethkenhagen, "Soviet–West German Economic Relations: The West German Perspective," in Stent, *Economic Relations*, pp. 69–89.

President Reagan laid responsibility for the action squarely on Moscow's doorstep and called for stringent economic sanctions against the Soviets and their allies. The new U.S. administration was particularly anxious to void the Soviet–West European pipeline project. The Europeans demurred.

American pressure on the allies to cancel the contracts intensified in 1982 as the administration took unusual legal steps to block the execution of those parts of the pipeline deal that involved European subsidiaries of U.S. firms. As charges of bad faith were leveled on both sides of the Atlantic, the Europeans stiffened their resolve to honor the contracts. Countering U.S. charges that West Germany risked falling into a dangerous energy dependence on the USSR, the Schmidt government affirmed that by the 1990s the FRG would be meeting no more than about 30 percent of its natural gas consumption and only 6 percent of its total energy needs from Soviet sources. The French made similar assertions.[19]

Faced with these and other arguments, the Reagan administration in November 1982 decided to back off from its attempts to compel the West Europeans to go along with a pipeline embargo. Though the immediate crisis in NATO began to subside, the pipeline controversy had revealed the wide gap that separated the United States from its Western allies on basic principles of East-West trade.[20] In the process, it also provided support for the view held by some members of the Soviet foreign policy establishment that "contradictions" between the United States and Western Europe could be expected to multiply even in periods of East-West confrontation, and not just under conditions of détente.

The continuing furor over Euromissiles exacerbated these conflicts. The Western Europeans had not greeted the two-track decision with unanimity. Influential segments of public opinion in the countries destined to receive the new American missiles were opposed to the planned deployments. The antimissile forces became particularly strong in West Germany. Though only a small minority rejected nuclear weapons or West German participation in NATO categorically, resistance to the impending installation of Pershing IIs and GLCMs fanned across a broad spectrum of the population. Even more alarming for the Schmidt government, opposition to the deployment scheme was spreading within the ranks of the SPD. Notable Social Democrats such as Willy Brandt and Egon Bahr increasingly equivocated in their support of the deployments, and others such as Erhard Eppler and Oskar Lafontaine were even more explicit in their objections to them. The

19. Otto Graf Lambsdorff, "The German Case for the Pipeline," *Washington Post*, July 28, 1982, p. A21. Lambsdorff was the FRG's minister of economics. For the French position, see Michael J. Sodaro, "Moscow and Mitterrand," *Problems of Communism* 31 (July–August 1982): 30.

20. For a survey, see Antony J. Blinken, *Ally vs. Ally: America, Europe, and the Siberian Pipeline Crisis* (New York: Praeger, 1987).

national SPD party organization, spurred by various local party bodies, voted to reconsider official support for the two-track policy.[21]

As the wave of public protests swelled across the Federal Republic in the early 1980s, the Soviets used their well-oiled propaganda machine to take advantage of the Schmidt government's internal difficulties. Moscow's mechanisms for playing upon antinuclear sentiments in the FRG and elsewhere had already had a trial run in the recent campaign against the neutron bomb. When it was revealed in 1977 that the Carter administration had asked the Schmidt government to deploy the enhanced radiation weapons, domestic opposition to the idea developed rapidly in the FRG. Gradually the Soviets awakened to the propaganda possibilities of the small but vocal protest movement. In 1978 the CPSU Central Committee established an International Information Department under Leonid Zamyatin to coordinate Soviet propaganda activities abroad. The department's first deputy chief was Valentin Falin, the former ambassador to the FRG. Although the neutron bomb issue blew over once Carter unilaterally decided to postpone his decision on deploying it, the International Information Department was ready for action once the INF controversy gained intensity.

As opposition to the planned NATO deployments unfurled throughout West Germany, Soviet propaganda skillfully played upon public fears that the United States was simply seeking to confine a future nuclear war to Europe.[22] Whether the Soviet leaders actually believed that the NATO missile deployments could be blocked through popular opposition to them is by no means certain, however. Although Helmut Schmidt's position was increasingly shaky, particularly within his own party, the Christian Democrats were largely united in favor of proceeding with the deployments on schedule. So were Foreign Minister Genscher and leading figures in the FDP. Moreover, the Soviets surely realized that, though their spokesmen in the FRG were given frequent opportunities to articulate their opposition to the NATO missiles in newspaper and magazine interviews and on television, Moscow had no control over the domestic antimissile groups, few of which were communist. There were even signs of Soviet skepticism about the antimissile movement's most outspoken elements. One commentator, a specialist on West Germany, denigrated the Greens as a group of disorganized and anti-Soviet utopians, unschooled in the realities of practical politics.[23]

21. Thomas Enders, *Die SPD and die äussere Sicherheit* (Melle: Ernst Knoth, 1987), pp. 251–75.

22. On Soviet propaganda efforts, see Elizabeth Pond, "Andropov, Kohl, and East-West Issues," *Problems of Communism* 32 (July–August 1983): 41–44.

23. I. Istyagin, "Partiya 'Zelenykh' v politicheskom landshafte FRG," *MEMO*, no. 2, 1983, pp. 129–33. For additional critical comments on the Greens, see the remarks by Nekrasov in FBIS, *Soviet Union*, Mar. 14, 1983, p. CC5.

In any event, the Kremlin displayed little inclination to reach a realistic compromise that might have obviated the installation of at least a portion of the 572 missiles slated for deployment while allowing the Soviets to keep a certain number of the SS-20s. The Soviets were just as quick as the Reagan administration to reject the "walk in the woods" formula that had been sketched out by the two chief negotiators in Geneva, Paul Nitze and Yulii Kvitsinskii, in the summer of 1982. The proposal would have canceled the deployment of the Pershing IIs, a significant concession that took account of the USSR's concern that the speed of this weapon (which could hit some Soviet targets in as little as six minutes) would provide the Kremlin with virtually no warning time.[24] Moscow's acceptance of a compromise of this sort might have severely complicated efforts by both the Schmidt government and the United States to maintain a firm front in favor of implementing the Brussels two-track decision. In the absence of such a forthcoming position on negotiations, the Kremlin was forced to fall back on the conceivable but unlikely prospect that the antimissile movement would succeed in forcing the West German government to abandon its support for the dual-track decision.

Nothing in postwar experience, however, would have encouraged the Soviets to believe that protest groups in West Germany could overcome the will of a majority of the members of the Bundestag. If anything, the Soviets were probably just as surprised as many West German officials by the dimensions of the protest against the NATO missiles. Moreover, as the INF crisis heated up, West German public opinion on the issue became increasingly ambiguous. Though opposition to the planned NATO deployments grew, a growing percentage of West Germans came around to the view that the Soviet threat was actually increasing, and that the Warsaw Pact was stronger than NATO. These conflicting trends in public opinion, while revealing widespread concern over NATO's two-track policy, also provided visible indications that Moscow's military policies were stimulating new fears of the USSR in the West German population.[25]

24. The Nitze-Kvitsinskii formula would have required the USSR to scale down its existing 225 SS-20s facing Europe to 75. In addition to refraining from deploying the Pershing IIs, the United States would deploy 75 GLCMs (each carrying four warheads). For an account, see Strobe Talbott, *Deadly Gambits* (New York: Knopf, 1984), pp. 116–51.

25. Responses by West Germans in public opinion surveys on the INF issue varied with the way the questions were phrased. Some polls showed a majority opposed to the planned deployments. But others, which deliberately included references to Soviet warheads or to arms-control negotiations, indicated that opposition to the NATO missiles fluctuated between 26% and 39% of West Germans between July 1981 and April 1982. See William K. Domke, Richard C. Eichenberg, and Catherine M. Kelleher, "Consensus Lost? Domestic Politics and the 'Crisis' in NATO," *World Politics* 39 (April 1987): 382–407. According to another poll, the percentage of FRG respondents who considered the Soviet military threat to be large grew from 41% to 50% between 1977 and 1981, before falling to 47% by 1984: *Der Spiegel*, June 12, 1989, p. 36. Other surveys reported that in 1983 the percentage of West Germans who considered the FRG to be militarily threatened was larger than the percentage that did not

Moreover, at least some of the wind was knocked out of the sails of the West German peace movement in November 1981, when President Reagan announced his "zero option" approach to the INF negotiations, which had just resumed in October. The proposal represented a new twist in NATO's response to Brezhnev's call earlier in the year for an immediate moratorium on INF deployments.[26] Responding directly to public concerns in Western Europe (and to a suggestion advanced by Schmidt), Reagan proposed a simple solution to the Euromissile problem: if Moscow agreed to destroy all of its SS-4s, SS-5s, and SS-20s (including those facing Asia), NATO would not deploy any of the 572 missiles envisioned in the dual-track decision. Though the antimissile opposition remained powerful, its momentum was temporarily interrupted.

The Kremlin's lack of flexibility grew all the more evident as relations with the Reagan administration withered. Moscow's long-standing desire to be acknowledged by the United States as an equal superpower met a rude reception in President Reagan's rhetorical swipes, particularly his condemnation of the USSR as an "evil empire." Soviet attitudes toward Reagan grew even more jaundiced when, in March 1983, he proposed the creation of an elaborate space-based antimissile system, the Strategic Defense Initiative (SDI). Kremlin spokesmen quickly assailed the idea as an American attempt to gain a first-strike capability. As Soviet-American relations plummeted to their lowest point in decades, it might have been only natural for the Soviets to shift their main overtures to Western Europe, and particularly to the FRG, where skepticism about Reagan's tactics and hopes for an early abatement of tensions were running high.

Yet the Brezhnev coalition did little to rescue Helmut Schmidt's floundering government in 1982. By the first part of the year it was increasingly evident that the SPD was losing its ability to govern effectively; the INF controversy was eating away at the fabric of its internal cohesion and disagreements over budgetary priorities were undermining its relationship with the Free Democrats. By summer Genscher was ready to switch the FDP's allegiance to the Christian Democrats. A new government under Helmut Kohl was formally established on October 1, with Genscher remaining as foreign minister. Kohl immediately announced his pledge to implement the NATO decision, and called for new elections to be held in March 1983.

Though it was highly uncertain that Moscow might have succeeded in

---

(46% to 40%) for the first time in several years. In 1982, 25% regarded NATO as stronger than the Warsaw Pact, 32% saw the Warsaw Pact as stronger, and 27% rated them as equally strong. In 1983 these figures were 13%, 36%, and 37%, respectively. See *The Germans and America: Current Attitudes* (Bonn: Friedrich Ebert Foundation, 1987), p. 43.

26. See Brezhnev's foreign policy remarks at the 26th CPSU Congress in *Pravda*, Feb. 24, 1981, pp. 2–4.

saving Schmidt's position, a mutually acceptable agreement on INF would surely have gone a long way toward shoring it up. Schmidt found the Soviets unbudgeable on the missile issue, however. Ever since 1974, Schmidt had consistently stated his objections to the SS-20s. The missiles had been the top item on the chancellor's agenda when he met with Brezhnev in 1978 and 1980. During Brezhnev's final trip to the FRG in November 1981, Schmidt told the visibly ailing Soviet leader that he would risk the survival of his own government to carry out the 1979 NATO deployment decision. The gravity of the Soviet missile deployments was also the central topic of a series of letters Schmidt exchanged with Brezhnev. In all of these personal exchanges, Schmidt found the general secretary to be personally affable and sincere in his wishes for good relations with the FRG, but unbending when it came to the SS-20s. Schmidt got an even more obstinate reception from Gromyko, who exercised a growing authority as Brezhnev's strength waned. At times the Soviets simply refused to discuss the INF issue with the West Germans, preferring to spend their moments with Schmidt berating the United States and China. Schmidt ultimately concluded that the Soviet leadership was not capable of appreciating Western concerns about Soviet military might, and would not negotiate on the INF issue with anyone but the United States.[27]

The public utterances of the Kremlin oligarchs confirmed these impressions. Brezhnev advanced various Soviet proposals for a freeze on INF deployments, and in March 1982 announced a moratorium on further SS-20 installations in the western USSR. At one point Brezhnev referred to the need of all Europeans to acknowledge that Europe was "our common home," a theme that Gorbachev would resuscitate and pursue even more vigorously.[28] Nevertheless, the general secretary also charged the West with making "material preparations for war," the accusation of such hard-liners as Ustinov and Ponomarev. Brezhnev promised military countermeasures in the event of the deployment of the U.S. missiles, and he reaffirmed the basic outlook of the wartime generation by stating in emotionally charged terms that the lessons of World War II continued to demand strong Soviet resistance to Western threats, economic blockades, and "military aggression." Once again, high-level Soviet officials sounded similar themes.[29]

The leadership changes that took place in Bonn and Moscow at the end

27. Schmidt, *Menschen und Mächte*, pp. 90, 92, 110–11, 127–28.
28. See Brezhnev's remarks while in Bonn in *Pravda*, Nov. 24, 1981, p. 2. On this theme, see Ye. Grigorev and V. Mikhailov, "Evropa—nash obshchii dom," ibid., Nov. 25, 1981, p. 4.
29. In *Pravda*, see Brezhnev, Feb. 23, 1980, pp. 1–2; May 10, 1981, p. 1; May 23, 1981, pp. 1–2; June 24, 1981, pp. 1–2; Mar. 17, 1981, pp. 1–2; and May 19, 1982, pp. 1–2; Gromyko, Feb. 19, 1980, p. 2; Suslov, Feb. 21, 1980, p. 2 (Suslov died in January 1982); Grishin, June 22, 1980, p. 3; Ustinov, Feb. 14, 1980, p. 2, and Feb. 22, 1980, pp. 2–3; and Ponomarev, Feb. 5, 1980, p. 3; Apr. 22, 1980, pp. 1–3; May 30, 1981, p. 4; and May 31, 1981, p. 4.

of 1982 (Brezhnev died on November 10) did little to change the situation. Although Helmut Kohl assumed office with a pledge to seek improved relations with the East on the basis of the treaties that the SPD-FDP governments had concluded with the USSR and other socialist states, the establishment of the new Christian Democratic–FDP government made the implementation of the NATO missile plan a virtual certainty. In Moscow, Yurii Andropov did little to change the essential conservatism of the Kremlin's foreign policy establishment, despite calls for economic reform and efforts to rejuvenate party cadres. Though he advanced new INF proposals that called for reductions in British and French missile forces, he consistently refused to negotiate on the basis of Reagan's proposed zero option.[30] Even when Kohl expressed support for the walk-in-the-woods formula as a possible basis for negotiation, the Soviets remained mum on the subject. As a result, they may have passed up a singular opportunity to drive a wedge between Kohl and President Reagan, who remained opposed to the Nitze-Kvitsinskii plan. The Soviets appeared to be equally unwilling to make any dramatic compromises that might have upset Kohl's chances in the 1983 Bundestag elections. On the contrary, a statement by Gromyko during the election campaign calling on West Europeans to display their "political maturity" by rejecting the U.S. negotiating strategy backfired on the Soviets, as it was widely regarded in the FRG as a crude attempt to intervene in the West German electoral process.[31] Although the Social Democrats, led by Hans-Jochen Vogel, favored unstinting efforts to negotiate an INF settlement at Geneva, the Soviet media blamed the SPD's "vacillations" for the reelection of the Kohl-Genscher coalition.[32]

A visit to Moscow by Chancellor Kohl in July failed to end the INF deadlock. Andropov bluntly warned the chancellor that Soviet countermeasures would inevitably follow in the wake of NATO's rearmament, compelling the Soviet Union and the Federal Republic to face each other through "pallisades of missiles." As the deadline neared for the scheduled NATO deployments, Andropov proposed the "liquidation" of all but about 140 SS-20s targeted on Western Europe.[33] The proposal required NATO

30. In November 1982, shortly after Andropov assumed power, the Soviets proposed a freeze on further INF deployments and a phased reduction of missiles and bombers to 600 on each side by 1985, to 300 by 1990, and eventually to zero. On December 21, during a visit by the SPD's Hans-Jochen Vogel, Andropov offered to reduce the SS-20 arsenal to 162, the same number as the British and French forces: *Pravda*, Dec. 22, 1982, pp. 1–2. This proposal implied that the USSR would move its remaining SS-20s eastward rather than destroy them.
31. *Pravda*, Feb. 24, 1983, p. 4.
32. See the comment made on Soviet TV in FBIS, *Soviet Union*, Mar. 8, 1983, p. G1. For another comment criticizing the SPD for not "firmly and decisively" declaring its opposition to the U.S. missile deployments, see ibid., Mar. 14, 1983, p. CC6. Falin maintained that Kohl had won the election largely on economic issues, arguing that the missile controversy was of secondary importance. See *Izvestiya*, Mar. 18, 1983, p. 5.
33. *Pravda*, Oct. 27, 1983, p. 1. A month later, the Soviets cut the figure to 129.

to desist from deploying any new missiles in Europe, however, and was promptly rejected by the United States.

By the end of 1983, with no effective compromise in sight, the stage was thus set for both sides to carry out their promised deployments. As the first NATO missiles were readied for their destinations, Moscow announced that it would proceed to install new shorter-range missiles in the GDR and Czechoslovakia. These "countermeasures" were accompanied by Moscow's decision to walk out of the Geneva negotiations, suspending further INF talks with the United States indefinitely.

But what other actions—if any—would the Soviets take to demonstrate their particular animus toward the Federal Republic? On this issue the Soviet elite appeared to be quite divided.

The Soviet Debate on West Germany

Three questions stood out as especially controversial in the USSR in this period. First, to what extent was the FRG responsible for the general deterioration of détente? Second, to what extent was Helmut Schmidt personally to blame for the NATO dual-track decision of 1979? And third, should Helmut Kohl's foreign policy be condemned as essentially "revanchist," or did it share some of the cooperative aims of the ostpolitik of Willy Brandt and Helmut Schmidt? Clear differences of opinion on these issues signaled uncertainty and disagreement among prominent Soviet foreign policy specialists on the tacit question whether Bonn should be singled out for special penalties in view of its stance on INF. All three of these questions were still open to debate in 1984, even after the Soviet daily press and propaganda organs had unleashed a vituperative campaign against West German "revanchism."

The first question separated those who believed that Bonn shared equal responsibility with the United States for the decline of détente from those who laid the blame primarily on Washington's shoulders. The first group usually stressed the bonds of "Atlantic solidarity" that knotted the two NATO allies firmly together. As we have seen, some writers frequently used this image of U.S.–West European partnership with a generally negative portrayal of the West's intentions to stress the dangers of the NATO threat and the obstacles to détente deliberately being erected by Western leaders. As employed in the evolving debate on West Germany in the 1980s, this argument made it very clear that Bonn could not be expected to exhibit any serious independence from its American partner, particularly in the military domain. Occasionally these writers would reinforce their analyses with quotations from Helmut Schmidt or other West German leaders suggesting that Bonn actually relished its status as the "chief ally" of the United States in Europe. By the same token, these authors held out little hope for a renewal of the spirit of détente in the United States. (Thus they could not be considered Americanists.) The overwhelming impression conveyed by these analysts was that the Kremlin should dig in its heels and refuse to make major concessions to either Bonn or Washington in the sharpening confrontation over Euromissiles. They also implied that West Germany should not be spared any "countermeasures" as a direct response to the stationing of the new American missiles.[34]

On the other side of this debate were those Soviets who tended to blame the United States "above all" for the erosion of détente. These analysts noticeably refrained from criticizing the West German government directly on this issue. In some cases they embellished their arguments with positive portrayals of Bonn's continuing desire for détente or for greater autonomy. Often these writers adopted an explicitly Europeanist outlook, stressing the primacy of contradictions in U.S.–West German relations (and, more broadly, in U.S.–West European ties). Some cited Helmut Schmidt or other West German officials approvingly to substantiate their claims about growing discord between Bonn and Washington. As might be expected, several of these writers had a field day detailing the bitter clashes between the United States and its West German allies over economic sanctions against the Soviet bloc. In their view, these economic disputes were bound to affect the entire range of U.S.–West German relations, including its military components. As a consequence, writers who took this approach made it rather obvious that Soviet decision makers should make a sharp distinction between Washington and Bonn when it came time to mete out penalties for intransigence in the INF controversy.[35]

34. In *MEMO*, A. Nikonov and R. Faramazyan, "Opasny kurs nagnetaniya voennoi napryazhennosti," no. 1, 1981, pp. 47–59; G. Sogomonyan, "Novy 'krestovy pokhod': Ideologiya i praktika," no. 5, 1983, pp. 37–48; V. Fyodorov, "V farvatere Vashingtona," no. 1, 1984, pp. 78–81, and "Zloveshchaya nostalgiya," no. 10, 1984, pp. 114–20; Yu. Melnikov, "Mirovoye sosushchestvovaniye i borba za pravo na zhizn," no. 11, 1984, pp. 3–14. Also, in *IA*, D. Yershov, "The Junior Partner in NATO's Military Harness," no. 3, 1980, pp. 28–37; A. Urban, "West Germany: Under Cover of 'Atlantic Solidarity,'" no. 5, 1980, pp. 61–69; Y. Konstantinov, "For Peace and Security in Europe," no. 5, 1981, pp. 48–58; and V. Shatrov, "Western Europe: New Military-Political Combinations in NATO," no. 8, 1984, pp. 41–49.

35. E.g., in *MEMO*, Bykov, "Glavnaya obshchechelovecheskaya problema," no. 3, 1980, pp. 3–16, and "V avangarde borby za uprocheniye mira," no. 10, 1980, pp. 3–16; V. Shamberg, "SShA v sovremennom mire," no. 7, 1980, pp. 43–57; L. Istyagin, "V rusle opasnoi strategii," no. 7, 1981, pp. 80–86; V. Lukov and A. Zagorskii, "Bely Dom protiv 'proekta veka,'" no. 3, 1982, pp. 104–7; V. Linnik, "SShA: Imperskiye ambitsii i realnost," no. 10, 1982, pp. 42–54; S. Madzoevskii and D. Tomashevskii, "Rost mezhdunarodnoi napryazhennosti i Zapadnaya Evropa," no. 11, 1982, pp. 42–51; G. Vorontsov, "Evropa: Proiski Vashingtona i imperativy bezopasnosti," no. 12, 1982, pp. 45–57; G. Yevgenev, "Initsiativa v polzu evropeiskovo i vseobshchevo mira," no. 7, 1983, pp. 23–31; V. Zagladin, "Sovremenny mezhdunarodny krizis v svete leninskovo ucheniya," no. 4, 1984, pp. 3–24; B. Shemyatenkov, "'Kholodnaya voina' ili razryadka: Dilemmy vneshnei politiki SShA," no. 5, 1984, pp. 3–14; V. Baranovskii, "NATO i EEC v politike imperializma," no. 6, 1984, pp. 27–38. In *IA*,

Meanwhile, several writers addressing the decline of détente adopted a mixture of positive and negative perceptions of the FRG. Usually their analyses combined criticism of West German policies in some areas (such as military policy) with support for the FRG in others (such as East-West trade). This somewhat flexible Atlanticist approach suggested that the Soviet Union should not back down from its differences with the FRG over the military balance in Europe, but it should nevertheless seek to improve its trade relationship with Bonn. It also implied that the Kremlin leadership should remain sensitive to the opportunities still available for playing upon existing strains within the U.S.–West German relationship without expecting a dramatic rupture between the two NATO allies. The main policy recommendation that appeared to follow from this line of reasoning was that Moscow should apply only a limited penalty at best to the FRG in the light of the Pershing II and GLCM deployments, one that would not preclude continuing cooperation with Bonn in the economic sphere or other areas.[36]

The second question at issue in these troubled years, the role played by Helmut Schmidt in the formative stages of NATO's decision to rearm, sparked an unusually frank exchange of opinions. Some analysts insisted that Schmidt's government had played a "particular role" in the elaboration of the NATO two-track decision. An unsigned article in *International Affairs* contended that the SPD-FDP government had won the support of Franz-Josef Strauss and other conservatives for a proposal to ask NATO to introduce new U.S. missiles into Western Europe.[37] Another article (also unsigned) argued that "it would be oversimplifying matters to see the stand taken by the NATO allies solely as a concession to U.S. pressure."[38] Other writers recalled Schmidt's London speech in the fall of 1977, in which the chancellor had suggested the desirability of a NATO response to the new Soviet SS-20 missiles. One of these specialists underscored Schmidt's "insistence" on new American missiles in Europe, while another stated that Schmidt still wanted the missiles even though he had earlier maintained

---

A. Akhtamzyan, "Leninist Policy of Peace," no. 4, 1980, pp. 3–12; V. Knyazhinsky, "The West's Foreign Policy Dead Ends," no. 3, 1981, pp. 6–14; N. Polyanov, "Atlanticists versus Europe," no. 4, 1982, pp. 105–12; V. Gorsky, "EEC-USA: Transatlantic Duel," no. 10, 1982, pp. 24–32; V. Zagladin, "The Peace Programme for the 1980s: Implementation and Follow-up," no. 3, 1983, pp. 35–42; and N. Shmelyov, "Economic Sanctions—An Instrument of US Hegemonistic Policy," no. 8, 1983, pp. 58–66.

36. E.g., G. Trofimenko, "Politika bez perspektivy," *MEMO*, no. 3, 1980, pp. 17–27; and in *IA*, L. Vidyasova, "US Imperialist Foreign Policy and the Modern World," no. 1, 1980, pp. 84–94; S. Tarov, "USSR-FRG: Dialogue Continues," no. 9, 1980, pp. 88–96; A. Sergeyev, "The Hypocritical Intrigues around Poland," no. 4, 1982, pp. 67–76; V. Nekrasov, "Europe in the Focus of World Politics," no. 3, 1983, pp. 86–94; L. Minayev, "American Hegemonism and Interimperialist Contradictions," no. 11, 1983, pp. 40–48.

37. "European Security and Military Détente," *IA*, no. 2, 1980, pp. 4, 6.

38. "Socialism and Peace in Europe," *IA*, no. 8, 1980, p. 6.

that nuclear parity already existed in Europe.[39] One scholar branded the Schmidt-Genscher government as "one of the initiators" of the 1979 NATO decision.[40]

Other writers advanced precisely the opposite view. They contended that plans for the deployment of the Pershing II and cruise missiles had been hatched in the United States and subsequently "imposed" on the FRG and other NATO allies. This view found favor among certain senior Soviet officials in the secondary elite, including Vadim Zagladin, the deputy head of the Central Committee's International Department. On the eve of the December 1979 NATO decision in Brussels, Zagladin accused the Pentagon of having worked out the deployment plans in advance, and alluded to U.S. "pressure" on the West Europeans to take the missiles.[41] A number of Soviet scholars shared these views, including representatives of both the positive and the mixed set of perceptions of the FRG.[42] One of them pointedly accused "NATO propaganda" of spreading the idea that it was the West European allies of the United States who had requested the deployment of the new American missiles in Europe, and concluded: "In fact, things were quite different."[43]

The Soviet discussion of the Schmidt government's complicity in the missile controversy continued well into 1983, long after Helmut Kohl's cabinet had replaced the SPD-FDP coalition and had emerged victorious in the elections of March 1983. As the scheduled deployment date for the first Pershing II and cruise missiles neared, advocates of the two positions pressed their opposing arguments with renewed insistence. Striking a negative note, one Soviet specialist wrote that responsibility for NATO's 1979 INF decision "must be shared by official Bonn," and quoted the *Frankfurter Rundschau* as reporting that this decision "was adopted in the past under pressure from the Federal Republic of Germany." Other writers adopted similar views.[44]

A contrary view was advanced by Valentin Falin, who maintained that,

39. A. Grigoryants, "The FRG: In the Snares of 'Nachrüstung,'" *IA*, no. 6, 1981, p. 101; N. Polyanov, "Washington's Fantasies and European Realities," *IA*, no. 11, 1982, pp. 99–100, 103–4.

40. E.g., V. Fyodorov, "Pered opasnym rubezhom," *MEMO*, no. 9, 1982, p. 112.

41. V. Zagladin, "Rabochy klass, sotsializm i mir," *MEMO*, no. 11, 1979, p. 17. In 1984 Zagladin asserted that it was "no secret" that the Pershing IIs and cruise missiles had been "imposed by the Americans" on Western Europe: FBIS, *Soviet Union*, July 3, 1984, p. CC8.

42. E.g., V. Davydov and N. Seregin, "'Evrorakety' protiv evropeiskoi bezopasnosti," *MEMO*, no. 9, 1980, pp. 137, 138; Y. Rakhmaninov, "Evropa na otvetstvennom rubezhe," ibid., no. 8, 1982, p. 9, and "For Peace and Fruitful Cooperation in Europe," *IA*, no. 7, 1980, p. 5; A. Platonov, "Yes to Dialogue, No to Confrontation," *IA*, no. 10, 1981, p. 25.

43. N. Yuryev, "Peace in Europe and US Militaristic Policy," *IA*, no. 6, 1984, p. 22.

44. A. Grigoryants, "FRG-USA: Subservient Relationship," *IA*, no. 11, 1983, p. 109. The author was *Izvestiya*'s correspondent in Bonn. See also S. Sokolskii, "Pervye shagi konservativnovo pravitelstva," *MEMO*, no. 7, 1983, p. 132, and the remarks of A. N. Yakovlev in *MEMO*, no. 12, 1984, p. 107.

though some people might locate the source of the two-track decision in Schmidt's 1977 speech, its roots were actually to be found in the earlier decision of the U.S. government to install a new generation of Pershing missiles in Europe. This American decision was taken, Falin alleged, even before the appearance of the first Soviet SS-20s.[45] Another authoritative Soviet international affairs specialist, Gennadii Vorontsov, expanded on this argument at considerable length. Vorontsov maintained that the NATO decision of 1979 (as well as the May 1978 decision on long-term modernization of NATO forces) originated in the determination of the Carter administration to move from détente to confrontation. The United States, Vorontsov said, had played "the decisive role" in the initiation of both these actions. He went out of his way to exculpate Helmut Schmidt, quoting the former chancellor as saying in 1981 that the two-track decision was "not my idea." At the end of 1984 Vorontsov noted that, though many people in the West assumed that the SPD leadership had joined in initiating the dual-track decision, the Social Democrats had now turned decisively against the deployment of the new American missiles.[46]

To be sure, efforts to portray Helmut Schmidt as bearing no responsibility whatever for NATO's missile plans represented a gross distortion of the actual events as prominently reported in the West. The Soviet international affairs experts who took part in these discussions were surely well aware of Western accounts of Schmidt's role. What mattered most in these debates, however, was not historical veracity but whether the FRG should suffer special sanctions once the NATO missiles were deployed. Those who stressed Schmidt's personal involvement in the deployment strategy seemed to be arguing in favor of punishing the FRG. Those who pinned the blame for the missiles directly on the United States were in effect arguing against the imposition of any severe, long-term penalties on Bonn which might ultimately redound to Moscow's disadvantage.

The third issue over which Soviet foreign affairs specialists squared off was how the Kohl government should be evaluated. Here again, manifest

45. Valentin Falin, "Podvodya itogi . . . ," *MEMO*, no. 12, 1983, pp. 10–11. At the height of the Soviet antirevanchism campaign in 1984, which featured numerous reminders of the Nazi invasion, Falin referred instead to *American* and *British* perfidy in their wartime dealings with the Soviet Union: "Front na dva fronta," ibid., no. 7, 1984, pp. 11–19.

46. Gennadii Vorontsov, "Bezopasnost Evropy i yadernoye oruzhiye srednei dalnosti," *MEMO*, no. 7, 1984, pp. 20–23, and "SShA, NATO i evrorakety," ibid., no. 11, 1984, p. 17. Vorontsov's reference was to a statement made by Schmidt before a group of American journalists indicating that it was President Carter who had made the formal proposal for the 572 new U.S. missiles at Guadeloupe. Schmidt claimed that he himself was "never enthusiastic" about the plan, an assertion that took U.S. officials by surprise. See *Washington Post*, Oct. 31, 1981, p. A12. For additional allegations that the decision to deploy new American missiles in Europe antedated the SS-20s, see G. Yevgenev and A. Aleksimov, "The Problem of Nuclear Arms Limitation in Europe: Why Does the USA Maintain an Impasse at the Geneva Talks?" *IA*, no. 11, 1983, p. 61; and V. Abarenkov, "Washington's Big Lie Concerning the Geneva Talks," *IA*, no. 5, 1984, pp. 96–102.

differences were discernible. Some commentators adopted a harshly critical tone toward the new government shortly after it was formed. Not only did they focus attention on Chancellor Kohl's determination to deploy the Pershing II and cruise missiles on schedule at the end of 1983; they took special aim at his government's encouragement of various expellee organizations, which provided a large bloc of support for Christian Democratic candidates. In 1983 and 1984 Chancellor Kohl and certain members of his cabinet addressed large gatherings organized by expellee groups, invariably invoking such themes as the enduring legitimacy of Germany's 1937 borders. Kohl himself proclaimed that the German question was still "open." While Soviet observers of West German political life had always been quick to condemn public manifestations of "revanchism" among private groups in the FRG, such as the irredentist *Landsmannschaften*, the attitudes of Helmut Kohl and his Christian Democratic colleagues now raised for the first time since the 1960s the question whether revanchist sentiments were being actively promoted by the government's highest-ranking officials.

The Kremlin's propaganda line against West German revanchism intensified into a militant crusade in the spring and summer of 1984, as we shall see. Several commentators, however, took potshots at the Kohl government's position on this issue much earlier. In the most strident of these attacks, *Izvestiya's* Vikentii Matveyev charged that the Federal Republic was on the verge of the "fascistization" of its domestic system. Britain and Italy, he warned, were also embarked on the same dangerous path, complete with their own versions of the Black Hundreds. Matveyev's dire forecast was considered so controversial that the editorial board of *Izvestiya*, in a move virtually without precedent, prefaced his article with a disclaimer asserting that it did not necessarily share the author's views.[47] In somewhat less hyperbolic terms, other journalists and academicians also directly linked the Kohl government with a resurgence of revanchist tendencies in the Federal Republic.[48]

Several analysts were much more sanguine about the Kohl-Genscher coalition. Some pointed out that, despite the chancellor's stated readiness to deploy the new American missiles at the end of 1983, the new government could not afford to ignore the views of antimissile voters, many of whom were Christian Democrats. It was also asserted that the United States was exerting strong pressure on Kohl and other NATO allies to install the missiles on time.[49] Aleksandr Bovin, a prominent foreign affairs expert on

47. *Izvestiya*, July 20, 1983, p. 5.
48. E.g., A. Grigoryants, "West German Militarists and Revanchists Become More Active," *IA*, no. 9, 1984, p. 90; G. Kirillov, "FRG: Reviving the 'Ewig Gestrige,'" *IA*, no. 10, 1984, pp. 39–48; and N. Polyanov, "Dangerous Revanchist March on the Rhine," *IA*, no. 12, 1984, pp. 80–83.
49. For a sampling, see the views of various Soviet commentators on television and radio broadcasts as reported in FBIS, *Soviet Union*, Mar. 7, 1983, p. CC3; Mar. 14, p. G1; Mar. 24, pp. G1–2; July 5, pp. G1–2; July 11, p. CC3.

the CPSU Central Committee, took exception to warnings that recent election results in West Germany, Britain, and Italy were part of a conservative tide sweeping over Western Europe. Europe was like a pendulum, he insisted; victories by the right in some countries would "inevitably" be followed by shifts in the opposite direction over time. Speaking specifically on the prospects of the Kohl government, Bovin maintained that only "minute alterations" were to be expected in Bonn's foreign policy. It did not matter who was chancellor, said Bovin, because the FRG's "real geopolitical situation" compelled it to pursue an active ostpolitik. "It cannot do otherwise."[50]

There were even moderate characterizations of the Kohl government's stance on the thorny issue of revanchism. At the height of the antirevanchism campaign of 1984, one Soviet author attributed revanchist goals primarily to private groups in West Germany rather than to the Kohl government. In an interview with a West German network, Vadim Zagladin criticized the appearances of West German officials at expellee rallies but refused to characterize the Kohl government's policy itself as revanchist. Indeed, Zagladin stated that there were actually fewer revanchists in the FRG at the present time than in the past.[51]

As in the case of the debate on Helmut Schmidt, the divergent images of Kohl's government were not intended to set a standard for analytical objectivity. Rather, the participants in the discussion were shading their portrayals of the FRG so as to convey where they stood on the question whether, or to what extent, the Soviet Union should freeze its relationship with West Germany in the aftermath of the NATO missile deployments.

These exchanges on West Germany were not the only ones taking place among Soviet specialists in this period. As in earlier years, discussions continued on the latest trends in U.S.–West European relations more generally and on the pros and cons of East-West trade.

On the whole, Soviet foreign affairs specialists continued to display a largely Atlanticist approach to the question of relations among the NATO allies in these years. One volume produced by a team of scholars connected with the Institute of the USA and Canada struck a careful balance between partnership and rivalry in U.S.–West European relations. While the states of Western Europe were portrayed as having increased their autonomy significantly in the 1970s, they were perceived as having no intention of breaking out of the Atlantic alliance. Instead they were viewed as increasing their leverage on American policy, which the United States was still in a position to counterbalance with its own levers of influence on Western Europe. One author made it very clear that the establishment of an integrated European nuclear force at any time in the future would be a dan-

50. FBIS, *Soviet Union,* June 2, 1983, p. CC4; July 5, p. CC6; May 6, pp. 2–3.

51. A. Vtorov, "Ot Khelsinki k Stokgolmy," *MEMO,* no. 8, 1984, pp. 22–32; FBIS, *Soviet Union,* Sept. 28, 1984, pp. CC21–23.

gerous development from the Soviet point of view, even if it did produce a greater degree of West European independence from the United States.[52]

Another collectively authored book that appeared at this time came to similar conclusions. A chapter devoted to U.S. relations with West Germany exemplified the prevailing tendency to adopt an evenhanded Atlanticist orientation. The authors placed great emphasis on the growing margin of foreign policy independence that the West German government had won ever since the start of the SPD-FDP coalition under Willy Brandt. They similarly detailed a wide array of diverging national interests between Bonn and Washington, above all in the conduct of East-West relations but also extending to such important areas as the Middle East and U.S.–West European economic links. However, the authors cited both Brandt and Helmut Schmidt as stating "unequivocally" that adherence to NATO remained a vital national security interest for the FRG. Under these two chancellors, they pointed out, Bonn had considerably strengthened its role as the principal military partner of the United States. In sum, the FRG in the 1970s had succeeded in overcoming its former subaltern status as a "junior partner" of the United States, and was now to be categorized as a " 'special' but . . . relatively independent American partner." As such, it was endowed with a greater capacity than ever before for influencing U.S. foreign policy in directions favorable to Bonn, but at the same time it was also reinforcing its "common class interests" and economic interdependence with the United States. Roughly similar conclusions characterized the book's analyses of France and Britain.[53]

Yet another multiauthored volume published in the late 1970s—this one by a group of IMEMO scholars—provided additional confirmation of the Atlanticist consensus shared by most Soviet academicians at this time. Western Europe emerged from this volume as more self-assured and self-motivated in its international engagements (especially with the East) than in the past, but still unqualifiedly faithful to its alliance commitments. Other books reached analogous conclusions, in some cases focusing specifically on West Germany.[54]

On either side of these Atlanticist images one could find analyses that

52. Yu. P. Davydov, ed., *SShA–Zapadnaya Evropa: Partnerstvo i sopernichestvo* (Moscow: Nauka, 1978).

53. V. F. Davydov, T. V. Oberemko, and A. I. Utkin, *SShA i Zapadnoevropeiskiye "tsentry sili"* (Moscow: Nauka, 1978).

54. E. S. Khesin, Yu. I. Yudanov, and Yu. I. Rubinskii, eds., *Zapadnaya Evropa v sisteme mezhdunarodykh otnoshenii* (Moscow: Mysl, 1979); I. N. Puzin and M. A. Balanchuk, *Mezhgosudarstvennye svyazi stran NATO* (Moscow: Mezhdunarodnye otnosheniya, 1979); G. A. Vorontsov, *SShA i Zapadnaya Evropa: Novy etap otnoshenii* (Moscow: Mezhdunarodnye otnosheniya, 1979); R. F. Alekseyev, *SSSR-FRG: Proshloye i nastoyashcheye* (Moscow: Izdatelstvo politicheskoi literatury, 1980); and V. N. Shenayev, M. Schmidt, and D. E. Melnikov, eds., *Federativnaya Respublika Germanii*, 2d ed. (Moscow: Mysl, 1983).

placed paramount emphasis on either the centrifugal or the centripetal trends in the U.S.–West European relationship. One Europeanist approach, for example, argued that the consolidation of Western Europe into a "power center" was an objective long-term tendency that would substantially increase Western Europe's economic and foreign policy independence. This favorable development, the author suggested, would not necessarily lead to an autonomous West European defense organization that could pose an additional military threat to the USSR. Even this pronouncedly Europeanist analysis, with its emphasis on U.S.–West European contradictions, took for granted the existence of NATO in the future.[55] On the opposite end of the discussion were arguments stressing partnership among the NATO allies as the overwhelming tendency in all aspects of U.S.–West European relations. Quite predictably, this approach was usually adopted by Soviet military officials in an attempt to rationalize support for greater Warsaw Pact defense efforts against a powerful and unified adversary.[56]

Americanist analyses were scarce in these years. In view of Moscow's contentious relationships with the Carter and Reagan administrations, this was hardly surprising.

In most of the academic analyses, particularly the Atlanticist and Europeanist ones, two central conclusions stand out. First, Moscow's opportunities for playing upon differences between the United States and Western Europe on a variety of issues remained abundant, but prospects for the dissolution of NATO, or for the neutralization of West Germany, were as good as nonexistent. Second, détente—defined specifically as the relaxation of tensions—promoted intercapitalist contradictions. Several authors underscored this point by adding that East-West confrontation only served to reduce frictions among the NATO allies, constricting Western Europe's capacity for independent action and enhancing the unifying role of military policy in U.S.–West European relations.[57] This was as explicit as Soviet scholars got in making a case for a less hostile international environment than the one that had been emerging since 1978. None of them publicly criticized the Soviet deployment of SS-20 missiles; this policy continued to be beyond reproach in open-source foreign policy discussions. Still, the defense of détente offered by these analysts represented a conspicuous critique of the leadership's dogged pursuit of confrontationist tactics.

55. V. P. Lukin, *"Tsentry sili": Kontseptsii i realnost* (Moscow: Mezhdunarodnye otnosheniya, 1983), chap. 2. For a work stressing the contradictions in U.S. relations with Europe's southern flank, see V. S. Shein, *SShA i Yuzhnaya Evropa: Krizis atlanticheskovo partnerstva* (Moscow: Nauka, 1979).

56. E.g., N. Petrov et al., *SShA i NATO: Istochniki voennoi ugrozy* (Moscow: Voennizdat, 1979).

57. Davydov et al., *SShA i Zapadnoevropeiskiye "tsentry sili,"* p. 282; Khesin et al., *Zapadnaya Evropa*, p. 82.

At the same time, however, voices continued to be heard in favor of the notion that it was Soviet military strength that actually promoted U.S.– West European contradictions. Without explicitly relating this point to the INF controversy, one prominent academician reiterated the long-standing Soviet view that military "parity" between the two superpowers had deprived the United States of "the means of pressure over its allies" which it had enjoyed in the days when it was practically invulnerable to Soviet attack.[58]

Soviet writers continued to diverge on the importance of East-West economic exchanges. The predominant outlook favored an expansion of trade and scientific interchanges with the West (above all with Western Europe), but it was occasionally suggested that East-West trade brought more benefits to such countries as West Germany than to the USSR. This notion was transparently intended to convince Bonn that the Soviet Union could get along quite comfortably even if it chose to curtail its trade with the FRG to punish the West Germans for emplacing new U.S. missiles on their territory.[59] Meanwhile, Soviet negotiators showed signs of improvisation and faulty coordination in their dealings with their Western counterparts, even in such critical bargaining situations as the pipeline negotiations. This behavior reflected lingering ambivalence in Moscow about the desirability of long-term economic relationships with the West, as well as bureaucratic infighting and antiquated organizational procedures within the Soviet economic system.[60] Once Andropov came to power, however, the debate on the USSR's economic future became more vibrant, with reformist, centrist, and conservative economists offering alternative visions of the domestic and international orientations of the Soviet economy.[61]

The discussions and debates that were taking place in Soviet publications at this time were thus directly related to identifiable policy options facing the Soviet leadership. The same was true in the GDR.

The GDR in the Crucible

As the Soviet–West German standoff on nuclear missiles hardened, the East German government found itself caught between its peren-

58. A. I. Utkin, *Doktriny atlantizma i evropeiskaya integratsiya* (Moscow: Nauka, 1979), p. 135.
59. E.g., N. Portugalov in *Sovetskaya Rossiya*, Mar. 28, 1978, p. 3; Yu. Zhukov in *Pravda*, Nov. 16, 1979, p. 4; V. Mikhailov in *Pravda*, Oct. 3, 1981, p. 4.
60. On these points, see Thane Gustafson, *Soviet Negotiating Strategy: The East-West Gas Pipeline Deal, 1980–1984* (Santa Monica, Calif.: Rand, 1985). Despite these problems, the Soviets managed to complete the construction of the pipeline ahead of schedule.
61. For a survey, see Ed A. Hewett, *Reforming the Soviet Economy* (Washington, D.C.: Brookings, 1988), pp. 274–302.

nial need to cultivate the Soviets and its burgeoning interest in détente with Bonn. Unquestionably the SED regime's paramount interest remained what it had always been: the perpetuation of stable party rule. Now as before, the Soviet Union retained an equally vital stake in the GDR's internal stability. The political and economic preconditions for this domestic tranquility, however, were shifting to Moscow's disadvantage. The tensions reverberating from the missile issue were beginning to stir up civil unrest in East Germany. By the early 1980s an active peace movement had sprung into being, stimulated by the antimissile protests in the Federal Republic and fueled by latent church-state antagonisms in the GDR and by a veritable war scare among segments of the population.[62]

In addition, the GDR's lingering economic weaknesses and pressures from the international economy were tightening the squeeze on budget planners. Rising energy prices were exerting a cancerous impact on the entire economic system. As the GDR's main petroleum supplier, the Soviet Union continued to make a major contribution of its own to the GDR's economic woes. Although Soviet oil prices remained well below world market prices, the burdens they imposed on the GDR were considerable.[63] By requiring increased output by East Germany's export sectors, the spiraling energy costs reduced the funds left over for infrastructural investments and for the politically all-important consumer welfare subsidies. The Honecker regime's commitment to stable prices for rent and groceries, together with its ambitious housing programs and other elements of the social contract, were carrying an increasingly expensive price tag.[64] Moreover, the necessity to shop in world markets for oil, technology, and other goods inevitably drove up the GDR's demand for hard currency, forcing the East Germans to incur mounting debts to Western creditors.[65]

These developments understandably reinforced the Honecker government's interest in a more placid international environment. If East Berlin

62. Ordinary East Berliners told me in 1980 and 1981 that "people think there will be war."

63. In 1970 the GDR was able to pay for its imports of Soviet oil with 7% of its total exports to the USSR; by 1980 this figure had risen to nearly 25%, and it was expected to climb to as much as 40% by 1985. In addition, the Soviets announced a freeze on future increases in oil exports to its allies: Deutsches Institut für Wirtschaftsforschung, "Handel DDR-UdSSR im Zeichen verminderten Wachstums," *Wochenbericht,* no. 7, 1980.

64. One estimate suggested that if the United States were to subsidize food and housing to the same extent as the GDR, the annual cost would be $120 billion for food and $24 billion for housing: *Washington Post,* Apr. 15, 1981, p. A30.

65. The GDR's net indebtedness to the West (including the FRG) in 1980 was between $10 and $11 billion; by the end of 1982 it was $12 billion. The net debt was cut to $8.5 billion by the end of 1983, in part by reductions of imports by upwards of 30% and by increases of exports by about 10%. See Thomas A. Baylis, "Explaining the GDR's Economic Strategy," *International Organization* 40 (Spring 1986): 381–420; Raimund Dietz, "Der Westhandel der DDR," *Deutschland Archiv,* no. 3, 1985, pp. 294–304; Maria Haendcke-Hoppe, "Konsolidierung in der Aussenwirtschaft," *Deutschland Archiv,* no. 10, 1984, pp. 1060–67.

could not lower East-West tensions on its own, it could at least try to keep the GDR as sheltered as possible from their harmful effects. At the same time, the SED leadership had to display continuing fidelity to Moscow's foreign policy, offering tangible support for Soviet activities in Afghanistan and the Third World and—above all—in the showdown with the West over intermediate-range missiles. Pursuing both of these tasks at once required the skills of a diplomatic tightrope walker; it also required a ruling coalition that was dedicated equally to steadfast bloc loyalty and to compromise with Bonn.

Since 1978 Honecker had let it be known that his desire for further collaboration with West Germany was undiminished. In an interview with the *Saarbrücker Zeitung* the SED chief affirmed that inter-German differences on a variety of problems posed "no obstacle" to continuing cooperation.[66] Honecker's manifest intention of shielding the positive aspects of the FRG-GDR relationship from the fallout of the missile dispute was particularly evident in his characterizations of the FRG. Even more explicitly than his Soviet comrades, Honecker portrayed the contemporary East-West scene as evenly divided between contradictory cooperative and conflictual tendencies. His preference for the cooperative side, however, was plainly evident in the way he phrased his remarks.[67] As the INF imbroglio worsened, the SED leader occasionally drew attention to Bonn's responsibility for the NATO dual-track decision, but generally refrained from harsh attacks on the West German government itself.[68]

On the whole, Hermann Axen adopted similar attitudes, as did the newly reappointed government head, Willi Stoph; Foreign Minister Oskar Fischer; and economics specialist Günter Mittag. Such lesser Politburo figures as Joachim Hermann, Werner Felfe, and Horst Dohlus also backed the delicately balanced pro-détente line. A more nuanced case was that of Kurt Hager, the keeper of the SED's ideological imprimatur. Hager offered repeated warnings about the subversive character of West Germany's bourgeois values, but unlike his Soviet opposite number, Suslov, he spoke out openly in favor of expanding economic ties with the West, including the FRG. Paul Verner also backed the Honecker line in public, but his position as the Secretariat's point man for internal security questions gave him the reputation of being a hard-liner.[69]

66. Reprinted in *ND*, July 7, 1978, pp. 3–4.
67. At a time when the Soviets were increasingly saying that the FRG talked about détente *but* was acting to promote tension, Honecker's order was the reverse: conflicts were indeed intensifying, *but* détente was still the "main trend." See, e.g., Honecker's remarks in *ND*, May 13–14, 1978, p. 3; May 25, 1978, p. 3; Dec. 5, 1979, p. 5. Honecker also said that the GDR "will not be deterred" by the NATO two-track decision "from doing all we can to continue the process of détente": *ND*, Dec. 14, 1979, pp. 3–4.
68. E.g., *ND*, Jan. 26–27, 1980, pp. 2–3; May 22, 1980, p. 3.
69. See, in *ND*, Axen: Apr. 27, 1979, pp. 5–7; Sept. 20–21, 1980, p. 6; Nov. 26, 1982, pp. 3–4; Stoph: Dec. 4, 1981, p. 3; Dec. 4, 1982, p. 3; Mittag: Dec. 12, 1980, pp. 3–4; Fischer: Apr. 14, 1981, pp. 6–7; Nov. 27–28, 1982, pp. 3–4; Hermann: Dec. 14, 1978, pp. 3–4;

In contrast to these essentially centrist views, more emphatically negative views on West Germany continued to be sounded. As in the past, the most vocal exponents of the harder line were Albert Norden and Defense Minister Heinz Hoffmann. They were joined by Konrad Naumann, the East Berlin party chief, who increasingly spoke out on foreign policy. All of them accentuated the growing danger of war emanating from Bonn's militaristic policies, and reissued the call to "vigilance" and "strengthening" of the Warsaw Pact's defense forces. Unlike the supporters of Honecker's line, the hard-liners usually failed to balance these appeals with affirmations of the desirability of détente.[70] Erich Mielke, the security minister, probably continued to cast his lot with these archconservatives.

Thus Erich Honecker had not only to negotiate the rocky shoals between Bonn and Moscow; he also had to be alert for potential opposition within his own ruling coalition to his policy of insulating the fragile inter-German détente from the impact of the Soviet–West German confrontation. The crosswinds buffeting Honecker's position were especially palpable in 1980. Honecker started the year determined to promote diplomatic and economic exchanges with the Schmidt government despite the NATO dual-track decision and the war in Afghanistan. Mittag visited West Germany in April, and shortly thereafter Honecker met with Schmidt at Tito's funeral in Yugoslavia. The leaders of the two German states declared that the FRG and the GDR shared a common responsibility for peace in Europe. By fall, however, more negative tones were in the air.

On October 13 in Gera Honecker delivered a speech that was unusually sharp in its critique of West German "revanchism" and of Bonn's role as "initiator" of the two-track decision. The centerpiece of the speech was a renewed call for West German concessions in settling four unresolved items on the inter-German agenda. Bonn was asked to recognize GDR state citizenship; to disband the Central Data Registration Office in Salzgitter (which kept files on East Germans for potential criminal proceedings); to elevate the permanent mission in each state's capital to a full-fledged embassy; and to define a disputed stretch of the inter-German boundary along the Elbe in the GDR's favor. Honecker accompanied his demands with a call to "revolutionary vigilance" on the part of the GDR and a vow to maintain defense spending "at the required level."[71] On the same day, an additional sting was added to Honecker's message with the entry into force of a recently announced quadrupling of the minimum exchange requirement for foreign visitors to East Germany.

Dohlus: June 16, 1983, pp. 3–4; Felfe: Nov. 25, 1983, pp. 3–4; Hager: Sept. 6–7, 1980, pp. 3–4; Nov. 27–28, 1982, p. 6; Verner: June 24, 1982, pp. 3–4.

70. For a sampling, see, in *ND*, Norden: Mar. 22–23, 1980, pp. 9–10; Naumann: Dec. 8, 1980, p. 6; Apr. 13, 1981, p. 3; Nov. 21–22, 1981, p. 5; and Nov. 27–28, 1982, p. 5; Hoffmann: Oct. 14–15, 1978, p. 3; Dec. 15–16, 1979, pp. 5–6; Apr. 13, 1981, p. 8.

71. *ND*, Oct. 14, 1980, p. 4.

The timing of Honecker's actions was instructive. The increase in the exchange requirement and the Gera speech both came after the SPD-FDP coalition had safely won reelection in the vote for the Bundestag on October 5. The SED had no interest in provoking the West German electorate into returning a Christian Democratic majority. Honecker may also have come under pressure from Moscow (and perhaps from inside his Politburo) to demonstrate greater firmness toward Bonn. Honecker was also visibly disturbed by the turmoil in Poland. The wave of strikes and the emergence of Solidarity in 1980 had shaken the flimsy basis of communist rule in that country to its foundations. The legalization of the free trade union and its sudden extension into practically every sector of Polish society inevitably threatened to arouse similar movements in the other socialist countries. Honecker and his lieutenants had swiftly moved to reduce the flow of Polish visitors to the GDR and made a strong case for decisive Soviet action, quite possibly military intervention.[72] Not surprisingly, Honecker's Gera speech was laced with warnings against interference in Poland's affairs by West Germans bent on "counterrevolution."

The new turn in Honecker's rhetoric did not signal a permanent change of course, however. In February 1981 Honecker told a British interviewer that the Gera demands were not intended to be preconditions for talks with the FRG on other issues. The SED leader also made highly publicized comments about the mutual benefits of inter-German trade during appearances at the Leipzig Trade Fair in March and September. Over the course of 1981, Honecker tended to spare the Schmidt government from polemical attack, reserving his most biting remarks for American foreign policy.[73] These obvious indications of Honecker's desire for a cooperative relationship with Bonn culminated in the long-awaited state visit to the GDR by Chancellor Schmidt and Foreign Minister Genscher in mid-December.

Throughout the year Honecker had been careful to couple his pro-détente outlook with strict observance of the Soviet line on INF. East German political leaders and mass media beamed a relentless stream of invective against the NATO two-track decision and the Reagan administration's refusal to accept Soviet proposals for arms reductions. Honecker clearly understood that the GDR was expected to play a pivotal role in Moscow's endeavors to pressure Bonn into backtracking from its support for NATO's rearmament scheme. Accordingly, his central message to Schmidt during their talks at Lake Werbellin carried a dire warning: "Good-neighborly relations cannot flourish," he said, "in the shadow of new U.S. nuclear missiles." The NATO deployments would "have an effect" on FRG-GDR relations, he warned, and he repeated Soviet threats about "countermea-

72. *Der Spiegel*, Apr. 13, 1981, p. 14.
73. *ND*, Feb. 13, 1981, pp. 3–4; Apr. 12, pp. 3–5; Aug. 31, p. 5; Nov. 20, pp. 3–6.

sures."[74] The somber overtones of the meeting were darkened all the more when the Polish government of General Jaruzelski, acting no doubt with Soviet connivance, chose that weekend to impose martial law on Poland. The timing appeared deliberately calculated to embarrass Schmidt, who had canceled a previously scheduled visit to the GDR in 1980 in part because of the volatile Polish situation.

Despite these intrusions from the international environment, the two negotiating teams managed to advance the cause of inter-German cooperation. Bonn agreed on a six-month extension of the "swing" arrangement, providing the GDR with a credit line of up to DM800 million. The West Germans made it clear, however, that they expected an amelioration of the latest currency exchange increase in the future. Plans were also set in motion to study a possible long-term trade agreement. For its part, the Schmidt-Genscher government was not inclined to extract propaganda advantages from Poland's troubles. Although the West German government had little inclination to join in a broad trade embargo against the East, as the Reagan administration demanded after Solidarity was banned, it later joined in EEC sanctions against the Jaruzelski regime.

With the arrival of the Kohl-Genscher government to power toward the end of 1982, the GDR made no substantial changes in its evenhanded policy toward the Federal Republic. Honecker was noticeably cordial in his initial comments on the Kohl government, after meetings with high-level CDU emissaries who assured him of the new chancellor's commitment to continuity in Bonn's policy toward the GDR. He also displayed a more optimistic assessment of the new administration than Gromyko. These indications of a positive attitude were simultaneously counterbalanced by a renewal of East Berlin's campaign against the impending NATO missile deployments. As the 1983 election contest took shape in the FRG, Honecker pressed Kohl to accept a version of Swedish Premier Olaf Palme's proposal for a zone extending 150 kilometers on either side of the inter-German border which would be free of battlefield nuclear weapons. The East Germans noted their preference for an even wider nuclear-free zone, but Kohl rejected the idea.[75]

With Kohl's reelection and the unbroken impasse in the U.S.–Soviet Geneva negotiations, NATO and the Warsaw Pact were heading full tilt toward nuclear escalation in Europe. The East Germans responded to the encroaching deadlines with a flurry of diplomatic activity. Mittag went back to Bonn in April, and Honecker spoke by telephone with Kohl. Later in the month the GDR sent word that Honecker would not be able to visit West Germany at the present time because of "the current situation," but

---

74. *ND*, Dec. 13, 1981, p. 3; Dec. 16, pp. 1–2.
75. *ND*, Nov. 27–28, 1982, pp. 3–4; Jan. 21, 1983, pp. 1–2; Feb. 9, 1983, p. 1.

Honecker let it be known that the visit was merely postponed, not canceled. Later the SED leader received such high-level visitors as Schmidt, Vogel, and Bahr of the SPD and West Berlin's Christian Democratic mayor, Richard von Weizsäcker.

By far the most unexpected of these meetings took place in July, when Franz-Josef Strauss showed up on a "private" visit. The conservative CSU chief had for decades been a rabid critic of the Soviet Union and East Germany. Strauss's trip followed the signing on July 1 of a DM1 billion credit arrangement between the GDR and a consortium of West German banks led by a Bavarian financial institution known to be close to Strauss.[76] The credit deal and Strauss's personal role in it dramatically illustrated the distance the FRG and the GDR had traversed over the last ten years. With such long-standing adversaries as Strauss and Honecker now shaking hands in East Berlin, it was evident that cooperation between the two German states, irrespective of existing differences, had become a fact of life in both countries.

Just as significant, it soon became evident that Honecker was willing to provide serious concessions to the West Germans in exchange for economic considerations. In late September it was reported that the GDR was beginning to dismantle certain automatic firing devices at the inter-German border. The removal of these weapons had long been demanded by various West Germans, particularly by conservatives such as Strauss, as a quid pro quo for improved ties between Bonn and East Berlin. As Honecker continued to move the GDR toward a more centrist foreign policy position, the ruling coalition's propensity to compromise was quite evidently on the rise.

Meanwhile, Honecker was placing renewed emphasis on the peace theme. At an international conference on Karl Marx organized by the SED in April, Honecker went so far as to admit that the "ways, forms, and methods of the struggle for peace" adopted by the various communist parties of the world differed. He left no doubt, however, about the GDR's commitment to peace as "the highest good of mankind," requiring cooperation across the East-West ideological divide. The presence of an SPD delegation at the conference reportedly raised the suspicions of Soviet officials about East Germany's foreign policy course.[77]

By autumn, however, the two German states were bracing themselves for the final surge toward nuclear arms deployments. Honecker mixed exhortations for continued negotiations with reminders of the inevitable Warsaw

---

76. Without the new credits, the GDR would have had to use more than half of its foreign exchange reserves to pay the interest on its foreign debts: *Washington Post*, Oct. 4, 1983, p. A12.

77. *ND*, Apr. 12, 1983, p. 2. On Soviet reactions, see A. James McAdams, "The New Logic in Soviet-GDR Relations," *Problems of Communism* 37 (September–October 1988): 53.

Pact "countermeasures," including new missiles in the GDR, in his eleventh-hour appeals to West German political leaders. In early October he told an Austrian broadcaster that there was "no chance to limit the damage" that the installation of the new Pershing and cruise missiles in the FRG would cause. In a letter to Kohl several days later he called for a "coalition of reason" between the two German states, and warned of a "new ice age" in inter-German relations if the missiles were deployed. Premier Stoph had issued similar warnings.[78] By the end of October, new missile complexes were being readied in East Germany for the promised Soviet shorter-range missiles. Honecker told a delegation of Greens that East German citizens would not "rejoice" at these countermeasures, but would nevertheless accept them.[79]

Meanwhile, in a mellower counterpoint to these warnings, Honecker announced that the firing devices at the border would eventually "disappear," and Mittag received Finance Minister Stoltenberg for a new round of talks on inter-German economic cooperation. Additional negotiations were launched with the West Berlin city government on outstanding issues.[80]

On November 22 the Bundestag voted 286 to 226, with one abstention, to deploy the Pershing II and cruise missiles. Three days earlier the SPD had rejected Helmut Schmidt's final plea to carry out the 1979 NATO dual-track decision, turning against the deployments by a vote of 383 to 14. The Soviets, who had offered last-minute proposals to reduce their SS-20s below previously indicated limits, staged their walkout at Geneva on November 23. Over the next two days the SED Central Committee met to mull over the implications of these events.

Honecker's address to the plenum captured headlines in the West when he asserted that the new Soviet missiles now being emplaced in East Germany "have caused no celebration in our country." Honecker insisted that the Soviet countermeasures, though unavoidable, would be kept "strictly" limited to those forces deemed "absolutely necessary" to maintain the military balance. Turning to relations with the Federal Republic, he said that the GDR was in favor of "limiting the damage as much as possible." Sooner or later, he assured his listeners, arms-control negotiations would bring positive results and détente would be continued. Later Honecker referred to the Soviet missiles on East German territory as "the devil's tool" (*Teufelzeug*), a term deliberately intended to communicate the GDR's consternation to Moscow.[81]

Honecker's plea for continued cooperation with the FRG despite the

---

78. *ND*, Oct. 6, 1983, p. 2; Oct. 10, p. 1; Sept. 12, pp. 3–4. The term "ice age" had been brought up by the Austrian interviewer. See FBIS, *Eastern Europe*, Oct. 6, 1983, pp. E1–2.
79. FBIS, *Eastern Europe*, Nov. 1, 1983, pp. E1–3.
80. See Honecker's interview in *ND*, Jan. 21, 1983, pp. 1–2.
81. *ND*, Nov. 26–27, 1983, p. 3; McAdams, "New Logic," p. 50.

missile controversy was starkly contradicted at the November plenum by Konrad Naumann. The East Berlin party leader blasted Helmut Kohl as "the nuclear chancellor" whose actions had proved the FRG's "bondage" to the United States and increased the danger of nuclear war. Naumann painted Kohl as an utterly untrustworthy negotiating partner and ridiculed his talk about adhering to Bonn's earlier treaties with the GDR and ensuring that war would never again emanate from German soil. Naumann unmistakably rejected Honecker's position. Only slightly less caustic were the comments of Heinz Hoffmann. The defense minister reasserted his oft-repeated warnings about West Germany's complicity in NATO's "large-scale preparations for war," and promised "new and improved" weapons on the Warsaw Pact side which would be able to deliver a "crushing counterstrike" to the enemy. Interestingly, however, Hoffmann acknowledged that the GDR would "not find it easy to take these measures," noting that they would have to be implemented within the framework of the national economy. Premier Stoph took a balanced position, repeating Honecker's pledge to limit the damage from the missile deployments but pointedly criticizing Bonn for pursuing policies opposed to East German interests.[82]

Thus as the missile controversy reached its apogee, it was abundantly evident that the SED leadership was divided over what to do next. So was the East German secondary elite.

The Debate on West Germany in the GDR

The years from 1978 to 1984 witnessed the most explicit and wide-ranging debate on foreign policy issues ever to take place in the East German specialized press. The main questions raised were very similar to those at issue in the USSR; several other points were more specific to the GDR's current predicament. All of these disputed questions were of immediate concern to policy makers.

The opportunity to debate these issues in the open derived from the two-sided centrist-conservative policy stance adopted by Honecker. By placing roughly equal stress on the need to support Moscow's efforts to pressure the West Germans on INF and on the desirability of maintaining the GDR's stake in détente with Bonn, Honecker in effect gave members of the secondary elite license to indicate which of the two policy orientations they preferred. Some writers, reflecting a more conservative point of view, supported what may loosely be called the "anti-Bonn" position; others leaned in the direction of détente. Still others supported both views simultaneously. A few specialists switched from one side to the other, evidently

82. *ND*, Nov. 25, 1983, pp. 7, 9; Dec. 9, pp. 3, 5.

trying to maintain the same precarious balance as Honecker himself. As time went on, however, it became increasingly apparent that Honecker could not pursue both ends at once; the tension in his double-edged policy would sooner or later turn out to be unsustainable. At some point a decision would have to be made in favor of either the anti-Bonn or the pro-Bonn position.

By 1983 it was becoming clear that Honecker was tilting heavily in the direction of détente. Accordingly, some analysts who had not yet fully committed themselves now shifted their emphasis decisively in support of inter-German cooperation and arms control. Others continued to cling to the hard-line position represented by Norden, Hoffmann, and Naumann.

The initial rounds of discussion took place in 1978 and 1979. One set of analysts adopted a cautious but generally positive attitude toward the Schmidt-Genscher ruling coalition, usually signaled by a reluctance to criticize it directly. Their main targets were prominent Christian Democrats or the United States (or NATO more generally). Schmidt and Genscher were not explicitly implicated in the NATO two-track decision.[83] On the critical question of inter-German relations, it was suggested that disagreements on particular issues did not preclude mutually beneficial cooperation in other areas.[84]

An even greater number of articles overtly denounced the policies of the Schmidt government. Frequently these denunciations centered on Bonn's military policies, with strong emphasis on West Germany's military spending increases in the 1970s and on the FRG's role as the "chief ally" of the United States.[85] These analysts characterized the Schmidt government's attitudes as "neo-revanchist" and warned that its position in such matters as the inter-German borders, GDR state citizenship, and the German ques-

83. E.g., in *DA*, Gerhard Scharschmidt and Siegfried Wenger, "Zur Kritik bürgerlicher Auffassungen in der BRD über 'Ost-West' Handel und -Kooperation," no. 3, 1978, pp. 42–59; Siegmar Quilitzsch, "Die Lüge von der 'Gefahr aus dem Osten'—Instrument wider Frieden, Sicherheit und Zusammenarbeit der Völker," no. 4, 1978, pp. 55–57; Stefan Doernberg, "Die Dynamik des Entspannungsprozesses und seine Prioritäten," no. 5, 1978, pp. 14–24, and "Die 'Anti-Entspannungskampagne' reaktionärer Kräfte, ihre Gefährlichkeit und Perspektivlösigkeit," no. 6, 1979, pp. 116–20; Egon Winkelmann, "Engere Zusammenarbeit für Frieden, Entspannung und Abrüstung," no. 9, 1979, pp. 5–9; and in *Einheit*, Peter Klein, "Abrüstung—Weltproblem erster Ordnung," no. 6, 1979, pp. 592–600, and Günter Kühne, "Strategie und Demagogie der NATO," no. 12, 1979, pp. 1257–65.
84. Stefan Doernberg, "Die DDR in der weltweiten Klassenauseinandersetzung der Gegenwart," *DA*, no. 10, 1979, pp. 34–51.
85. E.g., in *DA*, Gerhard Basler, "Das Bündnis BRD-USA in der NATO," no. 5, 1978, pp. 103–13; Werner Schulz, "Kontinuität und Wandel in der Westeuropapolitik der USA," no. 9, 1978, pp. 98–104; Jochen Dankert und Wilhelm Ersil, "Die NATO und Grundfragen der internationalen Politik," no. 11, 1978, pp. 73–88; Werner Nüblein, "Der internationale Einfluss des Sozialismus," no. 2, 1979, pp. 5–16; and in *Einheit*, Horst Fiedler und Alfred Preusse, "Kern der aggressiven Kräfte des Imperialismus," no. 2, 1979, pp. 121–29; Heinz Kessler, "Die NATO-Allianz gegen Frieden und Fortschritt," no. 4, 1979, pp. 381–89; and Bruno Mahlow, "Friedenspolitik und revolutionärer Kampf," no. 6, 1979, pp. 575–83.

tion, still allegedly unresolved, obstructed prospects for further collaboration.[86]

Both sets of views surfaced at a conference of East German foreign policy specialists in September 1979. Some participants acknowledged the self-evident resilience of West Germany's ties with the United States, including its support for NATO's upcoming INF decision, but they also noted (and in some cases stressed) the contradictions in U.S.–FRG relations, even on such sensitive questions as nuclear rearmament in Europe. The opposite view, put forward by a specialist on military affairs, admitted the centrifugal tendencies in intercapitalist relations, but insisted that centripetal trends were currently predominant. One participant, Stefan Doernberg, came forward with several ideas that in later years would be central elements of Gorbachev's "new political thinking." The socialist states, Doernberg said, were not seeking to base their own security on the insecurity of others, but favored equal security for all. In his view, the members of the socialist community should concentrate on reducing the military factor in international relations, and should seek to cooperate with all the countries of the world to solve the "global problems" created by energy shortages and threats to the environment.[87]

Meanwhile, several writers gave continuing evidence of nascent Atlanticist tendencies, presenting sophisticated descriptions of centrifugal and centripetal trends working simultaneously in ties between Washington and Bonn.[88]

These opening skirmishes were but a warmup for the clash of opinions that animated East German foreign policy discussions in 1980. As the Honecker government switched back and forth between cooperative and combative policies toward the Federal Republic, proponents of the most positive characterization of West German foreign policy insisted that it was the United States that was the prime instigator of the tensions now afflicting East-West relations. They ignored Bonn's role in such matters as the NATO

---

86. See Wilhelm Ersil's contribution to a discussion in *DA*, no. 4, 1979, p. 28; and Klaus Engelhardt, "Der Kampf der Völker für Frieden und Abrüstung," *Einheit*, no. 2, 1979, pp. 130–37.

87. See, in *IPW-Berichte*, no. 5, 1980, the contributions of P. Klein, S. Schwarz, and M. Winter, pp. 11ff.; A. Charisius, p. 13 (Charisius was a colonel on the staff of the GDR's Institute of Military History); and Stefan Doernberg, pp. 10, 15 (Doernberg was the director of the GDR's Institute for International Relations, which was closely connected with the Foreign Ministry). The Soviets themselves were beginning to explore the theme of global interdependence. See, e.g., V. V. Zagladin and I. T. Frolov, *Globalnye problemy sovremennosti: Nauchnye i sotsialnye aspekty* (Moscow: Mezhdunarodnye otnosheniya, 1981). According to an East German defector, this book had a great impact on academicians in the GDR. See Guntolf Herzberg, "Wann wir streiten Seit' an Seit' . . . ," *Deutschland Archiv*, no. 6, 1988, p. 606.

88. Otto Reinhold, "Die Ökonomische und die politische Krise des Imperialismus," *Einheit*, no. 10, 1978, pp. 1052–60. Also Claus Montag and Karl-Ernst Plagemann, "Zum gegenwärtigen USA-Globalstrategie," *DA*, no. 8, 1979, pp. 95–112. (Montag and Plagemann were specialists on U.S. foreign policy at the GDR's Institute for International Relations.)

two-track decision and the Western response to events in Afghanistan and Poland. On the contrary, several of them drew a clear contrast between American efforts to undermine détente and West German attempts to promote it. These authors portrayed the Schmidt government as under massive American pressure to adopt a more confrontationist stance toward the Warsaw Pact states than it actually wished.[89]

Several prominent analysts placed special stress on the contradictions eating away at U.S.–West European relations. Otto Reinhold, the rector of the SED Central Committee's Academy for Social Sciences, cited a passage from a West German publication suggesting that formerly weak states now increasingly followed their own interests while strong states were actually getting weaker. The allusion to the Federal Republic and the United States as the weak and the strong states was underscored by Reinhold's distinction between the Carter administration's confrontationist course and West Germany's desire for economic cooperation with the socialist countries. Gustav Hertzfeldt, editor in chief of *Deutsche Aussenpolitik*, also acknowledged this dichotomy between hard-line NATO states and those Western capitals urging compromise with the Soviet camp. Stefan Doernberg wrote that it was "especially the USA" that was working to torpedo détente at a time when various West European statesmen preferred the continuation of East-West cooperation and a limitation to the arms race. The "authors" (*Urheber*) of the NATO dual-track decision of December 1979, said Doernberg, were in Washington; he made no mention of Schmidt's role in requesting the introduction of new U.S. missiles in Western Europe.[90]

The same writers also emphasized the significance of the inter-German dialogue. Reinhold stated that many sectors of the West German economy were "indivisibly" linked with the socialist economies, and added that the USSR and the GDR would "do everything" to extend their commercial links with capitalist states and firms in the future. All the same, Reinhold felt compelled to attack the West German government for its indispensable role in the two-track decision and its anti-GDR policies.[91]

Doernberg broke new ground by boldly suggesting that the arms race

89. E.g., Gerhard Powik, "Konfrontationspolitik—ein Ausschlag auf die Arbeiterbewegung in den imperialistischen Ländern," *DA*, no. 9, 1980, pp. 65–77; Günter Kühne and Peter Stechmesser, "Die Lebenskraft der Leninschen Friedenspolitik," *Einheit*, no. 4, 1980, pp. 379–86; Ernst Krabatsch, "Frieden und Sicherheit," *Einheit*, no. 4, 1980, pp. 867–69 (Krabatsch worked in the Foreign Ministry); Peter Klein, "NATO forciert Rüstungskurs unter dem Druck der USA," *IPW-Berichte*, no. 9, 1980, pp. 44–48; Heinz Gambke, "Zusammenhalt und Zwietracht im 'Atlantischen Bündnis,' " *IPW-Berichte*, no. 11, 1980, pp. 1–9.

90. Otto Reinhold, "Zu einigen Problemen der internationalen Wirtschaftsbeziehungen unserer Zeit," *Einheit*, no. 6, 1980, pp. 603–10; Gustav Hertzfeldt, "Die Leninsche-Imperialismustheorie—ein Wegweiser im Kampf um Frieden und sozialen Fortschritt," *DA*, no. 4, 1980, pp. 23–38; Stefan Doernberg, "Ein Vierteljahrhundert im Dienste der Einheit der sozialistischen Gemeinschaft und der Festigung des Friedens," *DA*, no. 6, 1980, pp. 16–37, and "Friedenspolitik des Sozialismus," *Einheit*, nos. 7–8, 1980, pp. 691–98.

91. Reinhold, "Zu einigen Problemen," pp. 605–6; *IPW-Berichte*, no. 2, 1981, p. 16.

was imposing excessive costs on the Warsaw Pact states, and that the GDR did not necessarily have the same interests as the Soviet Union in relations with the West. He noted that there were limits to the use of force in the nuclear era and added that, for all its military prowess, NATO had not been able to win the cold war. He further asserted that increases in future military expenditures by the Warsaw Pact states would involve "no small sacrifices" and "certainly not easily solvable tasks." Just as explicitly, Doernberg reminded his readers that the Leninist notion of proletarian internationalism in no way excluded the pursuit of national interests by particular socialist states. The need for "harmony" and "coordination" among the socialist countries in their foreign policies "presupposes the development of one's own ideas," he said, and permits expanded possibilities on the part of the separate socialist states for participating in the "discussion and decision of important problems of international policy." Doernberg's reference to the sovereignty of the individual socialist states and of their capacity "to have a part in the realization of their own goals" represented a blunt affirmation of the GDR's right to follow its own state interests regardless of the Soviets' wishes.[92]

These pro-détente views did not go uncontested. Articles in such journals as *Deutsche Aussenpolitik, Einheit,* and *IPW-Berichte,* published by the SED's Institute for International Politics and Economics, were highly critical of West Germany's foreign and defense policy initiatives throughout 1980. They portrayed the FRG as coresponsible with the United States for the elaboration of NATO's political and military strategy against the Soviet bloc. Bonn's rising military expenditures and its expanding institutional role within NATO were also highlighted.[93] One writer described the FRG as the "whip" (*Einpeitscher*) behind NATO's conventional and nuclear arms programs, and others vilified West German Defense Minister Hans Apel as the "main whip" behind the two-track decision.[94] These writers acknowledged conflicts between the United States and Western Europe but declared that antisocialist unity was the predominant tendency within the Atlantic alliance. This view was especially popular among military specialists.[95] Bonn's "revanchist" foreign policy was attacked and the Schmidt

92. Doernberg, "Vierteljahrhundert," p. 17; "Friedenspolitik," pp. 694–95, 698; "Vierteljahrhundert," p. 33.

93. Max Schmidt, "Forschung für den Kampf gegen Imperialismus und Krieg," *Einheit,* no. 12, 1980, pp. 1271–80. Schmidt was the director of the SED's Institute for International Politics and Economics. See also the remarks of H. Gambke, as reported in *DA,* no. 6, 1980, p. 24.

94. Bruno Mahlow, "Die Sowjetunion—Hauptmacht des Friedens," *Einheit,* no. 11, 1980, p. 1119 (Mahlow was a deputy department head in the SED Central Committee). A similar charge was made by Max Schmidt in ibid., no. 12, 1980, p. 1278. Also Georg Grasnick and Heino Nolting in *IPW-Berichte,* no. 3, 1980, p. 61.

95. Albrecht Charisius, "NATO—Hauptinstrument der aggressiven Kräfte des Imperialismus," *Einheit,* no. 9, 1980, pp. 922, 926. See also Ruth Stoljarowa, "W. I. Lenin über

government was castigated for interference in the domestic affairs of the GDR, Poland, and other Warsaw Pact countries.[96]

Two well-defined imperatives emerged from these negatively oriented writings in 1980. The first was the need to maintain (or even increase) the Warsaw Pact's military strength, despite the "sacrifices" such efforts would entail. The second was the duty to close ranks behind the USSR. The anti-Bonn authors' interpretation of "proletarian internationalism" made no mention of the possibility of pursuing individual state interests.[97] Not surprisingly, most of these negatively inclined specialists also stressed the conflictual aspects of East-West relations, and rarely held out any hopes for the future of détente in Europe or for a broadening of cooperation with West Germany.

Though the positive and the negative orientations tended to dominate this discussion, a few writers adopted a middle position that recognized both favorable and unfavorable elements in Bonn's foreign policy.[98]

The "great debate" of 1980, coinciding with the Honecker coalition's zigzag approach to its ties with Bonn, did not die down over the next three years. Numerous articles appeared on both sides of the issue. On the whole, the participants used essentially the same arguments as before; if anything, writers in both camps became somewhat more explicit in their pronouncements. Those with a positive orientation toward détente with Bonn took special notice of West Germany's determination to move ahead with the gas pipeline agreements in the face of U.S. opposition to them.[99] Several analysts also expressed positive views of the antimissile movement as a factor that neither the Schmidt nor the Kohl government could ignore.[100] Nega-

---

objecktive Faktoren des proletarischen Internationalismus," *DA*, no. 4, 1980, pp. 6–22. On U.S.-FRG military cooperation, see Gerhard Basler, "Militärische Macht im entspannungsfeindlichen Konzept des Imperialismus," *IPW-Berichte*, no. 7, 1980, pp. 10–17.

96. Mahlow, "Sowjetunion," p. 1120; Schmidt, in *Einheit*, no. 12, 1980, p. 1278.

97. Egon Winkelmann, "Ein Bündnis neuen Typs," *Einheit*, no. 5, 1980, pp. 489–93 (Winkelmann was a department head in the SED Central Committee); Heinrich Homan, "Tag historischer Wahrheit und geschichtlicher Wirksamkeit," *DA*, no. 5, 1980, pp. 5–11.

98. E.g., Ernst Krabatsch, "Für Entspannung und Frieden entschlossen handeln," *Einheit*, no. 2, 1980, pp. 159–65; Helga Schirmeister, "Zur Bedeutung vertrauensbildender Massnahmen für die Festigung der Sicherheit und des Vertrauens in Europa," *DA*, no. 7, 1980, pp. 14–26; Günter Hillmann, "Die Aggressionskurs der NATO: Aktuelle Tendenzen," *DA*, no. 8, 1980, pp. 80–93.

99. Rudi Hacker, "Aktuelle Erscheinungen des imperialistischen Konfrontationskurses im Ost-West Handel," *DA*, no. 4, 1982, pp. 113–21; Christine Fiedler und Jürgen Nitz, "Missbrauch des Handels als Instrument imperialistischer Politik," *DA*, no. 6, 1982, pp. 73–89, and "Wirtschaftskrieg—ökonomische Komponente der USA-Konfrontationspolitik," *IPW-Berichte*, no. 10, 1982, pp. 9–15; Christine Fiedler, "Ost-West Wirtschaftsbeziehungen: Konfrontation oder Zusammenarbeit?" *IPW-Berichte*, no. 7, 1981, pp. 49–52; Klaus Benjowski, "Welche Ziele verfolgt Washingtons Droh- und Sanktionspolitik?" *Einheit*, no. 3, 1982, pp. 322–26.

100. E.g., Gerhard Lindner, "Zu einigen Aspekten der Friedensbewegung," *DA*, no. 6, 1982, pp. 5–12; Dieter Schuster, "Aktuelle Aspekte der Einheit von Aussen-, Sicherheits- und Militärpolitik," *DA*, no. 1, 1983, pp. 35–45.

tively inclined analysts zeroed in on Helmut Schmidt's seminal role in NATO military policy, denouncing him as the "inventor" (*Erfinder*) of the dual-track decision.[101] Charges of revanchism and avowals of East Germany's willingness to make "sacrifices" to keep up its end of the arms balance also echoed in the hard-liners' analyses.[102]

By contrast, a pronounced trend in the direction of the more positive set of images of the FRG manifested itself over time.[103] Some writers who had adopted negative or mixed views on West Germany earlier in this period came around to placing greater emphasis on such "positive" themes as U.S.–West German contradictions and the imperative of peace as the GDR's chief foreign policy priority.[104]

Through it all, the differentiation into positive and negative schools of thought seemed clearly related to the difficult choices facing the decision-making elite in these years. To raise the minimum currency exchange requirements for Western visitors or not; to accede to the FRG's requests for concessions on human rights or not; to continue down the path of economic cooperation with Bonn or not: these were real policy dilemmas.[105] As we know, similar questions were being discussed in Moscow. In fact, the foreign policy elites of the Soviet Union actively intervened in the East German debates, publishing articles and comments in the leading GDR journals. Conversely, analyses by East German specialists appeared in So-

---

101. Werner Flach, "BRD-Revanchismus gegen Entspannung," *Einheit*, no. 1, 1981, p. 8; Ernst Krabatsch, "Der Frieden braucht konkrete Taten," ibid., no. 3, 1981, p. 213. For similar appraisals, see Wolfram Neubert, "Die Grundfrage menschlichen Lebens in unserer Zeit," ibid., no. 11, 1981, p. 1086; Hans Zukunft, "Die Jahrhundertlüge," *DA*, no. 7, 1981, p. 21; Paul Heider, "Antifaschismus unter Waffen," *DA*, no. 9, 1981, p. 26. Even Stefan Doernberg stated in 1981 that Schmidt had "emphatically pleaded" for new U.S. missiles. See "Die Strategie des Friedens der sozialistischen Gemeinschaft," *DA*, no. 4, 1981, pp. 17–18.

102. Gregor Schirmer, "Friedensinitiativen des Sozialismus gegen antikommunistischen 'Kreuzzug,'" *Einheit*, no. 5, 1983, pp. 431–35; Rudolf Buhlmann and Dieter Hillebrenner, "NATO verschärft Konfrontationskurs," *DA*, no. 8, 1982, pp. 85–97.

103. I counted seventeen negatively oriented articles in *DA* and *Einheit* in 1981, against slightly more than half that number on the side of détente. There were also a few of the mixed variety. In 1982 and 1983 there was a marked shift to the positive. Ten articles in these journals were essentially negative, but more than three times as many were positive in their evaluations of the FRG. Once again there was a small sampling of mixed positive-negative images. In the spring of 1983 *DA* ceased publication.

104. See, e.g., the evolution in the views of Max Schmidt and Gerhard Basler of the Institute for International Politics and Economics (IPW). Compare Schmidt's anti-FRG views in *Einheit*, no. 12, 1980, pp. 1271–80, and his defense of the SS-20s in *IPW-Berichte*, no. 10, 1980, pp. 1–9, with his emphasis on U.S.-FRG contradictions in no. 12, 1981, pp. 1–13, and his criticisms leveled predominantly at the U.S. as opposed to West Germany in no. 10, 1982, pp. 1–8, 15; no. 9, 1983, pp. 1–9; and no. 10, 1983, pp. 1–10, 16. Basler attacked both the United States and the FRG in *IPW-Berichte*, no. 7, 1980, pp. 10–16, but edged toward a greater stress on their contradictions in no. 6, 1981, pp. 1–9.

105. Honecker reportedly was prepared to make more concessions to Bonn in the human rights area in 1983, but was prevented from doing so by hard-liners in the SED Politburo. See *Der Spiegel*, Oct. 3, 1983, p. 18.

viet publications. Both the Soviet and East German elites were internally divided on vital questions of the day, and specialists in one country were quite openly seeking to influence the debate in the other. Such a multi-faceted dialogue in public was unprecedented.[106]

To be sure, the distance separating the positive orientation from the negative one in East German and Soviet debates should not be exaggerated. Both sides appeared to acknowledge that relations with the West involved a mixture of conflict and cooperation, risks and rewards. While some specialists emphasized conflict and risk, others emphasized cooperation and reward. Nevertheless, the policy alternatives were clear enough, and it was evident in both Moscow and East Berlin that hard choices would have to be made.

1984

The disagreements between Honecker and the Soviet leadership burst into the open in 1984.[107] Honecker moved quickly after his damage-limitation speech to maintain the momentum in inter-German relations. He held a friendly two-hour meeting with Helmut Kohl after Yurii Andropov's funeral in February at which Kohl again invited Honecker to visit Bonn. Major economic accords followed with the obvious blessing of the West German government. Volkswagen signed agreements to manufacture autos in the GDR, and in July a group of West German banks concluded the second major credit agreement reached with East Germany in a year, this time to the tune of $330 million.

The GDR reciprocated with significant concessions to Bonn. Early in the year East Berlin worked quietly and effectively with the West German government to resolve the sensitive case of a group of East German citizens who were encamped at the FRG mission in East Berlin and the U.S. embassy in Prague, demanding the right to emigrate to West Germany. (One of them

106. Soviet authors writing in East German journals in these years included Viktor Belezkij, "Der revolutionäre Weltprozess an der Schwelle der 8oer Jahre," *DA*, no. 4, 1980, pp. 39–47; Jurij Strelzow, "Eine Mine unter dem Gebäude des europäischen Friedens," *DA*, no. 5, 1980, pp. 86–98; and Sergej G. Lapin, "Früchte des grossen Sieges," *Einheit*, no. 5, 1980, pp. 465–73. Belezkij and Strelzow presented positive views of the FRG, Lapin negative. A. Swetlow, in an article reprinted from *MEMO* in *IPW-Berichte*, no. 11, 1981, pp. 1–8, concentrated his attack on the United States. East German writers appearing in Soviet journals included H. Neubert and W. Paff, "Socialist Policy Is a Policy of Peace and Détente," and G. Kühne, "The Top Priority—to Eliminate the Threat of War," both in *IA*, no. 3, 1983, pp. 47–50 and 79–81, 113; and M. Schmidt, "FRG v sovremennom mire," *MEMO*, no. 4, 1982, pp. 41–52. The first two articles were positive in their evaluations of the FRG; the Schmidt piece was essentially negative.

107. For a comprehensive treatment, see Ronald A. Asmus, "The Dialectics of Détente and Discord: The Moscow–East Berlin–Bonn Triangle," *Orbis* 28 (Winter 1985): 743–74.

was Premier Stoph's niece.) Similar cases were amicably negotiated later in the year. In addition, the East Germans removed some 60,000 automatic scatter guns aimed at killing defectors, and defused land mines along a four-hundred-mile stretch of border. Upon the conclusion of the credit deal in July, the GDR announced a cutback in the minimum currency exchange requirements for certain categories of Western visitors, along with other measures designed to ease travel to East Germany. And most dramatic of all, the GDR displayed its readiness to meet one of Bonn's perennial demands by drastically increasing the number of East German citizens permitted to emigrate to the Federal Republic. By the end of the year nearly 35,000 East Germans have moved to the West legally, a substantial rise over the previous year's figure of little more than 7,700.

These unprecedented gestures of goodwill were manifestly intended to pave the way for Honecker's visit to the FRG. According to official West German sources, Honecker had received Chernenko's approval for the visit in February and then again in June.[108] All through the summer, officials from both German states busily prepared for the event. Then suddenly, on September 4, Honecker announced that the trip was off. Though he soon made it clear that this was once again a postponement rather than a flat cancellation, the extraordinary progress registered over the preceding months in inter-German relations had reached a turning point.

Honecker may have had reasons of his own for delaying the trip. The East Germans were visibly perturbed at Chancellor Kohl's decision to address an expellee rally on September 2, and at disparaging remarks about Honecker's upcoming visit made by Alfred Dregger, the conservative Christian Democratic Bundestag leader.[109] It was more than evident, however, that the Kremlin leadership had turned against Honecker's trip to Bonn at this time.

Since the start of the year, the differences between Erich Honecker and conservative Soviet officials had become a matter of public record. The simmering dispute over relations with West Germany soon fanned out into a blocwide debate. In January, Matyas Szuros, Hungary's former ambassador to the USSR and East Germany, now the party secretary responsible for international relations, declared that détente between the states of Europe should continue irrespective of the sharpening tensions in East-West relations. Except in extreme circumstances, he said, the national interests of the individual socialist states were more important than the unity of the socialist camp.[110]

This call to foreign policy independence in Eastern Europe was sternly re-

---

108. Ibid., pp. 753, 767.
109. Dregger said that the FRG's future "does not depend on Mr. Honecker's doing us the honor of a visit." See *ND*'s reactions, Aug. 25–26, 1984, pp. 1 and 2.
110. FBIS, *Eastern Europe*, Jan. 26, 1984, pp. F5–9, and Jan. 30, pp. F2–6.

butted in March in *Rude Pravo,* the flagship of the conservative party press in Czechoslovakia. The exchange unleashed an escalating war of words between proponents and opponents of détente. In response to Prague's criticisms, Szuros now urged the small and medium states of Europe to make their own contribution to the revival of détente. Szuros specifically mentioned inter-German relations in this context, and his remarks were prominently displayed in *Neues Deutschland.* The Soviets leaped into the fray in April. *Novoye Vremya* (New Times) printed a revised version of the *Rude Pravo* article and bluntly rejected the notion that the socialist countries should pursue their own foreign policy initiatives. The piece bore the name O. V. Borisov, the pseudonym of Oleg Rakhmanin, an influential foreign policy official in the CPSU Central Committee.[111]

It was precisely at this time, in the early spring of 1984, that Soviet media launched a full-scale propaganda assault against Bonn's "revanchism." Combining invective reminiscent of the 1950s with reminders of the horrors of World War II, the Kremlin made it very plain that it was not interested in an early upturn in its relationship with the FRG.[112] A visit to Moscow by Foreign Minister Genscher in May, his sixth meeting in a year with Soviet leaders, got him nowhere. TASS did not even take note of Genscher's acceptance of NATO-Warsaw Pact negotiations on the nonuse of force, a proposal advanced by Moscow a year earlier and still opposed by the Reagan administration. The Soviets did accept a $250 million credit from West German banks, however, shortly before Genscher's arrival.

The Kremlin's intransigence reflected the ascendancy of Andrei Gromyko, who had never been enthusiastic about West Germany, even in the salad days of détente. It also reflected an attempt to come to grips with a disintegrating leadership situation, as the aged Chernenko conveyed to the outside world an image of vacillation and decrepitude. The rifts in the Soviet elite were barely concealable. *Kommunist* warned at the end of 1982 against "factionalism" in the party. Although Mikhail Gorbachev had built considerable support in the upper reaches of the party for his accession to the post of general secretary, potential rivals to the dynamic young party secretary were still maneuvering for position. In January 1984 Grigorii Romanov, the Leningrad party chief, made a rare excursion to the West and delivered a hard-line foreign policy speech before members of the West

111. *Rude Pravo,* Mar. 30, 1984, p. 4, trans. in FBIS, *Eastern Europe,* Apr. 5, 1984, pp. D5–11; ND, Apr. 12, 1984, pp. 5–6; *New Times,* no. 16, 1984, pp. 12–14. Also O. V. Borisov, "Soyuz novova tipa," *Voprosii istorii KPSS,* no. 4, 1984, pp. 34–49. Rakhmanin was first deputy head of the Central Committee Department for Liaison with Communist and Workers' Parties of the Socialist Countries.

112. For an account of the antirevanchism campaign, see *Der Spiegel,* Aug. 13, 1984, pp. 19–27. The Soviets were also exercised by the West European Union's decision to permit Bonn to manufacture bombers. See V. Shatrov, "Western Europe: New Military-Political Combinations in NATO," *IA,* no. 8, 1984, pp. 41–49.

German Communist Party in Nuremberg, quite possibly in a bid to establish his foreign policy credentials.[113] A speech by Gorbachev was later censored in a collected volume. Tass publicly contradicted Chernenko's hint of flexibility on arms control.

Later in the year, however, the conservative forces appeared to lose ground. Marshal Ogarkov was removed from his post as chief of staff and Gorbachev made a highly successful trip to London, bearing a message of renewed détente in his talks with Margaret Thatcher.[114] Moreover, it was Gorbachev, not Romanov, who met with West German Communist leaders when they visited Moscow in late July.

These indications of disarray in the Kremlin's foreign policy were amply confirmed in the writings of the secondary elite. As we have already seen, the debate on West Germany's role in the East-West confrontation was still going strong in the leading Soviet foreign affairs journals in 1984.[115] It spilled out into the more widely read daily press as planning progressed for Honecker's trip to West Germany. On July 19 Aleksandr Bovin supported the GDR's drive for improved relations with Bonn in an interview with an East Berlin newspaper. Three days later *Pravda* took the opposite tack, accusing Bonn of "overstepping the mark" in demanding political concessions from the GDR in exchange for economic benefits. An even more pointed attack on East Germany's détente policy followed on July 27, two days after the announcement of the latest FRG-GDR credit agreement. Lev Bezymenskii, a German specialist who had been an interpreter for General Zhukov in the closing days of the war, accused the FRG of using "economic levers" to extract political concessions from the GDR. Borrowing the title of his article from Honecker's warning to Helmut Schmidt about "the shadow of the missiles," Bezymenskii recalled Honecker's Gera demands and noted that the Federal Republic continued to violate every one of them. The timing and content of the piece, which was eerily reminiscent of Ulbricht's notion that economic dependence would inevitably lead to political dependence, made it obvious that its intended audience was not in Bonn but in East Berlin. *Pravda* published an equally barbed critique of the East German position on August 2. On July 30, however, *Izvestiya* praised the notion of economic cooperation with the West. And in another indication that not everyone shared the tough *Pravda* line, Soviet international affairs

---

113. *Kommunist*, no. 18, 1982, p. 7; and see Elizabeth Teague, "Factions in the Kremlin?" *Radio Liberty Research*, RL 353, Sept. 18, 1984; Jerry F. Hough, "Gorbachëv Consolidating Power," *Problems of Communism* 36 (July–August 1987): 27–28; *Pravda*, Jan. 7, 1984, p. 3.

114. For an account of Ogarkov's dismissal and other political maneuverings in this period, see Dusko Doder, *Shadows and Whispers* (New York: Random House, 1986), chap. 8.

115. For additional examples, see Fred Oldenburg, "Werden Moskaus Schatten länger?" *Deutschland Archiv*, no. 8, 1984, pp. 834–43.

commentators on radio and television were strangely silent on German issues during the peak of the controversy in late summer.[116]

The East Germans countered by printing statements by Honecker and editorials in their own defense during August. They also published another friendly Hungarian article and excerpts from the *Izvestiya* piece of July 30.[117] It was all too obvious, however, that Soviet pressure on Honecker to postpone the trip was insurmountable. The SED chief's announcement on September 4 came almost exactly twenty years after the mustard gas attack on Horst Schwirkmann in Zagorsk.

The East Germans were quick to point out that the postponement of Honecker's trip did not put a halt to ongoing negotiations with the FRG and West Berlin on as many as fourteen separate issues. Moreover, the East Germans were noticeably reticent in their comments about West German "revanchism," falling far short of Soviet levels of opprobrium. Honecker and other SED officials made it clear that political and economic cooperation with Bonn would coexist with the GDR's undiminished loyalty to the Soviet Union.

In pursuit of a less conservative policy than Moscow's, Erich Honecker took the occasion to reinforce the centrist elements of his ruling coalition. In May 1984 the general secretary engineered important personnel changes in the Politburo and Secretariat. The conservative Paul Verner retired. An experienced specialist in inter-German relations, Herbert Häber, was brought in as a full member of the Politburo. To balance things out, however, Konrad Naumann, the outspoken hard-liner, was promoted.[118] These shifts followed the promotion in November 1983 of Egon Krenz, the head of the SED's Free German Youth movement (FDJ), both to the Secretariat

116. Bovin cited in Asmus, "Dialectics of Détente," p. 766n; *Pravda*, July 22, 1984, p. 5; July 27, p. 4; A. Drabkin, *Izvestiya*, July 30, 1984, p. 5 (on the same page B. Vinogradov criticized the Kohl government's stance on INF); FBIS, *Soviet Union*, Aug. 6, 1984, pp. CC1–14; Aug. 13, pp. CC1–13; Aug. 20, pp. CC1–14; Aug. 27, pp. CC1–18; Sept. 4, pp. CC1–7; Sept. 10, pp. CC1–12, and Sept. 24, pp. CC1–10. Bezymenskii was an editor of *Novoye vremya* (New Times) who had written books on Hitler's Germany, at times drawing sharp parallels with contemporary West Germany. For a favorable review at this time by a military writer, see *Krasnaya zvezda*, Aug. 29, 1984, p. 3.

117. See *ND*, July 30, 1984, p. 2, and July 31, p. 1. The same paper dutifully published the Bezymenskii broadside on July 28–29 (p. 5), but on July 30 took note of recent Soviet contracts with a West German firm (p. 5).

118. Other personnel changes at this time included the promotion of three candidate members of the Politburo to full membership (Werner Jarowinsky and Günther Kleiber, both specialists on economics, and Günter Schabowski, editor of *ND*). All three were regarded as supporters of Honecker's policies. In an effort to reassure conservatives, Honecker named Konrad Naumann to the SED Secretariat. Several weeks later Honecker promoted Egon Krenz and Günter Mittag, both outspoken supporters, to deputy chairmen of the State Council, and also named Naumann a member of this body. For an analysis of these shifts, see Peter Jochen Winters, "Personalentscheidungen und ihr politischer Hintergrund," *Deutschland Archiv*, no. 7, 1984, pp. 673–77.

312 / Moscow, Germany, and the West

and to full membership in the Politburo. Krenz soon came to be regarded as the likely successor to Honecker, who had also established his career as chief of the FDJ. Honecker also may have had a hand in getting the Soviets to recall their heavy-handed ambassador to the GDR, Pyotr Abrassimov, in the spring of 1984.[119] Maneuvers of this kind clearly strengthened Honecker's ability to proceed with his pro-détente policies while mollifying more conservative forces in the SED hierarchy. Meanwhile, key members of the East German secondary elite bolstered Honecker's line in 1984 with elaborate justifications for continuing cooperation with the West.[120]

At the same time, the SED's swing toward détente by no means implied the abandonment of East Berlin's responsibilities to its Soviet ally or an underestimation of the potential dangers of a close relationship with the West Germans. The GDR's military spending continued to rise.[121] Honecker actively promoted East Germany's expanding Third World engagements, making highly visible trips to the Middle East and Africa. Efforts to meet Bonn's human rights concerns were accompanied by periodic crackdowns on the local peace movement and by legislation designed to limit citizens' contacts with West German visitors. The GDR's manifest interest in greater economic contacts with the FRG and other Western states did not mitigate its ideological hostility to capitalism or its aversion to market-oriented domestic reforms. Between the attractions of détente and the imperatives of party rule, the Honecker coalition had found a centrist-conservative balance.

Conclusions

The missile crisis of the 1980s obviously had a severe effect on Moscow's relations with the Federal Republic of Germany. Moreover, it

119. Asmus, "Dialectics of Détente," p. 767.
120. See the discussion in *IPW-Berichte*, no. 6, 1984, pp. 1–13. One analyst (Ersil) continued to denounce the FRG, but Max Schmidt, Peter Klein, and others took a more positive view. See also Max Schmidt's article supporting such notions as a "coalition of reason" and a "security partnership" between the GDR and the FRG, ibid., no. 9, 1984, pp. 1–8. The concept of the security partnership had been advanced earlier by Kurt Hager in *ND*, May 25, 1984, p. 3. On SED-SPD cooperation, see Hans-Joachim Giessmann, "Gemeinsame Sicherheit statt Konfrontation," *ND*, no. 12, 1984, pp. 12–18, 23.
121. The GDR's own figures showed increases in defense spending of 5.7% in 1982, 5.8% in 1983, and 7.2% in 1984, with a rise of 6.7% planned for 1985; cited in Hans-Dieter Schulz's articles in *Deutschland Archiv*, no. 1, 1983, p. 5; no. 2, 1985, p. 113; and no. 3, 1986, p. 235. According to U.S. sources, GDR military spending reached an estimated total of $10.6 billion by 1984. The GDR also maintained a higher per capita military spending figure than the FRG and the other Warsaw Pact states (except for the USSR) throughout this period, reaching $636 in 1984. The comparable figure in the FRG was $329. See U.S. Arms Control and Disarmament Agency, *World Military Expenditures and Arms Transfers, 1987* (Washington, D.C.: U.S. Government Printing Office, 1988), p. 59. On the GDR's military shipbuild-

could not help but aggravate existing tensions with the United States. The INF controversy also had a highly divisive impact on the Soviet foreign policy elite. By 1980, if not earlier, key members of the Soviet secondary elite were openly divided in their depictions of West Germany's role in the missile issue, with harshly negative assessments contrasting brusquely with more positive images. The same divisions were present in the GDR.

The tensions provoked by the INF crisis in Soviet-GDR relations thus did not result in a simple case of a single Soviet position contraposed to a single East German position. The elites of both states were internally divided, and the competing sides within one state sought to influence the discussions and policy outcomes in the other state. In Moscow and East Berlin, the tacit question that seemed to underlie the public debates had immediate relevance for policy decisions that needed to be made in both capitals: Should cooperation with the FRG go forward in spite of the new American missiles to be deployed on West German soil, or should Bonn be penalized in some way for contributing to the reinforcement of NATO's European missile force?

In 1983 and 1984 the Soviet decision-making hierarchy opted to penalize Bonn. Moscow's decision to walk out of the Geneva talks in November 1983 was one indication of this choice; its military "countermeasures" in the form of new shorter-range missiles aimed primarily at the FRG were another.[122] A third penalty was manifest in the Kremlin's pressure on Erich Honecker to postpone his visit to the FRG in September 1984, a step heralded by the loud drumbeats of the antirevanchism campaign in the Soviet media. Similar pressures were placed on other members of the bloc who were also eager to court Bonn's political and economic goodwill. Less than a week after Honecker's announcement, Todor Zhivkov of Bulgaria put off his own trip to Bonn scheduled for later the same month. Moscow's hopes that the maverick Ceausescu might do likewise proved unavailing, however, and the Romanian chief went to Bonn in November.

Significantly, these Soviet attempts to impose a diplomatic freeze on the FRG did not exceed certain visible limits. The Kremlin never gave any indication of contemplating a more serious rupture in its ties with Bonn. On the contrary, the Soviets displayed their fundamental ambivalence toward West Germany by continuing to pursue their beneficial economic dealings with the FRG. On September 19, 1984, a scant two weeks after Honecker's announcement, Soviet officials in Frankfurt signed on to a $166 million

---

ing programs in these years, see Dale R. Herspring, "GDR Naval Buildup," *Problems of Communism* 33 (January–February 1984): 54–62.

122. Eventually the Soviets installed more than 60 SS-12/22 single-warhead Scaleboard missiles, with a range of about 550 miles, in the GDR and Czechoslovakia. In addition, some Soviet-based SS-23s, single-warhead missiles with a range of about 300 miles, were repositioned closer to the USSR's western borders.

loan offered by a consortium of nine western banks. This was the third credit deal consummated with the West Germans in the same year.[123] These agreements demonstrated that Soviet leaders could not go all out in an effort to punish Bonn without punishing the Soviet Union too.

Ultimately Soviet behavior toward the FRG in the years 1978–1984 followed the broad patterns that typified the conservative coalition put together under Brezhnev. Throughout this period Moscow's conception of détente remained narrowly confined to the maintenance of the European political status quo and to an expansion of East-West trade only insofar as it did not necessitate domestic economic reform. As the INF controversy gathered force, the Kremlin oligarchs evinced little willingness to reach out for a compromise that might have been acceptable to the West German government, if not to the United States. Even when it was evident that adherence to this course could only jeopardize the Soviet Union's painstakingly cultivated détente with West Germany, the Soviet leadership did not display the responsiveness required to arrest a rapidly deteriorating situation.

These tendencies were reinforced by the progressive disintegration of the ruling coalition's internal stability. The Brezhnev coalition was literally dying out. Andropov never had much of a chance to elaborate a more centrist foreign policy orientation; Chernenko was too weak, both physically and politically, and too innately conservative to offer a viable alternative. The clouded leadership picture in the Kremlin opened up opportunities for a more spirited foreign policy debate than had been possible in the mid-1970s. Members of the secondary elite, while mindful of their obligations as propagandists to back the general lines of the official foreign policy in public, nevertheless found greater room than in the recent past to perform their advisory function by engaging in an open debate on Germany. As subsequent events would verify, the divisions readily apparent in the Soviet secondary elite reflected strains and policy differences within the primary elite.

In the GDR, by contrast, the Honecker regime's movement from an emphasis on the more conservative aspects of Brezhnev's détente policy toward a stress on its more cooperative features grew even more pronounced during these years. Without in any way abandoning their alliance commitments, the East Germans displayed a greater propensity to seek compromise with Bonn than their Soviet counterparts, as well as a greater range of flexibility in responding to developing events. The personnel changes effected by Honecker in 1983 and 1984 reinforced these more

123. In January 1984 the Soviets obtained a $250 million credit arranged by Dresdner Bank, and later received a $125 million loan through the Deutsche Bank: *Washington Post*, Sept. 20, 1984, p. A38.

centrist leanings. On the critical question whether Bonn should be punished, the debate in East Germany in many respects duplicated the Soviet discussions. The competing positive and negative images of West Germany articulated by the secondary elite precisely mirrored the two sides, conservative and pro-détente, of Honecker's centrist-conservative coalition. They also reflected the dialectical balance in Honecker's own position, which combined a steadfast commitment to communist rule in the GDR with a growing political and economic stake in cooperation with the other Germany.

When it came time for the GDR to join the Soviets in penalizing the FRG, Honecker's response was to keep the punitive measures to a minimum, and to proceed along the path of inter-German cooperation in spite of the missiles. In the process, Honecker's clear signs of restiveness in the face of Soviet intransigence only complicated Moscow's problems. Moreover, like Walter Ulbricht in 1964, Honecker had taken advantage of a weakened leadership coalition in the Kremlin to make his own views known with outspoken bluntness.

In the end, the Soviet attempt to pursue a limited détente simultaneously with a strenuous arms buildup had failed in Europe, just as it had already failed with the United States. Instead of promoting insuperable contradictions among the NATO governments, the SS-20s and Moscow's confrontationist policies had only driven the allies, particularly the Americans and the West Germans, closer together, despite all the turmoil in the FRG created by the INF crisis and the NATO two-track decision. Moscow's once-promising cooperative relationship with West Germany now lay in shards. Conscious of its growing isolation, Moscow sought to revive its flagging relationship with the United States. At the end of September 1984 Gromyko was back in Washington, smiling wanly to reporters after a prolonged absence. Little progress resulted from his visit, however, as the Reagan administration held firm in its commitment to SDI. The main avenues to a less hostile relationship with both Washington and Bonn were now effectively blocked.

In these circumstances, a reevaluation of the Kremlin's entire foreign policy line of the past ten to fifteen years was in order. This, it seems, was the ultimate significance of the vigorous policy debate on Germany which had taken place in the heat of the INF controversy. As the developments of the next several years would demonstrate, those who now argued that Soviet interests were best served by a relaxation of tensions were in effect pleading for a redirection of Soviet foreign policy away from the fruitless paths of military self-aggrandizement and diplomatic-ideological confrontation. At a time of American self-assertiveness and international opposition to Soviet intervention in Afghanistan, these scholars and political figures recognized that Moscow's failure to preserve détente in Europe had only deepened the USSR's global isolation. And at a time of stagnating performance in the domestic economy, many of them also recognized that the Kremlin's punitive attitudes were jeopardizing the improvement of economic ties with the West, and especially with the Federal Republic.[124]

In short, the debate over Germany within the Soviet elite helped set the stage for the "new thinking" in Soviet foreign policy which was soon to be ushered in by Mikhail Gorbachev.

124. On the basis of a Soviet economist's assertion that the Soviet economy did not grow at all between 1978 and 1985, and a CIA estimate that military spending rose by 2% a year in the early 1980s, one Western analyst concluded that the military's share of GNP was growing in these years and that conflict over resource allocation presumably intensified as a result. See Anders Åslund, *Gorbachev's Struggle for Economic Reform* (Ithaca: Cornell University Press, 1989), p. 15.

CHAPTER TEN

New Thinking:
1985–1990

THE EXTRAORDINARY reform process set in motion by Mikhail
Gorbachev in the second half of the 1980s took most observers by surprise.
What began as a long-overdue industrial reorganization aimed at promoting economic "acceleration" soon swelled into an unexpectedly radical
program for transforming the political landscape of the USSR. Initially
Gorbachev appeared to be intent mainly on introducing a sweeping economic reform in an effort to jolt the Soviet economy out of an entire "era of
stagnation." Not only were annual growth rates lagging, but the USSR was
falling disastrously behind the Western world and the dynamic trading
nations of Asia in the high-technology sectors that set the pace for global
economic advancement.[1] Gorbachev inherited a retrograde industrial system, widespread food shortages, an unresponsive consumer sector, and a
proliferation of ecological disasters. These troubles, combined with the
absence of outlets for the expression of the popular will, were sapping the
productivity of a dispirited and cynical population.

The new Soviet leader decided early on that an economic *perestroika*
(restructuring) of the necessary magnitude would not be successful without
political reforms. At the very least, a measure of *glasnost* (a term that came
to mean an unprecedented level of openness in public discourse) would be
required to inform the Soviet people about the urgency of the problems
confronting them. This was especially the case after the Chernobyl catastro-
phe of April 1986. Having opened up the doors of a tightly guarded
political system by stretching the limits of censorship, Gorbachev next

1. Marshall I. Goldman, *Gorbachev's Challenge: Economic Reform in the Age of High
Technology* (New York: Norton, 1987).

embarked on an unprecedented quest for *demokratizatsiya*—the democratization of the Soviet system. His primary aim, to all appearances, was to give the Soviet population a greater say in the decisions affecting their lives, and in the process to direct public discontent at Brezhnev-style conservatives blocking the path to reform. A decisive step in this direction came with the openly contested elections to the newly established Congress of People's Deputies in March and April 1989.

Initially Gorbachev hoped to preside over a carefully channeled democratization process, a kind of "democratization from above" that could be orchestrated by reformists in the leadership to promote their policy preferences. But rising demands for even greater political change and faster economic progress soon overflowed the banks of the leadership's designs and surged into directions of their own. By the end of the decade, the Gorbachev regime stood confronted with widespread popular support for more radical reforms and a series of spontaneous strikes. It also faced the worrisome prospect of the internal dismemberment of the USSR as a host of national minorities demanded greater autonomy, or outright independence, in regions stretching from the Baltic to Central Asia, by way of Moldavia, Georgia and the Ukraine.

These developments inevitably raised serious questions about Gorbachev's ability to stay in power. The general secretary displayed remarkable forcefulness in dealing with his opponents, however. During the formative period of his regime, lasting about two years, Gorbachev managed to oust or demote a number of Brezhnev-era holdovers and to wrest control of foreign and military policy from conservative forces entrenched in the Foreign Ministry and the military establishment. Later he reduced the influence of Yegor Ligachev, a conservative leader committed to far more cautious reform. Despite Gorbachev's steady accretion of power, however, the leadership group assembled around him had all the markings of a Soviet-style coalition regime. Gorbachev clearly dominated this group, but as 1990 dawned, he still had to share power with other party oligarchs who did not necessarily subscribe to his vision of radical reform. Resistance to reform was particularly tenacious within the central party apparatus. Gorbachev accordingly sought to build a separate power base within the institutions of the Soviet state. By the end of the 1980s he was well on his way to transforming the largely ceremonial post of head of state into a powerful executive presidency endowed with constitutionally defined prerogatives and a more democratic source of legitimacy. This effort culminated in his election to the redesigned presidency by a majority of the Congress of People's Deputies in March 1990. At the 28th Party Congress in July he managed to oust Ligachev from the Politburo and to reshape the party leadership. Even these adroit maneuvers, however, did not eliminate Gorbachev's need to maintain viable coalitions at the highest levels of the party and state hierarchies to push along the laborious reform process. At no point during these years did he become the unchallengeable leader of a directive regime.

Throughout the years from 1985 to 1990, however, the prevailing policy thrust of Gorbachev's coalition was decidedly reformist. Despite the presence of Brezhnev-era conservatives (such as Gromyko and Vladimir Shcherbitskii) in the upper reaches of the leadership during much of this period, Gorbachev and his principal allies managed to keep Soviet policy on a reformist course. They did so even though they seemed to have no ready-made prescription for economic restructuring, an issue that produced sharp debate and protracted indecisiveness well into 1990.

These unprecedented internal developments were intimately connected with foreign policy. Gorbachev and his chief supporters announced at the outset that the restructuring of the Soviet domestic system would be accompanied by parallel efforts to effect a perestroika in international relations. In the beginning the Gorbachev coalition sought at the very least a *peredyshka* in its international engagements, a respite from the high tensions and burdensome costs of the USSR's previous foreign policy commitments. As might be expected of a reformist regime, the Gorbachev team's first priority was to set its own house in order by focusing on the internal requirements of economic growth and political change. These demanding domestic tasks required a more placid external environment and, not incidentally, a long-term reduction in military spending. Gorbachev's surprising decision in July 1985 to replace Foreign Minister Andrei Gromyko, the dour symbol of the Brezhnev era, with Eduard Shevardnadze, the party chief of Georgia, provided an early indication of the new regime's determination to subordinate foreign policy considerations to domestic priorities.

As time went on, however, it became increasingly evident that Gorbachev and his chief supporters were determined to seek a fundamental reorientation of Moscow's relations with the West. The INF Treaty of December 1987 marked a historic milestone in this direction. The startling events of 1988 and 1989 made it even more evident that Gorbachev wanted to de-Stalinize and demilitarize Soviet society, reduce the burdens of empire, and integrate the Soviet Union and its East European allies more effectively into the world trading system. The transformation of domestic policy required the transformation of foreign policy. These intentions militated for an early abatement of cold war tension.

They also reflected the outlooks of a new generation of Soviet leaders. Born in 1931, Gorbachev himself had come of age politically in the bracing years of Khrushchev's de-Stalinization campaign. Although he had witnessed the occupation of his homeland by the Germans as a boy, he had not invested his own career in the struggle against Nazi Germany or in the imposition of communism on Eastern Europe. These factors were bound to affect the outlook of Gorbachev and many of his contemporaries on both domestic and foreign policy.[2]

In keeping with its reformist orientation, the Gorbachev coalition thus held to a broadly defined concept of détente, centered above all in a significantly greater commitment to military détente than its conservative predecessors had ever exhibited. It also displayed far greater responsiveness and willingness to compromise, as well as a considerably more open approach to internal discussion and self-criticism on major foreign policy issues. Instead of having to speak in the oblique parlance of earlier decades, policy analysts now could state their views with greater candor. Specialists in the secondary elite were also accorded a more direct role in the shaping of policy decisions, thus enhancing their advisory function within the foreign policy establishment. Soviet foreign policy, in short, was once again being directly influenced by the nature of the decision-making regime in charge at the Kremlin. In this case, a regime pursuing radical reforms at home matched them with strikingly new departures in the USSR's external behavior.

Sooner or later, the "new political thinking" in Soviet foreign policy would have to come to grips with West Germany. Initially the Gorbachev regime seemed very reluctant to include Helmut Kohl in its widening web of direct contacts with Western leaders. But one of the major implications of the debate on Germany in the first half of the 1980s was that any attempt to exclude Bonn from the Soviet Union's evolving relationship with Western Europe would ultimately prove self-defeating. It was this "pro-Bonn" viewpoint that eventually prevailed in Kremlin deliberations once Gorbachev came to power. Proponents of a more punitive attitude toward the FRG, frozen in their confrontationist stance and dedicated to the continued "strengthening" of Soviet military might, were eventually discredited or replaced. Advocates of a less rigid policy option were more likely to be retained and even promoted.

As these events unfolded, the conceptual underpinnings of Soviet foreign and security policy underwent a thorough revision. The notion of a "common European home" extending from the Atlantic to the Urals became a central theme in the Kremlin's overtures to Western Europe. At the same time, Gorbachev and authoritative foreign policy spokesmen offered hints that the Kremlin might be rethinking the most axiomatic principles of its German policy. Assertions that the division of Germany might not last forever, and that the Berlin wall was not a "big problem," gave rise to fresh

2. Gorbachev's village of Privolnoye was in the Stavropol region occupied by the Germans in 1942. His father fought for five years in the Ukraine, and three of his uncles were killed. Aleksandr Yakovlev, one of Gorbachev's older supporters, suffered a permanent limp after being shot in the knee during the war: *Washington Post,* Feb. 12, 1990, pp. A13–14.

speculation in the West that Moscow might actually be contemplating Germany's unification in the foreseeable future.

These abrupt turnabouts in Moscow's domestic and foreign policies caught East Germany completely off guard. The political shock waves spreading from the Soviet Union rocked the complacent Honecker coalition, which was held together by a centrist-conservative consensus broadly shared among SED leaders. As we have already seen, centrist decision-making regimes in countries ruled by communist parties tended to pursue a mixture of policies combining relatively conservative leanings on some issues with a more flexible approach to others. In the GDR's case, a highly traditional affirmation of "the leading role of the party" in domestic affairs was combined with an explicit commitment to arms control and détente in Europe which grew ever more vocal as the INF crisis reached its peak in 1983 and 1984.

It was with considerable relief that the Honecker leadership greeted Mikhail Gorbachev's early efforts to promote significant East-West arms reductions. But the domestic components of Gorbachev's reform program significantly outran the GDR's capacity for change. Honecker and his key associates made it very clear that perestroika, glasnost, and demokratizatsia would not be translated into the East German political lexicon.

These domestically centered concerns were sharply aggravated by the foreign policy implications of Gorbachev's new course. Even the slightest hint, no matter how qualified, that the Soviets might no longer be committed unconditionally to the permanent existence of the GDR stirred anxieties in the Socialist Unity Party which bordered on paranoia.

Thus the Honecker regime was confronted with a double challenge from Moscow, one threatening its domestic raison d'être as a traditional neo-Stalinist one-party state, the other threatening its international raison d'être as the guarantor of the division of postwar Germany. In comparison with the Gorbachev regime, Honecker's stood out as a bastion of conservatism. Its conception of détente was considerably narrower, it was less prepared to adapt to changing conditions and less willing to compromise, and it permitted a narrower range of internal debate. Eventually both the internal and the foreign policy components of Gorbachev's reform program proved to be the Honecker regime's undoing.

In his foreign policy undertakings as in his domestic reforms, Gorbachev set loose forces for change that escaped his control and exceeded his initial ambitions. The result in East-Central Europe was the revolutionary outburst that swept conservative communist regimes from power in the fall of 1989 and opened the way, astonishingly, to the complete disappearance of the East German state. It is highly doubtful that Gorbachev expected such a rapid turn of events. To be sure, the Soviet leader and his Kremlin allies were determined to promote reform in the region and they were visibly inching their way toward a reconceptualization of their German policy. In all likelihood, however, they envisioned efforts by local party reformers to wrest power from the old guard and to deepen their domestic legitimacy through glasnost and democratization while widening their contacts with the West through market-oriented reforms. Such a strategy, if successful, would not only permit an orderly process of East-West disarmament and economic cooperation; it would also stabilize the division of Germany for an indefinite period by making a liberalized East German state more acceptable to its own population and more open to the West. While nudging their allies to move in these directions, Gorbachev and his followers were equally determined to avoid the interventionist policies of former Soviet leaders.

As popular participation reached new levels in the Soviet Union, hopes for similar—or even greater—opportunities rose throughout East-Central Europe. Hungary and Poland embraced multiparty systems while the GDR and other regimes bucked the tide of reform. When the dam burst at the end of 1989, the devastation was nearly total. As if by a relentless inner logic, the process that had begun with the restructuring of the Soviet domestic system ultimately led to the reconfiguration of postwar Europe.

Restructuring International Relations

For approximately the first two years of Gorbachev's tenure as general secretary, Soviet foreign policy was characterized primarily by its caution. As might be expected of a decision-making coalition in its formative stages, the Gorbachev leadership's conception of relations with the West was still in an exploratory phase; signs of growing adaptability and willingness to compromise were balanced by indications of uncertainty as to just how far the Kremlin should go to reduce tensions. The influence of conservative holdovers in the political and military hierarchies had yet to be decisively reduced. Evidence of serious debate on foreign policy issues therefore proliferated as the new regime sorted out its internal power structure and its policy priorities.

On the one hand, there was a cautious probing of the possibilities for ending the recriminatory atmosphere in East-West relations which the new Soviet leader had inherited from his predecessors. To this end, Gorbachev journeyed to Paris for meetings with François Mitterrand in October 1985, and held his first encounter with Ronald Reagan a month later in Geneva. In October 1986 the Soviet and American leaders met once again, in Reykjavik. These were the first U.S.-Soviet summits since 1979. On the other hand, Gorbachev was equally cautious in these years when it came to formulating Soviet arms-control proposals. Despite growing indications of flexibility in the Soviet position on the provocative INF issue, the new man in the Kremlin showed no signs of unconditionally accepting the West's zero option for liquidating intermediate-range missiles in 1985 or 1986.[3] In part for this reason, many Western observers remained skeptical about Gorbachev's ultimate motives.

Meanwhile, Gorbachev was guided during these first two years by one overriding security policy priority: stopping SDI. Ronald Reagan's determination to move ahead with plans to develop his "strategic defense initiative" constituted a major challenge to Gorbachev's domestic and foreign policy ambitions. The need to fashion some kind of military response to an effective American defensive system, even if it were limited to penetrating devices less costly than SDI itself, would impose severe strains on the Soviet budget at a time when Gorbachev was resolved to concentrate Soviet resources on economic modernization. Moscow's reformist leadership could ill afford a new round in the arms race, particularly one centered on expensive laser weapons, particle beam technology, and other space-age spinoffs of SDI research.

In addition, SDI interfered with Gorbachev's plans for a breakthrough in the political relationship with the West. With so much of his strategy for domestic restructuring hinging on a tranquil international environment and a renewed flow of Western economic assistance, SDI only complicated an otherwise visibly improving dialogue with the United States. Prime Minister Thatcher's government also lent its support to SDI research, while Mitterrand proposed a European program for civilian high-technology development, called "Eureka," which some Soviet observers believed to be adaptable to military uses.[4] Moscow's tortured relationship with West Germany gained yet anther irritant as the Kohl government signed an agreement with the United States in 1986 to facilitate the participation of West German firms in SDI research. The obstacle posed by SDI to improved East-West ties stood out with particular prominence at the Reykjavik summit, where a no-holds-barred discussion of potentially radical reductions in Soviet and American weapons systems foundered on Reagan's refusal to halt the "Star Wars" program.[5]

Nineteen-eighty-seven was a pivotal year in Moscow's evolving détente

3. While in Paris, Gorbachev continued to make Soviet acceptance of an INF accord contingent on a reduction in French and British nuclear arsenals. In early 1986 he stated that the "complete liquidation" of American and Soviet INF "in the European zone" would be possible in five to eight years if London and Paris would pledge not to "build up" their nuclear forces. See *Pravda*, Oct. 4, 1985, pp. 1–2; Oct. 6, pp. 1–2; Jan. 16, 1986, pp. 1–2.

4. Yu. Kovalenko in *Izvestiya*, Aug. 9, 1985, p. 5; also Aleksandr Bovin's remarks, FBIS, *Soviet Union*, Nov. 18, 1985, suppl. 001, pp. 12–13. While in Paris, Gorbachev said he wanted to find out if Eureka had "peaceful aims": FBIS, *Soviet Union*, Oct. 2, 1985, p. G7.

5. For a comprehensive assessment, see Bruce Parrott, *The Soviet Union and Ballistic Missile Defense* (Boulder, Colo.: Westview, 1987).

policy. After a Central Committee plenum in January heard Gorbachev call for "truly revolutionary and comprehensive transformations in society," the Soviet leader declared on February 28 that Moscow was now prepared to negotiate an INF accord with the United States without insisting that the Americans renounce SDI. The ensuing talks proceeded at a pace that can only be considered dazzling, in view of the complexity of the issues and the necessity for further concessions on major points by both sides. Gorbachev, quite obviously, was in a hurry. The treaty was ready for signature during his visit to Washington in December.

This landmark achievement in arms control provided clear evidence that the formative phase in Gorbachev's efforts to build a reformist coalition was largely over. While debate on a variety of issues continued (especially on domestic policy), it was apparent that Gorbachev had managed to assert his primacy over the foreign policy formulation process. The INF Treaty also ushered in a new phase in East-West relations. Gorbachev's acceptance of the West's terms for the accord had taken many Western observers by surprise, and some (such as Henry Kissinger) expressed misgivings about the treaty in view of the Warsaw Pact's continuing superiority in conventional weaponry. Moreover, the full extent of Gorbachev's readiness for unilateral arms reductions and for truly unprecedented levels of democratization in the Soviet Union and Eastern Europe had yet to be fully revealed by the end of 1987. Nevertheless, the INF Treaty led the way to a rapid improvement in East-West ties, resulting in previously unthinkable levels of cooperation between the two sides on a host of military, economic, and humanitarian issues. In the Soviet Union, meanwhile, the INF accord opened the gates to the most critical and comprehensive reappraisal of Soviet foreign policy to be conducted in open forums since the 1920s.

As these events took shape, the Soviet foreign policy elite elaborated a series of new concepts for gauging the prevailing trends in world politics and for guiding Soviet relations with the West in a period of extensive domestic reform. The main tenets of this reconceptualization were advanced by the middle of 1987, and their implications for past and future Soviet foreign policy were spelled out with increasing bluntness over the next two years. On virtually every count, the central ideas that guided the Gorbachev regime's "new thinking" on international relations conflicted directly with the conceptual rationales that structured the foreign policy activities of the Brezhnev-Andropov-Chernenko years:

1. The world is dialectically divided into two parts: the socialist and capitalist part, in which each social system develops according to its own laws, and a globally unified part, which embraces the whole of humanity. Both parts are characterized by growing interdependence and the need for greater cooperation as they face the common challenges of security, economic development, humanitarian concerns, science and technology, the

environment, energy, hunger, and simple survival. "Common human values," including self-determination, are more important than class values.

2. Peaceful coexistence is not a "specific form of the class struggle." Rather, it is a search for cooperation between socialism and capitalism which recognizes their differences and acknowledges that all states have certain objective interests. The differences between the two social systems constitute not a barrier to cooperation but a wealth of experience from which both sides can learn and benefit. Relations between socialist and capitalist states must at all times be "civilized" and conducted on the basis of mutual respect for their sovereignty and independence. Each side must work to eliminate its image of the other as the enemy.

3. Foreign policy is a reflection of domestic policy. Its main aim is to establish the conditions necessary for political, economic, and social development at home. The concept of national security should by no means be confined to military questions; economic progress and scientific-technological advancement are also essential ingredients of a nation's security.

4. The problem of security among states can be resolved not through military means but only through political means. Especially in the nuclear age, war must not be viewed as a continuation of politics. Nuclear war is unwinnable. The security of one state cannot be achieved at the expense of the security of others. It is therefore necessary to reduce the level of military confrontation both quantitatively and qualitatively, so as to achieve stable military parity at significantly lower levels of armaments, with each side having a reasonable sufficiency in military forces. Military strategy and force postures must be based on the concept of nonoffensive defense, which makes self-defense possible but significantly reduces and ultimately eliminates offensive capabilities and the possibility of surprise attack. The Soviet Union must assume its share of responsibility for the failure to achieve military détente in the past.

5. The horizontal spread of confrontation between the United States and the USSR, or between NATO and the Warsaw Pact, into regional conflicts in the Third World must be avoided.

These basic principles were articulated in a variety of official documents and were amplified and refined by such leading political figures as Gorbachev, Shevardnadze, Aleksandr Yakovlev, and Vadim Medvedev. Key members of the secondary elite also played a major role in the formulation and public exposition of these concepts, particularly Vadim Zagladin (who retained his position as first deputy chief of the Central Committee's International Department) and Yevgenii Primakov, who succeeded Yakovlev as head of IMEMO in 1985.[6] (Primakov stepped into the primary elite in

---

6. See also in *MEMO*, V. Petrovskii, "Sovetskaya kontseptsiya vseobshchei bezopasnosti," no. 6, 1985, pp. 3–13; V. Razmerov, "Realnosti i ikh osnovaniye v mirovoi politike,"

September 1989 when he was inducted into the Politburo as a candidate member.) The new concepts were bound to stir up controversy, however, especially among proponents of a more conservative approach to East-West relations. Although the main tenets of the Gorbachev world view carried the day and became enshrined as official policy in this period, they did not go unchallenged. The ensuing debates touched on topics that were intimately connected with Moscow's future policy moves toward West Germany.

This was especially the case with respect to military issues.[7] Starting with his speech at the April 1985 Central Committee plenum, which kicked off the drive for economic "acceleration," Gorbachev declared that the USSR would not "spare any effort . . . to reliably defend our fatherland," but this was not the same as an open-ended commitment to raise defense spending in the future. Two weeks later, on the fortieth anniversary of the defeat of Hitler's Germany, Gorbachev described the current international situation as "dangerous," but he quickly added that there were realistic opportunities for curbing militarism in the world. He went on to call for a détente that would be much greater than that of the 1970s.[8] In all his later speeches in 1985 and 1986, Gorbachev scrupulously refrained from promising to "strengthen" Soviet defense capabilities. In January 1986 he called for the elimination of all nuclear weapons by the year 2000. At the same time, Gorbachev left no doubt about his antipathy to SDI.[9]

When Gorbachev unveiled his new thinking on security policy at the 27th Party Congress, it was evident that critical military issues were by no means entirely resolved.[10] As in the past, proponents of a more conservative position stressed the unabated danger of war in the contemporary world, and insisted on military "vigilance" and on the need to "strengthen" the defense might of the USSR. These stock phrases were uttered at one time or another in 1985 and 1986 by such influential members of the primary elite as Ligachev, Gromyko, Shcherbitskii, Ponomarev, and Defense Minister Sergei Sokolov.[11] Their views were seconded by various military commanders.[12]

July 1986, pp. 3–12; and V. Kortunov, "Novoye politicheskoye myshleniye—imperativ sovremennosti," no. 10, 1986, pp. 16–25.

7. For an extensive overview, see Bruce Parrott, "Soviet National Security under Gorbachev," *Problems of Communism* 37 (November–December 1988): 1–36.

8. *Pravda*, Apr. 24, 1985, p. 2; May 9, pp. 1–3.

9. See, e.g., Gorbachev's positive assessment of the Geneva summit in *Pravda*, Nov. 28, 1985, pp. 1–2, and his arms-control proposals of Jan. 15, 1986, in ibid., Jan. 16, pp. 1–2.

10. *Pravda*, Feb. 26, 1986, pp. 2–3, 7–9.

11. Ligachev: FBIS, *Soviet Union*, June 20, 1985, p. R22; Gromyko: *Izvestiya*, Nov. 14, 1985, p. 2, and Apr. 12, 1986, p. 2; Shcherbitskii: *Isvestiya*, Nov. 28, 1985, p. 3; Ponomarev: *Pravda*, Dec. 29, 1985, p. 2, and FBIS, *Soviet Union*, Jan. 15, 1986, p. R10; Sokolov: *Pravda*, Nov. 8, 1985, pp. 1–2, and May 9, 1986, p. 2.

12. E.g., Maj. Gen. V. Khalilov, *Krasnaya zvezda*, Dec. 19, 1985, pp. 2–3; Gen. A. T. Altunin, *Ekonomicheskaya gazeta*, no. 9, 1986, p. 7; V. G. Kulikov, *Komsomolskaya pravda*,

Not all senior military figures shared these conservative views unreservedly. Marshal Sergei Akhromeyev, the new chief of staff, echoed some of the cardinal elements of Gorbachev's new military thinking more pronouncedly than other military figures.[13] He and like-minded officers apparently favored Gorbachev's goals of economic restructuring and a relaxation of tensions, possibly with a view to building a more modern and dynamic economic base for future Soviet military procurements.

The absence of a clear consensus on security policy in this period seemed to be confirmed at the 27th Party Congress. The resolution published at the end of the congress reflected Gorbachev's emphasis on arms control, reasonable sufficiency, and a defensive military strategy. The harshly worded new party program, however, coupled its call for peaceful coexistence with a stern reminder of "imperialism's aggressive policy" and of the advantages to be gained from "the strengthening of the country's defense capability."[14] Conservatives frequently cited these passages to demonstrate the party's support for their positions. Meanwhile, the growth in aggregate Soviet military spending in this period oscillated between 1 and 2 percent per year, a reflection of the dwindling resources available for defense.[15]

Another controversy emerged over Gorbachev's summit diplomacy. While Gorbachev hailed the positive elements of his first meeting with Reagan at Geneva, especially the joint statement in which the conservative American president had agreed that nuclear war was "unwinnable," members of the regime's conservative phalanx drew attention to the meeting's failures.[16] A similar exchange took place over the Reykjavik summit. Without minimizing his disappointment over Reagan's obduracy on SDI, Gorbachev described the meeting in Iceland as a "breakthrough." Ligachev, however, averred that the summit was a "failure" because it had shown

May 9, 1986, p. 1; Gen. Ye. Ivanovskii, FBIS, *Soviet Union*, May 13, 1986, pp. R4–7; Col. Gen. V. Verevkin-Rakhalskii, *Krasnaya zvezda*, May 13, 1986, p. 3; Gen. V. Shabanov, *Krasnaya zvezda*, Aug. 15, 1986, pp. 2–3.

13. *Izvestiya*, Nov. 28, 1985, p. 4; *Krasnaya zvezda*, Dec. 31, 1985, p. 5; *Izvestiya*, May 9, 1986, p. 3. In the latter VE Day speech, Akhromeyev referred to the "major contribution" of the United States, Britain, and France to the war against Hitler, an acknowledgment not repeated by more hawkish military leaders.

14. *Pravda*, Mar. 6, 1986, pp. 1–3; Mar. 7, p. 3. The final version of the party program failed to include a favorable reference to a "moderate faction" of Western politicians who were concerned about "all global problems," as proposed by a writer in *Kommunist*, no. 1, 1986, p. 81.

15. According to one estimate, real Soviet defense spending rose by 2% in 1985, by 1% in 1986, and by 2% in 1987. As a proportion of GNP, military expenditures fell from an estimated 12.6% in 1985 to 12.2% in 1986, then rose slightly to 12.3% in 1987. See U.S. Arms Control and Disarmament Agency, *World Military Expenditures and Arms Transfers, 1988* (Washington, D.C.: U.S. Government Printing Office, n.d.), p. 61.

16. For the joint statement, see *New York Times*, Nov. 22, 1985, p. A15. Gorbachev's remarks are in *Pravda*, Nov. 28, 1985, pp. 1–2. See also the views of Ponomarev in *Pravda*, Dec. 29, 1985, p. 2; Shcherbitskii in *Pravda Ukrainy*, Dec. 22, 1985, pp. 1–2; and Ligachev in *Izvestiya*, Jan. 22, 1986, p. 2.

"with all obviousness" that the Reagan administration was not interested in arms accords. Sokolov and Premier Nikolai Ryzhkov also drew attention to Reagan's military plans.[17]

It was in the immediate aftermath of Reykjavik that the wrangling over security policy appears to have come to a head, at least temporarily. In a remark that may have been at least partially intended for Soviet listeners, Gorbachev suggested that President Reagan was not taking sufficient measures "to control his hawks." A confrontation with Soviet hawks was now high on Gorbachev's agenda. At the January 1987 Central Committee plenum, Gorbachev devoted his full attention to quickening the pace of political and economic restructuring at home. The Central Committee resolution issued at the end of the plenum, however, contained a strongly worded statement on foreign policy which clashed openly with the spirit of Gorbachev's evolving arms diplomacy. It accused "warlike imperialist forces" in the United States of seeking nuclear superiority, thereby necessitating "the all-round strengthening of our country's military capability" and "constant vigilance" on the part of the Soviet armed forces. Over the course of the next several weeks, Sokolov reaffirmed his commitment to "strengthening" Soviet defense capabilities.[18]

These statements may have reflected indignation within the military at the sweeping disarmament proposals Gorbachev had brought to Reykjavik. Gorbachev was accordingly at pains to insist that the Reykjavik summit had been carefully prepared, involving full consultations with the Defense Ministry. Just as important, these skirmishes took place at a time when the linkage between a potential INF agreement and SDI was at the center of the Soviet leadership's attention. At Reykjavik the Soviets had insisted that no deal on intermediate-range forces in Europe could be reached unless the Reagan administration agreed at least to limit its SDI research programs. Gorbachev and several prominent Soviet spokesmen held to this position in the months that followed.[19]

There were indications, however, that the Kremlin was not so firmly committed to this linkage as it claimed. Several days after the conclusion of the Iceland summit, Viktor Karpov, the Soviet arms negotiator in Geneva, and Aleksandr Bessmertnykh of the Foreign Ministry stated that a deal on INF could be reached independently of an understanding on SDI. Karpov soon backed off from this position, but by mid-February Gorbachev himself

17. Gorbachev: *Pravda*, Feb. 17, 1987, p. 1; Ligachev: ibid., Oct. 17, 1986, p. 3, and Parrott, "Soviet National Security," p. 16; also *Pravda*, Nov. 14, 1986, p. 5; Sokolov: *Krasnaya zvezda*, Jan. 23, 1987, p. 3; Ryzhkov: *Pravda*, Oct. 22, 1986, p. 4, and Feb. 17, 1987, p. 2.

18. *Pravda*, Oct. 23, 1986, p. 2; Jan. 29, 1987, p. 2; Feb. 23, 1987, p. 2; *Krasnaya zvezda*, Feb. 12, 1987, p. 3.

19. *Pravda*, Oct. 15, 1986, p. 1; Oct. 23, pp. 1–2. See also the views of Akhromeyev in *Izvestiya*, Nov. 27, 1986, p. 4; Col. Gen. Nikolai Chervov in FBIS, *Soviet Union*, Oct. 29, 1986, pp. AA5–6; Deputy Foreign Minister Georgii Kornenko in FBIS, *Soviet Union*, Feb. 6, 1987, p. AA12; and Kvitsinskii in *General-Anzeiger* (Bonn), Feb. 7, 1987, p. 3.

no longer referred to the importance of a package approach to INF and SDI. Instead he called for a new level of confidence in international relations and warned against the danger of becoming "captives of the past." On February 26 the Soviet Union exploded its first atomic device since announcing in the summer of 1985 the first in a series of unilateral test moratoriums aimed at getting the Reagan administration to cease its nuclear testing program. Gorbachev's decision to end the moratorium at this time was possibly intended to mollify Soviet generals in advance of his next dramatic move. Two days later he announced that Moscow would no longer link a future INF accord to SDI.[20]

Gorbachev's desire for a speedy resolution of the INF problem was now apparent. With the road to domestic reform becoming rockier, Gorbachev needed a major foreign policy success that would transform Western perceptions of the Soviet Union and pave the way for future cuts in arms deployments and spending. Substantial concessions leading to an INF accord, it was believed, might also reduce support in the United States for the costly SDI program.[21] Gorbachev's haste was also prompted by fears that SDI might soon generate an irreversible cycle in the arms race, and that by 1988 major foreign policy decisions would be difficult to reach in Washington owing to the protracted presidential election campaign.[22] Within weeks of Gorbachev's announcement, a senior Soviet negotiator was forecasting an INF agreement within three to four months.[23]

Although it took somewhat longer than that to hammer out the INF accord (for reasons to be examined below), the historic agreement signed by Gorbachev and Reagan in Washington at the end of 1987 did not go down lightly with some elements of the Soviet elite. As the next round of INF negotiations got under way with fresh optimism, various members of the military hierarchy, including Defense Minister Sokolov, took a jaundiced view of U.S. intentions and said nothing to encourage hopes for an INF agreement. Several called openly for continuing efforts to "strengthen" Soviet defense capabilities.[24] In late May, however, Gorbachev dealt two successive blows to military hard-liners.

First, he presided over a session of the Warsaw Pact's political leadership which issued two documents adopting the Kremlin's new thinking on

20. *Washington Post*, Oct. 15, 1986, p. A23, and *New York Times*, Oct. 15, 1986, p. A13; *Pravda*, Feb. 17, 1987, pp. 1–2, and Mar. 1, p. 1.

21. See the remarks in FBIS, *Soviet Union*, by Georgii Arbatov and Roald Sagdeyev, Nov. 17, 1986, pp. AA8ff.; by Kornenko, Feb. 6, 1987, p. AA15; and by Falin, June 5, 1987, p. CC2.

22. Arbatov in FBIS, *Soviet Union*, Nov. 17, 1986, pp. AA6–7; Falin's comments in ibid., June 5, 1987, p. CC2; Gennadii Gerasimov's comments in *Sovetskaya kultura*, Jan. 24, 1987, p. 7; Vadim Zagladin's interview in *Frankfurter Rundschau*, Apr. 2, 1987, p. 8.

23. FBIS, *Soviet Union*, Mar. 16, 1987, p. AA3.

24. See Sokolov's VE Day address in *Pravda*, May 9, 1987, p. 2. Also the comments by Gen. Ye. Ivanovskii in *Sovetskaya Rossiya*, May 9, p. 2, and by Gens. P. Lushev and I. Tretyak, FBIS, *Soviet Union*, May 11, 1987, pp. 7–10.

security matters as the official policy of the alliance. Both statements affirmed that the Warsaw Pact's military doctrine had an exclusively defensive character, and that it was based on the quest for sufficiency at the lowest possible levels of arms deployments. They also acknowledged for the first time the existence of "asymmetries" in the European weapons balance, and proclaimed the Pact's readiness to remove them through lopsided reductions by each side in the appropriate categories. In addition to calling for "radical" arms reductions and strict on-site verification measures, the participants in the meeting also announced a moratorium on military expenditures of up to two years.[25]

Gorbachev's second blow came the next day. On May 30 he sacked Sokolov. Ostensibly the defense minister was blamed for the military's failure to prevent Matthias Rust, a young West German daredevil, from piloting his light plane through Soviet defenses and taxiing up to Red Square.[26] It was quite obvious, however, that the incident had provided a timely pretext for Gorbachev to remove an obstacle to his disarmament schemes and to serve notice on the Soviet military that the political leadership was firmly in command. Sokolov's replacement, Deputy Defense Minister Dmitrii T. Yazov, had recently confirmed that Soviet armed forces "have all they need" for defense, a position somewhat more in tune with Gorbachev's thinking.[27] Yazov was made a candidate member of the Politburo, rather than a full member, a position that reflected the military's reduced status in the Soviet hierarchy.

As negotiations on the INF treaty continued, critics within the military and foreign policy establishments warned against excessive enthusiasm and "delusions" about the West, while Gorbachev lambasted "skeptics, panic-mongers, and opponents of disarmament."[28] One of the central concerns of the conservatives was whether the Soviet Union was making too many concessions to the United States and its NATO allies in its pursuit of an INF treaty and other arms-reduction measures. This issue was raised directly in *Krasnaya zvezda* and other publications both before and after the signature of the INF accord. The fact that the treaty would require the Soviets to destroy twice as many missiles as the United States was particularly disturb-

25. See the communiqué and the "Document on the Military Doctrine of the Warsaw Pact States," issued May 29, 1987, in *Pravda*, May 30, pp. 1–2.

26. *Izvestiya*, June 1, 1987, p. 3, quoted Zbigniew Brzezinski to the effect that U.S. military leaders who commit mistakes should be fired.

27. FBIS, *Soviet Union*, Feb. 26, 1987, pp. V8–9. See Yazov's subsequent statements defending the new defensive doctrine and efforts to introduce perestroika into the Soviet armed forces, *Krasnaya zvezda*, July 19, 1987, p. 2, and *Pravda*, July 27, p. 5. See also the review of Sokolov's new book in *Krasnaya zvezda*, Oct. 30, 1987, p. 3.

28. *Pravda*, Oct. 7, 1987, p. 2. See also Gorbachev's speech in Murmansk, ibid., Oct. 2, pp. 2–3. For expressions of doubt about the impending INF agreement, see *Krasnaya zvezda*, Sept. 26, 1987, p. 2, and the article by Yurii Bandura in *Moskovskiye novosti*, Oct. 18, p. 5.

ing to some commentators.[29] As the treaty was sent to the Supreme Soviet for ratification, supporters and opponents of the agreement advertised their attitudes openly. Yazov, Akhromeyev, and Colonel General Nikolai Chervov, the Defense Ministry's senior arms-control adviser, spoke in favor of the treaty (albeit without enthusiasm), but Warsaw Pact Commander Viktor Kulikov called again for vigilance and military "strengthening."[30]

During the Supreme Soviet's deliberations, Yegor Ligachev supported the treaty but wondered aloud if the United States would abide by it, warning that "this cannot help but put us on our guard." Shevardnadze spoke out much more forcefully in the treaty's behalf. The foreign minister drew special attention to the treaty's potential economic benefits, and even admitted that the Soviet SS-20s possessed the same qualities of speed and accuracy that made the American Pershing IIs "one of the most dangerous kinds of weapons."[31] As the ratification process advanced in tandem with the U.S. Senate's consideration of the treaty, Soviet officials generally evaluated the agreement positively, but several acknowledged problems.[32]

The Supreme Soviet ratified the INF Treaty on May 29, 1988. The next day Ronald Reagan arrived in Moscow for his final summit as president.

The conclusion of the protracted INF crisis let loose a torrent of criticism of past Soviet policies that had led to the Euromissile imbroglio in the first place, as well as to such foreign policy misadventures as the war in Afghanistan. The intensified self-criticism added new impulses to a process of reevaluating Soviet foreign policy concepts and operating procedures which had actually begun even before the INF issue was settled. Starting with his decision to replace the implacable Gromyko with Shevardnadze in 1985, for example, Gorbachev had betrayed his intention of bringing the Soviet foreign policy apparatus under his personal control. Grigorii Romanov, the Leningrad hard-liner, was ejected from the party leadership at the same

29. *Krasnaya zvezda*, June 17, 1987, p. 3, and Oct. 9, 1987, p. 3; *Pravda*, Dec. 22, 1987, p. 5; *Izvestiya*, Mar. 1, 1988, p. 5, and Mar. 16, p. 3. See also *Krasnaya zvezda*, Apr. 5, 1988, p. 3, for a reference to "anxiety" on the part of many readers concerning the INF treaty, including one who offered to send "as much as we can from our family budget" to "strengthen our motherland's defense capability." The article was published in the wake of a conservative attack on Gorbachev's reforms spearheaded by a letter to *Sovetskaya Rossiya* by Nina Andreyeva, a chemistry teacher, on Mar. 13, 1988.

30. Yazov: *Krasnaya zvezda*, Dec. 13, 1987, p. 1, and Feb. 10, 1988, p. 2; Chervov: ibid., Dec. 19, 1987, pp. 1, 5; Akhromeyev: *Pravda*, Dec. 16, 1987, p. 4, and *Trud*, Feb. 21, 1988, pp. 1–2; Kulikov: *Sovetskaya Rossiya*, May 9, 1988, p. 1.

31. Ligachev: *Krasnaya zvezda*, Feb. 10, 1987, p. 1, and *Pravda*, May 29, 1988, p. 4; Shevardnadze: *Pravda*, Feb. 10, 1988, p. 2, and May 29, 1988, p. 4.

32. Akhromeyev took note of the "unequal" nuclear balance resulting from the British and French forces. Deputy Foreign Minister Kornenko admitted that, while the "overwhelming majority" of Soviet citizens favored the treaty, there were a few "equally unambiguous opinions" against it: *Pravda*, Feb. 20, 1988, p. 4. Earlier Zagladin had referred to a public opinion poll indicating that only 6% of the Soviet citizens interviewed had doubts about the treaty: FBIS, *Soviet Union*, Feb. 11, 1988, p. 3.

time. The removal of Boris Ponomarev as chief of the Central Committee's International Department in early 1986 and his replacement by the veteran diplomat Anatolii Dobrynin marked a further advance in this direction.

In May 1986, as the debates on security policy were intensifying, Gorbachev delivered a speech at the Foreign Ministry whose contents were not disclosed until the following year. The general secretary affirmed the need for new thinking in Soviet diplomacy, and placed special emphasis on the relationship between domestic restructuring and foreign policy. Rejecting "senseless stubbornness" in negotiating tactics, Gorbachev took a swipe at Andrei Gromyko by referring obliquely to the former foreign minister's reputation in the West as "Mr. Nyet." The Soviet leader also criticized the organizational habits and performance of the diplomatic service, making it clear that work style and personnel would have to change. A year later, Shevardnadze delivered a report to the Foreign Ministry which sharpened the leadership's critique of past practices. These remarks were accompanied by efforts to clarify the Kremlin's new conceptual approach to foreign and security policy by leading theoreticians such as Primakov.[33]

Once the INF issue was resolved, criticisms of past Soviet foreign policy actions became even more acerbic. Appropriately enough, one target of barbed comment was the decision to deploy the SS-20s. Prominent members of the secondary elite such as Aleksandr Bovin and Georgii Arbatov and Foreign Ministry officials such as Aleksandr Bessmertnykh and Viktor Karpov denounced the SS-20s on the grounds that they served no clear strategic purpose. Additional decisions on Soviet arms deployments and arms-control strategy over the previous two decades were also called into question. Some commentators took the Soviet government to task for overreacting to perceived threats, even to SDI. Arbatov questioned the reasoning behind Soviet superiority in tanks and other conventional weapons, and at one point admitted that the controversial radar station in Krasnoyarsk, the object of continuing U.S. protests, had been built even though it was "clear" that it violated the U.S.-Soviet ABM Treaty. Karpov confirmed that the MBFR talks had been "doomed to fail" because of their preoccupation with estimating troop numbers and their inability to tackle the question of on-site verification. By implication, the Soviet Union was responsible for these stalling tactics. Karpov also called for paring the Soviet military down to the size of a militia. The excessive economic costs of Soviet military spending were also criticized.[34]

33. *Vestnik Ministerstva Inostrannykh Del SSSR,* no. 1 (Aug. 5), 1987, pp. 4–6, 17–22 (an earlier account is in *Izvestiya,* May 6, 1987, p. 4); *Pravda,* July 9, 1987, p. 4.

34. Bovin: *Izvestiya,* June 16, 1988, p. 5, and *Moscow News,* no. 24 (June 12), 1988, p. 6. Arbatov: FBIS *Soviet Union,* Feb. 27, 1989, p. 17; *Krasnaya zvezda,* Dec. 31, 1988, p. 5; FBIS, *Soviet Union,* Feb. 27, 1989, p. 17. Karpov: FBIS, *Soviet Union,* Dec. 30, 1988, p. 9, and July 11, 1988, p. 9; *Der Spiegel,* Apr. 13, 1987, p. 47. Bessmertnykh: *New Times,* no. 46

The foreign policy of the pre-Gorbachev years was also attacked for its failure to recognize the magnitude of the USSR's economic and technological backwardness and to take effective measures to deal with it. Speaking at the 19th Party Conference in the summer of 1988, Arbatov deplored the internal processes of decline "which pushed us to the edge of an abyss into which it is terrifying to glance." Addressing the international aspects of this downslide, Yulii Kvitsinskii, Moscow's new ambassador in Bonn, told the conference that the most important determinant of a state's position in the modern world was its economic might, an area in which the USSR was so deficient that it was "embarrassing." He called for a parliament of the socialist countries, its members to be elected by their populations, to impart new dynamism to COMECON integration. Otherwise, he warned, "more and more European states will be sucked into the EEC, and via the EEC into NATO."[35]

The need for greater democratization in the formulation of foreign policy was another previously unexplored topic that now emerged. Aleksandr Bovin, for example, recommended placing "the whole of the diplomatic service in the zone of glasnost and control 'from below.'" To this end, he appealed for the participation of the broad public in the discussion of foreign policy issues, together with a greater reliance on feedback mechanisms as opposed to "complacent infallibility" in the elaboration of foreign policy alternatives. Zagladin also approved of greater public debate on international issues, provided that "certain norms" were observed. In the same spirit, the editors of IMEMO's *Mirovaya ekonomika i mezhdunarodnye otnosheniya* apologized to their readers for years of superficiality and inertia in the journal's treatment of topical issues. They promised new theoretical approaches and "the comparison of different concepts" in the future. Soviet television viewers also shared in the widening process of foreign policy glasnost as such Western politicians as Helmut Schmidt and Egon Bahr were invited to state their views before the cameras, often providing information and critical commentary on Soviet foreign policy activities that might otherwise have gone unreported in the official media.[36]

(Nov. 23), 1987, p. 7. For additional postmortems on the SS-20s, see the discussion in *SShA*, no. 12, 1988, pp. 23–41, and the anonymous article "Foreign Policy: Lessons of the Past," *IA*, no. 6, 1989, pp. 82–83. On overreaction: FBIS, *Soviet Union*, June 1, 1988, pp. 3–4, and Aug. 2, 1988, p. 11. Oleg Bogomolov estimated that the defense burden relative to national income was 250% greater for the Warsaw Pact than for NATO: *Literaturnaya gazeta*, June 29, 1988, p. 14.

35. *Pravda*, June 30, 1988, p. 6; July 3, p. 2.

36. Bovin: *Izvestiya*, June 16, 1988, p. 5. Zagladin: *Sovetskaya Rossiya*, June 23, 1988, p. 1, and FBIS, *Soviet Union*, Aug. 1, 1988, pp. 58–59. "K nashemu chitatelyu," *MEMO*, no. 7, 1987, pp. 3–5 (*Mezhdunarodnaya zhizn [IA]* changed editors in 1988). Transcripts of the *Studio 9* program in FBIS, *Soviet Union*, July 17, 1986, pp. CC1–19; Oct. 21, 1986, pp. AA1–8; and Apr. 9, 1987, pp. CC13–28.

One of the most far-reaching examples of foreign policy revisionism in this period focused on Soviet responsibility for the cold war itself. Vyacheslav Dashichev, a historian at Moscow's Institute of the Economics of the World Socialist System, took direct aim at the central tenets of Stalin's foreign policy. He also blamed the Kremlin for allowing military considerations to take precedence over political strategy in the 1960s, 1970s, and 1980s, thereby encouraging the emergence of a "front of great powers" against the USSR.[37]

Eduard Shevardnadze broached all of these themes. In a series of speeches and reports to the Foreign Ministry in 1988, Shevardnadze scored past Soviet military policies and negotiating strategies, reemphasized the decisive importance of national economic development, and blamed the "deformation" of domestic political life in the USSR for failing to prevent the iron curtain and the subsequent exacerbation of world tensions. He upbraided the Foreign Ministry for resisting democratic collegiality and insisted that Soviet diplomacy was "obliged to explain itself to the people." He called for legislative procedures for discussing and adopting foreign policy decisions and for exercising control over the military budget and the use of military force abroad. Consular workers were instructed to cooperate in expediting the settlement of humanitarian problems. In the fall of 1989 Shevardnadze himself admitted that the Krasnoyarsk radar station violated SALT I, and officially repudiated the decision to invade Afghanistan.[38]

At the Foreign Ministry in July 1988 Shevardnadze reiterated the notion expressed at the 27th Party Congress that peaceful coexistence must no longer be thought of as a "specific form of the class struggle." This idea was still controversial within Gorbachev's governing coalition. Less than two weeks later Yegor Ligachev challenged it. "We proceed from the class nature of international relations," Ligachev was reported as saying. "Any other formulation of the issue only introduces confusion into the thinking of the Soviet people and our friends abroad." The sensitivity of this ideological issue became evident once again in October. Only days after being elevated to full membership in the Politburo, Vadim Medvedev suggested that the distance between capitalism and socialism was not especially great. While explicitly rejecting the possible convergence of the two systems in some hybrid variant, Medvedev asserted that "the paths of their development inevitably intersect [peresekayutsya]," and that the two systems will continue to interact in the framework of one civilization. Medvedev, who had also just taken over the ideological portfolio from Ligachev in Gorbachev's latest reshuffling of the leadership, was presumably speaking for

37. *Literaturnaya gazeta*, May 18, 1988, p. 14. Also *Komsomolskaya pravda*, June 19, 1988, p. 3.

38. *Pravda*, July 26, 1988, p. 4; *Die Welt*, Oct. 21, 1988, p. 1; *Izvestiya*, Dec. 30, 1988, p.4; *Pravda*, Oct. 24, 1989, pp. 2–4.

the general secretary himself and others seeking a new definition of the ideological relationship between socialism and capitalism.[39]

These reassessments of past Soviet foreign policy and of the very nature of socialist ideology were accompanied by extensive revisions in Soviet military thinking. As debates proliferated among military officials and civilians on these questions, by the end of 1989 Soviet and Warsaw Pact forces had been repositioned to preclude the possibility of launching a surprise attack, and tank production was scheduled to be cut in half over the next five years.[40]

The "Common European Home"

Shortly after he assumed the office of general secretary, Gorbachev declared that Soviet foreign policy interests should no longer be viewed exclusively "through the prism of U.S.-Soviet relations." Western Europe, he insisted, must take its place among the principal foci of Soviet diplomacy. Several months later, during his visit to France, the new Soviet leader told French television viewers that the Soviets and the West Europeans lived in the "same house," and they needed to expand their cooperation accordingly.[41] This concept of the "common European home," purloined from the Brezhnev era, gained renewed emphasis at the 27th Party Congress and quickly became the main theme in Gorbachev's attempt to revive the diplomatic dialogue with Western Europe which had been so rudely interrupted by the INF controversy.

Although the Soviets persistently advertised their intention to upgrade Western Europe in Moscow's international priorities, this did not necessarily mean that the United States would now take a back seat in the revised foreign policy strategy emerging from the Kremlin. On the contrary, Gor-

---

39. *Pravda,* Aug. 6, 1988, p. 2; Oct. 5, p. 4. On these issues, see S. Pronin, "Ideologiya vo vzaimosvyazannom mire," *MEMO,* no. 10, 1988, pp. 5–15; Ye. Primakov et al., "Nekotorye problemy novovo myshleniya," ibid., no. 6, 1989, pp. 5–18; Georgii Shakhnazarov, "Vostok-Zapad: K voprosu o deideologizatsii mezhgosudarstvennykh otnoshenii," ibid., no. 3, 1989, pp. 67–78, and "Governability of the World," *IA,* no. 3, 1988, pp. 16–24. See also the article by a Soviet economist criticizing West German Social Democrats for questioning the desirability of market-based economies. The author urged her Soviet readers to avoid the SPD's errors and to study the writings of Milton Friedman and Friedrich Hayek: Larissa Piyasheva, "A Look at the Social Democrats' Experience," *IA,* no. 5, 1989, pp. 94–99, 136.

40. Raymond Garthoff, "New Thinking in Soviet Military Doctrine," *Washington Quarterly,* Summer 1988, pp. 131–38; Stephen M. Meyer, "The Sources and Prospects of Gorbachev's New Political Thinking on Security," *International Security* 13 (Fall 1988): 124–63; Harry Gelman, *The Soviet Military Leadership and the Question of Soviet Deployment Retreats* (Santa Monica, Calif.: Rand, 1988); Michael MccGwire, *Perestroika and Soviet National Security* (Washington, D.C.: Brookings, forthcoming). Also *Washington Post,* Oct. 25, 1989, p. A4, and Nov. 29, pp. A1, A22.

41. *Pravda,* Apr. 8, 1985, p. 1; Oct. 2, 1985, p. 1.

bachev and his chief aides made it very clear from the outset that the United States would have a central role to play in building Europe's future structure. As Moscow's new diplomacy evolved over the second half of the 1980s, the Gorbachev leadership carefully balanced its overtures to both the United States and the governments of Western Europe with a keen eye to existing realities and potential opportunities.

In this sense, Gorbachev took an Atlanticist approach to European affairs, steering a middle course between Europeanist and Americanist leanings. Thus the basic *direction* of Gorbachev's approach to U.S.–West European relations was the same as that of his predecessors ever since Nikita Khrushchev. They, too, in their own way, were Atlanticists rather than Europeanists or Americanists. Clearly, however, Gorbachev differed from earlier Soviet leaders (particularly Brezhnev, Andropov, and Chernenko) with respect to the *means* to be used to implement this policy. Gorbachev and his advisers believed that only a substantial moderation of Soviet policies stood any chance of improving Moscow's position vis-à-vis the West. As time went on, the very notion of "contradictions" among the NATO allies received progressively less attention as emphasis shifted to the need to work with all members of the Western alliance to resolve the issues that had kept the two camps divided.[42]

Indeed, the leading members of Gorbachev's foreign policy team were plainly aware that the Kremlin's European policy in the 1970s and 1980s had failed. Not only had it failed to break NATO's unity; it had also failed to enhance the Soviet Union's basic national security interests, leaving the country in a state of diplomatic isolation, exacerbated by costly overarmament and economic stagnation. The INF crisis contained particularly compelling lessons in this regard. The outcome of the crisis had essentially verified the view, voiced by some members of the Soviet secondary elite during the Brezhnev years, that East-West confrontation only reinforced NATO's unity. The contrary notion, that contradictions within the West would multiply even in periods of East-West confrontation, now stood revealed as fatally erroneous.

Meanwhile, as the Gorbachev decision-making elite embarked on its reexamined Atlanticist course, key members of the secondary elite continued to argue for more explicitly Europeanist or Americanist policies, while others provided rationales supporting the equilibrated Atlanticist approach. (Maximalists essentially contented themselves with accentuating the hard-line aspects of the conservative weltanschauung.) Here, too, there were both continuities with the recent past and new departures.

42. For traditionalist views on "interimperialist contradictions," see Gorbachev in *Pravda*, Dec. 11, 1984, p. 2, and his speech at the 27th Party Congress, ibid., Feb. 26, 1986, pp. 2–3; also A. Yakovlev, "Mezhimperialisticheskiye protivorechiya—sovremenny kontekst," *Kommunist*, no. 17, 1986, pp. 3–17; and the CPSU Party Program, *Pravda*, Mar. 7, 1986, p. 3.

As in the past, Europeanist and Americanist arguments stuck closely to the key tenets of the Atlanticist position, differing with it mainly in points of emphasis. Thus the Europeanists continued to regard Western Europe as more receptive to Soviet initiatives than the United States, but still acknowledged that "common class interests" among the transatlantic allies precluded the dissolution of the Western alliance. Americanists stressed that the United States remained the leader of the Western camp, and that the West Europeans themselves were not as independent as they seemed, while nevertheless recognizing that direct overtures to Western Europe could bring benefits to the Kremlin.

The novel element in these alternative views reflected the Gorbachev regime's new thinking on foreign policy. Instead of encasing their arguments within the conservative world view of the Brezhnev coalition, Soviet academicians, journalists, and lower-level officials now adjusted their positions to the conceptual guidelines underlying Moscow's foreign policy perestroika.

These developments were visible right from the earliest phases of Gorbachev's regime. Gorbachev himself made it immediately clear that the Soviets' relationship with the United States was critical for their future European initiatives. Above all, the key to breaking the deadlock over intermediate-range nuclear forces was in Washington rather than in London, Paris, or Bonn. Gorbachev's meetings with Thatcher in 1984 and Mitterrand in 1985 had only confirmed this fact. A face-to-face encounter with Ronald Reagan was therefore an early imperative.

Clues as to the new leader's thinking on the subject were provided in June 1985 by Vadim Zagladin and Aleksandr Yakovlev. In a discussion published in *Literaturnaya gazeta,* Zagladin rejected the view that Moscow should wait until Reagan left office before seeking improvement in relations with the United States. He further suggested that some American conservatives could be more open to improvements in U.S.-Soviet ties than liberals, pointing to Richard Nixon as an example. Yakovlev expressed deep disappointment over the "impotence and torpidity" of West European leaders in the face of American assertiveness, and he chided them for failing to dissociate themselves from the "blinding commonality of class interests" linking them to the United States. While Yakovlev was equally scathing in denouncing U.S. policy, he clearly held out little hope for a major improvement in Moscow's ties with Western Europe.[43]

Yakovlev's elevation to the post of chief of the Central Committee's Propaganda Department in August 1985, however, suggested that he was

43. *Literaturnaya gazeta,* June 26, 1985, p. 2. Yakovlev had denounced both the United States and West Germany in the first half of the 1980s. See, e.g., "Rakovaya opukhol imperskikh ambitsii v yaderny vek," *MEMO,* no. 1, 1984, pp. 3–17, and no. 12, 1984, pp. 106–10. See also "Opasnaya os amerikano-zapadnogermanskovo militarizma," *SShA,* July 1985, pp. 3–15.

prepared to back Gorbachev's emerging Atlanticist course. The tough stance he frequently took in his earlier public statements on the West soon mellowed, and Yakovlev gradually emerged as one of the chief supporters of Gorbachev's perestroika. Moreover, with Yakovlev's rapid rise into the Politburo and Secretariat in 1986 and Dobrynin's ascent, two of Gorbachev's key foreign policy advisers were specialists on North America. (Yakovlev had been ambassador to Canada from 1973 to 1983.) This fact was bound to affect the new leadership's overall foreign policy orientation.

Shades of a different opinion were expressed by Central Committee member Aleksandr Bovin. In the weeks before Gorbachev's first encounter with Reagan at Geneva, Bovin adopted a markedly Europeanist posture when he described Western Europe as far more interested in détente than the United States. At the same time, Bovin clearly defined the limits within which Soviet Europeanists viewed the continuing proliferation of U.S.– West European contradictions. "The social and class interests linking Western Europe to its transatlantic ally are so strong and constant," he wrote, "that to build a policy on the basis of wrecking those links would be unrealistic." Moscow's objective was the more modest one of using Western Europe, "via the transatlantic channel," to influence American policies on such pressing issues as SDI.[44]

After the Geneva summit, Bovin stuck to the position that major agreements with the Reagan administration were highly unlikely. This view was too pessimistic for Primakov. Bovin later admitted his mistake in underestimating Reagan's readiness for agreements, but he reaffirmed his essentially Europeanist outlook when he called for a "European Reykjavik."[45]

Another high-ranking Central Committee figure with strong Europeanist leanings was Valentin Falin. The former ambassador to the FRG had for years been an outspoken critic of U.S. foreign policy, and had cast his lot with the pro-Bonn group during the policy debates of the first half of the 1980s. Not long after Zagladin praised Richard Nixon, Falin denounced the former U.S. president, questioning his commitment to détente.[46] Like Bovin, however, Falin was keenly aware of the limits to the contradictions that perennially beset U.S.–West European relations. As he rose into Gorbachev's inner circle of foreign policy advisers, Falin affirmed the central importance of Moscow's relationship with the United States and acknowledged the strength of the Western Europeans' abiding solidarity with the Americans.[47] Following a stint as director of Novosti press, Falin became

44. FBIS, *Soviet Union*, Sept. 6, 1985, pp. CC1–4; *Izvestiya*, Sept. 25, 1985, p. 5.
45. FBIS, *Soviet Union*, Jan. 25, 1986, pp. CC8–9, and July 11, 1988, p. 10; *Izvestiya*, Feb. 3, 1989, p. 5.
46. *Izvestiya*, Aug. 6, 1985, p. 5.
47. See, e.g., Falin's interview in *Der Spiegel*, Oct. 20, 1986, pp. 173–79, and his remarks as reported in FBIS, *Soviet Union*, Feb. 6, 1986, pp. CC1–17.

chief of the Central Committee's International Department in the fall of
1988. He was an outspoken supporter of Gorbachev's domestic reforms.
Similar Europeanist tendencies were strongly represented in *Mirovaya
ekonomika i mezhdunarodnye otnosheniya* and *International Affairs* in the
first few Gorbachev years. As in pre-Gorbachev times, Europeanist authors
insisted that Western Europe cared more about détente than the United
States, and stressed the contradictions that vexed the U.S.–West European
relationship in a variety of political, economic, and military issues.[48] Quite
a few authors noted that the West Europeans were particularly interested in
expanding economic contacts with the Soviet Union, in part because they
were falling farther behind the United States and Japan in high-technology
development.[49] The continuing influence of peace movements and détente-
minded social democratic parties throughout Western Europe was seen as
offering still more opportunities for fruitful cooperation.[50]

While highlighting the advantages to be gained from the "Europeanist
thrust" in Soviet foreign policy, these Europeanist writers still did not see
much hope of pulling any West European countries away from their attachments to the United States. As in earlier years, the Europeanists perceived
Western Europe's accelerating steps toward independence as taking place

48. In *MEMO*, on détente: A. Lebedev, "Imperativy Khelsinki," no. 8, 1985, p. 13;
V. Shenayev's conference report, no. 11, 1985, p. 84; V. Falin, "Na poroge XXI veka," no. 1,
1986, pp. 96–103; A. Kundryavtsev, "Pressa Frantsii o sovetsko-frantszuskoi vstreche," no. 2,
1986, p. 116; O. Morgachev, no. 2, 1987, p. 104. In *IA*, no. 5, 1987: Aleksandr Bykov, "East-
West: Business Contacts," pp. 37–45, 63; Yuri Lebedev and Aleksei Podberyozkin, "A Historic Chance for Europe," pp. 3–11. On contradictions, see the remarks by E. Talyzina in
MEMO, no. 5, 1986, p. 101; A. Utkin, "O rasshirenii sferi deistviya NATO," *MEMO*, no. 5,
1987, pp. 32–42; and in *IA*, Yu. Shishkov, "Inter-Imperialist Rivalry Escalates," no. 5, 1986,
pp. 28–36; L. Vidyasova, "Inter-Imperialist Contradictions at the Present Stage," no. 7, 1986,
pp. 46–51; Yuri Karlov, "The Imperatives of Peaceful Cooperation in Europe," no. 5, 1987,
pp. 64–72.

49. In *MEMO*, Y. Yudanov, "O probleme 'tekhnologicheskoi otstalosti' FRG," no. 6,
1985, pp. 84–91; A. Dynkin, "Ekonomicheskiye problemy nauchno-tekhnicheskovo pro-
gressa v kapitalistichekikh stranakh," no. 7, 1985, pp. 26–37; M. Zibirova's remarks in no.
11, 1985, p. 96; I. Ponomareva and N. Smirnova, "SShA–Zapadnaya Evropa: Rozn ekonomicheskikh interesov," no. 8, 1986, pp. 131–36; "Problemy sotrudnichestva vostok-zapad,"
no. 11, 1986, pp. 123–25; V. Kuznetsov, " 'Velikaya mutatsiya' i Zapadnaya Evropa," no. 1,
1987, pp. 97–101; V. Tsirenshchikov in no. 2, 1987, p. 96; Y. Stolyarov and E. Khesin,
"Sovremenny kapitalizm i neravnomernost razvitiya," no. 5, 1987, pp. 17–31, and the remarks by V. Presnyakov in ibid., p. 96. M. Bunkina was one of the few Soviet economists who
contended that the technological gap separating Western Europe from the United States and
Japan was not growing; see ibid., p. 97.

50. In *MEMO*, E. Silin, "Anti-voennoye dvizheniye na sovremennom etape," no. 6, 1985,
pp. 21–32; S. Peregudov, "Sotsial-demokratsiya pered litsom novykh problem," no. 6, 1986,
pp. 16–30; V. Skorokhodov and A. Trukhan, "Massovye demokraticheskye dvizheniya sevodnya," no. 3, 1987, pp. 3–17; I. Shadrina, "Sotsintern v 'eru Brandta' i aktualnye problemy
mirovoi politiki," no. 6, 1987, pp. 14–28; V. Pankov, "Sotsialdemokraty ob ekonomicheskom
sotrudnichestve v Evrope," no. 10, 1987, pp. 121–27. In *IA*, E. Silin, "Ways of Safeguarding
European Security," no. 3, 1986, p. 87; Rudolf Vildanov, "Mass Democratic Movements—a
Component of the Peace Forces' Potential," no. 3, 1987, pp. 89–98.

within the framework of NATO and not outside of it. This notion was reinforced at the official level by Gorbachev's admonition at the 27th Party Congress that it was "difficult to expect" the Western alliance to be broken "in the real conditions of the contemporary world."[51]

Meanwhile, in keeping with the critical reappraisal of the Brezhnev era's foreign policy now under way, Europeanist-oriented analysts increasingly conceded that the Kremlin had made some costly errors in its policies toward the region. Several authors acknowledged that large segments of public opinion had turned against the Soviet Union in the early 1980s, as many West Europeans, and especially West Germans, had actually come to believe in the "myth of the Soviet threat."[52] Others observed that the problem with the earlier period of détente was that political and economic cooperation had not been accompanied by military détente, an omission that had to be rectified.[53] Economic cooperation with Western Europe, it was now admitted, had bogged down in part because of the Soviet Union's failure to restructure its own economy, a process that would require a careful study of the experiences of capitalist economies.[54]

Most important of all, Soviet analysts no longer reiterated the minatory Brezhnev-era notion that peaceful coexistence did not preclude East-West confrontation. In fact, this idea was sharply contradicted by prominent members of the secondary elite.[55] In addition, it was now acknowledged that the tensions of the past five to ten years had only brought the United States and Western Europe closer together.[56]

Europeanist writings were not the only ones represented in the specialist literature as the Gorbachev period advanced. More scrupulously balanced

51. See Gorbachev's speech in *Pravda*, Feb. 26, 1986, p. 3.
52. E.g., Nikolai Khomtov, "The FRG: In a Maze of Problems," *IA*, no. 2, 1987, p. 142.
53. See the remarks by V. Shenayev in *MEMO*, no. 11, 1986, p. 123; also A. Vtorov and Yu. Karelov, "The Dynamic European Policy of the USSR," *IA*, no. 4, 1986, pp. 86–87.
54. In *MEMO*, V. Volkov and S. Shmelev, "Strukturnye sdvigi v ekonomike kapitalizma," no. 8, 1985, p. 29; Ye. Primakov, "XXVII sezd KPSS i issledovaniye problem mirovoi ekonomiki i mezhdunarodnykh otnoshenii," no. 5, 1986, p. 6; V. Chistov's remarks in ibid., p. 103; the interview with Otto Wolff von Amerongen, no. 4, 1987, pp. 118–20; V. Zuyev in no. 5, 1987, p. 94; Yu. Yudanov, "Pozitsiya nauchnykh i delovykh krugov FRG," no. 10, 1987, pp. 75–83; V. Kuznetsov, "Zapadny opyt i nashi ekonomicheskiye reformy," no. 3, 1989, pp. 5–17 (pt. 1), and no. 7, 1989, pp. 5–17 (pt. 2). Also Ye. Primakov, "Kapitalizm vo vzaimosvyazannom mire," *Kommunist*, no. 13, 1987, pp. 101–10. See also the translation of sections of John Naisbitt and Patricia Aburdene's *Reinventing the Corporation*, in *SShA*, no. 1, 1987, pp. 80–89; no. 2, 1987, pp. 87–93; and no. 3, 1987, pp. 77–88; also N. V. Volkov, "O strukturnoi perestroike amerikanskoi ekonomiki," *SShA*, no. 3, 1987, pp. 14–25.
55. Anatolii Gromyko and Vladimir Lomeiko noted that, whereas in the past "peaceful coexistence could proceed in various forms of confrontation, now—only and exclusively in the form of peaceful cooperation and peaceful rivalry": "New Way of Thinking and 'New Globalism,' " *IA*, no. 5, 1986, p. 22.
56. See the remarks by G. Kolosova in *MEMO*, no. 5, 1986, p. 100; Yurii Zhukov, "Europe and NATO," *IA*, no. 10, 1986, p. 93; Igor Nechayev, "NATO's Drive for Military Superiority," *IA*, no. 4, 1987, p. 35. For an article accentuating the centripetal tendencies in intercapitalist relations in 1985, see V. Kudrov, "Tri tsentra imperializma—novye aspekty protivorechii," *Kommunist*, no. 13, 1985, pp. 104–14.

Atlanticist analyses, placing roughly equal stress on centripetal and centrifugal forces at work in U.S.–West European relations, were also in evidence.[57]

Americanist arguments could also be found. One of the most articulate proponents of the Americanist viewpoint was Yurii P. Davydov, chief of the section on U.S.–West European relations at the Institute of the United States and Canada. Davydov tended to throw cold water on Western Europe's alleged independence from the United States, providing damning evidence of the West Europeans' fidelity to the Atlantic alliance and their frequent coolness to Soviet proposals. Even Western Europe's social democratic parties, in his view, were more likely to oppose the United States when they were in the opposition than when they were in power. By contrast, Davydov took note of the Reagan administration's forthcoming positions on a variety of arms-control issues. At the same time, however, he acknowledged Western Europe's value as an occasionally positive influence on American policy. From these observations Yurii Davydov drew the conclusion that NATO was a self-sustaining structure, and that the United States had to be included in any future "all-European process."[58]

One issue bound to raise Soviet suspicions of Western Europe was the enduring question of military integration. To be sure, no one in the foreign policy establishment looked with favor on expanded West European cooperation on security. As in past years, however, some commentators tended to discount these prospects, emphasizing the difficulties of genuine military integration among the leading states in the region.[59] But others denounced West European defense initiatives as dangerous.[60] Significantly, one analyst

57. E.g., T. Parkhalina, "NATO—za fasadom 'Atlanticheskovo edinstva,' " *MEMO*, no. 7, 1986, pp. 104–10; A. Likhotal, "Na evropeiskom napravlenii," ibid., no. 7, 1987, pp. 6–19; S. A. Ulin, "Krisiznye yavleniya v NATO," *SShA*, no. 4, 1986, pp. 14–22; S. A. Karaganov, " 'Zvezdnye voiny' i Zapadnaya Evropa," *SShA*, no. 5, 1986, pp. 32–42; A. V. Kunitsyn, "Kokom: ambitsii Vashingtona i zdravy mysl," *SShA*, no. 7, 1987, pp. 80–86.

58. In *SShA*, Yu. P. Davydov, "Soedinennye Shtaty i obshcheevropeiskii protsess," no. 8, 1985, pp. 44–55; "Zapadnaya Evropa posle Zhenevy," no. 2, 1986, pp. 87–91; "SShA–Zapadnaya Evropa: Bremya partnerstva," no. 5, 1987, pp. 3–14; and "SShA, Zapadnaya Evropa i dogovor po RSD-RMD," no. 7, 1988, pp. 8–16. See also Davydov's edited volume *SShA–Zapadnaya Evropa i problema razryadki* (Moscow: Nauka, 1986). Although the Institute of the USA and Canada was the main center of Americanist opinion, some of its members also had more Atlanticist or Europeanist leanings (personal communications, Moscow, June 1987). See, e.g., V. F. Davydov, *Put k bezyadernoi Evrope* (Kiev: Izdatelstvo politicheskoi literatury, 1987).

59. N. Kishlova in *MEMO*, no. 11, 1985, p. 94; B. Vadimov, "Tekushchiye problemy mirovoi politiki," ibid., no. 1, 1986, p. 88; the remarks by G. Kolosova and by A. Chervyakov in ibid., no. 5, 1986, pp. 100, 101; Parkhalina, "NATO," p. 106; Yuri Zhukov, "What Kind of Dialogue for Europeans?" *IA*, no. 7, 1987, pp. 100–101. One writer took a relatively positive view of "Eureka," suggesting that it might increase Western Europe's economic independence from the United States. See Yu. Yudanov, " 'Evrika'—problemy sozdaniya zapadnoevropeiskovo tekhnologicheskovo soobshchestva," *MEMO*, no. 9, 1986, pp. 93–100.

60. In *IA*, V. Beletsky, "What Lies behind the 'European Defense Initiative' Project?" no. 7, 1986, pp. 49–55; Vladimir Stupishin, "Indeed, Nothing Is Simple in Europe," no. 5, 1988, pp. 69–73. In *MEMO*, A. Shakov and A. Mitropolskii, " 'Evropeiskaya oboronnaya ini-

in 1989 criticized Henry Kissinger, Zbigniew Brzezinski, and other Americans for wanting the West Europeans to increase defense cooperation among themselves as the United States prepared to reduce its own military presence in Europe. Noting "the stabilizing function of the U.S. presence," the author in effect urged the United States not only to "hold its position in Europe" but to put it on "more solid political foundations," so that disarmament and cooperation between East and West in Europe could proceed on an orderly basis in a period of rapid change. In a similar vein, another analyst suggested that it would be "a strategic miscalculation" for Moscow to play upon conflicts among the Western allies, arguing that a united NATO was more likely than a disunited one to promote East-West understanding.[61]

All of these strands of policy analysis ultimately found their way into the Gorbachev regime's notion of the "common European home." Europeanists were gladdened by its special emphasis on improving Moscow's ties with Western Europe; Americanists could rest assured that the Kremlin was not launching an unrealistic, and perhaps undesirable, effort to expel the United States from the region; and Atlanticists could join in applauding Gorbachev's attempt to deal opportunistically with both pillars of the Atlantic alliance while placing relations with Western Europe as well as the United States on a new foundation of détente.[62]

Accordingly, Gorbachev urged West Europeans to demonstrate greater independence from the United States, while at the same time reassuring them that the Soviet Union had no intention of "abducting Europa" away from its self-evident alliance commitments.[63] At the same time, the Soviet leader confirmed the "special responsibility" of the United States and the USSR for international developments, and even suggested that the United States would ultimately benefit from efforts to construct the common European home.[64]

Authoritative Soviet commentators supported these assertions by taking

tsiativa': Tsily, sredstva, posledstviya," no. 8, 1987, pp. 129–31; A. Rassidin, "Zapadnoevropeiskaya voennaya integratsiya—perspektivy i vozmozhnye posledstviya," no. 2, 1989, pp. 104–15; G. Burdili, "Vozrozhdeniye zapadnoevropeiskovo soyuza," no. 4, 1989, pp. 45–49. Also *Izvestiya*, Sept. 15, 1986, p. 5; Aleksandr Lebedev, "Bomb for Europe? The British and French Nuclear Arsenals," *New Times*, Jan. 26, 1987, pp. 20–23; *Krasnaya zvezda*, Nov. 27, 1988, p. 3.

61. Sergei Karaganov, "The USA and Common European Home," *IA*, no. 8, 1989, pp. 17–26 (Karaganov was deputy director of the new Institute on Europe); Stanislav Kondrashov in *Izvestiya*, May 6, 1989, p. 4.

62. On the ambiguities in the "common home" theme, see Fred Oldenburg, "Altes Denken im europäischen Gebäude?" *Rheinischer Merkur*, June 9, 1989, pp. 3, 8.

63. See Gorbachev's speech in Warsaw, *Pravda*, July 1, 1986, p. 1, and his speech in Prague, ibid., Apr. 11, 1987, p. 2. Also his book *Perestroika*, 2d ed. (New York: Harper & Row, 1988), p. 193.

64. *Pravda*, Nov. 28, 1985, pp. 1–2; Oct. 14, 1986, pp. 1–2. See also Primakov's remarks on the significance of U.S.–Soviet relations in FBIS, *Soviet Union*, Oct. 7, 1986, pp. CC9, CC12.

due cognizance of Western Europe's strong alliance ties and by repeatedly insisting that it would be highly unrealistic of the Soviet Union to think that it could induce the West Europeans to break them.[65] A striking reminder of Western Europe's enduring military dependence on the United States came to Moscow's attention shortly after the U.S.-Soviet summit in Reykjavik. Many West European political figures, including Helmut Kohl, expressed alarm at the breadth of the discussions on weapons systems essential to the defense of Western Europe. Although nothing came of these marathon sessions, the mere suggestion of a Soviet-American "condominium" arrangement negotiated behind the backs of West Europeans created an uproar in the region, requiring the U.S. government to reaffirm its nuclear and conventional security commitments to its NATO partners. Soviet observers took full account of these West European concerns. Meanwhile, the Soviets made it very clear that their concept of West European "independence" from the United States meant above all that the governments of Western Europe should be more flexible than the United States on a variety of political, economic, and security issues, and that they should take every opportunity to press their views on Washington.[66]

Perhaps no theme assured greater importance than the need for East-West economic cooperation. Without greater Soviet integration into the world economy, there could be no viable perestroika at home. Accordingly, in June 1988 Moscow formally established relations with the European Economic Community.[67]

The new Kremlin leadership's determination to bring the Soviet Union more actively into the international marketplace also applied to Eastern Europe. Soviet officials did not conceal their dissatisfaction with COMECON as a vehicle for promoting the economic development of either the Soviet Union or any of the organization's other members. Moscow's partners would therefore be urged to open their own economies to greater cooperation with the Common Market and the larger world trading system. Soviet analysts regarded these steps as crucial to addressing the economically motivated social tensions increasingly evident in various bloc countries.[68]

65. See, e.g., V. Kobish in *Literaturnaya gazeta*, no. 28, 1985, p. 9, and Zagladin's remarks in FBIS, *Soviet Union*, Aug. 2, 1985, p. G1; the *Studio 9* discussion with West German political figures in FBIS, *Soviet Union*, June 5, 1989, pp. 29–32. Also Nikolai Shishlin in *Sovetskaya Rossiya*, Jan. 21, 1986, p. 1; G. Vorontsov, "Ot Khelsinki k 'obshcheevropeiskomu domu,'" *MEMO*, no. 9, 1988, pp. 35–45.
66. E.g., see Arbatov's remarks in FBIS, *Soviet Union*, Oct. 20, 1986, p. AA12; Zagladin's in ibid., Feb. 10, 1988, pp. 11–12, and Jan. 15, 1986, pp. CC7–8; Bovin in *Izvestiya*, Mar. 16, 1988, p. 5; N. Spasov, "SShA-Zapadnaya Evropa: Novye vremena," *MEMO*, no. 10, 1989, pp. 110–28.
67. *Vestnik Ministerstva Inostrannykh Del SSSR*, no. 14 (Aug. 1), 1988, pp. 17–20.
68. See, e.g., the discussion among Soviet Foreign Ministry officials and others in *IA*, no. 1, 1989, pp. 123–32, 95. Also, in *Kommunist*, O. Bogomolov, "Sotsialisticheskiye strany na perelomnom etape mirovovo ekonomicheskovo razvitiya," no. 8, 1987, pp. 102–11, and "Mir sotsializma na puti perestroiki," no. 16, 1987, pp. 92–102.

Economic cooperation with Western Europe acquired even greater urgency as the nations of the EEC agreed to institute a single internal market starting in 1992. Soviet commentators were very sensitive to the possibility that the USSR and its economically ailing allies might be left to trail even farther behind Western Europe as the EEC's integration processes gained momentum.[69]

In short, Moscow's concept of the common European home was not intended to exclude the United States from Europe, but rather to include the Soviet Union and its allies more fully within it. Gorbachev himself pleaded that the Soviet Union should not be left out of Europe, and he called attention to the deep roots linking the Russians and other Soviet nationalities to European civilization.[70] Although the main addressees of the "European home" campaign were necessarily in Western Europe, Gorbachev and leading members of both the primary and secondary Soviet elites nevertheless made it very clear that a continuing American presence in Europe, including a military presence, was central to the whole idea. This Atlanticist approach was confirmed in December 1989, as Gorbachev proposed a thirty-five-nation summit conference involving the United States, Canada, and the other participants in the Helsinki process to discuss Europe's future.[71]

Bonn and the INF Treaty

Mikhail Gorbachev moved quickly to open up a dialogue with the chief leaders of the Western community, but the Kohl government was not on his initial list. His meetings with Thatcher and Reagan in 1984 and 1985 contrasted conspicuously with his unhurried approach to Bonn. During Gorbachev's first year or two in power the Kremlin was still inclined to punish West Germany for its critical role in the INF crisis. While the strident antirevanchism campaign tapered off appreciably, the FRG received distinctly secondhand treatment in the new Soviet government's emerging détente diplomacy. Economic ties between the two states also languished.[72]

69. See IMEMO's theses on this subject, "Evropeiskoye soobshchestvo sevodnya," *MEMO*, no. 12, 1988, pp. 5–18, and "Posledstviya formirovaniya edinovo rynka Evropeiskovo soobshchestva," no. 4, 1989, pp. 38–44. Also Zagladin's comments in *Die Welt*, June 6, 1989, p. 3.

70. Gorbachev, *Perestroika*, p. 177. See also, in *Pravda*, Gorbachev's speech at the Council of Europe in Strasbourg, July 7, 1989, pp. 1–2; Yakovlev's speech in Rome, Mar. 21, 1989, p. 4; and V. Zhurkin, "Obshchii dom dlya Evropy," May 17, p. 4.

71. *Pravda*, Dec. 1, 1989, pp. 1–2. For an extensive treatment of these issues, see Neil Malcolm, *Soviet Policy Perspectives on Western Europe* (London: Routledge, 1989).

72. West German imports from the USSR reached a peak of DM14.4 billion in 1984, then fell to 13.6 billion in 1985 and 9.3 billion in 1986. Exports dropped from DM10.8 billion in 1984 to 10.5 billion in 1985 and 9.4 billion in 1986: *Der Spiegel*, June 12, 1989, p. 109.

In addition, until 1987 Gorbachev showed no willingness to compromise on intermediate-range missiles unless the United States gave way on SDI, and he appeared even less eager to come to terms on the shorter-range rockets that had been installed in the GDR and Czechoslovakia as part of the "countermeasures" taken against the FRG in 1983 and 1984. Political and military conservatives would have been particularly indisposed to relax these punitive policies at this stage of the Gorbachev regime's development.

Kohl's support for SDI only exacerbated matters. Gorbachev and other authoritative spokesmen spent much of 1985 and 1986 trying to pressure the West Germans into rejecting participation in the Reagan administration's defense scheme in any form. This was a central item in Gorbachev's first letter to Chancellor Kohl; the issue also came up in Shevardnadze's meeting with Genscher in July 1985. At the same time, Soviet foreign affairs commentators took account of reservations on SDI within the governing coalition in Bonn, and some observed that Bonn might urge the United States to abandon "Star Wars" and disrupt Washington's plans to include Western Europe in the project.[73] Arguments of this kind supported the notion implicit in Europeanist, Americanist, and Atlanticist attitudes that the FRG was more valuable to the USSR as a member of the alliance than outside it.

The Soviets encouraged organized opposition to SDI in West Germany. The Social Democrats, who rejected the Reagan defense initiative, were warmly cultivated. Leading SPD figures such as Willy Brandt, Johannes Rau, Egon Bahr, and Oskar Lafontaine visited Moscow in 1985 and 1986, long before an invitation was extended to Chancellor Kohl. A joint SPD-CPSU working group was established to discuss topical political and security issues. The Soviets were particularly interested in probing the SPD's evolving attitudes on disarmament, which were drifting away from the prevailing NATO consensus under the influence of such party leaders as Lafontaine and Andreas von Bülow.[74] Some key concepts in Moscow's "new thinking" on security policy could in fact be traced to SPD strategists.[75] Delegations from the Greens were also accorded a warm welcome.

The cordial reception given these opponents of SDI contrasted starkly with the snub administered to CDU leader Philipp Jenninger, who led a

---

73. E.g., *Pravda*, Aug. 28, 1985, p. 3; FBIS, *Soviet Union*, Dec. 18, 1985, p. G4, and Dec. 20, pp. G1–2; Nikolai Portugalov in *Die Zeit*, Aug. 9, 1985, p. 4; in *Izvestiya*, Ye. Bovkun, Aug. 13, 1985, p. 5, and A. Grigoryants, Sept. 13, p. 5; in *Pravda*, Yu. Yakhontov, Oct. 31, 1985, p. 5, and Ye. Grigorev, Jan. 12, 1986, p. 5. A summary of Gorbachev's letter was published in *Bild Zeitung*, Nov. 4, 1985, pp. 1–2.

74. Stephen Padgett, "The West German Social Democrats in Opposition, 1982–86," *West European Politics* 10 (July 1987): 333–56; Matthew A. Weiller, "SPD Security Policy," *Survival* 30 (November–December 1988): 515–28.

75. Eberhard Schulz, "Das 'neue politische Denken' und die Deutschen," *Deutschland Archiv*, no. 9, 1988, pp. 972–73.

parliamentary delegation to Moscow at the end of 1985. Denied a meeting with Gorbachev or Shevardnadze, Jenninger broke off his visit a day ahead of schedule. These contrasting official attitudes toward the Kohl government and its critics were amply reflected in the specialist literature on the FRG at this time.[76]

Soviet pressure notwithstanding, the Kohl government moved steadily toward acceptance of participation in SDI. In April 1985 Kohl announced his approval of the American program. Although he agreed to join with Mitterrand in support of Eureka, Kohl declined to share the French president's aversion to SDI. In December the Kohl government formally declared its readiness to conclude an agreement with the United States permitting West German firms to take part in SDI research; the deal was signed in March 1986.

The Kremlin's disappointment in Kohl's actions was made clear by Boris Yeltsin, the future populist reformer, on a trip to the FRG. The Soviets were also concerned about West Germany's budding military partnership with France, which Kohl and Mitterrand took a personal interest in cultivating. Nevertheless, Gorbachev was determined to press ahead with his efforts to revive détente in Europe. Claiming to see "no logic" in West German foreign policy, Gorbachev unveiled a new initiative designed to get the permanently stalled MBFR talks moving again. Speaking at the 11th Congress of the SED in April 1986, he called for "substantial reductions" in land and airborne systems in Europe, with on-site inspection to verify compliance.[77]

This announcement was followed up by serious overtures to Bonn. In July 1986 Gorbachev and Shevardnadze met with Foreign Minister Genscher in Moscow. The meetings followed close on the heels of a visit by Mitterrand to the Soviet capital and a trip to Britain by Shevardnadze. At a time when U.S. officials were complaining of vagueness in Moscow's arms-control proposals and NATO countries were increasingly divided in their attitudes toward SDI and critical of such U.S. activities as the April bombing raid in Libya, Gorbachev and his lieutenants saw a need to inject greater momentum into the Kremlin's diplomacy toward Western Europe. These

76. For criticisms of Kohl in MEMO, see T. Panova et al., "Tekuschiye problemy mirovoi politiki," no. 4, 1985, p. 96; A. Svetlov, "Varshovskii dogovor na sluzhbe mira i bezopasnosti," no. 5, 1985, pp. 31–32; S. Tokhvinskii, "Potsdam: Kontury poslevoennovo mira," no. 8, 1985, p. 25; D. Melnikov's remarks in no. 11, 1985, p. 96; S. Sokolskii, "FRG i SOI," no. 8, 1986, pp. 111–14. Also G. Kirilov, "Bonn's Peaceable Rhetoric and Militaristic Practices," IA, no. 4, 1986, pp. 55–63. For a positive appraisal of the SPD, see G. Kirilov; for positive views of Genscher in MEMO, see A. Lebedev, "Imperativy Khelsinki," no. 8, 1985, p. 10, and B. Baranovskii et al., "Tekushchiye problemy mirovoi politiki," no. 4, 1986, p. 92. For positive views of the Greens, see Igor Borisov, "Bonn: Words and Deeds," IA, no. 10, 1987, p. 43.

77. Die Zeit, May 9, 1986, pp. 5–6; Pravda, Aug. 26, 1985, p. 5; and Apr. 19, 1986, pp. 1–2; Sovetskaya Rossiya, Feb. 15, 1986, p. 3. See also Robbin F. Laird, ed., Strangers and Friends: The Franco-German Security Relationship (New York: St. Martin's Press, 1989).

moves were coupled with new Warsaw Pact proposals on troop reductions in Europe.[78]

The Genscher visit resulted in the signature of an agreement on scientific-technical cooperation and the initialing of additional cooperative accords. More significant, Genscher reaffirmed Bonn's support for SALT I and SALT II, a matter of critical importance to the Soviets in view of the Reagan administration's tepid acceptance of the 1979 arms accord and its insistence that SDI did not violate the 1972 ABM treaty. Genscher also appealed to the Soviets to withdraw from Afghanistan and called for greater emigration opportunities for ethnic Germans residing in the USSR. For his part, Shevardnadze highlighted the "special unity" of the European continent, while denying any attempt to sever the "European wedge" from the Atlantic alliance. Soviet newspaper commentary presented both positive and negative portrayals of the West German ruling coalition around the time of the Genscher visit, testifying to continuing disagreements within the Soviet elite over the proper way to deal with the West Germans.[79]

The goodwill engendered by the revival of the Soviet–West German dialogue did not last very long. In October Chancellor Kohl obliquely likened Gorbachev's public relations abilities to those of Josef Goebbels. The remark drew a quick protest from Shevardnadze, and the Kremlin called off several official visits involving Soviet and West German delegations.[80] While Gorbachev refrained from responding publicly to Kohl's gaffe, he found highly visible ways to express his pique. As the Soviet–West German relationship took a turn for the better in 1987 and 1988, the Soviet leader entertained a steady stream of visitors from the FRG, including such prominent Christian Democrats as Richard von Weizsäcker, Franz–Josef Strauss, Lothar Späth, and Bernhard Vogel. Kohl would not be welcomed in Moscow until October 1988, two years after the Goebbels contretemps.

These personality disputes were not allowed to overshadow the pressing political interests of either the Soviet Union or the Federal Republic, however. After the Bundestag elections of January 25, 1987, reinstated the Kohl-Genscher coalition, Gorbachev got down to business, multiplying political and economic contacts at a variety of levels. Most important, the

78. *Pravda*, June 12, 1986, pp. 1–2. During Mitterrand's visit Gorbachev hinted at the Soviets' readiness to reduce their "surplus" of conventional forces in the European theater: ibid., July 8, p. 2. Soviet military figures continued to deny such asymmetries in Moscow's favor, however. See e.g., Col. Gen. Chervov's comments in FBIS, *Soviet Union*, Feb. 6, 1987, p. AA7.

79. *Pravda*, July 23, 1986, p. 4; *Izvestiya*, July 8, 1986, p. 4 (condemning the Kohl-Genscher coalition as favoring "militarists, revanchists, and extreme conservatives"), Aug. 11, p. 4 (stressing economic cooperation).

80. *Newsweek*, Oct. 27, 1986, p. 29. Shevardnadze said Kohl's "insulting" remarks "have angered us to the depths of our souls": FBIS, *Soviet Union*, Nov. 18, 1986, p. AA1. Also *Pravda*, Nov. 28, 1986, p. 5; *Washington Post*, Nov. 22, 1986, p. A15.

Soviet party chief was resolved to lift the ponderous INF millstone from the East-West relationship.

Gorbachev and Reagan had tentatively agreed at Reykjavik to eliminate all their intermediate-range missiles in Europe (that is, those having a range of 600 to 3,400 miles), while retaining 100 INF warheads each, to be based in the eastern USSR and in the United States. This agreement foundered on Moscow's insistence on linking it to SDI. No accord had been reached at the Iceland summit on shorter-range missiles, capable of traversing distances of 300 to 600 miles. The Soviets had approximately 130 such weapons in the European theater, including SS-12/22s in the GDR and Czechoslovakia and SS-23s in the western USSR. Though the United States had no similar systems, administration officials wanted to retain the option of converting the Pershing IIs to shorter-range Pershing IBs, with a view to establishing an equal ceiling with the Soviet Union for missiles of this range.

At first the Kremlin was not willing to include the shorter-range missiles in the INF treaty negotiations. Speaking in Prague on April 10, 1987, Gorbachev called for separate talks on these weapons.[81] Several days later he switched his position, informing Secretary of State George Shultz of Moscow's readiness to "eliminate" all its shorter-range missiles. The Soviets strongly objected to U.S. plans to build a contingent of Pershing IBs, and they were also sensitive to West German fears of Soviet shorter-range rockets aimed primarily at the FRG. At the same time, Gorbachev offered to eliminate Soviet battlefield (tactical) nuclear weapons, with a range of less than 300 miles, if the United States did likewise.

These proposals put the Kohl government in a quandary. On the one hand, the removal of intermediate-range weapons had widespread popular support in the FRG. On the other hand, leading members of the defense establishment feared that the removal of all the newly deployed Pershing II and cruise missiles, especially in combination with a U.S. pledge not to deploy shorter-range weapons, would leave the FRG vulnerable to the USSR's undiminished conventional superiority in tanks and artillery and to a potential nuclear exchange confined to battlefield weapons exploding in and around the FRG. This view was articulated most forcefully by Defense Minister Manfred Wörner, and was widely shared by other Christian Democratic politicians.

Hans-Dietrich Genscher, by contrast, leaned heavily in favor of a "double zero" agreement, aimed at eliminating all intermediate- and shorter-range missiles in Europe. Genscher had by this time emerged as an ardent advocate of Western efforts to take full advantage of Gorbachev's expressed interest in across-the-board arms reductions. At the World Economic Forum in Davos in early February 1987, Genscher urged the NATO states to

81. *Pravda*, Apr. 11, 1987, p. 2.

"take him at his word" by adopting, within the framework of the alliance's nuclear deterrence strategy, a negotiating posture aimed at achieving comprehensive disarmament at equal levels of security.[82] Genscher's motivations were not hard to fathom. As the key figure in a small centrist party perennially on the brink of electoral extinction, Genscher had to be sensitive to public demands for détente. At the same time, Genscher firmly believed it would be "a mistake of historic dimensions" if the West did not at least explore the possibility of ending the divisions on the continent and promoting human rights in the socialist states by encouraging Gorbachev's efforts to restructure Soviet foreign and domestic policy.

By the spring of 1987 Helmut Kohl was cornered into mediating between the Wörner and Genscher factions of his governing coalition. Public opinion polls did not make his task any easier. One sampling revealed that 92 percent of West Germans favored an INF treaty in general, but only a scant majority of 51 percent favored it without regard for a solution to the problem of the shorter-range missiles. American preferences also weighed heavily on Kohl's decision. After his conference with Gorbachev in April, Shultz advised the NATO allies either to accept the double-zero solution or reject it in favor of a buildup of intermediate- and/or shorter-range missiles. Shultz left little doubt that the United States favored the double-zero solution.[83]

Speaking to the Bundestag in early May, Kohl put off a final decision on the shorter-range missiles. Later, however, he agreed in principle that these weapons should be taken into consideration as part of a package deal with Moscow on INF.

In the meantime, another thorny issue threatened to shred the web of compromises now being woven into an INF accord. A Soviet draft treaty submitted shortly before Kohl's Bundestag address called for the elimination of American nuclear warheads reserved for use on the seventy-two aging Pershing IA missiles located in the FRG. Kohl objected to the proposal on the grounds that the Pershing IAs were owned by the Federal Republic, and therefore could not be included in negotiations confined to the two superpowers. The United States backed this position on the grounds that it did not wish to set a precedent for negotiating arms agreements with Moscow involving weapons owned by third states. The Soviets insisted that the Pershing IA missiles were not at issue; Bonn could keep the missiles (which the United States had signed over to the FRG in the 1970s), but the American-owned warheads had to be removed from Europe. In late July the United States confirmed that it was equally opposed to removing the warheads.

82. *Bulletin: Presse- und Informationsamt der Bundesregierung*, no. 13 (Feb. 4), 1987, pp. 93–97.
83. *Washington Post*, May 6, 1987, p. A31; Apr. 23, 1987, pp. A33–34.

Despite these and other obstacles to an accord (such as persisting disagreements over the extent of the on-site inspection regime), the march of events was moving almost inexorably toward compromise. Gorbachev revealed his responsiveness once again on July 22 when he announced that the Soviets were prepared to remove their SS-20s and intermediate-range warheads from the Asian rim of the USSR.[84] This sudden acceptance of a "global double zero" responded to West German concerns that these missiles could be transported to the European theater in time of war or crisis. While the Soviets held to their position on the Pershing IA warheads and on the possible conversion of the Pershing IIs into shorter-range rockets, Genscher let it be known toward the end of August that he favored dismantling the Pershing IA missiles and their warheads by the early 1990s, by which time the missiles would be obsolete. The Social Democrats and Greens, who were unconditionally opposed to retaining the West German missiles, demanded a Bundestag debate on the issue. The electoral fortunes of the CDU were also at stake in two upcoming regional elections. The Reagan administration took the view that the successful completion of an INF treaty now rested squarely on the shoulders of Helmut Kohl, adding insurmountable pressures on the chancellor to resolve the controversy.

This fact was fully appreciated in Moscow.[85] The moment offered a striking example of the United States' ability to persuade West Germany to adopt policies favored by Moscow. The significance of this event was surely not lost on analysts of U.S.–West European relations within the Soviet foreign policy elite.

Faced with overpowering domestic and external demands for compromise, Helmut Kohl pledged on August 26 that once the United States and the Soviet Union had completely eliminated their intermediate-range missiles, Bonn would destroy its Pershing IAs and would not seek to replace them. The statement removed the last major impediment to an INF treaty, and was praised by Soviet leaders.[86] On September 18 Shevardnadze agreed to drop Moscow's last-minute effort to mention the Pershing IAs in the treaty text, and Shultz pledged to remove the corresponding nuclear warheads. After several remaining issues were cleared up, the two foreign ministers agreed on the treaty's final terms at Geneva on November 24. The most radical nuclear-arms-reduction agreement in history was signed by Reagan and Gorbachev on December 8, 1987.[87]

84. *Pravda*, July 23, 1987, p. 2.

85. Nikolai Portugalov noted that Shultz had "passed the buck" to Bonn: FBIS, *Soviet Union*, Aug. 19, 1987, p. AA2. Another Soviet commentator likened the U.S. position to "Pilate washing his hands": ibid., Aug. 24, p. H3. Foreign Ministry spokesman Gerasimov hinted that the U.S. should pressure Bonn into compromising; ibid., Aug. 26, pp. CC1–2.

86. Shevardnadze said that Gorbachev "positively appreciated" Kohl's decision: *Izvestiya*, Sept. 20, 1987, p. 4.

87. The INF Treaty required the United States to destroy the 108 Pershing IIs and the 256 cruise missiles already emplaced in Western Europe. The USSR was to destroy all 441 SS-20s,

Caught up in the whirl of Soviet–West German cross-pressures as the INF negotiations proceeded was the hapless teenage aviator Matthias Rust. The Rust affair provided a timely opportunity for members of the Soviet secondary elite to voice their opinions on West Germany and the United States in 1987. Not everyone took the view that Bonn or Washington could be counted on as a reliable partner in détente.

One of the first comments on the case came from Valentin Falin, the chief of Novosti press. In an interview with a Hamburg daily several days after Rust's arrest, Falin said the pilot would be released "soon," perhaps after being tried and "thanked" for demonstrating where gaps existed in the Soviet air defense system. The next day Falin reportedly changed his mind, saying the matter was more serious than it had first appeared. Several weeks later Falin ascribed Rust's motives to personality factors rather than political ones (Rust himself claimed he was on a peace mission), and expressed hopes that the incident would not damage Soviet–West German ties. During President von Weizsäcker's stay in Moscow in early July, Falin was even more upbeat, predicting Rust's release within a few hours or days.[88]

Other commentators adopted a more negative tone. *Moscow News* and Tass on June 3 suggested that the Rust flight had been carefully prepared in West Germany, and hinted darkly at political purposes. Another writer referred to espionage maps aboard Rust's plane, and *Pravda* named the West German firm that had furnished the maps. One particularly exercised observer insisted that the United States had earlier used civilian aircraft for intelligence-gathering purposes. The anti-Soviet hysteria that had followed the 1983 KAL incident, he asserted, had been deliberately aimed at scuttling the INF talks then in progress. The author concluded that a similarly aimed provocation could not be ruled out in the Rust matter. As a two-month investigation of the case proceeded, a Soviet Foreign Ministry spokesman turned aside Falin's earlier comments about Rust's imminent release, calling them purely personal views.[89]

On July 28, the same day that high-level Soviet arms-control officials took a tough stance on the Pershing IA issue in an interview,[90] it was announced that Rust would stand trial. Fortunately for the young man, Rust was not formally charged with espionage. After pleading guilty to

112 SS-4s, 110 SS-12/22s, and 20 SS-23s. All warheads for these missiles were to be taken out of service. For the treaty text and excerpts from the protocols, see *New York Times,* Dec. 9, 1987, pp. A24–26.

88. FBIS, *Soviet Union,* June 2, 1987, pp. H7–8; June 3, p. H1; June 23, p. H1; *Washington Post,* July 9, p. A38. A close aide to the Kremlin leadership reportedly told *Bild am Sonntag* that Rust would not be put on trial. The next day a Soviet spokesman denied this rumor: FBIS, *Soviet Union,* July 7, 1987, p. H14.

89. FBIS, *Soviet Union,* June 3, 1987, p. H1; and June 4, pp. H1–2; July 10, p. CC2; A. Frenkin in *Literaturnaya gazeta,* June 17, 1987, p. 9; *Pravda,* June 5, 1987, p. 5; A. Savinov in *Komsomolskaya pravda,* June 28, 1987, p. 3.

90. *Washington Post,* July 29, 1987, pp. A1, A19.

charges of violating Soviet borders and hooliganism, he was sentenced on September 4 to four years in a labor camp. Rust was never removed from his Moscow prison, however, and later in the month Falin told a West German magazine that an appeal for clemency would be examined "benevolently." Nevertheless, in December Rust's request for a pardon was turned down.

There can be little doubt that Soviet authorities had good reason to regard Rust's intrusion into Soviet territory and his aerial circumnavigation of Red Square as crimes sufficiently serious to warrant some sort of punishment. But it also appears that Rust had fallen hostage to the still testy Soviet–West German political relationship. The Kremlin passed up several opportunities to reap public relations dividends in the FRG by releasing Rust in 1987. Hopes that Rust would be let go during President von Weizsäcker's visit in July or Strauss's trip in late December proved premature. Falin's consistent misreading of the prospects for a pardon suggests that the Soviet elite was divided over the matter. When Rust's sentence was finally suspended in August 1988, the timing provided evidence that political considerations had influenced the Kremlin's handling of his case. His release was announced immediately after a highly successful visit to Moscow by Foreign Minister Genscher, designed to set a positive tone for Chancellor Kohl's long-delayed meeting with Gorbachev in October.

Meanwhile, as relations between Bonn and Moscow gradually improved over the course of 1987 and 1988, the images of West Germany presented by members of the Soviet secondary elite reflected a continuing diversity of positive, negative, and mixed attitudes.[91]

A New German Policy?

Perhaps no issue in Soviet–West German relations in the latter half of the 1980s generated greater attention than the "German question" itself: Would the changes taking place in Soviet foreign and military policy, together with the extraordinary developments in Poland, Hungary, and the GDR, lead to Germany's unification at any time in the foreseeable future?

---

91. For predominantly negative images, see I. Borisov, "Voenno-promyshlenny kompleks FRG," *MEMO*, no. 8, 1987, pp. 121–28; for negative images of the CDU/CSU and positive images of the SPD, with no mention of the FDP, see Nikolai Khomtov, "The FRG: In a Maze of Problems," *IA*, no. 2, 1987, pp. 135–42; for a mixed view, noting differences between the CDU and the FDP on SDI, see G. Vorontsov, "Zapadnaya Evropa i SOI," *MEMO*, no. 3, 1987, pp. 41–48. For somewhat more positive views of the CDU/CSU, together with even greater praise for the SPD and Genscher, see Yu. Yudanov, "FRG vo vtoroi polovine 80-x godov—osnovnye problemy i poiski ikh resheniya," *MEMO*, no. 9, 1988, pp. 82–93. Largely positive views of the Kohl government's foreign policy are in M. Maksimova, "Raskryt potentsial sotrudnichestva," *MEMO*, no. 10, 1988, pp. 61–66. *MEMO* published the text of a talk given at IMEMO by the SPD's Hans-Jochen Vogel, no. 7, 1988, pp. 33–39.

Some Western observers were convinced that the Gorbachev regime was preparing monumental shifts in Soviet policy on Germany's status, with unification or some form of FRG-GDR confederation regarded as likely within a reasonably short time.[92]

To no small extent, well-placed Soviet commentators fanned these hopes with tantalizing hints of change. In early 1987 Nikolai Portugalov, one of the Central Committee's leading specialists on Germany, implied that the citizens of West and East Germany belonged to a single German nation. In September of the same year, Valentin Falin told West German television viewers that once the presence of foreign troops was substantially reduced in Europe, the 1971 Quadripartite Agreement "would not be the last word" on the subject of Berlin, and "more interesting models" could emerge. Several days later a Soviet diplomat in Geneva, Stanislav Chernyavskii, remarked to a conference of NATO military pastors that the Berlin wall had seen its "last days," and would disappear "soon." Vyacheslav Dashichev, the critic of Moscow's postwar foreign policy line, described the wall as a cold war legacy that would "have to disappear in time," and added that the USSR, the GDR, the FRG, and other interested states might reformulate their approach to Germany's division in ten or twenty years. In *Literaturnaya gazeta* the journalist Leonid Pochivalov observed that West and East Germans still had much in common.[93]

Statements of this kind provided unmistakable signs that the Soviet elite was indeed engaged in "new thinking" on the German question. Positive references to German national unity, or to the eventual disappearance of the Berlin wall, were simply not to be found in the pre-Gorbachev decades. Nevertheless, before the dramatic developments of late 1989 it was by no means certain that the Gorbachev leadership had come to any specific decision to modify the decades-old Soviet position on either the division of Germany or the division of Berlin. Ambiguities and reservations abounded in public discussions of these issues.

Portugalov, for example, coupled his comments about the unity of the German nation with references to the continuing existence of two German

92. In 1987 a West German Foreign Office official claimed that the USSR had established a commission to study a possible German confederation; the Soviets denied the report. Rumors of the imminent removal of the wall were also rife in the FRG at this time: *Washington Post*, Oct. 12, 1987, p. A30. On Soviet readiness to end the division of Germany, see Jerry F. Hough in ibid., May 21, 1989, p. C2.

93. *Moscow News*, March 8, 1987, p. 7. Portugalov had been the Novosti press representative in Bonn from 1972 to 1979, and had worked in the Central Committee's International Information Department until it was abolished in 1986; FBIS, *Soviet Union*, Sept. 24, 1987, pp. 49–50; Chernyavskii quoted in Fred Oldenburg, "Neues Denken in der sowjetischen Deutschlandpolitik," *Deutschland Archiv*, no. 11, 1987, pp. 1154–60; *Die Welt*, June 9, 1988, p. 5; *Der Spiegel*, July 4, 1988, p. 127; Ilse Spittmann, "SED setzt auf Zeitgewinn," *Deutschland Archiv*, no. 7, 1988, p. 691; Leonid Pochivalov, "Nemtsy i my," *Literaturnaya gazeta*, July 20, 1988, p. 14.

states.[94] Falin later remarked that the quadripartite agreement had not yet been "fully exhausted," and he criticized Bonn for failing to observe it strictly and consistently. He also defended the GDR's decision to build the wall in 1961, saying that it had been made "at the clear request" of East Germany's Warsaw Pact allies. Falin expressed understanding for East Berlin's belief that the time for "qualitative changes" had not yet arrived. (Curiously, however, Falin hinted that qualitative changes affecting the wall might be possible, and he cited Gorbachev as saying that the "wall of hatred" that existed before 1961 was harder to remove than a "wall of stone.") Falin denied that the Kremlin was studying reunification and insisted that it was a "waste of time" to consider the issue until both German states were ready to declare their military neutrality, a prospect he did not believe to be under consideration in Bonn. In the absence of a peace treaty, he said, one could speak of unification only "conditionally."[95]

Chernyavskii's prediction that the Berlin wall would fall was brushed aside by Foreign Ministry Spokesman Gennadii Gerasimov, who issued a ringing endorsement of both the construction of the wall and the quadripartite agreement. Dashichev qualified his remarks on the Berlin wall in 1988 by projecting an "evolutionary development" that would ensure certain economic and security guarantees to the GDR. A year later, he spoke of overcoming the barriers to human, cultural, and economic contacts between the FRG and the GDR, but added that this "by no means necessarily" meant either unification or a German confederation.[96]

Other authoritative members of the secondary elite reinforced the impression that the Soviets were engaged in a vigorous debate on critical German issues without having come to any firm decisions as to how or when to take definitive action. Aleksandr Bovin, for example, appeared to be rethinking his own position on these matters. In June 1987 Bovin lambasted President Reagan's speech at the Berlin wall, which called on Gorbachev to tear the structure down. He defended the "border installation" in the divided city as a precondition for disarmament and crisis

94. On this and related points, see Eberhard Schulz, "Sowjetische Deutschlandpolitik: Noch immer unentschlossen?" Deutschland Archiv, no. 9, 1987, pp. 940–49. For another article by Schulz stressing the continuities in the Kremlin's German policy, see ibid., no. 10, 1986, pp. 1053–63.

95. FBIS, Soviet Union, Mar. 1, 1988, pp. 32–33; Die Welt, Jan. 24, 1989, p. 6; ibid., suppl., Oct. 21, 1988, p. 3; FAZ, Oct. 1, 1987, p. 2; interviews with Austrian press in FBIS, Soviet Union, May 12, 1989, pp. 4–6; Der Spiegel, Oct. 23, 1989, p. 26.

96. FBIS, Soviet Union, Oct. 15, 1987, p. 16; Blätter für deutsche und internationale Politik, no. 6, 1989, p. 676. Dashichev was identified as the chairman of a research committee in the Soviet Foreign Ministry at the time of this interview. Dashichev later spoke of future cooperation between the two German states without mentioning the possibility of either unification or a confederation: quoted in Fred Oldenburg, "Sowjetische Deutschland-Politik nach den Treffen von Moskau und Bonn 1988/89," Berichte des Bundesinstituts für ostwissenschaftliche und internationale Studien, no. 63, 1989, pp. 46–47.

reduction in Central Europe. Bovin further asserted that the German question was closed as far as the "visible horizon" was concerned, adding that any attempt to reopen it would only reopen the question of war in Europe. Later, however, Bovin suggested that "variants" of Germany's status could come about in the future, as the blocs disappeared and Europe became "more European." In 1988 Vadim Zagladin told Der Spiegel that he saw no reason for the wall to come down "at present," and stated that reunification was "unrealistic today." Articles in Pravda dismissed the possibility of reunification in more explicit terms. At the end of 1988, however, two Soviet Foreign Ministry officials declared that it would be "incorrect" to assume that the question of Germany's reunification would not be raised in the future.[97]

As might be expected, these debates on Germany reflected ferment at the top of the Kremlin decision-making hierarchy. While indications of change in the Kremlin's position were delphic at best, between 1987 and 1989 the Gorbachev coalition was groping its way toward a new German policy more in keeping with the goals of political and economic restructuring in the socialist camp and more conducive to a cooperative relationship with the West.

Gorbachev and other Soviet decision makers were more firmly committed than some members of the secondary elite to the continuing division of Germany. Gorbachev told President von Weizsäcker in Moscow in July 1987 that statements suggesting that the German question was still open raised doubts about the FRG's adherence to the Soviet–West German treaty of August 1970 and other accords. The Soviet leader insisted that "one must proceed" from the fact that there were two German states with different social and political systems. "History will decide what will happen in 100 years," Gorbachev continued. "No other approach is acceptable." In Gorbachev's own account of this meeting he said he dismissed talk of "German unity" as "far from being 'Realpolitik' " and once again deferred to the judgment of history. "For the time being," Gorbachev warned, "one should proceed from the existing realities and not engage in incendiary speculations."[98]

The inflammability of the German question became even more apparent at this time as Pravda excised important sections of Weizsäcker's speech at a Kremlin reception hosted by Gromyko. Among the deleted passages was the president's statement that the Germans living in the FRG and the GDR "have not stopped, and will not stop, feeling as one nation." The CPSU

97. Bovin: Izvestiya, June 18, 1987, p. 3; MEMO, no. 1, 1989, p. 66. Zagladin: Der Spiegel, June 6, 1988, pp. 145–47, 149. In Pravda, B. Orekhov, June 13, 1986, p. 5; V. Mikhailov, Apr. 24, 1988, p. 4; Ye. Grigorev, Nov. 1, 1988, p. 4. Mikhail Amirdzhanov and Mikhail Cherkasov, "Our Common European Home," IA, no. 12, 1988, p. 32.
98. IA, July 5, 1987, pp. 1–2; Gorbachev, Perestroika, pp. 184–87.

daily also deleted Weizsäcker's insistence that "the unity of the nation shall and must be fulfilled within the freedom of its people." Also omitted were his pleas for liberalized emigration procedures for ethnic Germans who wished to leave the USSR.[99] When quizzed about the deletions the next day, Falin told Western journalists that the Soviet leadership was debating the matter.[100] The full text of Weizsäcker's speech was published later.[101] Gromyko, meanwhile, took advantage of Weizsäcker's presence to hand him a list of war criminals wanted by the Soviet Union for extradition.

Inevitably the issue of Germany's division surfaced once again during Chancellor Helmut Kohl's long-delayed visit to the USSR in October 1988. *Pravda* dutifully reported the chancellor's statement that the division of Germany was "unnatural," and that the German people should be able "to choose their fate freely and to come together in mutual freedom," as long as the four powers responsible for Germany agreed. On the eve of Kohl's arrival Gorbachev described attempts to erase the borders between the two German states as "disastrous." "There must be complete clarity on such questions," he insisted. He evaded a query about the Berlin wall. At a dinner given in Kohl's honor, Gorbachev called efforts to push through "unrealistic" policies on Germany a "dangerous matter," and referred to West Berlin's "special status."[102]

Despite these lingering disagreements, the Soviet–West German summit of 1988 proved rewarding for both sides. The meeting was preceded by Soviet concessions to Bonn on the inclusion of West Berlin in environmental and cultural agreements, a gesture that was accompanied by a Soviet rebuff to a U.S. request to expand airline traffic to the divided city.[103] Economic relations got a major boost as more than seventy West German businessmen accompanied Kohl to Moscow. Sixteen agreements were signed on the first day, followed by a framework accord designed to implement a DM3 billion credit that had been extended a week earlier by a consortium of West German banks. Intergovernmental agreements were signed on items ranging from joint space exploration to agricultural cooperation and cultural exchanges. Chancellor Kohl endorsed the "common European home" on condition that it permitted the free exchange of people and ideas, and hinted at a possible relaxation of the NATO embargo list. In Gorbachev's

99. *Pravda*, July 7, 1987, p. 4. The full text of Weizsäcker's speech is in FBIS, *Soviet Union*, July 7, 1987, pp. H6–10.

100. *Washington Post*, July 9, 1987, p. A38. Falin also noted the existence of "skeptics," "footdraggers," and "orthodox" opponents of Gorbachev's reforms: FBIS, *Soviet Union*, July 13, 1987, p. H9.

101. See Dettmar Cramer, "Der Bundespräsident in der Sowjetunion," *Deutschland Archiv*, no. 8, 1987, pp. 792–94. Also FBIS, *Soviet Union*, July 13, 1987, p. H8.

102. *Pravda*, Oct. 25, 1988, p. 2; *Der Spiegel*, Oct. 24, 1988, pp. 21, 30; *Pravda*, Oct. 25, 1988, p. 2.

103. *Washington Post*, Oct. 5, 1988, p. A29.

judgment, the summit had broken the ice between the USSR and the FRG, though he had not forgotten Kohl's reference to Goebbels two years earlier.[104]

The warming trend continued over the next months as the pace of East-West arms diplomacy quickened. In December 1988 at the United Nations, Gorbachev announced a unilateral cutback of 500,000 troops and of various categories of conventional weaponry over the next several years. Soviet commentators did not fail to point out that the number of troops to be decommissioned approximately equaled the size of the Bundeswehr.[105] In March 1989 a new forum for talks on the balance of conventional weapons was inaugurated as the Conventional Forces in Europe (CFE) negotiations began in Vienna. The revised format for NATO–Warsaw Pact discussions replaced the futile MBFR talks, and followed the publication for the first time in the Soviet press of figures on the conventional arms balance attesting to substantial Warsaw Pact superiority over NATO in tanks and other battlefield weapons.[106] Shevardnadze's speech at the CFE's opening session brought the Soviet stance on potential conventional force reductions even closer to NATO's position.[107] The mellowing atmosphere was lightened further in February 1989, as Soviet troops completed their pullout from Afghanistan. All these moves were accompanied by signs of Gorbachev's tightening grip on the Soviet military hierarchy, despite rumblings of discontent within the ranks.[108] They also stimulated highly favorable responses from the West German population, as upwards of 90 percent of FRG citizens believed the Soviet military threat to be receding.[109]

Gorbachev's long-awaited visit to Bonn was preceded by another dispute among the NATO partners on the implications of Moscow's accelerating disarmament measures. Gorbachev's earlier offer to eliminate all tactical nuclear weapons (battlefield devices having a range of less than 300 miles)

104. Gorbachev told *Der Spiegel* that "politicians should watch their words": Oct. 24, 1988, p. 22. For a review of the Kohl visit, see *MEMO*, no. 1, 1989, pp. 106–8.

105. *Pravda*, Dec. 8, 1988, pp. 1–2; Maj. Gen. V. Kuklov in *Krasnaya zvezda*, Dec. 28, 1988, p. 3.

106. *Pravda*, Jan. 30, 1989, p. 5. The revised Soviet figures still differed from NATO estimates in several categories: *Washington Post*, Jan. 31, 1989, pp. A1, A21.

107. *Pravda*, Mar. 7, 1989, p. 4; *Washington Post*, Mar. 7, 1989, pp. A1, A18.

108. In January 1989 Gorbachev announced a 14.2% reduction in the military budget. Marshal Viktor Kulikov was replaced as the Warsaw Pact commander in early February by Gen. Pyotr Lushev. The Soviet navy was forced to accept cutbacks later in the month. On March 7 Moscow announced it would remove 75% of its troops from the Mongolian border. On March 30 the Soviets ended conscription of students. Marshal Sergei Akhromeyev, who had earlier signaled his opposition to unilateral troop reductions, resigned as chief of staff at the time of Gorbachev's UN speech and was replaced by Col. Gen. Mikhail Moiseyev. Akhromeyev insisted that he had resigned for health reasons, but he remained as one of Gorbachev's military advisers. For evidence of the military's unease over the cutbacks, see *Washington Post*, Dec. 9, 1988, pp. A16, A18; Dec. 16, 1988, p. A37; Mar. 11, 1989, p. A19.

109. *Washington Post*, Mar. 18, 1989, p. A21.

found a significant resonance in the FRG. Doubts were growing about the wisdom of supporting American plans to introduce a new generation of these weapons in the mid-1990s, when the aging Lance missiles were due for replacement. (NATO had 88 reloadable Lance launchers in Western Europe, about two-thirds of them in the FRG, together with roughly 700 warheads. The Soviets had about 1,600 launchers and 3,100 warheads in this category in the European theater.)[110] A decision to proceed with the modernization scheme had to be made by 1992. With pressure mounting in the FRG to give the disarmament process a chance to prove itself, Helmut Kohl announced in February 1989 that his government would postpone its decision on Lance modernization until 1991 or 1992. The timing was transparently intended to remove the modernization issue from the next Bundestag elections, scheduled for the end of 1990.

Kohl's announcement created apprehension in the United States and Britain, as the Bush and Thatcher governments feared Bonn's abandonment of a common NATO position on nuclear modernization. Kohl himself was once again pinioned between contending viewpoints within his own cabinet. As the Defense Ministry warned of continuing Soviet conventional superiority in arguing for modernization, Foreign Minister Genscher— while rejecting a "third zero" solution—pleaded for immediate negotiations with Moscow on the issue. Some conservative elements within the Christian Democratic parties were also backing away from modernizing battlefield nuclear weapons, in part because their limited range would confine a nuclear engagement to areas populated by Germans. For their part, leading Social Democrats favored the removal of all nuclear artillery from Europe.[111] To add to Kohl's plight, his party was encountering a growing challenge from the far right as the chauvinist Republicans and their allies made unexpected inroads into CDU constituencies in West Berlin and Frankfurt. These electoral tremors prompted Kohl to reshuffle his cabinet in favor of Christian Democratic conservatives in April. But later in the month he challenged the United States by formally calling for negotiations with Moscow on battlefield nuclear weapons. In May, as the rift between the allies widened, Moscow announced that it would eliminate 500 nuclear warheads unilaterally from its European theater arsenal (out of an estimated total of more than 10,000) and proposed more generous cuts in conventional weapons at the CFE talks.

Finally, after intensive negotiations on the eve of NATO's fortieth anniversary summit at the end of May, American and West German negotiators resolved their differences. The United States agreed to hold talks with the Soviet Union on tactical nuclear weapons, and Bonn agreed that these

110. *Washington Post*, May 31, 1989, p. A18.
111. Ronald D. Asmus, "West Germany Faces Nuclear Modernization," *Survival* 33 (November–December 1988): 499–514.

negotiations should be deferred until after the implementation of an accord on conventional arms reduction to be worked out in the CFE framework. It was further stipulated that the prospective negotiations would aim at achieving a "partial reduction" in tactical nuclear weapons rather than their complete elimination. President Bush coupled this compromise agreement with a new conventional-arms proposal aimed at speeding up the timetable for achieving and carrying out a CFE accord. Bush was under heavy pressure to counter perceptions that he was losing ground to Gorbachev in the race for arms reductions.[112] *Pravda* expressed disappointment that Bonn had "failed to make the most of its possibilities" for influencing the U.S. position.[113]

Two weeks after the unexpectedly harmonious NATO summit, Mikhail Gorbachev arrived in Bonn. The Soviet leader tended to avoid referring directly to the German question in his prepared speeches. But remarks he made in response to questions, together with interesting nuances in statements made by the secondary elite, provided the most tangible suggestions thus far that the Gorbachev leadership might be preparing major changes in its German policy.

The timing of Gorbachev's visit was critical. It came as a succession of unprecedented events was shaking the communist world to its ideological core. Starting on May 25, the Congress of People's Deputies held its occasionally raucous opening session in Moscow. In early June, Gorbachev went to China for a visit that was eclipsed by the demonstrations in Tienanmen Square and their bloody aftermath. Meanwhile, the Hungarian communist party had already announced that multiparty elections would take place the following year. Democracy was also on the march in Poland, as pro-Solidarity candidates won massive victories in partially contested elections held throughout the country on June 4. These rapid strides toward democratic procedures in the USSR and Eastern Europe, together with the chilling lessons of the Chinese experience, could not help but have the most profound implications for Moscow's stance on a host of German issues, including the right of self-determination, the stability of the GDR, and the Berlin wall.

Gorbachev's visit was preceded by ambiguous but intriguing statements on German issues by leading members of the primary and secondary elites. Earlier in the year, Aleksandr Yakovlev had brushed aside questions about the wall while visiting the FRG, insisting that he did not represent East Germany.[114] In an article in *Der Spiegel* shortly before Gorbachev's visit, Portugalov put a positive spin on Gorbachev's remarks on Germany in

112. One poll showed that 47% of West Germans believed that the USSR was the "stronger force" for world peace, while 22% named the United States: *Washington Post*, May 30, 1989, p. A12.

113. June 1, 1989, p. 7.

114. *FAZ*, Jan. 10, 1989, p. 2.

Perestroika. Portugalov made no reference to the "hundred years" Gorbachev had suggested as the time frame for possible changes in Germany's divided status, but said that "these questions are open in the eyes of history." West Germans had not yet fully grasped the "programmatic depth" of Gorbachev's statements, he declared. Without clarifying Germany's long-term future any further, Portugalov added that the tasks of overcoming the division of Europe and building a common European home required "two German apartments, separate, with tenants who have equal rights and who are independent of each other, but still open to each other," in much the same way as Austria and Hungary. While Portugalov was clearly reaffirming the necessity of the division of Germany into two states for an indeterminate period, his hint about open borders was a curious twist, inasmuch as Hungary had recently begun to tear down the iron curtain separating it from Austria. Another member of the Soviet secondary elite, the editor of *Novoye vremya,* also affirmed the need for two German states, but he called the notion of two German nations "a contradiction in terms." Valentin Falin averred that a united Germany "wouldn't worry Moscow," though he once again noted that the West German government did not seem to be thinking in terms of a militarily neutral German state.[115]

Perhaps the most far-reaching recommendation for a new direction for Moscow's German policy at this time came from Vyacheslav Dashichev. In a memorandum prepared at the Institute of the Economy of the World Socialist System and given to the Soviet leadership on April 18, 1989, Dashichev ridiculed the Honecker regime for its "ideological primitivism" and declared that "one cannot conceive of a common European home without overcoming the division of Germany in its present form." He called for a "step-by-step, controlled reform" in the GDR and a progressive rapprochement between the two German states which might eventually lead to "reunification under the conditions of guaranteed security for all the countries of Europe." Rejecting a policy of confrontation with the West as incompatible with Soviet interests, Dashichev argued that the concept of neutralization would lose all meaning for the Federal Republic and the GDR ("or for a reunited Germany, if one arises") once East-West conflict situations disappeared. Even before that stage was reached, he believed that the two Germanies could withdraw from their military alliances. Dashichev felt that NATO and the Warsaw Pact should in any event cut their nuclear and conventional arsenals by 50 to 70 percent by the year 2000.

Dashichev made it clear, however, that Germany's unification "need not necessarily" occur anytime soon. It was "more realistic" in the near term to visualize "the gradual opening of the GDR's borders, the deepening of comprehensive cooperation with the FRG, and the guaranteeing of the right of Germans in East and West to unhindered contacts." In this initial phase each side would have to respect the social and political system of the other. Only in the "second phase," when East-West conflicts had dissolved and trust abounded, could a voluntary confederation of the two German states or some other arrangement (including unification) be expected. "It is very important that this process take place under conditions of internal and external stability," Dashichev added.[116]

Gorbachev himself did not go so far as these Soviet officials in his public comments on West Germany, but he was by no means so uncompromising as earlier Soviet leaders had been in regard to Germany's future. When queried about the possibility of a united Germany during a press conference in Bonn, Gorbachev conceded that "everything is possible," but he quickly alluded to "certain realities" and "obligations to the present" for which he hoped there would be "understanding" in the FRG and the GDR. In a similarly elliptical remark Gorbachev observed that "nothing is eternal in this world," and said that the Berlin wall could be removed as soon as the conditions that had led to its construction no longer existed. "I do not see a particularly big problem here," Gorbachev added.

An additional new wrinkle in Soviet language on Germany concerned the touchy issue of self-determination. At Bonn's insistence, the joint statement signed by Gorbachev and Kohl on June 13 affirmed "the right of all peoples and states to freely determine their fate," and acknowledged "unconditional respect . . . for . . . the peoples' right of self-determination." "Everyone," the document continued, "has the right to freely choose his own political and social system."[117]

Although these official and semiofficial statements appeared to indicate subtle shifts in Moscow's German policy, they were counterbalanced by more familiar positions. The joint statement also referred to the sovereignty of states, a rubric commonly used by Soviet and East European authorities to rationalize violations of popular self-determination. It called for the "strict observance" of the quadripartite agreement on Berlin. The interpretation of this agreement continued to be a sticking point, as the Soviets refused to sign navigation agreements to permit boats harbored in West Berlin to fly the FRG flag. Even Gorbachev's comments on the conditions for the removal of the Berlin wall simply echoed one of Erich Honecker's standard refrains in support of the wall's existence, as we shall see. Portugalov's suggestion that the goal of overcoming the division of Europe

---

116. The memo was published in *Der Spiegel*, Feb. 5, 1990, pp. 142–58. Dashichev regarded the FRG's economic attachments to Western Europe as an "irreversible reality" that was "no tragedy." He also made a strong case for market-oriented reforms and even called for converting the area around Kaliningrad, long barred to Western visitors, into a free-trade zone.

117. *Pravda*, June 14, 1989, pp. 1–2.

could be achieved without the unification of Germany reaffirmed a statement by Shevardnadze to this effect earlier in the year. Shevardnadze had also defended the Berlin wall.[118]

Though the Bonn summit appeared to offer only faint signs of movement on German issues, more tangible results were registered in other areas. Efforts to address the problems of ethnic Germans in the USSR were making progress.[119] So were plans to improve economic contacts. Both sides were aware that Soviet–West German trade was still barely recovering from its five-year slump. (West German exports had perked up from DM7.5 billion in 1987 to 9.4 billion in 1988, but imports from the Soviet Union continued to slide, from DM7.3 billion to 6.9 billion.)[120] Among the eleven agreements signed during Gorbachev's stay, one accord designed to stimulate and protect West German investments in the USSR and another aimed at training Soviet managerial personnel in the FRG were of particular economic importance.[121] Cooperation proceeded on some sixty joint ventures. Gorbachev's well-received speech before West German business leaders did not eliminate the reservations many of them felt about doing business with the Soviet Union, however. Persistent problems such as the nontransferability of the ruble, inadequately trained cadres, and the absence of Soviet manufactured goods capable of winning a share of Western markets continued to be singled out by the West Germans as barriers to a substantial upturn in Soviet–West German trade.[122]

Although the Bonn summit could be regarded as a success for Gorbachev, the visit did not result in any noticeable breakthroughs on the basic questions of German unification or West Germany's alliance commitments.[123] Neither side, moreover, showed any indication of expecting changes in

118. *Pravda*, Mar. 7, 1989, p. 4. When asked how he could condemn the iron curtain while supporting the Berlin wall, Shevardnadze replied, "These are two completely different things": *Washington Post*, Jan. 20, 1989, p. A1.

119. A record number of 45,000 Germans were allowed to leave the USSR in 1988; about 600,000 more were reported to want to leave. See Sven Steenberg, *Die Russland-Deutschen* (Munich: Langen Müller, 1989), pp. 202–3. For Soviet coverage of the "All-Union Association of Soviet Germans," see *Pravda*, Apr. 2, 1989, p. 1. Approximately 2.2 million Germans were living in the USSR. For rumors of the possible reestablishment of the Volga German Autonomous Republic, see *FAZ*, Mar. 3, 1989, p. 1. See also Gorbachev's remarks at a Central Committee plenum on the need to reestablish the rights of Soviet Germans, *Pravda*, Sept. 20, 1989, pp. 2–3.

120. *Der Spiegel*, June 12, 1989, p. 109. Also Heinrich Machowski, "Ost-West Handel stagniert weiter," *Deutschland Archiv*, no. 12, 1988, pp. 1313–20.

121. *FAZ*, June 13, 1989, p. 2.

122. See the interviews with Otto Wolff von Amerongen in *Süddeutsche Zeitung*, suppl., June 12, 1989, p. 45, and Axel Lebahn of Deutsche Bank in *Der Spiegel*, June 12, 1989, pp. 106–14. Also Nikolaus Piper, "Pommes frites für die Perestrojka," *Die Zeit*, June 9, 1989, pp. 37–38; *FAZ*, June 8, 1989, pp. 15–16; June 12, p. 13; and June 13, pp. 15–16; *Handelsblatt*, June 16–17, 1989, p. 2.

123. For a comprehensive analysis of the summit's results, see Oldenburg, "Sowjetische Deutschland-Politik," n. 96 above.

these areas. While Chancellor Kohl and the Christian Democrats remained committed to reunification in principle, they did not anticipate it in practice. Leading members of the SPD were increasingly urging the renunciation of the FRG's constitutional commitment to reunification, in hopes that formal recognition of the GDR might facilitate more open inter-German contacts and, over time, the liberalization of the East German regime. "Freedom instead of unity" (*Freiheit statt Einheit*) became their motto.[124] Public opinion polls continued to show strong support for reunification among older voters but less among younger ones; most West Germans indicated that they did not expect Germany to be reunified.[125]

Meanwhile, the Soviets remained as sensitive as always to U.S.–West German contradictions on such issues as nuclear modernization, but they recognized that these disputes were essentially about *how* NATO should defend West Germany, not whether it should do so. Public opinion polls showing 90 percent favorable ratings for Gorbachev in West Germany also showed consistently high levels of support for NATO.[126] Furthermore, the Kremlin displayed continuing concern that West Germany was perhaps moving too fast for comfort in the direction of West European integration. Repeated references by the Soviets to 1992 during Gorbachev's visit betrayed fears that intensified West European economic cooperation would leave the USSR and its allies stranded on the less developed side of the continent.

At the same time, however, the Soviets had good reason to cheer the effects of Gorbymania in West Germany. The perception that the USSR posed a threat to the FRG was dwindling, and support for the eventual withdrawal of both Soviet and American troops from German soil was rising rapidly.[127] Hopes that Gorbachev might be ready for including some

124. E.g., Egon Bahr, "Die Chancen der Geschichte in der Teilung suchen," *Deutschland Archiv*, no. 8, 1985, pp. 874–78; Klaus Bölling, "Deutsche Einheit? Deutsche Zweiheit!" *Die Zeit*, June 2, 1989, p. 47.

125. See Gerhard Herdegen, "Perspektiven und Begrenzungen," *Deutschland Archiv*, no. 12, 1987, pp. 1259–73; Richard Hilmer, "DDR und die deutsche Frage," ibid., no. 10, 1988, pp. 1091–1100.

126. A poll conducted in May 1988 suggested that only 5% of West Germans favored withdrawal from NATO, while 69% wanted to maintain the FRG's current status within the alliance; see Weiller, n. 74 above, p. 520. A 1986 survey showed a total 73% in favor of NATO membership, including 85% of Christian Democrats, 83% of the FDP, 68% of the SPD, and 25% of the Greens: *The Germans and America: Current Attitudes* (Bonn: Friedrich Ebert Foundation, 1987), pp. 21–22. For surveys of West German and Soviet attitudes on a range of issues, see Klaus Liedtke, ed., *Der neue Flirt* (Hamburg: Stern, 1989).

127. According to an Emnid survey, the percentage of West Germans who regarded the Soviet threat as "very large" or "large" had fallen from 50% in 1981 to 27% in May 1989, while those who saw the threat as "not so large" or "not to be taken seriously" rose from 48% to 72% in the same period: *Der Spiegel*, June 12, 1989, p. 36. Other polls reported that the percentage of West Germans who would "regret" a U.S. troop pullout had fallen from 59% in 1984 to 38% in 1988, while 76% would "welcome" a simultaneous U.S. and Soviet pullout: Liedtke, *Der neue Flirt*, pp. 141–42.

form of reunification were beginning to soar.[128] In the United States, Britain, and France, meanwhile, fears that the West Germans had an overly romanticized image of Gorbachev were proliferating.

Still, there were growing signs that the Kremlin was reexamining its attitudes on certain critical components of its German policy. There seemed to be unanimous agreement within the primary and secondary elites that Germany would have to remain divided for an indefinite period. As relations with the FRG improved over the course of 1988 and 1989, however, glimmers of change could be detected in Soviet statements on the unity of the German nation, the Berlin wall, self-determination, and the openness of the inter-German border. These statements were ambiguous, qualified, and occasionally conflicting, but it was evident that a serious discussion was going on, and that the Soviet elite might well abandon previously unbudgeable positions should circumstances make such changes necessary or opportune. Few people imagined, however, that the rush of events in the GDR would confront the Kremlin with unavoidable choices on these issues within a matter of months.

Resistance and Collapse in the GDR

From the outset, Gorbachev's reform program was meant to stimulate reformist impulses throughout the Soviet bloc, at least in the realm of economic policy. Gorbachev signaled his approval of economic restructuring in Eastern Europe by openly favoring General Wojciech Jaruzelski over the other bloc leaders. Jaruzelski's regime was slowly emerging from international ostracism after the formal cancellation of martial law in 1983, and was in the process of considering various proposals for economic decentralization. As Gorbachev's own reform drive took a more radical turn in 1987, the message to the other bloc leaders became clearer. Ligachev praised Hungary's economic experiments; Gerasimov, asked to explain the difference between Gorbachev's reforms and those of the Prague Spring, replied dryly, "Nineteen years."[129] Soviet theoreticians increasingly acknowledged differences in the interests of socialist states.[130]

While flashing these unambiguous signals in favor of change, the Gorbachev leadership was careful not to push its communist allies too hard.

128. E.g., see Günter Kiessling, *Neutralität ist kein Verrat* (Erlangen: Straube, 1989). Kiessling was a retired Bundesehr general and NATO official. Also Wolfgang Seiffert, *Die Deutschen und Gorbatschow* (Erlangen: Straube, 1989).

129. *Washington Post*, Apr. 26, 1987, p. A22; *New York Times*, Apr. 12, 1987, p. A12. See also the appeals by members of the Soviet secondary elite for a reconsideration of the Prague Spring in *Washington Post*, Nov. 5, 1987, pp. A1, A35, and Nov. 6, pp. A23–24.

130. Margot Light, *The Soviet Theory of International Relations* (New York: St. Martin's Press, 1988), pp. 305–8.

The Soviets wanted stability in the region, not disruption. Moreover, Gorbachev already had his hands full with the intractable reform process at home. The East Europeans were expected to assist the Soviets by revitalizing their own economies and by improving the quality of goods exported to the USSR. The Kremlin's directives to its COMECON partners on the latter score were precise. They applied with particular appropriateness to the GDR, Moscow's main trading partner.[131]

As the Soviet Union's reform effort swung from concentration on economic restructuring to a more radical political transformation, the pressures on the well-entrenched party elites in East-Central Europe to adopt similar measures intensified considerably. The Kremlin probably hoped that the democratization process in Eastern Europe, if undertaken promptly and managed skillfully, could be channeled in the directions the local party leaders desired.

The Soviets' experiences had revealed, however, that the beast of democracy, once released, was hard to control. Demands for independence in the Baltic republics represented only one troublesome aspect of what could happen when democratic aspirations were given free rein. Faced with the Soviet example, Hungarian leaders decided to race ahead of public opinion in the spring of 1989 by calling for free elections and a multiparty system, hoping to salvage some semblance of influence by reconstituting the communist party along social democratic lines. The Soviets made it clear that the USSR was not prepared to follow a similar course, but it would not interfere in Hungary's domestic affairs.[132] Jaruzelski gradually gave in to Solidarity's commanding position in Polish society by joining in a power-sharing arrangement based on partially contested elections held in June. Lacking any means short of violence to limit the scope of these democratic tendencies, the Soviet leadership reconciled itself to them, recognizing that any show of force would terminate the promising East-West détente and quite possibly jeopardize the reform process in the Soviet Union itself. Thus the Kremlin increasingly backed away from the Brezhnev doctrine on military intervention in socialist countries. Gorbachev affirmed his opposition to intervention "under any pretext whatsoever" on a visit to Yugoslavia in March 1988.[133] Similar statements would follow.

131. Siegfried Kupper, "Wachsender Druck—unterschiedliche Interessen," *Deutschland Archiv*, no. 1, 1987, pp. 56–61; Wolf Oschlies, "Heisst RGW 'Region Gegenseitigen Widerwillens'?" ibid., no. 4, 1987, pp. 415–20. For a report on Soviet dissatisfaction with East German imports, see *Die Welt*, Sept. 29, 1988, p. 8. Cf. Nikolai Ryzhkov's call for a "new qualitative level of cooperation" between the USSR and the GDR, and Stoph's noncommittal response, in *Pravda*, June 24, 1987, p. 4. Also Ryzhkov's critique of COMECON economies in *Pravda*, July 6, 1988, p. 4.
132. See the report on Aleksandr Yakovlev's meeting with Hungarian party chief Grosz in *Pravda*, Mar. 26, 1989, p. 4.
133. *Pravda*, Mar. 19, 1988, p. 1.

Although some members of the secondary elite openly suggested that a neutralized Eastern Europe might be an acceptable development,[134] Soviet leaders displayed no interest in pushing the pace of democratization in the region too quickly. Instead they preferred to let events take their natural course, apparently on the assumption that time was on the side of the reformers. Their optimal strategy was to save what could be saved of Soviet influence and party authority in the Warsaw Pact countries by encouraging local reforms and refraining from overt intervention. In view of the region's occasionally turbulent postwar history, however, this strategy inevitably courted the risk that if popular opinion were given free rein, nothing resembling Soviet-style rule could be saved, not even reformed socialist regimes.

No doubt in full awareness of these risks, the Honecker regime resisted Moscow's pressures for change. The East German leadership was determined to hold fast to the same centrist-conservative course that had managed to get the GDR through the rough waters of the first half of the 1980s with its political system intact and its international prestige flying at high mast. In practice, this meant pursuing an energetic diplomacy of détente and arms control externally and a firm but occasionally flexible policy of party domination internally. In comparison with the Brezhnev, Andropov, and Chernenko regimes, Honecker's was a model of progressive détente-oriented centrism. Once Gorbachev began pursuing his own brand of détente and lunged full tilt toward radical restructuring, however, the Honecker regime assumed the proportions of an ossified relic of communist conservatism.

As the Gorbachev challenge intensified, Honecker reaffirmed the centrist bearings of his ruling coalition by making some important personnel changes. In the fall of 1985 Konrad Naumann was stripped of all his official positions and was replaced as chief of the East Berlin party organization by Günter Schabowski, who now left his post as editor of *Neues Deutschland*. Stories circulated about Naumann's public inebriation and a stormy encounter with Honecker, but his outspoken opposition to political and economic cooperation with West Germany had already cast him as a critic of Honecker's policies. The military retained its place in the party hierarchy after the death of General Heinz Hoffmann in December 1985. The new defense minister, General Heinz Kessler, became a voting Politburo member several months later. Other personnel shifts in 1985 and 1986 further strengthened Honecker's hand.[135] Egon Krenz, the dauphin, also benefited

134. O. N. Bogomolov suggested that Hungarian neutrality might be acceptable, but he later backed off from this position, saying it was only "hypothetical": FBIS, *Soviet Union*, Apr. 26, 1989, p. 39. Gorbachev and Grosz rejected a neutral status for Hungary: ibid., Mar. 27, 1989, p. 25.

135. *Der Spiegel*, Dec. 9, 1985, p. 15. On the continuing importance of the East German military, see Dale R. Herspring, "The Military Factor in East German Soviet Policy," *Slavic*

from these moves. Conspicuous by their absence from Honecker's inner circle were any clearly identifiable Gorbachev-style reformers. Krenz hewed to the party line in public, as did Schabowski. Hans Modrow, already reputed to be a potential reformer, failed to break into the Politburo while Honecker was in charge. Modrow even drew an implicit rebuke in June 1989 when his Dresden party organization was criticized in the Politburo's report to the Central Committee.[136]

Honecker's confidence in his domestic and foreign policy course was undergirded by the stability of his own power base in the SED and by his awareness of opposition to Gorbachev's reform programs in the USSR.[137] Initially, however, Honecker welcomed Gorbachev's accession to power in the expectation that the GDR's détente policy might finally receive Moscow's blessing. The SED chief eagerly greeted Chancellor Kohl at Chernenko's funeral, and the two leaders reaffirmed their commitment to peace and cooperation.[138] Over the next several months, Honecker took a visibly more positive attitude toward the FRG than the Gorbachev regime.[139]

Once Gorbachev's diplomacy got into high gear, however, Honecker embraced it. The East German leadership enthusiastically supported most of the main arms-control initiatives advanced by Moscow in the latter half of the decade.[140] Honecker followed up most Soviet proposals with demarches of his own designed to pressure the Kohl government into responding positively to Moscow's suggestions. The SED leaders showed themselves to be particularly eager to rid their territory of the new missiles that had been installed as "countermeasures" to NATO's INF deployments.[141]

Review 47 (Spring 1988): 89–107. The first secretaries of the Bezirk party organizations of Magdeburg (Werner Eberlein), Karl-Marx-Stadt (Siegfried Lorenz), and Erfurt (Gerhard Müller) became candidate Politburo members in November 1985, and Herbert Häber retired because of illness. Eberlein and Lorenz became full Politburo members in April 1986, along with H.-J. Böhme, first secretary of Halle.

136. *ND,* June 23, 1989, p. 8. For conflicting views of Modrow at this time, see, in *Deutschland Archiv,* Frank Loeser, "Demokratisierung—auch in der DDR?" no. 9, 1987, p. 935, and Karl Wilhelm Fricke, "Die Nachfolge Honeckers komplizierte sich," no. 10, 1988, p. 1036.

137. A. James McAdams, "The New Logic in Soviet-GDR Relations," *Problems of Communism* 37 (September–October 1988): 47–70.

138. *ND,* Mar. 13, 1985, p. 2.

139. In an interview in *Le Monde* in June, Honecker trivialized West German appeals for reunification as an "obligatory exercise" for FRG politicians, "most of whom have no interest in the birth in Europe of a pan-German state": *ND,* June 8–9, 1985, p. 3. *Pravda's* report on the interview on June 9 did not refer to these remarks, but focused on Honecker's criticism of other aspects of West German policy. Earlier Gorbachev had warned of the "increased dangers of West German revanchism": *Pravda,* May 9, 1985, p. 3. See also Honecker's interview in the *Saarbrücker Zeitung,* reprinted in *ND,* Nov. 13, 1985, p. 3. Cf. also the articles by Honecker and Konstantin Rusakov in *Einheit,* nos. 4–5, 1985, pp. 291–305.

140. Reportedly a group of SED leaders led by Kurt Hager were opposed to Gorbachev's plans for unilateral Soviet and East German troop reductions in East Germany in the fall of 1988. See Oldenburg, "Sowjetsiche Deutschland-Politik," n. 96 above, p. 37.

141. See Honecker's interview in *Die Zeit,* Jan. 31, 1986, pp. 3–7.

Even such hard-liners as Erich Mielke touted the "securing of peace" (*Friedenssicherung*) as the overarching question in inter-German relations.[142] The East German secondary elite amplified these sentiments, stressing the need for a "security partnership" with West Germany and reasserting Honecker's call for a "worldwide coalition of reason."[143] In conjunction with this emphasis on the peace theme, the East German leaders provided explicit support for Gorbachev's summit meetings with President Reagan at a time when the Soviet leadership was divided on the issue.[144]

Unquestionably the Honecker coalition's unstinting emphasis on the twin themes of peace and disarmament served urgent domestic political ends. The peace movement that had sprung into existence in East Germany as the INF crisis gathered steam had grown by the middle of the decade into a vital component of the GDR's increasingly vocal oppositionist scene.[145] By co-opting the peace issue and encouraging Moscow to address it effectively, the Honecker leadership clearly hoped to stanch the spread of oppositionist activity and shore up the GDR's internal stability.

East Germany's peace policy also smoothed the path to economic cooperation with the FRG. Of all the factors motivating the GDR's policy of détente with Bonn, access to economic assistance of various kinds remained the single most important one. While the GDR could certainly have survived without the influx of West German trade, credits, lump-sum payments, and other forms of help, both its domestic economy and its international commercial and financial positions would have felt a significant pinch.[146] Internal economic conditions were deteriorating noticeably in the latter part of the decade. An aging industrial plant, runaway pollution, and a persistent inability to supply what Honecker himself called "the thousand little things" of daily life undercut the regime's achievements in housing and

---

142. *ND,* May 8, 1987, p. 2.

143. E.g., in *Horizont,* Max Schmidt and Gerhard Basler, "Weltweite Koalition der Vernunft—Überlebenschance der Menschheit," no. 6, 1985, pp. 3–4; Gerhard Zazworka, "Sowjetische Friedensoffensive weithin spürbar," no. 2, 1986, pp. 8–9; Gerhard Hahn, "DDR-Aussenpolitik—zuverlässig, berechenbar, initiativreich," no. 5, 1986, pp. 3–4. In *IPW-Berichte,* Max Schmidt and Wolfgang Schwarz, "Frieden und Sicherheit im nuklearkosmischen Zeitalter," no. 9, 1986, pp. 1–12 (pt. 1), and no. 10, 1986, pp. 1–9 (pt. 2). See Honecker's speech in *ND,* Apr. 29, 1985, p. 3.

144. See the statements by Honecker in *ND,* Nov. 23–24, 1985, p. 1; Dec. 31, p. 1; June 14–15, 1986, pp. 1–2; Nov. 22–23, pp. 3–4; Dec. 31, p. 1. Also the statements by Stoph, *ND,* Nov. 30–Dec. 1, 1985, pp. 3–5, and Fischer, Feb. 4, 1987, p. 3.

145. Vladimir Tismaneanu, "Nascent Civil Society in the German Democratic Republic," *Problems of Communism* 38 (March–June 1989): 90–111.

146. One estimate concluded that economic transfers from the FRG to the GDR exclusive of trade benefits now totaled approximately DM3.7 billion per year. Converted into East German marks, this amount roughly equaled 10% of the GDR's net material product, or two-thirds of its annual outlays for industrial investments. It also exceeded the GDR's published defense budget figure. See Jeffrey H. Michel, "Economic Exchanges Specific to the Two German States," *Studies in Comparative Communism* 20 (Spring 1987): 73–83.

social welfare, reinforcing the population's lingering sense that the GDR would continue to lag far behind West German living standards for a long time to come. The politically important state subsidies for rent and staple items, devouring nearly 20 percent of annual budgetary expenditures, were becoming increasingly onerous.[147] Although the GDR had managed to improve its debt position remarkably by the middle of the decade, its debts began increasing again as foreign currency surpluses declined.[148]

These and other economic considerations dictated a cooperative relationship with West Germany. However, the GDR's unwillingness to undertake significant economic reforms (particularly in its price system and trade practices) and its reluctance to invite West German firms to set up joint ventures stood in the way of a substantial improvement in inter-German economic relations. So did the GDR's costly import substitution policy for goods it preferred not to obtain primarily from West Germany.[149]

Moreover, the Honecker regime's outreach to Bonn was not without political complications. The Gera demands, for instance, were still on the table. Although the GDR did not make Bonn's acceptance of these demands a prerequisite for doing business on other issues (any more than it made cooperation with West Germany contingent on Bonn's rejection of SDI), it still insisted that the Kohl government formally recognize GDR citizenship and come to terms on the Elbe border, the Salzgitter registration center, and the establishment of full-scale embassies. (The SPD was moving in the GDR's direction on these issues.) In addition, the GDR stuck to its hard-and-fast positions on the status of Berlin, and temporarily complicated matters by increasing the outflow of asylum-seekers from third countries who wished to emigrate to West Berlin via East Germany.[150]

Even more fatefully, Honecker staked his political credibility on the preservation of the Berlin wall. Whenever the question of the wall came up,

147. On the GDR economy in this period, see, e.g., in *Deutschland Archiv,* Hans-Dieter Schulz, "Die DDR braucht 'ein kräftiges Wirtschaftswachstum,'" no. 3, 1986, pp. 233–36; Doris Cornelsen, "Zur Lage der DDR-Wirtschaft an der Jahreswende 1986/87," no. 3, 1987, pp. 292–98, and "DDR-Wirtschaft im ersten Halbjahr 1988," no. 10, 1988, pp. 1083–91; and Wolfgang Stinglwagner, "Kein Anlass zur Euphorie," no. 2, 1989, pp. 129–33.

148. *FAZ,* Aug. 5, 1987, p. 9. On the GDR's foreign debts, see Paul Frenzel, "Das sozialistische Geldsystem der DDR," *Deutschland Archiv,* no. 7, 1988, pp. 765–77.

149. Harry Maier and Siegrid Maier, "Möglichkeiten einer Intensivierung des innerdeutschen Handels," *Deutschland Archiv,* no. 2, 1989, pp. 180–91; Fritz Homann, "Innerdeutscher Handel und EG-Binnenmarkt," ibid., no. 3, 1989, pp. 301–8. See also the contributions by Arthur A. Stahnke and Irwin L. Collier, Jr., in Joint Economic Committee of the U.S. Congress, *Pressures for Reform in the East European Economies* (Washington, D.C.: U.S. Government Printing Office, 1989), 2:242–90. The GDR boasted that it produced 80% of the items in the world's assortment of manufactured goods.

150. See in *Deutschland Archiv,* Peter Jochen Winters, "Der Asylantenstrom als Hebel gegen Berlin," no. 9, 1986, pp. 913–15; Ilse Spittmann, "Eine vernünftige Entscheidung," no. 10, 1986, pp. 1025–27; and Wolfgang Seiffert, "Zur Rolle Berlins in der politischen Strategie der SED," no. 12, 1986, pp. 1273–74.

Honecker invariably insisted that the barrier would disappear only when the conditions that had required it to be built in the first place were eliminated.[151] He left little doubt that these conditions, which included the West's political infiltration and economic "plundering" of the GDR, were not expected to disappear soon. To drive home the point, Honecker declared in January 1989 that the wall "will still be there in 50 and 100 years."[152]

In response to West German pleas for an end to the killing of East Germans attempting to flee over the wall or the equally well-fortified inter-German frontier, the GDR continued to dismantle automatic firing devices at the borders. Honecker himself declared in a speech celebrating the Berlin wall's twenty-fifth anniversary that it was "better to negotiate with each other ten, yes, a hundred times than to shoot each other once." A year later, the East German border guards' standing shoot-to-kill orders were reportedly rescinded, a position confirmed by General Kessler in the fall of 1988. Nevertheless, an East German citizen was shot and killed at the Berlin wall while attempting to escape in February 1989, the seventy-eighth confirmed fatality since the structure went up in 1961.[153]

On the more positive side of the ledger, the GDR allowed tens of thousands of East Germans to emigrate permanently to the West, and eased travel restrictions on persons under retirement age who had relatives in West Germany.[154] Honecker and other key Politburo members met with government and opposition leaders from the FRG on a continuing basis. The culminating event in this flow of contacts was Erich Honecker's visit to the Federal Republic in September 1987.

By the time the SED chief was finally ready to embark on his first official trip to the FRG, the relationship between the GDR and the Soviet Union in the conduct of policy toward West Germany had changed dramatically. In September 1984, the last time Honecker had put off his trip, the Soviets were locked in a tense confrontation with Bonn, while the Honecker regime was straining to salvage what it could of détente. Soon after switching

151. See, e.g., Honecker's interviews reprinted in ND, June 8–9, 1985, p. 3; Jan. 14, 1986, p. 2; Jan. 31, 1986, p. 5; Mar. 19, 1986, p. 6; June 25, 1986, p. 3; and June 11, 1989, p. A30.

152. ND, Jan. 20, 1989, p. 5.

153. ND, Aug. 14, 1986, p. 1; FBIS, Eastern Europe, Aug. 24, 1987, p. G1; Kessler's interview in Die Zeit, reprinted in ND, Oct. 1–2, 1988, pp. 9–10; and Washington Post, Mar. 14, 1989, p. A20. Honecker denied the shooting incident and insisted there was no shoot-to-kill order: Ilse Spittmann, "Sozialismus in den Farben der DDR," Deutschland Archiv, no. 3, 1989, pp. 242–43.

154. After the wave of some 35,000 legal émigrés in 1984, the annual flow fell to 18,752 in 1985, 19,982 in 1986, 11,459 in 1987, and 29,033 in 1988. The number of East Germans below retirement age allowed to make short-term visits to the West increased from 66,000 in 1985 to 573,000 in 1986, 1.2 million in 1987, and more than 1.3 million in 1988. See the articles by Ilse Spittmann in Deutschland Archiv, no. 8, 1987, p. 786; no. 1, 1988, p. 2; and no. 1, 1989, p. 2; and by Thomas Ammer in ibid., no. 11, 1989, pp. 1206–8.

Soviet foreign policy onto the tracks of East-West cooperation, Mikhail Gorbachev reasserted the Soviet Union's primacy over the GDR in directing the Warsaw Pact's policy toward Bonn.[155] As a consequence, East Germany lost its privileged status as the savior of détente in the Soviet camp, and Honecker's room for more independent foreign policy maneuver was significantly constricted. More generally, as Moscow's relations with the United States and the leading West European states warmed up, the role of small and medium-sized states in preserving détente became superfluous. Honecker and other East German officials kept up an active exchange of visits with West European leaders after Gorbachev came to power, but these contacts were now relegated to the task of supporting Soviet initiatives instead of forging a relatively separate channel of East bloc diplomacy, as they had done during the confrontationist period in the Kremlin's relations with the West.[156]

In a similar vein, the Gorbachev regime expected the GDR to pursue its relations with the FRG in full conformity with Soviet priorities. Honecker did not get the green light from the Kremlin to go to West Germany until after Gorbachev's announcement in late February 1987 delinking an INF settlement from SDI. The Soviets may even have been responsible for preventing Honecker from joining with West Berlin Mayor Eberhard Diepgen in ceremonies scheduled to take place in both parts of the divided city in the spring of 1987 in commemoration of Berlin's 750th anniversary.[157]

The Honecker visit in September 1987 produced no major breakthroughs. Nevertheless, Honecker aroused interest with his comment that the day would eventually come when the common border would no longer divide the two German states but would unite them, much like the border between the GDR and Poland. Moscow's ambassador in Bonn, Yulii Kvitsinskii, said that he knew of no official Soviet reaction to Honecker's statement, but suggested that the character of the existing borders would change only after "a long process."[158]

One of the SED's most energetic efforts to retain a role for itself in the Gorbachev regime's evolving détente strategy was its dialogue with the SPD.[159] To the dismay of the Kohl government, which charged the opposition party with conducting its own foreign policy, the Social Democrats and the SED signed several agreements in this period. Most of them represented

155. On these points see Johannes Kuppe, "Marschroute zum XI. Parteitag festgelegt," *Deutschland Archiv*, no. 1, 1986, pp. 1–6.

156. Fred Oldenburg, "Die DDR im 'Haus Europa,'" *Berichte des Bundesinstituts für ostwissenschaftliche und internationale Studien*, no. 11, 1989, pp. 43–46.

157. *Washington Post*, Apr. 14, 1987, p. A15.

158. *ND*, Sept. 11, 1987, p. 5; FBIS, *Soviet Union*, Sept. 15, 1987, p. 24.

159. For an extensive analysis, see Ann L. Phillips, *Seeds of Change in the German Democratic Republic* (Washington, D.C.: American Institute for Contemporary German Studies, 1989).

proposed draft treaties on arms-control questions, including one on the establishment of a European zone free of chemical weapons, another proposing a nuclear-weapons-free zone, and another designed to establish a military "zone of trust" in Central Europe. The Czech Communist Party was included in additional talks with the SPD and SED.[160] Some of the ideas that emerged from these interchanges were proposed by the GDR to the West German government as a basis for negotiations at the official level.

While the Honecker regime pursued these initiatives with the dual purpose of enhancing its own reputation in the East-West arena and of rendering Moscow valuable assistance in advancing the aims of Soviet arms diplomacy, the Soviets reacted to the SPD-SED dialogue with a coolness that, in the eyes of one close observer, reflected their suspicions about inter-German cooperation.[161] One sign of the Kremlin's distrust came in June 1988, when the Soviets sent a low-level delegation headed by Minister of Culture Pyotr Demichev to a conference on nuclear-free zones in Europe which the Honecker regime had staged with great fanfare, and to which it had invited representatives from the SPD and other West European parties. Moscow's suspiciousness was more than amply matched by East Berlin's. Honecker kept a noticeable distance from the Soviet concept of the "common European home" until 1987, apparently out of uncertainty about the implications of the term for the Kremlin's German policy. On those occasions when Honecker or other GDR officials got around to invoking the "common home" theme, they usually emphasized its consistency with the need for all Europeans to recognize the postwar reality of the two German states.[162]

The East German elites were similarly reluctant to endorse certain other aspects of the Gorbachev regime's new thinking. Though they tended to favor the main tenets of Moscow's new security doctrines—Honecker himself pointedly reminded a Soviet audience of his own efforts as early as 1983 to promote military détente—they were clearly perturbed by recent Soviet efforts to minimize the ideological differences between socialism and capitalism. Honecker informed his hosts in Bonn that the two systems were as irreconcilable as fire and water.[163] Accordingly, members of the East

160. *ND*, June 20, 1985, p. 3; Oct. 22, 1986, p. 4; July 8, 1988, p. 5; Apr. 6, 1988, p. 1.
161. Heinz Timmermann, "Gorbatschow, die 'Eurolinke' und die SED," *Deutschland Archiv*, no. 3, 1987, pp. 285–92. Timmermann was a foreign policy adviser to the SPD. For a Soviet reaction to the dialogue with Social Democrats which stressed Soviet conceptions of new thinking and suggested that aspects of the SPD-SED dialogue were already outdated, see A. Galkin and Y. Krasin, "K novomu kachestvu dialoga," *MEMO*, no. 2, 1989, pp. 87–92.
162. See Honecker's speeches in *ND*, May 30–31, 1987, p. 3; Nov. 5, 1987, p. 3; Dec. 17, 1987, p. 1; Sept. 15, 1988, p. 3; Oct. 1–2, 1988, p. 3; and Fischer's speech in *ND*, Dec. 3–4, 1988, p. 15. Also Max Schmidt and Wolfgang Schwarz, "Das gemeinsame Haus Europa—Realitäten, Herausforderungen, Perspektiven," *IPW-Berichte*, no. 9, 1988, pp. 1–10 (pt. 1), and no. 10, 1988, pp. 1–11 (pt. 2).
163. *ND*, Nov. 5, 1987, p. 3; Sept. 8, 1987, p. 3.

German secondary elite gave considerable weight to the notion that disarmament and cooperation with the West by no means implied a slackening of the ideological struggle; socialism, in this view, retained not only its uniqueness but also its inherent superiority as a social system.[164]

The dangers of weakening the ideological dividing line between East and West became particularly acute for the SED as the result of a paper signed with the West German Social Democrats in 1987. Titled "The Clash of Ideologies and Common Security," the paper was intended to lay out a set of principles to guide future relations between the two parties. Drawing on memories of the historic disputes between the German Communists and the Social Democrats, the SPD and the SED acknowledged their continuing differences but each agreed to recognize the other as "capable of peace" (*friedensfähig*) and to eliminate reciprocal "enemy images." The paper aroused a positive response within the ranks of the SED. Before long, however, the SED hierarchy was reaffirming the class struggle. "Our image of the enemy is clear," intoned Kurt Hager, who added that "imperialism" was not by nature capable of peace. Otto Reinhold, who negotiated the paper for the SED, also sought to dampen its implications of ideological accommodation, and Honecker referred to the possibility of abrupt turnabouts in East-West relations, a warning not heard since the contentious first years of the decade.[165]

The ambivalence inherent in the SED leadership's approach to the West, with its two-sided emphasis on military-economic cooperation and ideological confrontation, provided a bit of latitude for members of the East German secondary elite to debate some of the key issues. While some stressed conservative notions, such as the unrelenting "aggressive essence of imperialism," others took advantage of the openings offered by Honecker's overtures to the Kohl government and by the SPD-SED paper to argue that "imperialism" was in fact capable of peace. Some analysts even viewed

164. See, e.g., the discussions in *IPW-Berichte*, no. 7, 1986, pp. 1–15; no. 10, 1986, pp. 42–48; no. 12, 1987, pp. 1–12. Also Gerhard Basler and Frank Berg, "Bedingungen, Erfordernisse und Tendenzen der Auseinandersetzung zwischen Sozialismus und Imperialismus," ibid., no. 6, 1987, pp. 14–21; Max Schmidt and Wolfgang Schwarz, "Neue Anforderungen an Sicherheitsdenken und Sicherheitspolitik—umfassende internationale Sicherheit als Erfordernis unserer Zeit," ibid., no. 9, 1987, pp. 1–11 (pt. 1), and no. 10, 1987, pp. 6–16 (pt. 2); and Hans Pirsch, "Antikommunismus in der aussenpolitischen Strategiebildung," ibid., no. 10, 1988, pp. 37–41.
165. *ND*, Aug. 28, 1987, p. 3; Oct. 28, 1987, p. 3; Nov. 11, 1987, p. 3 (Reinhold); Oct. 27, 1987, p. 3 (Honecker). See also, in *Einheit*, Otto Reinhold and Manfred Banaschak, "Der Streit der Ideologien und die gemeinsame Sicherheit," no. 9, 1987, pp. 771–80; and Reinhold, "Zur marxistisch-leninistischen Gesellschaftskonzeption unserer Partei," nos. 10–11, 1987, pp. 947–53, and "Authentische Auskünfte über die Politik der KPdSU," no. 4, 1988, pp. 341–47. Also Burkhard Koch, "Streit der Ideologien im nuklear-kosmischen Zeitalter," *IPW-Berichte*, no. 3, 1988, pp. 22–27; Harald Kleinschmid, "Ruckzugsgefechte der alten Männer," *Deutschland Archiv*, no. 11, 1987, pp. 1121–23; and Ilse Spittmann, "Irritationen zur Jahreswende," *Deutschland Archiv*, no. 1, 1988, pp. 1–4.

certain West German conservatives as well disposed to peace and cooperation.[166] The margins for foreign policy debate in open forums were growing
narrower in the GDR in these years as the Honecker regime increasingly
emphasized its conservative side. Within the limits of the prevailing centrist-conservative consensus, however, there was still room for some discussion within the secondary elite, some of whose members may have been
sympathetic to aspects of Gorbachev's reform program.[167]

While the SED leadership wrestled with the ideological challenge from
the Social Democrats, it was precisely these pressures for change emanating
from Moscow that represented the more urgent problem. The Honecker regime responded to the challenge of perestroika and democratization with a
reaffirmation of its own brand of socialism in terms that sharply demarcated it from developments in the Soviet Union.[168] When Gorbachev spoke
of the need for restructuring, the East Germans heralded the SED's success
in implementing "the unity of social and economic policy" ever since the
Eighth SED Congress of 1971. When queried about the relevance of the Soviet reforms for the GDR, Hager replied that it was not necessary to repaper
one's wall just because the neighbors were doing it.[169] Press coverage of Soviet events singled out the difficulties facing perestroika and the opposition
it was encountering, while glossing over or ignoring entirely the sweeping
changes it was bringing about. Certain Soviet publications were forbidden
to circulate in the GDR.[170] Meanwhile, East Germany's ruling coalition

---

166. In addition to the sources in n. 161, see Rolf Reissig, "Die Notwendigkeit des Friedens
und der heutige Kapitalismus," *Einheit,* no. 2, 1988, pp. 120–25 (on the "differentiation
process" in capitalism); and in *IPW-Berichte,* Lutz Maier, "Das Monopolkapital und die
Friedensfrage," no. 11, 1987, pp. 1–12, and "Aggressivität und Friedensfähigkeit des heutigen
Imperialismus," no. 9, 1988, pp. 11–19. For differentiated approaches noting both opponents
and proponents of détente among West German conservatives, see, in *IPW-Berichte,* Burkhard
Koch, "Der Einfluss politischer Ideologie auf die aussenpolitische Strategie im gegenwärtigen
Imperialismus," no. 12, 1985, pp. 14–19; "Konservatismus—Ideologie und Konzept gegen
gesellschaftlichen Fortschritt," no. 3, 1986, pp. 1–10; "Konservatismus der 80'er Jahre im
Widerstreit zu Frieden, Demokratie und sozialem Fortschritt," no. 11, 1986, pp. 38–40;
Steffen Mehlich, "BRD-Konservative zur Systemauseinandersetzung im Nuklearzeitalter," no.
3, 1987, pp. 19–24; "BRD-Konservatismus: Vom Abschreckungsdenken zur Akzeptanz
gegenseitiger Sicherheit," no. 2, 1988, pp. 10–15; Andre Helmer, "Widersprüchliche Posi-
tionen zur Abrüstung in der BRD-Regierungskoalition," no. 8, 1988, pp. 16–20.

167. For a reference to the GDR's readiness to compromise on human rights issues, see
Max Schmidt, "Die Aussenpolitik der DDR, die EG und die gesamteuropäischen Sicherheit-
sinteressen," *IPW-Berichte,* no. 2, 1987, pp. 1–8. On the need for adjustments in Marxist-
Leninist theory to explain capitalism's "capability for peace," see Dieter Klein, "Politö-
konomische Grundlagen für einen friedensfähigen Kapitalismus," ibid., no. 2, 1988, pp. 1–9.
For a positive view of joint ventures, see Christine Kulke-Fiedler and Paul Freiburg, "Joint
Ventures in der Ost-West-Wirtschaftszusammenarbeit," ibid., no. 6, 1988, pp. 44–47.

168. Fred Oldenburg, "The Impact of Gorbachev's Reforms in the GDR," *Berichte des
Bundesinstituts für ostwissenschaftliche und internationale Studien,* no. 25, 1988, and "Repair or Reform in the GDR?" ibid., no. 53, 1988.

169. Originally published in *Stern,* the interview was reprinted in *ND,* Apr. 10, 1987, p. 3.

170. Walter Süss, "Kein Vorbild für die DDR," *Deutschland Archiv,* no. 9, 1986, pp. 967–
88, and "Perestrojka oder Ausreise," ibid., no. 3, 1989, pp. 286–301.

formed a solid front of support for Honecker's centrist-conservative line, placing equal stress on both the desirability of arms reductions and the glories of "socialism in the colors of the GDR."[171] Even Walter Ulbricht was exhumed from his posthumous status as a nonperson and lauded in the pages of *Neues Deutschland*.[172]

By the end of 1988, the embattled Honecker was assuming a combative tone that testified to the enormous pressures confronting his regime. Rejecting any deviation from the SED's present course as "anarchy," Honecker offered an almost elegiac tribute to his entire generation of German communists, the generation that had survived fascism and built the GDR. While acknowledging haughtily that the GDR wore "no halo of infallibility," Honecker listed a string of achievements that reached bizarre lengths when he claimed that the GDR's living standards were basically higher than those of West Germany.[173] Other signs that the aging leader was losing touch with political reality would not be long in coming.

The threat to the SED leadership's conception of socialism was only one aspect of Gorbachev's challenge to the Honecker regime; the other came from Moscow's reactivated policy of rapprochement with West Germany. Honecker openly questioned Gorbachev's suggestion that Germany's divided status might be altered in a hundred years, and he invited Falin to renegotiate the quadripartite agreement if he felt it could be improved. The East Germans also reacted furiously to Dashichev's public comments on the Berlin wall, and they prevailed upon *Literaturnaya gazeta* to print a rejoinder to Pochivalov's article by Deputy Minister of Culture Klaus Höpcke, who stressed the differences between East and West Germans as opposed to what they had in common. To counter Soviet talk of the unity of the German nation, East German commentators resurrected the notion of two German nations.[174]

Matters reached an acute phase in East Berlin's ties with Moscow at the time of Gorbachev's visit to Bonn in the spring of 1989. *Neues Deutschland* played down the visit, and East German officials avoided any mention of "self-determination."[175] The Soviet leader's remarks on the Berlin wall

171. See, e.g., in *ND*, the speeches by Axen, Nov. 21, 1986, pp. 3–8; Dohlus, June 19, 1987, pp. 3–8, and Oct. 21, 1988, pp. 3–4; Felfe, Dec. 17, 1987, pp. 3–9; Hager, June 10, 1988, pp. 3–9, and Oct. 29–30, 1988, pp. 9–11; Hermann, June 21, 1985, pp. 6–11, and June 23, 1989, pp. 3–9; Jarowinsky, Nov. 23–24, 1985, pp. 3–7; Mittag, Dec. 15, 1988, pp. 5–6; and Stoph, June 18, 1986, pp. 4–5, and Dec. 2, 1988, pp. 3–10. See also Honecker's speech at the IXth SED Congress, Apr. 18, 1986, pp. 1–9; Feb. 7–8, 1987, pp. 3–4; and Feb. 13–14, 1988, pp. 3–11.

172. *ND*, June 30, 1988, p. 3.

173. *ND*, Dec. 2, 1988, pp. 3–10. Also Johannes L. Kuppe, "Offensiv in die Defensive," *Deutschland Archiv*, no. 1, 1989, pp. 1–7.

174. *ND*, Sept. 29, 1987, p. 4; June 10, 1988, p. 2; *Literaturnaya gazeta*, Oct. 12, 1988, p. 14; Gerhard Basler and Jürgen Hofmann, "Zwei deutsche Staaten und Nationen im europäischen Haus," *Einheit*, no. 2, 1989, pp. 170–76.

175. See Oskar Fischer's remarks during Shevardnadze's visit in *ND*, June 10, 1989, p. 10.

had created consternation and bewilderment in the GDR's foreign policy elite concerning Moscow's ultimate intentions; there was even uncertainty about whether the Soviets were reconsidering their position on unification. Communications between the two allies, severely damaged in 1983, had yet to be satisfactorily restored.[176]

Nor were the GDR's relations with its East European allies any better. Hungary, which had provided welcome sustenance for Honecker's détente policy earlier in the decade, was obliquely charged with risking "counter-revolution" as its political reforms advanced.[177] Jaruzelski's accommodation with Solidarity was hardly to the SED's liking. Worse still, Gorbachev's decision to tolerate these developments created a nightmare for the East German authorities. Of all the countries of the socialist bloc, the GDR was potentially the most easily democratized. In addition to the existing oppositionist groupings, political parties analogous to those in West Germany could be organized in rapid order. Signs of democratic yearnings surfaced openly in May, as church and oppositionist figures charged the SED with electoral fraud in the latest uncontested elections to the Volkskammer.

In a desperate grasp for allies, the Honecker regime latched on to China. East German leaders, including Egon Krenz, refrained from condemning the Beijing government's use of force against the pro-democracy demonstrators.[178] On June 12, the day Gorbachev arrived in Bonn, East Berlin welcomed Chinese Foreign Minister Qian Qichen. The GDR's diminishing assortment of friends in the rest of the socialist world was reduced to the antireformist regimes of Czechoslovakia and Romania and the likes of Albania, Nicaragua, and Ethiopia. Any hopes Honecker may have entertained for Gorbachev's removal from power were doused once again in September, as the Soviet leader maneuvered Shcherbitskii and several other figures out of the leadership. Similarly, a visit to East Berlin by Yegor Ligachev earlier in the month brought general assurances of the USSR's support for its East German ally, but no hints of possible military intervention to save Honecker's regime if need be. Ligachev also stated publicly that the Soviets had "no alternative" to perestroika, in spite of its difficulties.[179]

176. Personal communications, East Berlin, June 1989.

177. See the speech by Margot Honecker in *ND*, June 14, 1989, p. 4.

178. FBIS, *Eastern Europe*, June 9, 1989, p. 32. Krenz later claimed that his views were distorted by the West German press. See his *Wenn Mauern fallen* (Vienna: Neff, 1990), pp. 132–34.

179. See Ligachev's interview on East German television in FBIS, *Eastern Europe*, Sept. 19, 1989, pp. 18–22. See also *Pravda*'s muted account of his visit, Sept. 16, 1989, p. 4. Earlier in the summer, while in Hungary, Ligachev had said that the Czech government had requested Soviet intervention in 1968, but added that he supported the Warsaw Pact's recent statement "according to which we must not interfere" in the internal affairs of socialist states; quoted in Vladimir V. Kusin, "Gorbachev's Evolving Attitude towards Eastern Europe," Radio Liberty, *Report on the USSR*, Aug. 4, 1989, p. 12. For the Warsaw Pact declaration, see *Pravda*, July 9, 1989, pp. 1–2.

Thus by the summer of 1989, the GDR was all but isolated within the Soviet bloc. Outwardly, the regime adopted a defiant stance, epitomized by Education Minister Margot Honecker's exhortation to East German youth to defend socialism, "if necessary, with weapons." Inwardly, however, it was suffering from a dearth of new ideas, a superannuated leadership, and the physical impairment of Honecker himself. (The SED chief underwent a gall bladder operation in August.) As a mood of despair set in among the East German populace, rumors circulated that the Soviets were anticipating a major crisis in East Germany, and had already decided not to intervene. *Neues Deutschland* lent credence to the reports by publishing Moscow's official denial of the story, and by reminding the Soviets of their "duties as alliance partners" of the GDR.[180]

When it came, the crisis erupted with incredible rapidity. The catalyst was provided by the sudden exodus of thousands of East Germans to the West via the newly opened gates on the Austro-Hungarian border. Their numbers quickly mushroomed as thousands more, while vacationing in Hungary, crowded into makeshift camps demanding emigration. Over the GDR's protests, Budapest allowed more than 13,000 people to emigrate legally in one week. By late September, would-be émigrés swarmed into the West German embassy compounds in Prague and Warsaw, forcing the GDR to agree to their release. The process quickly repeated itself, and within a month more than 30,000 GDR residents had fled to the West via Eastern Europe. As these figures soared, approximately 90,000 others were already being permitted to leave the GDR by the authorities in East Berlin, who had recognized by early spring that the situation was becoming critical. As in the months before the construction of the Berlin wall, the GDR was bleeding to death.

On September 11 Tass blamed the West German government for fanning the crisis. According to a West German newspaper, however, Valentin Falin had already told Soviet political leaders in mid-August that the SED leadership itself was to blame for the growing exodus, and that it was "powerless and perplexed" as its citizens continued to leave.[181]

Into this deteriorating situation entered Gorbachev, whose speech in East Berlin on the GDR's fortieth anniversary contained statements that could be regarded only as incendiary. Gorbachev quoted President Reagan's appeal to tear down the Berlin wall without explicitly rejecting it. He also promised that as the East-West rapprochement progressed, "all walls of enmity, estrangement, and distrust between Europeans will fall." Twice in his speech the Soviet leader espoused "the sovereignty of the people" in

180. FBIS, *Eastern Europe*, June 14, 1989, p. 3; *Welt am Sonntag*, June 4, 1989, p. 1; *ND*, June 8, 1989, p. 2.

181. The report, citing West German intelligence sources, appeared in *Die Welt* Sept. 15 and was quoted in *Washington Post*, Sept. 15, 1989, p. A22.

socialist states, and he tweaked the Honecker leadership further by claiming that the Soviet Union's perestroika had aroused a great deal of interest in the GDR. Gorbachev also reiterated the standard Soviet position that the United States, not the USSR, had been responsible for dividing Germany. The speech amounted to a public rebuke of the Honecker regime and an outspoken appeal to the East German citizens to push for reform.[182] The next day, in a speech before the SED Politburo, Gorbachev uttered what turned out to be a prophetic warning: "Life punishes those who come too late."[183] As the GDR's predicament worsened, the ashen-faced Honecker responded to journalists' questions about the GDR's emigration problem by asking flippantly, "Is there an emigration problem?"

The wave of illegal demonstrations that preceded and accompanied Gorbachev's appearance in the GDR soon became a mass movement. Honecker held an ominous meeting with China's deputy prime minister, signaling the possible use of force, but the protests in Leipzig, Dresden, and elsewhere grew larger. Honecker resigned along with Mittag and Hermann on October 18, giving way to Egon Krenz.[184] Hundreds of thousands of East Germans filled the streets of East Berlin and other cities on the last weekend of October to demand democratic political reforms and the resignations of more communist officials. Meanwhile, the Warsaw Pact foreign ministers affirmed the right of "each and every people to self-determination . . . without external intervention," in effect countermanding the Brezhnev doctrine. Krenz flew to Moscow for consultations with Gorbachev on November 1. Gorbachev called for "pluralism of opinions" along with "the maximum degree of consolidation" among social forces in the GDR. He also warned Krenz that the communists should "not lag behind the course of events," but affirmed that the situation in the GDR was strictly an internal matter.[185]

Krenz returned home to find public skepticism mounting against his vague promises of reform. The refugee flow via Eastern Europe continued unabated. With power in the GDR shifting into the hands of an emboldened population, Krenz announced more Politburo resignations on November 3. Unappeased, more than 500,000 East Berliners took part in a legal antigovernment demonstration the next day. On November 5, the GDR declared that all East German citizens were free to leave the country via Czechoslovakia. As both German states braced themselves for the possibility of more than a million émigrés flooding into West Germany, Krenz made a desperate effort to gain public confidence by announcing the resignation of the entire Council of Ministers on November 7; another Politburo

182. *Pravda*, Oct. 7, 1989, pp. 4–5.

183. Krenz, *Wenn Mauern fallen*, pp. 86–87.

184. For Krenz's account of the transfer of power, see ibid., pp. 141–45.

185. *Pravda*, Oct. 28, 1989, p. 4; Nov. 2, 1989, pp. 1–2; Krenz, *Wenn Mauern fallen*, pp. 149–51, 191–92.

reshuffling followed the next day. Krenz also called for a new electoral law ensuring free and secret democratic elections in a speech to an emergency meeting of the SED Central Committee.

It was by now far too late, however, to pacify the East German population and reform-minded party members with stopgap promises of reform. On the evening of November 9 Schabowski announced on television that East German citizens would now be allowed to travel to the West without special permission; visas and passports would still be necessary, however. As the size of the crowds gathering at various crossing points in East Berlin during the next several hours swelled to potentially uncontrollable proportions, the barriers separating the two parts of the divided city were opened.[186] The Berlin wall, whose construction Erich Honecker had supervised in 1961 to keep East Germans from fleeing the GDR, was now coming down for precisely the same reason.

At least initially, the gamble appeared to be paying off. Freedom to travel had always been the main political demand of most East German citizens, and after their first weekend sprees in West Berlin and the Federal Republic, the overwhelming majority of East German visitors returned home. Their demands for a comprehensive political housecleaning in the GDR did not diminish, however; East Germany was in the throes of a popular revolution. Hans Modrow, who assumed the chairmanship of the Council of Ministers, appeared to enjoy public confidence, but Krenz and the entire SED Central Committee were forced to resign on December 3, after revelations of flagrant corruption on the part of Honecker and other party oligarchs. On December 9 a convulsed Socialist Unity Party, in one of its final acts under that name, chose Gregor Gysi, a young human rights lawyer, as its new leader. Gysi's task was to adapt the party—rebaptized the Party of Democratic Socialism—to a restructured political system in which it would no longer enjoy the "leading role," and to prepare it for elections to be held the following year.

These stormy events set off a chain reaction in Bulgaria, Czechoslovakia, and even Romania. Under Soviet pressure, Todor Zhivkov resigned on November 10. The recalcitrant Jakes regime was swept away several weeks later as huge demonstrations compelled the Czech communists to relinquish their leading role. A new government with a noncommunist majority was appointed in December. Most surprising of all, Ceausescu's seemingly invincible dictatorship was smashed to pieces in an outpouring of revolutionary rage.

For Moscow, the implications of these developments as the decade came

---

186. *Der Spiegel,* Nov. 13, 1989, p. 19. According to initial reports, Schabowski himself gave the order to lift the barriers after a personal inspection of the situation: *Der Spiegel,* Nov. 20, 1989, p. 20. Krenz later said that the new travel regulations were supposed to have been announced on Nov. 10, and Schabowski's premature announcement was a "slight mistake": *Wenn Mauern fallen,* p. 182.

to a crashing conclusion were ambiguous at best. There can be little doubt that Gorbachev had hoped for quite some time that the SED authorities themselves would find a way, without Soviet interference, to replace Honecker with a more reform-minded leadership. He probably calculated that the introduction of glasnost and democratization in the GDR, perhaps even as late as the spring of 1989, might have stabilized the SED's domestic position sufficiently to cool off popular discontent and obviate the need for drastic, hastily considered concessions to an angry population later on. Moreover, the timely introduction of a reformist regime in East Berlin, in Moscow's view, would also have served to stabilize the division of Germany. The pronouncements of Gorbachev himself and other authoritative Soviet spokesmen made it very plain that although the Kremlin was engaged in "new thinking" on Germany's future, it was not yet ready for a historic reversal of Germany's division. Even if the Gorbachev leadership might have been prepared to accept a modification of the status of the two German states at some future point—whether their unification in a single state or some form of confederation—it was not likely that even Gorbachev would have approved of such a development without first seeking some sort of quid pro quo from the West (such as a reduction or withdrawal of U.S. troops in Germany and significant economic assistance). The Soviet Union wanted to retain a direct role in German affairs as long as it possibly could.

This long-term vision required the long-term stability of the SED's role in East Germany. In the eyes of Soviet reformers, the SED could best preserve its authority by basing it on the consent of the governed rather than on repression. Democratization in the GDR, as in the USSR, would therefore aim above all to save the party by transforming it.

As Gorbachev was compelled to learn at home, however, the forces of popular democracy could escape the party's guiding hand and take off into avenues of their own choosing. In the GDR this risk was particularly grave. Honecker and his cohorts were convinced that unless East Germany remained a tightly controlled one-party system, its citizens would ultimately demand political freedoms and economic opportunities similar to those enjoyed by the West Germans. The absence of a demonstrable sense of separate nationhood compounded the problem. Under these circumstances, in the Honecker regime's view, a politically liberalized GDR would soon become indistinguishable from the Federal Republic, thus raising the possibility of its eventual absorption into an enlarged German state or into some form of confederative association.[187]

As it happened, Honecker's resistance to change only intensified de-

187. Otto Reinhold told a Western interviewer in August that "East Germany is only imaginable as an anti-fascist, socialist state, as a socialist alternative to West Germany. What reason for existence would a capitalist East Germany have next to a capitalist West Germany?": *Washington Post*, Sept. 24, 1989, p. A32.

mands for change in the East German populace. The cascade of events in the final months of 1989 also escaped Moscow's control. The Soviets were not willing to oust Honecker themselves, for fear that such heavyhanded tactics would contradict their repeated assurances of noninterference in the domestic affairs of socialist states. Although Soviet officials were in touch with Krenz and Modrow in hopes of encouraging an internal transformation in the SED,[188] the unexpectedly massive demonstrations in East Germany in the fall had shifted power to the streets. The opening of the Berlin wall and the promise of free elections were by this time the only means available to a desperate SED leadership to regain some vestige of authority.

Events had thus overtaken Moscow's evident preference for a more tranquil path to reform. Although Gorbachev himself and various members of the Soviet secondary elite had already signaled their willingness to reconsider the fate of the Berlin wall at some undisclosed future date, in all likelihood the Soviets were just as stunned by the suddenness of the occurrences in East Germany as the rest of the world.[189] Their immediate reaction was to assert that the opening of the inter-German borders by no means implied that unification was imminent.[190] Nevertheless, the possibility that the FRG and the GDR would ultimately be unified assumed an almost irresistible quality in the final weeks of the year as communist authority in East Germany continued to evaporate. Ordinary citizens demonstrating in the streets of East Germany proclaimed "one fatherland"; Helmut Kohl advanced a long-term proposal for unification; the EEC met to discuss Germany's future. Soviet politicians and commentators admitted that the prospect of unification was not to be dismissed.[191] Even Gorbachev soon appeared to hedge his bets. At the Malta summit meeting with President George Bush in December, Gorbachev warned against "artificial" attempts to "accelerate" change in the status of the two German states, but he did not explicitly rule out unification.[192]

The acceleration of the unification process needed no artificial stimulants, however. In the first three months of 1990, what remained of the

188. *Der Spiegel*, Nov. 13, 1989, p. 25, and Nov. 20, 1989, pp. 17–18; *Washington Post*, Nov. 11, 1989, pp. A1, A26.

189. See Zbigniew Brzezinski's report of his talks in Moscow in late October and early November in *Washington Post*, Nov. 12, 1989, pp. D1–2.

190. See, e.g., *Washington Post*, Gerasimov's comments, Nov. 11, 1989, p. A25; Gorbachev's remarks opposing reunification, Nov. 16, 1989, p. A44; Shevardnadze's comments, Nov. 18, 1989, p. A17; Ambassador Kvitsinskii's earlier statement favoring West German membership in NATO as a stabilizing factor in Europe, Mar. 18, 1989, p. A21. Also Fred Oldenburg, "Sowjetische Deutschland-Politik nach der Oktober-Revolution in der DDR," *Deutschland Archiv*, no. 1, 1990, pp. 68–76.

191. Boris Yeltsin, on a trip to the United States, stated that Germany should be reunified. The remark drew a sharp retort from the GDR: *ND*, Sept. 20, 1989, p. 2. See also the comments of R. Bogdanov in FBIS, *Soviet Union*, Nov. 8, 1989, p. 4.

192. *Washington Post*, Dec. 4, 1989, p. A23.

SED was subjected to a severe battering at the hands of noncommunist political forces in the GDR, most of whom were committed to some form of unity with the Federal Republic. After consultations in Moscow, Prime Minister Modrow proposed talks with Bonn on unification. On February 10 Helmut Kohl in Moscow received Gorbachev's assurance that he would respect whatever decision the German people made with regard to their future, provided that Germany's neighbors were involved in the unification process. Like the SED, the Soviet leader was acceding to realities that could no longer be contained. The depth of the East German population's feelings on the subject of German unity became clearly visible in the elections of March 18 as parties favoring unification amassed three-quarters of the vote.

Meanwhile, developments in East-Central Europe were having a boomerang effect in the Soviet Union. It was the democratization process inside the USSR that had sparked the long-pent-up demands for change in Eastern Europe. Gorbachev still cherished hopes of creating "socialism with a human face."[193] However, the tide of popular disaffection with Marxist-Leninist parties was so strong in Eastern Europe that Gorbachev's best-laid plans for a channeled democratization process quickly became submerged in a sea of demands for democratic freedoms, multiparty systems, and a westward-looking economic orientation. These stunning developments in Eastern Europe in turn gave a boost to similar sentiments in the Soviet Union. Before too long, calls were growing louder in the USSR for the abolition of the CPSU's constitutionally enshrined leading role and for the institution of a multiparty system. At a tense Central Committee plenum held in early February 1990, a majority voted with Gorbachev to give up the party's "leading role" as guaranteed in Article 6 of the Soviet constitution. Moreover, the sudden collapse of the political foundations of Moscow's East European empire added new impulses to separatist tendencies in the Baltic republics and elsewhere in the USSR. Deimperialization in East-Central Europe placed new strains on the cohesion of Russia's internal empire, the USSR.

As the twentieth century entered its final decade, one thing was clear: Gorbachev's attempt to conduct a reform from above had stirred up a revolution from below. The reverberations of this revolution shook virtually every aspect of Soviet domestic and foreign policy. Not since the first decade of the Bolshevik regime had the interaction between internal change and Moscow's involvement in world affairs been so tightly intertwined. Processes of reform that were initially aimed at stimulating the Soviet economy and revivifying the population's involvement in the country's political life had led to a dramatic turnabout in Moscow's relations with the

193. See Gorbachev's article in *Pravda*, Nov. 26, 1989, pp. 1–3.

West and to the transformation of the postwar political order. Germany's pending unification and the collapse of communism in Eastern Europe, like the unraveling of the USSR itself, were the products of Gorbachev's unintended revolution.

An entire era in Moscow's relationship with Germany was now over, and a new one was about to begin. The period that had commenced with Nikita Khrushchev's abortive attempt to improve relations with Bonn while keeping Germany divided had now concluded with the complete restructuring of Soviet-German relations under Mikhail Gorbachev.

CHAPTER ELEVEN

The Domestic Context
of Moscow's
German Policy

THE SUCCESSION of events from the early 1960s to the onset of the 1990s witnessed the passage from one political generation to another in Moscow and East Berlin. This transition was aptly symbolized by two sentimental journeys that took place in the waning stages of this period, at a time when the Soviet Union and East Germany were poised at the edge of fundamental but uncertain change. In the spring of 1987 Andrei Gromyko paid a visit to Cecilienhof, the castle in Potsdam where he had participated in the three-power conference that was held in the aftermath of the Grand Alliance's victory over Hitler's Germany. Two years later, in the early summer of 1989, a beleaguered Erich Honecker made what turned out to be his final trip to the USSR while he was in power. As if to round out a lifetime of dedication to the Marxist-Leninist cause, Honecker stopped in Magnitogorsk, the Stalin-era industrial city where he had worked on the construction of a metallurgical combine as an enthusiastic young communist in 1931.

Placed side by side, these snapshots of Gromyko in Potsdam and Honecker in the heartland of Soviet industry capture at a glance the central themes of Russian-German relations in the twentieth century: revolution, war, and postwar realignment. The careers of both men, with their roots in Stalinism and in the struggle against Hitler, ultimately found their guiding purpose in the creation and maintenance of what emerged as Europe's postwar order. Their mission, an all-consuming one, was to make sure that the past would not repeat itself, that Germany would never again rise in destructive wrath against its eastern neighbors. Above all, Soviet Russia was to be kept unassailably secure behind a shield of protective satellites. In accordance with this basic scheme, Gromyko and Honecker dedicated their

384

lives to maintaining a direct Soviet hand in German affairs, and to ensuring the hegemony of monolithic communist party rule throughout East-Central Europe. For more than four decades their efforts prevailed. But by the time they returned, in the twilight of their careers, to the scenes of earlier glories, the world they had helped create was beginning to come undone.

What factors accounted for the course taken by the Soviet Union's German policy in the decades after the war, and what accounted for the dramatic turnabout in Soviet behavior at the end of the 1980s?

To be sure, some observers would ascribe Moscow's conduct to the enduring great-power interests of the Russian state. And indeed, Soviet policy in the postwar period bore visible imprints of traditional great-power aims and operating procedures. Like any nation that had just suffered the horrors of invasion, the USSR required firm guarantees against a possible resurgence of German aggression. Endowed at the end of the war with tremendous military resources, the Soviets did not hesitate to use force to consolidate the East European buffer zone they demanded. At the same time, the Kremlin was acting out the centuries-old scenario of Russian imperial expansion. This time the sway of empire extended well beyond Poland to include nearly all the nations of Eastern Europe and parts of Germany, together with the formerly independent states of Lithuania, Latvia, and Estonia.

By the same token, the gradual erosion of Soviet controls in Eastern Europe over the decades, culminating in the sudden collapse of Soviet-imposed governments throughout the region in 1989, also bore a striking resemblance to processes that had occurred before in European history. All international systems have a tendency to atrophy. Old national antagonisms lose their intensity and the coalitions they brought into being dissolve. Empires fall apart as the burdens of control can no longer be sustained; as the center weakens, the forces of popular nationalism in the subjugated territories become irrepressible, bursting the bonds of domination. Viewed against the waxing and waning of alliances and empires in Europe's kaleidoscopic past, the dissolution of the interstate system established at the end of World War II may therefore be regarded as having been inevitable sooner or later. After nearly fifty years, its time was at an end.

It would be a mistake, however, to view the motivating forces of postwar Soviet foreign policy, whether in Europe or in its more globalized dimensions, exclusively or even predominantly in terms of traditional Russian great-power interests. In fact, the Soviet Union was never just a great power. It has also been an ideology in power, a state that has consistently defined itself in accordance with plainly articulated political and economic precepts. These ideological underpinnings have inevitably exerted a powerful influence on the USSR's foreign policy throughout the sweep of Soviet history.

Of course, this is not to say that Moscow's policy has been aimed primarily at fomenting revolution in the nonsocialist world. Far from it; Soviet leaders long ago reconciled themselves to the unlikelihood of revolutionary upheaval in the developed democratic states, and they generally refrained from compelling their Third World clients to adopt Soviet-style communist ideology as a condition of Moscow's support. Nevertheless, despite the USSR's loss of revolutionary élan, ideology continued to color the Soviet elite's vision of reality. Above all, the ideology defined the enemy.

As a consequence, the East-West conflict has never been simply a great power rivalry. At its core it has always been an ideologically propelled confrontation. Marxism-Leninism, as traditionally interpreted by Kremlin ideologues, axiomatically identifies capitalism and bourgeois democracy as the class enemy. Conversely, the West repudiates Soviet-style repression as morally reprehensible. The result has been hostility and mistrust in virtually all transactions between Moscow and the West from the outbreak of the Bolshevik revolution right up to the end of the 1980s. Only with Mikhail Gorbachev's promethean efforts to redefine socialism in its Soviet variant, and to reconcile it in some way with Western concepts of popular democracy and the rule of law, did the sharp political conflicts in East-West relations lose their edge. For more than forty years, however, ideological confrontation was the decisive factor in developing and sustaining the political and economic frictions that disrupted Moscow's ties with the market-oriented democracies of Europe, North America, and Asia.

This was especially the case immediately after the war, when the German question was high on the East-West agenda. If the nations that had fought against Hitler's juggernaut had acted strictly in accordance with traditional national interests, they would surely have had every reason to cooperate in the years and decades after the war. Their binding common interest would have been to prevent the reemergence of a German military machine and to encircle a reconstituted German state within a jointly constructed ring of security precautions. Classical balance-of-power logic, as well as elementary collective security concerns, would have dictated extensive collaboration, not dissension, among the nations of East and West.

The fact that matters did not develop in this way was due largely to ideological considerations. Stalin's determination to impose his own noxious brand of Marxism-Leninism on the states of East-Central Europe, instead of settling for some form of Finlandization for these countries, provided the principal casus belli of the cold war in the eyes of the Western democracies. The result was more than four decades of confrontation across a heavily fortified divide, the establishment of opposing alliance systems armed to the teeth with nuclear weapons, and the partition of Germany into two mutually hostile states, each eventually possessing considerable military capabilities.

Any effort to assess the motivations of Soviet policy toward Germany must therefore take full account of the ideologically based conceptions that have strongly influenced Moscow's actions. This task requires a concentrated focus on the domestic sources of foreign policy behavior, centering particularly on the perceptions and policy formulation patterns of the Soviet elite.

Variations in Soviet Policy

One advantage of such a focus is that it is especially sensitive to variations in Soviet behavior over time. Even slight differences between leaders have been of considerable consequence. The differences between the Khrushchev and Brezhnev regimes, at least during Brezhnev's first few years in power, are a case in point. Brezhnev and his colleagues eventually came around to pursuing a dialogue with the West German government, but not until Willy Brandt became chancellor were they prepared for serious negotiations. Khrushchev was ready much earlier to come to the table with Bonn, at a time when the Christian Democrats were in power. The course of Moscow's relations with both the FRG and the GDR might have been quite different had Khrushchev been allowed to proceed with his initiative in 1964 and later. Khrushchev might have succeeded, for example, in accelerating the development of the pro-détente wing of the CDU, and he might have forced the almost foreordained Soviet showdown with Ulbricht to take place much earlier than it actually did under Brezhnev. At the very least, Khrushchev might have pursued a wider economic relationship with the FRG than the Brezhnev coalition was ready to undertake, perhaps linking it with serious reforms in the Soviet domestic economy.

In addition, some intriguing "what if" questions can be raised about the implications of the differences between Khrushchev's and Brezhnev's attitudes toward the Soviet military. Would Khrushchev have embarked on the same vast development of conventional arms in the European theater as Brezhnev? Would he have initiated and continued the deployment of a new generation of intermediate-range nuclear weapons in the region, as Brezhnev did, after having already achieved a highly successful breakthrough toward expanded cooperation with the West Germans? Perhaps he would have; but it is equally plausible that Khrushchev, who showed no reluctance to take on the military hierarchy in an effort to restrain its appetite for manpower and weaponry, would not have risked jeopardizing the political and economic rewards of détente with Bonn by according as much deference as Brezhnev displayed toward the Soviet military command. A significantly different relationship between Moscow and Bonn, and between East and West, could well have been the result.

Equally significant differences existed in the policies toward West Germany adopted by Walter Ulbricht and Erich Honecker. And Mikhail Gorbachev demonstrated to even the most skeptical observer that truly radical shifts in the Kremlin's behavior were far from impossible.

Such variations can be attributed primarily to the nature of the decision-making regime that happened to be wielding power in Moscow or East Berlin. Key aspects of Soviet and East German foreign policy have been seen to depend on the *structure,* the *political direction,* and the *internal stability* of the decision-making elite. Much has depended on whether the structure was basically a directive regime (one-person rule) or a coalition. Variations in foreign policy behavior were especially affected by whether the regime's prevailing political direction was conservative, centrist, or reformist, and on the particular gradation of any of these orientations (as we have seen, Khrushchev's centrist-reformist regime differed in key respects from Honecker's centrist-conservative regime). The cohesiveness of the decision-making regime also had a visible effect on its ability to formulate and implement a coherent foreign policy. Khrushchev in 1964, Ulbricht in 1971, and the lame-duck regimes of Andropov in 1983 and Chernenko in 1984 were all too politically debile, for one reason or another, to prevent serious doubts from arising within the Soviet elite about the conduct of their policy toward West Germany.

These characteristics of the decision-making regime, in turn, had a visible impact on four critical aspects of foreign policy behavior: the regime's definition of the scope of détente; the regime's responsiveness in adapting to opportunities or problems in the international environment; the regime's willingness to effect significant compromises; and the degree to which the regime promoted or even tolerated public debate on tropical foreign policy issues. On the whole, conservative regimes (such as Brezhnev's and Ulbricht's) tended toward the lower end of the register with respect to all four of these variables, while Gorbachev's reformist regime soared to the higher end. The centrist regimes fell at various points between the two.

We have also observed how the influence of the regime's dominant political direction on any of these four behavioral variables can be reinforced or reduced by the degree of internal stability prevailing in the regime. The disintegration of a decision-making regime tends to narrow its conception of détente and reduces its adaptability and readiness for compromise. The cacophony of public debate usually rises in these cases, however, as opposition to the floundering leadership's policy line grows bolder and more open.

Another advantage of the internally oriented approach is that it can shed light on the political bargaining processes at the highest levels of the decision-making hierarchy. As we have seen, policy outcomes are at times affected by intense political conflict—a struggle for power itself—among the leading oligarchs. This was certainly the case throughout much of Khrushchev's tenure in office. But bargaining and coalition building can also be part of the normal give-and-take of Kremlin politics even when no serious effort is being made to topple the party chief or undercut his authority.

The Brezhnev period offers eighteen years of testimony to the fact that demonstrable differences can exist among key members of the leadership on important questions of policy without necessarily provoking or aggravating intense power struggles. At various times Brezhnev, Suslov, Kosygin, Podgorny, Shelepin, Shelest, Grechko, Ustinov, Gromyko, and Ponomarev each took public positions on foreign policy issues that were at variance with the views of fellow oligarchs without becoming involved in a plot to overthrow the governing leadership coalition. Of this group, only Shelepin, Shelest, and Podgorny were actually ousted from their positions for political reasons. Despite signs of rivalry or policy disputes with Brezhnev, none of these three figures ever appeared to pose a serious personal or factional challenge to him and his main supporters.

Of particular importance is the linkage between the discussions among the secondary elite—party and state officials, academicians, journalists—and the policy choices of the primary elite. Although this connection is frequently indirect and cannot be traced with unfailing accuracy, the two elites were intimately bound together in the period from 1963 to 1990. Most members of the secondary elite owed their jobs to the party-controlled *nomenklatura* system, and they owed whatever influence they had to carefully cultivated networks of personal and professional contacts. In judging how far they might go in their public utterances, they took their cues from the primary elites, who ultimately prescribed the scope and the limits of acceptable debate. (The foreign policy doctrines of the Brezhnev and Gorbachev regimes provide good examples of what these boundaries can be.) In the process, the members of the secondary elite exercised a dual function as advisers to the decision makers and as propagandists for the decision makers' chosen foreign policy lines.

In effect, the secondary elite acted as a sounding board for various analytical tendencies and foreign policy options, and provided arguments and conceptual rationales for a variety of alternative approaches to Bonn and its partners. With these divergent arguments in the air, members of the primary elite articulated their own assessments of the evolving international situation. Their publicly expressed perceptions and the policy decisions they made were very much in conformity with theoretical tendencies and policy arguments among the secondary elite. A positive correlation between words and deeds thus prevailed throughout the 1963–1989 period in Soviet policy toward the FRG. To a roughly similar extent, the same close correlation prevailed in the GDR.

Of course, these observable interconnections between words and deeds by no means suggests that the primary and secondary elites of the Soviet Union or even of the GDR were always united in their analyses of international processes or in their specific policy preferences. On the contrary, it is quite evident that serious differences divided both the Soviet and the East German elites on major issues affecting their attitudes and policies toward West Germany.

The sharpness of these differences tended to ebb and flow over the years. In the Soviet Union there were clear signs of policy differentiation within both the primary and the secondary elites in 1964, when Khrushchev launched his abortive German initiative; in 1969 and 1970, when the prospect of reaching major accords with the SPD arose; from 1980 to 1985, when the INF crisis led to debate on whether to punish Bonn; and in the first years of Gorbachev's tenure, as the Soviet leadership felt its way toward a reconceptualization of its policy toward the Western alliance. In the GDR, Ulbricht's iron grip on the foreign policy process gradually came unfastened in 1970 and 1971, permitting the expression of alternative views by both the primary and secondary elites. As in the Soviet Union, both sets of elites were at odds over the issue of détente versus confrontation with Bonn at the time of the INF controversy.

Meanwhile, sharp conflicts broke out between the Soviet and East German elites at various points along the way. In 1963–1964 and again between late 1966 and the spring of 1971 the Kremlin was engaged in a continuous battle of wills with Walter Ulbricht over the scope and content of relations with Bonn. An equally serious dispute ranged Mikhail Gorbachev against Erich Honecker in the late 1980s. In addition, as the INF issue divided opinions within the Soviet Union and East Germany earlier in the decade, members of each foreign policy establishment formed informal alliances with like-minded elites in the other state in a wide-ranging debate that cut across national boundaries.

At other times the elites seemed to be in relative agreement on the policy approach to be taken toward West Germany. A considerable degree of harmony seemed to prevail in the Soviet primary and secondary elites from late 1970 until the final years of the decade on the main contours of Moscow's approach toward Bonn. This approach, as we have seen, combined a limited amount of political and economic cooperation with the FRG with a significant amount of military modernization. At the same time, conflict between Moscow and East Berlin abated significantly in those years, as the East German elites developed a growing appreciation of the benefits of détente. Until 1970, of course, Walter Ulbricht managed to keep the East German secondary elite almost totally subservient to his own views.

Yet even in these periods of overarching policy consensus, conflicting views continued to be heard in both the Soviet Union and the GDR. Key members of the primary and secondary elites of both states took contrary positions on such basic issues as the trustworthiness of various West German political leaders, the degree of Bonn's independence from the United States, and the desirability of promoting economic cooperation with the FRG to still higher levels. Even in the suffocating atmosphere of Ulbricht's monolithic regime, occasional voices were raised in favor of reducing tensions and expanding cooperation with the Federal Republic.

The predominant Soviet outlook on West Germany throughout the entire period was therefore essentially ambivalent. At no point were the Soviet elites unanimous in their appraisals of West German foreign policy or in their assessments of the appropriate way for Moscow to proceed in its dealings with Bonn.

The end result of this ongoing tug-of-war was a hesitancy and caution that imposed distinct limits on cooperation with Bonn. Powerful elements of conflict and mistrust can be seen in virtually all of the Kremlin's dealings with the West Germans, at least until 1989. This constant tension between cooperation and conflict was internalized in the outlooks and policy preferences of individual members of the Soviet elite, particularly those in the highest decision-making organs of the party and the state. The outcome was a contradictory policy that oscillated between détente and discord while straining to have both at once. This uneasy balance could not be maintained indefinitely; eventually hard decisions had to be made. When forced to choose in the late 1970s and early 1980s, Brezhnev and his two immediate successors opted to pursue the burgeoning conflict to its ultimate conclusion. After several years of searching for a new approach, Gorbachev came out strongly for cooperation. But even Gorbachev exhibited tentativeness and ambivalence on critical German questions, such as the Berlin wall, until the cataclysmic events of 1989 made radical adjustments unavoidable.

The East Germans were similarly divided in their publicly articulated views on West Germany for most of the period if not quite all of it. There was considerably less room for open discussion in the grim Ulbricht decades, to be sure; but even here, as we have seen, contrary opinions sprouted to the surface now and then.

Constants in Soviet Policy

Of course, no full understanding of any of these divergent views can be achieved without a realistic appreciation of their limits. Throughout the period from 1963 to 1990, Soviet and East German leaders, together with their foreign policy advisers in the secondary elite, made it clear that their policies toward the Federal Republic were bounded by certain policy goals and analytical assumptions that never varied very much. Among these constants was the view that Germany had to be kept divided and the proposition that West Germany could not be neutralized.

During the first ten years or so after the war ended, Soviet policy on reunification displayed some traces of flexibility. Stalin, Beria, and Khrushchev all dropped hints that they might be willing to come to terms on establishing a greater German state, presumably by liquidating the GDR and allowing its territory to be attached to that of the Federal Republic. (At no time did Soviet leaders state that they would be willing to restore Germany to its borders of 1937.) Although the Western occupation powers did not display much interest in pursuing these feelers (any more than the Adenauer government), it was by no means evident that the Soviet leaders themselves were really ready to give up East Germany on the basis of Western proposals for free elections in the GDR. In any event, by the end of 1955, if not sooner, the Kremlin had decided to base its German policy on the premise that the division of Germany into two separate states would continue indefinitely.

The Soviet leadership's acceptance of a divided Germany reflected both its fundamental security interests and its ever-present ideological convictions. It was Germany, after all, that had unleashed World War II, and it was Germany that therefore had to be contained. Quite understandably, the generation of Soviet leaders that had suffered through the war were particularly committed to this outlook. At the same time, Germany's division at the Elbe and the imposition of communist party rule in the GDR provided a vital underpinning for Moscow's territorial and ideological control of Eastern Europe, as well as for its incorporation of Königsberg and the formerly independent Baltic republics. Any policy that might in any way lead to the establishment of an enlarged German state, even one confined to a merger of the FRG and the GDR, was viewed in Moscow as placing this entire edifice at risk.

Together these security concerns and ideological commitments provided Soviet leaders of the Stalin and Khrushchev generations with strong incentives to maintain Germany's division as long as possible. Although Khrushchev was prepared to resume the long-dormant dialogue with Bonn in 1964, his nascent détente with the Federal Republic was strictly circumscribed by his rejection of any change in Germany's territorial status. As it turned out, many of Khrushchev's contemporaries in both the Politburo and the secondary elite were not even prepared to go as far as their embattled party chief; for them, a summit with a Christian Democratic chancellor who placed reunification at the top of his negotiating agenda was simply out of the question.

Similarly, the Brezhnev coalition's circuitous route to détente with Bonn, which passed through Prague in 1968 and threaded its way through intricate internal bargaining processes in Moscow in 1969 and 1970, was always posited on the fundamental precondition of gaining West Germany's acceptance of Europe's postwar political order. The Brandt-Scheel government's willingness to meet the Kremlin halfway in this regard, by formally acknowledging the reality (though not the permanence) of the current situation, was the sine qua non of any Soviet–West German cooperation in the eyes of the Brezhnev leadership.

The Kremlin made it abundantly clear at the time, however, that it would not countenance Willy Brandt's abiding hope that a united Germany would one day emerge from the détente process. For Moscow, détente was intended to solidify the status quo, not overturn it; to provide a substitute for Bonn's desire for reunification, not encourage it. Bonn's "offensive détente" policy, however, kept Moscow on the defensive. While the United States pursued a policy of containment on the continent, Bonn pursued a policy of change. And while American energies centered on the military balance, West Germany's focused on political transformation. The two allies sought to coordinate their strategies, to be sure, but for Moscow the distinction was clear: far more directly than Washington, Bonn posed a serious challenge to Germany's divided status.

It was these political considerations perhaps more than any other that drove the Soviet hierarchy under Brezhnev to opt for the modernization and expansion of Soviet military capabilities in the European theater rather than to heed Brandt's appeals for a comprehensive military détente based on sweeping reductions in NATO and Warsaw Pact forces. Faced with incontrovertible evidence of Bonn's economic might and Eastern Europe's political fragility, the Soviet leadership had every reason to believe that a wholesale elimination of the military standoff might very well lead to the collapse of the political and ideological foundations of the communist imperium on the continent. Any serious demilitarization of the East-West conflict could only release the pent-up tensions that held the postwar order together, above all by undermining belief in the "myth of the German threat" among East Europeans. In these circumstances, a process of radical disarmament could indeed create a psychological climate in Europe conducive to Germany's unification, exactly as Brandt's grand design posited.

The Brezhnev coalition had no intention of heading down this perilous path. It therefore decided by the end of 1970 that political détente and economic cooperation with the SPD-FDP government must in no way preclude the reaffirmation of Soviet military strength. Statements by leading decision makers in the Kremlin, backed up by the writings of authoritative members of the secondary elite, provide clear confirmation of this fateful policy choice precisely at this critical moment. Images of West Germany were starkly divided between relatively positive views of its political and economic value and hostile portrayals of its unflagging military power. To a considerable degree, the relentless buildup of Soviet armor and the modernization of Moscow's intermediate-range missile arsenal were justified by this expressed perception of an inimical and dangerous West Germany, reinforced by visions of Bonn's enduring attachment to a powerful NATO alliance. The Brezhnev regime's unforthcoming position at the stillborn MBFR negotiations further confirmed its lack of interest in a serious military détente.

Of course, these conservative Soviet military policies were also rationalized by profuse references to American, British, and French military might. At the same time, some Soviet academicians insisted that the USSR's growing military strength was feeding West European doubts about the reliability of the American nuclear deterrent. Nevertheless, Moscow's decision to modernize its European arsenals in the Brezhnev years, rather than to join with the West in reducing them, cannot be ascribed solely to military considerations. Throughout the 1970s and well into the 1980s, these military policies represented above all a reaction to the political challenges posed by Bonn's dynamic ostpolitik.

The Kremlin leadership surely realized that war in the nuclear age was tantamount to suicide. They also plainly understood that, however great the "contradictions" over military strategy between Bonn and Washington may have been, the two allies were tightly linked and powerfully armed against the socialist camp. In these circumstances, the Kremlin had to regard the prospect of an attack by the West as unlikely, and the possibility of winning a war in Europe as hopeless. Even the mere threat of using force on the continent would probably galvanize Western resolve and set in motion a train of events whose course could be neither predicted nor controlled. For Moscow, war was neither an imminent danger nor a viable option.

A far more realistic consideration, however, was the need to maintain an element of confrontation in Europe in order to block the likely hazards of a runaway détente process. Kremlin decision makers seemed to understand that an all-embracing relaxation of tensions in the region, pushed onward by full-scale disarmament, would ultimately play into the West's hands. By spurring desires for East-West economic interdependence and even political liberalization in the countries of the Soviet bloc, it would above all play into West Germany's hands, chipping away at the rationale for the fortified barriers and repressive controls dividing the two halves of Europe. The events of the late 1960s, when Bucharest, Prague, Budapest, and Warsaw gradually turned toward Bonn, seemed to validate these apprehensions.

These events left an indelible mark on Soviet attitudes toward the West for the rest of the Brezhnev generation's term of office. Throughout the 1970s and the first half of the 1980s, Soviet leaders regarded the main threat emanating from West Germany as political, not military. But because they lacked effective political or economic countermeasures that might have held the socialist alliance together on the basis of popular approval, they responded with the one sure means at their disposal: military strength. Thus the motivations guiding Moscow's robust arms-development policies were themselves primarily political. For more than any other single reason, the Soviets armed in these years not because they expected war; they armed because they feared détente.

At the same time, Moscow's rejection of a unified Germany (a position reaffirmed by Gorbachev as late as the end of 1989) inevitably implied the Kremlin's acceptance of West Germany's membership in NATO. Once the Federal Republic formally joined the Atlantic alliance in 1955, the Soviets reconciled themselves to the impossibility of breaking up the Bonn-Washington partnership in the foreseeable future. Indeed, the two issues of reunification and alliance were tightly intertwined. The only card in Moscow's hand that might possibly have enticed the West Germans out of their alliance ties was a firm offer of unification. Past experience had shown, however, that Bonn would not necessarily reach for this card, especially when the Kremlin's intimations on the subject of reunification remained incomprehensibly vague. Over the ensuing decades, the Federal Republic's military and economic attachments to its allies had only grown stronger. So had the Kremlin leadership's determination to retain control of East Germany, which remained the forepost of the USSR's military position vis-à-vis the West and the linchpin of its empire in the East. West Germany's adherence to NATO, in fact, had come to be a blessing for the Soviets; it reinforced both the division of Germany into two states and the partition of Europe into ideologically incompatible blocs.

Thus neutralization of the FRG was a risky proposition to begin with; just as significant, Soviet elites perceived it as practically unachievable. It is at this juncture that the copious writings of the Soviet secondary elite assume critical significance. By revealing how the Soviets themselves assessed the shifting trends in "West-West" relations, these writings provide valuable insights into how they evaluated the prospects for various options in their dealings with the West.

Over the years Soviet observers became increasingly sophisticated in the way they described and evaluated prevailing trends in international politics. Until the late 1980s, however, this tendency toward analytical realism was accompanied by a dialectical vision of political life that was deeply ingrained in Marxist-Leninist modes of thought. Lenin's dictum that two simultaneously operating tendencies can always be found in relations among capitalist states—one toward unity, the other toward "contradictions"— was a fundamental premise that directly informed the world view of Soviet analysts and political leaders. However practical their approach to realpolitik might be, the Soviets' view of reality was filtered through this and other ideologically colored lenses.

The main import of Lenin's teaching was that capitalist states were always in conflict with one another, but that these conflicts could not be expected to surmount certain "common class interests." The unifying tendencies were especially strong in consolidating the capitalists' opposition to the socialist world. These postulates suggested to Soviet leaders that they had ample opportunities to exploit differences among the NATO allies, but that it would be unrealistic to expect the Atlantic alliance to disintegrate completely. Though Moscow could "drive wedges" between the Western states, it could not definitively break them apart.

These theoretical perspectives had a direct bearing on the Soviet elite's attitude toward the neutralization of West Germany. Presumably, if any Soviets might be at all inclined toward neutralization, they would most likely be found among those of the Europeanist orientation. It was the Europeanists who stressed the salience of the contradictions corroding Western unity and accentuated the West Europeans' search for greater independence from the United States. And yet the overwhelming majority of Europeanist analysts explicitly rejected the neutralization of any West European ally of the United States as highly unrealistic. Time and again Soviet Europeanists stressed that West Germany's attempts to carve out a wider margin of foreign policy independence were always strictly contained within the structures of the NATO alliance. In their view, Moscow should indeed make special efforts to promote such "centrifugal" tendencies within the alliance by cultivating the West Germans and other Europeans, but on no account should anything resembling the Finlandization of America's European allies be anticipated. These prevailing assumptions help explain why the Soviets were so unprepared to deal with the issue of Germany's unification once the GDR fell apart at the start of 1990.

Americanist analysts called attention to Western Europe's abiding reliance on the United States and America's undiminished importance as a major player in European affairs. Still, they abjured any thought of favoring a bipolar "condominium" arrangement forged by the two superpowers over the heads of the Europeans. Both the Americanist and the Europeanist outlooks had much in common with the Atlanticist tendency, which placed roughly equal stress on centripetal and centrifugal trends in U.S.–West European relations. All three orientations advocated policies designed to play upon Western contradictions, such as the use of West European "levers" to influence U.S. policy and vice versa. All three also urged that due account be taken of NATO's indissoluble unity. Finally, all three positions had institutional bases in the leading foreign affairs think tanks.[1]

1. Europeanists were especially well represented at IMEMO and at the Institute of European affairs established in 1987; Americanists tended to cluster at the Institute of the USA and Canada. Atlanticists could be found in all three institutions. Consequently *Mirovaya ekonomika i mezhdunarodnye otnosheniya* tended to showcase Europeanist and Atlanticist views while Americanist and Atlanticist arguments predominated in *SShA*. All three orientations, along with the maximalist point of view, could be found in *International Affairs*.

The Soviet leaders themselves, from Khrushchev to Gorbachev, basically adopted the balanced and opportunistic Atlanticist strategy. All eschewed the uncompromising message of maximalism (a policy approach more favored by Walter Ulbricht); and all of them tended to avoid placing exclusive or excessive reliance on either the American or the West European pole of the Atlantic alliance. To be sure, there were times when the Soviet leadership appeared to swing decisively in the direction of the Europeans. Such attempts were particularly obvious in the late 1960s, when Gaullism and other trends in the Western alliance appeared to augur a long-term dissipation of American influence on the continent. It was in those years that Moscow refloated its proposal for an "all-European" security conference and called for the simultaneous dissolution of NATO and the Warsaw Pact.

The Soviets did not appear to be excessively optimistic about the prospects for those proposals, however. The likelihood of a decisive rupture between Western Europe and the United States (indeed, even between de Gaulle and the United States) was categorically discounted by just about all the main Soviet specialists who analyzed these events at the time. As its actions soon demonstrated, the Kremlin held out little hope for luring Western Europe into an "all-European security system" that excluded the United States. Similarly, Moscow's repeated appeals for the abrogation of the two alliances came to assume a purely ritualistic character. The Soviets recognized that America was in Europe to stay, and that the West Europeans—and in particular the West Germans—wanted it that way.

Furthermore, Moscow's track record in driving wedges between the United States and West Germany was mixed at best. On the whole, the Soviets were relatively successful at exploiting contradictions between Bonn and Washington on economic issues; they were considerably less successful in loosening their all-important military partnership.[2] Moscow demonstrably counted on Bonn to use its "levers" (a favorite Soviet term) to influence American policy in positive directions, but at times the United States could perform an equally valuable service by pressuring the West Germans into adopting policies favorable to Soviet interests.[3]

2. West Germany induced the United States to compromise its position in regard to the Harmel Report in 1967 and the NATO embargo lists in the 1970s; resisted the Carter administration's proposals for an economic embargo after the invasion of Afghanistan; and successfully resisted pressures by the Reagan administration to cancel the pipeline agreements of the early 1980s. The Soviets failed to persuade the West German government to distance itself significantly from the U.S. position during the quadripartite negotiations on Berlin in the early 1970s; during the CSCE talks in Helsinki; during the MBFR talks; during the INF crisis of 1978–1983; and with respect to SDI and battlefield nuclear weapons in the late 1980s. The Soviets applauded official West German statements in support of U.S. ratification of SALT II, but Reagan did not submit the treaty for ratification.

3. The United States supported West German ratification of the Nuclear Nonproliferation Treaty, pressured the Christian Democrats to go along with ratification of the eastern treaties in 1972, and pressured Kohl to yield on the Pershing IA issue in 1987.

This Atlanticist course was another constant in Soviet decision-making with respect to West Germany. Important differences, however, separated the various Soviet leadership coalitions on the all-important question *how* Moscow's Atlanticist policy toward the NATO alliance should be implemented.

Khrushchev's centrist-reformist coalition was fatally divided on its German policy, as on so many other things. By the time the more conservative Brezhnev coalition was ready to deal with the West Germans, the Kremlin oligarchs were basically in agreement that Moscow's outreach to Western Europe and the United States had to be conducted in accordance with a highly conflictual and ideologized outlook on East-West relations. The result was a tepid approach to East-West cooperation which was eventually eclipsed by a much stronger commitment to military self-assertiveness.

Even the military aspects of the Brezhnev regime's approach to the West displayed distinctly Atlanticist tendencies. The Kremlin made no serious attempt to woo the West Europeans away from their reliance on American protection by *reducing* the Warsaw Pact's military potential in the European theater. As a consequence, Moscow may have missed an opportunity to bring the security partnership between the United States and Western Europe to the brink of a potential rupture. Conceivably, by drawing down its nuclear and conventional forces in the area in a massive way, while at the same time building up Soviet strategic forces aimed at the United States, the USSR might well have maneuvered the NATO allies into adopting two radically divergent assessments of the Soviet threat. The Europeans, looking across a significantly demilitarized zone extending deep into the USSR, might have perceived very little real threat to their security; the Americans, facing a growing arsenal of long-range missiles, would have felt considerably more endangered. In these circumstances the differences between the Western allies on policy toward the USSR could have intensified appreciably, and many West Europeans might have been ready for a major reappraisal of their transatlantic attachments. Just how far these divisive tendencies might have gone can only be imagined. In fact, however, Soviet leaders showed no signs of even considering the possibilities of such a "Europeanist" military deployment strategy. Their unwillingness to do so provides one more indication that they never regarded the prospects of a decisive breakup of NATO with much seriousness. Instead they held to a manipulative Atlanticist course by playing off one side of the alliance against the other while simultaneously increasing the military threat to both.

The failure of this conservative policy became increasingly evident as the INF crisis unfolded in the late 1970s and early 1980s. Having determined that more was better when it came to military procurements, the Soviet leadership had no measure for determining how much was enough. Convinced that "contradictions" were bound to occur among the NATO allies in any event, the Brezhnev coalition further assumed that these conflicts would proliferate even in times of acute East-West confrontation, and not just under conditions of détente. Various members of the secondary elite provided theoretical sustenance for this view, but other analysts clearly favored a return to détente. Proponents of a more cooperative relationship with the West, and especially with the FRG, made it plain that they wanted no part of a punitive policy toward Bonn, particularly one that would punish the Soviet Union and its allies economically and drive the USSR even deeper into a fruitless and self-defeating isolation. These debates grew sharper as the aging Soviet leadership lost its grip on power. In many respects, the antirevanchism campaign of 1984 was the last battle cry of the World War II generation.

Mikhail Gorbachev thus ascended to the post of general secretary in the midst of a foreign policy crisis. The problems he faced were compounded by a host of economic problems that had been accumulating for decades. The Soviet Union's economic lability had immediate implications for Gorbachev's attitudes toward West Germany, the GDR, and socialist ideology itself. It was also the driving force behind his far more cooperative Atlanticist policy.

Economic Issues and the GDR

One of Nikita Khrushchev's principal aims in seeking to open up contacts with the FRG was to pull the USSR once and for all out of its Stalinist autarkic traditions and to draw the West Germans into a long-term involvement in the modernization of the Soviet economy. These efforts were accompanied by modest but politically significant attempts to reform some of the structures of the Soviet command system.

Brezhnev quietly shelved Khrushchev's domestic reforms, and it was several years before he shifted to a more favorable view of East-West trade. Ultimately the need for technology and credits from the West proved too powerful to ignore. Not all members of the Brezhnev coalition were favorably disposed to expanding economic ties with the capitalist states, however, and Brezhnev himself saw to it that Moscow's economic liaisons with the West would serve more as a substitute for domestic reforms than as a stimulant for them, as many of the Kremlin's business partners urged.

Although it was not until Gorbachev's accession to power that the dimensions of the Soviet Union's technological backwardness became public knowledge, in fact the magnitude and foreign policy implications of the Soviet bloc's economic dilemmas were foreshadowed nearly two decades earlier. Walter Ulbricht's appeals for intensified efforts to accelerate the socialist camp's technological modernization were driven by urgent foreign policy considerations. Ulbricht's reading of the Czech crisis of 1968 had convinced him that Eastern Europe would fall an easy victim to Western—and especially West German—economic blackmail if serious efforts were not undertaken immediately to narrow the gap in technological proficiency that even then threatened to doom the socialist states to disastrous economic inferiority to the West. In Ulbricht's view, the East's economic dependence on the West could only lead to political dependence.

In retrospect, Ulbricht was at least partially right. Although the West did not acquire the capability to dictate terms to the socialist bloc, in fact the economic backwardness of the Warsaw Pact states could not help but weaken their political position both internally and internationally. As it happened, Ulbricht had no success in his attempts to rectify the situation. His long-term program to develop advanced technology in the socialist camp "by our own means" found little resonance in Moscow or in the capitals of Eastern Europe. His quixotic attempt to accelerate high-technology development in the GDR foundered on the East German economy's limited resources and systemic inadequacies. The GDR ran a distant second to West Germany as an attractive source of modern technology even in the eyes of its COMECON partners.

With these failures, Ulbricht not only suffered a fatal personal defeat; he also provided a lesson to Erich Honecker, Leonid Brezhnev, and other Eastern bloc leaders on the endemic insufficiencies of the socialist economic system. Faced with the collapse of Ulbricht's grand design, these leaders turned to the West for assistance, but always kept in mind the potential perils of excessive economic dependence on their Western partners.

For the post-Ulbricht leadership in the GDR, the foreign policy consequences of economic retardation were inescapable. It was economic self-interest more than anything else that sustained the Honecker coalition's stake in détente with the FRG throughout the 1970s and 1980s. The benefits to be gained from inter-German cooperation, however, inevitably required a series of compromises on human rights and other questions singled out by Bonn for special consideration. Although both sides found ways to maintain a constructive attitude, the GDR, as the supplicant in this relationship, was at a distinct disadvantage. Only the SED leadership's control over the number of East Germans allowed to leave the GDR and its ability to limit the Westerners who entered East Germany to those willing to pay a steep admission price gave the Honecker regime any leverage in its dealings with Bonn. Without the wall, East Berlin could not bargain.

The Soviet Union did not provide much help. The Kremlin supported the GDR's existence but otherwise treated its trusted ally with imperial hauteur. The Soviets never gave Walter Ulbricht the veto over German policy that he coveted in the 1950s and 1960s. In the early 1970s they compelled the GDR to open its doors to a stream of Western visitors, an action that could only undermine the SED's efforts to bolster its legitimacy at home. With the daily opportunity to compare their lives with those of West Germans and others from the outside world, large numbers of East Germans were bound to direct their frustrations at the SED leadership, further weakening the party's domestic authority and creating the basis for potential instability. The Soviets compounded these problems in the middle of the decade by jacking up the price of Soviet oil. Soon thereafter they jolted the SED once again by forcing it to support Moscow's confrontationist INF policy, thereby complicating Honecker's ties with West Germany and aggravating political unrest in the GDR. Then came Gorbachev.

By contrast, West Germany supported the political and economic stability of the GDR in the years when Moscow was increasing its demands on the Honecker government. One of the great ironies of Soviet-German relations in the 1970s and 1980s was that Bonn was propping up East Germany at the very time that Moscow—however unintentionally—was undermining it. By granting the GDR de facto recognition, Bonn conferred international legitimacy on the East German state; and by keeping up a steady flow of credits, transfer payments, and trade benefits, the West Germans helped ease the Honecker regime's mounting economic and political predicaments.

The Federal Republic's cooperativeness, of course, was by no means intended to stabilize communist rule in East Germany over the long term. The West German government wanted stability in the GDR primarily as a means of encouraging the SED leadership to feel secure enough to liberalize its travel restrictions and ultimately its political system. "Change through rapprochement," after all, was the original credo of the SPD's détente policy toward East Germany. In later years, when some of the initial exponents of this proposition began calling for the juridical recognition of the GDR, they did so for the express purpose of facilitating democratic political change in East Germany. "*Freiheit statt Einheit*"—freedom instead of unity—was intended by many Social Democrats to be just as corrosive of East German totalitarianism over time as "*Wandel durch Annäherung.*" The Christian Democrats were even more insistent on gaining humanitarian concessions from the SED in exchange for economic benefits. On top of these political calculations, the Federal Republic posed a standing psychological threat to the GDR government simply by virtue of its attractiveness to millions of East Germans.

The SED leadership thus lived under a state of permanent siege. It stood confronted by an imperious ally, a disaffected population, and an economically superior "class enemy." Its ideological conservatism, moreover, was the source of internal economic problems and political tensions that could not help but weaken the GDR's international position. This connection between domestic factors and foreign policy was to be exposed with particular force in the Soviet Union under Mikhail Gorbachev.

Perestroika

Gorbachev's determination to reform the Soviet system reflected the primacy of domestic policy over foreign policy on the new leader's political agenda—a sharp reversal of the Brezhnevites' priorities. For them, consumer needs were strictly subordinate to the requirements of the military, and a tight lid had to be clamped on all forms of political dissidence at home if the Soviet Union was to preserve its image as an international superpower. Moreover, the imposition of a static neo-Stalinist ideology on the USSR, as reflected in "the leading role of the party" and a petrified central planning system, reinforced the Kremlin's grip on East-Central Europe.

Gorbachev's recognition that radical reforms were imperative was a candid admission of the failure of this neo-Stalinist variant of Marxism. It also represented a sharp setback in Moscow's ideological confrontation with the United States. As Khrushchev had insisted decades earlier, at a time when the nuclear age was growing more perilous, the East-West conflict could be conducted only through peaceful means, above all through a competitive quest for economic superiority. Reduced to its essence, this competition came down to two practical questions: Which system was better able to promote economic growth? Which system could afford the next round in the arms race?

On both counts Gorbachev conceded defeat. Faced with an unproductive industrial sector and a plethora of consumer-related problems, he recognized that only a fundamental overhaul of the Soviet Union's economic and political institutions could save the country from irreversible decline. Although Gorbachev's reformist coalition had not come up with a comprehensive economic reform program after nearly five years in office, it nonetheless acknowledged the need for a new approach.

Moreover, the readiness of key Western states to raise the stakes in the arms race (despite their own economic woes) had a profound impact on Moscow's decision to move toward mutual disarmament. NATO's resolve to counter the SS-20s with new missiles of its own was of fundamental importance in convincing Gorbachev to seek a halt to the resource-draining arms spiral. The Soviets themselves amply testified to this fact. As the INF crisis escalated in the first half of the 1980s, the foreign policy elite became embroiled in a heated debate over the consequences of the arms race. NATO's two-track decision, and above all the Federal Republic's critical role in its adoption and implementation, made it clear that the Kremlin could not have both a cooperative détente and a one-sided arms buildup. Some Soviet foreign policy experts clearly sought to rescue the Soviet–West German relationship from further deterioration. They argued that confrontation with the FRG was simply not in Moscow's political or economic interest.

Later, as Mikhail Gorbachev beamed the light of glasnost on foreign policy discussions, Soviet officials and academicians voiced sharp criticisms of previous Soviet arms policies. Leading foreign ministry spokesmen, including Eduard Shevardnadze himself, condemned the SS-20s along with the USSR's excessive conventional arsenals and its foot-dragging negotiating tactics. Prominent members of the foreign policy establishment attested to the impact of Western rearmament efforts on Moscow's decision to call off the military confrontation.[4] Some admitted that the prospect of a breakthrough in SDI research had accelerated the Gorbachev regime's quest for a breakthrough in U.S.-Soviet arms reductions. The Soviets simply could not afford a high-technology arms race while dangling on the precipice of economic collapse. Gorbachev's progressive retreat from earlier positions linking an INF accord to the Reagan administration's renunciation of SDI provided even more graphic evidence of the pressures western policies—and NATO unity—had placed on Soviet decision makers. Unable to sustain confrontation, the Kremlin sued for cooperation.

This historic turnabout in Moscow's relationship with the West reflected the impact of domestic processes on the USSR's foreign policy behavior. The INF agreement, the adoption of unilateral measures of conventional disarmament, and a host of unprecedented concessions on human rights and other issues had not been forced upon Moscow by its adversaries in typical great-power fashion. On the contrary, when these changes began, the USSR was at the peak of its military power. It was internal economic decay, stemming from a moribund neo-Stalinist ideology, that had generated these transformations in external policy.

By the same token, it was the ideological reassessment taking place in the USSR, not a military clash or some grand NATO–Warsaw Pact bargain, that brought about the liquidation of Moscow's East European empire. Glasnost and democratization in the Soviet Union had an ineluctable ripple effect in East-Central Europe. If Gorbachev ever entertained any illusions about being able to rein in this liberalization process, he surely had to discard them by the second half of 1989 as events in the other Warsaw Pact

4. E.g., Ambassador Kvitskinskii noted that some people in the West attributed the INF agreement to NATO's counterarmament efforts, an opinion he did not contradict. ("It's not worth polemicizing about it. What matters is the result"): *Frankfurter Rundschau*, May 7, 1988, p. 10. Dashichev declared that the Reagan administration's arms policies imposed "an incredible burden" on the Soviet economy: *Komsomolskaya pravda*, June 19, 1988, p. 3.

countries whirled out of control. The game was finally lost as Moscow decided to withhold the one reliable method at its disposal for keeping Eastern Europe in check: the use of force. This decision, too, had ulterior domestic motivations. Armed intervention abroad might strangle the reform effort in the Soviet Union. And it would most assuredly wreck Soviet hopes for Western economic assistance, particularly within the "common European home."

As things turned out, Gorbachev overestimated the prospects for a reformed socialism in East-Central Europe and underestimated the revulsion the local populations felt for the entire political system. The swiftness of the GDR's collapse was especially shocking. According to an SED Politburo member, one of the reasons Gorbachev did not press more vigorously for Honecker's ouster earlier was his confidence that a reformist regime would be able to win over the population once the aging Honecker passed from the scene.[5] (Even Dashichev, in his memorandum of April 1989, assumed that the GDR would survive for an indeterminate period after the Berlin wall was opened.) The Soviets also underestimated the longings for unification that continued to beat in the breasts of most East Germans.

In retrospect, it appears that the German Democratic Republic could never have survived on its own under conditions of internal democracy and openness to the West unless political and economic conditions were at least as good as those in the Federal Republic. Failing these prerequisites, the GDR could be maintained only by force. A creation of the postwar settlement (or lack of one), it possessed no raison d'être other than that of keeping Germany divided and partially under Soviet control. The SED never succeeded in building a viable national identity among the people and it never came close to providing them with Western freedoms or material living standards. On the contrary, it alienated them irreconcilably by walling them off from the West and subjecting them to constant surveillance by the state security police, the ubiquitous Stasi. In the end, the GDR's demise reflected the absence of nationhood and the failure of neo-Stalinist ideology.

The Kremlin's willingness to permit the opening of the Berlin wall undermined communist authority throughout Eastern Europe. As power in East Germany slipped rapidly from the Socialist Unity Party's hands without any signs of Soviet intervention, it was instantly apparent to the rulers and populations of Czechoslovakia, Bulgaria, and even Romania that the Gorbachev Politburo would not lift a finger to protect Moscow's floundering empire. Having started out in 1985 with the intention of saving what could be saved in Eastern Europe through reform, the new Kremlin leadership was resigned to saving nothing when it was confronted by revolution in

---

5. Personal communication, East Berlin, June 1990.

1989. Saving perestroika in the Soviet Union was Gorbachev's overriding priority.

In letting East-Central Europe go its own way, Gorbachev put his own authority in the Soviet Union on the line. The magnitude of what the Kremlin had just given up became increasingly evident in the early months of 1990 as the GDR dissolved from within and Germany's unification became unavoidable. Moscow had in effect surrendered its most valuable conquest from World War II without an explicit quid pro quo from the West. The Warsaw Pact was turning into an empty shell while Washington and Bonn insisted on keeping the new Germany in NATO. As the Soviets risked being bystanders in what was once their strategic stronghold in Europe, Gorbachev was publicly taken to task for his policies. At a series of party forums in 1990, conservative critics roundly criticized the Soviet leader for having lost Eastern Europe and above all East Germany. These criticisms of Gorbachev's foreign policy were part of a mounting conservative attack on perestroika as such, a campaign that gained intensity at the 28th CPSU Congress in July.[6]

Despite these rebukes, Mikhail Gorbachev displayed an uncanny ability to turn the system's defeats into personal victories. A master at the art of strategic retreat, Gorbachev managed to convert the loss of Eastern Europe into a major gain in relations with the West. By the end of 1989 virtually everyone in the NATO countries was convinced of Gorbachev's good faith in seeking a radical transformation in East-West relations. As a result, the Western allies reconsidered NATO doctrine and force postures and discussed the possibility of extending significant amounts of assistance to the Soviet economy. Domestically, Gorbachev and his principal supporters weathered the storm of conservative criticism and emerged from the 28th Party Congress with their foreign policy intact. Ligachev himself was pushed out of the political leadership.

The problem of how Moscow should deal with the new Germany would remain, however. As in the past, several alternative approaches suggested themselves. One option was to retain an element of conflict in Moscow's dealings with the West, a choice clearly favored by Soviet conservatives. While the days of rock-ribbed maximalism might be over, a return to a more distrustful attitude toward the West, reflecting "class" differences and the need for military strength, was a central plank in the conservatives' platform.

6. See, e.g., Ligachev's remarks about the danger posed by the FRG's "swallowing up" of the GDR in *Pravda,* Feb. 7, 1990, p. 6, and General A. M. Makashov's comments at the founding meeting of the Russian Communist Party implying the possibility of war as a result of Germany's unification and inclusion in NATO, ibid., June 20, 1990, p. 4. Ligachev repeated his views at the 28th Party Congress: ibid., July 11, 1990, p. 6. For additional criticisms of Gorbachev's European policy at the congress, see FBIS, *Soviet Union,* July 6, 1990, pp. 10, 13–16.

Another option would be a redefined Europeanism. Now that Germany was unified and the Warsaw Pact mortally weakened, the time might be ripe, in this view, for insisting on NATO's disbandment. At the very least, Moscow might insist on Germany's exclusion from the NATO alliance and push for the withdrawal of American military forces from Europe. (Elements of this line of reasoning were foreshadowed in Dashichev's 1989 memorandum.) For many Europeanists, achieving these goals would maximize Soviet security in the region while enhancing Moscow's ability to deal directly with the West Europeans without undue American interference.

Americanists may argue, by contrast, that some kind of United States presence in Europe will remain in Moscow's interest for a long time to come. Drawing on arguments advanced in previous decades, exponents of this position will likely refer to America's stabilizing effect in Europe as a whole and its restraining effect on Germany in particular. Germany's unification, Americanists may contend, makes the continuing involvement of the United States in Europe's affairs more necessary than ever, since no one can foresee what path a powerful German state will take and only the United States is strong enough to provide a counterweight to Germany or to a German-dominated Europe. Moreover, uncertainty about Germany's future will be aggravated by uncertainty about the future of nuclear weapons. If NATO disbands and Germany is cast adrift from its American ally, will it seek to acquire a nuclear capability of its own (or in concert with Britain and France)? Will America's military withdrawal prompt the British and French to augment their own nuclear potential? These questions will quite probably continue to be raised in the Soviet Union at least until NATO and the USSR agree to eliminate their nuclear arsenals completely. Even if this landmark accord can be reached, fears may still persist that no one can ever put the nuclear genie back in the bottle once and for all.

With due regard for Europeanist and Americanist arguments, some Soviets will opt for the intermediate Atlanticist position. Accordingly, they will tend to see the benefits of preserving an American role on the continent (including a military role) while seeking to reduce that role to a comfortable minimum so as to free up Western Europe for direct contacts and agreements. Some Atlanticists may continue to speak in terms of playing upon Western "contradictions," but as the East-West conflict unwinds, most will abandon these conflict-laden concepts of pre-Gorbachev days and seek to maximize cooperation with both Western Europe and the United States.

As we have observed, Atlanticism in one form or another has been the traditional preference of the Soviet leadership. In the aftermath of the events of 1989, Gorbachev's reformist regime seemed intent on maintaining the cooperative Atlanticist tendency it had pursued since shortly after coming to power. Moscow joined with the Western occupation powers and the two German states in a series of "two plus four" meetings designed to pave the way for German unity. After first insisting that the new Germany must not be in NATO, the Soviets accepted a package of arrangements that kept all of Germany in the Atlantic alliance but allowed Soviet troops to stay in former GDR territory during a transition period. On July 16, 1990, Gorbachev informed Chancellor Kohl that the Soviet Union would no longer object to Germany's inclusion in NATO once unification took place. Kohl, in return, pledged major reductions in the size of the Bundeswehr. For the longer haul, Moscow voiced interest in a new European security system built around the CSCE nations, a group that included the United States and Canada. In keeping with the Atlanticist contours of the "common European home," the Gorbachev leadership showed every sign of favoring continued American involvement in Europe.

However, the Soviets in 1990 also sought to encourage West German (and, more broadly, West European) proposals to provide massive economic aid and to reduce NATO's military potential as rapidly as possible. On both points, some West Germans were more amenable than the Bush administration to accommodating Soviet wishes. (Chancellor Kohl, along with President Mitterrand, favored a $15 billion aid package, while SPD leaders pushed for Germany's denuclearization.) Once again, as so often in the past, the Soviets hoped to get the Europeans to influence Washington's stance. In true Atlanticist fashion, however, Moscow also sought to induce the United States to exert favorable pressures on Western Europe. Another example of these American levers arose in the spring of 1990, as President Bush backed away from the modernization of short-range missiles, leaving Prime Minister Thatcher virtually isolated within NATO on this issue. At the NATO summit in July, Bush was considerably more receptive to the idea of using nuclear weapons only as a "last resort" than either Thatcher or François Mitterrand.

How these general orientations are defined and implemented in the future will ultimately depend on developments inside the USSR. Although Mikhail Gorbachev captured the world's attention with his daring political high-wire act, the forces that were reshaping Soviet politics were far more powerful than just one man. The clash between the old guard and proponents of radical reform intensified in 1990. The fragmentation of the Union was proceeding at a frenetic pace as the Baltic nations and others demanded independence. The remaining republics insisted on greater sovereignty. The Communist Party of the Soviet Union itself was on the brink of disintegration. Fears of famine, civil war, and a military coup hung in the air. The outcome of these internal processes could not help but have a profound effect on the course of Soviet foreign policy.

However these trends evolve, the Soviet Union is bound to be absorbed in a prolonged quest for a new political order. And yet the main sources of Moscow's international behavior in the years ahead are likely to be found in the same components of the domestic system as in previous years. The decision-making regime, the perceptions of the foreign policy elites, and the specific features of economic policy will all contribute to the making of the Kremlin's external policies. So will public opinion, to a far greater degree than ever before.

At the highest decision-making level, much will depend on the institutional power structure and the political coloration of the primary elite. New state institutions, such as the executive presidency and the Federation Council, will have to be tested while the leading party organs—the Politburo and the Secretariat—redefine their roles. Conservatism, centrism, and reformism will take on new meanings as conditions change and the Soviet political spectrum expands or contracts with them. (At the start of the 1990s Gorbachev seemed to be holding the center against centrifugal forces on his right and left.) Meanwhile, members of the secondary elite will probably seek to extend their newly won latitude to debate foreign policy issues openly and candidly, and to deepen their influence on the decision makers themselves. If the democratization process advances, the secondary elite's membership will be widened to include new recruits from parliamentary bodies and noncommunist political groupings, while foreign policy specialists representing a greater diversity of opinions than before will be drawn from the elite's traditional breeding grounds in academia and journalism. Finally, domestic economic policies will directly affect foreign policy decisions to the extent that the economy adapts itself to international market conditions. Cutting across all of these factors, of course, is the fateful question of the future of the USSR itself: will Moscow's foreign policy speak for the whole Soviet Union, for only part of it, or strictly for Russia?

Germany will also have to go through an internal process of adjusting to the new realities brought on by unification and the democratization of the East. Most citizens of the new Germany will surely wish to maintain strong political and economic ties to the West European community, but the role of the United States and NATO in Germany's future will probably be the subject of lively debate. So will the question how deeply Germany should be involved in the political and economic development of the Soviet Union and Eastern Europe. Though the days of Bismarck's *Schaukelpolitik* may be over, Germany's status as *das Land in der Mitte* is not. More than at any other time since the end of World War II, the opportunities and problems associated with this pivotal position in Europe will stimulate vigorous discussion within Germany over the country's future course and, indeed, its very identity.

Whatever the outcome of these developments, a decisive watershed has clearly been reached in Moscow's ties with Germany as the twentieth century enters its last decade. In a century of ideologies, ideological change is transfiguring the Soviet Union and sweeping across Eastern Europe. In a century of pain, the fears and hatreds bred by two brutal wars are giving way to a quest for reconciliation and mutual understanding. How these processes unfold will of course depend significantly on the evolution of interstate relations between East and West. But perhaps to an even greater degree, the future of this historic relationship will be affected by internal processes. For both nations, foreign policy will begin at home. In the future as in the past, how the Soviets and the Germans govern their relations with each other will depend in large measure on how they govern themselves.

Index

MICHAEL JOSEPH SODARO is Associate Professor of Political Science and International Affairs at The George Washington University, where he has been a member of the Institute for Sino-Soviet Studies since 1977. He received his B.A. from Fordham University, his M.A. from the School of Advanced International Studies (SAIS) of The Johns Hopkins University, and his Ph.D. from Columbia University. He also studied at the Institut d'Études Politiques, Paris, and has taught at SAIS, Georgetown University, and the United States Foreign Service Institute.